The City & Guilds textbook

Level 5

Diploma in Leadership and Management for Adult Care

▌Tina Tilmouth
▌Jan Quallington

HODDER
EDUCATION
AN HACHETTE UK COMPANY

The Publishers would like to thank the following for permission to reproduce copyright material.

Photo credits: p.3 © John Wildgoose/Caiaimage/Getty Images; **p.78** © Jacob Lund/stock.adobe.com; **p.87 top** © Stratol – iStock via Thinkstock/Getty Images; **p.87 bottom** © CandyBox Images – Fotolia.com; **p.88** © Gstockstudio/stock.adobe.com; **p.110** © Syda Productions/stock.adobe.com; **p.111** © Jules Selmes/Hodder Education; **p.134** © B. Boissonnet/BSIP SA/Alamy Stock Photo; **p.136** © Stockbyte via Thinkstock/Getty Images; **p.151** © Jacob Lund/stock.adobe.com; **p.154** © Nirat makjantuk/123RF; **p.197** © JPC-PROD – Fotolia; **p.256** © Barry Diomede/Alamy Stock Photo; **p.269** © Andrzej Tokarski/stock.adobe.com; **p.304** © Denise Hager/Catchlight Visual Services/Alamy Stock Photo; **p.307** © contrastwerkstatt/stock.adobe.com; **p.313** © Syda Productions/stock.adobe.com; **p.328** © JackF/stock.adobe.com; **p.346** © Alexander Raths/stock.adobe.com

Credits for quotations: p.182 © Copyright Chartered Institute of Personnel and Development 2018; from Carroll (2007) on p.196 Copyright © Psychotherapy in Australia 2011; p.198 © Copyright General Social Care Council 2010; pp.204–5 © Skills for Care & CWDC, 2013, 2007; p.231 © Skills for Care 2018; pp.237–8 Copyright © 2018 Sustainable Development Unit; Table 8.1 p.265 © ADSS, October 2005; p.261 © Skills for Care 2018; p.269 © 2007 Commission for Social Care Inspection (CSCI); p.301 © Copyright Chartered Institute of Personnel and Development 2018; p.333 © The King's Fund 2011. Crown copyright material is reproduced under Open Government Licence v3.0.

Although every effort has been made to ensure that website addresses are correct at time of going to press, Hodder Gibson cannot be held responsible for the content of any website mentioned in this book. It is sometimes possible to find a relocated web page by typing in the address of the home page for a website in the URL window of your browser.

Hachette UK's policy is to use papers that are natural, renewable and recyclable products and made from wood grown in well-managed forests and other controlled sources. The logging and manufacturing processes are expected to conform to the environmental regulations of the country of origin.

Orders: please contact Bookpoint Ltd, 130 Park Drive, Milton Park, Abingdon, Oxon OX14 4SE. Telephone: (44) 01235 827827. Fax: (44) 01235 400454. Email education@bookpoint.co.uk Lines are open from 9 a.m. to 5 p.m., Monday to Saturday, with a 24-hour message answering service. You can also order through our website: www.hoddereducation.co.uk

© Tina Tilmouth 2019

First published in 2016

This second edition published in 2019 by

Hodder Education

An Hachette UK Company

Carmelite House

50 Victoria Embankment

London, EC4Y 0DZ

www.hoddereducation.co.uk

Impression number   5 4 3 2 1

Year   2023 2022 2021 2020 2019

Cover photo © Juanmonino/E+/Getty Images

Illustrations by Integra Software Services Pvt. Ltd.

Typeset in India by Integra Software Services Pvt. Ltd.

Printed in Slovenia

A catalogue record for this title is available from the British Library.

ISBN: 978 1 5104 2907 9

Contents

How to use this book

This textbook covers all eleven mandatory units for the City & Guilds Level 5 Diploma in Leadership and Management for Adult Care.

Key features of the book

Learning outcomes: learn about what you are going to cover in each unit.

Learning outcomes and assessment criteria are clearly stated and fully mapped to the specification. Examples given in the topic sections are not intended to be an exhaustive or prescriptive list, but to provide guidance.

Getting started: a short activity or discussion to introduce you to the topic.

Key terms: understand important terms and concepts.

Reflect on it: learn to reflect on your own experiences, skills and practice, and develop the skills necessary to become a reflective practitioner.

Research it: enhance your understanding of topics with research-led activities encouraging you to explore an area in more detail.

In practice: test your understanding of the assessment criteria, apply your knowledge and generate evidence.

Case studies: learn about real-life scenarios and think about issues you may face in the workplace.

Reflective exemplars: explore examples of reflective accounts tailored to the content of the unit and understand how you can write your own accounts.

Summaries of legislation relevant to the study of each unit. You must be aware that legislation and guidance are frequently updated so it is important to ensure you keep up to date with the most recent and applicable version of legislation and national and local regulations.

References to books, websites and other sources for further reading and research.

More information about adult care

You can find more information about this City & Guilds qualification and specification by searching for 'Level 5 Adult Care' or '3080' on the website: www.cityandguilds.com

Note: Those who use adult care services have been referred to as service users and individuals. However, they all refer to the/a person in receipt of services.

Unit 501

Leadership and management in adult care

GLH 30

About this unit

Effective team performance requires the development of a positive and supportive culture in an organisation. Only in this way can we expect staff to be supportive of a shared vision to meet the agreed objectives for a health and social care setting. The most important person in your team will be the service user or client and they need to be central to any team working.

The unit will introduce you to the roles of the manager and leader of teams in the adult care sector and the models of management and leadership which are relevant to this type of work. You will be encouraged to examine strategies of leading and managing teams in order to identify your own strengths, responsibilities and learning needs, and to reflect on best practice within the care context.

Your understanding of this unit should help you to develop your skills in leadership and management, your vision for the service you manage, and how to involve others in driving forward a strategy that will be successful for all those you care for and support in your setting.

The unit will help you to develop an understanding of the importance of leadership and management in ensuring the implementation of required policies and procedures, the development of existing and new strategies in service design and delivery, the management of quality outcomes, and ways to support and develop your teams in creating a shared vision for all.

As part of this unit, you will critically evaluate your own effectiveness as leader and manager, be aware of your strengths and areas for further development, and learn how to adapt and apply your skill sets to varying needs, situations and circumstances within your role.

Underpinned by theories and models of leadership and management practice, you will explore how these apply in your practice to include some of the barriers and challenges faced in a leadership and management role in adult care settings.

Learning outcomes

By the end of this unit you will:

1 Understand the application of theories of leadership and management
2 Understand the importance of leadership and management in adult care settings
3 Lead commitment to a vision for the service
4 Provide leadership for a team in an adult care setting
5 Manage team working

Getting started

Before you study the unit, think about the following:

● What is the difference between a leader and a manager and how do these differences apply to your practice?

● What qualities contribute to making a good leader and how could you evaluate whether you/others fulfil these qualities?

● What and who might be the potential barriers to effective leadership and management?

● Does a good manager mean you have to be an effective administrator?

LO1 Understand the application of theories of leadership and management

AC 1.1 Theories and models of management and leadership

In this section, you will be required to critically analyse theories and models of management and leadership, including the ones we cover here.

Leadership and management are terms often used simultaneously, but they are different. Management is concerned with process and developing systems that relate to organisational aims and objectives and communicating those systems across the organisation. Leadership, meanwhile, is about the behaviour and personal style of the person leading and their ability to influence others towards goals (Stewart, 1997). In this section, we will focus on various theories and models of management and leadership.

Urwick's Ten Principles of Management

Lyndall Urwick (1943) compiled a list of ten general principles for being an effective manager. These ten principles are:

- The **objective** or the overall purpose of an organisation: as a manager your objectives will reflect those of the organisation and you will have to ensure that the team you lead are working to meet them. This will require that they also invest in what the organisation wants to achieve so your leadership to that end is crucial.

- **Specialisation**, that is one group having one function. If you know the strengths and weaknesses of each of your staff members, you will be in a good position to be able to ensure that you can choose the right person for the task. For example, sometimes you may need to choose a specialist group to handle a situation or task. You may need more senior members of staff who are specialists in, say, teaching roles to help newer members of staff in training.

- **Coordination**, to organise the team to facilitate 'unity of effort'. Every effort in a team project needs to be coordinated and as a manager you must be able to organise this. Tasks and jobs will be done only if there is a clear coordinated plan of action and all are aware of it.

- **Authority**, in that there should be a clear line of authority in every organised group. Although you have overall authority within the team, there are times when you may delegate this to a group member in order to get a job done. For example, you may delegate the training of staff to one member of the group who has the authority to book and organise training.

- **Responsibility**, so that somebody is accountable for the actions of subordinates. All team members are accountable for the jobs they do and the actions they take in the course of their duty. As a manager you need to make it clear that this is expected of staff and to explain clearly what that means in practice.

- **Definition**, to ensure that all roles, jobs and relationships are clearly defined. As a manager you should ensure that all job descriptions are up to date and clear.

- **Correspondence**, which demands that in every position, responsibility and authority correspond with one another. Team work demands that every member is aware of what others do. This enables people to know how their role affects the work of others. For example, a healthcare assistant working in a department may be responsible for stocking shelves with equipment and ensuring that supplies are available. If this is not carried out, then it has a direct effect on those who are in need of those supplies and equipment and can make their job more difficult. Your managerial role is to see that all members of the team are aware of that effect.

- **Span of control**, to ensure that no person supervises more than 5–6 **line reports** whose work is **interlinked**. As a manager you should ensure that no staff member is overwhelmed by the number of duties they have to perform or the number of staff they are responsible for.

KEY TERMS

Line reports are those members of staff who report to you.
Interlinked work is work that is connected and that has similar objectives.

- **Balance**, which is the requirement to maintain the units of an organisation in balance. Each part of the organisation can run well only when there is balance. If one team is not functioning well this will have a detrimental effect on others. For example, the 2016 strikes by junior doctors upset the balance of the way in which the NHS runs. The waiting lists got longer as scheduled operations had to be cancelled.

- **Continuity** to ensure that reorganisation is a continuous process and provision is made for it. As a manager you should ensure that when things are not working well and continuity in the service is upset for whatever reason, there is a contingency plan which might be put into place.

    Adapted from: www.open.edu/openlearn/money-management/management/leadership-and-management/discovering-management/content-section-1.1.1 Accessed on 27/5/17

Reflect on it

1.1 Urwick's ten principles

How do the ten principles fit with your experience of being a manager? Do they still work for you today or are they outdated?

You may recognise some of the above principles as being a part of your role and it is useful for you to take a critical look at what you do in each instance. For example, in analysing the above theory you might ask why such principles are useful, if they are, and give examples from your own practice to demonstrate your understanding.

How can you demonstrate balance in your own workplace? What about coordination and authority? How do you ensure that this is a part of the team function and how useful is it?

Write a short piece giving examples of your experience.

Trait theory

Whereas Urwick's ten principles were developed for managers, Gordon Allport's trait theory (Allport and Odbert, 1936) is a leadership model which describes characteristics of good leaders. The idea that 'leaders are born rather than made' asserts that by identifying those characteristics in a person, we could identify who might be an effective leader. On the other hand, behavioural theory suggests that leadership can be learned, and that people may be taught to display the appropriate behaviours. In this theory, the assumption is that 'leaders are made, not born. Some theorists argue that by learning to behave in a manner which makes you a 'good' leader, it is possible to become a good leader.

What do you think about trait theory? We might criticise it for being too general and subjective. For example, the belief that a person is born with certain traits and remains the same means that people are either born to leadership or not. If you do not have the traits identified in Allport's theory, this implies you will not be a good leader. On the other hand, behavioural theory suggests the opposite: that we are able to learn how to lead and can develop the characteristics needed.

Lewin's leadership styles

In 1939, Kurt Lewin described leadership styles and, although somewhat dated, they remain relevant to team leadership and management today. He identified three very different leadership styles (Lewin et al., 1939). You may be familiar with the terms authoritarian, democratic and laissez faire applied to styles of leadership. The traits of these styles and their advantages and disadvantages are as follows:

Autocratic/Authoritarian or 'I want you to...'

- The leader/manager makes decisions on their own without consulting the team.
- They expect the team to follow the decision exactly.
- The task is to be accomplished in the least amount of time possible.
- Instructions have to be clear and concise.
- Team members may become dissatisfied when they have ideas but are unable to voice these.
- Team members are not consulted on decisions being made.
- This can make them feel less involved and their commitment to the task is likely to be lukewarm.
- This type of leadership is good in situations requiring immediate or emergency action – for example, in emergency departments or in a crisis situation decisions have to be made quickly.

Democratic/participative or 'Let's work together to solve this'

- Involving the team in the decision-making process leads to the team members feeling they have ownership of the task.
- This style is democratic and is the most popular style of leadership.
- The drawback is that teams are made up of individuals with vastly different opinions and decision making can therefore be a lengthy process. The leader must be prepared in this case to make the final decision in a collaborative way.

▲ **Figure 1.1** A collaborative leader values participation from employees

Laissez faire or 'You two take care of the problem while I go'

- Team members are allowed to make their own decisions and get on with the tasks.
- This works well when people are capable and motivated in making their own decisions.
- The problem with this style is the tendency to go off task, with the result that the outcome is never achieved. It may lead to the team becoming impatient with the amount of time it takes to make a decision.

Goleman's leadership styles and emotional intelligence (EI)

Daniel Goleman (1995) stated that emotional intelligence is:

'the capacity for recognising our own feelings and those of others for motivating ourselves, for managing emotions well in ourselves as well as others.'

Source: Goleman, 1995, p.137

For Goleman, self-awareness is about knowing our own emotions and recognising those feelings as they happen. So, we may feel angry at something somebody has said, but as a manager and leader, showing that anger inappropriately will have a negative effect on relationships.

Social awareness refers to the empathy and concern we have for others' feelings; the acknowledgement that people under threat in an organisation may show aggression and anger. Decisions affecting people's jobs may have to be made, and the manager who sees only the task at hand is failing to acknowledge the effect this is having on those at risk and those who have to continue to work in such a climate of change.

Relationship management is the ability to handle relationships competently in order to best deal with conflict, and to develop collaboration in the workforce.

Finally, Goleman refers to motivation, particularly of ourselves, to enable the workforce to meet goals.

In a management situation our awareness of the impact of our actions and responses can go a long way towards defusing situations that might be potentially threatening. We may not be feeling very happy or friendly ourselves, but being in a position of authority demands that we have some awareness of the feelings of others. A good manager has a level of emotional intelligence.

Emotional intelligence as a theory has been criticised for being unscientific and some writers question how we can measure accurately the traits of 'emotional stability', 'agreeableness', 'extraversion' and 'conscientiousness' which are often referred to in the theory. Self-report personality-based questionnaires can be falsified (were you truly honest the last time you completed a questionnaire in a magazine?) so the measurement is potentially flawed.

On the other hand, Goleman's research showed that leaders with EI performed better than those who did not have this ability. He also suggested that EI in leaders was more useful than just having technical expertise or a high IQ.

Maslow's Hierarchy of Needs

Abraham Maslow's (1908–1970) work has been influential in many disciplines and you may be aware of his hierarchy of needs theory, which outlined the things that contribute to a person's wellbeing (see Figure 1.2). According to this theory, we are motivated by unsatisfied needs. For example, our physiological need for food and water, once satisfied, is no longer a motivator and leaves us free to pursue the next level in the hierarchy, that of safety and security, and so on. The theory has been used in health and social care settings, when managers have recognised the impact that motivation has on workplace success. The biggest resource, and the most expensive, in any organisation is its employees and therefore motivation theory has become a valuable tool for managers.

Case study

1.1 Managing difficult situations

A member of staff has recently undergone a traumatic separation from her husband. She has three small children and is struggling to make ends meet. She finds it difficult to get to work on time and has been late a number of times recently. You know she does not have family to help her get the children to school.

When you ask to see her to try to resolve some of her issues, she is aggressive and quite rude. This may make you feel angry, particularly when you are trying to come up with a solution. However, fighting anger with anger does not work and you need to consider how you might approach this problem in a different manner.

How might you deal with this situation?

Perhaps you will have empathised with the staff member's plight and asked her how she might see a way forward. It is likely she has been unable to take time out to note the decline in her work or her lateness. You might suggest a change in hours to help her to get to work on time, or a reduction in her hours of work until she can settle her children into a more favourable routine. Perhaps she might work the same number of hours but at times when the children are at school.

The way you deal with the situation will have an effect on the whole workforce.

What do you think are the main issues in this case study? For example, how would you deal with your anger and your staff member's aggression to resolve the situation? How would emotional intelligence help here?

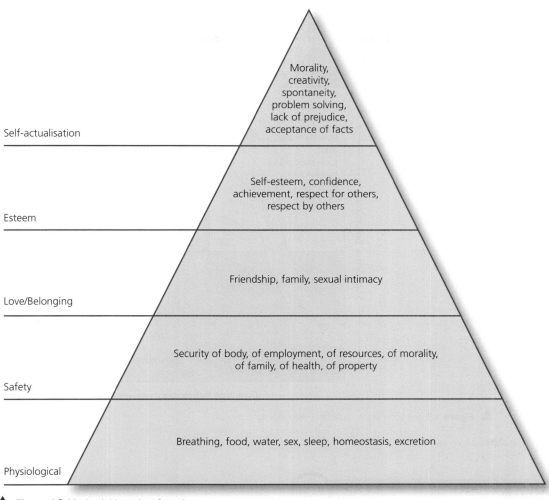

▲ **Figure 1.2** Maslow's hierarchy of needs

Contemporaries of Maslow – Herzberg and McGregor – were developing motivation theories alongside Maslow's in an attempt to determine how to motivate people in the workplace.

Criticisms of Maslow's theory (and other theories of motivation) include the lack of empirical research to support its conclusions, the assumption that all employees are alike and will therefore respond in similar ways, and that all situations are alike. Another criticism is the assumption that the lower needs must be satisfied before a person can reach self-actualisation. For example, there are cultures in which large numbers live in poverty, but people may still be capable of higher order needs such as love and belongingness. Also, history tells us of many creative people, such as authors and artists, who manage to reach their potential despite living an impoverished life.

Hersey and Blanchard – situational leadership

Situational leadership theory, devised by Paul Hersey and Ken Blanchard, describes leadership as being led by the situation that is presented to you and adapting the leadership style to that situation. This approach depends upon the leader having the ability to adapt to the task in hand by evaluating the competence and commitment of the workforce to accomplish that task (Northouse, 2018). For example, if during your daily routine an emergency situation were to arise, situational leadership would require you to adapt to this and you would have to decide at that moment the best course of action. To be a situational leader requires an ability to adjust according to what is happening.

It further classifies leadership style into four different behaviours of the leader, which are shown in Figure 1.3.

Here we see the leadership behaviours, directing and supporting, which can be shown to be high or low.

- The team receiving instructions and carrying them out is the High Directive–Low Supportive function (S1).
- The leader handing over control to the workforce but facilitating their development to help them to achieve the goal is the High Supportive–Low Directive approach (S3).

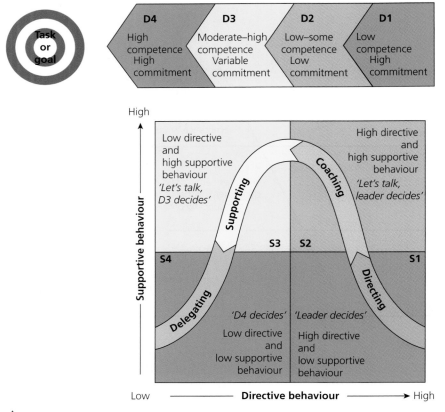

▲ **Figure 1.3** The company's situational self-leadership model

1.1 Situational Theory

Research Hersey and Blanchard's situational theory using Figure 1.3. Show how the S2 High Directive–High Supportive style and the S4 Low Directive–Low Supportive style of management of tasks might work in your workplace.

Read more about this at www.leadership-central.com/situational-leadership-theory.html#ixzz4iS7WYgct

Contingency theories put forward the view that situations lend themselves to different styles of leadership and that the team leader's flexibility to adapt in response to those situations is key (Fiedler, 1967; Martin et al., 2010; McKibbon et al., 2008). Successful outcomes in this respect depend on the leader adopting a style based on several variables: the job in hand, the qualities of those in the team and the context in which the team is working.

KEY TERM

Contingency theories state that there is no one best style of leadership. In this case the leader's effectiveness is based on the situation.

Kouzes and Posner – the leadership challenge

James Kouzes and Barry Posner's (2003) Leadership Challenge model identifies character traits that are generally associated with good leaders:

- Honest
- Inspiring
- Forward-looking
- Competent
- Intelligent
- Dominant
- Consciousness

- Enthusiastic
- Sense of humour
- Integrity
- Courageous
- Visionary.

The bottom line is that good leaders and managers are able to generate enthusiasm and commitment in others. They lead by example with consistent values and break down barriers which stand in the way of achievement. Kouzes and Posner (2003, in Tilmouth et al., 2011) argue:

- A good leader will also inspire a shared vision and enlist the commitment of others.
- A good leader will promote collaborative working which builds trust and empowers others.
- A good leader recognises others' achievements and celebrates accomplishments.

If, however, you do not fully believe in what you are asking others to do then this will affect performance. This model demands that you, as a manager, model the practice and behaviours you wish your staff to portray. A criticism might be that if you are unable to do this, then this type of leadership will prove fruitless.

Reflect on it

1.1 Unpopular decisions

Some decisions which are made at senior management level may be unpopular and yet as a manager you are asked to ensure they are followed. How might you do this? What if you believe it to be a bad decision? How will you motivate staff to undertake the unpopular outcome?

Belbin – team roles

Meredith Belbin's research (1981) on the various roles needed in an effective team looked at determining how problems in teams could be predicted and avoided by controlling the dynamics of the group.

The results revealed that the difference between a team's success and failure was dependent not on factors such as intellect but on behaviour. The research team began to identify separate clusters of behaviour, each of which formed distinct team contributions or team roles. Belbin identified nine team roles. Briefly summarised, these are:

- **Shaper**: task focused and generates action in a team
- **Implementer** (company worker): the person who carries forward the strategies and gets the task done
- **Completer-finisher**: the perfectionist of the team
- **Coordinator** (chairman): the delegator who clarifies what needs to be done
- **Team worker**: they carry out the work and turn ideas into action
- **Resource investigator**: they explore what is happening locally and nationally and develop contacts
- **Plant**: creative, lateral thinker/problem solver
- **Monitor evaluator**: focused, logical, dispassionate and able to see all options
- **Specialist**: they focus on their own subject area rather than being team focused.

Belbin came up with an additional team role called the specialist, for example those who focus on their own subject or expertise only. They can be seen as independent and not really part of the team but contribute their particular knowledge when required.

Each role has its strengths and weaknesses, and effective performance is encouraged if you are aware of the roles each of your staff exhibits and assign them duties that fit that role.

KEY TERMS

Conflict is a disagreement or an argument.
Trust is having confidence in something or someone.

Research it

1.1 Belbin's team roles

Go to www.belbin.com/about/belbin-teamroles/ and find out more about the roles listed above and the strengths and weaknesses of each.

Think about your setting. How do these relate to the members of your team? How do these present a challenge?

You may wish to use this to write your own reflective account and use it as an example of how to evidence this assessment criterion.

I am a perfectionist. I need to see the job done. I like to make sure every 't' is crossed and 'i' is dotted and that the detail is attended to. Errors and gaps leave me feeling a little out of control and occasionally cross. With respect to Belbin's categories, I guess that makes me a completer-finisher: 'conscientious, anxious' and 'inclined to worry'.

At the team meeting last week I asked the staff to work on the rota for the client's activities for July. We had anticipated that there would be some visits out of the care environment and I had asked two of the staff to arrange these and the others to arrange for external speakers to attend on other days.

At the team meeting this week I got quite irritated when A said he had not quite finished the task. I felt at first that he was irresponsible and lazy since he knows very well that I like to get the job done on time and I felt he had been unreasonable in asking for more time. J had completed the task and presented her work to the team, but I became aware of an atmosphere developing and I feel she may have irritated some of the staff. I noticed the other team members were looking a little cross at some of the suggestions being put forward.

I had to think about what this all meant and reflected on the task, the team and the individuals I had specifically asked to do the job.

J is creative and comes up with some really good ideas, which is why I had chosen her to lead on the activity rota. In Belbin's roles I guess she is 'the plant'. She solves difficult problems with some real 'out of the box' thinking, which I like. But I think she may have got carried away with all these wonderful activities and was not communicating this well to the rest of the team. The team were therefore unable to put forward some of the downsides of her suggestions.

With A, I simply did not read the situation well. I think A takes on the role of the coordinator and was able to clarify the task to others and set the goals but then tried to get the team to do the work for him! When they did not, he realised he had run out of time.

So I learned a lesson this week about my team and went away to consider how I can support them.

Management by wandering around (MBWA)

In this style of management, the manager sets aside time to walk through their departments to make themselves visible and available to staff. They see the problems the staff face and have time to listen to concerns. This is the sort of manager who operates an 'open door' policy. This means that you do not have to make an appointment to see the manager; you simply go to them when you need to.

In his book written with Nancy Austin *A Passion for Excellence* (1985), Tom Peters stated that as leaders and managers wander about, three things should be going on:

● Managers should be listening to what people are saying.
● They should be using the opportunity to transmit the company's values.
● They should be able to give people on-the-spot help.

This theory seems to have much to commend it, but do you have the time to 'wander around'? Some managers may find they can spend a whole day just answering emails and fail to get out into the setting. It would require a general rethink of how you use your time to facilitate this way of working.

Power and empowerment
Dimensions and sources of power

In most organisations, there will be people who have more power than others simply because they are in a higher position in a hierarchy. This power can be used in a positive way, but often the concept of power brings to mind negative connotations of abuse and harassment and this kind of thinking can lead us to distrust anybody who is in such a position of power. In this way, power can be perceived as influencing or controlling somebody in a negative way.

If you are the manager in a work setting, you are already in a position of power. You may have recruited the people you manage. You have influence and authority over those people. Furthermore, the concept of 'master–apprentice' in any work situation evokes a hierarchy of power that favours the master, and this is likely to affect the working relationship.

Reflecting on power

It is useful to consider the power you hold in your position and to reflect on how you use it. For example, do you get a sense that people in your employ are wary of you? Could this be because of the way they perceive you? Do they think you try to control them? Or perhaps you do not exercise your power at all and find that maybe the team take you for granted and often fail to deliver on deadlines?

Reflect on it

1.1 Reflecting on power

Think about the sorts of power that you may have come across during your work life. Write an account of how they affected you.

Defining empowerment

KEY TERM

Empowerment is giving someone authority.

Empowerment is 'a process by which people, organisations and communities gain mastery over their affairs' (Rappaport, 1987) and in order to do this, individuals need to have more control over what they are doing and should be encouraged to work autonomously.

Leadership in this instance is not about control and making decisions on behalf of staff but is more about empowering staff to lead on ideas and innovations to make the workplace more efficient. This approach links in with motivation theories (such as Maslow's theory, see page 4) but this is not an easy approach to take.

Essentially, the leader refrains from directing the staff and telling them what to do and how to do it. Rather, they allow the team to do it on their own. They give staff the problem to solve and then allow them to work through solutions without stepping in and giving the answers. Staff should feel more motivated when they work in this way.

Care and control

Empowering staff means you are relinquishing control of some of your power to some extent in terms of management. Care should be taken to support staff so that they feel safe to carry out the tasks and make decisions, and to seek help if they need it.

Evidence opportunity

1.1 Theories and models of management and leadership

Provide a written account critically analysing theories and models of management and leadership, including the ones we have covered in this section.

You may wish to also consider how these apply to adult care practice.

Explore the evidence for and against each theory.

AC 1.2 How theoretical models are applied to practice

In this section, you will be required to evaluate how three theories and/or models of management and leadership (that you learned about in AC 1.1) apply to adult care practice.

You will need to critically evaluate how three theories and/or models of management and leadership apply to adult care practice and will need to explore the sections we cover below. You should explain in your critical evaluation to what extent you agree with the three management styles you cover. You will research them well, argue 'for' and 'against' each of the styles as to their use in your own workplace and provide evidence from a range of sources.

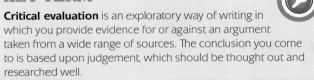

KEY TERM

Critical evaluation is an exploratory way of writing in which you provide evidence for or against an argument taken from a wide range of sources. The conclusion you come to is based upon judgement, which should be thought out and researched well.

Defining what makes a great leader and manager

Leadership and management are different and as Stewart (1997) stated: 'Management is essentially about people with responsibility for the work of others and what they actually do operationally, whereas leadership is concerned with the ability to influence others towards a goal.'

A leader inspires others to work towards a shared vision for the future and is able to empower and motivate people. A manager, on the other hand, may simply give out tasks and ensure that the day-to-day operations of the organisation are running smoothly. However, good managers also inspire staff to perform and command respect. They show empathy and consideration for the staff and have good communication skills and discipline.

Figure 1.4 highlights some of the traits of a good leader, including confidence, good interpersonal skills and charisma.

You should also look back at the Kouzes and Posner's Leadership Challenge model, which identifies character traits associated with good leaders, that we covered in AC 1.1, especially if you want to use this as one of the theories on which to base your critical evaluation. See page 6.

▲ **Figure 1.4** Some traits of a good leader

Research it

1.2 Characteristics of a good leader

What do you think are the characteristics of a good leader/manager?

Conduct some primary research and ask your peers and colleagues for their views. Figure 1.4 outlines some of these. All these are correct, of course, and there are many more you may have included.

The following may be helpful for secondary research and will help you to gain a greater understanding of the traits of good leadership and management:

Adair, J. (2009) *Effective Leadership: How to be a successful leader*. New York: Pan Macmillan.

Tilmouth, T., Davies-Ward, E. and Williams, B. (2011) *Foundation Degree in Health and Social Care*. London: Hodder Education.

www.businessballs.com/dtiresources/TQM_development_people_teams.pdf

Your role as a leader and manager

Adair (1983), an influential writer on leadership and management, identified three key roles for leaders:

1   Achieving the task.
2   Developing team members.
3   Maintaining the team.

These may sound obvious but how often do we become so task orientated that we forget the needs of the team?

Team members need to understand the task and be given the resources to achieve that task if the outcome is to be successful. In this respect, team and individual development is critical to ensure that individuals can perform in the team (Martin et al., 2010).

Reflect on it

1.2 Your own role

How would you define your own role in the workplace?

How is your role different from those you lead or manage?

Make some notes for your portfolio.

How you identify and understand your own management style(s)

Different leadership styles

As a manager in a care setting, it is important that you identify and understand your own management style so that you can adjust your style to the different people in your team. Not everyone responds well to a direct approach. Some may wish to be allowed to use their own initiative and to feed back to you. Others may require gentle handling, so you may need to adjust to this.

Think about the managers you worked for in your first few roles. Reflect on what you either liked or disliked about them. Was it purely their friendly nature or were you a little in awe of them? Did they inspire you with confidence or were you a bit scared of them? Did they show an interest in you as a person or were they more task-focused? Your style of leadership will be more effective if you are wise in your choice and adjust to each person.

Adjusting styles

The American Management Association in 2011 collected data on the managerial effectiveness of 622 leaders across hundreds of organisations and highlighted three competencies that spanned all industries. This is reflected in work by Terry (1993) and George (2003) on authentic leadership.

The three competencies are as follows:

1   **Building trust and demonstrating personal accountability**: A leader who keeps their promises and honours commitments to the staff will be regarded by the staff as somebody who can be trusted. Far from being weak, the leader/manager who accepts

responsibility for their actions and communicates honestly is seen as accountable and trustworthy.

2 **Action orientation**: Staff want somebody to act decisively and to suggest a solution in a crisis, so **action orientation** is about maintaining the momentum and sense of urgency about a project or a piece of work.

3 **Flexibility and agility**: Working for somebody who has fixed ideas can be demoralising, so if you are able to adjust to the situation and change your behaviour according to the change in circumstances, you demonstrate that you are open to new ways of doing things.

By being authentic in this way, you develop a sense of trust with the staff and they can then be held accountable for their actions, and by adjusting the way in which we manage and lead we can be more effective in our role.

> ## KEY TERM
>
> **Action orientation** is a type of leadership in which practical action is taken to deal with a problem or situation.

Lewin et al. (1939) explored different leadership styles and it would be a good idea to return to AC 1.1 if you would like to use this as one of the theories for your critical evaluation. Likewise, Allport also looked at leadership styles and you should revisit the section on Allport in AC 1.1 if you'd like to base your critical evaluation on this.

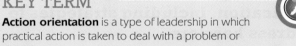

Evidence opportunity

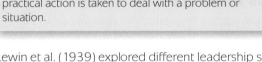

1.2 **Management styles**

1 Interview your manager and ask about their own style of management. Perhaps arrange to shadow them for a day.

2 Comment upon your own style and how it is similar to or different from that of your manager.

3 Analyse how different management styles may influence outcomes of team performance.

Write this up as a reflective account for your journal.

Adapting management styles to meet requirements of role and with individuals and teams

The social skills needed in different leadership roles vary, and leaders need to adjust their styles at different times to facilitate or help group process (Wheelan, 2005).

At times we may need to be more directive and assertive to address and reduce any anxiety in team members,

but this needs to be accomplished in a positive and open way. Supplying the resources needed to get the job done helps the team to accomplish their tasks and feel supported. When the team start to work well and demand to participate more, a good leader will recognise this and step back rather than risk resentment due to the undue influence from the leader. At times the leader's competence is questioned and it is important not to take the attacks personally. Ultimately you want the team to take the leadership role on themselves to become more autonomous and responsible.

Whatever qualities we possess or need to develop, we will use these in various ways and adopt certain styles with respect to how we lead and manage.

Part of a manager's role is to encourage others to work effectively and whichever style you adopt, you need to be able to rationalise why you chose that way to work. The outcomes will be affected if you fail to recognise the effect your style of leadership is having on the team. In AC 1.1, we looked at Goleman's style of leadership which emphasises the role of **emotional intelligence** in managing people. If we become more attuned to our own emotions and can see how they affect others, we will be in a better position to handle situations which may require empathy and an understanding of the other person's feelings.

An effective team is committed to working towards the same goals and the team members will cooperate with decisions. In well-managed teams, results are produced quickly and economically where there is a free exchange of ideas and information (Tilmouth et al., 2011).

You will have a particular management style that you favour, but the ability to adapt to different situations is good practice. Every individual we manage is unique and, as with our service users, we need to treat people as such. Our style of management must adapt to the unique nature of each person in our team and we should try to draw upon different styles of management to accommodate this.

Positive and negative emotions impact our behaviour and the behaviours of those we lead and manage. Our awareness of this and our ability to manage our emotions will lead to more positive outcomes in pressured situations.

> ## KEY TERM
>
> **Emotional intelligence** is being aware of and having the ability to control our own emotions, so as to handle interpersonal relationships empathetically (to think about and understand how others are feeling and see things from their point of view).

Senior colleagues/team managers – roles as managers and others

Your role as manager will also impact upon others in the wider team and you need to be aware of how your behaviour and the way in which you manage impacts these individuals.

Senior colleagues/team managers

Deputy: Your deputy needs to work closely with you and adopt the same values and attitudes towards the organisation as you. There should be a strong link between how you both manage the team and a clear understanding of the tasks or operations you wish them to undertake.

Team leaders/supervisors: It might be that a delegated task for your deputy will be to manage the team leaders and supervisors. If this is the case, then your responsibility will be to ensure that you support the deputy in this role. You may take a step back from the line management of these people, but you should always be aware of what is happening at this level by getting regular updates from your deputy.

Others

Home owners: These might be the people who own your setting, particularly if you are in a residential care setting or care home. Sometimes home owners only want to know that their business is in safe hands. As the manager you will need to keep them well informed about all aspects of the running of the service, but this can be handled at a regular meeting.

Company directors: These people have a financial interest in the business and may also make strategic decisions. As a manager it is your responsibility to ensure they are aware of the day-to-day running of the setting and any related issues.

Trustees: They serve on the board of an institution, charity or local government. They are not normally paid for their role but have control over how the organisation is run. They will need to be aware of the administrative and legal side of the business and will want assurance that the setting is running in compliance with the law and that high-quality care is a top priority.

> ### Reflect on it
>
>
> #### 1.2 Adjusting your management style
>
> Take some time to consider how you might adjust your style when talking to your deputy, team leaders/supervisors, home owners, directors and trustees.

> ### Evidence opportunity
>
> #### 1.2 How theoretical models are applied to practice
>
> Using the models that we have discussed in AC 1.1 and 1.2, write a critical evaluation about how three theories and/or models of management and leadership apply to adult care practice. Think about the things that we discussed in this section. For example, how might Kouzes and Posner's leadership challenge apply to your own setting and how would you compare it to the use of Daniel Goleman's EI theory?
>
> Give examples of how you would demonstrate emotional intelligence or leadership traits in your work and how you apply these to your practice.

AC 1.3 Barriers between leadership and management theory and their application, including strategies to address barriers

In this section, you will be required to analyse barriers to applying leadership and management theory in respect of the topics we discuss here.

It is important to learn about and understand all the different theories around leadership and management which will inform your role and help you to become a good manager. However, you will encounter situations and barriers that will make it difficult to put the theory into practice and in this section we will address some of these.

Managing is about planning, coordinating and implementing policies and procedures which are often imposed from higher management. It is about directing people and resources to meet the principles and values of an organisation.

Leadership on the other hand is about inspiring others to follow you and motivating them to reach new goals. It is about having ideas and working towards new visions and plans and motivating others to move with you.

Strategic management

Strategic management is about how an organisation will meet its goals and involves setting objectives, looking at the competition and making an analysis of the internal organisation.

For any organisation to run efficiently, a strategic management plan requires goals and objectives for the workforce. These are monitored and analysed on a regular basis to audit or check where the organisation is meeting or failing to meet its targets. This requires managing individuals and their performance, managing teams, and managing the changes that the team will experience as a result of the strategic plan.

A new strategic plan applies changes throughout the organisation, so you need to manage change in a sensitive way in order to keep the staff and team focused on the vision and the strategic direction. Barriers and conflict occur when staff feel unsure about this direction and are simply expected to make the change happen. For example, a great idea can be forgotten if it is not implemented in a sensitive manner. New ways of working need to be introduced carefully, with staff being given an opportunity to question, and to come to terms with what is expected of them. Training and talking things through are invaluable.

Managing individuals/performance management

Any business relies upon staff to do the jobs they are paid to do and to do them well. One barrier is that people will not always conform. People are unique. Some work hard, others are lazy, some communicate well and others don't. Some are moody and demoralised, whereas some are always upbeat and motivated. Managing people requires you to hold them to account for their performance. The process involves setting objectives for the employee which are linked to business plans, and discussing ways in which success can be measured.

The Institute of NHS Quality states:

'Performance management enables organisations to articulate their business strategy, align their business to that strategy, identify their key performance indicators (KPIs) and track progress, delivering the information to decision-makers.'

It also provides a performance management tool which may be downloaded from its website to help the process.

Go to: www.nhsemployers.org/case-studies-and-resources/2018/04/people-performance-management-toolkit

Trust to build good relationships and maintaining communication are a useful start. Praise for jobs well done rather than pointing out the errors that have been made is also a good strategy. If you want a professional approach to work and a hardworking force then you need to set an example.

Managing teams

Teams are groups of individuals who are all unique in their own way. They have different values, attitudes and abilities. Some will feel challenged by tasks you give them and need support, but others will find these tasks easy to do. Barriers

to team success are a result of not knowing what motivates your staff and poor communication. By applying different styles of leadership and management theory you can help the team to become better at what they do. Adapting your style to the situation and the person will show a greater understanding about their needs to perform well as a team.

Managing change

In health and social care, change happens for various reasons:

- new research in practice becomes available
- new policies and regulations
- overspending on budgets
- the need to update premises disrupts the working day
- turnover of staff.

Any change is a challenge and can cause anxiety for some, becoming a barrier to the achievement of goals and objectives. Managers need to be aware of how to minimise this and keep the team focused. Managing change requires a planned and systematic approach to ensure that the team's motivation is maintained.

John Kotter (1996) devised 'eight steps to successful change', which provide a useful starting point. Each stage recognises how individuals respond to and approach change, and Kotter identifies this through how we see, feel and then act towards change.

Kotter's model shows well how managers can motivate people to buy into the change by 'owning' the change and this is the important element of any successful change.

We can reduce the eight-steps model to four major factors:

- **The urgency factor**: the pressure to change is on the organisation. You need to get the team behind you to ensure successful outcomes.
- **The vision factor**: a clear shared vision is an imperative and, as manager, it is necessary to ensure that team members are with you and not against you. Motivation is the key here and you need to be aware of what motivates your team.
- **The resource factor**: the resources you need to implement change have to be identified before you proceed, and you need to ensure these are provided. Without the necessary tools, your team cannot be expected to do the job.
- **The action factor**: when all else is in place, the next part of any change is to act. Having planned for change and implemented it, you then need to check that it is working and act if it is not.

If the change is working, then maintaining the effectiveness and appropriateness of the change is good practice. By monitoring and analysing data produced you are in a position to evaluate the success or otherwise and to keep the team informed of progress.

Managing quality

Quality assurance within the NHS is made up of three components – patient safety, patient experience and clinical effectiveness – and all healthcare systems in the UK are required to provide safe and good-quality healthcare, improving the patient experience, as well as continually updating practice in the light of evidence from research. All this happens through the system of clinical governance. Scally and Donaldson defined clinical governance as

> *'a system through which NHS organisations are accountable for continuously improving the quality of their services and safeguarding high standards of care by creating an environment in which excellence in clinical care will flourish.'*
>
> **Source:** Scally and Donaldson, 1998, p. 61

A core responsibility in delivering healthcare, in any setting whether it is the NHS or social care, is to ensure that all who receive care are safeguarded, and we must examine and analyse how we manage such performance. The essential standards of health and safety, as set out by the Care Quality Commission, and relevant legislative requirements must be met.

To maintain such high-quality care in your organisation you need to create a performance management system which:

● identifies areas of best practice and focuses on continuous improvement

● delivers better outcomes to patients

● improves health services by acting upon new initiatives and information

● ensures that organisational activities are linked to the overall goals of the organisation.

Throughout the last 20 years or so, reviews and policies have attempted to address quality in social care and in the NHS. The emergence, in October 2014, of the Five Year Forward View was an attempt to bring together organisations which had a part in quality assurance and to establish a National Quality Board (NQB). This board is made up of the CQC, NHS England, NHS Improvement, Public Health England, NICE and Health Education England and the Department of Health. The review continues and, in 2017, 'Next steps on the NHS five year forward view' was published. In April 2009, the CQC was established to regulate the quality of health and social care and was under the Health and Social

Research it

1.3 Policies

Research some of the new quality policies that have been published from the list below.

● Gov.uk 2017 Next steps on the NHS five year forward view Supporting NHS providers to deliver the right staff, with the right skills, in the right place at the right time: Safe, sustainable and productive staffing. www.england.nhs.uk/wp-content/uploads/2013/04/nqb-guidance.pdf

● Improving experiences of care: Our shared understanding and ambition http://webarchive.nationalarchives.gov.uk/20161103235253 www.england.nhs.uk/wp-content/uploads/2015/01/improving-experiences-of-care.pdf

● How to organise and run a risk summit (second edition) www.england.nhs.uk/wp-content/uploads/2017/07/risk-summit-guidance-july-2017.pdf

● Revised guidance for QSGs – 'How to run an effective QSG' www.england.nhs.uk/wp-content/uploads/2014/03/quality-surv-grp-effective.pdf

● National Data Quality Review www.england.nhs.uk/wp-content/uploads/2013/04/1ndqr-exec-sum.pdf

● Care Quality Commission fundamental standards www.cqc.org.uk/what-we-do/how-we-do-our-job/fundamental-standards

● Care Quality Commission regulations www.cqc.org.uk/guidance-providers/regulations-enforcement/regulations-service-providers-managers

Care Act 2008. Each adult social care provider and NHS trust became legally responsible for ensuring the new essential standards of quality and safety were met.

Strategies to overcome barriers

Conflict within teams can lead to barriers forming within the workforce. These barriers can include poor staff morale, a lack of communication between team members and an increase in reported sickness as staff avoid coming to work. Conflict is unpleasant and leads to disruption in performance. However, when resolved effectively, conflict can lead to personal and professional growth if you are able to have discussions about areas of concern and reasons for the conflict. Conflict and conflict resolution can therefore be creative and productive.

Individual professional development

Resolution and a reduction in barriers can be dealt with by having in place a good system of staff or professional development within the workplace, and strategies by which you might encourage good dialogue between the team.

Individual SWOT analysis of service delivery and teams

Individual staff development can involve staff undertaking **SWOT analysis** in which they identify their strengths, weaknesses, opportunities and threats within their role and then by reflecting upon how they would like to develop both as an individual in the workplace and as a team member. This can help overcome barriers as staff will feel more valued as they are encouraged to develop in their chosen career. As the manager you might help by adopting coaching and mentoring as a form of on-the-job development and you could also help staff access other training courses, perhaps aiding them in financing the course. See the coaching and management section below.

SWOT analysis will help you to identify things that you are good at and doing well, things that you are not doing so well and could improve, areas that present opportunities and things that could threaten or are troublesome. The aim is to improve performance and the quality of care.

KEY TERM

SWOT analysis involves defining strengths, weaknesses, opportunities and threats and can be undertaken as part of your professional development, to evaluate your setting or a particular project you are working on.

Individual self-reflection

Reflection is part of revalidation for all staff and is therefore a requirement, but it can be a valuable learning resource. The barrier to undertaking this activity is often expressed as lack of time so as a manager you need to be able to give staff the time to step back and reflect, perhaps during team meetings or individual appraisal sessions or supervision.

By looking back at significant events in our work we can start to work on our skills of evaluation as we first describe what happened and then think about our feelings about the event. We then start to look at what was good or bad about the situation and can analyse how we might have reacted differently. We can then plan what we might do in the future if a similar situation arises. Mistakes can happen in our work but by undertaking a reflective approach we are able to think things through and then plan how to change in the future.

Individual and team action planning

Staff appraisal, supervision sessions and team meetings are all areas where planning can take place. You might also organise times off site when teams can engage in planning sessions. Planning is an important activity in managing health settings and one barrier to this is the lack of time. To expect your team to make a change or complete a

project without giving them time to do so is unrealistic and they will fail.

Individual management coaching and mentoring

Coaching and mentoring are becoming important parts of staff development in the support of healthcare staff and it is useful here to define the two terms.

A coach is somebody who, while not having direct experience of a client's formal occupational role, has knowledge and understanding of processes within the workplace which they can use to help the staff member to make the changes they desire. A mentor, on the other hand, is somebody with direct knowledge about the person's role and can work with them to give them the benefit of their own experience.

Barriers to this type of working include not investing in staff to undertake these roles. The mentor system works well when staff are trained and time is invested in their development. With well-trained mentors, work in the area flourishes and staff are supported. As a manager, you do not have time to take on this role, so you need to delegate it to staff by identifying those who have potential and wish to train in these roles and then investing time and finance into the training.

Evidence opportunity

1.3 Barriers between leadership and management theory and their application

Provide a written account analysing barriers to applying leadership and management theory in respect of the topics we have discussed in this section. Look at strategies that could be used to address these barriers.

AC 1.4 How different leadership styles can impact on working culture and delivery of service

Here, you will be required to evaluate different leadership styles and their impact on working culture and service delivery, including the topics we cover in this section.

We addressed different leadership styles in AC 1.1 of this unit and it would be a good idea to recap these now.

Inclusive vs exclusive

Inclusive versus exclusive approaches to leadership and management refer to the way in which recruitment to the workforce is managed. You may have come across the term 'talent management', which is about finding the right person for the job by employing individuals who are considered to be particularly valuable to an organisation because of the qualities they possess.

(www.cipd.co.uk/knowledge/strategy/resourcing/talent-factsheet)

Some organisations approach their workforce planning inclusively by investing in the current staff they have and developing them according to the specific needs of the organisation. In this way the 'whole workforce' is developed. In this approach, there is an acknowledgement that talent exists at all levels of the organisation and the focus is on developing existing staff to the needs of the company or setting. This type of approach is very motivating as staff feel valued and this will impact upon morale.

An exclusive approach is the recruitment to the workforce of staff from outside the organisation with specific skills and knowledge according to the needs of the organisation at the time.

Open vs closed

A manager who adopts an open style seeks to develop relationships of trust with their staff which are based upon mutual respect. This will have a positive impact upon the workforce since there will be more trust. A disadvantage is that on some occasions there is a need for a more direct approach to get a job done.

A closed style of management is more directive and autocratic. While this is necessary when, for example, somebody has to take the lead in an emergency situation, in everyday management this may have a negative impact upon staff morale.

Positive vs negative

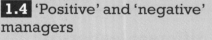

Reflect on it

1.4 'Positive' and 'negative' managers

What do you think would be the difference between a positive manager and a negative one?

A positive manager will take time to support the team and help them to achieve the goals of the organisation. They will be upbeat and highlight strengths and the things that the team is doing well rather than focus on the things that have gone badly. Adopting a positive style will motivate people and they will be inspired to do their best.

A negative manager will focus on failures rather than the achievements of the team and may resort to punishment when the goals are not met. Under a negative regime your team are likely to feel demoralised, where staff are not inspired to or may not feel supported to do their best.

Democratic, paternalistic, affiliative, laissez faire, commanding and visionary approaches to management

Democratic: staff are able to participate in the decision-making process. The democratic manager is open and allows everyone to put forward ideas and discuss options. While this has its advantages, without some control on the part of the manager it can be chaotic and sometimes a consensus is never reached. It may also be time consuming.

Paternalistic: a more controlling type of leadership in which a fatherly approach is adopted to control and protect staff. Staff are expected to be loyal to the manager and will obediently follow orders. The disadvantage lies in its assumption that the leader knows best and will make decisions on behalf of the workers. At best this might be seen as patronising to some, at worst it can be damaging if the leader has strong opinions and a tendency to have dictatorial ideas.

Affiliative: put forward by Daniel Goleman as one of his six leadership styles. This leader wants teams to feel connected and work in harmony. Praise ensures that the team is cohesive. A disadvantage is that there may be a tendency to ignore poor performance, preferring to keep upbeat and positive.

Laissez faire: the leader allows the staff to have free rein and lets them make their own decisions while the manager takes a back seat.

Commanding: this is the opposite of laissez faire and takes control, giving clear directions. It is useful in crisis situations where clear thinking and direction are needed.

Visionary: these leaders enable people to move towards a shared vision, motivating them but not necessarily telling them how to reach that vision. They adopt an open style, sharing information and power.

Evidence opportunity

1.4 How different leadership styles can impact on working culture and service delivery

Provide a written account evaluating different leadership styles and their impact on working culture and service delivery.

You may wish to determine when you might use certain types of leadership. In what situations might you change your leadership/management style? Give examples.

When evaluating, make sure that you give two sides to your argument. Look for example at the advantages and the disadvantages of an approach and then say when it might be a useful approach to use or not.

LO2 Understand the importance of leadership and management in adult care settings

AC 2.1 Impacts of policy drivers on leadership and management in adult care services

You will be required to evaluate current national and local **policy drivers** *and how these impact on your leadership and management role, including the ones we discuss in this section.*

National and local policy drives the way in which healthcare is delivered and managed in this country. In this section, we shall look at some of the current initiatives which you need to be aware of in your leadership and managerial role.

KEY TERM

Policy drivers are documents, research, acts of parliament and information that can lead to change in practice and drive forward new types of treatment and procedures.

Health and Social Care Act Regulations 2014 and fit and proper persons

The Health and Social Care Act 2008 (Regulated Activities) Regulations 2014 were introduced following the Francis Report into care at Mid Staffordshire NHS Foundation Trust (Francis, 2013) and established new fundamental standards for care. Should care not reach those standards, provision is made within the guidelines to take enforcement action.

As a result of this Report, there have been changes to the way in which adult social services are led and managed. New practices are being introduced all the time and change to the way in which care is delivered and monitored is part of this. In part 5 of the regulations, Section 1 introduces requirements relating to persons carrying out or managing a regulated activity and these are termed the fit and proper person requirements for directors and determine that directors of care are of 'good character' and 'have the qualifications, competence, skills and experience necessary for the relevant position' (DoH, 2014).

The Equality Act

The Equality Act 2010 brought together four major EU Equal Treatment Directives and replaced previous anti-discrimination laws, simplifying the law and making it easier to understand. It is an umbrella act bringing together legislation that deals with race, disability and gender.

It highlighted protected characteristics of age, gender reassignment, pregnancy, religion, marriage and civil partnerships, and sexual orientation in an attempt to end discrimination. Additionally, it strengthened protection by setting out the different ways in which unlawful treatment may occur. Individuals are now fully protected from discrimination in the workplace and in wider society.

Additionally, it clearly identifies that if a health or social care organisation provides goods, facilities, services or functions to the public then it must make sure that it does so within the requirements of the law. The Act brings together a number of individual pieces of legislation into one law in order to make the law on equality, diversity and discrimination much clearer and simpler.

The Equality Act 2010 applies to any organisation that provides goods, facilities or services to the public, or to a section of the public. The act applies to private, statutory and voluntary organisations, no matter what the size. Equality law affects everyone running an organisation as well as applying to the staff and volunteers who might do something on behalf of the organisation.

The impact of this act has been to enable protected groups to gain employment and to not be discriminated against. There has also been a positive move to address the gender pay gap and equal pay and fair pay for all are also being addressed.

The Care Act 2014

The Care Act 2014 sets out the key responsibilities of local authorities in meeting the needs of individuals who require help and support to promote their wellbeing. The main aim was to provide integrated care and to introduce the right to an assessment for anyone in order to offer more control in their care and to help people to stay as independent as possible. www.legislation.gov.uk/ukpga/2014/23/contents/enacted/data.htm

The impact of these acts of parliament in the adult care sector has led to change to the way in which care is delivered and paid for, and will also impact upon the way in which care is managed and led. Leadership and management have to change to meet new needs in the care sector. For example, the changes to the way in which the Care Quality Commission will inspect your service will drive forward change to your policies and the way in which staff deliver their care.

CQC Key Lines of Enquiry

The Care Quality Commission's Key Lines of Enquiry (KLOEs) were introduced in 2013 and highlight how healthcare providers will be inspected and judged against five key questions:

● Are they safe?
● Are they effective?

- Are they caring?
- Are they responsive to people's needs?
- Are they well led?

The KLOEs direct the focus of inspection so as to make sure that there is a consistent and standardised approach to inspection. The impact has been to ensure that all inspections of health premises are carried out fairly and consistently. For managers, it means that there is a more transparent approach to inspection as the five key questions provide clear and concise guidelines as to what is being looked at.

Research it

2.1 Policies and your setting

Look at the CQC document, A new start: Consultation on changes to the way CQC regulates, inspects and monitors care (2013), to identify how this might change the way in which your provision is inspected.

Fit and proper person

As mentioned on page 17, the fit and proper person, as detailed in regulation 5 of the Health and Social Care Act 2008 (Regulated Activities) Regulations 2014, applies to people employed in management roles in the care setting satisfying requirements that they:

- are of good character
- have the qualifications, competence, skills and experience that are necessary for the position
- can perform the function and tasks for which they are employed
- are not responsible for any serious misconduct or mismanagement.

The Care Certificate

Any new care worker must be trained and inducted into the role. The Care Certificate was developed by Skills for Care, Health Education England and Skills for Health and provides a set of standards that social care and health workers should cover as part of their training. It links to National Occupational Standards and units in other former qualifications such as NVQs and diplomas for new staff as well as those who want to undertake training yet may have been in post for some time. It covers various areas about what care actually is and gives workers a good basis from which they can develop their knowledge and skills.

As a manager you must be aware of what is on offer for your staff and be clear about what you will require them to do to access training. This is likely to impact upon your training budget as you put people through new qualifications.

Evidence opportunity

2.1 How policies impact leadership and management

Provide a written account evaluating the current national and local policy drivers and how these impact on the leadership and management role, including the ones we have covered in this section.

You may need to do some research around the current national and local policy drivers.

Research it

2.1 Policies and your setting

1 Download the Care Quality Commission's standards and say how your organisation is meeting this particular requirement for staff.
2 How have the policies shown above affected your role as a manager and leader?

Think in terms of the positive and negative impact upon your setting of these policies. Show the arguments for and against the changes and how they have impacted in your own setting.

AC 2.2 Reasons managers in adult care settings need both leadership and management skills

Here, you will be required to explain why it is important for managers in adult care to have both leadership and management skills.

Is there a difference between a leader and a manager? As we have already seen (page 9), many writers have debated this concept. Fayol, in 1916, identified the functions of a manager as being planning, organising, staffing and controlling. Kotter (1990), on the other hand, believed leadership to have a more far-reaching effect, being a role that sought change and movement. Clearly though there is a need for both and ideally a manager should possess leadership qualities as well as managerial qualities.

As a manager you will be expected to coordinate the staff to ensure they carry out their tasks well and deal with any underperformance if it happens. You will ensure that the daily routines are carried out and the service functions well and delivers its strategic plan.

However, as a leader you will ensure that in the course of their work the staff are taken care of. Leaders inspire others to want to do their best and you can do this by ensuring that you always follow through on any promise you have made and assume responsibility for the team. If, as the manager, you are good at inspiring your team then you are also coming close to being a good leader.

There is much more information about the difference between management and leadership in AC 1.3 (page 12).

in AC 1.3 (page 12)

Evidence opportunity

2.2 **Reasons managers in adult care settings need both leadership and management skills**

Explain to your assessor why it is important for managers in adult care to have both leadership and management skills. Or you could provide a written account.

Reflect on it

2.2 **Leadership and management skills**

Look at the table below and evaluate your own job description against it. Are you a leader or a manager and how might you change to adapt to both roles? Reflect on the reasons why.

Leaders	Managers
Have ideas	Move people to develop those ideas
Inspire people	Coordinate people
Create opportunity	React to situations
Create vision	Provide resources to achieve the vision
Have followers	Show people the way

AC 2.3 Interactions between leadership and the values/culture of an organisation

In this section, you will be required to analyse both internal and external factors that impact your leadership and management role and related interactions considering the topics we discuss in this section.

Organisational culture and values

The term 'culture' is a complex one but refers to the rules, norms, values or beliefs that are shared by a group. In the context of an organisation then, culture is about the professional values and beliefs shared by that group. As a manager, one of your roles is to ensure that staff have clarity about what is expected of them with respect to the values of the organisation.

An effective organisation works towards the same goals and the members will cooperate with the decisions made. When properly managed and developed, team work improves processes and produces results quickly and economically through the free exchange of ideas and information.

Your personal values and those of others

A positive culture is when team members all work towards the same goals and vision of the organisation. They must have a clear understanding of their own responsibility within the workplace and be able to reflect upon the practice in order to monitor their performance. Your management style will impact upon how well the team are able to work together to meet the aims and objectives of the organisation.

Effective teamwork requires all team members to relate well to each other and as a manager you need to recognise the similarities as well as the differences in the individuals who make up your team. Your challenge is to respect those differences in personality and to work with them to ensure the team members do not clash or that the team does not become dysfunctional.

Team work also requires a good knowledge of the individuals who make up your team and the roles they play. Team work is not about getting people together and dictating your orders but rather about developing a commitment to the goals by establishing trust and cohesion and recognising everyone's efforts and work.

Openness and transparency with others and inclusion of staff and others

The organisation which promotes openness and creativity, encouraging the team members to share information, to innovate and take calculated risks, will provide a positive climate in which to work and will enable staff to feel included in decision making. By ensuring that all your staff are included in making decisions, you will help them to feel valued and respected. One of your roles as a manager will also be to include those who work as your partners and families and friends of your clients in moving the organisation forward in a positive way. By encouraging open discussion and ideas, a more transparent and open culture will develop.

Managing conflicting values and addressing difficulties

There are two types of conflicts:

- those which revolve around the disagreements in relation to approaches to work
- those which may arise between individuals, stemming from differences in personal values and beliefs.

Badly managed conflict leads to ineffective team work. People start to avoid each other and rifts develop. This inevitably leads to ineffectual or weak care of service users, clients and patients.

LaFasto and Larson (2001) suggest an effective way of solving this sort of conflict in Unit 504 AC 3.4, with their CONECT model, and it would be useful for you to look at this to achieve this outcome.

Thompson's (2006) RED approach to managing conflict is for situations with a high degree of tension associated with them.

See pages 14–15 for more about resolving conflicts. This is also covered in Unit 504 AC 3.4 and you should refer to these models now.

Reflect on it

2.3 Conflict and your managerial role

Show how the points above have impacted your work as a manager and leader and give examples.

How have you dealt with conflict within the work setting which may have arisen as a result of differing personal and organisational values?

Positive engagement of colleagues and those receiving care and support

Supervision of staff has been introduced into practice to provide professional support and learning to enable them to develop knowledge, skills and competence in their work and additionally to safeguard those receiving care. It is during these sessions that you as a manager can promote the values of the organisation and this in turn will enhance the experience of the service user and improves quality and safety in the care setting.

Reflect on it

2.3 Supporting staff

As a manager, how do you undertake this responsibility of providing professional supervision for staff to ensure they are supported in their roles and to enhance their skills and performance?

Giving and receiving positive and negative feedback

Feedback is an open two-way communication between two or more parties. Feedback to staff should be regular and is a daily part of your work as a manager. In formal feedback sessions, the best way to approach this task is to first ask the member of staff how they perceived their performance of a task. By linking the feedback to their

professional development, the person will be able to focus more on what they need to change. You can see what they understand about how well they are doing their job and you are also encouraging them to be reflective about their performance.

Sometimes positive feedback is not given, yet genuine positive feedback is motivating for staff. Thanking somebody at the end of the day for a job well done or acknowledging a person's work during a shift builds respect and ensures that the member of staff is secure in their work.

How, though, do we approach giving bad news with respect to their role or performance? We cannot go through life without making any mistakes and without requiring some guidance on aspects of our work, and although the content of feedback may be negative, it can always be given in a constructive and encouraging manner. You can help the member of staff to solve a problem, or to address a part of their behaviour and work towards organisational goals so they develop, grow and improve.

So how do you go about giving constructive feedback? You may have heard of the 'feedback sandwich'. This is a three-step procedure to help provide constructive feedback, consisting of praise, followed by the problem area or criticism, followed by more praise. In this way, the unpalatable news is sandwiched by good news and the blow of receiving it is softened.

Although it has come in for criticism (ironically) from some writers, it is a good way for new managers and supervisors to help to deliver news that may otherwise be seen as negative.

▲ **Figure 1.5** The praise sandwich

Level of experience in management role and related responsibilities

The transition from employee to manager is a challenge because now you are the one in charge and being looked to for advice and guidance. Ultimately, you are responsible for how the team is working.

The following points might help:

● First, you need to establish your style and authority by ensuring you understand your own values and priorities in the role. For example, if communication and trust are important to you then you need to ensure that staff are aware of this and you stick to these values at all times.

- Be a good listener. By listening to others, you learn about them.
- Recognise that change happens slowly and affects staff morale.
- Attribute success to the team and not just to you.

Evidence opportunity

2.3 Interactions between leadership and the values/culture of an organisation

Internal and external factors impact leadership and management roles. Provide a written account analysing both internal and external factors that impact your leadership and management role and related interactions and consider the topics we have covered in this section.

You may wish to use some of the headings in this section and identify how you intend to minimise the impact of these on your own role and your interactions. For example, say how you would develop a new manager or how you would ensure that you are able to give positive or negative feedback.

AC 2.4 Systems that establish a culture of continual learning and development in the care setting

Here, you will be required to evaluate the importance of learning and development in your care setting, to include the topics we cover here.

Manager induction standards

In previous sections, we talked about the induction standards for staff and the Care Certificate. Standards are a tool to develop a consistent approach to care and as such ensure that those who work in the care sector meet a high level of quality in their work.

The Skills for Care website (www.skillsforcare.org.uk) is a useful resource for checking the standards and for guidance on how they must be met. It is on this website that you will find the Manager Induction Standards (MIS) which identify what a manager needs to know and understand to perform well in their role. Updated in 2016, they link to the Care Certificate and the Leadership Qualities Framework.

Building on the old version of the Manager Induction Standards (from 2012), the standards are:

1 Leadership and management
2 Governance and regulatory processes
3 Communication
4 Relationships and partnership working

5 Person-centred practice for positive outcomes
6 Professional development, supervision and performance management
7 Resources
8 Safeguarding, protection and risk
9 Manage self (new standard)
10 Decision making (new standard)
11 Entrepreneurial skills and innovation (new standard) (www.skillsforcare.org.uk)

In your own setting you need to look at how effective the learning and development strategy is and what can be improved. Evaluating this strategy by looking at the strengths and weaknesses of how you engage with developing your own skills as a leader and manager will strengthen the culture of learning in your setting and set a good example to staff.

By undertaking to engage with this training, you will be enhancing your own learning but also setting excellent examples for your staff. Your care setting will benefit as you bring new ideas into practice.

Research it

2.4 Management Induction Standards

Go to the following link and check the new standards: www.skillsforcare.org.uk/Standards-legislation/Manager-Induction-Standards/Manager-Induction-Standards.aspx

Remember if the link no longer works, then try searching for the Management Induction Standards in your browser.

Reflection and reflective practice

Reflective practice is an essential element of personal development and continual learning. It provides an opportunity to stop and take stock. Bolton (2010, p. 4) identifies a number of applications for reflective practice. Reflective practice enables you to:

- identify what you know but do not know that you know
- identify what you want to know but do not know
- reflect on what you think, feel, believe, value
- examine how well actions match up to beliefs
- reflect on barriers to practising the way that you would wish to practise
- think about what you should/can change in your work context and how this could be achieved
- learn how to value others' perspectives even when they differ from your own
- examine your personal behaviours and responses and seek ways to make these more productive (Tilmouth and Quallington, 2016).

Your role as a manager

As a manager, teaching and encouraging staff to be self-reflecting is very important. However, reflection need not relate just to isolated and specific incidents. Reflection in action can be a powerful tool. It can be used to improve practice by supporting individuals to question their routine work as they carry it out. They may measure their behaviour against their values and the values of the organisation to ensure that these are consistent. Or they may try a new approach to an activity and evaluate its success. Encouraging staff to become self-governing and to take responsibility for their work standards is an important element of a successful learning organisation. Reflective practice provides an opportunity for all practitioners to check their own standards of work and enhance practice (Tilmouth and Quallington, 2016).

Continuing training and development for themselves and others

See Unit 506, AC 1.1 for information on the importance of continually improving your own knowledge and practice and that of the team.

Evidence opportunity

2.4 Systems that establish a culture of continual learning and development

The Manager Induction Standards, reflection and reflective practice and continuing training and development are all systems that establish a culture of continual learning and development in the care setting. Prepare a PowerPoint presentation for staff evaluating the importance of learning and development in your care setting, including the areas we have discussed in this section.

You may wish to show how you address the Manager Induction Standards, reflection and reflective practice, and continuing training and development for yourself and others in your workplace.

Reflect on it

2.4 Importance of learning and development

Write a reflective account about the importance of the Manager Induction Standards, reflection and reflective practice, and continuing training and development for maintaining professional quality. Look at something you have learned and how it has changed your practice. Show why we need to develop and undertake continual learning in our roles as care professionals.

AC 2.5 Methods of creating an atmosphere which inspires a culture that is open, positive and inclusive

Here, you will be required to evaluate communication strategies for creating an open atmosphere, including the ones we discuss here.

Duty of Candour – openness and honesty

The Duty of Candour refers to the practice of being honest with patients, employers and colleagues when things go wrong and is part of the GMC (General Medical Council) and NMC (Nursing and Midwifery Council) Codes of Practice.

Regulation 20 of the Health and Social Care Act 2008 (Regulated Activities) Regulations 2014 ensures that care providers are open and transparent with people who use the services and other 'relevant persons' who may be acting for the person in care. Specific requirements that providers must follow when things go wrong with care and treatment include informing people about the incident, and providing reasonable support, truthful information together with an apology when things go wrong.

Creating an atmosphere of open communication enables workers to feel able to trust the system and ensures that processes for honest and transparent communication are in place. The team should feel able to share any concerns or ideas they have and should have clear indications about what you expect their behaviour should be.

Whistle blowing

Whistle blowing means making a disclosure or revealing information that is in the public interest if we see or hear anything that might cause harm to a patient or another person in our care. For example, we are legally and morally obliged to report any poor practice or abuse we witness.

This can be daunting for employees who have to continue to work in an organisation in which an investigation, suspension or prosecution occurs as a result of the challenge. While the expectation is that individuals should raise challenges and concerns, it is imperative that they can do this in a supportive and protective environment. It should be possible to deal with most challenges inside the organisation, which should, with appropriate guidance, allow you to resolve the situation or support sanctions. However, there are occasions when a practice is so widespread and resistant to change, or of such a serious nature, that a more radical approach is required. In such circumstances, staff who witness such activities will be protected by law for making this public. However, this does not mean that the individual has a right to go to the press or other public forum to expose an organisation without trying to resolve issues internally first.

The policies and systems discussed apply to staff as well as service users.

A whistle blower is protected by law for disclosure if they:

- are a 'worker'
- believe that malpractice in the workplace is happening, has happened in the past or will happen in the future
- are revealing information of the right type (a 'qualifying disclosure'), which refers to information that the worker believes is a criminal offence, a miscarriage of justice or failure to comply with a legal obligation. This may have taken place in the past, or may happen in the future
- reveal it to the right person and in the right way (making it a 'protected disclosure'). This is where workers bring information about a wrongdoing to the attention of their employers or a relevant organisation, and in doing so they are protected in certain circumstances under the Public Interest Disclosure Act 1998.

See Unit 205 AC 4.2 for further details.

If a worker feels unable to make a disclosure to their employer, there are other 'prescribed people' to whom a disclosure can be made. Disclosure can be made to the person responsible for the area of concern such as a team leader or mentor.

To make a protected disclosure to 'others' rather than the employer, the whistle blower must:

1 Reasonably believe their employer would treat them unfairly if the disclosure was made to the employer or a prescribed person.
2 Reasonably believe that the disclosure to the employer would result in the destruction or concealment of information about the wrongdoing.
3 Have previously disclosed the same or similar information to the employer or a prescribed person (Tilmouth and Quallington, 2016).

Concerns and complaints procedures

A reflective, learning organisation tries to identify issues before they become grievances or complaints. Consequently, a well-publicised and confidential opportunity to access advice, support and counselling should be a feature of how organisations engage with concerns and complaints. When a complaint is made or a concern is raised it is useful to provide time to talk through the issue. Being believed and supported is sometimes enough to enable the individual to draw on their own reserves and tackle the issue directly or change the situation indirectly. This level of support must be independent of line management, which involves a different level of formality and responsibility, and independent of anyone who may subsequently be asked to investigate an issue if it is escalated. It must also utilise individuals who can be relied on to be impartial to provide

information about available options but not to make decisions on behalf of the complainant. Confidentiality is essential. The decision whether or not to progress a complaint should normally rest with the individual; however, managers may need to do so on behalf of another when the complainant is in a subordinate role.

Constructive criticism

Giving **constructive criticism** when an individual is not performing well in a role is probably one of the hardest jobs of the manager and one which may be done badly. Being too negative can destroy trust and a previously good working relationship, so the issue must be handled with sensitivity. You need to support your claims or criticism with facts and examples and then say what you would want in the future and why. It is also helpful to give the person target dates for completion of a task so that the person has something to work towards.

> ### KEY TERM
>
> **Constructive criticism** is offering positive and negative comments about another person's work in a friendly rather than a confrontational way. In doing so, we want to improve the outcome so well-reasoned and valid facts are given to help the person to change.

> ### Case study
>
> #### 2.5 Constructive criticism
>
> Jacob is Steve's manager. He has noticed that Steve, a care worker who is supervising other staff, is struggling with the new induction course for staff and has been unable to complete his work. Some of the staff have not been trained and are now working without any guidance and this is causing a rift in the team.
>
> How might you handle this?
>
> Jacob might simply inform Steve that staff are unhappy and that he needs to sort it out as soon as possible. A constructive way of dealing with it would be if Jacob approached Steve as follows:
>
> 'How are things with the new staff inductions? I note that there have been some difficulties with some of the staff and they are a little lost currently. How might we improve things for them do you think? Is there anything I might do to help move this along?'

Commitment to equal opportunities

See Unit 505, LO4 for more information on this before you read this section here.

As a manager you have a key role in ensuring that equality of opportunity is promoted as a key organisational value and that the law is complied with. Public sector organisations and other organisations that carry out public functions, such as in the health and social care sector, must consider how they will eliminate conduct that is prohibited under the Equality Act.

The Equality Act (2010) provides for the protection of people and their characteristics, with specific protections for:

● age
● disability
● gender reassignment
● pregnancy and maternity/paternity
● race
● religion or belief
● sex/gender
● sexual orientation.

Promoting, implementing and monitoring good equality practices will reduce the likelihood of unlawful discrimination and legal challenge. We want to create a workplace in which there is open communication and a positive culture for all who set foot into the setting.

Evidence opportunity

2.5 Methods of creating an open, positive and inclusive culture

Provide a written account evaluating communication strategies for creating an open atmosphere, including the topics we have covered in this section.

Reflect on it

2.5 Open, positive and inclusive culture

For each of the headings shown below, provide evidence in your portfolio of how your organisation creates an atmosphere which inspires an open, positive and inclusive culture. What communication strategies do you use?

● Duty of Candour – openness and honesty
● Whistle blowing
● Concerns and complaints procedures
● Constructive criticism
● Commitment to equal opportunities.

Say what the positives and negatives of each one are. For example, what are the strengths of your whistle-blowing policy? What might the weaknesses be?

How do you feed back constructive criticism to staff? What effect does this have on them?

AC 2.6 Methods of promoting a service which encourages innovation and creativity in a positive and realistic manner

You will be required to explain methods of promoting a service, including the topics we discuss here.

To create innovation and creativity in the workplace, all individuals who have a connection with that organisation should be encouraged to engage in exploring new ways to develop and change the way in which it works.

There are a number of ways in which the internal systems might help this.

Here you will be required to explain methods of promoting a service which encourages innovation and creativity in a positive and realistic manner.

Feedback and suggestions procedures

Feedback comes by way of complaints and compliments, and these provide a good indication of the areas of practice that are working well or badly. In a climate in which people feel able to complain without fear of recrimination, this is a useful way to check practice and to act upon the areas that require some work.

You need to be aware that a low number of complaints does not necessarily mean that there are no issues. It may be that individuals feel unable to comment for fear of being victimised and this in itself needs investigation. We often get commended for the way in which staff have carried out their work and this needs to be rewarded in some way. A compliments system where service users and visitors can leave a small note to compliment a member of staff may be a useful way in which staff can be recognised for their work. Some organisations have a 'staff member of the month' scheme and this is a nice way to recognise good work. This can lead to creative ways by which staff might be praised for their work and innovative schemes to reward their positive work.

'Community' involvement – both internal and external and community impact and related communications to others

Additionally, people in the community may wish to become involved in the workings of organisations. The NHS, for example, has community involvement through Clinical Commissioning Groups, inviting members of the public to be part of these groups and enabling them to be at the forefront of what happens in their NHS. For smaller organisations, the use of focus groups comprised of service users and relatives or other interested parties may also be a useful way of maintaining quality within a service and promoting change.

Focus groups can be set up to look at areas of practice and to give feedback on procedures or systems. These may be made up of staff, service users and even visitors or family, and are a way of gathering opinions in an open environment. These sorts of meetings are useful for gathering information that is crucial for the running of your setting and as such should be well conducted, with members of the group being clear about what they are being asked to do in a climate that is positive and welcoming. It is important to keep the members informed of the outcomes of the meeting.

The impact of such groups and meetings is that the community is informed about what is happening within the care systems and is a part of the decision-making process.

Creativity is about new ideas and exploring these. It is about having an original or unusual thought or idea. Innovation, though, is the act of getting that idea implemented and used. Your staff may have good ideas but will not verbalise them because they cannot see how the idea might work. Others, however, may not be quite so creative but may be innovators who are able to able to put into practice the idea. As a manager you will want to build a team culture of positive responses to creative ideas and innovative ways of moving these forward.

Evidence opportunity

2.6 Methods of promoting a service that encourages innovation and creativity

Explain to your assessor the methods you use to promote a service that encourages innovation and creativity in a positive and realistic manner and consider the topics we have covered in this section. Or you could provide a written account.

Reflect on it

2.6 Encouraging innovation and creativity

How is your own service promoted in ways that encourage innovation and creativity? Provide evidence for your portfolio.

LO3 Lead commitment to a vision for the service

AC 3.1 Communicate forward thinking vision and strategy confidently to inspire and engage others

Here, you will be required to communicate forward thinking vision and strategy with consideration of your own strengths in motivational thinking/speaking, in management and staff meetings, meetings with those in receipt of care, their carers and relevant others, and at internal and external activities/events.

> *'If I really want to improve my situation, I can work on the one thing over which I have control – myself.'*
>
> **Source:** Covey, 2004

In order to engage others, we must be able to communicate the way forward for them and to be a force for change ourselves. A lot of the time this requires us to work first on ourselves. We need to develop a sense of self and an awareness of how we conduct ourselves and respond to others. For example, we need to know what our strengths and weaknesses are and have a fair understanding about our own beliefs, attitudes and emotions. By having this level of self-awareness we can start to understand other people.

In this section, you will be expected to know how to communicate forward thinking vision and strategy confidently and engagingly, and inspire others to follow and consider the things that we discuss below.

Own strengths in motivational thinking/speaking

Leading a group requires the ability to motivate them. Where do we start?

Think back to some of the leadership models we looked at in the first section and in particular Maslow. His theory demanded that certain needs are met before somebody may be able to undertake a task. For example, if someone is hungry they may not be in the best place to undertake a task you want them to. So send them for lunch first! This is a simple way of making a difference to somebody, but what else might you need to do to motivate them further?

Reflect on it

3.1 What motivates you?

1 List the things that enhance your job for you and give some examples about what makes you want to do them.

You may have put down things like being treated with kindness and fairness, and being listened to. Being praised is also highly motivating. Showing an interest in your staff and encouraging them by giving them additional responsibility is also a way to motivate people.

2 What strengths do you have in motivational thinking/speaking, and how do you inspire others to follow?

Evidence opportunity

3.1 Communicating forward thinking vision and strategy

Communicate (to your assessor) forward thinking vision and strategy with consideration of the topics we have discussed in this section.

You could also prepare a presentation to staff to inform them of a change of practice. Pay close attention to how you will deliver the new initiative and how you will motivate them to accept the change.

Write an evaluative account of how your presentation was received.

When staff are being requested to buy into something new, communication and transparency of purpose are crucial to success.

Team meetings with agendas giving team members opportunities to contribute should be set up and other forms of communication such as email or using a mobile phone may also be useful to communicate care changes or other practice enquiries. Team meetings are a good vehicle to communicate how the organisation is moving forward towards its vision.

Suggestions from staff should be encouraged and considered.

You also need to ensure that the people in your care and their families are well informed about how the organisation is striving to meet their needs. Meetings will be an opportunity to communicate this.

In management and staff meetings and meetings with those in receipt of care, carers and relevant others

In communicating an organizational vision to your team and those in receipt of care, you need firstly to target your message to your audience and inform the staff as to what they are working towards. Talking to staff about where the organization is heading helps to create a shared vision and purpose.

Internal and external activities/events

Many teams and organisations arrange events to keep people informed of what is happening and link these in with awards evenings and socials. This can really help workers to feel part of a bigger organisation and feel that any contribution they make is valued and respected.

Being confident and engaging others

As a manager you need to be confident about the work of your organisation and its vision in order to be able to inspire

others. This requires you to have a good understanding about the strategies of the organisation and how it intends to move forward.

AC 3.2 Engage with internal and external stakeholders to create awareness of forward thinking

Here, you will be required to evidence that all stakeholders are aware of service expectations, using appropriate communication strategies, such as individual meetings, group meetings and marketing/digital methods.

Individual meetings

Stakeholders need to engage with the work of the setting to be fully informed of the vision and the way forward with respect to the service. They have an interest and an investment in the business and as such require to be fully aware of ways in which the service is developing.

Stakeholders

Your organisation is a part of a much wider community and groups of professionals and you will be liaising with and calling on the services of those who work in social work, community nursing staff, infection control teams, the justice system and education staff. You may also come into contact with carers, service users and their significant others.

Meetings and marketing/digital

Your communication with groups may be via individual meetings in which you liaise with and meet with one person from a group or it may be in the form of regular group meetings.

Additionally, there may be shared marketing and other ways in which you communicate. You need to ensure that stakeholders are made aware of how the organisation is moving forward and what the expectations for the service are. The digital age has meant we have at our disposal many ways in which we can now link with other groups which may be at a distance. Skype, FaceTime, conference calls and computer links are all valuable digital methods by which we can link with stakeholders.

Evidence opportunity

3.2 Engage with internal and external stakeholders to create awareness of vision

Provide evidence for your assessor and portfolio that all stakeholders (internal and external) are aware of service expectations, using appropriate communication strategies such as the ones we have discussed in this section.

Reflect on it

3.2 Creating awareness of forward thinking

1 Construct a spider diagram which shows the internal and external stakeholders you work with.

2 Write an account of how you engage with internal and external stakeholders to create awareness of forward thinking.

AC 3.3 Create service development plans to support the vision ensuring it is both shared and owned by those implementing and communicating the vision

Here, you will be required to create service development plans, including management meetings, staff supervision, strategic planning, and research and development activities.

Service development planning is concerned with change and the way in which individuals in the service and the stakeholders external to it are involved in this is crucial to its successful implementation.

A service development plan includes an analysis of the health needs of a population and identifies how these needs can be met using the resources available.

Your own service development plan will feed into a much larger document but may just be about your own setting. For example, you will be asked to develop a plan of how

your service will meet the objectives of the organisation as a whole and this will then be linked into the wider organisation plan and ultimately into the plans of the Health and Wellbeing Board (HWB).

Management meetings and staff supervision

Planning inevitably involves a cycle of events and it is crucial that staff are kept aware of change through meetings and supervision sessions.

The first step in any process for planning is to assess the current situation and then to demonstrate the reasons as to why a change is needed. Staff need to be sure that the decision to change is necessary to support the organisation in moving forward. Your service development plan will be useful here to communicate the vision of the service both in term of your own setting and how partners and stakeholders fit into that vision.

Strategic planning

Strategic planning will sometimes involve changes to job roles, processes, policy changes and structural re-organisation. Staff therefore must be aware of the impact this is likely to have on them.

Priorities need to be set and then objectives and targets developed.

Research and development

This may be an opportunity for staff to be involved in research and development activities such as surveys or fact-finding projects to identify how change will be effective or how it might impact upon current work.

Once more evidence, such as data which has been gathered, is forthcoming, budgets can be assessed and a programme of how the change will be implemented and monitored can be drawn up. The final stage will be to evaluate how well the change has embedded into the organisation.

The service development plan is likely to include evidence you have collected from various aspects of your work. For example, there may be data collected from staff surveys and service user surveys that may be used to argue for more resources in certain areas. Staff may have undertaken research in the form of projects or literature reviews which again may support requests for changes to practice or simply show how the service is working to move the wider organisation forward.

Evidence opportunity

3.3 Create service development plans to support the vision

Show your assessor service development plans you have created including the ones we have discussed in this section. How do you ensure they support the vision and that it is both shared and owned by those implementing and communicating the vision, such as your staff?

You could also obtain a copy of the organisation's strategic plan/service development plan and show how you have used staff meetings, supervision, strategic planning and research and development to implement and communicate the vision within the plan to staff. You might look at how you as a team have addressed some of the strategies in the plan through the conduct of staff meetings or training. For example, one of the national objectives has been to reduce infection and to improve cleanliness in healthcare settings. What evidence can you provide that your service plan has addressed this?

AC 3.4 Implement strategies for involving stakeholders and others in decisions about service delivery

In this section, you will be required to implement strategies for involving stakeholders and others in decisions about service delivery, including the ones we discuss in this section. Decisions may include positive change management, and the future vision for the service (this is a way in which organisations are helped to thrive through change).

KEY TERM

Partnership working is the use of inclusive and mutually beneficial relationships in care work that improve the quality and experience of care.

When we talk about **partnership working** we are referring to the relationships between individuals with long-term care conditions, their carers, and service providers and care professionals. You should refer to Unit 504 for more information on relationships and partnership working.

Communication strategy – internal/external

See Unit 503, AC 1.4 for more information on partnership working and effective communication.

Stakeholders need to be part of the decision making about service delivery because they have a vested interest in how the service works. By effectively communicating with them we can ensure that they receive information that is relevant to their needs so that they can continue to support the service users.

Reflect on it

3.4 Communication systems

Think about the communication systems discussed and reflect on how they might be misused or how they might fail.

The types of communication systems the partnerships are likely to rely upon include:

- written records, such as email and letters
- electronic databases
- service users' personal notes
- daily records of care and nursing/medical notes.

We want to ensure that the service we offer improves the experience and outcomes of the people who use that service. This can only be done by minimising the barriers between different services and ensuring that the lines of communication are not blurred.

Community meetings – internal/external

One method of communicating is to involve stakeholders in community meetings. These may be a regular way of ensuring that all in the community are kept up to date with change, innovation and the way in which the organisation is moving forward.

Team/individual meetings

Regular staff meetings are also part of the communication strategy in care organisations.

Feedback processes and procedures in respect of service provision

We often engage in one-way communication; this means the way in which information is transferred from one person to another with little opportunity to give feedback to the sender. Sometimes we do this to transmit a fact, or to instruct somebody to do something. One-way communication is not effective and there need to be reciprocal methods by which individuals are able to give feedback about the process. Stakeholders and staff are entitled to personal, two-way communication, and face-to-face meetings are essential to progress being positive.

Positive change management and future vision for the service

By having a positive change management plan in place, everyone in your setting will have a vision of what the change looks like and how it will be reached. This means you can check how successful your project is at various stages, and it also means you can motivate your staff along the way.

Evidence opportunity

3.4 Strategies for involving stakeholders and others in decisions about service delivery

Develop a flow diagram to show how you would involve stakeholders and others in decisions about service delivery.

What strategies would you implement for involving the various stakeholders and others in decisions about service delivery? How would you use the strategies we have discussed in this section?

LO4 Provide leadership for a team in an adult care setting

AC 4.1 Adapt leadership and management styles to reflect different situations and stages in a care team's development

Here, you will be required to show that you can adopt relevant leadership and management styles.

In AC 1.1 and 1.2, we covered various theories and models of management and leadership. It would be useful for you to recap your learning from those ACs.

The leadership and management style you adopt can be changed according to the situation that presents itself or the individual you are dealing with. For example, some members of the team may require a more hands-on leadership style or one in which you are more authoritarian. In other situations, you may want to delegate tasks and leave the team to make their own decisions. Your ability to adapt and change will enhance the development of the team.

Evidence opportunity

4.1 Adapt leadership and management styles to reflect different situations and stages

Explain to your assessor and show them how you adopt relevant leadership and management styles. How do you adapt leadership and management styles to reflect different situations and stages in a care team's development?

Reflect on it

4.1 Your preferred style of leadership

Say which is your preferred style of leadership and management and provide an example for your portfolio.

AC 4.2 Develop trust and accountability within the team

Here, you will be required to show you can build positive relationships within the team(s) with consideration of the topics we discuss here.

Active listening skills

Developing trust in any relationship is about respect and being transparent and honest in what we are thinking and doing. We show ourselves to be trustworthy managers by being consistent and the sort of person who can be relied upon. Communication and listening are at the heart of this.

Think about it.

Think of a time when you know that you were not being listened to and heard.

- What was going on at that time?
- How did it affect the interaction?
- What do you think was going on for the person you were trying to communicate with at that time?

KEY TERM

Active listening is listening clearly and ensuring that you understand what the sender intends to communicate and the content of the message.

Active listening shows that our staff and service users have been heard and the way in which we do this is with the following skills:

- acknowledging and reflecting feelings
- body language
- restating
- paraphrasing
- summarising
- questioning.

Team cultures

In addition to improving the way we communicate, we can address the sort of culture we wish to develop in the team as this will have a powerful and pervasive influence over the behaviour and practices of the people within that team (Mullins, 2009).

The wider organisation in which you work is complicated and complex interactions occur between individuals. The complexity and interdependency of relationships support an environment in which conflicts of interest and power differentials can be abused if appropriate policies, practices and guards are not in place to counteract this. This will have an effect upon your team and its culture. The way in which you approach the leadership and management of the team will impact upon the way it works. Where this is a positive, value-based influence it can be invaluable to the manager in spreading good practice. As a manager, you might use your position to encourage your staff to adopt anti-discriminatory and non-judgemental attitudes in their work by challenging discrimination that may come to your notice.

Team values and values-based culture

Culture is developed and built by the values, beliefs and attitudes that people bring to it and these are often deeply ingrained and are acquired through learning and our upbringing. We are encouraged to believe that certain attitudes and behaviours are acceptable. It is only when these values, beliefs and attitudes are challenged, by either new information or different experiences, that they may be seen to be flawed. Even when individuals' views can be shown to be discriminatory, deeply held beliefs may be resistant to change and this is termed prejudice.

A prejudice is an attitude or belief that is based on a faulty and inflexible generalisation/belief which can lead to negative emotions and discriminatory actions. Prejudice does not necessarily cause someone to discriminate unfairly, but examining such beliefs and values and questioning them is a first step in recognising and tackling prejudice.

To eliminate prejudice requires us to redefine beliefs and attitudes in the light of new information and then to change our behaviour in the light of that information. Furthermore, we need to challenge others who articulate similar prejudices. None of this is easy to do, particularly the latter; however, challenging others can have a significant impact on breaking down discrimination and prejudice. Often prejudice is not only an individual issue but represents views that might be more widely held within a group or specific context. When a strong, widespread belief is apparent, challenging it is difficult and individuals who try to do so may fear ridicule, victimisation or reprisals if they stand up against the prevailing beliefs and practices. In an organisation or team, it is important that everyone is aware that prejudice and discriminatory practice cannot be tolerated. Individuals who become aware of such practice must be supported and protected to speak out and not to feel excluded because of it. Creating a culture of discussion and tolerance is important in developing an open-minded community and in preventing abusive practice.

The first step in supporting others to challenge discrimination and exclusion is to accept that they exist and to acknowledge that discrimination is a significant factor in inhibiting equality.

Prejudice can lead to unacceptable behaviours, including harassment, bullying and victimisation, as well as poor standards and abuse of power over others. Harassment, bullying and victimisation are all behaviours that individuals are protected against under the Equality Act (2010); it is important to remember that it is not just individuals and groups that can be prejudiced and discriminatory (adapted from Tilmouth and Quallington, 2016).

KEY TERM

A **values-based** culture is one in which the goal is to work by a common set of values that guides behaviours.

Team diversity, roles and responsibilities

We are all products of our culture, our experiences and our education and, as such, our teams are likely to comprise a diverse mix of people. While discrimination and exclusion may not be intentional, they may come about as a result of the belief that everyone experiences life in the same way.

As managers it is necessary to communicate to staff that we need to respect the diverse nature of the team and to respect the differences in the experience, skills and knowledge that people bring to the mix. We should develop a culture of zero tolerance for negative behaviour if the values people have are different to our own. One of the ways in which this might be done would be to promote policies that set out expectations of behaviour to others and that remind staff of disciplinary sanctions should they breach the policy. Another may be to look at the roles of each member of the team and to set out clearly the responsibilities they have.

Team activities – internal and external

Regular team activity will help to develop trust within the team. One useful way would be to get staff involved in planning by allowing time during the regular team meeting for the team to express their views and to communicate their opinions or ideas. So often, our team meetings become a mere information-giving session and this does not provide an adequate venue for the exchange of ideas. If this is the case, then valuable expertise, the skills and knowledge of the staff will not be accessed. Through the use of a mentoring process, team members can learn a great deal from each other and the expertise each one possesses through their experience and training can be used as a valuable resource for planning.

Other team activities such as peer teaching may also be an influential way to ensure that a cohesive team is developed.

Individual and team accountability, and feedback on team performance and achievement

> ### KEY TERM
>
>
> **Accountability** is taking responsibility and being liable or answerable for something.

Good management demands that we hold people accountable for what they do or don't do and the way in which you do this can make or break the relationship.

When goals were not met due to something the employee has failed to do, then it is appropriate for them to be held accountable for this failure. But if we are trying to hold employees accountable for things that are out of their control, this is unreasonable and we will lose the trust we have with the staff.

Be consistent: The key ingredient is consistency and your staff will expect to be called to account if goals are not met or jobs are not done. The way in which you do this is also important and it is much better to deal with an individual in a firm but kind way in private about a performance error than to berate or criticise them in public for a misdemeanour or mistake. Additionally, it is important that all staff are dealt with in the same way; otherwise the sense of injustice is great and trust is lost.

Build relationships: As a manager, there is a distance between yourself and the staff. But the leaders and managers who take the time to build relationships with staff will gain their trust. It is a wise manager who takes time to find out a little about their staff and to share a little about their own life. You are likely to remember a manager who takes an interest and asks about your family or is happy to share a few words.

Be honest: Trust builds respect and it is this that gets results.

Provide constructive feedback to allow staff to make the changes they need to. Highlighting achievements can empower your staff and motivate them to improve their practice even further.

Service users require staff who are confident and happy in their work and this can be achieved only if managers are able to encourage this in their workforce.

> ### Evidence opportunity
>
> **4.2** Developing trust and accountability within the team
>
> Show your assessor how you develop trust and accountability and build positive relationships within your team(s), considering the topics we have discussed in this section.

> ### Reflect on it
>
>
> **4.2** Developing trust and accountability
>
> Write a reflective account of the methods you use to develop trust and accountability within the team.
>
> Include a **critical incident** which demonstrates the way in which you maintain accountability and trust in your work.

> ### KEY TERM
>
>
> A **critical incident** is an unintended event that occurs when an individual in healthcare is involved in something that results in a consequence to him or her; for example, a fall.

AC 4.3 Build team commitment to the service and its values

Here, you will need to show that you can build the team's commitment to the service and its values by consistently demonstrating your own commitment and expressing the vision.

As a manager your commitment to the vision and values within the service must be demonstrated by action and the way in which you behave. You must become a role model for your team if you are to help them to commit to the same values and vision. This will inspire the team to follow your lead.

> ### Reflect on it
>
>
> **4.3** Mission statement
>
> Write a short piece that expresses your commitment to the vision and mission statement of the organisation for which you work.

> ### Evidence opportunity
>
> **4.3** Leading by example
>
> Show your assessor how you build the team's commitment to the service and its values by consistently demonstrating your own commitment and expressing your own vision.

AC 4.4 Develop, implement and review strategies that support positive values-based cultures in teams

Here, you will be required to develop, implement and review strategies that include:

- *action planning and reviewing of team(s) against service vision and related achievements*
- *commitment by all to a values-based team culture in support of the service vision.*

Have you heard of Airbnb? Etsy? Netflix? Chances are you have, and one of the reasons is because they are all successful companies that deliver a service. Why are they successful? A major influence has been the development in these companies of a positive values-based culture, one in which employees share the whole ethos and vision of the company and are rewarded for it in diverse ways. All these companies demonstrate real passion for what they do and engender this in their employees by involving them in decisions and giving staff significant time to help them to develop and be involved in change and to be rewarded for their input.

Action planning and reviewing of team against service vision and related achievements

In devising an action plan, you first need to get together a planning group made up of individuals from the community that are involved in making the change. These can be the team in the setting and also other stakeholders. The first step is to describe the vision or what needs to be done and then say what success would look like.

> ### Reflect on it
>
> **4.4** Positive values-based culture
>
> High-performance teams demonstrate willingness to change, passion for what they do and a positive can-do spirit (adapted from www.jump4biz.com/Culture_Corporate_Cohesiveness_faq_Culture.php).
>
> How might you plan for a culture change in your own team to make it clear that you are developing a positive values culture?

Commitment by all to a values-based team culture in support of the service vision

Commitment by the team means that they can accomplish great things and move effortlessly towards the vision of the setting. Teams that self-manage and that are empowered to make their own decisions get the jobs done on their own terms and are willing to go the extra mile to support the service vision.

> ### Evidence opportunity
>
> **4.4** Strategies that support positive values-based cultures in teams
>
> Show your assessor how you develop, implement and review strategies that include:
>
> - action planning and reviewing of team(s) against service vision and related achievements
> - commitment by all to a values-based team culture in support of the service vision.

> ### Reflect on it
>
>
>
> **4.4** Strategies that support positive values-based cultures in teams
>
> How do you intend to go about ensuring that you have all your staff committed to this?

AC 4.5 Manage workloads effectively

Here, you will be required to show that you can manage workloads using standard working procedures including time management, delegation, setting priorities, and demonstrating and promoting a work–life balance for self and others.

Time management

Time management is an important component of developing an effective staff team as it takes time to identify individual needs and interests and to assess what will bring about most benefit to the culture of the organisation. If done effectively, this will be time well spent. It is important to account for interests as well as organisational needs, although the latter may take priority. If staff feel their individual interests are supported, it will help maintain motivation and morale in the team. In addition, staff need to feel that the activity is valued for its own sake and is not just another chore to be squeezed in around more important routine activities. Consequently, staff need the encouragement to put their learning into practice and this is where delegation is an important skill.

Delegation

By delegating certain tasks to individuals in your team you are showing trust and respect for their ability and are also saving yourself time. It is a huge motivator for staff and is a useful personal development tool. It enables your staff to take on more responsibility and to have a greater interest in the job you do.

Setting priorities

To enable the achievement of a 'shared vision', the team will need to work to a set of objectives. Aims are the goals you hope to achieve or, in this case, may be the overall shared vision. Objectives are the activities you undertake in order to reach those goals.

Demonstrating and promoting a work–life balance for self and others

By being mindful of time management, delegation and the priorities for the team you will be able to demonstrate that you are mindful of a work–life balance.

Sometimes work can get very busy and we can lose sight of the important things in life. In some team cultures, individuals may feel they need to be seen to be staying on at work in order to feel valued. They may not take a lunch break but rather work at their desk and eat lunch. They may not leave work on time for fear of being seen to be lazy. People need to be encouraged to take their leisure time seriously and to put in the hours when at work and then leave it behind until the next day.

> ### Evidence opportunity
> **4.5** Manage workloads effectively
>
> Show your assessor that you can manage workloads using standard working procedures including time management, delegation, setting priorities, and demonstrating and promoting a work–life balance for self and others.

> ### Reflect on it
>
> **4.5** Managing your workload
>
> Prepare a mind map that shows how you manage your workload. Use the headings we have covered above.

LO5 Manage team working

AC 5.1 Facilitate inclusion of team members when agreeing team objectives

Here, you will be required to show you can facilitate inclusion when agreeing team objectives to support strategy and vision.

Effective teams share a commitment to achieving the common objectives of the organisation and work well together. The overall objectives that need to be achieved should be clearly identified and defined in terms that each team member understands. Participation of each team member is encouraged, and they are given free rein to contribute ideas.

> ### Evidence opportunity
> **5.1** Facilitate inclusion of team members when agreeing team objectives
>
> Show your assessor how you facilitate inclusion when agreeing team objectives to support strategy and vision.
>
> Or you could ask a team member to write a detailed testimonial for you to show how they were included in agreeing team objectives on a project.

AC 5.2 Develop and support innovation and creativity while planning team objectives and ensuring collective agreement

Here, you will need to show that you can develop and support innovation and creativity while planning team objectives and ensuring collective agreement.

There are a number of ways in which innovative and creative strategies might be used to encourage staff to contribute to change. Some hospitals are changing their organisational culture by adopting new ways of working with problems.

The philosophies of Kaizen and lean management describe a culture of continuous improvement where all employees improve the organisation by being actively involved in the change.

Kaizen is part action plan and part philosophy and has been adopted by some hospital trusts in this country to engage in continuous improvement in a meaningful way. One such hospital trust, the Shrewsbury and Telford Hospital Trust (SaTH), has engaged with the Virginia Mason Institute in Seattle, USA, in order to develop this culture and to become the best and safest hospital in the world. Using the Kaizen approach, the trust set up week-long Rapid Process Improvement Workshops (RPIW) where staff at all levels, particularly those engaged in the actual practice under scrutiny, take part in a process of change in a given area. At these events, an initial review of the current state of the practice is looked at and a plan for improvements developed. Initial visits and then follow-ups to the area are undertaken and staff are involved in implementing the improvements and reviewing and adjusting them to find out what works. When the changed process is in place, staff report their findings to the public with the results after 30 days, 60 days and 90 days. For example, a most successful RPIW was that carried out on reducing the time it took to treat sepsis patients on arrival at the trust.

The philosophy behind Kaizen is to build a culture where all employees become actively engaged in suggesting and implementing improvements to the company.

Research it

5.2 Lean management principles

Look at the Kaizen philosophy and lean management principles and make notes on them. How might you incorporate such an approach in your work?

AC 5.3 Assign roles, detailing responsibilities and personal work objectives with team members

Here, you will need to show that you acknowledge individual skill sets, interest, knowledge, expertise and development needs while motivating all individuals, including the topics we cover here.

The success of a team will depend on bringing together people with diverse skills and knowledge and if they lack these, encouraging them to undertake training and education. For example, the skills of doctors, nurses, occupational therapists and physiotherapists working together in an orthopaedic ward to best meet the needs of the patients on the ward is called a multidisciplinary team (MDT).

Reflect on it

5.3 Motivating your staff

As a manager, knowing what each individual in your team has to offer will aid the success of the team. You need to know what motivates each member of staff and how to ensure they continue to give of their best. How, though, might you deal with the following:

- those who are not assigned their first choice of role?
- those who might disengage with the process?
- those who might show less motivation and/or enthusiasm than others?
- those who demonstrate complacency and/or disengagement?

Recognising the diversity of skills within the staff may be a useful starting point. Some staff will have experience which they can pass on to others and they can be asked to take on more responsibility to help and support these.

Listen to what it is the employee wants and needs to help them to do their job and then acknowledge that by showing your appreciation. A simple word of praise for what they are doing may be all that is needed. If they require additional support or training, then this might be more readily available through redeploying other staff to help them. The point is to listen to the staff member and identify the reason for their demotivation. Only then might you be able to offer the solution they need.

Those who are not assigned their first choice of role

Members of staff may apply for one role within the setting and then be offered another and this may fall outside of their comfort zone. Discussion about what support they require and any additional training may be helpful here to re-motivate them.

Those who might disengage with the process

These people, also known as plateaued performers, have reached points in their work where they no longer engage well with work. They may feel bored by what they are doing or are showing less motivation and/or enthusiasm than others. A conversation about what is happening for them at work and how they believe they might feel more re-energised to find some motivation at work would be useful. They may simply feel unchallenged and need a new focus.

Those who might demonstrate complacency and/or disengagement

Much like the above, these staff members may need a new challenge in their work to get them to re-engage with the team. Maybe they have been passed over for promotion or a training course and are finding it hard to continue in the same role.

What could you do? We can never overestimate the importance of good communication in such situations and you will need to listen and get involved with staff to determine how to move forward.

All of the above categories show staff who have been demotivated in some way. Some may be disappointed about not being given an additional responsibility or a promotion. Others may simply be less enthusiastic about a project and start to disengage from it. These sorts of behaviours can quickly escalate and others on the staff may pick up on the mood and start to feel the same. As a manager you need to be aware of the mood and deal with it before it grows.

5.3 Assign roles, detailing responsibilities and personal work objectives

Show your assessor how you have assigned roles to team members and detail the responsibilities and personal work objectives with team members.

Show how you acknowledge individual skill sets, interest, knowledge, expertise and development needs while motivating all individuals, for example:

- those who are not assigned their first choice of role
- those who might disengage with the process
- those who might show less motivation and/or enthusiasm than others
- those who might demonstrate complacency and/or disengagement.

You could also discuss how you assess the skills and knowledge of your staff and use them to the advantage of the team.

AC 5.4 Implement systems to support team members working towards personal and team objectives and monitor progress

Here, you will be required to show how you implement systems that enable team members to match their personal goals to the overall objectives of the service.

Health and social care workers are subject to performance reviews, supervision and appraisal, and a review or appraisal is the ideal time to set objectives for the coming year and for change in their workload or requests for training. '**SMART**' targets are a useful way of identifying personal objectives.

Staff must ensure they remain 'fit for practice' by undertaking professional development activities regularly (training for example) and updating their own portfolio of evidence to show how they have developed. By undertaking this course and carrying out the activities throughout this book you are engaging in **continuing professional development (CPD)** and providing evidence through the activities you complete. Your staff also require development and in supervision or appraisal sessions you need to work with them to identify their own strategies for development.

KEY TERMS

Continuing professional development (CPD) is training and education activity to ensure staff remain fit for practice.
SMART targets are those objectives which are specific, measurable, achievable, realistic/relevant and time-related.

Case study

5.4 Workload and training and development

Meeting with Jasmine

Workload – Jasmine feels that currently her workload level is fine and she is enjoying the work with the newer clients. She feels the changes the team made by allocating a named staff member to a group of clients is useful. Jasmine feels her confidence has grown and she is relishing the more independent way of working. I commented that as her team leader I had noticed that she was making appropriate decisions for her clients and was working well in the team.

Training and development

So far this year Jasmine has attended the Health and Safety update and two further in-house training courses. She seems very keen to undertake a foundation degree in Health and Social Care at her local sixth form college. We discussed what this would entail and Jasmine mentioned that it was one day a week in college for two years with additional days off to undertake further work placement activity. We devised the following action plan:

- Jasmine to advise of fees and days required out of work by 17/10/19.
- Jasmine to approach the college and to get an application form and start the process of applying by 20/11/19.
- TT (the team leader) will approach the area manager to obtain permission in principle for attendance and to inform Jasmine of the decision by 20/11/19.
- Further meeting to take place on 21/11/19 to discuss next steps.

Evidence opportunity

5.4 Implement systems to support team members to work towards objectives and monitor progress

Show your assessor how you implement systems that enable team members to match their personal goals to the overall objectives of the service.

Case study 5.4 shows one way in which we might set objectives. You may wish to show or discuss with your manager how you set your personal work objectives for the coming year and discuss this with your manager. You could also discuss with them how you work with a member of your own team to identify opportunities for their development and growth.

AC 5.5 Provide feedback on performance for individuals and the whole team

In this section, you will need to show how you provide feedback and the methods you use, including for example the ones we discuss here.

We all like to know what we are doing well and what we might be able to improve upon so being given some feedback is useful.

Team-based feedback

At a team level this might be during meetings when organisational performance is looked at and feedback is provided to demonstrate how productive projects have been. Feedback, of course, may also be of a more negative nature and the team may be made aware of improvements that need to be made.

360 degree feedback

360 degree feedback is a method of performance appraisal which gathers feedback from a number of sources, including peers, direct reports, more senior colleagues and customers. This variety of feedback can offer line managers a wide-ranging perspective and help to make performance management a more objective and fair process.

Constructive criticism

Occasionally, it is necessary to give negative feedback to staff in order to address issues with unsatisfactory performance. This can inevitably cause conflict and can be quite uncomfortable.

Individuals receive criticism in different ways and you need to ensure that you are sensitive to how they will be feeling at this time.

A good approach is to provide a positive point initially and to say clearly what was good about it. You can stress how well they did and what you liked about their performance. When critiquing their performance, you could highlight this as 'an area for improvement'. Again, you must specifically draw attention to what you expect the team member to do and give a clear indication of how they might achieve this. You can then constructively give advice on how they can change. Finally, by ending with a positive point you can do much to rebuild self-esteem in what can often be a rather uncomfortable situation.

Supervision(s) and appraisal

Supervision is a practice that should provide regular, ongoing support for staff and as such time should be set aside for it. Staff need to be clear about what supervision is for and also given space to discuss issues in a confidential and safe environment.

Supervision supports practice, enabling staff to maintain and improve standards of care and to reflect upon their practice. Similarly, appraisal is about giving staff a place to reflect on their work and learning needs in order to improve their performance and usually results in a personal development plan. This can be achieved through discussing their development and feedback on their job performance in a way that is constructive and motivational. It should result in an effective personal development plan which can be revisited and updated continually.

Mentoring and coaching

Coaching and mentoring are similar in nature, so we should be clear about what they refer to. Both are used to enable individuals to flourish in their work and also their personal lives.

Gallwey defined coaching as unlocking a person's potential to maximise their performance. It is helping them to learn rather than teaching them (Gallwey, 1986; Whitmore, 2002).

Successful coaches, according to Parsloe (1999), require knowledge and understanding of process and have at their disposal a variety of styles, skills and techniques. A coach therefore may not have direct experience of a client's formal occupational role, but will be able to use a process to help them to make the changes they desire.

On the other hand, mentoring is a professional relationship and is about following in the route of a colleague who can pass on knowledge and experience of a role.

Sometimes, however, training on the job in new skills and techniques or simply to update the staff in new policies, practices and procedures is required. The use of coaching as a strategy to advise and support team members and to enhance team performance is now a well-respected factor in team development.

Parsloe and Wray (2000) defined coaching as:

'a process that enables learning and development to occur and thus performance to improve. To be successful, a coach requires a knowledge and understanding of process as well as the variety of styles, skills and techniques that are appropriate to the context in which the coaching takes place.'

Compliments and complaints – both internal and external

See page 24.

> ### Evidence opportunity
> **5.5** Provide feedback on performance for individuals and the whole team
> Using the above headings, provide evidence in your portfolio of how you provide and receive feedback on performance for individuals and the whole team.

AC 5.6 Identify performance issues within the team addressing issues positively for ongoing development

Here, you will be required to show that you use constructive evaluation and feedback to inform individual action plans for continued professional development and ongoing learning for the team(s).

Reflect on it

5.6 Individual development

Being mindful of confidentiality and anonymising your records, provide evidence of a meeting with a member of your staff. Describe how you prepared for the meeting and how you approached the subject of the individual's continuing development. Show how you used constructive evaluation and feedback to inform individual action plans for CPD and ongoing learning for them and the team.

Evaluate your own performance by writing a reflective account of what you did, why you did it in that way and the outcome of the whole meeting.

AC 5.7 Recognise progress achieved towards team and personal work objectives

Here, you will be required to show how you recognise progress achieved towards team and personal work objectives through some of the topics we discuss in this section.

Evidence opportunity

5.7 Recognise progress achieved towards team and personal work objectives

Provide evidence in your portfolio of how you recognise the progress that has been achieved towards the team's and your personal work objectives.

How do you recognise the progress that has been made/achieved through feedback and the topics that we have covered in this section?

You might include copies of paperwork that is useful for auditing such feedback.

Individual and team feedback

Feedback to the team should relate to the objectives set and to the work they are doing. This sort of feedback can be done at team briefings or in meetings.

Individuals' supervision – self and others

During supervision with individual staff members, you can highlight where the team is in achieving group goals and can then pinpoint how the staff member has been a part of that achievement. This can be a good way to motivate staff when they can see that what they are doing is having a positive impact upon the team and the setting. This might also be an opportunity to praise and reward somebody for their good work.

Individual appraisal – self and others

As above, staff appraisal can be an opportunity for growth and self-development. Encouraging staff to reflect upon the objectives and then appraising their performance can be motivating if they can see how their work impacts upon the setting.

As the manager you need to recognise the progress that is being made and reward staff for their performance.

Individual/team observations – formal and informal

Observing the way in which a practice is carried out is a useful way to check progress of staff and to determine whether practice is of its best. Informal observations occur when you happen to observe a member of staff carrying out their daily duty. Formal observations are those which are arranged in advance for a particular date and time. Teachers are very aware of this type of observation as it is the means by which inspections are carried out.

Auditing processes and procedures

There are many types of audits, which are simply systematic reviews of care measured against criteria and designed to improve service user care.

The policies within a care organisation can be checked as to their effectiveness if an audit is carried out. For example, we might trace a service user's complaint from the time the letter was received to the time when it had been dealt with. By going through the complaints policy, we can tell whether the stages had been followed or not. Other forms of audit are financial, internal and organisational.

Informal and formal inspection processes

The thought of undergoing an inspection is often an area of concern for staff but if informal inspections are part of a daily routine, whereby the conditions within the workplace are looked at for safety and efficiency reasons, this need not be the case. More formal inspections may be carried out by external bodies simply with the intention of checking that the workplace is fit for purpose and doing what it should be doing to protect service users' safety.

Feedback from those in receipt of care and support

In 2013 the NHS launched its Friends and Family Test (FFT) to help service providers to ascertain whether their patients are happy with the service provided or whether improvements are needed. A simple leaflet which is quick to fill in is given to patients, friends and family.

Your care organisation may use a similar tool to measure service user satisfaction.

Evidence opportunity

5.7 Inspection, observations, audit and feedback

Show how you deal with inspection, observations, audit and feedback from others to check the progress of your team.

Legislation

Legislation	
Health & Social Care Act 2008 (Regulated Activities) Regulations 2014	These outline the fundamental standards for care.
Five Year Forward View (2014)	This was an attempt to bring together organisations that had a part in quality assurance and to establish a National Quality Board (NQB)
The Equality Act 2010	This is an umbrella act bringing together legislation that deals with race, disability and gender. It highlights protected characteristics of age, gender reassignment, pregnancy, religion, marriage and civil partnerships, and sexual orientation in an attempt to end discrimination.
The Care Act 2014	This act sets out the key responsibilities of local authorities in meeting the needs of individuals who require help and support to promote their wellbeing. The main aim was to provide integrated care and to introduce the right to an assessment for all.
The Care Quality Commission's Key Lines of Enquiry (KLOEs) 2013	These present the key criteria against which health care providers are inspected and judged.

Suggestions for using the activities	
This table summarises all the activities in the unit that are relevant to each assessment criterion. Here, we also suggest other, different methods that you may want to use to present your knowledge and skills by using the activities. These are just suggestions, and you should refer to the introduction section at the start of the book, and more importantly the City & Guilds specification, and your assessor, who will be able to provide more guidance on how you can evidence your knowledge and skills. When you need to be observed during your assessment, this can be done by your assessor, or your manager can provide a witness testimony.	
Assessment criteria and accompanying activities	**Suggested methods to show your knowledge/skills**
LO1 Understand the application of theories of leadership and management	
1.1 Reflect on it (page 3)	How do the ten principles fit with your experience of being a manager? Write a short piece giving examples of your experience.
1.1 Research it (page 6)	Research Hersey and Blanchard's situational theory using Figure 1.3. Show how the S2 High Directive–High Supportive style and the S4 Low Directive–Low Supportive style of management of tasks might be used in your workplace.
1.1 Reflect on it (page 7)	Some decisions made at senior management level may be unpopular and yet as a manager you are asked to ensure they are followed. How might you do this?

Suggestions for using the activities	
1.1 Research it (page 7)	Go to www.belbin.com/about/belbin-teamroles and find out more about the roles listed on page 7 and the strengths and weaknesses of each. Think about each of them in connection with your setting.
1.1 Reflect on it (page 9)	Think about the sorts of power that you may have come across during your work life. Write an account of how they affected you.
1.1 Evidence opportunity (page 9)	Provide a written account critically analysing theories and models of management and leadership, including the ones we have covered in this section. Explore the evidence for and against each theory.
1.2 Research it (page 10)	What do you think are the characteristics of a good leader/manager? Conduct some primary research and ask your peers and colleagues for their views.
1.2 Reflect on it (page 10)	How would you define your own role in the workplace? How is your role different from those you lead or manage? Make some notes for your portfolio.
1.2 Evidence opportunity (page 11)	Interview your manager and ask about their style of management. How is your style similar to or different from theirs? Analyse how different management styles may influence outcomes of team performance. Write this up as a reflective account for your journal.
1.2 Reflect on it (page 12)	Consider how you might adjust your style when talking to your deputy, team leaders/supervisors, home owners, directors and trustees.
1.2 Evidence opportunity (page 12)	Using the models discussed in AC 1.1 and 1.2, write a critical evaluation about how three theories and/or models of management and leadership apply to adult care practice. Give examples of how you would demonstrate emotional intelligence or leadership traits in your work and how you apply these to your practice.
1.3 Research it (page 14)	Research some of the new quality policies that have been published from the list on page 14.
1.3 Evidence opportunity (page 15)	Analyse barriers to applying leadership and management theory in respect of the topics discussed in this section. Look at strategies that could be used to address these barriers.
1.4 Reflect on it (page 16)	Explain what you think would be the difference between a positive manager and a negative one.
1.4 Evidence opportunity (page 16)	Provide a written account evaluating different leadership styles and their impact on working culture and service delivery.
LO2 Understand the importance of leadership and management in adult care settings	
2.1 Research it (page 18)	Look at the CQC document *A New Start: Consultation on changes to the way CQC regulates, inspects and monitors care* (2013) to identify how this might change the way in which your provision is inspected.
2.1 Evidence opportunity (page 18)	Evaluate the current national and local policy drivers and how these impact on the leadership and management role, including the ones we have covered in this section.
2.1 Research it (page 18)	Download the CQC's standards and say how your organisation is meeting this particular requirement for staff. How have the policies shown in this section affected your role as a manager and leader?
2.2 Evidence opportunity (page 19)	Explain why it is important for managers in adult care to have both leadership and management skills.
2.2 Reflect on it (page 19)	Consider whether you are a leader or a manager and how you might change to adapt to both roles. Reflect on the reasons why.
2.3 Reflect on it (page 20)	Consider how you have dealt with conflict within the work setting, which may have arisen as a result of differing personal and organisational values.
2.3 Reflect on it (page 20)	As a manager, consider how you undertake the responsibility of providing professional supervision for staff to ensure they are supported in their roles and to enhance their skills and performance.

Suggestions for using the activities	
2.3 Evidence opportunity (page 21)	Provide a written account analysing both internal and external factors that impact your leadership and management role and related interactions. Consider the topics covered in this section.
2.4 Research it (page 21)	Check the new standards at the link given. If the link no longer works, try searching for the Manager Induction Standards in your browser.
2.4 Evidence opportunity (page 22)	Prepare a PowerPoint presentation for staff evaluating the importance of learning and development in your care setting, including the areas discussed in this section.
2.4 Reflect on it (page 22)	Write a reflective account about the importance of Manager Induction Standards, reflection and reflective practice, and continuing training and development for maintaining professional quality.
2.5 Evidence opportunity (page 24)	Provide a written account evaluating communication strategies for creating an open atmosphere, including the topics covered in this section.
2.5 Reflect on it (page 24)	How does your organisation create an atmosphere that inspires an open, positive and inclusive culture? What communication strategies do you use? Consider how you feed back constructive criticism to staff.
2.6 Evidence opportunity (page 25)	Explain the methods you use to promote a service that encourages innovation and creativity in a positive and realistic manner.
2.6 Reflect on it (page 25)	Consider how your service is promoted in ways that encourage innovation and creativity.
LO3 Lead commitment to a vision for the service	
3.1 Reflect on it (page 26)	List the things that enhance your job for you and give some examples about what makes you want to do them. Outline your strengths in motivational thinking/speaking and how you inspire others to follow.
3.1 Evidence opportunity (page 26)	Prepare a presentation to staff to inform them of a change of practice.
3.2 Evidence opportunity (page 27)	Provide evidence that all stakeholders (internal and external) are aware of service expectations, using appropriate communication strategies such as the ones discussed in this section.
3.2 Reflect on it (page 27)	Construct a spider diagram showing the internal and external stakeholders you work with. Write an account of how you engage with these stakeholders to create awareness of forward thinking.
3.3 Evidence opportunity (page 28)	Show your assessor service development plans you have created, including the ones discussed in this section.
3.4 Reflect on it (page 28)	Think about the communication systems discussed and reflect on how they might be misused or might fail.
3.4 Evidence opportunity (page 29)	Develop a flow diagram to show how you would involve stakeholders and others in decisions about service delivery.
LO4 Provide leadership for a team in an adult care setting	
4.1 Evidence opportunity (page 29)	Explain how you adapt leadership and management styles to reflect different situations and stages in a care team's development.
4.1 Reflect on it (page 29)	Say which is your preferred style of leadership and management.
4.2 Evidence opportunity (page 31)	Show how you develop trust and accountability and build positive relationships within your team(s), considering the topics discussed in this section.
4.2 Reflect on it (page 31)	Write a reflective account of the methods you use to develop trust and accountability within your team.

→

Suggestions for using the activities	
4.3 Reflect on it (page 31)	Write a short piece that expresses your commitment to the vision and mission statement of your organisation.
4.3 Evidence opportunity (page 31)	Consider how you build your team's commitment to the service and its values by consistently demonstrating your commitment and expressing your vision.
4.4 Reflect on it (page 32)	Think about how you might plan for a culture change in your team to make it clear that you are developing a positive values culture.
4.4 Evidence opportunity (page 32)	Explain how you develop, implement and review strategies that include action planning and reviewing of team(s) against service vision and related achievements, plus commitment by all to a values-based team culture in support of the service vision.
4.4 Reflect on it (page 32)	How do you intend to go about ensuring that you have all your staff committed to this?
4.5 Evidence opportunity (page 33)	Show that you can manage workloads using standard working procedures, including time management, delegation, setting priorities, and demonstrating and promoting a work–life balance for yourself and others.
4.5 Reflect on it (page 33)	Prepare a mind map that shows how you manage your workload.
LO5 Manage team working	
5.1 Evidence opportunity (page 33)	Show how you facilitate inclusion when agreeing team objectives to support strategy and vision.
5.2 Research it (page 34)	Look at the Kaizen philosophy and lean management principles and make notes on them.
5.3 Reflect on it (page 34)	Consider what motivates each member of staff and how to ensure they continue to give of their best.
5.3 Evidence opportunity (page 35)	Explain how you have assigned roles to team members and detail their responsibilities and personal work objectives.
5.4 Evidence opportunity (page 35)	Consider how you implement systems that enable team members to match their personal goals to the overall objectives of the service.
5.5 Evidence opportunity (page 36)	Using the headings in this section, show how you provide and receive feedback on performance for individuals and the whole team.
5.6 Reflect on it (page 37)	Consider a meeting with a member of your staff. How did you prepare and how did you approach the subject of the individuals continuing development? Evaluate your performance.
5.7 Evidence opportunity (page 37)	Explain how you recognise the progress that has been achieved towards the team's and your personal work objectives.
5.7 Evidence opportunity (page 38)	Show how you deal with inspection, observations, audit and feedback from others to check the progress of your team.

References

Allport, G.W. and Odbert, H.S. (1936) Trait-names: A psycho-lexical study, *Psychological Monographs*, 47(211).

Belbin, M. (1981) *Management Teams: Why they succeed or fail.* London: Heinemann.

Bolton, G. (2010) *Reflective Practice: Writing and professional development* (3e). London: Sage Publishing.

Covey, S.R. (2004) *The 7 Habits of Highly Effective People.* London: Simon & Schuster.

Care Quality Commission (2013) *A New Start: Consultation on changes to the way CQC regulates, inspects and monitors care.* London: CQC.

Care Quality Commission (2015) Regulation Five: Fit and proper persons: Directors. Information for NHS bodies. Newcastle Upon Tyne: CQC.

Department of Health (2014) The Health and Social Care Act 2008 (Regulated Activities) Regulations. London: TSO.

Fayol, H. (1916) *General and Industrial Management.* London: Pitman.

Fiedler, F.E. (1967) *A Theory of Leadership Effectiveness.* New York: McGraw-Hill.

Francis, R. (2013) Report of the Mid Staffordshire NHS Foundation Trust Public Inquiry. London: TSO.

Gallwey, T. (1986) *The Inner Game of Tennis.* London: Pan.

George, B. (2003) *Authentic Leadership: Rediscovering the secrets to creating lasting value.* San Francisco, CA: Jossey-Bass.

Goleman, D. (1995) *Emotional Intelligence.* New York: Bantam Books.

Kotter, J.P. (1990) *A Force for Change: How leadership differs from management.* New York: Free Press.

Kotter, J.P. (1996) *Leading Change.* Brighton, MA: Harvard Business School Press.

Kouzes, J.M. and Posner, B.Z. (2003) *The Leadership Challenge* (3e). San Francisco, CA: Jossey-Bass.

LaFasto, F.M.J. and Larson, C.E. (2001) *When Teams Work Best: 6,000 team members and leaders tell what it takes to succeed.* Thousand Oaks, CA: Sage Publications.

Lewin, K., Lippit, R. and White, R.K. (1939) Patterns of aggressive behavior in experimentally created social climates, *Journal of Social Psychology*, 10: 271–301.

Martin, V., Charlesworth, J. and Henderson, E. (2010) *Managing in Health and Social Care.* Abingdon: Routledge.

McKibbon, J., Walton, A. and Mason, L. (2008) *Leadership and Management in Health and Social Care.* London: Heinemann.

Mullins, L. (2009) *Management and Organisational Behaviour* (8e). Harlow: Prentice Hall.

Northouse, P.G. (2018) *Leadership: Theory and practice* (8e). Thousand Oaks, CA: Sage.

Parsloe, E. (1999) *The Manager as Coach and Mentor.* London: Chartered Institute of Personnel & Development, p. 8.

Parsloe, E. and Wray, M. (2000) *Coaching and Mentoring: Practical methods to improve learning.* London: Kegan Paul.

Peters, T. and Austin, N. (1985) *A Passion for Excellence: The leadership difference.* London: Collins.

Rappaport, J. (1987) Terms of empowerment/exemplars of prevention: toward a theory for community psychology, *American Journal of Community Psychology*, 15(2): 121–48.

Scally, G. and Donaldson, L.J. (1998) Clinical governance and the drive for quality improvement in the new NHS in England, *British Medical Journal*, 317(7150): 61–5.

Skills for Care (2016) *Manager Induction Standards; Reviewed Edition.* London: SFC.

Stewart, R. (1997) *The Reality of Management* (3e). Oxford: Butterworth-Heinemann.

Terry, R.W. (1993) *Authentic Leadership: Courage in action.* Jossey Bass: Wiley and Sons.

Thompson, N. (2006) *Anti-Discriminatory Practice: (British Association of Social Workers (BASW) Practical Social Work) (Practical Social Work Series)* (4e). London: Palgrave Macmillan.

Tilmouth, T., Davies-Ward, E. and Williams, B. (2011) *Foundation Degree in Health and Social Care.* London: Hodder Education.

Tilmouth, T. and Quallington, J. (2016) *Diploma in Leadership (2e) for Health and Social Care.* London: Hodder Education.

Wheelan, S.A. (2005) *Creating Effective Teams: A guide for members and leaders* (2e). London: Sage.

Whitmore, J. (2002) *Coaching for Performance: GROWing people, performance and purpose.* London: Nicholas Brealey.

Useful resources and further reading

Cavazotte, F., Moreno, V. and Hickmann, M. (2012) Effects of leader intelligence, personality and emotional intelligence on transformational leadership and managerial performance, *The Leadership Quarterly*, 23(3): 443–55.

Care Quality Commission (2015) Guidance for Providers on Meeting the Regulations, available on the CQC website.

Care Quality Commission (2015) How CQC Regulates: Residential Adult Social Care Services – Provider Handbook, available on the CQC website.

Care Quality Commission (2015) How CQC Regulates: Residential Adult Social Care Services – Appendices to the Provider Handbook, available on the CQC website.

Department of Health (2006) *Our Health, Our Care, Our Say: A new direction for community services.* London: HMSO.

Department of Health, Skills for Care and Skills for Health (2013) Code of Conduct for Health Care Support Workers and Adult Social Care Workers in England, available on the Skills for Health website.

Leadership Starts with Me (2013), National Skills Academy for Social Care, available on the NSA website.

Manager Induction Standards, Skills for Care, available on the Skills for Care website.

Managing a 'Skills for Health Home from Home'. A Companion to 'Creating a Home from Home', A Guide to Standards, The Residential Forum.

Meeting the Workforce Regulations: Skills for Care Advice on CQC's Workforce-specific Outcomes (Version 1.7: October 2011), Skills for Care, available on the Skills for Care website.

Outstanding Leadership in Social Care (2012), National Skills Academy for Social Care, available on the NSA website.

A Vision for Adult Social Care: Capable Communities and Active Citizens, Department of Health (2010), available on the Department of Health website.

Books

Goleman, D. (1998) *Working with Emotional Intelligence.* New York: Bantam Books.

Gopee, N. and Galloway, J. (2009) *Leadership and Management in Health Care.* London: Sage.

Leitch, S. (2006) *Leitch Review of Skills*. London: HM Treasury.

Maslow, A. (1987) *Motivation and Personality* (2e). New York: Harper & Row (1970, 3rd revised edition published by Longman).

McClean, S. (2012) *Power and Empowerment in Health and Social Care*. London: City & Guilds.

McGrath, J. and Bates, B. (2017) *The Little Book of Big Management Theories and How to Use Them* (2e). London: Pearson.

National Voices (2014) *Person-centred Care 2020: Calls and contributions from health and social care charities*, accessed from www.nationalvoices.org.uk/sites/default/files/public/publications/person-centred-care-2020.pdf

Newton. R. (2011) *The Management Book: How to manage your team to deliver outstanding results.* Upper Saddle River, NJ: Prentice Hall/Financial Times.

Owen, J. (2015) *The Mindset of Success: From good management to great leadership*. London: Kogan Page.

Peters, S. (2012) The *Chimp Paradox: The mind management programme to help you achieve success, confidence and happiness*. London: Vermilion.

Reynolds, M. and Holwell, S. (eds) *Systems Approaches to Managing Change: A practical guide*. London: Springer.

Journals and magazines

CMM Care Management Matters
Caring Times
Care Talk
Skills for Care, Care Magazine
Care Home Management
Expert Care Manager Magazine
The British Journal of Healthcare Management
Community Care
Caring UK

Websites

www.open.edu/openlearn/moneymanagement/management/leadership-and-management/discovering-management/content-section-1.1.1

www.leadership-central.com/situational-leadership-theory.html#axzz4iS7NGw92

http://webarchive.nationalarchives.gov.uk/20161103235253

www.legislation.gov.uk/ukpga/2014/23/contents/enacted/data.htm

www.cipd.co.uk/knowledge/strategy/resourcing/talent-factsheet)

www.jump4biz.com/Culture_Corporate_Cohesiveness_faq_Culture.php

Age UK – www.ageuk.org.uk

Equality and Human Rights Commission (EHRC) – www.equalityhumanrights.com

Health & Care Professions Council (HCPC) – www.hcpc-uk.co.uk

National Skills Academy for Social Care – www.nsasocialcare.co.uk

Social Care Institute for Excellence – www.scie.org.uk

Skills for Care – www.skillsforcare.org.uk.

Governance and regulatory processes

About this unit

Scally and Donaldson (1998) defined clinical governance as:

'a system through which NHS organisations are accountable for continuously improving the quality of their services and safeguarding high standards of care by creating an environment in which excellence in clinical care will flourish.'

Source: Scally and Donaldson, 1998, p. 61

All adult care and health care systems in this country are required to provide safe and good-quality care, improving the service user experience, as well as continually updating practice in the light of evidence from research. The scandal relating to the Mid-Staffordshire Healthcare Trust, for example, highlighted the treatment of patients and led to an inquiry into failings in the system. The Francis Report and a response by the government to improve the safeguarding and the quality of care is another example of the need to monitor performance in a structured and effective manner.

This unit is about the responsibility to deliver safe adult care. As a manager of care services, you are responsible for the safety and wellbeing of service users. To do this, performance management systems need to be put into place which not only identify best practice and focus on continuous improvement but also deliver better outcomes for service users by acting upon new initiatives, legislation and information.

Learning outcomes

By the end of this unit, you will:

1 Understand legislation and statutory requirements that underpin adult care provision

2 Understand internal governance arrangements within your own organisation

3 Understand systems and requirements for regulation of adult care services

4 Understand roles, remits and responsibilities in registered services

5 Understand inspection processes

6 Understand wider ranges of regulatory requirements that apply to services

Getting started

Before you study the unit, think about the following:

● What do the terms 'governance' and 'regulation' mean?

● Do you understand why these are so important for your organisation and for all adult care?

● What are the internal arrangements for governance within your organisation?

● Do you know your role and responsibilities in the inspection process?

LO1 Understand legislation and statutory requirements that underpin adult care provision

AC 1.1 Legislation and statutory frameworks

*Here, you will be required to investigate the current UK legislation and statutory frameworks that apply to **social care providers**, **NHS providers** and **voluntary sector providers**, including the ones we discuss in this section.*

KEY TERMS

Social care providers are healthcare providers who operate on one or more sites; these settings vary and can range from individuals' homes to specialised care settings to hospitals.
NHS providers: these are health professionals who provide care services within the NHS.
Voluntary sector providers: these are part of charitable trusts or groups who simply volunteer services to support health and/or social care services.

This section highlights the main legislation that impacts upon health and social care provision in this country and which applies to social care, the NHS and voluntary care sectors.

Legislation must be applied to all practice. Tragic incidents can happen when the legal aspects of care work are either not followed correctly or ignored altogether. Failure to uphold the law will inevitably lead to consequences not only to service users but also to staff and the care establishment as a whole.

The Health and Social Care Act 2008 (Regulated Activities) Regulations 2014

The regulations were introduced following the Francis Report into care at Mid-Staffordshire NHS Foundation Trust (Francis, 2013) and introduced new fundamental standards for care. These standards of care included a new 'professional duty of candour' outlining the need for health and social care professionals to be open and honest when things go wrong and to be honest about reporting adverse incidents or near misses that may have led to harm.

Other standards highlight the needs for treating people with dignity, respect, with their consent and in a safe way by engaging competent and qualified staff of good character. For more on these standards see Unit 501.

Should care not reach those standards, provision is made within the guidelines to take enforcement action.

Fit and proper person

Part 3 of Section 1 of the Regulations introduces requirements relating to people carrying on or managing a regulated activity. These are termed the 'fit and proper person requirements' for directors and determine that directors of care are of 'good character' and 'have the qualifications, competence, skills and experience necessary for the relevant position' (DH, 2014).

The Equality Act

The Equality Act (2010) brings together legislation that deals with race, disability and gender, replacing and simplifying previous anti-discrimination laws, making them easier to understand. It highlights protected characteristics of age, gender reassignment, pregnancy, religion, marriage and civil partnerships, and sexual orientation in an attempt to end discrimination. It strengthened protection by setting out the different ways in which unlawful treatment may happen to someone. Individuals are now fully protected from discrimination in the workplace and in wider society.

The Care Act (2014)

This sets out the key responsibilities of local authorities in meeting the needs of individuals who require help and support to promote their wellbeing. The main aim was to provide integrated care and to introduce the right to an assessment for anyone in order to offer more control in their care and to help people to stay as independent as possible.

The act simplified and improved the existing legislation for care, changing the way in which care was accessed and financed. People requiring care are now able to access care and support from local authorities or other organisations in the community and have more choice about the type of support and care they receive.

Under this legislation, service users receiving care and support from any regulated provider are covered by the Human Rights Act (1998), and local authorities are responsible for helping the service user to access independent financial advice to help them with care funding.

The Care Quality Commission (CQC)

Regulations

Section 23 of the Health and Social Care Act 2008 (HSCA 2008) instructed the Care Quality Commission to produce guidance to help care providers meet the changes required by the Health and Social Care Act 2008 (Regulated Activities) Regulations 2014. This document replaced CQC's 'Guidance about Compliance: Essential standards of quality and safety' and its 28 outcomes. The regulations apply to providers and managers registered with the CQC who carry on regulated activities in any sector.

Fundamental standards

The guidance lays down fundamental standards that must be met by registered persons. Care services must never fall below these standards, and every person who uses a care service has the right to expect such high-quality care. These are stated on the CQC's website and include the following:

- **Person-centred care**: Treatment is individualised to meet the service user's needs and preferences.
- **Dignity and respect**: Service users have equality, privacy and support to help them remain independent and involved in the local community.
- **Consent**: Prior to any care or treatment, the service user (or anybody legally acting on their behalf) gives their consent.
- **Safety**: Risks are evaluated during any care or treatment pathway, ensuring staff are qualified and competent to keep clients safe.
- **Safeguarding from abuse**: Neglect, degrading treatment, unnecessary or disproportionate restraint or inappropriate limits on freedom are unacceptable.
- **Food and drink**: Anyone receiving care and treatment has enough to eat and drink to keep them in good health.
- **Premises and equipment**: Settings and items used for care services are suitable, secure and looked after properly.
- **Complaints**: Systems should be in place to handle and respond to client complaints, with a thorough investigation and action being taken if problems are identified.
- **Good governance**: Quality and safety of care must be monitored to help the service improve and reduce any risks to health, safety and welfare for service users.
- **Staffing**: Qualified, competent and experienced staff are in place and receive the support, training and supervision that they need to help them do their job.
- **Fit and proper staff**: Staff can provide the care and treatment appropriate to their role, recruited via efficient recruitment procedures and after relevant checks (e.g. DBS, formerly CRB) have been implemented.
- **Duty of Candour**: Settings are open and transparent about clients' care and treatment. If something goes wrong, the setting offers support and an apology.

- **Display of ratings**: The CQC rating is displayed where stakeholders can see it, and should also appear on the organisation's website.

KLOEs

CQC's Key Lines of Enquiry were introduced in 2013 and highlight how healthcare providers will be inspected and judged against five key questions:

- Are they safe?
- Are they effective?
- Are they caring?
- Are they responsive to people's needs?
- Are they well led?

The Key Lines of Enquiry direct the focus of inspections to ensure that scrutiny is consistent.

Mental Capacity Act

The Mental Capacity Act 2005 protects and supports people who do not have the ability or capacity to make decisions for themselves. The act applies to people aged 16 and over in England and Wales and makes provision in a number of different conditions for those whose capacity is affected.

A person with capacity is able to understand information that is relevant to the decision they want to make and can retain that information long enough to make the decision. They will also be able to weigh up the information they have been given and to communicate their decision by means such as talking, using sign language, or through simple muscle movements such as blinking of an eye or squeezing a hand. If a person is deemed to lack capacity then any decision made must be in their best interests – we look at how this is enacted later.

See Unit 504, AC 2.3 and Unit 508, AC 2.8 for more about the Mental Capacity Act.

Mental Health Act 1983

The 1983 Mental Health Act laid down provision for the compulsory detention and treatment of people with mental health problems in England and Wales and focused upon strengthening patients' rights to review their treatment.

Mental Health Act 2007

The Mental Health Act (MHA) was amended in 2007 and focused on public protection and **risk management**. The amended legislation extends the powers of compulsion and introduces compulsory community treatment orders, making patients' compliance with treatment a statutory requirement.

The main changes outlined in the 2007 MHA are as follows:

- **Definition of mental disorder**: A single definition replaced categories of disorder found in the 1983 MHA. The definition covers 'any disorder or disability of the mind'. Individuals with learning disabilities are exempt here as they are not suffering from a mental disorder unless the disability is associated with aggressive or irresponsible conduct.

- **Criteria for detention**: For detention to be put into place a relevant health professional must guarantee that medical treatment, including psychological intervention, is available. This is 'the appropriate treatment test' and replaces the former 'treatability test'.

- **Professional roles**: Anyone with experience in supporting people with mental health problems, such as nurses, occupational therapists and psychologists, can now make assessments and referrals as there have been changes to the roles of professionals. The former title 'approved social worker' has been replaced by 'approved mental health professional'.

- **Responsible clinician role**: This replaced the responsible medical officer and social workers or other clinicians can now fill this role. Recommendations for detentions under Sections 2 and 3 of the 1983 MHA still have to be made by two 'registered medical practitioners'.

- **Nearest relatives**: Service users can remove their nominated nearest relative if they feel that person is unsuitable. Civil partners have the same status as husband and wife on the list of eligible relatives.

- **Community treatment orders**: Provided people who are discharged from hospital continue the medical treatment they need they can live at home under supervision. This is called the Community Treatment Order (CTO) and replaces the 'supervised discharge' of the 1983 MHA. Failing to comply with the conditions of the CTO may result in the person being recalled to hospital under Section 17E.

- **Mental health review tribunals**: A community patient is referred to a Mental Health Review Tribunal (MHRT) to determine whether he or she can receive a formal discharge.

- **Age-appropriate services**: Anyone under 18 who is admitted to hospital for a mental disorder must be accommodated a suitable setting for his or her age.

- **Electro-convulsive therapy (ECT)**: This should be given to a patient without their consent only in an emergency. If the patient lacks capacity to consent, the treatment can be given only if it is appropriate and does not conflict with the safeguards set out in the 2005 Mental Capacity Act.

- **Advocacy**: The UK government in England and the Welsh Assembly are responsible for providing an independent mental health advocate to a person who is liable to be detained.

Deprivation of Liberty Safeguards

In 2007, the MHA introduced Deprivation of Liberty Safeguards (DoLS) by amending the 2005 Mental Capacity Act, and the rights of victims were extended by amending the Domestic Violence, Crime and Victims Act 2004.

According to the Human Rights Act: 'Everyone has the right to liberty and security of person. No one shall be deprived of his liberty [unless] in accordance with a procedure prescribed in law'.

If a person lacks capacity to make decisions and cannot therefore consent to necessary treatment, then the Deprivation of Liberty Safeguards are put into place to keep them safe from harm. It is important that if the restrictions are put into place, they are in the patient's best interest.

The Safeguarding Vulnerable Groups Act 2006

The Safeguarding Vulnerable Groups Act (SVGA) 2006 was passed to protect children and vulnerable adults from harm, or risk of harm, from people who are deemed unsuitable to work with such groups. As a result of this act, the Independent Safeguarding Authority was established and merged with the Criminal Records Bureau to become the Disclosure and Barring Service (DBS).

Protection of Freedoms Bill

The Protection of Freedoms Bill amends the SVGA 2006. It abolished registration and monitoring requirements but retained the national barring function.

Health and Safety at Work Act 1974 and associated regulations

You will be familiar with the Health and Safety at Work Act 1974 (HASAWA), which is the main piece of UK health and safety legislation. It places a duty on all employers 'to ensure, so far as is reasonably practicable, the health, safety and welfare at work' of all their employees. Additionally, it requires:

- the safe operation and maintenance of the working environment, plant (equipment) and systems
- maintenance of safe access and egress to the workplace
- safe use, handling and storage of dangerous substances
- adequate training of staff to ensure health and safety
- adequate welfare provisions for staff at work.

Source: www.hse.gov.uk/legislation/trace.htm

The Management of Health and Safety at Work Regulations 1999 (the Management Regulations) further highlights and details in greater depth what employers are required to do to manage health and safety under the Health and Safety at Work Act. The main requirement is the need to carry out a risk assessment. Employers with five or more employees need to record the significant findings of the risk assessment.

Evidence opportunity

1.1 Legislation and statutory frameworks

Investigate the current UK legislation and statutory frameworks that apply to social care workers, NHS providers and voluntary sector providers, including the ones that we have covered in this section. You could provide a written account of your findings for your portfolio.

Research it

1.1 Legislation, policies and procedures

Look at the 2015 CQC document 'Social care: Recent changes to the CQC's regulation of adult residential care (care homes)' to identify how this has changed/might change the way in which your provision is inspected.

Which pieces of legislation listed above apply to your setting? For each one, find out its purpose and investigate the related policies and procedures in your setting.

What are your responsibilities with respect to how legislation is implemented in your setting?

AC 1.2 Effects of legislation and policy on practice

Here, you will be required to analyse the association between legislation and policy on person-centred care and positive outcomes-based procedures and practice. This should include effects on a range of policies relevant to your own area of provision.

There is a strong association between legislation and **policy** on person-centred care and positive outcomes-based **procedures** and practice. All these laws will be enshrined in the policies and procedures you are required to have in your workplace.

Policies set out the arrangements you have for complying with the law and procedures identify the activity surrounding practice needed to implement the policy. As a manager, one of

KEY TERMS

Policy is a plan or principle of action proposed by an organisation, also known as guidelines or codes.
Procedures state how policies will be carried out or actioned in the setting.
Risk management is the forecasting of potential risks and minimising them or avoiding them altogether. Your policies should identify how you undertake risk assessment in your area and how you intend to manage risks that arise.

your roles is to ensure that staff are aware of the importance of carrying out practice according to policy. Failure to do so can have major consequences for the client, the organisation and the member of staff, as we shall see in the next section.

Person-centred care

The Health Foundation (2014) explain person-centred care as:

- giving people dignity, compassion and respect
- offering coordinated and personalised care, support or treatment
- supporting people to recognise and develop their own strengths and abilities to live independent and fulfilling lives.

It is therefore about making the individual requiring the care the central figure in the process. The government publication Putting People First: A Shared Vision and Commitment to the Transformation of Adult Social Care was published in 2007 and outlined its personalisation agenda – the government's vision of enabling individuals to live independently with complete choice and control over their lives.

Personalisation is about allowing individuals to build a system of care and support tailored to meet their needs and designed with their full involvement. It is about ensuring that the individual has their choices taken into account and their culture and ethnicity respected, with care tailored to these factors. Historically, a 'one size fits all' approach to care was in practice and this meant the individual had to fit into and access existing care services, whether they were appropriate or not.

The term 'person-centred care' is now used to describe care which is user focused, promoting independence and autonomy. Collaborative and partnership approaches to care often use the term 'person-centred' to describe their ethos (Innes et al., 2006).

Table 2.1 outlines some of the legislation, white papers, reports and guidance that affect person-centred care. The legislation from AC 1.1 may also be relevant here.

Table 2.1 Documentation and its relevance to person-centred care

Date	Act/guidance	Purpose and effect
2000	The NHS Plan	Highlighted the need for personalisation and coordination of services, to streamline and improve services and waiting times.
2001	The Valuing People White Paper	Made direct payments available to more people with a learning disability and introduced the term 'person-centred planning'. The effect has been movement on the personalisation agenda.
2002 (updated 2008)	The Wanless Report: Securing Good Health for the Whole Population	Focused on enablement and empowerment, with patients being partners in care.
2005	The Mental Capacity Act	Highlighted the patient's right to make choices and have their preferences respected, even if others (advocates) make decisions on their behalf. This has had an effect on enabling people with mental health problems to have greater control.
2005	SCIE and the Department of Health, Independence, Well-being and Choice: Our Vision for the Future of Social Care for Adults in England	Stated that a social model approach to care which 'supports people to be independent by ensuring they have the support to live as they wish' was favoured, affecting the way in which care is delivered.
2005	Improving the Life Chances of Disabled People	Individual budgets to improve choice and control over the mix of care and support.
2005	Independence, Well-being and Choice	Social care services help people to maintain their independence by 'giving them greater choice and control over the way their needs are met'.
2006	Our Health, Our Care, Our Say: A new direction for community service	Developed the concept of personalised care.
2007	Putting People First: A shared vision and commitment to transformation of adult social care	A commitment to enable people to manage and control their own support through individual/personal budgets.
2008	Lord Darzi's report, 'High Quality Care for All'	Highlighted the need to change public expectations of services. It included the importance of people being involved in decisions about their care.
2009	The first NHS Constitution in England	Described what people could expect from the NHS and brought policy statements of intent to form a rights framework which reflects the needs and preferences of patients, their families and their carers. Also patients, families and carers would be involved in and consulted on all decisions about their care and treatment.
2009	Care Support Independence: Shaping the future of care together	A consultation on how personalised social care and support can be delivered and funded.
2009	Personal Health Budgets: 'First steps'	Introduced the personal health budget to allow people to have more choice, flexibility and control over the health services and care they receive.
2010	The Francis Report	The failings in care at Mid Staffordshire NHS Foundation Trust between 2005 and 2009 forced the person-centred care agenda back into the public awareness. It focused sharply on dignity, compassion and respect.
2010	A Vision for Adult Social Care: Capable communities and active citizens	Set out the plans for a new direction for adult social care, putting personalised services and outcomes centre stage, based on six principles, personalisation being one such principle.
2012	The Health and Social Care Act	Requires the Clinical Commissioning Groups to promote the involvement of every patient.

➡

Date	Act/guidance	Purpose and effect
2013	The Berwick Advisory Group	Greater involvement of patients and their carers at every level of the health service in order to deliver safe, meaningful and appropriate healthcare.
2014	The Care Act	Requires local authorities to involve adults in their assessment, care and support planning and review.
2017	New framework to promote person-centred approaches in healthcare	Framework commissioned by Health Education England to promote the support, care and advice given to suit individuals' needs. It supports those in care to manage their own health and wellbeing and encourages shared decision making, ensuring information is personalised and accessible.

As we can see from the laws and guidance published since 2000, there has been a major revamp of adult social care law in England, all with the intention of seeking to transform care. The Care Act 2014 was a move to a single piece of legislation so people were clear about their rights.

Evidence opportunity

1.2 Effects of legislation and policy on practice

Provide a written account analysing the association between legislation and policy on person-centred care and positive outcomes-based procedures and practice. This should include effects on a range of policies relevant to own area of provision. Think about the things that we have discussed in this section.

Reflect on it

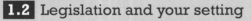

1.2 Legislation and your setting

Reflect on the ways in which the laws and papers in Table 2.1 have affected the way in which your setting delivers its care.

List five procedures or policies in your work setting which have developed as a result of legislation.

For example, you might look at how the Mental Capacity Act 2005 has impacted your work and comment on the changes the setting has made.

AC 1.3 Drawing attention to potential conflicts

Here, you will be required to evaluate the benefits of using local and/or national forums to draw attention to potential conflicts between statutory frameworks and values/ principles for good practice.

In trying to adhere to and meet the requirements of legislation we occasionally find there are areas of conflict.

For example, the Care Act requires that all service users are involved in their care planning and assessment processes. While we would agree this is excellent practice, lack of time, staffing resources and finance may make this difficult to achieve. The Francis Report also commented upon the need to treat patients with dignity and this has become enshrined in the Care Act. The waiting times at hospitals and the nursing of patients in corridors while beds are sought also brings this into question.

It is imperative that local and national forums are consulted when there is a potential for misunderstandings to occur. For example, if we find that care which conforms to the legal requirements cannot be given, this needs to be honestly dealt with and brought to the attention of groups such as the Health and Wellbeing Board and Care Commissioning Groups.

These local forums may be able to supply us with helpful information.

It is important that a positive organisational culture is developed which reflects and reinforces a commitment to delivering excellent standards of care in line with the law. The challenge which may otherwise lead to conflict is to ensure that everybody knows what the values and resulting policies of the organisation are and how they are expected to adopt these in their work. Staff cannot be expected to enact values that they are not aware of. An explicit and transparent statement of values must be discussed with staff and made available to the public, thus providing a clear indication of expectations of behaviour. Second, discussion of what this actually means in practice is important in helping staff to make the link from expressed values, which may seem intangible, into real practice. In successful organisations, there is a clear correlation between espoused values and the ethical leadership of that organisation's leaders on the successful realisation of values within an organisation (Renz and Eddy, 1996). That is to say, it is essential that the leaders are seen to live and enact the values.

Evidence opportunity

1.3 Drawing attention to potential conflicts

Provide a written account evaluating the benefits of using local and/or national forums to draw attention to potential conflicts between statutory frameworks and values/principles for good practice.

You might like to consider, for example, what potential conflicts between statutory frameworks and values/principles for good practice you are currently experiencing in your care setting. What are the local groups to which you can turn for support?

If you work with other managers (on the same or a different level to you), how do you ensure that these are made known to them?

How easy is it for staff to come to you with their concerns and have them dealt with? Give an example of an incident in which this has happened and document the outcome.

LO2 Understand internal governance arrangements within your own organisation

AC 2.1 Governance mechanisms

*Here, you will be required to describe your own organisation's **governance procedures** and mechanisms. You will be required to critically evaluate your own organisation's governance mechanisms to be able to identify how these relate to the identity of the organisation. This will include the topics we discuss in this section.*

KEY TERM

Governance procedures and **mechanisms** refer to the monitoring of actions, practices and policies which guide the decisions of organisations and their stakeholders.

Governance concepts

Scally and Donaldson (1998) defined clinical governance as

> 'a system through which NHS organisations are accountable for continuously improving the quality of their services and safeguarding high standards of care by creating an environment in which excellence in clinical care will flourish.'
>
> **Source:** Scally and Donaldson, 1998, p. 61

We want adult social care to be safe and of good quality. Care governance provides a framework through which this can be assured.

Governance processes

Risk management

This is about making sure the risks to service users for whatever reason are minimal. We need to check that we identify what can go wrong in care and ensure that if something does happen we learn from it and change it for the future. For example, sepsis is a big problem for the NHS and to reduce the numbers of fatalities, trusts have been working to reduce the risks associated with it by looking at past practice and speeding up current practice.

Clinical audit

An audit compares one thing against another to check its quality. For example, you may be required to audit the compliance with handwashing in the setting. There would be certain standards expected with handwashing and by monitoring our performance against such standards we are able to check efficiency. The audit on handwashing would therefore check and identify if we are not meeting the standards and we can make changes to practice. Auditing may be a local practice but there are also national audits into which all care organisations put data.

Education, training and continuing professional development

Our staff are a major resource so time and money spent in upskilling those people and ensuring they have the knowledge to do excellent work are required under the governance principles. This can range from mentoring to formal training courses. All upskilling activities should be recorded.

Your staff need to be aware of the responsibility they have to update their knowledge and to attend health and safety training on a regular basis. It is your responsibility to ensure that the opportunity to do this is available and that staff are encouraged to take time to attend training courses so that there is no reason for not complying with health, safety and risk management policies and procedures. Failure to comply could mean the staff member would be put at risk of losing their job and there will also be consequences for the organisation.

Evidence-based care and effectiveness

We should give care based upon researched evidence that it is the best practice. The National Institute of Clinical Excellence provides guidelines for practice which care organisations must follow. To go back to our earlier example on handwashing, this activity has been researched and nationally accepted guidelines as to the most effective way in which to carry out the procedure are available.

Service user and carer experience and involvement

Complaints and compliments are a vital link to how others feel about the service and we should take these on board. We need close partnerships with families, friends and others who work with the service user in our care. Governance is about establishing policies and procedures and also monitoring the processes to ensure that the organisation meets the needs of the people who use it. Efficient monitoring of complaints is a necessary part of the process.

Staffing and staff management

Highly skilled people working to provide quality care need to be supported and motivated. Part of governance is training and upskilling of staff. Additionally, we need to ensure that staff are motivated to encourage them to stay with the organisation.

Roles and responsibilities within the governance process

As managers of health services, we are responsible for the safety and wellbeing of our service users, and for ensuring that the components of clinical governance are in place and being worked towards.

As a manager and leader in adult care, your knowledge of the law and how it is translated into practice through policy and implemented by your staff must underpin your practice. Undoubtedly, you will already have a good working knowledge and practice related to the legal aspects of care work, but it is wise to revisit this from time to time. You will need to ensure you offer strong induction activities and training for staff. Staff need to understand their roles and responsibilities about health and safety record-keeping and reporting and must also be aware of the necessity of complying with policies and procedures and practice. Any breaches must be dealt with effectively and quickly to avoid unsafe practice. By monitoring compliance to the policies and procedures and ensuring that checks/audits take place and that risk assessments are updated, you will be practising safely with respect to this part of your management role.

To maintain such high-quality care in your organisation you need to create a performance management system which:

● identifies areas of best practice and focuses on continuous improvement

● delivers better outcomes to service users

● improves adult care services by acting upon new initiatives and information

● ensures that organisational activities are linked to the overall goals of the organisation.

The NHS Institute for Innovation and Improvement states:

> *'Performance management enables organisations to articulate their business strategy, align their business to that strategy, identify their key performance indicators (KPIs) and track progress, delivering the information to decision-makers.'*

It also provides a performance management tool which may be downloaded from its website to help the process.

www.nhsemployers.org/case-studies-and-resources/2018/04/people-performance-management-toolkit

For more information on performance management see AC 1.3 on critical reviews and inquiries.

Understanding of the governance process within the organisation

We need adult care that is standardised, of good quality and good reputation, and that conforms to government legislation. Above all, we want to work in organisations that are accountable for what they do and are transparent so that all involved can see the decisions being made and understand why they are needed. Governance also requires that we work in partnership with other sectors, including the private and voluntary sectors. This requires that service users and their families, as well as the partners we work with, all participate in the decision-making process.

See the WHO guidance on governance within health systems at: www.who.int/healthsystems/topics/stewardship/en/

Evidence opportunity

2.1 Governance mechanisms

Provide a written account describing your organisation's governance procedures and mechanisms. Then, critically evaluate your organisation's governance mechanisms, so that you can identify how these relate to the identity of the organisation. Include governance concepts, governance processes, roles and responsibilities within the governance process, and understanding of the governance process within the organisation.

Reflect on it

2.1 Governance mechanisms

1 Describe your organisation's governance procedures and mechanisms, saying how you evidence the following:

- risk management
- clinical audit
- education, training and continuing professional development
- evidence-based care and effectiveness
- service user and carer experience and involvement
- staffing and staff management.

Pick three of these aspects and critically evaluate how successfully your organisation uses these procedures and mechanisms to ensure positive outcomes. In evaluating it is a good idea to question why you do certain things and what is good or otherwise about what you do. For example, if you undertake a clinical audit of handwashing and find that staff are not complying with the practice, what do you do about this? Ask questions such as 'Why are staff non-compliant?', 'What else is happening?' and 'What might be done to change this?'

2 What are your roles and responsibilities within these areas of work?

AC 2.2 Personal accountability

Here, you will be required to evaluate your accountability and role within your organisation's governance structure.

If we are accountable for something, then we are said to take responsibility for it and in adult care this means we should always ensure that we are competent to carry out tasks and procedures while being acutely aware of the service user's safety. For example, adult care workers are expected to undertake annual training on manual handling to protect themselves and their service users. There are standards such as the use of hoists, slide sheets and other manual handling equipment. But what happens in the workplace? Perhaps you do not have the equipment or perhaps staff simply are not using it, feeling it is too time consuming.

Being 'accountable' means we must be able to justify what we are doing and why we are doing it, and also justify that we are competent to carry out the task in question.

Staff must be clear that they will be held accountable for errors, mistakes or problems so they should be able to feel confident to speak up if they can't or shouldn't do something.

Evidence opportunity

2.2 Personal accountability

Provide a written account evaluating your accountability and role within your organisation's governance structure.

You might like to consider what you are accountable for. For example, what actions and processes are you responsible for and entrusted to complete? Give an example of an area of your work for which you are accountable and discuss the positives and negatives of this situation.

As a manager you are accountable for the whole team too and need to be aware of what it is your staff are doing and how they are doing it.

We owe our service users a duty of care to deliver their care in a safe and kind manner and to ensure that we abide by the code of conduct laid down by our particular professional body.

Hay system

Read more at: www.businessdictionary.com/definition/accountability.html

Reflect on it

2.2 What are you accountable for?

What are you accountable for in your role as manager?

Evaluate how your role and accountabilities help you to ensure you maintain your organisation's governance structure. Give an example from practice and demonstrate how you are accountable in practice. Show the pros and cons of your role with respect to accountability. For example, how do you ensure staff are upholding practice policy and how do you deal with those who do not conform?

AC 2.3 Protocols, policies and procedures

*Here, you will be required to critically review how your own organisation's **agreed ways of working**, **protocols**, policies and procedures relate to governance and accountability and the link to quality of care provision. This will include feedback from those using services, those acting on their behalf and other stakeholders so that you can continually drive improvement.*

KEY TERMS

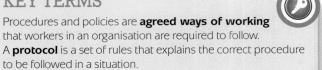

Procedures and policies are **agreed ways of working** that workers in an organisation are required to follow.

A **protocol** is a set of rules that explains the correct procedure to be followed in a situation.

The difference between procedures and policies lies in the fact that policies are designed to help an organisation meet its objectives and so may grow and change. A protocol is a standardised way of doing something and is generally a step-by-step directive to be followed to help accomplish a task. Not following a protocol leads to misunderstandings or sometimes miscommunications. For example, there are protocols medical professionals follow in dealing with patients who present with certain illnesses, and these indicate regimes of treatment to be given. These protocols are based on evidence and research and are followed in a specific way. Policies, on the other hand, are different in that they assist in decision making and grow and change over time.

When we refer to agreed ways of working we are really talking about the culture of the organisation in which we work and the policies and procedures which are laid down in that culture.

A culture is the way in which things are done and will be reflected in the values and attitudes of the staff who work in that organisation. For example, a culture of safety within your organisation will be reflected in everything that you do – if you work in a high-pressure environment you may be aware that there are in-house counsellors who can be contacted easily should you require psychological or emotional help to stay safe.

Your staff will be educated about patient safety and your policies and procedures will have patient safety at the heart of their practice.

Additionally, the stakeholders and those who use the service or are in partnership with you will be aware of your agreed ways of working.

Evidence opportunity

2.3 Protocols, policies and procedures

Provide a written account to critically review how your own organisation's agreed ways of working, protocols, policies and procedures relate to governance and accountability and the link to quality of care provision. This will include feedback from those using services, those acting on their behalf and other stakeholders so that you can continually drive improvement.

Your organisation's agreed ways of working, the protocols, policies and procedures all relate to governance and accountability and link to quality of care provision. For example, failure of staff to work within a policy or to follow a strict protocol could have a detrimental effect to the service and a service user may suffer as a consequence. This will lead to the service being accountable for errors.

In evaluating your own service's protocols and policies, look at the positive and negative effects of the ways of working and how they impact upon the service. What is good about having such practices in place? Are there any limitations?

Reflect on it

2.3 Agreed ways of working, protocols, policies and procedures

1 What are your organisation's agreed ways of working, protocols, policies and procedures? Do these reflect a particular culture, for example of safety or person-centred care?

2 Review how these relate to governance and accountability and to quality of care provision.

3 Provide evidence for your portfolio by looking at feedback from those using services, those acting on their behalf and other stakeholders.

4 Explain how this evidence can be used to continually drive improvement.

LO3 Understand systems and requirements for regulation of adult care services

AC 3.1 The inspection system in England

Here, you will be required to explain the key drivers and impacts of legislation for the inspection system, including the topics we discuss in this section.

The Health and Social Care Act and the Care Act

The HSCA and the Care Act both set out key responsibilities of local authorities to meet the needs of individuals who require help and support to promote their wellbeing and the HSCA set out the CQC's statutory powers and duties. The CQC is the lead inspection and enforcement body for safety and quality of treatment and care matters involving service users in receipt of a health or adult social care service from a provider registered with the CQC.

The Health and Safety Executive (HSE)/local authorities are the lead inspection and enforcement bodies for health and safety matters involving service users who are in receipt of a health or care service from providers not registered with the CQC.

The process recognises that certain bodies may be more appropriate to deal with specific cases. So, for example, the CQC will be called to investigate an incident where a service user is seriously injured or dying after being physically restrained by staff, but the HSE and local authority may be asked to investigate a manual handling injury to an employee.

Both pieces of legislation focus upon quality and standards in care to address some of the catastrophic failings within the care sector (see below) which resulted in neglect and abuse of service users in a number of settings. As a result of these laws, the inspection framework for care settings has changed.

Recent local/national queries and findings from serious case review

As a manager you are required to have in place policy and procedure to protect service users, staff and visitors from breaches of health and safety law. The Francis Report, published in 2013, reported on the Mid Staffs NHS Foundation Trust where a major failure in patient care was uncovered. As a result, an important change was introduced in April 2015, giving new enforcement powers to the CQC with respect to health and safety in the care sector. The main purpose of the group is to monitor, inspect and regulate services to ensure standards of quality and safety are being met. Failure to do so would result in prosecution.

The change ensures that there is effective and coordinated regulation of health and safety for service users, workers and members of the public and a shared responsibility between the CQC, the HSE and local authorities to ensure safety.

Other appropriate topical reviews and reports

Examples of findings that have led to reform

In May 2011, a BBC Panorama documentary showed shocking undercover footage of abuse and humiliation carried out by a team of carers at Winterbourne View hospital in South Gloucestershire, which was owned and operated by a private company, Castlebeck. As a result of this programme, a **serious case review** led to 11 employees being charged and the closure of Winterbourne View, as well as criticism of the CQC for its failure to act when complaints had been made. Lessons learned from this serious breach of human rights led to a review of Castlebeck's management structures and they were eventually sold in 2013 and in 2016 the CQC launched a new strategy for quality.

In another example, Orchid View was a West Sussex private nursing home registered as a care home with nursing for up to 87 people in the categories of old age and dementia. Opened in November 2009, it closed in October 2011 following revelations of several safeguarding alerts and investigations and possible criminal offences. In October 2013, an inquest found that five people had 'died from natural causes attributed to neglect' and that several other people 'died as a result of natural causes' with 'insufficient evidence before me [the coroner Penelope Schofield] to show that this suboptimal care was directly causative' of

their deaths.... This suboptimal care caused distress, poor care and discomfort to residents and the families of people who were not the subject of the Inquest' (Orchid View Serious Case Review, June 2014).

A further example was the case of Simon Willson in 2010 who was found hanged in a hospital toilet after being transferred out of the A&E department of Kent and Canterbury hospital following a drug overdose. Despite being resuscitated he suffered brain damage and subsequently died. The patient had been to Canterbury police station that morning and asked to be sectioned, clearly stating his suicidal thoughts and admissions of previous attempts to hang himself. He had a history of depression.

Despite the trust having policies in place, these had not been followed on this occasion and the trust had therefore been found guilty of breaching the Health and Safety at Work Act (1974).

These cases highlight the need for quality assurance, regulation and inspection procedures to be in place and monitored to ensure that safeguarding is foremost in our care giving.

As a result of these reviews, from April 2015 fundamental standards for the quality of health and adult social care have been introduced together with a radical reform to CQC's regulatory and inspection approach. Chief Inspectors of Hospitals, Adult Social Care and General Practice have also been appointed.

The inspection process brought about by legislative changes has meant that hospitals have come under greater scrutiny, with some failing to meet basic standards of care. These were put into 'special measures' and given additional support to make fundamental and necessary changes to practice.

Evidence opportunity

3.1 The inspection system in England
Provide a written account explaining the key drivers and impact of legislation for the inspection system, including the Health and Social Care Act, the Care Act, recent local/national findings from Safeguarding Adults Reviews and other appropriate topical reviews and reports. You could also explain this to your assessor.

Reflect on it

3.1 Impact of legislation

Write a short piece explaining the impact of legislation such as the Health and Social Care Act and the Care Act and any other recent local/national queries and findings from Safeguarding Adults Reviews that may have impacted on the way your service is inspected. In evaluating such cases, ask yourself some questions such as:

- What might have been the cause of the breach of the policy?
- What lessons can your service learn from these incidents?
- How does your service ensure staff are aware of their duty with respect to adhering to policy?

AC 3.2 Services subject to registration and to inspection

Here, you will be required to identify services subject to registration and inspection, covering a range of provision for all adult services. To include service provision in social care and acute care.

The CQC is responsible for the inspection and regulation of all social and acute care providers including prisons, GPs, health centres, childminders and nurseries, NHS and independent hospitals and care homes. It inspects and reports upon the standards found in the setting.

Social care

Social care is a generic term relating to services available from health and social care providers. It relates to the provision of social work, including social support services and personal care, and protects adults at risk or adults with needs arising from illness, disability, old age or poverty. It also includes caring for children in these circumstances.

Acute care

Acute care is secondary healthcare in which short-term treatment for an injury or an illness is given. If somebody requires urgent treatment for a medical condition or an operation, this is acute care.

Evidence opportunity

3.2 Services subject to registration and to inspection

Identify services that are subject to registration and inspection, covering a range of provision for all adult services, including service provision in social care and acute care.

List the services you are aware of in the sphere of adult social services that require registration and inspection. Which are acute services and social care services?

You may wish to identify the settings you work in partnership with and try to find out what their CQC ratings are. The ratings should be displayed on their websites.

AC 3.3 Key areas of enquiry for inspection

Here, you will be required to identify the key areas for enquiry and how the evidence for these build towards ratings, including: safe, effective, caring, responsive and well-led.

The CQC uses KLOEs during inspections to assess how care providers are performing against five key questions:

- Are they safe?
- Are they effective?
- Are they caring?
- Are they responsive to people's needs?
- Are they well-led?

Each KLOE is accompanied by several questions that inspection teams consider during inspection. These are known as 'prompts 'and are designed to gather and record evidence to answer each KLOE. For example, a prompt for 'Are they safe?' is about safeguarding and protection from abuse: 'How do systems, processes and practices keep people safe and safeguarded from abuse?' A prompt for 'Are they effective?' regards governance: 'Are there clear responsibilities, roles and systems of accountability to support good governance and management?' The answers lead to a set of further questions so that inspectors can really understand how the services are performing.

This is a standardised framework with a standardised rating system and as the service provider you are in more control of the evidence you present. For example, having knowledge of what is going to be inspected means you are able to check systems, policies and protocols are in place and to provide evidence of how you meet the KLOE. By accessing the CQC's Good and outstanding care guide (available online at www.skillsforcare.org.uk) you can also gain a clearer idea about what constitutes good or outstanding care. Subjectivity plays a part in any inspection process so while you may feel your organisation covers the outstanding criteria on the day, you cannot expect all inspectors to agree, particularly if other service providers are achieving the same standard. Asking the inspectors what further evidence is needed will help.

Research it

3.3 CQC's Key Lines of Enquiry (KLOEs)

Look at the KLOEs set out on www.cqc.org.uk/guidance-providers/nhs-trusts/key-lines-enquiry-nhs-trusts. Identify the key areas for enquiry and identify how you would evidence that you cover these areas.

Look now at the positive aspects of this way of inspecting.

AC 3.4 Grading system and implications

Here, you will be required to describe and differentiate between the different grades available at inspection and evaluate the implications of each grade on a service.

The CQC will rate or grade each of the five key questions and will give an overall rating as either outstanding, good, requires improvement or inadequate.

Outstanding means that the service is performing exceptionally well, while good means the service is performing well and meeting expectations. If a service requires improvement this shows that the service must improve as it is not performing well enough according to standards.

An inadequate service is performing badly and actions against the person or organisation are put into place. An inadequate service is likely to be closed down until radical changes are made.

Evidence opportunity

3.4 Inspection grades and boundaries

Provide a written account that describes and differentiates between the different grades available at inspection and evaluate the implications of each grade for a service. Try to use an example from your own service to show the differences between the grade boundaries. For example, if in your last inspection you received a good for leadership and management, how are you improving your practice to ensure you receive outstanding next time?

 Outstanding means the service is performing exceptionally well.

 Good means the service is performing well and meeting CQC expectations.

 Requires improvement means the service is not performing well and CQC has indicated where improvements need to be made.

 Inadequate means the service is performing badly and CQC is taking action against the person or organisation that runs it.

Research it

3.4 Grading system and implications

Locate your last inspection report and look at the grading for each of the five key questions. Evaluate the implications of the grades for the services you offer.

How will you as a manager address each rating to ensure an improvement is made for the next inspection?

Compare the grades to those of a similar setting or service in your area. Explain the implications for your service when comparing the grades.

AC 3.5 Sources of information and support

Here, you will be required to critically evaluate sources of support and information available. These will include local, regional, national and professional networks.

Local and regional

Your local Clinical Commissioning Group (CCG), a clinically led statutory NHS body responsible for the planning and commissioning of healthcare services in local areas, will be able to provide guidance with healthcare issues. CCGs work closely with the local authority, safeguarding boards and providers and service user groups.

Local authorities promote the wellbeing of the public by carrying out care and support functions. Safeguarding boards are responsible for safeguarding adults and children with care and support needs by ensuring that local safeguarding arrangements are in place as defined by the Care Act 2014. Providers refer to anybody who delivers healthcare or social care and service user groups are patients, service users, carers or families who have an interest in the health and social care services and wish to provide additional help or advice to the statutory services.

If you are practising in Wales, it is the Care Inspectorate for Wales that provides information and Scotland also has its own inspectorate.

National

There are a number of websites and organisations where you can access support for your care sector. Overseeing health and social care nationally is the Department of Health, which provides information on the latest legislation and policies regarding all aspects of health and social care.

This department then delegates responsibility to regional and local health authorities and the CQC. This is the main health and social care regulator and the government has given the CQC the responsibility for inspecting and regulating health and social care in England and for compiling reports for providers of health and social care.

Additionally, the National Institute of Clinical Excellence (NICE) provides guidance on current best clinical practice and you can access a wealth of information from its website.

UK-wide, the following societies and organisations are also available for support:

- UK Online provides government information and services.
- Government Carer Information.
- Skills for Care.
- Skills for Health.
- Age UK.
- Alzheimer's Society.
- Bettercaring helps care professionals and consumers find care homes in the UK.
- Careaware is a public information and advisory service specialising in the issues relating to long-term care.
- Care Directions is an internet guide to care and the rights of older people.
- Centre for Policy on Ageing is an independent organisation promoting social policies that allow older people to achieve their full potential in later life.
- Action on Elder Abuse aims to prevent the abuse of older people.
- Help the Aged provides practical support to help older people to lead independent lives, especially those who are frail, isolated and poor.
- The Princess Royal Trust for Carers.
- Carers UK offers advice on benefits and services available to carers.

Professional networks

Professional bodies such as the British Medical Association, the Nursing and Midwifery Council and the British Association of Social Workers can provide much-needed guidance on medical and legal processes. In addition to these, local professional networks were set up following the NHS Commissioning Board's report on 'Securing excellence in commissioning primary care' (2012). They cover dentistry, pharmacy and eye health, and encourage service improvements to reduce health inequalities for local communities.

LO4 Understand roles, remits and responsibilities in registered services

AC 4.1 Roles and responsibilities of key people

Here, you will be required to review and evaluate the different functions for the specified roles within your own organisation and the wider responsibilities of key people in the inspection of registered services. You will need to specifically refer to governance and consider the roles and responsibilities of some of the people we discuss in this section.

There will be specified roles within your organisation and externally that cover specific tasks to enable governance. You also need to be aware of the wider responsibilities of key people in the inspection of registered services.

The registered manager

It is a legal requirement under the Health and Social Care Act 2008 to nominate a registered manager, as set out in Regulation 7: requirements relating to registered managers. This person must:

- be of good character
- be able to properly perform tasks that are intrinsic to their role
- have the necessary qualifications, competence, skills and experience to manage the regulated activity
- have supplied their employers with documents that confirm their suitability.

Adapted from: www.cqc.org.uk/guidance-providers

All providers must have a registered manager with the exceptions of some GP services and NHS trusts. The person undertaking this role must apply for a CQC counter-signed DBS check and demonstrate their fitness to be registered as a manager.

The registered manager will be expected to take appropriate action to address any shortfalls in practice and also to improve the situation. This means your role will be to look to the teams with which you work and ensure that they take responsibility for updating their knowledge and continually improving their practice.

The nominated individual (and who may be appointed to this role)

To register as a care organisation you need to nominate an individual to act as the main point of contact with the CQC. This may be the registered manager but is more usually another person in the organisation who can support the manager. They will have overall responsibility for supervising the management of the regulated activity and ensuring the quality of the services. Therefore, they must be a senior person, with authority to speak on behalf of the organisation. The role of this person is to supervise and take responsibility for the management of the service and to show how it provides quality of life for the people who use it.

The 'fit and proper person'

This person has met the criteria to be a Registered Provider, Nominated Individual or Registered Manager in terms of character and qualifications but does not have a specific role. It is a term that is becoming increasingly familiar in the sector. We would want all of our employees to be classified as 'fit and proper' persons, who are responsible for the quality and safety of care, and for meeting the fundamental standards.

Inspectors

These are the individuals who are employed by the CQC to monitor, inspect and regulate health and social care services. They will be independent of your organisation to ensure inspections remain fair and objective.

The governance tasks that inspectors might undertake are to ensure that you are complying with the fundamental standards of quality and safety and that the people in your care are receiving the right care. They will ensure that your service is open and honest about the way in which the care is delivered.

Auditors

NHS England and the Healthcare Quality Improvement Partnership (HQIP) commission auditors who collect and analyse data supplied by local clinicians to provide a national picture of care standards for a specific condition. On a local level, auditors provide local trusts with tailored reports on how they are their complying with standards and performing against them. They also highlight any necessary improvements that need to be made. (www.england.nhs. uk/ourwork/qual-clin-lead/clinaudit/)

Board members

These people are appointed to run the day-to-day affairs of an organisation and are elected to represent, and be accountable to, the shareholders or trustees. They must supply a yearly report on the performance of the organisation.

The governance tasks board members might undertake are to establish policies related to quality and to ensure that structures such as committees are in place to undertake to deliver a plan for quality. They also delegate tasks to the chief executive and other senior management. They jointly oversee organisation activities and define the organisation values.

Non-executive directors

These are individuals who are not part of the management team within the organisation but are essentially 'outsiders' who can give a different perspective and insight into the setting. They are not members of the day-to-day management team but are likely to be involved in strategy, policy and planning.

One governance task that non-executive directors might undertake is to check that the performance of management is meeting agreed goals and objectives. They may also ensure that the financial information is correct and that financial controls and systems are in place and managed appropriately.

Trustees of adult social care businesses and charities

Trustees may also be known as board members or directors but whatever the title, they control an organisation or charity and are responsible for making sure it does what it is set up to do.

The governance tasks that trustees might undertake are to make sure that the charity is carrying out the purposes for which it is set up and also to understand how the charity benefits the setting. Trustees also need to be aware of how charity funds are being spent.

> ## Evidence opportunity
>
> ### 4.1 Roles and responsibilities of key people
>
> Who in your organisation holds the specified roles outlined above?
>
> What are their roles and responsibilities?
>
> Identify the key external people involved in the inspection of your registered services.
>
> What is the benefit of this role to the governance of the organisation?

LO5 Understand inspection processes

AC 5.1 Persons involved in inspection processes

Here, you will be required to identify the different people and organisations that need to be informed of any pending inspection and understand the importance of ensuring a culture of inspection readiness.

It would be useful to look at the next three sections together but for this part you need to identify who will undertake key roles in an inspection and what will be expected of others in the organisation and the team.

As the registered manager you will take a lead role in ensuring paperwork is easy to access and up to date, and having a list of people to contact if any of the nominated people are unavailable at short notice. If you are fortunate to have a nominated person in place then you can support this individual in his or her preparations as they will take the lead.

News of a pending inspection can sometimes cause unnecessary stress, but if good practice is the norm in your service you can reduce this anxiety by helping staff to see and appreciate that they are doing the best they can do and that they are supported.

How to prepare for an inspection

Read the CQC guidance about compliance and encourage your service users to complete the 'please tell us your experience' evaluation surveys you undertake. Ensure that staff understand the role of the CQC and what happens during an inspection visit, and that they have received training that is appropriate for their role.

> ## Evidence opportunity
>
> ### 5.1 How to prepare for an inspection
>
> Using the list of people from activity 4.1, tell your assessor who will need to be informed about a pending inspection. You should include organisations that need to be informed of any pending inspection. Then tell your assessor about the importance of ensuring a culture of inspection readiness, i.e. working in a setting that is ready for inspection at all times.

AC 5.2 How to prepare for an inspection

Here, you will be required to review organisational readiness for an inspection using the five key questions.

There are five key questions that you will need to review to make sure that you are prepared for an inspection.

Is the service SAFE?

Inspectors will want to check that people are being protected from abuse and harm and that risks are carefully monitored.

Evidence for this can be provided by looking at safeguarding notifications, for example complaints, concerns and incidents. Inspectors may also approach staff and patients to ask questions about how safe they feel. Observations of care in the service can also provide detail about how staff approach people and how they interact and deal with difficult situations.

Is the service EFFECTIVE?

An effective service is one in which people's care, treatment and support achieve good outcomes. This can be assessed by looking at evaluation forms and service users' and families' feedback. By talking to staff and stakeholders, the inspection team can gain evidence of training and support. The inspector may also want to be present at handover when staff discuss the patient to determine their level of knowledge about the service and their service users.

Is the service CARING?

A caring service is one which treats people with compassion, dignity, respect and kindness. The inspectors may need to access care plans and files and also to see what others say about the care they have received. Communication is also looked at and evidence of types of systems in use shows whether staff are communicating with patients effectively and with kindness.

Is the service RESPONSIVE?

A responsive service is organised and meets people's needs in a well-structured manner. Observation of care will quickly show whether a task-orientated approach is used or whether person-centred care is truly practised. The inspection teams again may wish to view service user satisfaction surveys and staff training records.

Is the service WELL-LED?

A service that is well-led will show that it is open and fair and delivers high-quality person-centred and innovative care. Staff will be well-trained and morale is likely to be good. The general atmosphere of the service will immediately show how well you as a manager have performed to engage staff to ensure that they deliver care that is excellent. Inspectors will look at how staff interact with each other and how this is taken into service user care. Unhappy staff are unlikely to be motivated to do a good job and this will reflect in how they approach the care.

The inspection team may also wish to access team meeting minutes and staff training and supervision records.

Evidence opportunity

5.2 How to prepare for an inspection

Are you inspection ready?

Using the five key questions, prepare evidence folders for each of the questions. What evidence will you need for each folder?

AC 5.3 Inspection process and information required

Here, you will be required to explain how the regulators prepare for an inspection, the role of the inspection team and the sources of information used for inspection of adult care services, to include the topics we discuss here.

At the start of an inspection, the inspection team will contact the senior staff and set up a meeting at which they will explain who the team is and what they intend to do. In some care sectors, they will expect to see a presentation where the care provider gives its own view of its performance.

There is then a period of gathering views and information from the staff, service users, families and carers. This may include face-to-face discussions, emails or surveys.

The team collects evidence towards the KLOEs by observing care, looking at care plans, checking policies and how they are working, and looking at where the care is given.

At the end of the inspection, a feedback meeting is held with senior staff and the findings are summarised. Any issues that have been highlighted are discussed and subsequent actions are planned. These findings are then published in a report, quality assured and a grading of the service is given according to the grading given on page 57.

- **Local information**: inspectors will be informed about the setting and the location within the community by looking at local information. They may also look at complaints and gather information from staff, carers and people who use services.

- **Information collected before the inspection** and **information from people who use services, their families and carers, staff and other professionals**: the CQC will collect information from the service provider and from any records they already have. They will also look at local and national data.

- **The inspection**: includes observing care and looking at records and documents and for adult social care they will also look at local information and any data they have collected from people who use services, their families, carers, staff and other professionals.

- **Reports that are quality assured, graded and published**: at the end of an inspection, a report is produced with ratings shown. This provides an overall judgement of the quality of care on each of the five key questions. Quality assurance panels are set up to look at samples of inspection reports to check consistency.

Evidence opportunity

5.3 Inspection process and information required

Prepare a written account explaining how regulators prepare for an inspection, the role of the inspection team and the sources of information used for inspection of adult care services, to include the areas covered in the bullets.

AC 5.4 Ways to address the outcome and impact of an inspection

Here, you will be required to explain the ways to address the outcome and impact of an inspection.

Responding to areas of concern

Any areas that require improvement need to be addressed urgently. You and your team will need to develop an action plan to address them and make improvements.

Acknowledging the areas of good practice

This is the positive outcome of inspection and clearly staff, service users and the stakeholders should celebrate the areas of good practice. This should be part of your website and promotional materials.

Developing an action plan

An action plan to address areas of concern and the improvements to be made should be developed immediately as there will be a follow-up on any action by a focused inspection.

Follow-up focused inspections

The inspectors will return to check that action plans have been completed and that areas of concern have been addressed.

LO6 Understand wider ranges of regulatory requirements that apply to services

AC 6.1 Regulation processes that apply to the service or aspects of it

Here, you will be required to explain the range of different regulatory requirements applying to the service, including current legislation.

Health and safety

The Health and Safety at Work Act 1974 (also referred to as HSWA, the HSW Act, the 1974 Act or HASAWA) is the primary piece of legislation covering occupational health and safety in Great Britain. The Health and Safety Executive, with local authorities (and other enforcing authorities), is responsible for enforcing the act and a number of other acts and statutory instruments relevant to the working environment.

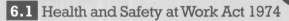

> **Research it**
>
> **6.1 Health and Safety at Work Act 1974**
>
> Go to legislation.gov.uk and download a copy of the act. Make short notes so that you can explain your responsibility and role in relation to the act.

The Care Quality Commission in England became the lead investigator of incidents in care services in 2015. The CQC, the Health and Safety Executive and local authorities in England have all worked together since 2015 to ensure 'there is effective, coordinated and comprehensive regulation of health and safety for patients, service users, workers and members of the public visiting these premises. It is one of the measures taken by Government to close the "regulatory gap" identified by the Francis Report into failings at the Mid Staffordshire NHS Foundation Trust' (Memorandum of Understanding between CQC, the HSE and local authorities in England).

The memorandum outlines the responsibility of each of the parties involved. The CQC is the lead inspector and enforcement body for the safety and quality of treatment and care involving patients and service users in receipt of a health or adult social care service from a provider registered with the CQC.

The HSE sets out an overall public safety policy and undertakes investigation of a non-clinical nature where the accident or incident is reportable under the Reporting of Injuries, Diseases and Dangerous Occurrences Regulations 1995 (RIDDOR). These would include trips and falls, scalding and those arising from people handling. It will also investigate non-RIDDOR accidents where an incident has happened because of standards not being achieved and where there has been failure in management systems. Sometimes this has resulted in serious injury or death. Such failures may be linked to the absence of arrangements for assessing risks to health and safety, inadequate control of health and safety risks, or inadequate monitoring of the procedures or equipment needed to control the risk.

The HSE/local authorities are the lead inspection and enforcement bodies for health and safety matters involving patients and service users who are in receipt of a health or care service from providers not registered with the CQC. As a manager your role requires knowledge of the HSE policy and its implications for your own setting. Your staff need to be trained to ensure compliance.

> **Reflect on it**
>
> **6.1 Health and Safety at Work Act**
>
> The Memorandum of Understanding between the CQC, the HSE and local authorities in England provides examples of the service they provide. Find the memorandum online and read it. Prepare a fact sheet for your staff showing the responsibility you all have under the Health and Safety at Work Act.

Employment law

Employment law regulates relationships between employers and employees and sets out the rights for both. As the manager you are required to ensure that your disciplinary and grievance policies contain reference to these laws and follow the guidance within them. For example, if a disciplinary process with a member of staff is started then employment law dictates that a letter setting out the issue is sent to the staff member and a chance to attend a meeting is given before decisions to proceed are made.

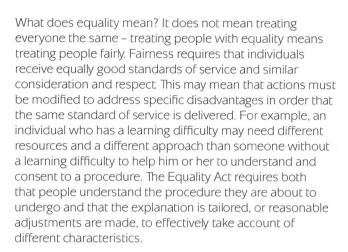

Research it

6.1 Employment law

Check out the range of different employment law regulatory requirements applying to your service and write a short piece showing how your service complies with regulatory requirements.

www.gov.uk/browse/employing-people/contracts is a useful resource covering topics such as contracts, pensions, dismissal and recruitment and hiring of staff. As a manager of staff, you need to be aware of the legal aspects of recruiting people to posts in a fair and non-discriminatory way and should also understand about criminal record checks and the right to work in the UK.

www.cipd.co.uk/knowledge/fundamentals/emp-law/employees is also a useful resource.

Equal opportunities

The manager is key in ensuring that equality and anti-discriminatory practice are promoted within the organisation and that the law is complied with. (See page 23 for more on this.)

But what are the models of practice that underpin **equality**, **diversity** and **inclusion** in your area of responsibility?

People possess different characteristics – being different is what makes us all so interesting. Some characteristics can pose particular challenges for individuals or can be seen as a challenge by others. The law makes it explicit that these characteristics are not an excuse for substandard treatment by services and requires that reasonable adjustments are made to ensure **equal opportunity**. If care workers are to meet needs effectively, they must engage with people as unique individuals and recognise their differences in order to plan to address their specific needs. An aim of good care is that people are treated with equality regardless of their differences.

KEY TERMS

Equality means treating individuals or groups of individuals fairly and equally irrespective of race, gender, disability, religion or belief, sexual orientation and age.
Diversity is equal respect for people who are from different backgrounds.
Inclusion is positive behaviour to ensure all people have an opportunity to be included and not be unfairly excluded because of their individual characteristics.
Equal opportunity is the principle of having fair and similar opportunities in life to those of other people and ensuring people are not discriminated against based on individual characteristics.

What does equality mean? It does not mean treating everyone the same – treating people with equality means treating people fairly. Fairness requires that individuals receive equally good standards of service and similar consideration and respect. This may mean that actions must be modified to address specific disadvantages in order that the same standard of service is delivered. For example, an individual who has a learning difficulty may need different resources and a different approach than someone without a learning difficulty to help him or her to understand and consent to a procedure. The Equality Act requires both that people understand the procedure they are about to undergo and that the explanation is tailored, or reasonable adjustments are made, to effectively take account of different characteristics.

More recently

You will also need to ensure that you keep up to date with the latest changes in legislation, as well as issues such as the gender pay gap, to ensure that you are following best practice in upholding everyone's rights.

Any other laws or policies appropriate to the setting

The Employment Act (2002) ensures that workers are provided with written evidence by means of a letter on the issue under investigation in a disciplinary hearing and are invited to meetings and appeals procedures. The ACAS (Advisory, Conciliation and Arbitration Service) Code of Practice (2015), while not a law, provides useful guidance as to the procedures to follow in cases of grievance and discipline. Failure to follow the guidance can result in hefty fines for an organisation.

The Employment Rights Act (1996) ensures that each contract of employment makes reference to a grievance procedure.

Evidence opportunity

6.1 Regulation processes that apply to the service or aspects of it

Provide a written account explaining the range of different regulatory requirements applying to the service, including current legislation and the areas we have covered here.

Reflect on it

6.1 Other laws and policies

Are there any other laws or policies which are appropriate to your setting? For example, if you are working with people with learning difficulties, what laws might you need to apply?

AC 6.2 Types of information required for regulation processes

Here, you will review the different types of information that the organisation is required to keep and reflect on the quality of the information stored.

If we are to deliver adult care that is safe, fair and of high quality we must ensure that information systems within our organisation are sound and that the records we keep are safe.

Your own setting will have custody of many forms of information about the patients, the staff, the organisation itself as well as the stakeholders and the partners you work with. For example, you will have records of satisfaction surveys and reports of how you have managed complaints and concerns.

Letters from patients and families can also provide information about the service and its delivery. Your staff supervision, appraisal and training records are also key pieces of information which show how well you meet the statutory standards. Care records and meeting minutes provide valuable evidence of how well care aims are achieved. To integrate this information, you will need to train staff in how to use it. Additionally, you will have policies which detail how you work with others to deliver care, meet health and safety regulations, and manage information within the system.

If your care setting wishes to continue to provide care, it must be accountable for its practices and must be able to show evidence of the care it is providing.

The quality of the information stored can be assessed by looking at the source of the material gained and its reliability. Surveys from service users, for example, in which only five people answered a questionnaire are not a good source of information to recommend a change in service delivery.

Evidence opportunity

6.2 Types of information required for regulation processes

Speak to your assessor and review the different types of information that the organisation is required to keep. Then reflect on the quality of the information stored.

Reflect on it

6.2 KLOEs and information

Go back to the CQC's KLOEs about services. These are:

- Are they safe?
- Are they effective?
- Are they caring?
- Are they responsive to people's needs?
- Are they well-led?

Under each question, list the information you can supply to support your organisation in answering these questions.

For example, under 'Are they safe?', you may supply accident records, your health and safety policy, confidentiality policy and maintenance records.

AC 6.3 Regulatory frameworks presenting conflicting requirements

Here, you will be required to analyse where conflict between regulatory requirements may occur. You will need to include how to overcome these conflicts. Conflicts can include the areas we cover here.

Partnership working is an important means of making improvements in adult care and this depends on effective partnerships between the different professions and organisations involved in commissioning and delivering services and interventions. It requires shared communication systems, including shared databases, records and files, to ensure that consistency in care is maintained and decision-making processes are clear, otherwise conflict can occur.

Communication and the use of information between partners have to be firmly established to ensure that all parties are talking to each other and have the service user at the heart of the care.

Occasionally there is conflict between partners in the delivery of a person-centred service. For example, Regulation 9: Person-centred care of the Health and Social Care Act 2008 (Regulated Activities) Regulations 2014 ensures that care or treatment is personalised specifically for individuals based on an assessment of their needs and preferences. It is possible that partners may disagree about the care needed and conflict may therefore arise.

Case study

6.3 Conflicting requirements

Judith Bowler is a widow aged 75 years who lives alone. She suffers from chronic lung disease and has restricted mobility. She has had several respiratory infections resulting in admission to hospital. Her daughter Joan visits and helps her with practical care and shopping and she also has supportive neighbours. Her two main needs are:

● maintaining her independence in her own home

● maintaining and managing nutrition.

Due to her lung problem Judith cannot meet her first need and requires help to keep her home clean and safe.

While Judith is able to eat food and drink, she cannot fully prepare her meals herself and relies on her daughter to do this.

What kinds of conflicts may occur here?

Here we have a situation where a person wants to remain independent but it may be unsafe to do so. Without additional help for both Judith and her daughter there is a possibility that both may suffer a negative outcome if Judith is insistent upon remaining in her own home. Judith, of course, may also suffer a negative outcome if she is forced to leave her own home for residential care. Conflict here may arise with partners in care who cannot meet her requirements.

For more on conflict during partnership working, see Unit 504.

For many reasons, it is not always easy to carry out regulatory requirements in practice. It is up to you, your team and your partners to find ways of overcoming these barriers so that you can both meet the requirements and deliver high-quality care.

The effectiveness of the work you do with others, whether in your team or at a local authority level, depends upon having shared aims and objectives and goals, with all parties working together to achieve the same ends. Without this, breakdown in communication and conflict is likely to occur so there need to be shared policies, procedures and, in some cases, resources that are implemented and used effectively.

Potential for the duplication of regulatory activities by local councils and national regulators

Conflicts can occur in a number of areas when agencies from different disciplines are working together to deliver care. Each will have its own way of managing care and there may be potential for the duplication of regulatory activities by authorities and national regulators. Occasionally there will be unnecessary duplication in inspections, or visits to service users, paperwork and data requests. It is crucial therefore to ensure that roles and responsibilities for tasks are clear and that information is coordinated in an efficient manner. For example, a community nurse

may visit on a daily basis at the same time as another care worker undertaking perhaps a slightly different role. Careful coordination of the visits may reduce work or improve the quality of the service to the patient.

● **Limits of authority**: As with boundaries, all partners must know where their authority ends and is taken up by another service. Again, there is a management structure in each partnership and service and as such this is a potential conflict area. If managers do not agree as to where their authority ends and others' begins, tasks may be left unfinished or there may be disagreement arising as to who takes responsibility for work being done. A useful example is that of the work of the police and the health services. For example, very often the police accompany patients to hospital who may also be under arrest or who may be being detained for their own safety. There must be clear guidelines as to how this arrangement will work within the care system and where each jurisdiction ends. A clear protocol will help with this.

● **Decision making**: Clarity with respect to who makes final decisions in certain areas of the service should be established at the outset of the partnership. For example, when the police are involved, meetings between police and health professionals should clarify the arrangements that must be in place when a patient is in hospital. Hospital staff will be aware that they have the final decision as to when the patient is medically fit to be taken from the hospital. The case will then pass to the police who will then take decisions on the patient's behalf.

● **Areas of responsibility**: Like boundaries, each partnership member needs to be clear about what they are responsible for with respect to the care the service user requires. You will need to have an understanding of all of these areas.

Conflict need not always be viewed as a negative occurrence. It may highlight an important issue and lead to a better outcome for all concerned. For example, in healthcare settings conflict between partners may arise if resources are threatened due to the introduction of another service. If staff feel that their role is undermined in any way by another service, this can lead to conflict. The main aims in any conflict resolution are to communicate, listen and keep an open mind about the situation.

The Research Briefing 41, commissioned by SCIE (2012), 'Factors that promote and hinder joint and integrated working between health and social care services' (Cameron, 2012), is a useful resource that comments upon the findings from a large study about integrated (partnership) working.

In order to avoid conflict it is useful to understand where it might occur and to address these areas. Conflict can happen in the following situations:

- There is a lack of understanding about joint aims and objectives or failure to establish a shared purpose so it is imperative that all are aware of what you are hoping to achieve in the delivery of care.

- Individuals have little clarity about the roles and responsibilities or there are difficulties in role boundaries. This can be remedied by ensuring that all staff have job descriptions to which they may refer and that they are clear about their role boundaries.

- There is confusion about policies and procedures underpinning the new service or way of working. An open door policy where all staff can approach the manager to discuss any confusion can help this.

- There are organisational differences or competing 'organisational visions' and lack of agreement about which organisation should lead. It is likely that the organisations you partner with may have very different mission statements and visions so recognising this and ensuring that there is a lead organisation in the partnership will help.

- There is an absence of a pooled or shared budget and differences in resources and spending or there is financial uncertainty. Finance can be a real problem if it is not clearly defined. For example, budgets devolved to services within a hospital will be managed by the head of the department. If resources are being used by others who enter the service, this can have an effect on patient care. If others are regularly using resources in the area then a shared budget might need to be negotiated.

- Communicating across professional or agency boundaries, particularly when they are not located on the same site. This can be an issue, but the use of social media, Skype, conference calls and computers can help to resolve this.

- There is difficulty sharing information, lack of access to information and incompatible IT systems. The NHS has promised a widely compatible computer system for a number of years but this has yet to be delivered. However, discussion about how information will be shared in a safe way will certainly improve the patient outcome.

- There is a lack of strong and appropriate managerial support. Training might be of use in this instance and managers can also be encouraged to work together to gain peer support.

Lack of coordination of information by the regulator and local care commissioners

There have been a few initiatives to break down barriers and one way is to address the communication systems between professional groups. Successful collaboration depends on open and transparent discussion. Traditionally, communication has relied on written formats – referral forms, feedback forms, case notes, care plans, letters and faxes. However, while quality record keeping and evidence-based policies and procedures are necessary, there does need to be more one-to-one collaboration and **active participation** in meeting with partners on a regular basis.

There must be a safe way of sharing information and confidentiality must not be breached. Systems need to be in place to ensure that all partners are aware of how they may accomplish this. Record keeping should also be standardised where possible across the partnership so that records are consistent. A review into the regulatory environment facing care homes in 2013 reported that there was significant duplication of activities by local authorities and the CQC, leading staff to 'provide paperwork not care'. The excessive focus on paperwork rather than quality was cited as an issue and the government identified a need to cut red tape in the industry.

KEY TERM

Active participation refers to enabling individuals to be included in their care and being able to voice how they wish to live their life and obtain their own care.

Health and safety responsibilities versus person-centred planning

See Unit 504 AC 1.1 for information on health and safety responsibilities versus person-centred planning. The Care Act 2014 encourages 'person-centred care' and this requires complete recognition of the needs and choices of the person receiving care. By ensuring that support is available to families and the service user, and by listening to those on the receiving end of care, a better quality of life can be expected.

As care professionals, we also have to weigh up the risks involved in allowing patients to undertake some activities which we deem to be risky to their health and safety and this can cause conflict and seem to go against person-centred care.

Safeguarding

Local Safeguarding Adults Boards are made up of the local social services authority, the police, the NHS and all groups involved in protecting at-risk adults. To ensure that the public are able to have a say in decision making, the boards also include members of the local community.

The standards outlined in the Safeguarding Adults national framework detail how the partnerships should work and be set up. The onus is on the local authority to establish a multi-agency partnership to lead 'safeguarding adults' work and to include representation from all the appropriate statutory agencies such as adult social services, housing, welfare rights/benefits, education services, legal services, primary care trusts, other NHS care trusts, the Commission for Social Care Inspection, the Healthcare Commission, the Strategic Health Authority and the Department for Work and Pensions.

Boundaries are in place in care work to ensure there is clarity about what your role and responsibilities are. With clear boundaries all members of staff in the partnership will be clear about where their roles begin and end and the potential for any conflict to occur will be minimised. Sometimes professional disagreements about the way in which safeguarding cases are handled may erupt. This may happen when a challenge is presented to other agencies or partners about the way in which a claim has been handled or dealt with. If a vulnerable person's safety is at stake, it is the professional's duty to act in the person's best interests with the aim of resolving any conflict at an early stage. We must be aware that sometimes we may disagree with colleagues' decisions but that resolving the conflict and cooperating with others must be carried out at the earliest stages so as not to disadvantage the at-risk individual.

Reflect on it

6.3 Overcoming conflicts

Write a reflective account explaining how you have managed to overcome conflicts, using the topic headings to show how you have dealt with each of these areas within local partnerships.

Evidence opportunity

6.3 Regulatory frameworks presenting conflicting requirements

Provide a written account analysing where conflicting requirements between regulatory requirements may occur.

You will need to include how to overcome these conflicts. You could, for example, cover the ones we have discussed in this section.

The Care Act (2014) simplified and improved the existing legislation in care, changing the way in which access and financing care were carried out. People requiring care are now able to access the care and support from local councils or other organisations in the community and have more choice about the type of support and care they need.

Under this legislation service users receiving care and support from any regulated provider will now be covered by the Human Rights Act and local councils are responsible for helping the service user to access independent financial advice to help them with care funding.

- The Human Rights Act (1998) protects the human rights of individuals to privacy, among other rights.
- The Data Protection Act (1998) deals with the processing and protection of data on individuals.
- The Freedom of Information Act (2000) allows individuals to see all the information of a personal nature held about them.
- The Equality Act (2010) is an umbrella act bringing together legislation that deals with race, disability and gender. It highlighted protected characteristics of age, gender reassignment, pregnancy, religion, marriage and civil partnerships, and sexual orientation in an attempt to end discrimination.
- The Public Interest Disclosure Act (1999) safeguards individuals by providing them with the means to speak out about issues of negligence, miscarriages of justice, crime and dangers to health. It is commonly referred to as the 'Whistle Blowing Act'.

Suggestions for using the activities

This table summarises all the activities in the unit that are relevant to each assessment criterion.

Here, we also suggest other, different methods that you may want to use to present your knowledge and skills by using the activities. These are just suggestions, and you should refer to the Introduction section at the start of the book, and more importantly the City & Guilds specification, and your assessor, who will be able to provide more guidance on how you can evidence your knowledge and skills. When you need to be observed during your assessment, this can be done by your assessor, or your manager can provide a witness testimony.

Assessment criteria and accompanying activities	Suggested methods to show your knowledge/skills
LO1 Understand legislation and statutory requirements that underpin adult care provision	
1.1 Evidence opportunity (page 48)	Investigate current UK legislation and statutory frameworks that apply to social care workers, NHS providers and voluntary sector providers, including the ones covered in this section.
1.1 Research it (page 48)	Which pieces of legislation listed in this section apply to your setting?
1.2 Evidence opportunity (page 50)	Analyse the association between legislation and policy on person-centred care and positive outcomes-based procedures and practice.
1.2 Reflect on it (page 50)	Reflect on the ways in which the laws and papers in Table 2.1 have affected the way in which your setting delivers its care.
1.3 Evidence opportunity (page 51)	Evaluate the benefits of using local and/or national forums to draw attention to potential conflicts between statutory frameworks and values/principles for good practice.
LO2 Understand internal governance arrangements within your own organisation	
2.1 Evidence opportunity (page 52)	Evaluate your organisation's governance mechanisms. Identify how these relate to the identity of the organisation.
2.1 Reflect on it (page 53)	Describe your organisation's governance procedures and mechanisms. Evaluate how successfully your organisation uses these to ensure positive outcomes.
2.2 Evidence opportunity (page 53)	Evaluate your accountability and role within your organisation's governance structure.
2.2 Reflect on it (page 53)	What are you accountable for in your role as manager?
2.3 Evidence opportunity (page 54)	Review how your organisation's agreed ways of working, protocols, policies and procedures relate to governance and accountability and the link to quality of care provision.
2.3 Reflect on it (page 54)	What are your organisation's agreed ways of working, protocols, policies and procedures? How do these relate to governance and accountability and to quality of care provision?
LO3 Understand systems and requirements for regulation of adult care services	
3.1 Evidence opportunity (page 55)	Explain the key drivers and impact of legislation for the inspection system, including the Health and Social Care Act, the Care Act, recent local/national inquiries and findings from serious case reviews, and other appropriate topical reviews and reports.
3.1 Reflect on it (page 56)	Reflect on the impact of legislation that may have impacted the way your service is inspected.
3.2 Evidence opportunity (page 56)	List the services you are aware of in the sphere of adult social services that require registration and inspection. Which are acute services and social care services?
3.3 Research it (page 56)	Look at the CQC's KLOEs. Identify the key areas for enquiry and identify how you would evidence that you cover these areas.

→

Suggestions for using the activities	
3.4 Evidence opportunity (page 57)	Provide a written account that describes and differentiates between the various grades available at inspection and evaluate the implications of each grade for a service.
3.4 Research it (page 57)	Locate your last inspection report and look at the grading for each of the five key questions. Evaluate the implications of the grades for the services you offer.
3.5 Evidence opportunity (page 58)	Provide a written account critically evaluating sources of support and information available. These will include local, regional, national and professional networks.
3.5 Research it (page 58)	Make a list of the local areas of support that are available to help improve the service you give.
3.5 Research it (page 58)	Find out more about your local Clinical Commissioning Group and prepare to attend a meeting to evaluate what it does and how it might be useful.
LO4 Understand roles, remits and responsibilities in registered services	
4.1 Evidence opportunity (page 60)	Identify the key internal and external people involved in the inspection of your registered services. What are their roles and responsibilities?
LO5 Understand inspection processes	
5.1 Evidence opportunity (page 60)	Using the list of people from Evidence opportunity 4.1, identify who will need to be informed about a pending inspection.
5.2 Evidence opportunity (page 61)	Using the five key questions in this section, prepare evidence folders for each of the questions.
5.3 Evidence opportunity (page 61)	Give a written account explaining how regulators prepare for an inspection, the role of the inspection team and the sources of information used for inspection of adult care services.
LO6 Understand wider ranges of regulatory requirements that apply to services	
6.1 Research it (page 62)	Go to legislation.gov.uk and download a copy of the Health and Safety at Work Act. Make short notes so that you can explain your responsibility and role in relation to the act.
6.1 Reflect on it (page 62)	Prepare a fact sheet for your staff showing the responsibility you all have under the Health and Safety at Work Act.
6.1 Research it (page 63)	Check out the different employment law and regulatory requirements applying to your service and write a short piece showing how your service complies with regulatory requirements.
6.1 Evidence opportunity (page 63)	Explain the range of regulatory requirements applying to the service, including current legislation and the areas covered in this section.
6.1 Reflect on it (page 64)	Are there any other laws or policies that are appropriate to your setting? For example, if you are working with people with learning difficulties, what laws might you need to apply?
6.2 Evidence opportunity (page 64)	Review the different types of information that the organisation is required to keep to meet requirements.
6.2 Reflect on it (page 64)	Go back to the CQC's KLOEs. Consider whether they are safe, effective, caring, responsive to people's needs, well-led.
6.3 Reflect on it (page 67)	Explain how you have managed to overcome conflicts, using the topic headings in this section to show how you have dealt with each of these areas within local partnerships.
6.3 Evidence opportunity (page 67)	Give a written account analysing where conflict between regulatory requirements may occur.

References

Cameron, A., Lart, R., Bostock, L. and Coomber, C. (2012) Factors that promote and hinder joint and integrated working between health and social care services,' *Research Briefing 41*, SCIE.

Department of Health (2000) *The NHS Plan: A plan for investment, a plan for reform*. Cm 4818-I. Norwich: HMSO.

Department of Health (2001) *Valuing People: A new strategy for learning disability for the 21st century; planning with people; towards person-centred approaches – accessible guide*. London: HMSO.

Department of Health (2007) *Putting People First: A shared vision and commitment to the transformation of adult social care*. London: HMSO.

Department of Health (2008) *The Wanless Report: Securing good health for the whole population*. London: HMSO.

Department of Health (2014) *The Health and Social Care Act 2008 (Regulated Activities) Regulations 2014*. London: TSO.

Francis, R. (2013) *Report of the Mid Staffordshire NHS Foundation Trust Public Inquiry*. London: TSO. www.midstaffspublicinquiry.com/report

Health Foundation (2014) *Person-centred Care Made Simple*, accessed from www.health.org.uk/publications/person-centred-care-made-simple

HM Government (2009) *Shaping the Future of Care Together*. Green Paper.

Innes, A., Macpherson, S. and McCabe, I. (2006) *Promoting Person-Centred Care at the Front Line*. York: Joseph Rowntree Foundation/SCIE.

Renz, D. and Eddy, W. (1996) Organisations, ethics and healthcare: Building an ethics infrastructure for a new era, *Bioethics Forum*, 12(2): 29–39.

Scally, G. and Donaldson, L.J. (1998) Clinical governance and the drive for quality improvement in the new NHS in England, *British Medical Journal*, 317, 4 July: 61–5.

Useful resources and further reading

Care Quality Commission (2014) *The State of Health Care and Adult Social Care in England 2013/14*, www.qcs.co.uk/cqc-fundamental-standards/?utm_source=bing-ppc&utm_medium=cpc&utm_campaign=bingppc1 accessed on 16/6/17

Department of Health (2014) *Hard Truths: The journey to putting patients first. Volume One of the Government Response to the Mid Staffordshire NHS Foundation Trust Public Inquiry*, 2 volumes. London: TSO.

Health and Social Care Act 2012, section 13H.

Wanless, D. (2002) *Securing Our Future Health: Taking a long-term view*. London: HM Treasury.

Websites

www.cqc.org.uk/guidance-providers/regulations-enforcement/about-guidance

www.health.org.uk/sites/health/files/PersonCentredCareMadeSimple.pdf

www.england.nhs.uk/ourwork/qual-clin-lead/clinaudit

www.nhsemployers.org/case-studies-and-resources/2018/04/people-performance-management-toolkit

Communication and information management in adult care

GLH 10

About this unit

Effective communication and information management demands that we know ourselves well, are aware of what we bring to our communication, and how we might impact on those we communicate with.

The purpose of this unit is to revisit the systems of communication we use in care work and in particular when managing information in a care setting. In any relationship, be it personal or working, effective communication skills play an essential part, and being able to communicate well is one of the most important aspects of your role as a leader and manager.

Misunderstanding and misinterpreting the message can lead to team conflict and disrupt the smooth running of the organisation. It can, moreover, lead to ineffective delivery of services and unproductive team work. Being an effective communicator, then, is the key to successful working.

In this unit, we'll explore the different models of communication, how to develop communication systems and practices which will support positive outcomes, understand how we can implement systems for effective information management and support others to communicate effectively.

Learning outcomes

By the end of this unit, you will:

1. Understand models of communication
2. Develop communication systems and practices which support positive outcomes
3. Implement systems for effective information management
4. Support others with effective communication strategies

Getting started

Before you study the unit, think about the following:

- What different models of communication are there in your setting, and how might they apply to your management practice?
- What systems do you have in place to ensure all staff fully understand the policies and procedures that apply to their practice and how is this monitored?
- What are the barriers to effective communication within **service delivery teams**?
- Why is it important to lead others in maintaining accuracy in record keeping?

KEY TERMS

Service delivery teams are teams within the **multidisciplinary groups** such as the primary care team, social care team, hospital, housing and other services used within your own setting.

Multidisciplinary groups have people with different specialist skills. For example, the group may have people with medical and care expertise, and there may be people who have specialist knowledge on housing and other services.

LO1 Understand models of communication

Defining communication

To be skilled in communication requires us to be able to use a variety of interpersonal techniques and to be able to adapt the way in which we communicate according to a variety of factors. As a manager, your skills lie in listening actively to staff and other people you meet in your work in order to make decisions and to negotiate issues that may arise. Your role requires you to deliver information and provide feedback. You will use several methods to do this, including attending meetings, training staff, assessing service users and writing reports.

Crawford et al. (2006) suggest that:

> 'Communication is something we do in our internal world of thoughts and in our external world by speaking, writing, gestures, drawing, making images and symbols or receiving messages from others.'

Effective communication is the means by which we deliver and receive a message and both need to be consistent in order for the communication to work.

Communication is the basis of interaction, so skills in speaking, writing and, in particular, listening are essential in health and social care. As a manager, you will be interacting and communicating with a range of people within health and social care settings, including service users (who may be vulnerable) and their families as well as staff, visitors and other professionals. You may sometimes communicate with individuals who are going through a personal crisis or are feeling upset, for example, and this therefore requires skill in making sure they feel supported and valued.

The effectiveness of your communication skills as a manager and leader within the care setting will undoubtedly lead to the success of the organisation and the team with which you work.

AC 1.1 Theoretical models of communication and their relevance to practice

In this section, you will be required to explain theoretical models of communication and assess their application in the service provision, including the ones we discuss here.

Linear models

The Shannon and Weaver model of communication (1949) is one of the earliest linear models of communication (see Figure 3.1); in a linear model the communication process and the transfer of information are in one direction.

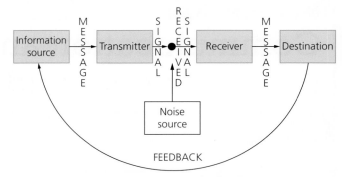

▲ **Figure 3.1** Shannon and Weaver's model of communication

Source: www.businesstopia.net/communication/ shannon-and-weaver-model-communication

In the Shannon and Weaver model (Figure 3.1):

- the information source or the sender has a message to deliver
- the transmitter is the sender who transmits the message by the method (channel) they have chosen, e.g. voice, machine, text, email
- the receiver or decoder receives or hears the message as a series of signals and translates it
- the destination is the means by which the message is received, e.g. ears during face-to-face communication, phone, computer, etc.
- noise refers to any physical disturbances in the environment which may prevent the message getting through. Noise can occur at any stage in the transmission.

An example of linear communication being used in service provision is when a manager issues instructions in an emergency. The transmitter asks the receiver to phone for an ambulance. The receiver is not expected to offer their own ideas. The feedback from the receiver may be agreeing and then making the phone call.

Transactional models

Transactional models of communication describe the exchange of messages between sender and receiver. Both take turns to send or receive messages, so that every part of the communication process (such as the transmitter, receiver, environment and medium) is constantly changing. This model requires the receiver to listen to the sender for successful communication, and both sender and receiver are regarded as communicators.

Wood's (2004) transactional model (see Figure 3.2) offers a more complex communication process than Shannon and Weaver's linear model. In it, messages are being sent back and forth, with a focus on interpretation of their meaning. As language develops, we notice that different meanings may be assigned to the same word. From a cultural point of view, this may result in miscommunication because we cannot always be sure that a word has the same meaning for two people. For example, words such as 'wicked' and 'bad' mean something very different to the youth of today than they may have done to older generations. There are many more examples of how words change. The words we use alter depending on the situation and the people involved and because of this, we can never be sure that a word has the same meaning for two people (Porritt, 1990). This is particularly important when communicating feelings, as the strength of the word may differ between people.

This model recognises the differences in social, cultural and relational contexts and that understanding communication depends upon a shared response. Communication depends upon various physical, cultural, environmental, social, psychological and emotional factors, so we cannot always predict the response of another person.

An example of transactional communication in service provision may be talking to a service user about their food preferences in a face-to-face context. The sender (staff member) asks the receiver (service user) what they like to eat. The receiver feeds back by telling them (so becomes the sender, while the staff member becomes the receiver). The original sender may then clarify by asking more questions, and taking into account non-verbal communication. It is very much a two-way process. In a managerial position, you may speak to the person that you manage about training needs in an appraisal meeting or receive feedback on your own performance.

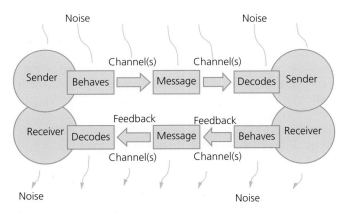

▲ **Figure 3.2** Transactional model of communication

Source: www.businesstopia.net/communication/ transactional-model-communication

Interactive models

Schramm's interactive model (1954) is similar to the transactional model in that there is a two-way process of communication and it includes an 'interpreter' to address the problem of meaning (see Figure 3.3). This model recognises the psychological frame in which interaction occurs.

For example, our attitude towards the sender may influence our understanding of the message. As a manager, you may react differently to a complaint from a service provider you know well because you are more familiar with the way they communicate, than to a complaint from a new service user. The context in which the message is sent is also important. Shouting the word 'fire' in a crowded area will receive a very different response than if it is shouted on a firing range.

The difference in meanings between cultures is also addressed in this model. When we come into contact with people from different cultures we are often confronted with new meanings for familiar words, and also different behaviours and gestures. This can quickly become a barrier to communication due to misunderstanding. For example, staff members who have grown up in the UK may be put off by the direct way of speaking which some cultures favour and others may find the lack of eye contact which is a sign of respect in some cultures misleading and even believe it to be disrespectful.

As service providers, and as managers, we should be aware of, and make allowances for, changes to communication due to cultural differences.

Schramm's model of communication suggests that messages need to be decoded and interpreted before they can be understood. Decoding and interpreting may result in a different understanding from that intended by the encoder (sender of the message).

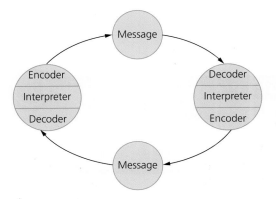

▲ **Figure 3.3** Schramm's model of communication

SOLER/SURETY models

SOLER was a model developed by Egan in 1975 and is used widely in a variety of settings. It provides an acronym that can be used for non-verbal communication, for example between a therapist and their client. Table 3.1 shows how wordless messages can be given and received. This can be applied equally well to the roles of manager and team member.

Table 3.1 Explanation of Egan's SOLER model

S	Sit squarely	Sit at an angle to the other person so that you are either side of an imaginary corner. This allows you to see all aspects of their non-verbal communication, which you might not see if you were sitting side by side. This position is less threatening than sitting face on.
O	Open position	Sit with uncrossed arms and legs to convey to the client that you are open and not defensive.
L	Lean slightly towards the client	Leaning towards the client shows that you are interested and want to understand their problem.
E	Eye contact	It is important to get the balance right. The client will feel uncomfortable if you stare and will think that you are not interested if you do not look at them at all.
R	Relax	If you are relaxed, you can concentrate on listening rather than worrying about how to respond to the service users.

Source: Tilmouth and Quallington 2015

A new acronym developed by Stickley (2011) is SURETY. It adds to the SOLER model by including touch and the importance of individual intuition, encouraging us to think about therapeutic space.

S: Sit at an angle

U: Uncross legs and arms

R: Relax

E: Eye contact

T: Touch

Y: Your intuition

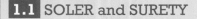

Research it

1.1 SOLER and SURETY

Give three examples of when SOLER or SURETY could be useful models to use in your own setting and practice.

In management roles, we communicate with people who may be in a subordinate position to ourselves, those in more senior roles, peers and others such as visitors or other service providers, and they may have different communication needs. The way you communicate may differ based on the different people you communicate with. However, it will be useful to make sure that you apply principles of SOLER and SURETY as these will help you to be an effective communicator.

The role of phatic communication

This is simply 'small talk' or the type of speech which we use to be sociable. So, for example, you might say to somebody 'take care', 'have a nice day' or simply mention the weather. We are not necessarily stating a fact or passing on information; we are just moving the conversation along.

Burgess (1964) defined it as speech to promote human warmth and in care work this certainly has a place. Although it is sometimes thought to be trivial, it helps to establish a human touch to our communication. For example, you might ask a team member how they are or ask how their daughter got on in her football match at the weekend. Think about the last time somebody remembered a personal fact about you and how it made you feel. As a manager, you need to take an interest in your workers.

Also bear in mind that people who struggle with phatic communication often come across as very direct, so it's useful to be prepared, and not to use small talk if they will become impatient with what they regard as 'unnecessary' communication.

Formal communication vs informal communication

Formal communication is official communication that passes through a setting, whereas informal communication is usually on a smaller scale and less official, such as telling a colleague about an immediate issue when you pass them in the corridor. We see formal communication happening when there are hierarchies in place and there is a chain of command. It comes generally in written form, such as via email, and there is evidence that such communication has actually happened. It might also be giving a PowerPoint presentation to staff or a safety talk. Informal communication is generally oral in nature and tends to happen in an ad hoc manner. There may be little to support what has been said. You may, for example, tell a colleague where they can find the service user they're looking for. It might also be the general conversation between team members and service users.

The type of communication we use in our personal communication with members of staff and friends will be different to that we might use in an organisational context. For example, our language may be more formal when we speak to service users or other members of the multidisciplinary team and less formal in our everyday lives.

Self-awareness and perception awareness in communication

KEY TERMS

Self-awareness is the ability to notice the self and to be able to recognise our own behaviour and personality. It is to be aware of our own character and feelings and sometimes this can be difficult for us. Being self-aware means knowing our own emotions and recognising the feelings arising from those emotions when they happen. We are therefore in control of what is going on within us and we are able to use our emotions appropriately. We may feel angry or sad at times but it might be inappropriate to show those feelings at work.

Perception awareness is our ability to recognise how and what we are communicating to others through our non-verbal communication. How we present ourselves to others can communicate much about us.

One of the things that we often do not pay enough attention to is our body language. Argyle (1978) pointed out that non-verbal communication can have as much as five times the impact on a person's understanding compared with the words spoken, so if we are displaying negative non-verbal signals this can prove problematic. Communication can be broken down as follows:

- 7 per cent is what you say in words.
- 38 per cent is contributed by how you say it (volume, pitch, tone, rhythm, etc.).
- 55 per cent reflects your body language (facial expressions, gestures, posture, etc.).

It is also useful to remember that service users in a health and social care setting may have communication difficulties and may not pick up the non-verbal cues communicated (Crawford et al., 2006).

The way in which we present ourselves can have as much if not more impact on whether our message is listened to and understood.

When communicating:

> *'Our attention is focused on words rather than body language. But our judgement includes both. An audience is simultaneously processing both verbal and non-verbal cues. Body movements are not usually positive or negative in and of themselves; rather, the situation and the message will determine the appraisal.'*

Source: Givens, 2000, p. 4

It is vital to ensure that our behaviour and bodily actions match our speech. Awareness of the way in which we conduct our non-verbal communication is just as important as what we say in some cases.

Evidence opportunity

1.1 Theoretical models of communication and their relevance to practice

Provide a written account explaining theoretical models of communication and assess their application in the service provision, including the ones we discuss here.

Reflect on it

1.1 Non-verbal communication

How do you use non-verbal communication? Take a few minutes to look at the people around you. Even if they are unaware of you watching them, they are still communicating to you. Can you, for example, tell how somebody is feeling by the way they are standing? Are they smiling? How are they dressed? What is their walk like? All these things are communicating something.

Now apply this exercise to yourself. How do you communicate with your staff when you are not speaking to them? What are you conveying? Do you always feel like a professional? How do you convey that to your staff? What actions show this? Write a short reflective account and think about how models of communication apply to this.

Reflect on it

1.1 Communication models and practice

How do you present yourself to your staff and what do they actually see?

Write a short reflective piece about your own body language and check it out with your manager.

Look at how some people command respect in a room or demonstrate their presence. They are not necessarily the loudest person or even the most senior but there is something about them that attracts respect and attention. Do some research on how they communicate in non-verbal ways.

Compile a table which explains these models of communication and give new examples of how they might be applied in your service provision. How might you use the Shannon and Weaver model of communication, Wood's (2004) transactional model and the SOLER/SURETY model?

AC 1.2 Workplace models and methods of communication and their importance

Here, you will be required to analyse the effectiveness of communication models and methods within practice and their impact on service delivery to include written, electronic/digital, pictorial, signage, social media.

The means of communication you use to meet different needs will include verbal and non-verbal. It may be:

- written
- electronic/digital
- pictorial
- sign

and may include communication through social media. The information may be:

- personal
- organisational
- formal
- informal
- public (information/promotional).

In the study of communication, we might come across the following three terms:

- **interpersonal communication**, which involves non-verbal, paralinguistic (see AC 1.5, page 83) and verbal communication
- **environmental communication**, which involves the way in which our environment affects our interactions
- **intra-personal communication**, which takes place within ourselves, or 'self-talk'.

Before we discuss written, electronic, pictorial, sign and communication through social media, it is worth exploring the different communication methods generally, and what they may mean in practice.

Verbal communication

Verbal communication can be complex since the meaning of words changes between cultures and generations. On its own it can be ineffective because we can never be sure that a word has the same meaning for two people (Porritt, 1990), especially when we are talking about feelings.

Choose words carefully: We need to be careful not to use jargon and abbreviations or language that is too complex, that our service users or staff may not understand. Keep in mind the person you are speaking to and tailor your language to them. We need to be aware of cultural differences in

language and conscious of the diverse nature of our service users. Similarly, we should avoid euphemisms, such as saying someone has 'passed away' instead of died. One example is of a student nurse who, for weeks, thought that the term 'gone to Rose Cottage' meant that the patients she had nursed had all been taken to a care home of that name! In fact, they had died.

- **Avoid clichés and alienating language**: One of the things that might alienate your staff is the use of cliché and 'management-type' speak. Terms such as 'thinking outside the box', 'blue-sky thinking', 'scoping' can sound overused and inauthentic and may also be misunderstood.

- **Be culturally sensitive and speak clearly**: For example, ensuring that you are not covering your mouth or turning away from a person when speaking will help those who need to lip read or listen carefully due to hearing problems. It is also important to consider cultural sensitivities around communication.

- **Be aware of paralinguistic communication**: When we moderate our speech, for example changing the pitch, volume, rhythm, tone of voice and timing, occasional grunts, 'ums' and 'ahs', we are using paralinguistic communication. The way we say something can affect how our message is perceived. Yawning, sighing, coughing, tutting, laughing and groaning are also forms of paralinguistic communication. How do we communicate these aspects of language in non-verbal written communication though? In such cases we may change the colour or size of the font, or use capital letters and exclamation marks. Paralinguistic communication can offer us a clue to how a person is feeling and this can help in our dealings with them. Also see AC 1.5 page 83 for more information on paralinguistic communication.

Non-verbal communication

Table 3.2 shows the types of non-verbal communication we use.

> ### KEY TERM
>
> **Culture** is the customs, attitudes and beliefs that distinguish one group of people from another.

Table 3.2 Non-verbal communication

Facial expression	Our facial expression communicates emotions unless we train ourselves to mask our feelings. If you say you are angry while smiling, it gives a confusing message.
Eye contact and gaze	The way you look into another person's eyes during conversation is called eye contact. If somebody can hold eye contact throughout a conversation, it can communicate a level of confidence and willingness to communicate fully. Some of the people you communicate with will have a low level of eye contact, which might communicate a lack of ease with the conversation or a lack of confidence. It is a good idea to reduce the level of your eye contact to reflect theirs, otherwise it can feel threatening. The appropriateness of maintaining eye contact differs according to **culture**.

Gestures	Gestures are movements of your arms and hands that accompany speech. Gestures can help communication – for example, pointing in the direction in which a person needs to go can add emphasis to the communication. However, too much gesturing can be distracting.
Body position, posture and movement	The body position of a client can tell you a lot about how they are feeling – if they are hunched over, with arms and legs crossed, they are probably feeling quite anxious. Rogers (2002) recommends that we relax and it is important not to appear too formal and distant. However, if we are too laid back in our posture, we could appear uninterested. Sitting with our arms and legs crossed can appear closed off and defensive. In some circumstances, it may be a good idea to mirror the body posture of the person we are with.
Personal space and proximity	Two to three feet in distance between the chairs is about right for me; however, you may notice that some service users push their chairs back as soon as they sit down in the prearranged chairs. This may be because the space does not feel comfortable to them. People seem to have their own invisible boundaries, which change according to who they are interacting with and how comfortable they feel. Porritt (1990) calls it a bubble that surrounds us.
Clothes	The clothes you choose to wear say a lot about you. Dressing too informally or too formally may alienate you from service users.
Therapeutic touch	Touch can be a contentious subject. On the one hand, there is evidence of touch having therapeutic benefits; on the other, it can be misinterpreted and seen as an invasion of a person's personal space. Bonham (2004) suggests it may be appropriate and supportive for staff to touch when service users are distressed as it may validate the degree of their suffering. He suggests that appropriate places to touch in this situation are hands, forearms, upper arms and shoulders.

Source: Tilmouth et al. (2011)

Written

Written reports, notes, email and other forms of electronic communication are all important, and being able to maintain clear and accurate records is a legal requirement. As Donnelly and Neville (2008) point out, written communications should be accurate, detailed, up to date, non-judgemental and legible so that others are able to read and understand them. Confidentiality guidelines and, as such, all forms of written communication must be kept safely and should conform to the Data Protection Act (1998) and the slightly different requirements of the General Data Protection Regulation (**GDPR**), introduced in May 2018.

> ## KEY TERM
>
> **GDPR** refers to the General Data Protection Regulation. This is a set of data protection laws that protects individuals' personal information. This superseded the Data Protection Act 1998 in May 2018.

Electronic/digital

Email is a quick and convenient method of communication with the bonus that people can respond immediately or when it is suitable for them. As a written record of a communication, it can be accessed afterwards for evidence in a way that a telephone communication cannot. We can also add attachments and links to relevant websites into the email, allowing the respondent to go straight to the information. There is no postage and it can save on journey time to and from meetings.

There are disadvantages with emails, however, due to their impersonal nature and the inability to pick up paralinguistic and non-verbal signals. Short and to-the-point emails can sometimes

appear rude and people tend not to reply to emails they do not understand, so you could be waiting for an answer for a while.

Confidentiality is another important consideration, with the potential for confidential information going to the wrong person by mistake or accidentally forwarded on by the respondent to someone who would not be included by the first writer.

Pictorial

Pictorial (or assisted) communication refers to use of aids such as picture and symbol communication boards and electronic devices, which help individuals who have difficulty with speech or language problems to express themselves.

Signage

Sign language, Braille, Makaton, assisted technology and other non-verbal methods of communication are useful aids for those service users who cannot communicate verbally and, as a manager, you will need to ensure that staff are equipped to support service users who may need to use such methods. Everyone in the setting also needs to know the meanings of signs such as at fire exits or smoking areas.

> ## Evidence opportunity
>
> **1.2** **Workplace models and methods of communication and their importance**
>
> Provide a written account analysing the effectiveness of communication models and methods within the practice and their impact on service delivery to include:
>
> - written
> - verbal and non-verbal
> - electronic/digital
> - pictorial
> - signage
> - social media.

▲ **Figure 3.4** Mobile phones have made it easier to access social media and communicate using various social media websites and platforms

Social media

Facebook, Twitter, WhatsApp and blogs have changed the way in which we communicate. Businesses and organisations use these methods for marketing and informing others about what they do. While these are useful tools for getting our message out there, we need to be aware of what we write and who might read our posts. As a manager, you may wish to restrict your personal accounts to friends and family only and not allow your staff to access them. These forms of media can never be deleted and an unprofessional post or personal opinion may be viewed by staff or others and could prove detrimental to your own business or the way in which you are perceived as a manager of staff.

Reflect on it

1.2 Methods of communication

Which different means of communication do you use in your role? Provide a reflective account and list the types of communication you use at work and comment on how effective each type is in your span of duty. You might address when and how you use verbal, non-verbal, sign, pictorial, written, electronic and assisted methods. The means of communication may be personal, organisational, formal, informal or public (information/promotional).

AC 1.3 Reasons for applying different systems of communication

Here, you will be required to critically evaluate the use and application of different types of communications within your working environments, for example with individuals who have various illnesses and needs, including the ones we discuss here.

The use and application of different types of communications within working environments

We communicate daily with diverse groups. Figure 3.5 shows the different types of people you will deal with as part of your role. You may need to use particular skills to get your message across to some of these people. Recognising this is paramount since many barriers to communication arise from inappropriate language and terminology, which effectively means the message is lost. For example, the delivery of factual information can be quite impersonal and may be inappropriate when dealing with a vulnerable child or adult with complex needs or learning difficulties, or someone who is depressed or autistic and therefore requires a more empathetic response. However, a member of the medical staff may require a factual response.

Therefore, for the message to be received and understood, you must match your communication with the individual you are speaking to and the circumstances in which the interaction takes place. For example, a person you manage may be distressed after dealing with a stressful situation, they may not be listening to what you are trying to say and may therefore need information to be written down or to have another conversation at a better time.

Davis and Fallowfield (1991) reported on failure of communication and lack of empathy, and Graham (1991) described how a breakdown in respectful relationships leads to poor communication. Hewison, in 1995, highlighted the power relationships and barriers to communications.

Research it

1.3 Communication and interpersonal skills

It would be useful to research further and explore more recent texts dealing with communication and interpersonal skills by Burnard (1996) and Donnelly and Neville (2008), or to watch relevant TED talks on the internet. TED talks are usually 20-minute instructive talks from leaders in their field and often cover communication, among other topics.

How to communicate with individuals with different care needs

- **Depression**: A person with depression needs to be spoken to in a clear and concise way as they may be slower in response and activity.
- **Dysarthria**: (difficulty in articulating due to a brain condition). This sort of condition can be very frustrating for a person as they try to communicate but often fail to find words. The use of electronic aids, picture cards or symbols may help.

- **Language difficulties**: Again, this is frustrating and if an interpreter is unavailable then pictures and drawings can be used.

- **Dementia**: Speak clearly and slowly and use short sentences. Maintain eye contact and giving the person time to respond. They must not feel patronised or a nuisance and patience is needed here.

- **Complex needs**: The form of communication which is best depends on the person's needs. For example, multiple sensory loss may require electronic forms of communication.

- **Sensory loss**: If the person has lost hearing ability or is partially sighted we can employ hearing loops, Braille or other forms of communication the person is familiar with.

- **Autistic spectrum needs**: Too much information can be a barrier to communication, so any extraneous information needs to be filtered out. It is best to use the person's name and to ask for their attention before talking to them and giving instructions. Saying less and speaking slowly will aid communication. The use of symbols and pictures may help.

- **Learning difficulties/differences**: Mencap compiled 'Your guide to communicating with people with a learning disability'. This would be useful for you to find online and read.

In a nutshell, people with a learning disability feel that the best way to communicate with them is face to face and one to one, using easily understandable words.

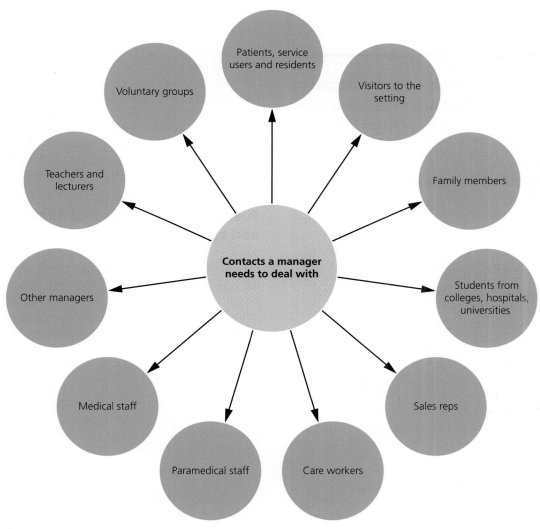

▲ **Figure 3.5** As a manager, you will need to deal with a range of people

Evidence opportunity

1.3 Reasons for applying different systems of communication

Provide a written account critically evaluating how you used and applied different types of communications within your working environment, for example with individuals who have the different care needs we have discussed in this section.

You might like to consider what was successful and what you would do differently next time.

How can you support the people you manage to communicate with individuals with different care needs?

Remember when we critically evaluate something we are asking questions on the subject area – 'why' and 'how', not just 'what'. It is therefore not about just describing your communication methods here but about considering how valid and reliable you are and what strengths and weaknesses you have. You might also question why the results may differ depending on the circumstances.

AC 1.4 Ways in which communication underpins effective service operation

Here, you will be required to explain how communication impacts on effective service operation in relation to the topics we discuss.

Sustainable relationships – internal and external

Effective health and social care is provided in collaboration and partnership with others, either in the same team (internally) or across a range of agencies and disciplines within the care sector (externally).

We spend time building personal and organisational or partnership relationships and trust within those relationships matters. The success of our business or team depends upon the ability to collaborate and build effective working partnerships with both internal staff and those who work outside the organisation. Building sustainable relationships is also a useful indicator of how successful you are as a leader because good relationships will motivate staff and others to do their best.

All partnership working depends on effective communication and good working relationships. As part of a care team that goes beyond the boundaries of your own organisation, you need to be aware of the need to build team links with external bodies.

KEY TERM

Partnership working is the use of inclusive and mutually beneficial relationships in care work that improve the quality and experience of care. It refers to the relationships between individuals with long-term care conditions, their carers, and service providers and care professionals.

Partnership working

Partnership working is an important means of making improvements in health care. It depends on effective partnerships between the different professions and organisations involved in commissioning and delivering services and interventions. It requires shared communication systems, including shared databases, records and files, to ensure that consistency in care is maintained and decision-making processes are clear. In 2014, the Care Act brought about national changes to care and support in England.

The Care Act 2014 simplified and improved the existing legislation in care and the changes mean that more people are now able to access care and support, from local councils or other organisations in the community. They also have more choice about the type of support and care they need. In addition, different ways to pay for care and support are now available. This meant that communication between partners had to be firmly established to ensure that all parties were talking to each other and had the service user at the heart of the care.

Positive outcomes for individuals, families and carers

We want our service users, patients, their family and friends to experience the best care possible and yet we are constantly made aware of how communication fails in healthcare. McDonald, in a 2016 report for NICE, states that while great improvements in communication have been made, proposals now are focusing on 'objectives which can save costs, improve health outcomes and enhance the quality of patients' experience of healthcare' (McDonald, 2016).

Miscommunication must be avoided, and we need to ensure that messages are clear and understood. Good communication enables us to make decisions and promote rights, and give choice to service users. This means we can promote a person-centred service. Good communication also ensures that staff and service users are empowered and can support each other well in their work.

Leadership and management of teams

There are a number of reasons for communicating as a manager and leader, including:

- delegation of work
- conducting meetings
- presentations
- supervision and appraisal
- report writing
- building the team
- negotiation
- interviewing.

All these tasks in themselves are detailed and can be further broken down to reveal more complex levels. For example, before undertaking supervisory roles, we need to be aware of what they entail. Our list might look like this:

- function of supervision
- who requires it?
- mechanics of how it is carried out
- record-keeping policies
- conduct of the interview
- evaluating the process.

Meeting communication needs

Whatever the communication need or type, a good working relationship is essential and demands that there is trust and the ability to talk openly and honestly. The other person may need to feed back to you, to report complaints of abuse, for example, and as a manager you should ensure you equip them with the skills to do so. During your daily work you will undertake a variety of roles and will need to adjust your communication to each circumstance. Effective communicators make appropriate choices when it comes to deciding how they intend to interact and when they are clear about the purpose of the interaction. The different people to which you will have access will require different types of communication and you may find yourself advising, instructing, welcoming, assessing, observing, informing and counselling.

See AC 2.3 for information on how you can support effective communication as a manager.

Conflict management/resolution

When we come across a situation that is causing some **conflict**, this may cause us to have negative feelings about a person, which in turn may become a barrier to communication.

KEY TERM

Conflict is a disagreement or argument.

Case study

1.4 Sophie

Sophie is the union representative for Unison. She is trying to encourage union members into action over spending cuts in the setting as a result of the recent recession and the potential redundancy situation that has arisen. There have also been government cutbacks on staffing and this has meant that you, as a manager, have had to look closely at the workforce and make hard decisions about reducing the number of staff. Five people are now at risk of losing their jobs.

Sophie has sent an email to all Unison members and is seeking the following commitment from union members:

- one-day strike action and protest outside the workplace
- non-cooperation at meetings, with all the Unison members turning their chairs to face the back of the room, staging a protest while being present.

Think about the following:

1. Comment honestly on how this makes you feel about Sophie and her potentially disruptive influence.
2. What is your initial response to the actions as a manager?
3. Now reflect on the above and say why you reacted this way and how you will respond to the situation.

It is possible that your thoughts about Sophie in the case study are negative and at the moment it would be difficult to have any sort of dialogue with her that could be positive. Perhaps you feel her actions are unjust and unfair; the cuts are not your fault, after all, but a result of a drive in the organisation to reduce costs. You may even take this stance personally.

Your reactions are perfectly reasonable, but as a manager you have to detach yourself from the subjective emotions of the situation, that is your personal feelings about Sophie, and deal in a more objective way with the task at hand, which is reducing the impact of these actions and raising staff morale. A tall order!

Conflict is often viewed as a negative issue and it becomes a problem when it affects our work, causes inappropriate behaviour and lowers morale, impacting on the workforce and the service users. John Adair, in his book *Effective Teambuilding* (2000), came up with the following five strategies for dealing with conflict:

1. Competing – forcing your own ideas through because you believe your way is right.
2. Confronting/collaborating – bringing all the issues into the open and exploring all feasible options you are showing an openness to change.
3. Compromise – negotiating to meet halfway.
4. Avoid – opting out altogether and avoiding taking up any position.
5. Accommodate – allowing the change to happen so as not to hurt feelings.

In case study 1.4, the conflict is about budget cuts impacting on your workforce. This situation is unavoidable and therefore you are unable to change it. But the way in which you approach the inevitable redundancies and unrest will go a long way to securing a happier outcome in the long run. The strategy that appears to be most useful will be collaboration and confronting the issue, and employing the views of the entire workforce in exploring all the options.

The people in the organisation face a loss in a small way. If you are faced with the same or a similar situation, understanding their emotions will help you to address the changes in an effective way.

With effective communication that encourages the person or team within the institution to accept and understand the reason for the change, you can move to a new way of working that is embraced by everyone (Cole, 2011).

Information sharing

The way we work with others demands that we are open about what we do and effective in sharing information. As an integral way of working, local strategic partnerships have been able to share information and sometimes services to enable service users to be cared for more effectively. You need to ensure that, as a manager, you are aware of the policy in place for partnership working. This policy will detail how information is to be shared and stored to protect the confidentiality of clients as well as detailing referral processes and recording procedures.

For effective partnership, communication systems must be robust, confidential and standardised so that all staff who need to access records understand how they can do this without compromising confidentiality. All partners need to be involved in improvements to the ways in which this is done. Clear protocols as to who is responsible for updating information and who is allowed access to data need to be in place to ensure effective use.

Working environments

Different communication systems are likely to be used within working environments. For example, you might find that different staff carry out record keeping in different ways, or some staff may present nursing or care assessments differently to others. This can lead to communication issues, particularly if staff do not clearly understand how records are being stored and shared. Confidentiality may be compromised when there is confusion about how the records are sent between several partners.

Also, the actual setting may be a form of environmental barrier. For example, excessive noise, poor layout or even the way in which people work in a setting can be detrimental to communication. These issues can be addressed by making changes to the fabric of the environment and improving the layout of the place in which communication is to occur.

As a manager, you should critically examine the environment where you and staff engage with visitors and other staff, when you communicate bad news for example, or where supervision and team meetings are held. If you feel uncomfortable and unsettled in this setting then the chances are that your staff and visitors will too.

Also see AC 2.3 on supportive environments to promote effective communication.

Evidence opportunity

1.4 Ways in which communication underpins effective service operation

Write an account explaining how communication impacts on effective service operation in relation to the topics we have discussed in this section.

Research it

1.4 Communication in your setting and partnerships

Design a questionnaire to obtain feedback from the following groups of people about your communication systems in place at this time:

- service users
- staff
- visitors
- other professionals you deal with.

You may have collected information from personal files and care plans, minutes of meetings, diaries, staff communication systems and emails. Then reflect on your findings. Focus on how you maintain positive outcomes for individuals and families and how you manage conflict within the workplace.

The following questions may be helpful:

- How is information shared within your organisation and among your team and partners?
- Where does communication break down?
- What is good about your communication?
- What needs to be changed?
- Is there anything missing?

When you believe you have the information you need, set down some proposals to improve the communication systems.

AC 1.5 The written word versus the spoken word

Here, you will be required to analyse why the accurate interpretation of written and spoken words is key to effective communication when managing and delivering a care service with reference to the topics we discuss.

Before you begin this section, it may be useful for you to recap types of communication in AC 1.1.

Interpretation versus misinterpretation

You will use both written and verbal communication to provide instructions and feedback and to discuss issues with the people you manage. However, just because we are speaking the same language, it does not follow that we clearly understand what is being said, yet often we make the mistake of assuming we do understand. How many times have you said to somebody, 'but that is not what I meant'? Perhaps your written communication has been taken out of context and somebody has felt angry about what you have proposed?

When we are face-to-face with a person there are other senses at play. We are better able to clarify meanings, for example by using the other person's body language to recognise that we may have been misunderstood. The values and beliefs that a person brings to the communication may also affect the way in which they receive the message.

Written communication is even more likely to be misunderstood or misinterpreted because it is not supported by body language and often we are not present with the reader to explain exactly what we mean. Writing loses some of the nuances of verbal conversation and this can lead to the message being misinterpreted. It is therefore useful after the message has been read to ask for clarification that what has been communicated has been understood.

Language, pitch, tone, inflection and its potential impact on others

We discussed paralinguistic communication in AC 1.2 (page 76). Table 3.3 shows how specific aspects of this can have an impact on understanding.

Burnard (2005) argues that we must be careful of making assumptions about how someone is feeling and paralinguistic communication can offer us clues. It can also impact upon others and cause them to feel differently about our message. As a manager, we need to be aware of our paralinguistic signals, for example when giving feedback to a member of staff. Even if the words are positive, the person may feel they are being criticised if you haven't taken into account your tone and inflection.

Record keeping/reports

Working as a manager in an adult setting means you will be responsible for keeping records and reports. Accurately documenting events and care provides an account of what actually took place. Records form an account of the patient's experience and this helps to provide continuity of care. We rely on these records if, later on, we need to remind ourselves of what was done at the time. Records must be:

- clear
- legible
- accurate
- honest.

Records may be handwritten or computer based, but staff must comply with whichever method the workplace requires. They should know how to use the systems and tools in the workplace and how to maintain confidentiality. Records must comply with legal requirements such as the Data Protection Act 1998 and GDPR.

Table 3.3 Paralinguistic communication

Tone of voice	Our tone of voice carries information about our feelings. It can add emphasis to the words we use.
Speed of speech	Speaking quickly can indicate that we are nervous. However, speech that is particularly slow may communicate that we are unsure about how we are being received by the listeners.
Volume	We may intentionally speak at a low volume (quietly) so that only the person closest to us hears. A person may mumble a reply when leaving the room so that you know they disagree with you but are unsure what they have said.
Inflection	Inflection is the movement of our voice. The emphasis we place on certain words can change the meaning of our sentences. For example, saying 'Do you WANT a drink?' can sound impatient and suggest that the person being asked is slow to respond, whereas 'Do you want a DRINK?' could suggest that things other than drink are on offer, such as food.
Pitch	A high pitch may communicate nervousness whereas a low pitch can be associated with authority.
Hesitations	Ums and ahs sometimes communicate uncertainty or fear, or can be used as clues that the other person wants to take a turn in the communication.
Accent	This communicates where we are from. It is important for a health and social care worker to be understood so we may have to learn to modify a strong regional accent if recipients are unused to it.

Source: Adapted from Tilmouth et al. (2011)

Legally, we are all responsible for what we write and should be aware that what we have written becomes a public record. If a complaint is made, those records may become part of an inquiry and you may be asked to explain what you have written.

Digital: emails, texts and social media

Digital communication is becoming more widespread and we often text to send personal or professional instant messages.

Emails to people we work with may include e-newsletters, or information relevant to all employees. The email may apply only to the person who receives it. We may email people outside the setting, such as GPs and healthcare staff, to convey information about the individuals we care for.

Using emails has advantages and disadvantages. It is a very quick and instant form of communication and you can send various documents to one person or multiple people. However, they may be ignored or lost if the person has hundreds of emails in their inbox. They can also be inadvertently sent to the wrong person or may be misunderstood.

Any emails that are sent between service providers must be encrypted if they contain information about patients or are of a confidential nature.

Social media is useful when it is for a closed group which is intended for staff in a setting. However, again messages may be misconstrued or fail to get through so it is important to recognise that not all staff may use this as a means of communication. Texts and posts on social media must not refer to workplace incidents or patients.

When using such methods, it is important to remember that they form written records of your practice that may be read by anyone or used as evidence in the future. All of this is important when managing and delivering a care service because accurate interpretation of communication is so important. If somebody misconstrues your meaning, for example if they think you are not respecting service providers, there could be serious consequences for you and your business.

Future recommendations to inform best practice

NICE has published numerous guidelines on communication in various parts of the health service. We mentioned one earlier: McDonald (2016). Effective communication can help a vulnerable person feel safe and secure and we need to take time to ensure that they are able to express their needs clearly to us. Some ways to do this are to:

- communicate with the service user when they are alert and able to respond
- give time for the conversation and to allow breaks so the service user can take stock of what is being said
- ensure the environment is conducive to communication and communication isn't being conducted in a noisy or poorly lit area
- ensure that you face the person, maintain eye contact and speak clearly
- use simple language and regularly check understanding.

You will not only need to know this when communicating with service users, but also, as a manager, you will need to ensure that the members of staff that you manage are aware of the different forms of communication, and are supported to be effective communicators to deliver the best possible service to service users.

See AC 2.4 for more information on recommending and implementing improvements to communication systems and practices.

Evidence opportunity

1.5 The written word versus the spoken word

Provide a written account analysing why the accurate interpretation of written and spoken words is key to effective communication when managing and delivering a care service. Refer to the topics we have discussed in this section.

Reflect on it

1.5 Written and spoken language

Think about the uses for written and spoken language in your own setting. Which do you consider to be the more accurate way of communicating and why? Give examples of both written communication and the spoken word to demonstrate your understanding.

Reflect on it

1.5 Evaluating effectiveness of communication systems and practices

How do you evaluate the effectiveness, quality and performance of communication systems in your setting? What standards do you use? Why is it important to ensure accurate communication?

Choose one of the communication systems in your setting (the complaints procedure, for example) and write an account reflecting on and evaluating the quality of the organisation's performance relating to that system.

Research it

1.5 NICE

Look at the above paper on the NICE website (ww.evidence.nhs.uk/document). Read it and make notes about how you might develop some of the points within your own workplace.

LO2 Develop communication systems and practices which support positive outcomes

It is important to develop communication systems and practices which support positive outcomes. Positive outcomes are any beneficial outcomes for adults which lead to improved health, emotional wellbeing and quality of life. As a manager you will ensure that your service provides safe care free from discrimination and harassment where services users and staff can have choice and control, dignity and respect.

AC 2.1 Monitor and evaluate efficiency of internal and external communication systems and practices

Here, you will be required to monitor communication systems and practices currently in use within the workplace, identifying potential issues and barriers, with relation to specific needs of people providing and using adult care services.

It is important to monitor the internal communication systems and practices within your workplace, identifying potential issues and barriers that relate to the specific needs of people providing and using adult care services.

Internal communication refers to the way in which staff communicate, for example via one-to-one discussions with managers or informal discussions with each other. Emails, memos, texting, social media, annual reports and printed materials such as newsletters also convey messages throughout an organisation.

External communication is for organisations and people operating outside the organisation and focuses on spreading news and information to the public, service users and other stakeholders to reflect the ethos and values of the organisation.

Monitoring

In monitoring something, we look at whether there are any deficiencies we need to address and whether changes need to be made to address new initiatives. We can do this in two ways:

1 Search for information to support the current level of function with respect to communication.

2 Analyse and interpret that information to decide on a plan of action.

Our communication systems need to be monitored for effectiveness. The policy on record keeping, for example, may state how staff should record complaints but this needs to be monitored as to how the process is being used and whether in fact it is efficient and maintains confidentiality. You may have a system of checks in place to determine how well staff are managing to record the complaints in line with the policy.

In determining the effectiveness of a system or practice it is essential to monitor its use and review it regularly.

Evaluating

Having collected the information, you now need to analyse and evaluate it. To do this you should examine all the data you have and then determine its positive and negative aspects.

One way this can be carried out is on an informal basis where you obtain casual feedback from individuals as to how well your systems work. However, it is far better to collect information that may be used in auditing your service and can provide evidence to external bodies of your continual progress and quality assurance in the organisation.

There are a number of useful ways in which you can formally ask for feedback. For example, you may use service user forums (groups of service users who meet to discuss the quality of the service) and meetings when the quality of these services can be discussed and minuted. This provides valuable information as to how the service users feel about the organisation. Other ways may be through a complaint and compliment system, questionnaires, appraisal and focus groups.

The care you give and the way you deliver the care have a significant impact, not only on the users of the service but also on staff morale, and as such, any feedback is essential in measuring the quality of the care you provide.

Evidence opportunity

2.1 Monitor and evaluate efficiency

Here, you will be required to show your assessor how you monitor and evaluate the efficiency of internal and external communication systems and practices.

You will be required to show them how you monitor communication systems and practices currently in use within your workplace, identifying potential issues and barriers, with relation to specific needs of people providing and using adult care services.

AC 2.2 Recommend and implement improvements to communication systems and practices

Here, you will be required to make recommendations and implement change in a timely manner.

Improving communication can be done through staff and service user meetings and reports. For example, if a member of staff suggests a change to current practice, it is important that the idea is considered and discussed at a team meeting. The change may be useful but may require some refinement before full implementation.

Any proposed change will require you, as the manager, to ensure that all staff are aware of what needs to be done and that a plan of action is in place. Any revised working practice must be discussed and fully understood by staff and others involved in the setting. New responsibilities may arise that may require training and time. By communicating all the information to staff and having guidelines in place, the changes can be presented in a clear and efficient way to ensure success.

Evidence opportunity

2.2 Recommend and implement improvements to communication systems and practices

Speak to your assessor and show them how you make recommendations and implement change in a timely manner.

Research it

2.2 Improving communication systems

Safeguarding Adults Reviews, when used, often comment upon poor communication as requiring attention to improve care. Undertake a small-scale study to monitor the communication practice within your own setting and comment upon and evaluate how effective it is. Identify any improvements to the practices and make recommendations for revised systems.

Reflect on it

2.2 Revised communication systems and practice

Reflect on the way in which you led the implementation of a revised practice of your communication systems in your setting.

1 Which communication practice in your setting did you change and why?

2 How did you recommend this change to your team? Make notes to document your thoughts.

Reflect on it

2.1 2.2 Communication systems and practices

Using the responses obtained from the questionnaire you compiled for Research it 1.4, answer the following questions.

1 What methods did you use to collect the information?

2 What barriers and potential issues did you identify within your organisation's communication system? (See page 89 for examples of barriers.)

3 How did you identify these issues?

4 How did you determine which practices should stay, and why?

5 Who was involved in the decision?

6 What will you do to change the systems and lead the implementation?

AC 2.3 Create supportive environments to promote effective communication

Physical (noise, light, space, furniture, comfort, colour)

An area where communication is likely to break down is an inappropriate environment. Have a look around the room in which you are sitting. How does it make you feel? Think about it for a moment. Is it welcoming, untidy, busy, crammed, too large, are the chairs too far apart? Also take a good look at where and when you conduct important communications with staff. The initial impact of a room or building can have a huge effect on how people feel and can influence the success of an interaction.

As a manager, you will need to be aware of the environments in which you hold meetings such as appraisals to ensure that these are suitable for the desired

Reflect on it

2.3 Environments and communication

'I remember attending an informal interview where I was asked to sit in an easy chair. The interviewer sat in an upright chair next to me and towered over me. The effect this had on me, as I sank down into the soft cushions, was of being vulnerable. I am sure the interviewer had not intended for me to feel that way but it certainly changed the way in which I responded to his questions.'

What might your response have been in this situation? Have you ever had a similar experience where the actual setting was inappropriate for the situation?

purpose, and will promote effective communication between you and others. Noisy environments may mean your message is not heard, impacting on the outcomes you may have expected. A room that is poorly lit may mean that you are unable to clearly read the other person's body language, or make eye contact. Where furniture is placed can impact communication: in meeting rooms, even the position of the chairs can affect the interactions. For example, look at the two photographs of different types of classroom set-ups in Figure 3.6. Which classroom set-up do you prefer? Does the set-up in the first image bring up memories of school? Perhaps those memories are less than happy? The way that our environment communicates with us is extremely important.

How cold or warm the room is and even the colour on the walls can affect how comfortable we feel, and how and what we choose to communicate.

You will be aware of the need for privacy when carrying out sensitive types of communication, such as breaking bad news or reprimanding someone. But have you thought about the impact your own setting will have on others? Thinking about these things will allow you to create, choose and work in environments well suited to the needs of the people you work with, and manage, and ultimately those that you provide care and support for.

▲ **Figure 3.6** Different types of classroom set-ups

Staff attitudes and stigma

Staff have their own beliefs, attitudes and prejudices and, as managers, we need to be aware of this in order to encourage their cultural awareness and the need to communicate in a non-judgemental way. **Stigma** and **discrimination** trap individuals in a cycle of illness so we need to ensure that staff are aware of this and are not failing the service users by their own failure to communicate fairly. If we always accept and value the people with whom we interact by expressing warmth and a non-judgemental attitude, we will improve our communication skills no end.

Have you ever felt judged or that the other person was not listening to you? In this sort of situation it is very difficult to be open and honest about our feelings and needs. If we judge the people with whom we are interacting, whether they are staff or service users, they may feel they are unable to open up to us, which might be detrimental to the organisation's aims and objectives. In other words, your failure to communicate effectively or ingrain this principle in your staff will lead to lack of success.

We regularly come into contact with all types of people, who all have their own feelings, values and attitudes. Sometimes these may clash with how we see the world. We may not share their views or particularly like the stance the person takes, but managers and leaders of a setting have to show tolerance of these views (providing they are not contravening any anti-discrimination policy). We need to be fully aware of how we come across to those we are communicating with. It is possible that we may communicate our dislike of somebody through our body language or the way we speak to them; this will have a negative effect on the interaction and may lead to conflict in the workplace.

Approaches which support effective communication

Effective communicators adapt their communication style to the situation and respond in sensitive and empathetic ways to the needs of those they are communicating to. In supporting others to become effective communicators, you, as a leader, must be an effective role model and, where you are able, reflect effectively on how you are communicating your messages.

Effective communicators are just as much aware of the skills and types of communication as they are of the need to affirm the self-worth of the person with whom they are interacting. What do we mean by this?

Be empathetic

Rogers (1980) referred to the term 'empathy', which is the ability to 'put yourself in the shoes of others' or to understand the client's frame of reference. Active listening skills are the best way to show **empathy**. This is different from showing sympathy, which might make a person feel pitied.

> ## KEY TERM
>
> **Empathy** is being able to understand and share the feelings of another person or having the ability to experience another person's condition from their perspective.

Daniel Goleman (1995, p. 137) stated that emotional intelligence is:

> *'the capacity for recognising our own feelings and those of others for motivating ourselves, for managing emotions well in ourselves as well as others.'*

For Goleman, self-awareness is about knowing our own emotions and recognising those feelings as they happen. So, we may feel angry at something somebody has said, but as a manager and leader, showing that anger inappropriately will have a negative effect on relationships.

Social awareness refers to the empathy and concern we have for others' feelings; the acknowledgement that people under threat in an organisation may show aggression and anger. Decisions affecting people's jobs may have to be made, and the manager who sees only the task at hand is failing to acknowledge the effect this is having on those

at risk and those who have to continue to work in such a climate of change.

Relationship management is the ability to handle relationships competently in order to best deal with conflict, and to develop collaboration in the workforce.

Finally, Goleman refers to motivation, particularly of ourselves, to enable the workforce to meet goals.

In a management situation our awareness of the impact of our actions and responses can go a long way towards defusing situations that might be potentially threatening. We may not be feeling very happy or friendly ourselves, but being in a position of authority demands that we have some awareness of the feelings of others. A good manager is one who has a level of emotional intelligence.

Take a non-judgemental approach and listen

If we support all our communication by accepting and valuing the people with whom we interact through the expression of warmth and a non-judgemental attitude, we will improve our communication skills no end.

Have you ever felt judged or that the other person was not listening to you? In this sort of situation, it is very difficult to be open and honest about our feelings and needs. If we judge the people with whom we are interacting, whether they are staff or service users, they may feel they are unable to open up to us, which might be detrimental to the organisation's aims and objectives. In other words, your failure to communicate effectively or ingrain this principle in your staff will lead to lack of success.

Help staff to support communication with service users

As a manager and leader, you can support effective communication by ensuring that your staff are aware of the need to be flexible in how they communicate within different contexts and to engage in communication that is empathetic and values the people they are interacting with. It is also useful if staff understand any communication plans

▲ **Figure 3.7** How do you ensure that you communicate effectively?

that are developed in partnership with speech and language therapists to enable continuity of care. Service users will have different communication needs and it is important that staff can address these needs by having a firm understanding of different communication methods such as sign language. They may need to have specialist training in these.

Staff need to be mindful of how to communicate verbally with certain individuals in ways which show a respect for their differences and needs. Non-verbal communication may also pose barriers to effective communication so staff need to be sure they are aware of how this may affect the interaction. For example, when communicating with somebody who is angry we need to ensure that we approach the conversation in a way which will not escalate the situation. Staff will need advice on how to do this and may also require training in dealing with this sort of situation. Also see LO1 for more information about communication skills that both you and staff you manage will need.

Assistive technology

This is a term for devices that can assist a person with a disability to lead a more independent life. There are a number of devices that can aid hearing and make communicating more accessible. These might include easy-to-use telephones and 'memory' phones which have photos of contacts with pre-programmed numbers, large print and tactile keyboards to enable the person to communicate by computer. Loop systems enhance hearing and a range of hearing aids is available to suit individual needs.

As a manager, you will need to ensure that your staff are aware of what clients require and arrange for adaptions to be made.

KEY TERM

Assistive technology refers to the use of aids such as picture and symbol communication boards and electronic devices, which help individuals who have difficulty with speech or language problems to express themselves.
Your staff must be aware of all the options available and need to be able to give out that information in an unbiased way. You may be asked, 'What would you do or what would you choose?' In most cases the answer has to be, 'I am not you and it is for you to decide.'

Reflect on it

2.3 Barriers to communication

List two issues (one internal and one external factor) that may have been the reasons for the blocks or barriers in communication. For example, an external barrier may be a poor environment for the communication which lacks privacy, leading to an internal barrier in that you are unsafe talking about a matter.

You may have come up with some of the following:

● Difference in culture, values and language.

● Dealing with different viewpoints and values/negative feelings about the person you are speaking to or getting upset about what they are saying, leading to conflict.

● Body language and non-verbal communication (NVC), as well as general personality issues where some people will be more confident communicators than others.

● Conflict and resistance to change causing upset.

● Personal issues which may make it difficult to concentrate and communicate effectively.

● Power dynamics, that is where some people are perceived to be in higher/lower levels of power, affecting their ability to communicate/how they are expected to communicate.

● Self-esteem may affect confidence and thus someone's ability to communicate.

● Tiredness, personal issues or other health issues or disabilities, including sensory loss. Health issues may include people who suffer from depression and anxiety, for example, which may affect their ability to communicate.

● Environmental issues, including noise and/or poor lighting.

● Feeling unsafe, due to the person's demeanour or behaviour.

● Not listening effectively.

Evidence opportunity

2.3 Supportive environments to promote effective communication

Prepare a written account for your assessor and staff explaining how different environments impact on the promotion of effective communication. Use the headings in this section to help you.

AC 2.4 Evaluate benchmarking techniques used for effective communication and reviewing purposes

Here, you will be required to evaluate benchmarking techniques used in your own service area, which could include auditing records, action plans and CPD records to evaluate the effectiveness of your communication systems and processes, to include the topics we discuss in this section.

What do we mean by benchmarking? It is the practice of making comparisons either within or between organisations/settings. Various measures can be used to check how well one organisation or setting is competing with another.

The DoH's paper 'Essence of Care' (2010) defined benchmarking as 'a systematic process in which current practice and care are compared to, and amended to attain, best practice and care'.

Benchmarking techniques could include auditing of records, action plans and continuing professional development records, such as appraisal forms, to evaluate the effectiveness of communication systems and processes. Auditing refers to an examination of books, accounts, statutory records and documents to determine the financial state of an organisation.

'Essence of Care' laid down benchmarks for various aspects of care in response to evidence collected from patients. The benchmarks identified 12 topics which patients were unhappy about. These were: bladder, bowel and continence care, care environment, communication, food and drink, prevention and management of pain, personal hygiene, prevention and management of pressure ulcers, promoting health and wellbeing, record keeping, respect and dignity, safety, self-care.

Recommendations to and for new and existing staff

New staff and existing staff need to be aware of the term benchmarking and should have some knowledge about how it affects the area in which they work. Staff from different settings can help to compare their former settings and may be able to bring in new ideas.

Recommendations to and for those in receipt of care and support

The 'Essence of Care' document collected evidence from service users as to various aspects of care. Your own service users might be made aware of these findings and may even add to them.

How leadership and management practice impacts on effective communication(s)

Good leaders and managers want to accomplish improvements in any ineffective part of their setting so good communication skills that empower staff and service users to challenge ideas and to make comparisons about the systems in place for communication in the setting are admirable. As a manager you will need to role model good communication to achieve this.

Evidence opportunity

2.4 Evaluate benchmarking techniques used for effective communication and reviewing purposes

Provide a written account evaluating benchmarking techniques that are used in your own service area: these could include auditing records, action plans and CPD records to evaluate the effectiveness of your communication systems and processes. Address the areas we have covered in this section.

Research it

2.4 Benchmarking techniques for effective communication and reviewing

The table below shows the benchmark for communication as laid down in 'Essence of Care'. Complete the final column to show evidence of how best practice benchmarks are achieved in your own setting, using auditing records, action plans, CPD records and other relevant documentation.

Then use this information to prepare a report that evaluates the effectiveness of benchmarking techniques in care. Consider what is done well and what could be done better.

Content	Best practice	Evidenced by
Interpersonal skills	All staff demonstrate effective interpersonal skills	
Opportunity for communication	Communication takes place at a time and in an environment that is acceptable to all parties	
Assessment of communication needs	All communication needs are assessed on initial contact and are regularly reassessed. Additional communication support is negotiated and provided when a need is identified or requested	
Information sharing	Information is accessible, acceptable, accurate and meets needs, is shared actively and consistently with all who need it, and is widely promoted across all communities	
Resources to aid communication and understanding	Appropriate and effective methods are used to enable communication	

Content	Best practice	Evidenced by
Identification and assessment of principal carer	The principal carer is identified at all times. Their needs, involvement, willingness and ability to collaborate with staff in order to provide care are assessed	
Empowerment to perform role	Staff and carers are continuously supported and fully enabled to perform their roles safely	
Coordination of care	All staff communicate fully and effectively with each other to ensure that service users and carers benefit from a comprehensive and agreed plan of care which is regularly updated and evaluated	
Empowerment to communicate needs	Staff, service users and carers are enabled to communicate their individual needs and preferences at all times	
Valuing staff, service users and carers' expertise and contribution	Effective communication ensures that the people's and carers' expert contributions to care are valued, recorded and acted upon and reviewed with staff	
Service user's and/or carers' education needs	Service user's and carers' information, support and education needs are jointly identified, agreed, met and regularly reviewed	

LO3 Implement systems for effective information management

AC 3.1 Implement effective information management systems meeting all legal and ethical requirements

Here, you will be required to show that you can support others to understand and adhere to the legal and ethical requirements of information management systems in relation to your own service.

Any system of information management is required to be legally sound. Information shared in organisations has to be kept confidential and staff need to be aware of their role in this. Beauchamp and Childress (1994) define confidentiality as 'keeping secret' information given to a person by another. It is infringed when that information is disclosed to someone else without the giver's consent (see page 46 for a definition and more information on consent).

Health and social care staff are required to fulfil their duty of care and maintain confidences obtained via their work and you, as a manager, need to respect this requirement. However, if a public interest issue is at stake, then confidence may be broken. For example:

- if a crime has been committed or you believe it is about to be
- if malpractice has occurred
- if abuse is suspected

- to prevent harm to self or to others
- if professional misconduct has occurred.

If there is a breach of confidentiality within your workplace, then you as the manager are obliged to take disciplinary action and/or legal action. From a legal point of view, you are obliged to follow the laws associated with maintaining confidentiality, including:

- The Care Act 2014
- Data Protection Act (1998) and GDPR (2018)
- Human Rights Act (1998)
- The Freedom of Information Act (2000)
- The Equality Act (2010)
- Public Interest Disclosure Act (1999) (often referred to as the 'Whistle Blowing Act').

Other guidelines are:

- setting-specific guidelines, drawn up for a setting's unique circumstances
- clinical governance requirements
- essential standards for quality and safety (CQC)
- Caldicott Report recommendations
- Skills for Care guidelines
- Disability Discrimination Act (1995).

From an ethical point of view, in maintaining confidentiality, health professionals explicitly or implicitly make a promise to their service users to keep their information confidential, thus respecting the autonomy of the client. But problems arise when decisions need to be made that require the sharing of certain personal information. For example, Article 10 of the Convention on Human Rights and Biomedicine states: 'Everyone has the right to respect for private life in relation to information about his/her health care' (European Parliament & Council of the European Union, 1995).

As a manager you need to ensure that you have implemented effective information management systems which meet all legal and ethical requirements and are safe with respect to confidentiality and data protection. Unfortunately, the NHS became a victim of computer hackers in October 2016 when the personal information of thousands of medical staff at NHS Wales was stolen. This included their names, dates of birth, national insurance numbers and data on radiation exposure of staff who worked with x-ray equipment. The data had been stored and processed by a private IT contractor until its security was compromised. Encrypted systems and not sharing codes or passwords increase data security.

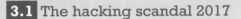

Research it

3.1 The hacking scandal 2017

Research and read up about the hacking scandal that affected the NHS. Go to www.telegraph.co.uk/news/2017/05/12/nhs-hit-major-cyber-attack-hackers-demanding-ransom/to read about the 2017 hacking scandal.

How does this help you to understand the importance of effective information management systems and security?

Evidence opportunity

3.1 Effective information management systems

Write a short report which explains how you support your staff to understand and adhere to the legal and ethical requirements of information management systems in relation to the services you provide, and implement such systems. Or you could show this to your assessor.

AC 3.2 Lead practice to address legal and ethical conflicts that arise between maintaining confidentiality and information sharing

Here, you will be required to show you lead practice that considers both legal and ethical conflicts relating to the area of service, and consider the areas we cover in this section.

One of the tensions with respect to confidentiality lies with the use of information and its safekeeping. This is an important issue on a national scale. For example, in 2013, the Health and Social Care Information Centre (HSCIC; now called NHS Digital) was established to improve health and

care by providing national information, data and IT systems for patients, researchers, commissioners, analysts and clinicians in health and social care. It aims to let everyone say whether they are happy for their personal data to be shared beyond their personal contact with a health and social care professional, and to allow people to find out when and why their data has been used for purposes other than direct care.

Health and Social Care (2015) Information and technology for better care. Information Centre Strategy 2015–2020 outlines the requirement to keep safe information about patients and clients, which can sometimes be a contentious issue.

As a manager of a setting, you and the individuals that you manage may come across various obstacles when trying to ensure confidentiality and keeping information safe. There will be legal and ethical conflicts that may arise, some of which we explore below. It is your duty to ensure that the people you manage are aware of the actions to follow and that they are clearly outlined in the policies and procedures for your setting.

Relatives expecting information without consent

Occasionally a relative will call and ask for information about a service user. Our first duty is always to the service user or individual in our care. If the patient or service user has not given consent, then as a care professional you will not be able to discuss their care with the relative.

Information may be shared with the consent of the patient or service user. Some hospitals and care organisations will write in the patient's notes the details of those who may have access to information. If it is kept digitally, this information may be password protected and the person asking about the service user may be asked to declare the password before information can be shared. When the people you manage come across an issue like this, they will approach you for advice and the best course of action. You should be able to advise them as to best practice here, and also advise them of any occasions when confidentiality may be breached. This is covered in the section on consent on page 93.

Capacity issues

The Mental Capacity Act (MCA) 2005 was designed to empower individuals who may lack the mental capacity to make their own decisions about their care and treatment. Capacity refers to having sufficient or enough understanding and memory to understand the situation that a person finds themselves in. Those who may lack capacity are individuals who have dementia, a severe learning disability, a brain injury or a mental health condition, or may be affected by a stroke or unconsciousness caused by an anaesthetic or accident.

The act contends that health professionals must assume that somebody has mental capacity unless a capacity assessment proves otherwise and also that individuals must be given help to make decisions based on information that they understand.

There is also provision within this law for an **advocate** or another trusted person to make a decision on behalf of the person if they lack capacity at a future date. When a person is judged not to have capacity the decision can be made for them, but it must be in their best interests. Confidentiality must always be maintained and a person needs to give **consent** before information about them is shared.

KEY TERMS

An **advocate** is an individual who acts for or on behalf of another, particularly if the person lacks capacity in some way or simply requires help to speak out.
Consent means to give permission for something to happen. It may be verbal, written or implied but always needs to be addressed.

Consent issues

As a manager, you will also need to ensure that the people you manage are aware of consent issues when working with the individuals that they care for. They must be aware that before any treatment can be given to a patient or service user, their consent must be obtained. This may simply be asking the service user if what you are planning to do is OK to go ahead with. For example, if you are going to help a service user with their personal needs, consent is gained by explaining what you are going to help them with and then asking them if they agree to this.

Consent has to be a voluntary action agreed by the service user themselves and not one which has been influenced by another person. It also has to be 'informed' – all information, including benefits and risks, must be explained and any alternative treatments described. The person also has to have capacity.

There are occasions when confidentiality can be breached and the care professional is duty-bound to share personal information without the service user's or patient's consent. This may happen for two reasons: first, when the professional feels that information must be shared in the public interest. If the patient or service user is a risk to others then police may be involved. Second, if a court orders information to be disclosed for whatever reason. If either happens then the care professional needs to inform the client and their relatives.

Next of kin versus nearest relative

Next of kin is different to the nearest relative. The next of kin is usually a relative or close friend chosen by the client/patient soon after they are admitted to health or social care. This person is documented on patient notes and care plans.

The term 'nearest relative' is defined in the Mental Health Act 1983 and this person may not always be the same as the next of kin. Your next of kin may be your mother but the partner you live with may be your nearest relative. Section 26 of the Mental Health Act gives a list of people who might undertake this role. The general rule is that the nearest relative will be the person who comes highest on this list, although this is not always the case. The nearest relative has certain rights under the Mental Health Act. The nearest relative can, for example, ask for a Mental Health Act assessment from social services to decide whether the individual might be detained, and they also have the power to discharge the client/patient from a section of the Mental Health Act.

The next of kin has no legal powers under the Mental Health Act.

Reflect on it

3.2 Breaching confidentiality

Think about when you might have to breach a service user's confidentiality. Under what circumstances would you be prepared to do this and how would you go about it?

Research it

3.2 Nearest relatives

Go to www.rethink.org/carers-family-friends/what-you-need-to-know/nearest-relative and make notes about the nearest relative rules.

How might you handle a next of kin wanting to hold a mental health assessment for a person when the next of kin isn't a nearest relative?

Power of attorney – lasting versus enduring

The role of the **Lasting Power of Attorney (LPA)** replaced Enduring Power of Attorney (EPA) in 2007. An EPA made before then is still valid. The difference is that an LPA enables an individual with capacity (this wasn't the case for EPAs) to appoint a person or persons to make decisions about their health and welfare, property and financial affairs should they become unable to do so themselves, without being subjected to pressure or fraud. Each of these decisions is made with legal documentation to support them.

KEY TERM

Lasting Power of Attorney (LPA) is a legal document which allows anybody over the age of 18 to appoint one or more people to support the decision-making process should the individual become unable to do so. The person must have the mental capacity to undertake this step. This has replaced the Enduring Power of Attorney (EPA) which was a legal document that appointed one or more people to make financial decisions.

AC 3.3 Implement systems to monitor and review accuracy and reliability of information

Here, you will be required to evaluate a range of systems to ensure that information is captured, monitored and reviewed to meet legal and organisational requirements.

As a manager, one of your responsibilities is to ensure that information is accurate, reliable and captured, monitored and reviewed to meet legal and organisational requirements relating to such information. In order to gain accurate and reliable data you will need to ensure that systems are in place in which sufficient evidence is examined. For example, if you want to make a change to practice you should collect evidence and facts from various sources to ensure that you have enough information to monitor. You may collect surveys from staff and service users, interview stakeholders and then compare the results to other areas and use secondary information from another source to gain an informed, accurate and reliable set of data.

Accurate information refers to facts that define the truth about something and reliable information is that which can be trusted, that is coming from a trusted source.

It should be accessible only to the relevant people and staff need to understand how the information is to be used. The service user must be aware of how the information about them is used and how such use conforms to legal and ethical principles.

One of the main legal requirements deals with the quality of the reports collected and the way in which the system is implemented. As a manager, there are four key areas which you need to monitor and evaluate:

1 **Purpose** – clarity about why you need to collect data.
2 **Collection** – the processes by which data is collected.
3 **Storage** – the processes and systems used to store and maintain patient information and notes.

4 **Analysis** – the process of translating data into information that can be used to improve the organisation and its care-giving.

Taking this a step further, the information that is collected must also comply with legal requirements of accuracy to provide an account of what actually took place.

LO4 Support others with effective communication strategies

AC 4.1 Establish effective monitoring systems for communication within services

Here, you will be required to establish effective communication/information delivery systems with staff and others using adult care services, with consideration of the topics we discuss.

You will need to ensure that you not only effectively communicate with the people that you manage, but monitor the systems that you have in place. You will need to ensure that you have systems in place. We discuss some of the ways in which you could do this below.

Staff induction processes and procedures

In your role as manager you will need to ensure you offer strong induction activities and training for staff. Staff need to understand their roles and responsibilities with regard to health and safety record keeping and reporting and must also be aware of the necessity of complying with policies and procedures and practice. Any breaches must be dealt with effectively and quickly to avoid unsafe practice. By monitoring compliance to the policies and procedures and ensuring that checks/audits take place and that risk assessments are updated you will be practising safely with respect to this part of your management role.

The Common Induction Standards were replaced by the Care Certificate on 1 April 2015, which was designed for non-regulated workers who give care. The process enables new members of your team to gain confidence in their role and, as a manager, you can be assured that your staff are obtaining the skills and knowledge needed to provide compassionate, safe care.

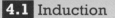

Reflect on it

4.1 Induction

How do you ensure that your staff are being adequately inducted into their roles as care workers? What audit trail or records do you have that show this?

An audit trail refers to the records, information and set of data that provide evidence of the activities that have been carried out.

Staff supervision across all staff teams irrespective of employment hours, formal and informal

In 2013 CQC published a paper entitled 'Supporting information and guidance: supporting effective clinical supervision' following the recommendations from the Winterbourne View Serious Case Review. It sets out what effective clinical supervision should look like, and although it was developed primarily for supporting people with a learning disability, it provides a useful guide for all care sectors and settings. As a result of this case, codes of practice have changed and ways of working mean that staff are required to undertake realistic workloads and are entitled to training and regular skills updates.

From a legal point of view, supervision is a requirement for all staff. Skills for Care in its document 'Providing Effective Supervision' (2007) states that:

> 'High quality supervision is one of the most important drivers in ensuring positive outcomes for people who use social care and children's services. It also has a crucial role to play in the development, retention and motivation of the workforce.'

As a manager you are responsible for the effectiveness of the work your team undertakes and for the quality of that work. By focusing more on the outcomes for the organisation and not, for example, on the supervisee and their development, supervision becomes a tick-box exercise, checking compliance with policy and procedure. At worst, supervision may not be done at all and may be left out of your role.

Formal supervision requires a regular meeting with staff at a set time in which discussion is recorded. Informal supervision can happen at any time when a member

of staff seeks advice or guidance. This sort of support may be unplanned and delivered in response to the supervisee's needs. It is wise to record all discussions, even if they are informal.

Supervision is a vital management tool for improving the practice in a team and questioning practice. SCIE (2012) carried out research to evidence the worth of supervision. The findings suggested that:

- good supervision is associated with job satisfaction, commitment and retention
- supervision helps to reduce staff turnover and is significantly linked to employees' perceptions of the support
- for service users, anecdotal evidence suggests that supervision may promote empowerment, fewer complaints and more positive feedback.

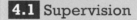

Reflect on it

4.1 Supervision

Identify the systems for supervision in your own setting. Are you happy with them? What could be improved? How do you communicate their use with your staff?

Mentoring/coaching opportunities for the manager and colleagues and internal and external training events

Continuing professional development and lifelong learning are particular requirements for any care professional, and are essential for the development and improvement of safe and effective care services, improving staff retention and contributing to good management practice. As a manager you will need to make sure that systems are in place that ensure staff get the knowledge, skills and training they need.

Coaching and mentoring in the workplace mean that every opportunity where learning may be required can become an informal learning opportunity and, unlike conventional training, the focus is on individual and organisational goals or sharing experiences to help a staff member develop new skills while working. This type of activity contributes to the learning culture of the workplace.

Even if it's on-the-job advice, mentoring and coaching must be measurable and recorded, and to that end any internal or external training events that staff attend should be documented in personal development files. Staff should be given measurable (SMART – specific, measurable, attainable, realistic and timely) objectives so that their personal development can be objectively identified.

Skills for Care in 'Keeping Up the Good Work – A practical guide to implementing continuing professional development in the adult social care workforce' (2010) highlights the fact that, traditionally, the formal training offered to staff ignored a range of other activities such as coaching and mentoring. It states:

> 'CPD for the social care workforce ought also to include any development opportunity which contributes directly to improving the quality of service and improved outcomes for people who use services. This may include work-based learning through supervision and other opportunities supported and provided by employers, such as in-house courses, job-shadowing, secondment, mentoring, coaching' (2010, p. 1).

There is much to commend coaching and mentoring in the workplace and this has become a major way in which learning takes place.

As methods for staff development, coaching and mentoring should be seen to complement traditional training. While attendance at training courses is a necessary and useful way to develop staff, one-to-one support through coaching and mentoring can help to focus on developing specific new skills that benefit both the individual and the work setting.

Clutterbuck (2011), an authority on coaching and mentoring, argues that significant studies of effective managers reveal that those managers who spend a high proportion of their time and energy coaching or mentoring others get the best results from their teams.

Reflect on it

4.1 Training

Identify evidence of the ways in which your staff are trained in order to keep their knowledge and skills up to date. Reflect on the following:

How do you monitor the skills of your staff? How would you become aware of gaps in skills in the workforce? What monitoring systems are in place to ensure staff receive the training they need? Show any documents you have as evidence.

Individual and team goal setting in supporting positive outcomes

An effective team works towards the same goals and the team members will cooperate with the decisions made. When properly managed and developed, team work improves processes and produces results quickly and economically through the free exchange of ideas and information. For example, in establishing systems which monitor the accomplishment of goals you may use an appraisal system in which staff are expected to identify their own SMART targets. Managers may also set goals relating to the team as a whole, so that together staff can work to a successful outcome.

Any organisation that promotes openness and creativity, encouraging the team members to share information, to innovate and take calculated risks, will provide a positive climate in which to work.

Reflect on it

4.1 Goal setting

Explain how you set goals within your team to produce positive outcomes for the service users.

Action planning, e.g. care planning, recovery planning, support planning

Developing an action plan for the team in line with the organisation's strategic plan will enable the team to successfully meet outcomes for staff and service users. In your team meetings, a creative option is enabling staff to contribute to those plans. Any plans made at a higher management tier must be communicated sensitively to the staff who are expected to put them into action.

The staff will be most familiar with the idea of care planning to support the journey of the patient or service user through the care organisation and then onto recovery.

Risk assessment

In supporting the use of risk assessments, we need to feel safe about the decisions made. One way to do this is to ensure that you can defend each decision you make with respect to the assessment of the individual.

You might think about the following questions to guide your assessment:

- Have you taken all reasonable steps in the process?
- Have you used reliable methods?
- Have you collected enough information and looked at it in an evaluative manner?
- Are you working within policy and law?
- Have you recorded all the decisions that were made?

In addition to the above, you might actually take a purely health and safety approach to risk:

- Step 1: Look for hazards.
- Step 2: Identify who could be harmed and how.
- Step 3: Evaluate the risk.
- Step 4: Record the findings.
- Step 5: Assess the effectiveness of the precautions in place.

Your role as a manager will be to effectively monitor the systems you have in place for assessing risk and supporting staff in their risk assessments, ensuring they have taken into account these factors and recorded all the findings. Risk assessments should be made available to all relevant people (while taking into account confidentiality), perhaps on a computer database or in a paper file. They should be checked and updated regularly.

Review current policies in line with legislative and regulatory requirements

The Home Office website (www.gov.uk/government/ organisations/home-office) provides details of the relevant legislation relating to information and communication and how to keep them secure. Have a look at some of the following:

- Data Protection Act 1998
- Freedom of Information Act 2000
- Human Rights Act 1998
- Equality Act 2010
- Terrorism Act 2006
- Official Secrets Act 1989
- Malicious Communications Act 1988
- Privacy and Electronic Communications (EC Directive) (Amendment) Regulations 2011
- Police and Justice Act 2006.

You need to establish that systems are in place to ensure that significant changes to the law are identified and processes are implemented to cover them. You need to make your staff aware of changes to legislation that will affect their practice, for example the ways in which GDPR is different to the

Data Protection Act 1998. One way of keeping up to date with legislative and regulatory requirements is to read sector news, blogs and websites, and to undertake regular training. If you model this and encourage it as good practice, your team might do the same.

AC 4.2 Evaluate monitoring systems for communication

Here, you will be required to critically evaluate your existing communication/information delivery systems and make relevant recommendations for change.

It is important to be critical of the way in which you communicate in your setting as poor communication is often held up to be the cause of inadequate care being delivered and/or staff being unhappy in their work.

Evidence opportunity

4.2 Evaluating monitoring systems for communication

Using the documentation you collected and evaluated for Evidence opportunity 3.3, critically evaluate your existing communication/information delivery systems and then recommend relevant changes to the systems to ensure they are safe and fit for purpose. You could look at:

- staff induction processes and procedures
- staff supervision
- mentoring, coaching
- training
- individual and team goal setting
- action planning
- risk assessment
- how policies are reviewed to meet legislative and regulatory requirements.

You could provide a written account or speak to your assessor.

Reflective exemplar

Write a reflective account of how three of your current policies have changed due to legal changes and how this has affected work practice. Give one example from each policy.

Legislation

See ACs 1.5, 3.1, 3.2, 4.1 for more information on legislation relevant to this unit.

Legislation	
Employment Act 2002	This act addressed the minimum statutory disciplinary and grievance procedures.
Employment rights Act 1996	This act addressed dismissal, unfair dismissal, parental leave, and redundancy and the rights of employees.

Suggestions for using the activities	

This table summarises all the activities in the unit that are relevant to each assessment criterion.
Here, we also suggest other, different methods that you may want to use to present your knowledge and skills by using the activities. These are just suggestions, and you should refer to the Introduction section at the start of the book, and more importantly the City & Guilds specification, and your assessor, who will be able to provide more guidance on how you can evidence your knowledge and skills. When you need to be observed during your assessment, this can be done by your assessor, or your manager can provide a witness testimony.

Assessment criteria and accompanying activities	Suggested methods to show your knowledge/skills
LO1 Understand models of communication	
1.1 Reflect on it (page 73)	Write a short reflective account about how your communication may change according to the people you meet who may have a different outlook on life or values to yourself.
1.1 Research it (page 74)	Give three examples of when SOLER or SURETY could be useful models to use in your own setting and practice.
1.1 Evidence opportunity (page 75)	Provide a written account explaining theoretical models of communication and assess their application in their service provision, including the ones we discuss here.
1.1 Reflect on it (page 75)	Consider how you use non-verbal communication. Write a short reflective account and think about how models of communication apply to this.
1.1 Reflect on it (page 75)	Write a short reflective piece about your body language and check it out with your manager.
1.2 Evidence opportunity (page 77)	Provide a written account analysing the effectiveness of communication models and methods within your practice.
1.2 Reflect on it (page 78)	Provide a reflective account and list the types of communication you use at work and comment on how effective each type is in your span of duty.
1.3 Research it (page 78)	Explore more recent texts dealing with communication and interpersonal skills by Burnard (1996) and Donnelly and Neville (2008), or watch relevant TED talks on the internet.
1.3 Evidence opportunity (page 80)	Provide a written account critically evaluating how you used and applied different types of communications within your working environment.
1.4 Evidence opportunity (page 82)	Write an account explaining how communication impacts on effective service operation in relation to the topics we have discussed in this section.
1.4 Research it (page 82)	Design a questionnaire to obtain feedback from service users, staff, visitors and other professionals about your communication systems in place at this time.
1.5 Evidence opportunity (page 84)	Provide a written account analysing why the accurate interpretation of written and spoken words is key to effective communication when managing and delivering a care service.
1.5 Reflect on it (page 84)	Think about the uses for written and spoken language in your setting.
1.5 Reflect on it (page 84)	Choose one of the communication systems in your setting (the complaints procedure, for example) and write an account reflecting on and evaluating the quality of the organisation's performance relating to that system.
1.5 Research it (page 85)	Read the paper on the NICE website and make notes about how you might develop some of the points within your own workplace.
LO2 Develop communication systems and practises which support positive outcomes	
2.1 Evidence opportunity (page 85)	Show your assessor how you monitor and the evaluate the efficiency of internal and external communication systems and practices.
2.2 Evidence opportunity (page 86)	Speak to your assessor and show them how you make recommendations and implement change in a timely manner.
2.2 Research it (page 86)	Undertake a small-scale study to monitor the communication practice within your setting. Identify any improvements to the practices and make recommendations for revised systems.

Suggestions for using the activities	
2.2 Reflect on it (page 86)	Reflect on the way in which you led the implementation of a revised practice of your communication systems in your setting.
2.2 Reflect on it (page 86)	Answer the questions using the responses obtained from the questionnaire.
2.3 Reflect on it (page 86)	Have you ever had an experience where the setting was inappropriate for the situation?
2.3 Evidence opportunity (page 87)	Consider three different types of communication. For each example, explain how your environment impacts on the promotion of effective communication.
2.3 Reflect on it (page 89)	List two reasons (one internal and one external factor) that may have been the reasons for the blocks or barriers in communication.
2.3 Evidence opportunity (page 89)	Prepare a written account for your assessor and staff explaining how different environments impact on the promotion of effective communication.
2.4 Evidence opportunity (page 90)	Provide a written account evaluating benchmarking techniques used in own service area.
2.4 Research it (page 90)	Complete the final column of the table to show evidence of how best practice benchmarks are achieved in your setting.
LO3 Implement systems for effective information management	
3.1 Research it (page 92)	Research and read up about the hacking scandal that affected the NHS.
3.1 Evidence opportunity (page 92)	Write a short report that explains how you support your staff to understand and adhere to the legal and ethical requirements of information management systems. Or you could show this to your assessor.
3.2 Reflect on it (page 93)	Think about when you might have to breach a service user's confidentiality. Under what circumstances would you be prepared to do this and how would you go about it?
3.2 Research it (page 93)	How might you handle a next of kin wanting to hold a mental health assessment for a person when the next of kin isn't a nearest relative?
3.2 Evidence opportunity (page 94)	What are the legal and ethical conflicts relating your own area of service? Show your assessor.
3.3 Evidence opportunity (page 94)	Evaluate the effectiveness of the systems for communication in your work setting.
LO4 Support others with effective communication strategies	
4.1 Reflect on it (page 95)	How do you ensure that your staff are being adequately inducted into their roles as care workers? What audit trail or records do you have that shows this?
4.1 Reflect on it (page 95)	Identify the systems for supervision in your setting.
4.1 Reflect on it (page 96)	Identify evidence of the ways in which your staff are trained in order to keep their knowledge and skills up to date.
4.1 Reflect on it (page 96)	Explain how you set goals within your team to produce positive outcomes for service users.
4.2 Evidence opportunity (page 97)	Critically evaluate your existing communication/information delivery systems and then recommend relevant changes to the systems to ensure they are safe and fit for purpose.

References

Adair, J. (2000) *Effective Teambuilding: How to make a winning team*. London: Pan Macmillan.

Argyle, M. (1978) *The psychology of interpersonal behaviour*. London: Penguin.

Beauchamp, T.L. and Childress, J.F. (1994) *Principles of Biomedical Ethics*. Oxford: Oxford University Press.

Bonham, P. (2004) *Communication as a Mental Health Carer*. Cheltenham: Nelson Thornes.

Burgess, A. (1964) *Language Made Plain*. London: English Universities Press.

Burnard, P. (2005) *Counselling Skills for Health Professions* (4e). Cheltenham: Nelson Thornes.

Care Quality Commission (2013) Supporting information and guidance: Supporting effective clinical supervision, accessed from www.cqc.org.uk/sites/default/files/documents/20130625_800734_v1_00_supporting_information-effective_clinical_supervision_for_publication.pdf

Clutterbuck, D. (2011) *Creating a Coaching and Mentoring Culture*, accessed from www.gpstrategiesltd.com/downloads/Creating-a-coaching-and-mentoring-culture-v2.0-June-2011[23].pdf

Cole, J. (2011) We know why, but do we know how? Unpublished essay submitted for MSc.

Crawford, P., Brown, B. and Bonham, P. (2006) *Communication in Clinical Settings*. Cheltenham: Nelson Thornes.

Davis, H. and Fallowfield, L. (eds) (1991) *Counselling and Communication in Health Care*. Cirencester: Wiley.

Department of Health (2010) Essence of Care: 2010 benchmarks for the fundamental aspects of care. London: TSO.

European Parliament & Council of the European Union (1995) Directive 95/46/EC of the European Parliament and of the Council of 24 October 1995 on the protection of individuals with regard to the processing of personal data and on the free movement of such data. Official Journal, L281, pp. 31–50.

Givens, D.B. (2000) *The Nonverbal Dictionary of Gestures, Signs and Body Language Cues*. Washington: Center for Nonverbal Studies Press.

Goleman, D. (1995) *Emotional Intelligence*. New York: Bantam Books.

Graham, R.J. (1991) Understanding the beliefs of poor communication, *Interface*, 11, pp.80–2.

Hewison, A. (1995) Nurses' power in interactions with patients, *Journal of Advanced Nursing*, 21: 75–82.

McDonald, A. (2016) *A Long and Winding Road: Improving communication with patients in the NHS*. London: Marie Curie.

Porritt, L. (1990) *Interaction Strategies: An introduction for health professionals*. London: Churchill Livingstone.

Rogers, C. (2002) *Client Centred Therapy*. London: Constable.

Rogers, C. (1980) *A Way of Being*. New York: Houghton Mifflin.

Schramm, W. (1954) 'How Communication Works', in W. Schramm (ed.) *The Process and Effects of Communication*. Urbana, IL: University of Illinois Press, pp. 3–26.

Shannon, C. and Weaver, W. (1949) *The Mathematical theory of Communication*. Urbana, IL: University of Illinois Press.

Skills for Care (2010) *Keeping Up the Good Work – A practical guide to implementing continuing professional development in the adult social care workforce*. Leeds: West Gate, www.skillsforcare.org.uk.

Skills for Care and CWDC (2007) Providing effective supervision: A workforce development tool, including a unit of competence and supporting guidance. SCF01/0607, accessed from www.skillsforcare.org.uk/Document-library/Finding-and-keeping-workers/Supervision/Providing-Effective-Supervision.pdf

Stickley, T. (2011) From SOLER to SURETY for effective non-verbal communication, *Nurse Education in Practice*, 11: 395–8.

Tilmouth, T. and Quallington, J. (2015) *Diploma in Leadership for Health and Social Care* (2e). London: Hodder Education.

Tilmouth, T., Davies-Ward, E. and Williams, B. (2011) *Foundation Degree in Health and Social Care*. London: Hodder Education.

Wood, J. (2004) *Communication Theories in Action: An introduction*. Belmont, CA: Wadsworth/Thomson Learning.

Further reading and useful resources

CWDC and SfC (2012) *Providing Effective Supervision*. Leeds: Children's Workforce Development Council and Skills for Care.

Care Quality Commission (2015) Guidance for Providers on Meeting the Regulations, available on the CQC website.

Care Quality Commission (2015) How CQC Regulates: Residential Adult Social Care Services – Provider Handbook, available on the CQC website.

Care Quality Commission (2015) How CQC Regulates: Residential Adult Social Care Services – Appendices to the Provider Handbook, available on the CQC website.

Code of Conduct for Health Care Support Workers and Adult Social Care Workers in England, Department of Health, Skills for Care and Skills for Health, 2013, available on the Skills for Health website.

Delivering Dignity: Securing dignity in care for older people in hospitals and care homes (2012), Commission on Improving Dignity in Care, available on the NHS Confederation website.

Francis Report (2013) (Report of the Mid Staffordshire NHS Foundation Trust Public Inquiry). Available at: www.midstaffspublicinquiry.com

Residential Forum (1997) *Creating a Home from Home: A Guide to Standards*. London: Residential Forum.

SCIE (2012) The Research Briefing 43. Effective supervision in social work and social care. London: TSO.

SCIE (2016) *Dignity in Care, Social Care Institute for Excellence Practice Guide 9*. London: SCIE.

Books

Burnard, P. (1996) *Acquiring Interpersonal Skills; A handbook of experiential learning for health professionals* (2e). London: Chapman and Hall.

Donnelly, E. and Neville, L. (2008) *Communication and Interpersonal Skills*. Exeter: Reflect Press.

Egan, G.E. (2002) *The Skilled Helper* (9e). Belmont, CA: Brooks/Cole.

Kuhnke, E. (2012) *Communication Skills for Dummies*. London: John Wiley & Sons.

Moss, B. (2015) *Communication Skills in Health and Social Care* (3e). London: Sage Publications.

Peters, S. (2012) The *Chimp Paradox: The mind management programme to help you achieve success, confidence and happiness*. London: Vermilion.

Journals and magazines

The Journal of Dementia Care
Living with Dementia Magazine
CMM Care Management Matters
Caring Times
Care Talk
Skills for Care, Care Magazine
Care Home Management
Expert Care Manager Magazine
The British Journal of Healthcare Management
Community Care
Caring UK

Websites

www.rethink.org/carers-family-friends/what-you-need-to-know/nearest-relative

www.businesstopia.net/communication/shannon-and-weaver-model-communication

http://keydifferences.com/difference-between-formal-and-informal-communication.html#ixzz4jVGbLqRl accessed on 9/6/17

http://rcnhca.org.uk/top-page-001/record-keeping/ accessed on 11/6/17

Health and Social Care (2015) Information and technology for better care. Information Centre Strategy 2015–2020.

Social Care Institute for Excellence: www.scie.org.uk

Age UK: www.ageuk.org.uk

Dignity in Care Campaign: www.nhsconfed.org/priorities/Quality/Partnership-on-dignity/Pages/Commission-on-dignity.aspx

Skills for Care: www.skillsforcare.org.uk

Unit 504

Relationships and partnership working

GLH 20

About this unit

Working in partnership defines a joint working arrangement where the partners from different services all agree to aim to achieve a common goal for the service user, despite being independent bodies. In a health and social care setting, and in your leadership role, this means sharing relevant information and creating a culture of shared ownership and common working arrangements across organisational and professional boundaries.

One of the aims of government in recent years has been to ensure that health and care services work together to provide care that is integrated and personalised. This requires services from a variety of settings to work as partners to ensure the service user receives the best possible care. It also means that building good relationships between the services is imperative.

Joint health and care managed networks have been put forward as best practice for ensuring service users with complex health needs benefit from services that share information and work towards common goals. In this unit, we will look at how we can promote effective partnership working by establishing good working relationships with all care services we deal with, as well as with our colleagues and the families of the people we care for. We will cover the ways in which legislation and regulation influence our working partnerships and how the relationships we have with stakeholders underpin person-centred practice and the achievement of positive outcomes.

Learning outcomes

By the end of this unit, you will:

1 Understand the context of relationships and partnership working
2 Lead effective relationships with those using adult care services and their families
3 Manage working relationships with colleagues in the organisation
4 Work in partnership with professionals in other agencies

Getting started

Before you study the unit, think about the following:

- How many different agencies/individuals does your team work with on a daily basis? For example, dental services, physiotherapy or support groups such as Age Concern.
- What percentage of these interactions do you think are positive?
- What, in your view, are the roles and responsibilities of managers in developing good working relationships?
- How do you think innovative procedures can be developed to engage colleagues and promote effective partnership working? Innovative procedures might include new and improved ways of working.

LO1 Understand the context of relationships and partnership working

AC 1.1 Ways legislation and regulation influences relationships with others

Here, you will be required to critically analyse national, local and your own organisation's guidelines, legislations and policies that relate to partnership working.

The idea of partnership working developed as a result of acknowledging that it was impossible for one healthcare provider to provide all care for a service user. Partnership working, then, describes the relationships between services that have a responsibility for supplying a variety of care services. In order to work as partners, services need to create new organisational structures or processes that are separate from their own organisation and in which they plan and implement a jointly agreed programme, sometimes with joint staff or resources.

To work effectively as a partnership there are certain features that need to be in place:

- joint agreement that the service user is the central figure in the process and must be empowered through the process
- good communication
- strong leadership
- adequate resources
- trust between partners
- shared policies and guidelines.

You will find that there are numerous national, local and organisational guidelines, legislation and policies that relate to partnership working. As a manager, you must be aware of these and how they may influence your relationship with others.

For more details about current UK legislation and statutory frameworks, see Unit 501, AC 1.1.

Working in partnership – the NHS and the Health and Social Care Act 2012

With more than 1.3 million staff, the NHS is the biggest health service provider in Europe. Within such a large organisation there will be many different types of groups and teams working together in an effort to ensure that the best service is achieved.

The Health and Social Care Act 2012 brought new structures and working arrangements for the NHS in England. Primary care trusts (PCTs) and strategic health authorities (SHAs) were dispensed with and new bodies such as NHS England (known previously as the NHS Commissioning Board) and Clinical Commissioning Groups (CCGs) were brought in with responsibility for commissioning NHS services. Local authorities took on the task of new public health commissioning.

As an effective way to deliver integrated care, health and wellbeing boards (HWBs) are the one forum that brings together elected members, clinicians and other members of the local community to discuss the integration of care and budgets.

Working in partnership with other professionals has significantly changed the experience of the service users, putting them firmly at the centre of the care given, with greater access to shared resources, improved communication between teams and a more streamlined care service.

NHS England has worked to ensure that health strategy includes the voluntary, community and social enterprise (VCSE) sector, which plays a key role in improving health, wellbeing and care outcomes. The role of VCSE organisations in service provision has been promoted in recent legislation and strategy documents, such as the Health and Social Care Act 2012, Care Act 2014 and Five Year Forward View 2014, all of which recognise the focus of the VCSE as providing expertise to public service delivery.

Other key partners that work with NHS England are:

- the Care Quality Commission (CQC)
- the Department of Health
- Health Education England
- Healthwatch England
- the pharmaceutical industry
- local government
- NHS Improvement
- National Quality Board
- professional groups
- providers
- Public Health England
- trade unions.

List adapted from information on www.england.nhs.uk/ourwork/part-rel/

An advisory group set up in 2015 was tasked with reviewing how the statutory services and the VCSE groups could work together in a more meaningful way to 'maximise their partnership'.

The influence of the changes in the law and the more structured inclusion of VCSE organisations have meant that more effective relationships have been forged between statutory and voluntary services, private providers and charities. This has resulted in better outcomes for individuals who have complex needs. Access to specialist expertise in the community and a focus on early action allow preventative services to contribute to improving health outcomes and take pressure off secondary care services. Complex needs can be met in the community in which the individual lives, helping to prevent unnecessary hospital admissions. This ultimately provides a cost-effective way in which to treat people and relieves pressure on much-stretched services in the statutory sector.

Examples of statutory services such as the National Health Service or local government while voluntary services include charities such as the Red Cross, Age Concern or faith-based organisations that can provide support. Private providers such as nursing or residential care homes are also included here, and charities often provide care homes and hospice care. For example, the charity Marie Curie has numerous hospices throughout the UK.

Research it

1.1 VCSE Review

Go to www.england.nhs.uk/ourwork/part-rel/# and have a look at 'VCSE Review. Investing in partnerships for health and wellbeing; Joint review of investment in Voluntary, Community and Social Enterprise organisations in health and care sector' (2016). Read about the work on NHS England and the partnerships they have forged. Explain how these examples and ways of working could be applied to your setting.

Examples of guidelines, legislation and policies relating to partnership working

All the changes that we have discussed above have been a result of the need to focus on cooperation between services to provide 'joined up' healthcare and to streamline the services to reduce cost and use of resources. Other policy changes included the need to focus more on wellbeing and personalising care to ensure that the service user was at the heart of their own care.

The Health and Social Care Act 2012 established HWBs in an attempt to reduce health inequality in local areas. These inequalities are due to living conditions and wider social, economic, environmental, cultural and political factors known as the wider determinants of health. 'Health in All Policies' (HiAP) is a collaborative approach across sectors, policy and service areas, to improve the health of all people by incorporating health considerations into decisions made (PHE, 2016).

Board members from all areas of voluntary and statutory services work in partnership to look at local community needs and determine how services can work together to provide a seamless system of care. For example, some hospital emergency departments throughout the country experience 'winter pressures' with more service users coming through the departments leading to extensive waiting times. As a care

manager this is likely to impact upon your own service, as the secondary care services look to you to provide ongoing care for these individuals when they leave the hospitals.

The HWB would look at ways in which primary and secondary care services might work together to reduce these pressures. By working with staff from a range of services such as the ambulance service, primary healthcare services, such as GPs, community health teams and pharmacies, can put strategies in place to deal with the increase in patient numbers due to ill health. The setting up of urgent care centres, preventative flu jab campaigns, an increase in availability of GP appointments are all ways in which the flow of patients through emergency departments and the secondary services offered in hospitals may be reduced.

Case study

1.1 Working in partnership

A study by Hunter et al. in 2018 evaluated the leadership role of HWBs across England and commented upon their effectiveness in driving health initiatives. The findings showed that HWBs, although valued and representing a place where the system can come together, in their current form have little power to hold partners and organisations to account: Sustainability and Transformation Plans (STPs) were viewed by study participants as 'eclipsing' HWBs.

It was commented that HWBs were at a crossroads with two possible future scenarios: that of assuming responsibility as the accountable organisations for the delivery of place-based population health in an area, or with STPS taking over their role and function.

As a manager, comment on how your local HWB works and how it ensures that all services link up.

What are your views on the approach put forward by the research? How does your HWB meet its objectives?

You can find the Hunter research at: https://research.ncl.ac.uk/media/sites/researchwebsites/davidhunter/Evaluating%20HWBs%20FINAL%20REPORT%20-%20April%202018%20Final.pdf

---

Other legislation and White Papers which relate to partnership working are:

- Health and Social Care (Safety and Quality) Act 2015
- Government White Paper 'Our Health, Our Care, Our Say: A New Direction for Community Services' (2006)
- The White Paper 'Equity and Excellence: Liberating the NHS' (2010)
- The Five Year Forward View: Policy changes to implement the NHS five year forward view: a progress report (2016).

For our **colleagues** and health professionals, partnership working has improved the quality of the service offered and has proved to be more cost effective, thus securing jobs. By recognising common goals, a 'whole person' approach to care can be taken; there has been a growth in the understanding of other care professionals' roles and mutual respect is therefore built. The personalisation agenda has put service users firmly in charge of ensuring that the care and support they require have been designed with their involvement to meet their unique needs.

Evidence opportunity

1.1 Ways legislation and regulation influences relationships with others

Think about how legislation and regulation influence relationships with others. Critically analyse national, local and your own organisation's guidelines, legislation and policies that relate to partnership working.

You might like to consider how these guidelines, legislation and policies have enabled partnership working and affected care outcomes overall.

In order to critically analyse, you could ask questions such as why the partnership was needed, how it developed and what impact it has had on your way of working and the outcomes for the clients. You should not fall into the trap of merely describing what happened but need to analyse the strengths and weaknesses of the outcomes and make comparisons with other services.

AC 1.2 How relationships with stakeholders underpin person-centred practice and affect the achievement of positive outcomes

Here, you will be required to analyse the association between person-centred care and positive outcomes with the ability to engage in partnership working. This should include effects on a range of stakeholders relevant to own area of provision.

Before reading this section, go to Unit 505 1.1 and read the text on The Health Foundation.

The importance of partnership working with **colleagues**, **other professionals** and **others** should not be underestimated.

Partnership working has been set up to improve the experience and outcomes of people who use the service by minimising barriers between different services.

As far back as 2002, the National Service Framework recommended 'more formalised structures and systems for achieving joint aims'. Through the use of Health Improvement and Modernisation Plans (HIMPs), partnership working between the NHS, local agencies and communities became the main focus. More recently, the Health and Social Care Act 2012 has developed the need for a more integrated way of working through partnerships and HWBs.

KEY TERMS

Colleagues are people you work with to provide care services, or can be health professionals or others in the workplace. They may be in similar job roles to you or may have a different status. For colleagues to work in partnership, there needs to be collaboration and commitment to the service user to ensure best practice.

Other professionals include people who are from different agencies and disciplines but still part of the wider healthcare team. They may be advocates for the service user or from social care agencies or other health disciplines such as physiotherapists and mental health workers, etc.

Others refers to those people who may not come under the umbrella of health professionals. They could be family, carers and friends, or children and young people.

Relationships with 'stakeholders', person-centred practice and how this helps to achieve positive outcomes for individuals

Health and social care professionals work together at three levels (Department of Health, 1998):

- strategic – planning and sharing information
- operational management – policies that demonstrate partnership
- individual care – joint training and a single point of access to healthcare.

However, all these working arrangements involve individuals from different professional backgrounds and locations, with different funding and resources and philosophies of care, and as such are potentially prone to challenges.

Armistead and Pettigrew (2004), argued that:

> 'It is important to recognise that the very term "partnership" might increasingly be perceived pejoratively, synonymous with lengthy, fruitless meetings, forced upon unwilling organisations by … government policy.'

This way of working has benefits for all **stakeholders** involved in the care process. Likewise, the relationships between the different stakeholders underpin person-centred practice and help to ensure that service users remain at the centre of care and that positive outcomes can be achieved for individuals.

KEY TERM

Stakeholders include any person, or group, that has an interest in what is happening in your organisation. For example, in a care home for older adults, stakeholders may be relatives, the residents themselves, local businesses and the board of directors.

Individuals receiving care

For service users it has meant a more 'joined up' approach to their care. For example, having a single assessment process instead of multiple assessments by different agencies has been well received by service users and extends their choice. The Single Assessment Process is a way in which health and social care organisations work together to assess and plan care for people in need of a care service. This care must be person-centred, effective and coordinated.

The service users are ultimately our customers and they are at the centre of designing and delivering health and social care services. The Department of Health has actively promoted the involvement of service users and the public in decisions about the planning, design, development and delivery of local services, and service users see themselves as having a particular role to play, not least because they are 'experts in their own experience'.

Colleagues and other professionals

For our colleagues and health professionals, partnership working has improved the quality of the service and has proved to be more cost effective, thus securing jobs. By recognising common goals, a 'whole person' approach to care can be taken, resulting in a greater understanding of other care professionals' roles and building mutual respect.

Establishing good relationships within the workplace between health professionals and other services underpins good person-centred care. For example, the housekeeping or catering teams may have little to do with the physical care of service users but they play an important part in ensuring the environment is clean and well-resourced and that service users are well-nourished. They are, thus, an important part of the holistic approach to care and the positive outcome for service users is that they are being cared for in safe, clean environments.

As a manager, your role is to recognise the part that other teams and services play in care delivery. Your leadership role does not stop with the team of people who deliver the care but extends to others in the work setting who all have a job to do. By establishing good relationships with these services the team will all work together to ensure the service user in the setting has a good experience.

Family and other carers

Family carers also play a huge role in caring for their family members and are a major part of the partnership in care. It is important for care professionals to recognise and respect the role of lay carers and to support the role. Over the last 20 years or so, there has been greater recognition of the benefits of family members providing care, particularly if it helps to keep the family member in their own home. With detailed knowledge of their loved ones' preferences, illness, culture and value systems, these 'lay carers' (those with no care qualifications) are better equipped to provide the loving support the service user needs. In the past, however, lay carers were rather neglected and felt isolated and unsupported. Care professionals therefore need to ensure that the relatives of service users are involved in care planning processes and assessments.

The impact of newer ways of working and the recognition these lay carers now have ensured that service users can now stay at home for longer with better resources and more support. Families are now able to stay together with support from health professionals whereas in the past people with complex needs always had to be cared for in settings away from the home.

Better outcomes

Your role as a manager and leader in adult care is to ensure that every person your organisation cares for has a good experience of care and should experience good outcomes from the service.

Partnership working enables the strategic goals and vision of the organisation in which we work to be jointly discussed and understood. It enables agreement to be reached on how the care for a service user can be implemented in the best interests of that service user and their family, as well as staff.

The Social Partnership Forum's website highlights the benefits of good partnership working as being:

- trust and mutual respect
- openness, honesty and transparency
- top-level commitment
- a positive and constructive approach
- commitment to work with and learn from each other
- early discussion – no surprises
- confidentiality when needed.

Source: www.socialpartnershipforum.org/1111

Working in partnership therefore provides safe, quality care from a range of providers who have the client/service user at the centre of the whole process.

Outcome-based practice

You will find it useful to read Unit 505 AC 1.1 on outcome-based practice before you start to read this section.

A different approach

The idea of 'outcomes' in care was seen to be focused on achievement and was regarded as a more meaningful way to assist with care.

In using this approach, the care worker takes on the role of assisting the service user to identify immediate, medium-term and long-term goals. Rather than leading the client's care, the health professional:

> 'steers, guides, (and) pronounces the identification of "needs" and the proposed "intervention" towards practice driven by the service user, who is encouraged and facilitated to identify their "outcomes", a set of immediate, medium- and long-term goals that they wish to achieve. The focus on outcomes overcomes many of the deficiencies of the "needs" model described above.'

> **Source:** Qureshi et al., 2000, quoted in Barnes and Mercer, 2004

Care work becomes target driven and specific, with a goal in mind, and it is the service user in this type of care who sets review dates and monitors their achievement, thus moving away from the care professionals' 'assessment of the service user's needs'.

The service user then remains in complete control of the entire process, from the identification of outcomes to their achievement and evaluation of the success or failure of the venture. In this type of approach, the role of the care professional is to assist the service user in the achievement of their outcomes only.

While this approach would seem to provide the ultimate in person-centred care, it is not without its critics and a critical evaluation of the approach by Qureshi et al. in 2000 for York University highlighted some of the issues with it.

Care professionals seemed to struggle with the concept of outcomes as they lacked understanding of what the outcomes' focus actually was.

A further area of concern was with the notion of 'expert power'. Putting the service user at the centre of the assessment process, identifying their own aims and objectives in negotiation with care professionals, meant that the professional felt their role had been reduced to one of facilitator as the control and responsibility for the achievement sat very much with the service user. For some professionals this did not sit well with the belief that as experts, they should have a bigger part in the decision-making process.

This somewhat radical approach to care meant that professionals needed to change their perceptions of care and embrace a newer way of working. The move to using the term 'outcome' rather than 'need' was one which helped to change perceptions, although the research showed this was not easy.

The role of the care professional

Further issues with this type of approach seemed to stem from the care professionals' need to reach a service solution instead of listening to the service user's desired outcomes. This was reported as a need to take responsibility on the part of the professional and was also linked to pressure of work. A number of professional practice issues have been noted in the research and the challenge of introducing an outcomes approach has been raised. These were:

- the tendency of the care professionals to fall back into a provider service mode instead of thinking and acting creatively with service users
- the inability of care staff to grasp the outcomes concept.

Interestingly, the research showed that service users valued the outcomes approach and 'appear comfortable with setting goals and working towards them'.

How outcome-based practice can result in positive changes in individuals' lives

Outcome-based care puts the person firmly at the centre of the care service and delivers meaningful individual outcomes. Go to Unit 505, 1.1 to read about how a results-based accountability culture can lead to positive changes in service users' lives, and what the key benefits of this care are.

Evidence opportunity

1.2 How relationships with stakeholders underpin person-centred practice and affect the achievement of positive outcomes

Provide a written account analysing the association between person-centred care and positive outcomes with the ability to engage in partnership working. This should include effects on a range of stakeholders relevant to your own area of provision.

Reflect on it

1.2 Person-centred care, stakeholders, positive outcomes

How has person-centred care affected the work of the partners you work with? Give an example of how partners work together to improve service user care.

For example, you may wish to comment on how you work with the housekeeping team in your setting or perhaps an external partner such as the GP service. Comment upon a change in policy which included your partners. An example might be how your service has managed the 'winter pressures' that may have affected the number of people coming to your service. Or perhaps you have made changes to the assessment process of the service users, which might have affected other partners' work with the service user. Analyse the association between person-centred care, working in partnership and the outcomes in this example. In this case talk about how the partnership changed or how you worked together and why it needed to change.

AC 1.3 Benefits of networking with other agencies and community groups

Here, you will be required to critically evaluate the impact of working with other agencies and community groups within the local area and relevant to the service. This will include analysis of a range of potential benefits to both those accessing adult care services and the organisation.

In person-centred care, health and social care professionals work collaboratively with people who use services (Health Foundation, 2014) and support them to make informed decisions about their own health.

The government White Paper 'Improving health and care: the role of the outcomes frameworks', published in 2012, made a pledge to enable people to live better for longer and put forward a number of outcomes for enabling this. With three outcomes frameworks, for public health, adult social care and the NHS, published since 2010 the intention was to focus on improving all aspects of healthcare across the system, one focus of which was the strengthening of joint or partnership working. One of the ways in which these might be achieved is through 'networking'.

What is meant by 'networking' and what are the benefits of networking with agencies and community groups?

Networking is the process of linking with professional contacts and sharing information with them. It can be a formal or informal process, with meetings being set up or simply having a conversation with another professional.

The benefits are that solutions to problems can be shared if everybody works towards a common purpose or goal.

For example, you may notice that service user satisfaction within your service has started to fall but the solution is far from easy as there are many stakeholders who feed into the service and have an impact on the service users within it. You discuss it with others in the network and they agree to work towards a common goal, that of reversing the current trend. Your first step might be to invite interested parties such as other care professionals from various settings, maybe GP groups or members of the HWB, service users in the setting and their families, and community members such as schools, councils or other settings similar to your own to a meeting to share their experiences and to discuss possible ways forward. Once established, this group can then feed into other groups in the local area to gain more data about the problem and bring their findings back to the core group. By working in such a way you are able to access many more people who will all have ideas about how the quality in the service can be improved.

What are the potential benefits to those accessing adult care services, and the organisation?

The benefits of working in this way will mean that those accessing care services in the future will be experiencing a more informed quality service which is at the heart of a community network. The organisation itself will be able to work through its problems by accessing expertise from others external to the setting.

The Social Partnership Forum's list highlights the benefits of good partnership working in AC 1.2. Trust and mutual respect, openness, honesty and transparency all benefit those accessing care. Top-level commitment and the adoption of a positive and constructive approach, with a commitment to work with and learn from each other in the partnership, is also a potential benefit for the agencies involved.

Evidence opportunity

1.3 Benefits of networking

Critically evaluate the impact of working with other agencies and community groups within your local area and relevant to your service. Analyse a range of potential benefits to both those accessing adult care services and the organisation.

You might, for example, like to consider how you have engaged with networking to ensure that you are able to access the expertise of a wide group of settings. If you work in the statutory care sector, say how working with partners in the voluntary sector has helped your service users to have better outcomes of care.

Include an example from your own practice which shows how partnership working has delivered better outcomes.

AC 1.4 How integrated working with other agencies delivers better outcomes for those using adult care services

Here, you will be required to explain the benefits of integrated working.

Benefits of integrated working

Integration of care is seen as the assimilation of organisations and/or services into single entities, allowing for greater transparency between partners as well as enhanced benefits for service users (Tilmouth et al., 2011).

The 2013 DOH document *Integrated Care: Our Shared Commitment; A framework that outlines ways to improve health and social care integration* outlined a five-year plan in which integrated care and support would become the norm, improving outcomes for all people who use services.

In this document, Sustainability and Transformation Partnerships (STPs) to improve integrated working were introduced with a remit to accelerate the use of partnerships in all aspects of care. With a specific commitment to person-centred care and support, the vision was to address the fragmented care many people had experienced. It highlighted the need to communicate better, to work more effectively as teams and to treat people as individuals. There was a commitment to end delay and duplication of services, thus achieving better outcomes for all (DOH, 2013).

In 2017, the NHS published an update on the five-year plan to show what progress had been made on STPs. With some areas investing in STPS, the plan now is to push forward the initiative to more areas and encourage the integration of services and funding by working together with patients, the public, NHS commissioners and providers, local authorities and other providers of health and care services. **Source:** NHS, 2017, Next Steps on the NHS Five Year Forward View

The Better Care Fund has also been introduced: this is an initiative attempting to join up health and care services across the NHS and local government. NHS England, Department for Communities and Local Government, Department of Health and the Local Government Association (LGA) are all working together to help local areas plan and implement integrated health and social care services across England. **Source:** www.england.nhs.uk/ourwork/part-rel/transformation-fund/bcf-plan/Better Care Fund

The benefits of integrated working can be seen in the delivery of better all-round care for service users. 'Integration' means working together to achieve better outcomes and it ensures higher levels of satisfaction.

> ### Evidence opportunity
> #### 1.4 Integrated working and better outcomes
> Explain to your assessor the benefits of integrated working, and how integrated working with other agencies delivers better outcomes for those using adult care services.

Effective integration, for example, means that you analyse, plan and deliver fully integrated services with colleagues from other disciplines, which reduces the overlapping of services, thus reducing costs and delivering a more seamless care package.

AC 1.5 Features of effective partnership working across agencies and ways to overcome barriers

Here, you will be required to describe features of effective partnership working that minimise barriers.

The increasing pressure put on health and care services has resulted in barriers to working and the policy goal of 'putting people first' has been slow to achieve. To help overcome this, the charity coalition National Voices wants the health and care systems to set an ambition to achieve genuinely person-centred care by 2020. This would improve the quality of life, health and wellbeing of people, and make care systems more sustainable.

Many of the features of effective partnership working are covered in ACs 1.1 and 1.2. Essentially, effective partnership working requires a commitment to sharing expertise and knowledge with our colleagues in order to deliver services to those who need them.

Some of the barriers to effective partnership can be reduced if a good partnership agreement is in place. This agreement should state the features of effective partnership working, such as a clear shared vision, clarification of role descriptions and lines of accountability, and details of reporting and complaints procedures.

All these features can minimise the barriers to effective partnerships. However, you are likely to come across barriers when you work with others. Some barriers to effective partnership working are described below.

Barriers to partnership working

Lack of role clarity

The various roles that come together in partnerships can make joint working difficult, particularly where there are perceived differences in status between occupational groups.

For example, many health professionals do not have the title 'Dr' in front of their name and sometimes they can feel they are not listened to or not taken seriously. Some practitioners may feel that their professional status is threatened and this can lead to problems in coming to joint decisions.

Joint employment

Joint employment, or co-employment, refers to the employment of a person in two related companies that are separate entities. It also applies to companies that provide employees to others even though they are financially separate and pay workers individually. Barriers may arise when working conditions between organisations are different, particularly where new patterns of working are being requested at the same time. In order for a partnership to work, it may require changes to an employee's terms and conditions or to the hours they work and the employee may well perceive this as unfavourable.

This can lead to resistance to change, resulting in poor morale among staff and other partners, particularly service users and other professionals and colleagues.

Financial barriers

When professionals who work in partnership have different pay scales according to their professional group and their role within it, this can cause conflict. Additionally, there may be resentment if staff notice that money is used to employ staff from one group to provide a service normally provided by their own staff. Staff shortages can also damage interaction and the groups will start to withdraw from partnership working in an attempt to limit demands that are being made. If money is in short supply, establishing budgets and costs for various initiatives across partnerships can cause problems as there may be costs involved. Expenses, mileage payments and overtime all need to be found; this can be frustrating and may also become a barrier.

Difficulties in sharing information

There may be reluctance to share data and also difficulties in linking incompatible IT systems and the way in which records are kept in each organisation.

Limited time

With increasing numbers of partnerships developing, the time spent in meetings and travelling can be significant, so that less time is spent in practice. This may lead to the outcomes being far less successful than originally planned.

Different priorities and cultures

Staff working in different disciplines prioritise the care they give in a variety of ways. If we lack understanding about how a service works and constantly question the way staff carry out care, this can lead to barriers forming. Staff who have to spend time explaining themselves may become resentful. In addition, our whole ethos of working may be vastly different to that of the partner and this can lead to us questioning the care they give. An underlying lack of understanding about how care can be delivered in different ways could damage the partnership.

Features of effective partnership working across agencies

Effective partnerships work when there are shared values and goals and a commitment to providing a first-class service for the service users. Drawing up a partnership agreement that outlines a clear shared vision, and clearly defines roles and lines of accountability, will help. The reporting and complaints procedures should also be highlighted and shared.

Overcoming barriers

Overcoming barriers requires a commitment to working together in a professional way and this might be achieved by looking at the following.

Improving communication systems

Poor communication is an area which is consistently cited as a reason for underperformance and can also lead to conflict (Yoder-Wise, 2007). Therefore, as a manager and leader of a team, you need to hone these skills and improve any deficit or shortfall where you can. It is also important to communicate a clear vision to staff, and what teams are expected to achieve in their timeframes, a point that West (1994) emphasises.

A key factor in developing good team working and overcoming challenges is the manager's ability to develop positive relationships with the wide range of staff from different disciplines. This requires the ability to communicate effectively with people at all levels within the organisation.

Successful collaboration depends on open and transparent discussion. Traditionally, communication has relied on written formats such as referral forms, feedback forms, case notes, care plans, letters and faxes. However, while quality record keeping and evidence-based policies and procedures are necessary, there does need to be one-to-one collaboration and **active participation** via regular meetings with partners.

> ## KEY TERM
>
> **Active participation** in this context refers to enabling individuals to be included in their care and to be able to voice how they wish to live their life and obtain their own care.

Engaging families and putting interests of service users first

Engaging the service user's family in all decision making and supporting them in their aims to help their loved ones

▲ **Figure 4.1** What methods do you use to overcome barriers to effective partnership working?

means barriers to the partnership can become a thing of the past because everyone is working towards a common aim and purpose. The Care Act 2014 encourages 'person-centred care' and this requires complete recognition of the needs and choices of the person receiving care. By ensuring that support is available to families and the service user, and by listening to those on the receiving end of care, a better quality of life can be expected.

Families are partners in the care process as much as professionals, and as such need to be informed of and clear about their role.

Retaining momentum

Effective partnerships work because they comprise groups of people who complement each other in the roles they undertake within the service.

In order to overcome barriers, it is important to retain momentum, and to ensure that everyone knows where the project is heading and what they need to do to get there. As a manager you need to be aware that any partners in the groups that fall behind schedule or fail to complete a task will have a negative effect on the team's momentum as a whole. Task sharing is one way this can be reduced. Time allocation is also important in maintaining momentum: too little and team members can get stressed, too much and the momentum can flag.

Engaging different professionals and working as a team

There is also a potential for conflict in partnerships between adult care staff working alongside medical staff, for example, who may be separated by geographical boundaries. Also, working in external settings, communication barriers and status inequalities may frustrate things and make the completion of tasks difficult. In addition, the mismatch of cultures, behaviours and understanding of services as well as a lack of understanding of each other's roles in the

setting can be challenging and may affect the work we do. In order to overcome such challenges, joint working between professionals is critical and meetings need to be set up on a regular basis with members of the multi-disciplinary team to jointly plan and deliver services.

One key factor in developing good partnerships is the manager's ability to develop positive relationships with the wide range of staff from different disciplines. This requires the ability to communicate effectively with people at all levels within the organisation.

Reflect on it

1.5 Features of effective partnerships and barriers

Think about a partnership you have set up in your setting and reflect on the effective features within it. What did you find particularly difficult? How have you worked to improve the barriers you experienced, if any?

Evidence opportunity

1.5 Effective partnership working and overcoming barriers

Write a report describing the features of effective partnership working that have helped you to minimise and overcome barriers within your work area.

AC 1.6 Your own role and responsibilities in establishing positive relationships within and beyond the organisation

Here, you will be required to evaluate your own role as a leader in adult care services to ensure that the service creates and maintains positive relationships with all those that come into contact with the service.

The Authentic Leadership approach developed by George (2003) focuses on characteristics of good leaders. He found that authentic leaders have a strong desire to serve others and demonstrate five basic characteristics:

1 They have a purpose.
2 They have strong values and are clear about the right thing to do.
3 They establish trusting relationships.
4 They demonstrate self-discipline.
5 They are passionate about their mission.

As we have learned, working in partnership means you will be working alongside different people from a variety of disciplines, as well as colleagues within your own team and members of the service user's family. One of the responsibilities you have is to maintain an open mind about the way in which other services work and to respect the roles of others in the care they give. For your colleagues, you also need to create a working environment which promotes national policies with respect to partnership working.

As a leader in adult care services, you must evaluate the way you carry out your own role to ensure that the service creates and maintains positive relationships with all those that come into contact with it.

Respect other roles

When we work with partners, we work alongside different people from a variety of disciplines, as well as colleagues within our own team and members of the service user's family. One of the responsibilities of a manager is to maintain an open mind about the way in which other services work and to respect the roles of others in the care they give.

Create a positive working environment

You also need to create a working environment for your colleagues which promotes national policies with respect to partnership working. All partners need to be reminded that their working together brings better outcomes for the service user and is at the heart of this initiative.

Prioritise person-centred care

An emphasis upon collaborative working will ensure that the service users in your care are provided with the support they require to live the lives they want with dignity. This is stressed in the Care Act 2014 and highlighted in the White Paper 'Equity and Excellence: Liberating the NHS' (2010).

Link stakeholders

Effective team work also enhances service user care and safety because members of the team coordinate and communicate their activities with the common aim of ensuring the service user is at the centre of the care. One of your main roles will be to act as a link person in the partnership, whether it is with families or other professionals, and also to develop a climate of trust between all partners.

Build trust

Trust is such an important issue in management and leadership and is at a premium in today's working climate. If partnerships are to work, you need to ensure that you have created trust in your organisation by being open and reliable in your decision making and by articulating a commitment to the way in which the partnership is to work. Jobs are being lost on a daily basis, there is a climate of downsizing and outsourcing of work, and this will have had an effect on your workforce and the partners with whom you work.

When there is a lack of trust, the result is fear, suspicion and insecurity, leading to lowering of morale in general, with resultant resistance to change and reduced productivity.

George (2003) noted that individuals wanted their leaders to be open with them and to become more transparent, thus softening the boundary between roles. A trusting relationship with the leader leads to greater commitment to the mission and also loyalty. The document 'Partnerships: A literature review' (2007) published by the Institute of Public Health in Ireland also highlighted that 'building trust between partners is the most important ingredient in success'. Therefore, as a manager, your role is to create a high-trust culture which ensures that your staff and the people in the partnership feel safe and valued.

Open communication

Communication is important and in an atmosphere where trust is central to the workings of the team, individuals will feel free to be able to contribute fully. Staff should feel able to be part of negotiations within an organisation. External stakeholders and partners are also part of the communication process and must be invited to engage in discussion about the work that is being done.

▲ **Figure 4.2** How do you ensure there is open communication when working in partnership?

Evidence opportunity

1.6 **Your role and responsibilities in establishing positive relationships**

Find and evaluate evidence for your portfolio to show that, as a leader in adult care services, you ensure that the service creates and maintains positive relationships with all those that come into contact with the service.

You might like to include the ways in which you ensure there is open communication when working in partnership. For example, say how you communicate with external partners and what methods you use. How do you ensure that all partners are kept informed of changes?

It might be useful for you to ask partners how they feel the work they are doing with you is helping service users in their care. You might also try to gauge whether they feel some change might be useful.

LO2 Lead effective relationships with those using adult care services and their families

AC 2.1 Model open, respectful and supportive relationships

Here, you will be required to show you model open, respectful and supportive relationships and communicate to establish effective partnership working.

In an atmosphere where trust is central to the working of the team, open communication is important and individuals will feel free to be able to contribute fully. Staff should feel able to be part of negotiations within an organisation. One way to encourage this is for you, as the manager, to be a role model for encouraging mutual support and respect. For example, the way you treat your staff will be under scrutiny by others who come in to work in the service. If they observe a lack of respect, there may be some resistance to communicating with you.

The most important thing you can do to develop effective supportive working relationships is to build your reputation as a professional who is trustworthy and inspires confidence and respect in your team as well as between all team members. In this way you can show that you provide other professionals with information, advice and support within the boundaries of your role and expertise and, as such, can develop procedures for partnership working that are fair to all parties involved.

By being honest and open with staff you can develop a more cooperative way of working. Actively listening to the problems your staff and others have, and attempting to come to a mutual resolution when conflict arises, will go a long way to ensuring that the workforce remains positive. Your policy on communication, for example, can help effective working relationships by being robust and up to date.

Colleagues

You will be familiar with the notion of setting objectives in order to achieve aims. Part of your role as a manager and leader will be to educate your staff and, as such, you set objectives as to what you hope the people attending your session will gain from being there. So, too, with partnership working – there needs to be a good balance between developing the partnership and its objectives in order for it to be successful. We must ensure that we recognise and respect the differences that might exist between all concerned and not make assumptions about the way in which other organisations or individuals work and lose sight of what we are actually there for. By being open and respectful in the relationship, we can improve the trust among the wider partnership and thus enable a more effective way of working.

Individuals you care for

Individuals must also be treated in a most respectful manner. One way in which this might be done is to ensure that all staff respectfully address their service users and give them choices about their care. As a manager you can help staff to do this by ensuring training sessions are available and arrange supervision sessions whereby ways of working can be checked and discussed.

Families

The families, carers, advocates and friends of the service user are an important part of the care team surrounding the service user and so must be included in setting the objectives for care. These people are at the heart of the service user's life and as such can often see things like imbalances in the care being planned. They should be aware of the way in which each part of the team communicates and the relationship between the specialists and other workers involved in the care. They are then better placed to see where the boundaries between partners lie and who is accountable for the care in the setting.

You will need to ensure that both you and your staff establish good open relationships, ones that are transparent so that everyone who comes into the organisation can see that this way of working has been adopted and practised by all staff. You will need to ensure you effectively communicate information and that staff are willing to listen and to put into practice that which has been agreed. You and the staff you manage will need to ensure they are respectful, not only to the service user but to all who come into contact with the organisation and with each other.

In working with families and carers, service users and their advocates, there are a number of ways that health and social care organisations develop their procedures to ensure they meet the needs of carers. Some of these may be:

- identifying a mentor within the organisation who will be the first point of contact for carers and will take primary responsibility for making sure that carers' needs are considered
- providing 'carer awareness' training for all staff to ensure they understand what role the carer will be taking
- developing links to local carers' organisations to explore ways of working together
- developing a carers' charter to ensure that best practice guidelines for working with carers and staff are identified and that staff are aware of these
- starting up a staff–carers' network

- making sure information for carers is available and well-publicised
- involving carers in service planning and development
- providing training for carers in areas such as lifting and handling, intimate care, use of equipment, stress management and maximising their own health and wellbeing.

The HSE and voluntary agencies supported by the HSE, such as Caring for Carers and The Carers Association, provide a national certified training course, 'Care in the Home', for carers and people working in the caring profession. This course covers practical caring skills such as feeding, washing and dressing, and personal skills such as communication, stress management and coping skills. (For more information on this, see www.hse.ie/eng/services/list/4/olderpeople/carersrelatives/Support_for_Carers.html)

Other professionals

Open and respectful relationships with our partners will ensure that all involved will feel valued and want to make the partnership work, and as the manager you need to model this type of behaviour. For example, engaging with joint objectives and acknowledging the potential areas of conflict within a partnership may be useful and is one way to achieve cooperation to work towards a common goal. Your role will be to ensure that conflict is dealt with effectively and that you manage the partnership workers respectfully.

Evidence opportunity

2.1 Model open, respectful and supportive relationships

Show your assessor how you model open, respectful and supportive relationships, and how you communicate to establish effective partnership working.

Reflect on it

2.1 Communication; open, respectful and supportive relationships

How do you ensure there is open communication when working in partnership? Supply some evidence to demonstrate how you do this in your setting.

How can you ensure you model open, respectful and supportive relationships? Make a list and provide this as evidence for your portfolio.

Make sure that you think about this in relation to partnership working.

AC 2.2 Support others to recognise the values of co-production and the contribution and expertise of those using adult care services and relevant others

Here, you will be required to engage the team in a way that enables them to understand the values and importance of co-production.

Co-production

As a manager, you must engage your team in a way that enables them to understand the values and importance of co-production.

The guide 'Co-production in social care', from the Social Care Institute for Excellence (SCIE), provides a definition of co-production as a relationship between professionals and service users in which power is shared and the partnership is equal, leading to better planning and delivery of services.

The Care Act 2014 introduced the concept in its guidance to define a more meaningful relationship with care planning for the service user than just involvement. It is about moving the power to change things to the service user.

The values within co-production are set out in the guide as follows:

- Equality – everyone has assets and no one person is more important than another.
- Diversity – inclusivity and the efforts of groups who are from diverse backgrounds and who may be under-represented in care should be heard.
- Accessibility and equal opportunity – for all to participate in any way they can.
- Reciprocity – or the getting of something back for putting something in.

As a manager you need to ensure that your staff and others in partnership with your setting understand the concept and importance of co-production. Co-production supports those who use social care services by improving their experience of services. In the past failure to listen to the people who use services and their carers has led in some cases to abuse and neglect. There have been numerous inquiries into such abuse and recommendations to develop more equal and meaningful relationships with people who use services. Co-production describes ways of working in partnership with people who use services, carers and citizens to improve the services to find a shared solution to the problems our service users face. For example, those who use the service need to be consulted and included at the start of any project that affects them.

Staff and partners need to be clear that a meaningful care relationship is one in which professionals and service users are all empowered to plan and deliver support together. Everyone in the care partnership has contributions to make and co-production values this approach.

Reflect on it

2.2 Co-production

Think about the term co-production and what it actually means for you. Can you come up with examples that show how you, in your role, have shared this concept with your staff?

For example, using the four headings shown above – Equality, Diversity, Accessibility and equal opportunity, and Reciprocity – say how you have demonstrated this is your setting.

Evidence opportunity

2.2 Support others to recognise the values of co-production

Show your assessor how you engage the team in a way that enables them to understand the values and importance of co-production. Show your assessor how you support others to recognise the values of co-production and the contribution and expertise of those using adult care services and relevant others.

Research it

2.2 Co-production

Read the SCIE guide about co-production.

Read the recommendations in the SCIE's co-production guide at:

www.scie.org.uk/publications/guides/guide51/files/guide51.pdf

For each heading (Culture, Structure, Practice and Review) describe at least one way in which you can engage your team to enable them to understand the values and importance of co-production.

Reflect on it

2.2 Values of co-production

Think about the values of co-production. Write about the values to the team of this way of working.

You might use the headings:

- equality
- diversity
- accessibility and equal opportunity
- reciprocity.

How have these been embedded in adult care? For example, with inclusivity you might discuss how service users from diverse backgrounds and who may be under-represented in care have been given a voice.

AC 2.3 Ensure those using adult care services and relevant others are aware of their statutory rights

Here, you will be required to implement procedures to ensure that everyone is aware of their statutory rights. These could include procedures based on aspects of the following pieces of legislation and areas we discuss in this section.

It is important that service users, their carers, families and any other people involved in their care are aware of their statutory rights. These are their legal rights, which are designed to protect them when using the services. For example, many people who come into care settings are not aware of their rights with respect to data protection and consent and so need to be shown what they can expect from us as care providers. You might take the opportunity to issue the relevant forms at this time and to ask service users to appoint people with powers of attorney if they have not done so and also determine next of kin and nearest relatives.

Perhaps in your admission procedure you might discuss rights and responsibilities with the service users so that they can be more informed of these.

There are a number of pieces of legislation that they should be aware of, some of which we discuss below.

The Mental Capacity Act 2005

The Mental Capacity Act 2005 (MCA) is a law that protects and supports people who do not have the ability to make decisions for themselves. The act applies to people aged 16 and over in England and Wales and makes provision for those whose **capacity** is affected. It defines what it means for an adult to have the mental capacity to consent to or refuse treatment and describes the process of the capacity assessment.

> ## KEY TERM
>
> **Capacity** in this context refers to the ability of a person to do or understand something.

To have capacity a person must be able to:

- understand the information that is relevant to the decision they want to make
- retain the information long enough to be able to make the decision
- weigh up the information available to make the decision
- communicate their decision by any possible means, including talking, using sign language or through simple muscle movements, such as blinking or squeezing a hand.

If capacity is diminished, then decisions may be taken for the service user with their best interests in mind. If capacity is likely to diminish in the future, then the MCA advises the appointment of a trusted person to make a decision on their behalf.

Your knowledge of the MCA will be useful to enable you to manage decision making for service users. It allows people over the age of 16 to appoint a proxy decision maker who has the legal power to give consent to medical treatment when the service user loses the capacity to consent. In the case of a person who is detained under mental health legislation, the principles of consent continue to apply, and care staff must ensure that the individual is aware of the circumstances and safeguards needed for providing treatment and care without consent. The decision as to whether the individual lacks capacity must be made with the medical staff providing the treatment or care and in consultation with family and care staff. In an emergency situation when an individual requires treatment but is unconscious, treatment to preserve life may be given, as long as it is in the best interests of that individual.

Refusal of treatment by a person with capacity should be respected and a record made. If the person who has refused treatment or care is confused or mentally incapacitated in some way, care staff must make a full and frank assessment of their care and ensure that the individual is safeguarded.

A referral to court to obtain permission to treat may sometimes be necessary.

If you are dealing with a child, then obtaining consent is complex as young people under the age of 16 are considered to lack the capacity to consent or to refuse treatment. Parents or those with parental responsibility must give consent. If the child is considered to have significant understanding and intelligence to make up his or her own mind about what is happening to them, that may be waived. (Although we are dealing with adult care here, this may be relevant if children are involved with the adult undergoing care.)

A child of 16 or 17 is considered to be able to consent for themselves, but good practice demands that parents or guardians are involved. Refusal of consent by a child of any age up to 18 years can be overridden by the parents or in exceptional circumstances an order from the court.

There are a couple of exceptions where a capable individual may be treated without first obtaining their consent. For example, a magistrate can order detention in hospital if a person has an infectious disease that presents a risk to public health, for example rabies, cholera or anthrax (Public Health (Control of Disease) Act 1984).

The Mental Health Act

The 1983 Mental Health Act laid down provision for the compulsory detention and treatment of people with mental health problems in England and Wales and focused upon strengthening patients' rights to review their treatment.

The act was amended in 2007 and focused on public protection and risk management. The amended legislation extends the powers of compulsion and introduces compulsory community treatment orders, making patients' compliance with treatment a statutory requirement. In other words, it would be lawful to insist upon the patient having treatment in this case, particularly if they pose a risk to themselves or others in not doing so.

The main changes contained in the 2007 MHA can be found in Unit 502.

Deprivation of Liberty Safeguards 2007

In 2007 the MHA introduced deprivation of liberty safeguards (DoLS) through amending the 2005 Mental Capacity Act, and the rights of victims were extended by amending the Domestic Violence, Crime and Victims Act 2004.

The Human Rights Act states that 'everyone has the right to liberty and security of person. No one shall be deprived of his or her liberty [unless] in accordance with a procedure prescribed in law'.

The deprivation of liberty safeguards are put in place when it is necessary to deprive a resident or patient who lacks capacity to consent to their care and treatment of their liberty in order to keep them safe from harm. In other words, if a person lacks capacity to make a decision, the restrictions may be put in place without their consent as long as it is in their best interest.

The Equality Act 2010

The Equality Act 2010 brought together four major EU Equal Treatment Directives and replaced previous anti-discrimination laws, simplifying the law and making it easier to understand. Additionally, it strengthened protection by setting out the different ways in which unlawful treatment may occur. Individuals are now fully protected from discrimination in the workplace and in wider society.

Power of attorney

Anyone making a decision on behalf of a person they believe to lack mental capacity must do so in that person's best interests. The Mental Capacity Act introduced a new type of power of attorney known as a Lasting Power of Attorney (LPA). An LPA allows people to choose someone who can make decisions about their health and welfare, as well as their finances and property, if they become unable to do so for themselves. Often they choose a member of their family or a close friend but this should be done before the loss of capacity and documented with the patient's knowledge and consent long before it might be used.

Care Act 2014

This act put people and their carers in control of their care and support, and in combining existing legislation made it easier for the public to understand social and healthcare. It changed the way in which support to vulnerable people is given and aimed to ensure that greater control and influence are given to those in need of support. Changes were also made to the way in which local authorities provide support to people, and ensured a fairer national system to reach those most in need.

The Care Act sets out some 'key principles' on how health and social care professionals should work with people, putting service users at the centre of care, with their views, wishes, feelings and beliefs always being considered first.

As the manager of a setting, it is important to ensure that everybody is aware of their statutory rights. Staff, service users, visitors and those you work in partnership with need to be fully informed of how your setting demonstrates an awareness of the legal aspects of care work and operates within the legislation. The policies you develop in the setting will reflect the legal requirements and help to make the legal aspect more accessible. For example, your safeguarding policy may refer to aspects of the MCA and DOLs to ensure that service users are safeguarded with respect to their legal rights. The setting website should have a section that demonstrates to others your commitment to the law, and staff induction needs to include reference to the importance of working within policy and what this looks like in your setting.

The legislation that we have discussed is correct at the time of writing. However, there may be changes to legislation as a result of **Brexit**.

KEY TERM

Brexit is a term that has been used to denote the United Kingdom leaving the European Union. In 2016, UK voters decided that they no longer wanted the UK to be a member of the EU. There are a number of 'EU' laws that are in place in the UK. At the time of print, it is uncertain how these laws will be affected when the UK finally leaves the EU.

Evidence opportunity

2.3 Statutory rights and making sure everyone is aware

Show your assessor how you implement procedures to ensure that everyone is aware of their statutory rights. These could include procedures based on aspects of the following:

- The Mental Capacity Act
- The Mental Health Act
- Deprivation of Liberty Safeguards
- The Equality Act
- Power of Attorney
- The Care Act

AC 2.4 Implement systems that encourage engagement

Here, you will be required to implement systems that encourage and enable engagement in decision making and reviews.

Engaging staff

Service users/patients must be able to make their own decisions with respect to the care they need and want so the staff should be prepared to ensure they are able to do this. Occasionally, staff may find it difficult to step back from simply giving care which they, the staff, deem necessary, disempowering the service user in the process. For example, it might speed up the process of giving care if staff simply stepped in and carried out the care the service user needs, but this may not be in the best interest of the service user. As a manager you will need to support your staff in this and recognise that sometimes more time for care may be needed. You may need to develop a plan of action to give staff access to training to ensure they fully appreciate all the issues surrounding outcome-based care.

Engaging individuals and families

As mentioned above, the service user and their family need to be given correct information with respect to the rights of the individual in care. During the admission process, it is useful to engage with the family and individual and inform them of the various acts which may have a bearing on the service user's wellbeing. For example, you may like to discuss the concept of capacity and the need to be aware of what might happen should the service user be unable to make a decision about their care in the future.

It is most important that as staff we do not underestimate the input from carers, family and others in the care of an individual. Should a carer become ill themselves, making them unable to continue in the caring role for a while, there must be a procedure in place to ensure that care for the service user can be continued in the way it has been planned.

As a manager you need to be able to help staff to engage with families to ensure that they feel included in the care planning process and that they have somebody they can access should they ever feel the need to. Families and other carers can sometimes experience great isolation socially so it is useful if there are systems in place that can ensure they are informed of groups and help they can expect when they feel this way.

One system that might be implemented could be for carers to have access to a monthly meeting to discuss and review the progress of the care being given to the service user and to suggest any changes should they feel these are needed. There might also be a system in place whereby a carer can telephone a direct number to speak to a staff member who can help them with queries regarding the care.

Empowering the individual

For individuals to have more control over their care and more engagement with the care process, they need to be actively engaged with the whole process so they can understand all the options and not merely attend meetings where their care is being discussed.

The person who is at the centre of making a decision has to feel they are actively doing so. We may take for granted administration, meetings and bureaucracy but service users may be overwhelmed by this and it would take a lot of confidence on their part to question anything you may put forward. The following steps may help:

Step 1: Identify the choices available

The service user needs to be clear about who they want involved in their care and about the choices they have but may rely on you or your staff members to help them to identify the specialist help. For example, a service user who is being cared for at home by their spouse may not realise that special equipment such as hoists for bathing is available to help her and her husband cope and so they may fail to realise they have a choice.

Step 2: Ensure ongoing communication

Monitor the process of the care arrangements as you go along and check that the service user is clear about what has happened so far. It is important that the communication method is suitable for service users. If, for example, service users have trouble reading small print, you need to ensure that they have access to large-print versions of documents. Service users may also need extra assistance if English is not their first language and interpreters may be required at each meeting.

Step 3: Gain additional information if necessary

It may be that service users have previous case notes with another agency and in this step, you need to obtain your service user's consent to obtain those notes. Service users need to be informed of all aspects of their care, including the need to contact others for additional information.

Step 4: Ensure consent

Recording the above step is necessary and your service user may be asked to sign to confirm that they have agreed for certain information to be released. If at any point your service user does not give consent for any action, this must be respected.

Step 5: Obtain feedback

Just as you need to monitor the process throughout, you must also ensure that feedback from the service user and family and friends is forthcoming regularly. Positive feedback will mean that, of course, the process is working well. However, any concerns must always be dealt with in an efficient and non-judgemental way. If the service user wishes to make a complaint, it is up to you to support them in accessing the correct procedures to do so.

Research it

2.4 Systems that encourage engagement

For your portfolio, find out about the systems that are in place in your setting which encourage and enable engagement in decision making and reviews. List and evaluate these.

Systems are simply ways of carrying out certain procedures. You might look at the admission process and the paperwork involved that encourages the service user to be an active participant in their care. In evaluating such a system, you could comment upon the strengths and weaknesses within the process and say how it might be improved.

Another system you might look at is the way in which medication is handled in the setting. Are staff responsible for giving out medication or are service users encouraged to look after and administer their own? Do they have a choice? Again in evaluating this sort of system you need to question the practice in place and determine whether it might be changed to benefit the service user.

LO3 Manage working relationships with colleagues in the organisation

3.1 Develop procedures to facilitate effective working relationships with colleagues

Here, you will be required to develop procedures to facilitate effective working relationships with colleagues.

Effective team performance requires the development of procedures which enable a positive and supportive culture and good relationships between staff in an organisation. Only in this way can we expect staff to be supportive of a shared vision to meet the agreed objectives for a health and social care setting. The most important person in your team will be the service user or client and they need to be central to any team working. In the next section, we will look at procedures such as team formation, appraisal systems and outcome measures.

Imagine a group of footballers who have little idea about the rules of the game, what the objectives of the game are and how the position they play works with the rest of the team. Picture the first match and guess the outcome. Of course, it is likely to be a mess, isn't it? With nobody working together and without any direction, the game will be lost.

In total contrast to the example above, effective teams in your setting work together towards common goals and objectives and it is important you know what the features of effective team performance are.

The reality of modern health and social services is that the care available depends as much on how health and social care employees work with each other as on their individual competence within their field of expertise (Tilmouth et al., 2011).

All teams need to go through a development process and well-established teams have to be motivated to perform in roles in which they fit comfortably. Effective teams are those which comprise people who complement each other in their roles and who are managed and led in an efficient way.

Staff relationships within the team should be nurtured to encourage a cohesive atmosphere at work. A key factor in developing good team working and overcoming challenges is the manager's ability to develop positive relationships with the wide range of staff from different disciplines. This requires the ability to communicate effectively with people at all levels within the organisation.

Procedures

Pearson and Spencer (1997) suggest that teams are formed because of a belief that having people work on shared goals interdependently will lead to synergy (or cooperation and interaction) and the aggregate or total of individuals' performances will be exceeded by the work group's performance (Tilmouth et al., 2011). In other words, individuals who work together can achieve more than individuals who work on their own.

Effective teams display certain features and the following are eight characteristics identified by LaFasto and Larson (1989) in their book *Teamwork: What Must Go Right/What Can Go Wrong*. According to Larson and LaFasto, the team must have:

- a clear goal
- a results–driven structure
- competent team members
- unified commitment
- a collaborative climate
- high standards that are understood by all
- external support and encouragement
- principled leadership.

To sum up, goals, roles, procedure, relationships and leadership are the essential pre-requisites for effective team working (McKibbon et al., 2008). The members of a team need to be able to communicate and collaborate to function effectively. If we coordinate the work of a group of people and develop shared goals, working towards a common aim, then we are almost there.

It is important to be able to measure how effective each of your work partnerships is and to do so requires appraisal systems and outcomes measures.

Work performance appraisal systems can be used to assess how effective the partnership has been as well as the quality of the work produced. The evaluation methods used can take various forms and largely depend on the type of career professional being appraised. For example, doctors are required to undertake an annual medical appraisal to demonstrate to the GMC that they are up to date and fit to practise, and a specific process is followed. In health and social care work, evaluation of work performance may well rest on several basic techniques such as supervision and performance appraisals.

In evaluating your working relationship with your staff, it might be useful to use a self-assessment tool in which staff are able to provide anonymous feedback about various aspects of the working relationship.

In evaluating procedures outside assessment, other professionals and teams may be asked to observe the workplace on a formal and informal basis, providing independent feedback. This can then be measured against the in-house evaluations by staff and service users.

Evaluation can also be gained through the use of written comment forms, telephone surveys or online questionnaires. Families and friends and others who may be supporting the service user may be included in evaluation and asked to comment upon the service provision. We may also ask advocates to evaluate the service and comment on whether and how they have been included in discussions and planning regarding the service user.

Undertaking such measures can identify the successes of team working as well as the failures and can provide evidence for change. By making an evaluation of the way in which partnerships are working it is possible to assess the effectiveness of the care provided and make changes accordingly.

Develop processes to accommodate different types of working relationships and a range of colleagues

All relationships are different, but we may forget this and expect people to think and behave like we do, which is not always the case. Respecting the differences brought to the setting by diverse groups of people will not only enrich the process but will also help to create a rapport. Different ways of working can be evaluated in the setting and the development of procedures might be a useful way of accommodating different working methods.

Develop and lead the implementation of communication strategies when working with all internal stakeholders

Communication strategies play a role in developing high-performance partnerships and are necessary for change and improvement to take place. Effective strategies include ensuring that clear and consistent messages are sent to all parts of the organisation in a simple and direct way. As a manager in the setting it is wise to spend time thinking about what it is you want to say and how you will say it, as this can set the tone for developing an atmosphere of trust and openness.

Demonstrate trustworthiness when colleagues divulge personal confidences

To divulge a personal confidence takes a lot of courage and as the manager you need to be able to show you can be trusted with such information and that you will deal with

it appropriately. If the confidence is troubling and you are concerned about any consequences to the person, you will need to discuss this with them and encourage them to open up further to others. For example, a person who may be being abused at home may require further support from other agencies and you should encourage them to seek out support with your help.

Demonstrate a range of communication skills for effective working relationships

Verbal skills: involve more than just talking. How you deliver messages and feedback and also how you receive them requires an ability to speak clearly and effectively. Interpreting messages and acting upon the information gained is a skill. The ability to empathise, summarise, paraphrase and speak in a calm way is a skill that engages people and encourages them to open up in conversation.

Active listening: involves asking questions, rephrasing the conversation to gain better understanding and paying attention to what the other person is saying. Sometimes you just need to remain silent and this can be a difficult thing to do. Develop skills to listen and try not to jump in with a solution. Look at the other person's body language and learn from their actions. A good listener will do only that and not try to formulate their next question or their next response. In doing so you are not listening actively.

Questioning: in an open way is more effective than asking a lot of closed questions that require only a yes or no response. More information can be gained if the person is asked to expand their response.

Written/electronic means: include emails and texts which are good ways to send and receive messages, but we need to be aware of the tone and the way in which the message might be received. Because we cannot convey emotion within a text or show our body language, we must prepare the message in a clear and professional way. Some messages should not be delivered in this way as they can be perceived as cold and may damage a relationship.

Manage meetings to explore different aspects of working relationships and team meetings

People who attend a meeting wish to know it will not drag on and that their time will be well spent. By setting out ground rules you can ensure that the meeting will be well-run and you can then keep control of proceedings. If the attendees are aware of how the agenda will be set and addressed and how long they are going to be in the meeting you can ensure that the relevant aspects of the working relationship can be explored in a timely and efficient way. In team meetings you may need to ensure that everyone has an opportunity to respond if they need to and you may also have to keep general chat to a minimum.

Face-to-face meetings

These are most useful in imparting information that is too important to leave to an email or is sensitive in nature. If you are giving feedback to a member of staff or are meeting with a visitor or service user, this is the most appropriate way to talk. You then engage with verbal, non-verbal and listening communication, which enables you to gain a greater amount of information.

Digital conference/webinar

These represent a most useful way in which to keep in touch with external stakeholders and partners in other locations. The same advice applies here as for meetings but prior to this sort of meeting you will need to make additional checks to ensure the WiFi is working and you have the correct equipment in place to participate.

Evidence opportunity

3.1 Develop procedures to facilitate effective working relationships with colleagues

Show your assessor, and discuss with them, how you develop procedures to facilitate effective working relationships with colleagues. Consider the topics you have covered in this section.

Research it

3.1 Procedures to facilitate effective working relationships with colleagues

Study the team you work with over the next couple of days and try to get to know the members in a little more detail. How do the features of effective team performance present themselves in your team?

Evaluate the effectiveness of current procedures in your setting that relate to working relationships with colleagues. For example, look at the appraisal systems and measures you have in place and use within supervision sessions. What do you think is good about the procedures and what might you change?

Think about how these were developed and say how they enable staff to develop effective working relationships. Supply evidence of this for your portfolio using relevant examples.

AC 3.2 Develop and agree common objectives

Here, you will be required to develop and agree common objectives when working with colleagues.

Agree objectives that are SMART when working with colleagues

See Unit 506, AC 2.5 for more information on SMART objectives.

Use negotiation skills to ensure colleagues agree with any work-based targets to achieve objectives

Not everybody will agree with objectives or work targets that have been set so you will need to develop skills of negotiation to help in any situation where this happens.

Negotiating requires a planned approach and, in ensuring that colleagues are in agreement with the targets set, you will need to prepare to meet with them to discuss and clarify the objectives, then look for a solution in which both parties are happy with the outcome.

Maintain focus on the overall aim of the working relationship

It is important to remember the reasons why we are in a working relationship and to focus staff on the need to provide a care service that puts the service user first and staff issues second. Reminding our colleagues about our commitment to the provision of a quality service may help.

Evidence opportunity

3.2 Develop and agree common objectives

Show and explain to your assessor how you develop and agree common objectives when working with colleagues, addressing the areas we have discussed here.

AC 3.3 Allow colleagues to make appropriate contributions

Here, you will be required to implement systems and practices that allow colleagues to make appropriate contributions using their specific expertise.

Demonstrate they value the time taken to discuss issues relating to the objectives

Meetings may be viewed as wasting time and taking staff away from the jobs they are doing. There may be some truth in this if the meetings are not well run, are lengthy and seem to achieve nothing. As the manager, it is important to ensure that your meetings are valued by staff. This is achieved by having a regular time set for discussion, and an agenda that is specific and achievable in the time allocated. If you say the meeting will last one hour it is important to ensure this happens. By setting out such boundaries, colleagues will start to value the time spent and will contribute.

Demonstrate flexibility to allow creativity and individual expression while not compromising effective work practice and objectives

Quality in the work we do is essential and must never be compromised; however, occasionally a creative approach can be offered that may prove to be a useful solution to a care issue. Sometimes our immediate reaction to a suggested change is to dismiss it and carry on with previous practice. However, just because somebody does the work in an alternative way does not make it wrong and we need to have some flexibility to accept individual expression and working style.

Show respect for contributions made by colleagues and demonstrate leadership

No contribution should ever be dismissed even if it does not fully meet the objective. Too often new ideas are ignored simply because we are focused on the objective we need to achieve. Colleagues may be expressing excellent ideas and a good leader and manager will respectfully consider these and ask for clarification on the idea. Even if an idea is not immediately moving an objective forward, it may prove useful later.

Show how they accommodate the specific expertise of others in the decision-making process

The humility to accept that there are colleagues who have expertise in certain areas is a quality in good leaders and managers; seeking input from colleagues to help with a decision is good practice. We should respect the fact that our colleagues have a wealth of experience from other employment and from the training and education they have undertaken, and as such can be a source of ideas and solutions. Their help to make decisions should not be underestimated or missed.

Evidence opportunity

3.3 Allow colleagues to make appropriate contributions

Show your assessor how you implement systems and practices that allow colleagues to make appropriate contributions using their specific expertise. You could address, for example, the topics we covered in this section.

AC 3.4 Deal constructively with conflicts or dilemmas

Here, you will be required to show you can manage conflicts or dilemmas that occur among colleagues.

Conflict

Conflict within teams is not uncommon but it can be unpleasant and lead to disruption in performance. Badly managed conflict leads to ineffective team work and people start to avoid each other and rifts develop. This inevitably leads to ineffectual or weak care of service users, clients and patients. However, when resolved effectively, conflict can be creative and productive, leading to personal and professional growth.

It is imperative to handle such conflict effectively since bad handling of these situations will lead to an ineffective team. Staff start to avoid each other and rifts occur, with staff taking sides. The ultimate downside of this happening is that this most certainly leads to poor and ineffectual care of service users. It is important to be assertive and provide fair feedback on problems or areas of conflict.

Conflict should not always be viewed as a negative occurrence. It may highlight an important issue and lead to a better outcome for all concerned. For example, in healthcare settings conflict between partners may arise if resources are threatened due to the introduction of another service. If staff feel that their role is undermined in any way by another service, this can lead to conflict. The main aims in any conflict resolution are to communicate, listen and keep an open mind about the situation.

The Research Briefing 41, commissioned by SCIE (2012), 'Factors that promote and hinder joint and integrated working between health and social care services', is a useful read and comments upon the findings from a large study about integrated (partnership) working.

The factors that cause conflict include some of the following:

- lack of understanding about joint aims and objectives or failure to establish a shared purpose
- lack of clarity about the roles and responsibilities
- confusion about policies and procedures underpinning the new service or way of working
- organisational difference or competing 'organisational visions' and lack of agreement about which organisation should lead
- absence of a pooled or shared budget and differences in resources and spending
- communicating across professional or agency boundaries, particularly when they are not located on the same site
- information sharing – difficulty sharing information, lack of access to information and incompatible IT systems
- lack of strong and appropriate managerial support (thought to undermine attempts to work across agencies and professional boundaries)
- different professional philosophies

- lack of trust, respect and control
- difficulties in role boundaries
- constant reorganisation
- financial uncertainty
- difficulty in recruiting staff.

Occasionally others involved in care, family members or members of the wider multidisciplinary team may disagree about something in the setting and this needs to be dealt with in a sensitive and professional manner. There may be disagreements among other professionals or the family about the way in which care is given and this may be due to a lack of understanding about certain features of the care role. For example, the family or others involved in care may not understand the risk involved in certain lifestyle choices such as eating unhealthily or the importance of ensuring that medication is given on time. This can lead to the service user being compromised and may lead to conflict. The way in which this is handled needs to be specific to the person you are dealing with and will require a different approach to those who are health professionals.

Dealing constructively with conflicts or dilemmas

A conflict may fall into two categories:

1 Conflict that revolves around the disagreements in relation to approaches to work.
2 Conflict that arises between individual members of the team stemming from differences in personal values and beliefs.

Thompson's (2006) RED model suggests an effective way of solving and managing conflict. He suggests:

R – Recognise the conflict; do not sweep it under the carpet.

E – Evaluate the conflict to see how detrimental it would be if it was allowed to develop.

D – Deal with the conflict; keep communication open.

The two destructive extremes, either pretending the conflict does not exist or overreacting to the situation, are best avoided, according to Thompson.

The most effective way of solving conflict in a team is for the people concerned to have a constructive conversation (LaFasto and Larson, 2001). By doing so, each person will be helped to see the other person's perspective and will gain some understanding about the way the other person feels about the situation. The conversation must result in each party committing to making improvements in the relationship (Tilmouth et al., 2011). These conversations might be initiated by the staff members themselves or they may require the services of a neutral facilitator or another person to mediate in the situation. This can be set up in supervision.

LaFasto and Larson's (2001) CONECT model for resolving conflict by conversation is useful:

- Commit to the relationship by discussing the relationship and not the problem causing concern. Each person should say why they feel change should occur and what they hope to gain.
- Optimise safety, with both parties committing to maintain confidentiality and create an atmosphere of trust.
- Neutralise defensiveness, with each person explaining what they have observed, how it made them feel and the long-term effects of the other person's actions.
- Explain each perspective or each side of the argument.
- Change one behaviour and ask each person to change.
- Track the change and decide how improvements will be measured. Agree to meet to discuss whether changes have been successful (Tilmouth et al., 2011).

Appropriate ways in which to deal with any barriers and conflicts which arise can be on a one-to-one basis or in group discussion. Providing information to enable service users and the team involved in their care to make informed decisions may also help the process and reduce the conflict. Conflict may sometimes be the result of lack of information, which causes distress and may lead to angry outbursts.

We might also instigate contracts between people to highlight expectations with respect to roles and behaviour. This can then help to resolve potential conflict areas.

Another way in which conflict may be managed is through a mentoring system. By allocating a mentor to each staff member, conflicts can be brought to them for discussion and mediation.

The way in which you deal with and resolve conflict comes from your favoured leadership approach. The skills approach developed by Mumford et al. (2000) lists, within its five components, social judgement skills as one of the competencies required in dealing with conflict. The capacity to understand people and social systems serves to enable leaders to work with others to solve problems and to implement change. Part of this competency is social performance and this refers to the skill in persuasion in communicating with others. Any conflict can be resolved if the leader acts as a mediator in the process.

Poor communication is often cited as a reason for underperformance and can also lead to conflict. Therefore, as a manager and leader of a team, you need to hone your communication skills and improve any deficit or shortfall where you can.

One aspect of communication is that of **negotiation**. Much of a manager's day is spent in negotiation with other people and it can become an almost unconscious activity. We may

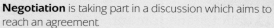

KEY TERM

Negotiation is taking part in a discussion which aims to reach an agreement.

simply be setting up a meeting or planning care with a member of staff, but the way in which this is carried out can mean the difference between an effective outcome or a failed one. Successful negotiation is linked to assertiveness and we aim to negotiate in an open and flexible manner in order to achieve a positive outcome.

Conflict can also arise when staff are faced with dilemmas. When an incident occurs which goes against your own values and beliefs, you are faced with an ethical dilemma. For example, a dilemma may arise when you feel you are obliged to break confidentiality. You may feel that a member of the team is acting in a way that is not respectful to service users. The dilemma you have is what to do with this information. You need to safeguard the service users and you will be required to follow your organisation's vulnerable adults' procedure, but this means that the member of staff in question will need to be held accountable and this can have a detrimental effect on team morale.

Another example may include actions taken when you observe poor practice in the setting. While it is the correct course of action to report such matters, it may be difficult to do so if you believe somebody may lose their job as a result of this.

Case study

3.4 Deal constructively with conflicts or dilemmas

Here are some other examples of situations where duty of care and responsibilities come into conflict. How might you deal with each of these dilemmas? Should they be supported and on what basis is this justified?

- a service user who does not want confidential information to be shared with his or her daughter
- a service user you see being treated disrespectfully by one of your colleagues does not want the incident reported
- a staff member who wants time to attend mass when on duty on a Sunday
- a carer who refuses to undertake any further training on the basis that he or she has little time to do so.

The dilemma that you as a manager need to reconcile is how far someone's right to make decisions for themselves

can be supported when it conflicts with a professional obligation. The duty of the care worker is not to control others' lives but to inform them and support them in order that they can make good decisions for themselves, whether they are staff members or service users.

We might consider the following points when addressing a challenge to the team's effectiveness, whether it be due to a conflict or an ethical dilemma:

- Are we empathetic? Have we really considered what it feels like to be in the shoes of the particular team worker with a problem?
- Can we seek clarification to make sure that we fully understand the other person's position and their needs?
- Are we calm or taking things personally?
- Are we prepared to support our case?
- Can we keep to the point and not allow ourselves to be side-tracked?
- Can we offer a compromise?

Demonstrate calmness and acknowledge the feelings of colleagues

We may feel that we have little or no control over conflicts that arise, and faced with a colleague who is angry or upset we will react with the fight or flight response, as we might with any kind of perceived threat. Our bodies will flood with adrenaline and this will make it more difficult to remain calm. By taking a moment to breathe we start to control and calm those hormones and can make a more considered response.

Respond promptly when requested to provide support

To prevent a situation escalating we need to respond quickly and to treat all parties with respect. Care should be taken not to display behaviours that suggest we are criticising the parties involved or showing a lack of concern about them.

Take time to establish the causes of the conflict

Arguments may arise because of simple misunderstandings or poor communication. Listening to both parties helps you to understand how each person is feeling.

Demonstrate a non-judgemental approach to enable an equalisation of power

It is important to remain impartial and not to take sides. We need to listen to both parties' explanations and take care to keep our judgement to ourselves until fully explored.

Support colleagues to come to an amicable outcome, ensuring their duty of care is not compromised

If we can get our colleagues to look at the bigger picture, they may start to gain a different perspective. They may begin to see the other's point of view in a disagreement and this can then lead to a solution that is agreeable to both parties. Reminding colleagues of their duty of care to service users and also to the organisation may help them to reprioritise the way they are dealing with the situation and to look again at what has led to the conflict.

Show leadership when conflicts or dilemmas cannot be resolved amicably

If a solution is not agreeable to both parties, you may need to escalate it to another person. If you have a Human Resources department, they can help to negotiate a solution. Otherwise you will need to look at what can be agreed on, and then ask the parties to either agree to differ or negotiate a plan to move forward in some way.

> ### Evidence opportunity
>
> **3.4** Deal constructively with conflicts or dilemmas
>
> Show your assessor how you manage and deal constructively with conflicts or dilemmas that occur among colleagues. Address the topics we have discussed in this section.

Reflecting on practice

In resolving conflict, when people's needs are discovered then a solution can be found. We may be tempted to compromise, but compromise means that people's needs are still not fully met and this can lead to resentment (West, 2004).

Ensuring that conflicts are addressed in the right manner means that relationships are maintained and can function smoothly.

A conflict situation is never pleasant but by reflecting on the circumstances that led to the event and thinking about how it might have been handled in a different way we can sometimes find more useful ways of managing conflict should it arise again.

> ### Research it
>
>
> **3.4** Conflict management
>
> At your next team meeting, table an agenda item on conflict management.
>
> Collect information about how staff manage conflict in their roles with service users and with other staff members.
>
> Collect the information to provide a record of types of conflict experienced and ways in which it is managed.

> ### Reflect on it
>
>
> **3.4** Conflict with colleagues and other professionals
>
> Write a reflective account about a conflict or a dilemma that has arisen in the workplace, detailing how you dealt with it and what solutions you put forward. Did you experience any conflict throughout the process of working with others? Reflect on how you dealt with it and what you learned from this.
>
> Or you could write a reflective account about how you would use the following approaches to address conflicts and dilemmas that may arise between service users, staff and carers, families and significant others:
>
> - one-to-one discussion
> - group discussion
> - using contracts
> - providing information to inform choices
> - mentoring for conflict resolution.

> ### Reflect on it
>
>
> **3.4**
>
> Explain how you have managed conflicts or dilemmas that occur among colleagues within the work setting and evaluate the impact of your style of conflict resolution. Describe how a different way of dealing with the same conflict might have changed the outcome.
>
> How might you apply Thompson's RED model in relation to how you dealt with your situation?

AC 3.5 **Evaluate working relationships with colleagues**

Here, you will be required to evaluate your own working relationships with colleagues.

Demonstrate self-reflection on performance in work role and engage in self-appraisal

Taking a step back and reflecting upon our aims and objectives, and occasionally on the way we do our jobs, can be refreshing and help us to gain a better picture of ourselves. Self-reflection and appraisal are ways of gaining a better insight into our thoughts and behaviours and our performance and motivation. It helps us to look at the experiences we have and learn from them, making changes where necessary.

Engage colleagues in providing feedback on your performance and value feedback

Encouraging colleagues to give you feedback on how you are performing is a useful way to check your own evaluations. In teams where the culture of trust operates, your colleagues will be honest and you can accept the feedback and work it into future plans. Sometimes it may be a challenge to accept negative feedback but in reflecting upon what has been said you benefit from making changes that will lead to better working relationships.

Evidence opportunity

3.5 Evaluate working relationships with colleagues

Evaluate your own working relationships with colleagues. Address the topics we have covered in this section.

LO4 Work in partnership with professionals and other agencies

AC 4.1 **Negotiate with other agencies for a specific task or area of work**

Here, you will negotiate with professionals in other agencies to agree a specific task or area of work, including the topics we cover in this section.

Understand the range of professionals and other agencies you may work with

We work with many different people in the course of our duties including those from the healthcare system such as GPs, community nurses and care workers, physiotherapists, pharmacists and those from the local council, advocacy services, mental health workers and also charitable organisations such as Age Concern or Citizens Advice.

Formal partnerships are funded by the government to give care and are bound by contracts and policies, whereas informal partnerships are those which exist within families and friends who are not paid to provide care and work together unbound by contracts.

Formal partnerships

This includes formal care professionals who are contracted and paid. These may be community care workers, community nurses or hospital nursing staff, physiotherapists or care home staff as well as other paid contracted health professionals. Your partnerships with other paid professionals such as the GP service also come under this heading. These partnerships are in place by law and the way in which you relate to and communicate with these people will be more structured and bound by policy and procedure.

Informal partnerships

These are people who provide care but are unpaid. These include family members or friends. They could also be voluntary carers or support groups or church groups that provide care for no fee. The informality of the partnership means a different relationship is experienced and the way in which you communicate here will differ from your communication with formal partners. For example, it is unlikely that the informal carer will be expected to attend many meetings or be subject to audit and appraisal. Your relationship is likely to be more friendly and supportive.

Work collaboratively to agree objectives of any partnership and how tasks and responsibilities will be allocated

All partnerships thrive on effective communication and good relationships. Collaborating with professionals from external agencies should include agreeing shared objectives and responsibilities and tasks so that there is no overlap of duties and each partner has a clear idea of the way forward with the work.

Ensure that objectives are SMART and agree procedures

For any objective to produce a successful outcome, it should be SMART. SMART objectives define the end result in a clear manner and the way in which this can be reached. Being specific about what is wanted and having a measure by which to check the outcome means that everyone working to the objective will have a better understanding about what is required to achieve the goal.

Work with professionals and other agencies to agree timelines for monitoring progress

Alongside the SMART objectives, clear timelines can show exactly when the project is to end and where progress needs to be shown at various points along the way. In this way success of short-term targets can be celebrated as well as final ones, and the achievement of the project so far can be evaluated.

AC 4.2 Use agreed ways of working

Here, you will be required to use agreed ways of working to carry out your own role and support others to carry out their responsibilities.

Establish agreed ways of working that meet agreed objectives

As with the previous section, when working with other professionals it is important that agreed ways of working are established at the outset so that consistency may be maintained.

Establish boundaries of role and responsibilities and agree timelines

While you are the manager in your setting, you may well be working alongside the manager of another similar setting and this will therefore require boundaries to be set as to the role and responsibility each of you will have for a project. These need to be agreed at the outset when you are setting agenda and review dates for the work. Doing so will aid the process to clearly describe each person's part of the management of the project.

AC 4.3 Deal with challenges

We have seen from the previous sections that the primary purpose of partnership working is to improve the experience and outcomes of people who use services, and this is achieved by minimising organisational barriers between different services. In addition, partnerships work by:

- delivering coordinated packages of services to individuals

- reducing the impact of organisational fragmentation
- bidding for, or gaining access to, new resources
- meeting a statutory requirement

Partnership working is central to the care of service users and brings together a variety of other services such as those in the voluntary sector. The DOH launched the Voluntary Sector Strategic Partner Programme in April 2009 to improve communication between the department and voluntary health and social care organisations. It enabled voluntary sector organisations to work in equal partnership with the Department of Health, the NHS and social care for the benefit of the sector and has improved health and wellbeing outcomes.

You may also be working with other agencies within the wider multidisciplinary team such as advocacy agencies or other healthcare teams.

An advantage of working closely with other organisations is that they may be able to offer advice on specific issues. A disadvantage of relying purely on other organisations is that some may be affected by lack of funding which may make it difficult for the sector to finance its work.

However, there will be challenges that you will face and as a manager it will be your responsibility to manage.

Challenges

As we have seen on page 121, while partnership working has many advantages, its success depends on dealing constructively with challenges. With more formal partnerships such as with medical professionals, the challenges will be different than those with family members and may involve difficulties with time and scheduling meetings to engage everybody involved. There may also be professional challenges in which procedures or practice are questioned. For example, it might be difficult for a nurse to challenge the practice of, say, a GP even though the nurse may have more knowledge about the practice. The hierarchy within some services may therefore be a challenge.

 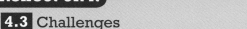

Dealing constructively with challenges within partnership working

Systems leadership may be a starting point for addressing the challenge of partnership working. Changes to the NHS and to adult care over the last 50 years have meant that a different approach to leadership has to be employed. One of the changes is that care organisations and the staff must work across services to meet the needs of the growing elderly population and the number of people with complex medical conditions who need care and support from different services.

> ### KEY TERM
>
> **Systems leadership** is the way in which the best resources from other settings and disciplines can be used to bring about improvement and beneficial change across partnership systems in other organisations.
> The style of leadership is characterised by a belief that leadership is the responsibility of teams, rather than individuals, and is collaborative in nature.

The King's Fund has researched the value of systems leaders, which describe a type of collective leadership with 'everyone taking responsibility for the success of the organisations and systems in which they work' (King's Fund, 2015).

This approach focuses on the belief that leadership is the responsibility of teams and not just the managers in an organisation.

The report shows that effective systems leaders are people who lead through influence and persuasion and who recognise the need to engage their peers in decision making. They recognise that improvements take time and that obstacles and resistance occur. One of the leaders interviewed stated that systems leaders succeed by 'being comfortable with chaos' (Timmins, 2015).

Timmins described systems leadership as 'an act of persuasion that needs to have an evidence base for change'. He stated that leaders can achieve anything as long they 'give away ownership' and 'don't want to take the credit for it' (Timmins, 2015).

This approach may cause conflict with some partners or other professionals who are not fully in tune with a different way of working.

By entering into dialogue and taking time to explain how such a system may work you can deal constructively with some of the criticism that you may receive. With family members, it may be a simple case of discussing with them what they want for their loved one and how they believe

this will be of benefit. By seeking a better understanding of their dilemma, you are more able to get a better picture of their needs and can then start to show how the service may be able to accommodate those needs.

Agree ways of working to establish common ground

We all wish to provide a service that achieves a positive outcome for our service users and so we need to work towards establishing a mutual understanding about what is best for all.

When conflicts or dilemmas arise learners take time to identify the causes and issues in a non-judgemental manner

Trying to establish common ground may lead to conflict and as a manager you may be required to take a step back and identify what is the cause and how it is best managed. Laying blame on one party will be destructive and a non-judgemental and impartial approach must be taken here.

Provide support and information, and demonstrate calmness and acknowledge the feelings of professionals and other agencies

Working in a calm, respectful manner with other agencies and professionals enables you to identify the information needed to support the outcome. You need to recognise that sometimes feelings run high, particularly when it comes to ways of working, and people may want to defend their profession's input into a project. This will require careful and considerate handling, acknowledging how others feel while negotiating a shared outcome.

> ### Research it
>
>
> **4.3** Timmins Report
>
> Go to www.kingsfund.org.uk/sites/files/kf/field/field_publication_file/System-leadership-Kings-Fund-May-2015.pdf and read the Timmins report. Explain how you could integrate system leadership into your own style of leading the staff through partnership working.

> ### Evidence opportunity
>
> **4.3** Dealing with challenges
>
> Show your assessor how you deal constructively with challenges to partnership working. Consider the topics we have covered in this section.

AC 4.4 Implement communication and recording systems

Here, you will be required to implement communication and recording systems that comply with current legislation for information sharing between agencies.

Establish shared ways of working to support effective communication

Effective communication among partners needs to have a clear statement of purpose that outlines to all how it will help to achieve overall organisational objectives and how it will engage everybody effectively.

Support a problem-solving approach to communication issues

As a manager you will appreciate that communication problems can be detrimental to effective care delivery so will want to minimise these. Adopting a problem-solving approach, whereby transparent communication processes are preferred, enables all staff to freely express themselves. Effective communication opens up dialogue between people in environments of trust and safety.

Professionals and other agencies meet current legislative requirements for the recording and storage of information

Care work demands the keeping of records and their safe storage. When we are working with partners across locations this may become difficult. It is important that each partner agrees on the best way to record and store data and that this meets legislative requirements.

Establish regular meetings with professionals and other agencies to ensure objectives remain focused on benefits to the service user

A regular meeting whereby all partners can discuss the objectives and the current achievement of objectives against performance indicators will ensure that the focus remains firmly with the service user. The meeting, which may be fortnightly, monthly or quarterly, should be one in which representatives from all areas of the partnership can contribute and then feed back to the wider team.

Evidence opportunity

4.4 Implement communication and recording systems

Show your assessor how you implement communication and recording systems that comply with current legislation for information sharing between agencies. Consider the topics we have discussed here.

AC 4.5 Challenge poor practice or failure to work in agreed ways

Here, you will be required to challenge, in ways to promote change, any poor practice or failure to work in agreed ways.

Agree ways of working that support the duty of care in line with legislative requirements (law of tort)

As care professionals we have a duty to provide a standard of reasonable care, and failure to do so is punishable in law. In English tort law, the duty of care is a legal obligation and the absence of it must be established to proceed with any action in a claim for negligence. Anybody claiming against a care professional for negligence must be able to show a duty of care has been breached. As a manager you must determine with other care professionals that the duty of care is clearly understood and that any poor practice is dealt with quickly and efficiently.

Agree ways of recording and reporting poor practice

There should be agreement among partners over standard ways of reporting poor practice across all organisations and partners.

Challenge when actions that could cause harm or fail to support the best interest of the individual in receipt of care are identified or reported

Any poor practice needs to be challenged and brought to the attention of the manager. Therefore whistle-blowing policies must be agreed. All poor practice needs to be challenged and a common agreement as to how this will be dealt with should be drawn up. For example, a designated safeguarding officer who works with all the partners and to whom everyone can come with issues might be a way forward.

Evidence opportunity

4.5 Challenge poor practice or failure to work in agreed ways

Show your assessor how you challenge, in ways to promote change, any poor practice or failure to work in agreed ways. Consider the topics we have discussed in this section.

AC 4.6 Evaluate the effectiveness of partnership work

Here, you will be required to evaluate the effectiveness of partnership work and processes that underpin it and see agreement for improvements.

Agree with professionals and other agencies timelines for evaluating work objectives

Evaluation is an essential part of quality improvement and is how we determine the merit or value of the care being given. In evaluating objectives, we engage in a process to improve the care and to enhance decisions being made, and this needs to be done at regular times throughout the work rather than at one end point. As the manager in a setting, it is useful to agree a timeline with other agencies to check this is done.

Agree processes for evaluating work objectives and the impact on service users

Agreeing the type of evaluation to be carried out will impact upon the way in which the evaluation data can be used. For example, a summative evaluation 'sums up' the effect of the intervention and comes at the end, helping the team to determine whether the objective has been met or not. It is useful for judging the overall worth of an intervention. Alternatively, you may decide that formative evaluation should be used, as this approach provides information about how things are developing as the project is happening, and helps the

team to see whether improvement has been achieved. It also helps to see how it has occurred in their particular environment.

Agree how reflection from all parties will contribute to any evaluative process

Evaluating the ways of working with partnerships is a crucial process to ensure that quality improvement in care is ongoing. Successful care can be celebrated, and lessons can also be learned from mistakes that may have happened. Poor evaluation can undermine service user care. It should be agreed with professionals and other agencies that the outcomes of evaluations and reflection will be recorded and reported to all parties.

Evidence opportunity

4.6 Evaluate the effectiveness of partnership work

Speak to your assessor or provide a written account evaluating the effectiveness of partnership work and processes that underpin it. Seek agreement for improvements. Consider the topics we have covered in this section.

Legislation

Legislation	
The Health and Social Care Act 2012 brings together the White Papers which led to its development	This introduced the Care Quality Commission (CQC).
The Care Act (2014)	Replaces previous laws to provide a 'coherent' approach to adult social care. It set out new duties for local authorities and partners, and new rights for service users and carers. It aims to ensure that: • fairer care and support are given to individuals • support for physical, mental and emotional wellbeing is offered to the person needing care and their carer • prevention and delay of the need for care and support are avoided • people are in control of their care.
Health and Social Care (Safety and Quality) Act 2015	Confers a duty on health and adult social care providers to share information about a person's care with other health and care professionals. It also makes provision about the safety of health and social care services in England, particularly with respect to the integration of information relating to users of health and social care services in England.
Government White Paper 'Our Health, Our Care, Our Say: A New Direction for Community Services' (2006)	Set out the Government's proposals to reform and expansion of community health and social care services to meet local needs, in poorer deprived communities. It highlighted four key objectives: better health prevention services and earlier intervention; increased patient choice; tackling inequalities and improving access to community services; and increased support for people with long-term needs to live independently.

→

Legislation	
The White Paper 'Equity and Excellence: Liberating the NHS' (2010)	Set out the Government's long-term vision for the future of the NHS. Main outcomes to be: • patients at the heart of everything the NHS does • focus on continual improvement of things that really matter to patients - the outcome of their healthcare • empower and liberate clinicians to innovate, having the freedom to focus on improving healthcare services.
The Five Year Forward View (2014)	This made a commitment to give more power to individuals to manage their own care and support to make their own informed decisions.

Suggestions for using the activities

This table summarises all the activities in the unit that are relevant to each assessment criterion.

Here, we also suggest other, different methods that you may want to use to present your knowledge and skills by using the activities. These are just suggestions, and you should refer to the Introduction section at the start of the book, and more importantly the City & Guilds specification, and your assessor, who will be able to provide more guidance on how you can evidence your knowledge and skills. When you need to be observed during your assessment, this can be done by your assessor, or your manager can provide a witness testimony.

Assessment criteria and accompanying activities	Suggested methods to show your knowledge/skills
LO1 Understand the context of relationships and partnership working	
1.1 Research it (page 103)	Read about the work on NHS England and the partnerships it has forged. Explain how these examples and ways of working could be applied to your setting.
1.1 Evidence opportunity (page 104)	Think about how legislation and regulation influences relationships with others. Critically analyse national, local and your own organisation's guidelines, legislations and policies that relate to partnership working.
1.2 Evidence opportunity (page 106)	Provide a written account analysing the association between person-centred care and positive outcomes and the ability to engage in partnership working.
1.2 Reflect on it (page 107)	How has person-centred care affected the work of the partners you work with? Give an example of how partners work together to improve service user care.
1.3 Evidence opportunity (page 107)	Critically evaluate the impact of working with other agencies and community groups within your local area and relevant to your service. Analyse a range of potential benefits to both those accessing adult care services and the organisation.
1.4 Evidence opportunity (page 108)	Explain to your assessor the benefits of integrated working, and how integrated working with other agencies delivers better outcomes for those using adult care services.
1.5 Reflect on it (page 110)	Think about a partnership you have set up in your setting and reflect on the effective features within it.
1.5 Evidence opportunity (page 110)	Write a report describing the features of effective partnership working that have helped you to minimise and overcome barriers within your work area.
1.6 Evidence opportunity (page 111)	Find and evaluate evidence for your portfolio to show that, as a leader in adult care services, you ensure that the service creates and maintains positive relationships with all those that come into contact with the service.
LO2 Lead effective relationships with those using adult care services and their families	
2.1 Evidence opportunity (page 113)	Show your assessor how you model open, respectful and supportive relationships, and how you communicate to establish effective partnership working.
2.1 Reflect on it (page 113)	How do you ensure there is open communication when working in partnership? Supply some evidence to demonstrate how you do this in your setting.
2.2 Reflect on it (page 114)	Think about the term co-production and what it actually means for you. Give examples that show how you, in your role, have shared this concept with your staff.
2.2 Evidence opportunity (page 114)	Show your assessor how you engage your team members in a way that enables them to understand the values and importance of co-production.

Suggestions for using the activities	
2.2 Research it (page 114)	Read the SCIE guide about co-production. For each heading (Culture, Structure, Practice and Review), describe at least one way in which you can engage your team to enable them to understand the values and importance of co-production.
2.2 Reflect on it (page 114)	Think about the values of co-production. Write about the values to the team of this way of working.
2.3 Evidence opportunity (page 116)	Show your assessor how you implement procedures to ensure that everyone is aware of their statutory rights.
2.4 Research it (page 117)	List and evaluate the systems that are in place in your setting which encourage and enable engagement in decision making and reviews.
2.4 Evidence opportunity (page 118)	Show your assessor how you implement systems that encourage and enable engagement in decision making and reviews.
LO3 Manage working relationships with colleagues in the organisation	
3.1 Evidence opportunity (page 120)	Show your assessor, and discuss with them, how you develop procedures to facilitate effective working relationships with colleagues.
3.1 Research it (page 120)	Evaluate the effectiveness of procedures in your setting that relate to working relationships with colleagues.
3.2 Evidence opportunity (page 120)	Show and explain to your assessor how you develop and agree common objectives when working with colleagues.
3.3 Evidence opportunity (page 121)	Show your assessor how you implement systems and practices that allow colleagues to make appropriate contributions using their specific expertise.
3.4 Evidence opportunity (page 124)	Show your assessor how you manage and deal constructively with conflicts or dilemmas that occur among colleagues. Address the topics discussed in this section.
3.4 Research it (page 124)	Collect information about how staff manage conflict in their roles with service users and with other staff members. Provide a record of types of conflict experienced and ways in which conflict is managed.
3.4 Reflect on it (page 124)	Write a reflective account about a conflict or a dilemma that has arisen in the workplace, detailing how you dealt with it and what solutions you put forward.
3.4 Reflect on it (page 124)	Explain how you have managed conflicts or dilemmas that occur among colleagues within the work setting and evaluate the impact of your style of conflict resolution.
3.5 Evidence opportunity (page 125)	Evaluate your working relationships with colleagues. Address the topics covered in this section.
LO4 Work in partnership with professionals and other agencies	
4.1 Evidence opportunity (page 126)	Show your assessor how you negotiate with professionals in other agencies to agree a specific task or area of work. Include the topics covered in this section.
4.2 Evidence opportunity (page 126)	Show your assessor how you use agreed ways of working to carry out your own role and support others to carry out their responsibilities, addressing the topics covered in this section.
4.3 Reflect on it (page 126)	Think about your job role and that of one of your partners. How do you feel when you need to challenge a decision a GP may have made or if a healthcare support worker challenges a practice you have put into place?
4.3 Research it (page 127)	Explain how you could integrate system leadership into your own style of leading the staff through partnership working.
4.3 Evidence opportunity (page 127)	Show your assessor how you deal constructively with challenges to partnership working.
4.4 Evidence opportunity (page 128)	Show your assessor how you implement communication and recording systems that comply with current legislation for information sharing between agencies.
4.5 Evidence opportunity (page 128)	Show your assessor how you challenge, in ways to promote change, any poor practice or failure to work in agreed ways.
4.6 Evidence opportunity (page 129)	Speak to your assessor or provide a written account evaluating the effectiveness of partnership work and processes that underpin it.

References

Armistead, C.G. and Pettigrew, P. (2004) 'Effective partnerships: Building a sub-regional network of reflective practitioners.' *The international journal of Public Sector Management*, 17(7): 571–85.

Barnes, C. and Mercer, G. (eds) (2004) *Disability Policy and Practice: Applying the Social Model*. Leeds: The Disability Press.

Department of Health (2010) *Equity and Excellence: Liberating the NHS*. London: HMSO.

Department of Health (2012) *Improving Health and Care: The role of the outcomes framework*. Government Publications.

Department of Health (2013) *Integrated Care: Our shared commitment; A framework that outlines ways to improve health and social care integration*. London: TSO.

George, B. (2003) *Authentic Leadership: Rediscovering the secrets to creating lasting value*. San Francisco, CA: Jossey-Bass.

Health Foundation (2014) *Person-centred Care Made Simple*. www.health.org.uk/sites/health/files/PersonCentredCareMadeSimple.pdf

Joint Review of Investment in Voluntary, Community and Social Enterprise Organisations in Health and Care Sector (2016); co-produced by representatives of the VCSE sector and the Department of Health, NHS England and Public Health England. London: NHS England. www.gov.uk/government/uploads/system/uploads/attachment_data/file/524243/VCSE_Investment_Review_A.pdf

LaFasto, F.M.J. and Larson, C.E. (1989) *Teamwork: What Must Go Right/What Can Go Wrong*. London: Sage Publications.

LaFasto, F.M.J. and Larson, C.E. (2001) *When Teams Work Best: 6,000 team members and leaders tell what it takes to succeed*. Thousand Oaks, CA: Sage Publications.

McKibbon, J., Walton, A. and Mason, L. (2008) *Leadership and Management in Health and Social Care*. London: Heinemann.

Mumford, M.D., Zaccharo, S.J., Connolly, M.S. and Marks, M.A. (2000) Leadership skill: conclusions and future directions, *Leadership Quarterly*, 11(1): 155–70.

NHS England (2016) VCSE Review. VCSE Review. Investing in partnerships for health and wellbeing; Joint review of investment in Voluntary, Community and Social Enterprise organisations in health and care sector, accessed from https://assets.publishing.service.gov.uk/government/uploads/system/uploads/attachment_data/file/524243/VCSE_Investment_Review_A.pdf

NHS England (2017) *Next Steps on the NHS Five Year Forward View*. London: TSO.

Pearson, P. and Spencer, J. (1997) *Promoting Teamwork in Primary Care: A research-based approach*. London: Arnold.

Qureshi, H., Bamford, C., Nicholas, E., Patmore, C. and Harris, J. (2000) *Outcomes in Social Care Practice: Developing an outcome focus in care management and user surveys*. York: Social Policy Research Unit, University of York.

SCIE (2012) The Research Briefing 41. Factors that promote and hinder joint and integrated working between health and social care services. London: TSO.

SCIE (2015) Co-production in social care: What it is and how to do it, Guide 51; accessed from www.scie.org.uk/publications/guides/guide51/index.asp on 11/7/17

Thompson, N. (2006) *People Problems*. Basingstoke: Palgrave Macmillan.

Tilmouth, T., Davies-Ward, E. and Williams, B. (2011) *Foundation Degree in Health and Social Care*. London: Hodder Education.

Timmins, N. (2015) *The Practice of System Leadership. Being comfortable with chaos*. London: The King's Fund. www.nhs.uk/Conditions/social-care-and-support-guide/Pages/mental-capacity.aspx

West, M. (1994) *Effective Teamwork: Personal and Professional Development*. London: Blackwell.

West, M. (2004) *Effective Teamwork: Practical lessons from organizational research*. London: Wiley and Sons.

Yoder-Wise, P.S. (2007) *Leading and Managing in Nursing*. St. Louis: Mosby/Elsevier.

Further reading and useful resources

Boydell, L. (2007) *Partnerships: A literature review*. Dublin: Institute of Public Health in Ireland.

Department of Health (2006) Our health, our care, our say: A new direction for community services. London: HMSO.

Griffith, R. (2015) Understanding the Code: Working in partnership, *British Journal of Community Nursing*, 20(5): 250–2.

Hunter, D. and Perkins, N. (2014) *Partnership Working in Public Health*. Bristol: Policy Press.

Innes, A., Macpherson, S. and McCabe, I. (2006) *Promoting Person-Centred Care at the Front Line*. York: Joseph Rowntree Foundation/SCIE.

Johns, C. (2000) *Becoming a Reflective Practitioner*. Oxford: Blackwell.

National Voices (2014) Person-centred Care 2020: Calls and contributions from health and social care charities, accessed from www.nationalvoices.org.uk/sites/default/files/public/publications/person-centred-care-2020.pdf

Nursing and Midwifery Council (2015) The Code: Professional standards of practice and behaviour for nurses and midwives [online]. Available at: www.nmc-uk.org/code

Reed, J., MacFarlane, A. and Clarke, C. (2011) *Nursing Older Adults: Partnership Working*. Maidenhead: McGraw-Hill.

Rolfe, G., Jasper, M. and Freshwater, D. (2011) *Critical Reflection in Practice. Generating knowledge for care* (2e). London: Palgrave Macmillan.

Social Care Institute for Excellence, www.scie.org.uk

Unit 505

Person-centred practice for positive outcomes

GLH 30

About this unit

The purpose of this unit is to enhance the manager's knowledge of the theory and principles, understanding and skills required to promote and implement person-centred practice and to lead the implementation of active participation of individuals.

We look at how the development of the personalisation agenda from a service-led provision has changed the face of care in the UK.

We also deal with consent in practice and what this means for service users. This addresses the issue of active participation as a way of working that recognises an individual's right to participate in the activities and relationships of everyday life as independently as possible. The individual as an active partner in their own care or support is given a voice in today's health and care service provisions and is no longer regarded as a passive recipient. You will be introduced to various models of person-centred practice to enable you to lead and encourage the active participation of your service users.

Learning outcomes

By the end of this unit, you will:

1 Understand the principles and values of person-centred outcome-based practice
2 Manage resources to facilitate positive outcomes for individuals
3 Lead practice in health and care methods to achieve person-centred outcomes
4 Champion equality, diversity and inclusion to achieve positive outcomes
5 Lead continuous improvement in carrying out health and care procedures where required
6 Develop community relationships to provide integrated services
7 Managing concerns and complaints in adult care

Getting started

Before you study the unit, think about the following:

- How do you think services can be managed to meet best practice guidelines and benchmarks for person-centred practice?
- What training and support do staff need to ensure services achieve positive outcomes for individuals who use services?
- What kinds of integrated services are currently provided to facilitate the achievement of positive outcomes for individuals who use services?
- How can services be improved to ensure individuals receive a person-centred approach to their care package?

These are just things you should start to think about, and you will find out more about these throughout the unit. It would also be useful to come back to these questions as you study the unit.

LO1 Understand the principles and values of person-centred outcome-based practice

AC 1.1 Theories and values of positive practice

Here, you will be required to critically evaluate the principles, theories and values of positive outcomes-based practice relating to the wellbeing of individuals, to include the topics we cover here.

What is person-centred care?

The Health Foundation (2014) explains person-centred care as:

- giving people dignity, compassion and respect
- offering coordinated and personalised care, support or treatment
- supporting people to recognise and develop their own strengths and abilities to live independent and fulfilling lives.

The Care Act 2014 further moved this agenda on by making it a main focus in care and identifying the outcomes that matter to the individual.

'Outcomes' are defined as the end-results of services for individuals, so an outcomes-focused service would be one which prioritises the care that the service user identifies as the most important to them.

For individuals this means they can specify the care which will have a greater impact for them on their wellbeing. For example, a positive outcome for somebody might be that they are able to stay in their own home with carers and professionals coming in to deliver personal and medical care rather than them being taken into hospital or long-term social care. We could argue that treatment in hospital might still have a positive outcome in terms of them getting physically better but for this particular individual the impact upon wellbeing and emotional health may be huge.

Person-centred care is, therefore, about making the individual requiring the care the central figure in the process. The government publication *Putting People First: A Shared Vision and Commitment to the Transformation of Adult Social Care* was published in 2007 and outlined its personalisation agenda – the government's vision of enabling individuals to live independently with complete choice and control over their lives (DOH, 2007).

Personalisation allows individuals to build a system of care and support tailored to meet their needs and designed with their full involvement. It is about ensuring that the individual has their choices taken into account and their culture and ethnicity respected, with care tailored to these factors. Historically, a 'one size fits all' approach to care was used and this meant the individual had to fit into and access already existing care services, whether those services were appropriate or not.

The term 'person-centred care' is now used to describe care which is user-focused, promoting independence and autonomy (see Figure 5.1). Collaborative and partnership approaches to care often use the term 'person-centred' to describe their ethos (Innes et al., 2006).

Positive practice then is about treating people in a compassionate manner with dignity and kindness. It is a means of truly embedding person-centred care with its focus on the individual and their specific needs and not just paying lip service to this by undertaking a tick box exercise.

▲ **Figure 5.1** A care plan is user-focused, taking into account individual needs and wishes

Principles, theories and values of person-centred practice relating to choice and control

In this section, we will be discussing the principles, theories and values of positive outcomes-based and person-centred practice, and how these relate to the wellbeing of individuals, and how they are given choice and control.

We give several examples of the different approaches that care providers have tried and show how these contemporary approaches to health and social care delivery enable the empowerment of individuals to personalise their own care. The person-centred approach to care has involved a positive shift away from a 'one size fits all' service in which individuals had to accept the way the service worked and fit into it by changing their lifestyle and putting aside their own choices to services which are now designed to fit around the needs of individuals. The changes have put the person at the centre of the care and give more freedom of choice.

The Dimensions approach

Dimensions is a company that provides evidence-based support that helps people with complex needs to become actively involved in their communities. It provides a training tool which describes person-centred thinking as well as practice. It is also concerned with developing values, skills and tools designed to get to know the individuals in our care. The aim is to ensure that the person is kept at the centre of the decision-making process and feels listened to.

The training course has a number of tools:

- One Page Profiling

  This is a one-page document which details the important information about a person. There are usually three headings:

  - what people appreciate or like about me
  - what's important to me
  - how best you can support me.

  Your care setting may use a similar plan such as a care passport.

- Relationship circle

  This is a means of identifying who a person knows, how they know them and how they help them. It shows us who is important to the individual and how they support and might be involved in planning. Furthermore it helps to discover which relationships can be strengthened or supported.

  Your own relationship circle may include some of your family but you might also include significant others such as friends or work colleagues.

- What's working/not working

  This helps to understand what works for the individual and what doesn't work from looking at different perspectives. It is a means of analysing what is happening in the person's life and can help them to identify what is important to them and whether they are being supported in a good way. In this way problems can be identified and solved.

Research it

1.1 The Dimensions approach

Go to the Dimensions website at www.dimensions-uk.org/initiative/person-centred-thinking/ and access the training page. There is an online training course for staff in care.

Evaluate the package and determine whether it would be useful in your setting.

Also go to www.thinkandplan.com where you will find practical examples of the tools we have discussed. Evaluate the tools and worksheets you find.

The building blocks framework

The WHO (World Health Organization) Health Systems Framework identifies a system of building blocks which make up health systems that are fit for purpose. The prime function is to maintain the health of individuals. The building blocks are:

- the provision of high-quality, effective, safe, personal and non-personal health services
- a well-performing health workforce where there are sufficient numbers and a mix of competent and responsive staff
- reliable health information systems which can produce useful information
- access to safe, efficient, cost-effective and good quality essential medical products, vaccines and technologies
- a good health finance system with adequate funds, so that people can use the services they need when they need them
- accountable leadership and governance with effective oversight of strategic policy frameworks, coalition building, the provision of appropriate regulations and incentives and attention to system design.

Source: Adapted from /www.wpro.who.int/health_services/health_systems_framework/en/

As a manager you can implement such systems by ensuring that the policies and procedures which relate to the service are up-to-date and that quality assurance is practised. The staff you manage need to be able to deliver care to the highest standard and receive excellent support from management to make this possible.

Research it

WHO

Go to the WHO website (www.who.int) and research the Health Systems Framework.

Undertake a small study to show how your own setting is 'fit for purpose'.

Use the building blocks as headings and give examples of your own input to each part.

The Common Core Principles to support self-care

The Common Core Principles were published by Skills for Care in 2015 to help people support self-care in order to live healthier and more independent lives. The seven principles are:

- **Principle 1** Person-centred practice that engages, supports, encourages and facilitates involvement and helps individuals to make decisions that are right for them.

- **Principle 2** Effective communication enables individuals to identify their strengths, assess their needs, and develop and gain the confidence to self-care.

- **Principle 3** For individuals to make well-informed decisions about their self-care they must have access to appropriate information and understand the range of options available to them.

- **Principle 4** Developing skills and confidence in self-care requires access to a range of learning and development opportunities, formal and informal.

- **Principle 5** New technology is an important aspect of enabling people to self-care.

- **Principle 6** Individuals are enabled to access support networks and participate in the planning, development and evaluation of services.

- **Principle 7** Risk taking is a normal part of everyday life, so supported risk management and risk taking is an important element of maximising independence and choice.

Evidence opportunity

1.1 Common Core Principles

Give an example of how your setting uses each of the Common Core Principles to support the wellbeing of your service users.

Evaluate their success and describe how the application of each principle can be improved.

For example, for Principle 3 show how you help people to make well-informed choices about their self-care needs by giving examples of the process used.

Research it

1.1 Approaches to person-centred practice

Research the reablement approach and biographical or life-story work. Critically review these approaches. What are the advantages and disadvantages of each?

Historical approaches to care work

We can clearly see the benefits of the philosophy behind person-centred care, but despite extensive support by government, policy makers, practitioners, and clients and their families, there remain difficulties with implementation.

Person-centred practice has resulted from 30 years of investigation into the development of quality care, the origins of which can be traced to changes that took place in the early 1970s as part of a move to 'normalisation' (when long-stay institutions for disabled people began to close down). Normalisation is about 'normalising' the environment and not the individual, and aims to enable individuals to lead 'normal patterns' of life rather than forcing them to conform to societal norms (see Figure 5.2).

Unfortunately, the planned changes with respect to moving service users to community care did not have the desired effects. They were expected to fit into the available care services for all and very little personalisation of care was evident then. In addition to the discrimination and the stigma attached to being a physically or learning disabled person or mentally ill person in the community, the health care system systematically failed these individuals and this led to further criticism of the social care agenda. Research into the problems being encountered at the time revealed major change was needed to the way in which care was being delivered. One critical debate was about two models of care, the Medical Model and the Social Model.

▲ **Figure 5.2** Normalisation is about 'normalising' the environment, and not the individual

Medical Model vs Social Model

The Medical Model of care described the disabling condition and focused on the impairment the individual suffers and how that impairment reduces the individual's quality of life, causing disadvantage. In this model, the emphasis then was on identifying the disability, understanding it and learning to treat and change its course if possible, or preventing further deterioration.

The Social Model of care took the opposite view and looked at the environment and its disabling impact on individuals. The Social Model supported the notion that society creates disability and that barriers and prejudice, together with the subsequent exclusion by society, are the defining factors for who is disabled and who is not in a particular society. The lack of resources, facilities or the environment which restricted mobility meant that individuals with disabilities were unable to participate in work or education.

This model reflected the view that while physical or mental impairment poses problems, these do not necessarily have to lead to disability unless society fails to accommodate these differences.

This led to a change in the way in which disability was viewed and politicians were forced to address the issues. It was clear that in order to improve care, changes to the way in which it was being delivered would need to be high on the agenda.

Over time, there was marked improvement in how society accepted people with disabilities, those with learning disabilities, as well as people with mental health problems and older people as equal members of the community. The Social Model of care forced the view that society was in fact the problem for such groups because it failed to provide adequate services to meet their needs. The model was hailed as a more person-centred approach to care than the Medical Model.

As we have seen above, the approach to person-centred care has involved a shift in the way in which care is delivered and rather than a 'one size fits all' design, services were designed to fit around the needs of individuals.

The changes haves not only put the person at the centre of the care process but also shifted power towards them, enabling them to have more freedom of choice. The principles guiding this agenda centre on the notions of equality, choice, independence and inclusion. In order to meet these needs, the services we supply in healthcare must challenge the unequal power structures that have been evident between service providers and service users. Sanderson (2003, p. 20) talks about this change as being the need to operate from a position where service providers have 'power with' service users rather than 'power over' them.

In trying to implement person-centred care, managers need to be clear about how the support to service users will be delivered; it is not merely a case of including service users and families and asking them what they think or what they want. There are processes to guide practice and six of these approaches are mentioned below:

1   The McGill Action Planning System (MAPS) is a planning process for children with disabilities to enable their integration into the school community. The team in this process includes the child, family members, friends, and regular and special education personnel.

2   ELP, or Essential Lifestyle Planning, uses detailed plans to get to know what is important to someone. When using these types of plans, the assumptions behind them are that:
    - the individual will have a lifestyle that works for them
    - our quality of life depends on how well or badly we achieve that lifestyle.

    As care workers we should help people to live their chosen lifestyle – not try to change the person to fit in with our view of life.

3   Personal Futures Planning involves getting to know the person to determine what their life is like now and developing ideas about what they would like to do in the future. Action is then taken to help them to implement this and to explore possibilities within the community to see what needs to change within services (Mount, 1990 and O'Brien, 1987).

4   The PATH (Planning Alternative Tomorrows and Hope) system was developed by Jack Pearpoint, Marsha Forest and John O'Brien and features a person's dreams for the future (termed 'their north star') and puts it into action, reviewing the plan 1–2 years later.

5   In the collaborative care and support planning model, what matters to the person is explored along with the best treatment, care and support. Additionally, the service user is encouraged to set goals and think about actions they can take to reach them.

The charity National Voices has identified four stages of the approach:

- preparing for a discussion
- having the discussion (with the care and support worker)
- writing down the main points from the discussion
- review.

See www.nationalvoices.org.uk/what-care-and-support-planning for more information.

6   In the person- and family-centred care approach the focus is on the way in which the care is organised and the way staff interact with service users and their families.

This approach incorporates 'shadowing' service users in order to develop knowledge of their perspective and to gain a shared vision for the ideal service user experience, and working through individual improvements.

Go to www.kingsfund.org.uk/projects/PFCC and www.health.org.uk/areas-of-work/programmes/family-patient-centred-care for more information.

We may see the positives in care being given using these approaches. The person is at the centre of decision making and their choice and wishes are paramount. However, negative factors include time to undertake the approach and funding, which may be a scarce resource. Also staff may require additional training to initiate these models.

Health and social care has come a considerable distance in terms of person-centred care. Traditional views of service users as passive recipients of care are now being challenged and the way in which the 'needs of the disabled' were determined, without reference to the individual, has largely disappeared. Today, person-centred planning has taken centre stage in services, although it has not been fully adopted or implemented across social care provision and there needs to be more work carried out to ensure that it is.

> ### Reflect on it
> **1.1** Person-centred care
>
> Person-centred care reflects the values of empowerment and personalisation that underlie contemporary approaches to health and social care in England. Write a reflective account of your own views on this subject and describe how you meet these needs in your organisation.

> ### Evidence opportunity
> **1.1** Approaches to person-centred care
>
> Which approaches to person-centred practice do you favour? Give an account, evaluating its use. Which other model might be appropriate?

Ways outcome-based practice and person-centred practice interlink to support positive change

Outcomes-based practice

Outcomes-based practice specifies what the person at the centre of the care process needs to do to achieve their health care aims. This has created a results-based accountability culture, which relies on data-driven decision-making processes to help to improve the lives of citizens and the community as a whole. Being accountable in this way means evidence is provided for the outcomes achieved for service users and services can be judged on whether service users are better off as a result of the services' input.

The key benefits of such care are:

- Service users can choose care preferred and needed to improve their quality of life.
- They can have more flexibility in choice and any changes to need can be responded to more quickly.
- Care workers can work closely with service users to enable them to become more independent.
- It strengthens partnership working.
- Evaluating the effectiveness of services is easier where outcomes measures are set out.

Several approaches to outcomes-based practice have been identified. These include the following:

- **Results-based accountability** is also known as outcomes-based accountability. It uses data-driven decision-making processes to help solve problems and is a way of thinking and acting that improves the lives of people in the community. It has been developed to improve the performance of an organisation's services.
- **Outcomes management** is the means to help service users and providers make care-related choices based on knowledge of the effects those choices may have on the service user's life.
- **Outcomes into practice** focuses on the outcomes people value.
- **The logic model** is a logical framework and theory of change used by funders, managers and evaluators of programmes to evaluate effectiveness.

Whichever model is used, the basic premise is that outcomes-based practice is a new way of working which replaces the needs-led approach that tended to focus on the immediate situation and support requirements that would be provided by the care professional.

See AC 1.2 in this unit, where there is more information on outcomes.

Person-centred practice

In person-centred care, a good outcome will enable the person not only to have their needs addressed but to move towards what they aspire to in the future.

The link between the two

Helen Sanderson Associates demonstrates the link between the two terms by describing person-centred outcomes as:

- being a personal and not a service perspective
- controlled and influenced by the person
- specific to the person and able to be measured (HSA, 2015).

In an attempt to ensure that all individuals requiring care have their needs met holistically, the **'personalisation'** agenda has been introduced into a lot of recent government documentation.

Your role as a manager

We can see that to support positive change for individuals outcomes-based and person-centred practice need to be interlinked. It is possible to have an outcomes-based service which is purely service-led and not person-centred at all. In other words, it meets the needs of the setting rather than the individual. However, by linking the two, the individual is able to choose the care preferred to fit their own lifestyle and needs. As a manager, your role will be to ensure that the staff are fully open to allowing choice and autonomy with respect to how the individuals they care for can become more independent and empowered in their own care setting. This will require training and supervision of staff to ensure they have the service users at the heart of everything they do.

Ways active participation contributes to relationships, wellbeing and the achievement of positive outcomes for individuals

Reflect on it

1.1 Active participation

Consider for a moment how you might feel if you were a patient in hospital and never consulted about your treatment. You merely had to accept the decisions made and do as you were told. It would not be very long before you were completely switched off and passive in whatever was being done to you. You might even feel that you were being undervalued with respect to any of your wishes. It would also have a detrimental effect on your relationships with others, both personal and professional, and this would affect your wellbeing, hardly a positive outcome.

The Nursing and Midwifery Council standards of conduct make it very clear that healthcare workers should listen to the people in their care and respond to their needs as individuals. They should be aware of their preferences and act in accordance with these. The Skills for Health Code of Conduct for Healthcare Support Workers and Adult Social Care Workers echoes this, outlining the behaviour and attitudes expected of those who work in the sector. Although the code is voluntary, it is accepted as best practice.

In evaluating how active participation has enhanced the wellbeing and quality of life of our service users, we may ask for feedback via questionnaires.

Standard 7 of the Care Certificate is about privacy and dignity and references active participation as a way of ensuring that individuals have a right to participate in activities and relationships as independently as possible. Rather than a passive onlooker the individual should be encouraged to be an active partner in their own care as they alone know what matters most to them in life. We, as carers, can never assume anything about a person and what we think they might like to do.

Positive relations with others: Loving relationships and friendships in which care and trust are apparent are so important to all of us and yet there may be a tendency to forget this in the workplace. Just as we value closeness and support of others, so too will our service users, but this can be neglected when we merely attend to physical needs. The need to be able to connect with others and have the opportunity to make friends is just as important in long-term care for service users (who may not see family or friends daily) as it is to us who can return home to our families every night.

Autonomy: Being free to make choices and our own decisions is a liberating feeling. Being in control of our destiny is what autonomy refers to. When a person goes into a care home or is ill for a long period of time, often choice is removed from them and well-meaning care workers may think this is the right thing to do. As unique people with our own identity, values and goals in life, we need to be able to maintain the ability to think and act for ourselves and as care workers we must empower our service users to do the same.

Mastery: Autonomy is about making decisions for ourselves and keeping control of our lives. Being masters of our own environment and adapting to and modifying our situations in order to progress and achieve what we need is a vital part of this concept. In long-term care, this may seem to be difficult to achieve, but as care professionals it is imperative to keep the lines of communication open and to access the service user's desires as to how they wish to live and what they need to do to control their circumstances as much as possible.

This in turn will give them confidence and belief in our abilities, which brings with it a sense of pride and success.

By being an active partner in care the individual is able to continue with relationships which will enhance their wellbeing and independence.

See AC 3.2 for more information on promoting wellbeing and positive outcomes.

Research it

1.1 Active participation, wellbeing and quality of life

Undertake a small-scale study of a group of individuals in your care and ask them to comment on how well active participation in their own care enhances their wellbeing and quality of life.

Ways of working with individuals to ensure choice and control over decisions affecting them

How can you work with individuals to ensure that they are in control of their choices? Care planning may be one way in which this can be achieved. For example, think about this case.

The staff at the local hospital emergency department have a particular person who regularly attends because their blood sugar levels are uncontrolled. They treat the person each time and send them home again until the next incident. This is clearly not a good plan for the individual as they are not in control of their care in this way. A care plan is needed in which the specific problem is addressed and the outcome they want can be put into place to give the individual more choice and autonomy. In this case, it would be useful to ask what their preferences are for this treatment and to try to work with this. For this person, education about their care is clearly needed here, so a plan to educate them about their health issue and how they can help themselves can be advised and the person can be taught how they can best manage their condition.

Integrated service provision for creating seamless care

All care settings and professional disciplines need to be supported and guided in obtaining information from service users to ensure that their wishes and choices are taken into account and this will require shared systems of working across traditional boundaries. So, for example, the physiotherapy team in an older adult care facility will need to have access to records and care plans. In developing ways of working which involve many teams, the following points to remember are:

- The central figure in the process is the service user.
- Family and friends are partners in the care process.
- The care plan is a guide to what is important for the service user and shows what support they need.
- A care plan helps the person to be a part of the community and is not merely about what services they need.

The plan is a continuous process and does not stop when it has been written. The people involved continue to evaluate and act within the plan to help the service user to achieve the best quality care (DOH, 2003).

In reviewing care, we need feedback about how the needs and preferences of the service user have been met and whether changes may be required. The supervision process you have in place is a good way to gain feedback from staff and time can be given to review which approaches worked well and which did not. Additionally, the team meeting and a multidisciplinary meeting can be useful forums for discussing this. For others such as family members, friends, advocates and other professionals, reviews of care need to be planned and there should be regular meetings or perhaps forums to enable this.

The manager's role is to ensure that guidelines for practice are available for staff that highlight the care for service users to ensure that seamless care is provided. Decisions about the care to be given are made during the assessment process with the service user and are then translated into treatment plans, procedures, medical notes and care plans. Care plans ensure that care given is standardised to reduce the risk of variation throughout the day. For example, a staff member on a night shift who may not have been involved in the initial assessment needs to be aware of how a service user is cared for during the day and how they wish to be treated so that the same care can be continued. Practice protocols are there for guidance and as a manager you are responsible for ensuring they are upheld and also implemented. Sometimes it may be necessary to involve other members of the wider disciplinary team to provide a different area of expertise so staff need to know how the referral to other professionals can be made.

Evidence opportunity

1.1 Wellbeing

In your own care setting, how do you promote a culture among the workforce which shows consideration of all aspects of individuals' wellbeing? Write a case study which shows the systems and processes in place that promote individual wellbeing.

LO2 Manage resources to facilitate positive outcomes for individuals

AC 2.1 Facilitate an organisational culture that values positive outcomes and person-centred practice

Here, you will be required to reflect on how you drive an organisational culture which values positive outcomes and person-centred practice.

It is important that a positive organisational culture is developed that reflects and reinforces a commitment to valuing positive outcomes and person-centred practice. The challenge is to ensure that everybody knows what the values and resulting policies of the organisation are and how they are expected to adopt these in their work. Staff cannot be expected to enact values that they are not aware of. An explicit and transparent statement of values must be discussed with staff and made available to the public, thus providing a clear indication of expectations of behaviours. Second, discussion of what this actually means in practice is important in helping staff to make the link from expressed values, which may seem intangible, into real practice. In successful organisations, there is a clear correlation between espoused values and the ethical leadership of that organisation's leaders and the successful realisation of values within an organisation (Renz and Eddy, 1996). That is to say, it is essential that the leaders are seen to live and enact the values.

Applying the principle of equality is an active way to ensure that systems, processes and practices do not inadvertently disadvantage anyone. In this way, you drive the culture towards ensuring that person-centred practice is the norm in your own setting.

In promoting equality as a value, staff will understand that all individuals should be afforded **equal opportunities** to achieve positive outcomes. The equal opportunities approach to equality strives to cancel out disadvantage. This means that barriers must be removed, where possible, or that positive interventions are implemented to invalidate those things that create disadvantage.

An equal opportunities approach requires that all individuals are offered the same or similar opportunities. This is known as reasonable adjustment. The law requires that reasonable adjustments are anticipated in advance rather than met only when an issue arises. Legal enforcement of equal opportunity has been very effective in significantly changing behaviours in respect of tolerance and engagement with difference and diversity and has had significant success in improving equality and inclusion.

See LO4 for more information on championing equality, diversity and inclusion to achieve positive outcomes.

Driving an organisational culture that values positive outcomes and person-centred care

Culture is the behaviour, values, thoughts and norms of an organisation – the unspoken rules. In a health and social care setting, this refers to the staff's beliefs about care and how these might affect the way in which they work.

In order to promote psychological wellbeing, let's take as our starting point Ryff's 1989 Psychological Wellbeing Inventory. In engendering a culture that promotes wellbeing in our day-to-day practice, as managers we need to ensure we have an awareness of aspects of wellbeing and what it is service users may need.

By valuing the concept of positive wellbeing for service users, you can ensure that staff are reminded about the need for positive outcomes for people in their care. Training and ongoing staff development during supervision can also ensure that staff fully appreciate the need to constantly raise their awareness about how wellbeing for service users can be improved. There are certain factors you should consider to promote a culture of wellbeing in day-to-day practice:

Self-acceptance

The way we view our lives and ourselves is a major source of wellbeing. Self-acceptance is about coming to terms with what we can't change or control. If we are satisfied with who we are, and can live with our experiences without bitterness or regret, we can find contentment with our current situation.

Positive relations with others

Relationships and friendships are important to all of us, even in the workplace. We and the people in our care have an innate need to connect with others and to establish friendships.

Autonomy

The freedom to make choices is a liberating feeling and removing that choice just because somebody is in long-term care is damaging and soul-destroying. We are all unique people with an identity, values and goals in life, and we must empower our clients to maintain the ability to think and act for themselves.

See page 139 for information on 'mastery'.

KEY TERM

Equal opportunity is the principle of having opportunities in life that are fair and similar to those of other people and ensuring people are not discriminated against on the basis of individual characteristics.

Purpose in life

Can you imagine a life without a purpose? Some service users may feel that once they are in long-term care or have a disability that prevents them from living the way they used to, life is not worth living. They need to be empowered to feel that there is something to strive for, even in changed circumstances. By enabling the client to continue to use their strengths and talents, to develop relationships and to pursue their goals, they can find real purpose in living.

Personal growth

We never stop learning so long as we are willing to be open to new experiences and seek out our potential. Service users may be elderly or in long-term care, yet we as care professionals need to encourage them to continue to be curious about aspects of life and to seek out opportunities to grow as a person.

The whole concept of wellbeing is about being comfortable in our lives where everything has come together. But the question is, how can you enable the people you care for to feel this way?

Evidence opportunity

2.1 Organisational culture, positive outcomes and person-centred practice

Provide a reflective account of how you drive an organisational culture that values positive outcomes and person-centred practice. How do you manage resources to facilitate positive outcomes for individuals?

You might, for example, like to think about how you ensure that the people in your care have autonomy. Give an example to show how you encourage their personal growth. What sort of activities and choices do you offer?

AC 2.2 Develop, implement and evaluate plans to ensure team members have appropriate training, development and support to promote person-centred practice

Here, you will be required to develop, implement and evaluate plans to ensure colleagues have appropriate training, development and support to promote person-centred practice.

Managers are responsible for planning for the future and this will require you to estimate what you will require in terms of staffing and training, for example, so that the service is ready for any changes on the horizon. Your plan will identify how the service intends to meet the needs of its service users and how it will develop the service provision for the future.

Your planning for the future needs to ensure that the staff are fully aware of how the organisation values training which upskills its staff and enables them to recognise individual health and care needs.

For example, staff may need to be encouraged to undertake the Care Certificate training. Supervision and appraisal sessions may also be an opportunity for staff to demonstrate what they understand by person-centred care and they can be encouraged to reflect on the organisation's values and their own practice. However, there may be constraints on how far staff are able to enable clients to live full and purposeful lives when it comes to service delivery, and of course some things may be difficult to achieve. Positive outcomes for individuals are possible only if they are fully involved in deciding what that positive outcome will be. In planning an individual's care, we need to have systems in place which allow them to be at the centre of that care and be an equal partner in the decisions made. It may, therefore, require a change to the ethos and values of the setting, so that:

- there are systems in place which do something more for the client than simply allowing them to have choice. They are those in which the person is valued, has dignity and is treated as the unique person they truly are
- there is demonstrable respect for the person and care staff take the time to really get to know the person and take into account all their cultural and religious choices, and values and preferences
- there is equality in a relationship and support for the client to live the life they want in the circumstances they find themselves in. It's about them, not us!

Evidence opportunity

2.2 Develop, implement and evaluate plans to ensure team members have appropriate training, development and support to promote person-centred practice

Show your assessor how you develop, implement and evaluate plans to ensure colleagues have appropriate training, development and support to promote person-centred practice.

AC 2.3 Manage others to work with individuals, ensuring that they adapt their approaches to meet an individual's changing needs

Here, you will be required to provide evidence of how you manage others to work with those in receipt of care and support, ensuring that you adapt your approaches to meet an individual's changing needs.

The person who is at the centre of decision making has to feel they are actively involved. Too often a client may feel they are merely a passive attendant at a meeting, with little say in what goes on. We take for granted the work we do, with all its related administration, meetings and bureaucracy. For service users, this may seem rather overwhelming and it would take a lot of confidence on their part to question anything put forward. You need to enable your staff to ensure that individuals are happy to participate in their care. This may require managing them in following a set process that ensures needs are consistently met. For example, you could manage the implementation of a step-by-step process. This is covered in Unit 504 LO2 AC 2.4.

In adapting approaches to account for emerging or changing needs, there needs to be an evaluation of the care process that has been undertaken. Sometimes emergencies happen and we need to review the care. A service user may deteriorate overnight, for example, and require a more hands-on approach to care. Person-centred practice recognises that needs change over time and plans for a change in the service provision. We may need to inform family, friends, advocates and other professionals of the changes that have occurred and which may affect the part they play in the care.

Reflect on it

2.3 Changing needs

Reflect on an incident in which you and the team needed to adapt the care approach in response to one of your service user's changing needs or preferences. How did this affect the person-centred approach?

Evidence opportunity

2.3 Managing others to adapt approaches

Provide evidence of how you manage the staff to work with those in receipt of care and support, ensuring that they adapt their approaches to meet an individual's changing needs.

For example, during supervision you might 'action plan' staff to provide examples of how they react to a client's changing needs. You may ask them what strategies they use to give their clients the confidence to speak up.

Perhaps they could provide a sample care plan with annotations to show where each step has been accomplished.

AC 2.4 Manage resources to ensure that reviews of individuals' preferences, wishes, needs and strengths are valued within the achievement of positive outcomes

Here, you will be required to manage resources to ensure that reviews of individuals' preferences, wishes, needs and strengths are valued within the achievement of positive outcomes.

As the manager you are sometimes limited with respect to the resources you have at your disposal. Individual needs and wishes should, however, be a priority and you will need to look carefully at the resources you have to achieve this where possible. For example, it may simply require some clever redeployment of staff to ensure that a service user is able to engage with a hobby or a group meeting outside of the setting.

Evidence opportunity

2.4 Manage resources to ensure that reviews of individuals' preferences, wishes, needs and strengths are valued within the achievement of positive outcomes

Show your assessor how you manage resources to ensure that reviews of individuals' preferences, wishes, needs and strengths are valued within the achievement of positive outcomes.

AC 2.5 Manage resources to ensure that individuals are actively supported to make healthy choices through a person-centred approach

Here, you will be required to manage resources to ensure that individuals are actively informed and supported to make healthy choices through a person-centred approach in maintaining their wellbeing.

Resources

Funding and services

To ensure that our service users have positive outcomes, we need to be clear about the resources at our disposal and how they will be used. Any plan of care produced needs to be financially resourced and to consider the availability of services, which of course may change over time. This is why there needs to be a continual check on what is happening with the service user's care. As a manager, your role is to ensure that the budget you are given is used wisely and you may have to identify where savings may be made elsewhere to ensure financial resources are being put to good use for service user care.

Funding may be reduced or demand for a particular service may increase, making it more difficult for your client to access the service. Adjustments to the plan should be made in accordance with how it is progressing.

When we audit or monitor a provision, we make a judgement as to how the resources have been used and whether there has been a positive impact on the service user. For example, we may have decided that by 'inputting' more funding into a community outing (output), service users will experience improved quality of life, which will result in a positive outcome. The resources here would be seen to be well-used and effective.

We may also monitor the effects of the way in which the programme of activities we have planned for the service users has improved their wellbeing. A simple evaluation questionnaire can provide feedback on whether the service users enjoyed a session to help determine whether we would repeat it. It is likely that you have in place an evaluation system to enable everyone involved in the care to comment and document how that care is working.

Lay carers, the client themselves and the service care providers all need to provide regular feedback about the care package and any need for adjustment. At the start of the whole care planning process, you will have put into place a means for providing feedback. You will also have identified some key people in the process:

● Individual receiving the care.

Being the central figure in the care process, there needs to be a clear process for service users to record how they experience the care receive. This can be achieved by the use of a checklist, perhaps on a weekly or monthly basis, regular contact via email, telephone or meetings with the care manager or the person facilitating the care, and recording the care given on a daily basis on the care plan.

● Family and friends involved in the care.

Feedback from these individuals is valuable, but form filling can be laborious and time consuming. They may feel overwhelmed with having to provide a regular feedback form, so you need to be able to obtain their views in different ways. Perhaps a weekly phone call may be the solution.

● Healthcare professionals and service providers.

It is important that at meetings and in discussion with colleagues and service providers we can determine how the resources are being managed and how well the budget is being used. At these meetings we can also undertake a review of how the care package for the individual is meeting their preferences and achieving a positive outcome for them.

KEY TERM

Lay carer is a person who is not a health professional but gives care to somebody, usually in their own home.

Your staff

The biggest resource at your disposal are your staff and by ensuring they are well-equipped in terms of the training they require to promote good health and healthy choices for service users, you will be able to lead a practice that promotes health.

Care work requires research in terms of well-trained staff and budget being used appropriately. In planning, care staff must be aware that the promotion of good health and giving service users information to help them to make healthier lifestyle choices are as important as managing long-term chronic conditions.

Evidence opportunity

2.5 Manage resources to ensure that individuals are actively supported to make healthy choices through a person-centred approach

Show your assessor how you manage resources to ensure that individuals are actively informed and supported to make healthy choices through a person-centred approach that maintains their wellbeing.

Reflect on it

2.5 Health and healthy choices

Write a short reflective account of how you have promoted the notion of good health and healthy choices in one aspect of your provision and how you engaged the staff with it. For example, how did you promote the idea of nutrition?

Reflect on

2.4, **2.5** Managing resources

1   Give an example of how you have managed resources so that individuals can achieve positive outcomes in your setting.

2   In your workplace how do you promote good health and healthy choices in all aspects of the provision?

3   How does your organisation monitor the resources and evaluate progress towards the achievement of outcomes for your clients? Write a reflective account of the process undertaken and place copies of relevant documentation into your portfolio.

AC 2.6 Implement systems and processes for recording healthcare interventions

Here, you will be required to critically review and evaluate operational systems and processes for recording health and care interventions with those in receipt of care and support.

The process of monitoring and evaluating the care package is about recognising and documenting changes to circumstances. You will already have systems in place that record the care to be provided and to evaluate that care. As a service provider, you are also duty-bound to regularly ask for feedback from clients and their families about how well you do in the delivery of your service.

Records should monitor the progress of the service user towards their outcome so that all staff are able to observe progress and gain information. In order to record the progress, there must be a clear statement of the outcome, a plan of how the outcome will be achieved and regular feedback about progress.

Care assessment and **care plans** are useful systems for documenting care. Handwritten records and notes are still used extensively but increasingly we are favouring electronic formats for storing records. We may, therefore, find that our partners may send information with respect to the individuals we care for in this way. Electronic records may include:

- care plans
- hospital nursing and medical records
- GP and primary healthcare team records
- outpatient records
- test results, including photographs of the patient, X-rays, pathology and other laboratory records.

We may also have letters to and from the patient or their GP, emails, texts and recordings.

All of these records describe the care the individual is receiving and are, therefore, of a confidential nature. As a manager, you must ensure that the systems and processes in place conform to the Data Protection Act (1998) and now GDPR 2018.

It is most important that we do not underestimate the input from carers, family and others in the care of an individual. Should a carer become too ill themselves to continue in the caring role for a while, there must be a procedure in place to ensure that care for the service user can be continued in the way it has been planned.

As a manager, you need to engage with families to ensure that they feel included in the care-planning process and that they have somebody they can access if they need to. Families and other carers can sometimes feel socially isolated so it is useful to have systems in place to inform them about support groups and help that is available.

Another system could be for carers to have a monthly meeting to discuss the progress of the care being given to the service user and to suggest any changes if necessary. There might also be a system in place whereby a carer can telephone a direct number to speak to a staff member about the care.

> **KEY TERM**
>
> A **care or support plan** is a written document or something recorded in service user notes which is an agreement between a service user and an adult care professional to help manage their day-to-day health and care needs.

> **Evidence opportunity**
>
> **2.6 Implementing systems, processes, procedures and practices**
>
> Provide a written account critically reviewing the systems in place by commenting upon the strengths and the weaknesses of the processes.
>
> You may find it useful to collect together the documentation you use to show how you go about recording progress in care and the achievement of client outcomes. Do you think the process and the system you use are useful? Give reasons for your answer.
>
> Also what systems and practices are in place to address the needs of family and other carers?

LO3 Lead practice in health and care methods to achieve person-centred outcomes

AC 3.1 Manage systems and processes which enable early identification and assessment of an individual's current and emerging health needs

Here, you will be required to critically analyse your management systems and processes which enable early identification and assessment of an individual's current and emerging health and care needs, to include the topics we cover here.

In recent years, there have been media articles about the need for early assessment with respect to memory loss and signs of stroke in patients. The National Institute for Health and Care Excellence (NICE) recommends that early assessment should take place to enable planning for the future or, if treatment is to be given, to enable its institution at an early stage. In the case of stroke, the quicker the condition is assessed, the sooner the individual can access treatment and there is the possibility of full recovery. In these cases, then, early assessment is crucial to enable a better outcome for the client.

In all other cases of need, the assessment process should be initiated immediately or as soon as the care requirements of the client change. Early assessment enables the care plan to be implemented with speed and to meet the needs of the client as they arise.

When the assessment takes place, the client needs to be the central figure in the negotiation and this is recognised in legislation as being the optimum process for care planning. Others in the process, including other care workers, family or informal carers, should be clear about their roles and need to know how to record and report on the process.

Any delay that occurs in the assessment process will mean that risk and needs increase and this could lead to care not being given and the service user suffering as a result. The Care Act 2014 clearly states the obligations of the local authority to ensure that service users and carers have access to care services together with an assessment of their circumstances, needs and risks, and also early identification of needs and support.

Recognising and recording individuals' current and emerging health and care needs

During a care assessment, you determine what care needs the individual has, together with the level and type of care and support required to meet those needs. This is a fundamental role of the care worker and a manager. You also need to ensure that the relatives of service users are involved in care planning processes and assessments. The care plan is a continuous process and does not stop when it has been written. The people involved continue to evaluate and act within the plan to help the client to achieve the best quality care.

Understanding the importance of early identification and assessment

The importance of early identification

The health of service users can change at any time and it is good practice to ensure that there are systems in place that can identify these changes early so that treatment and care can be given to accommodate this. For example, a client or service user who develops a chest infection or a urinary tract infection can quickly deteriorate and may be at risk of sepsis, which is a life-threatening condition. Using a system by which staff can easily check the current health status will enable them to escalate their concerns more quickly.

One such system is the National Early Warning Score (NEWS) 2015, which was developed by the Royal College of Physicians to help staff in hospitals recognise symptoms of deterioration. Widely used in acute settings, it is a scoring system which looks at basic physiological measures such as respiratory rate, oxygen saturations, temperature, systolic blood pressure, pulse rate and level of consciousness.

A score is given and any observation that is out of normal parameters is given a higher score. For example, a respiratory rate of 12–20 scores 0 on the scale as this is considered to be within normal range. If the person is showing a respiratory rate of 9–11 respirations per minute (rpm) they score a 1, less than 8 rpm and more than 25 rpm scores a 3. Scoring a 3 will indicate that a major change has occurred and that something is wrong.

It would then be up to the member of staff to inform somebody of this change and to seek help for the client or service user.

The role of the manager

The manager's role here is to ensure that all staff understand the system they are using and are documenting and reporting changes to the trained staff. Some managers conduct 'care rounds' on each shift to keep updated about the service users'/clients' progress. The rounds may take only a few minutes but ensure that the manager remains well-informed about individuals' current and emerging health needs.

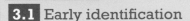

Research it

3.1 Early identification

What early warning system is available for your staff? How are they required to document such changes?

Understanding the importance of assessment

The Social Care Institute for Excellence (2003) states:

> 'Although assessment has been recognised as a core skill in social work and should underpin all social work interventions, there is no singular theory or understanding as to what the purpose of assessment is and what the process should entail.'

With no one theory to support it, the process of assessment then becomes a huge subject and one which potentially might differ with each service in a partnership group. This is why when working with partners we bring together people who know the service user well and can contribute to the care positively. These people may be from other services but may also include family, friends and informal carers.

When this type of working is not done well, this can lead to fragmentation of a service user's care, with many differing approaches to assessing their needs being used at the same time. It becomes imperative, then, to determine how we as care providers will assess the service user and to simplify the process.

Care planning

The care planning process is a good place to start. In any assessment of a client's needs the 'basic helping cycle' shown in Figure 5.3, as suggested by Taylor and Devine (1993), is useful.

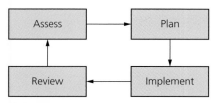

▲ **Figure 5.3** The basic care cycle (based on Taylor and Devine, 1993)

In this basic cycle, the service user and the care professional work together to assess the needs, resources and potential risks for the service user. In doing this, we are responding to the needs of the service user and are also working in conjunction with policy to ensure, for example, that we are providing individualised care and maintaining independence. The care to meet those needs is then planned and put into action at the third stage and finally evaluated or 'reviewed', starting the cycle again.

In 2006 Thompson described what he called the 'ASIRT' model of care planning:

AS – Assessment phase, which is the start of the process and the first part of an action plan leading onto the …

I – Intervention stage when aims and objectives for the intervention are selected

R – Review when the evaluation of what has happened takes place, before finally

T – Termination, when the intervention is no longer needed and can be stopped.

Models of assessment and purpose

The care planning process, however we approach it, is just one part of assessment. Three different models of assessment have been suggested in research by Smale et al. (1993):

- The Questioning Model – in which the care worker leads the process and questions and listens, before processing the information. This means that the process is service led.

- The Procedural Model – in which information is gathered by the care professional who then makes a judgement as to 'best fit' for the service. This is criterion based and a range of checklists is used to determine which service is best for the service user.

- The Exchange Model – in which the care worker views the service user as the expert in their own care needs. This is really the most person-centred approach of the three. This model seems to describe the most holistic form of assessment, with the care professional managing a more client-centred approach.

The types of assessment we carry out will differ according to the setting we are in or according to the types of needs the person has. If the person living in their own home is having difficulty with their personal care, they might consider getting support by having a community care assessment of their needs. These assessments are carried out by social services and can vary, depending on the particular needs of the person being assessed.

Older people

Community care assessments for older people are carried out under the single assessment process.

People with mental health problems

Assessments for people in need of mental health services are carried out under the Care Programme Approach (CPA), which assesses:

- risk and safety
- psychiatric symptoms and experiences
- psychological thoughts and behaviours.

Mental health issues require the help of mental health care professionals and the community care assessment entitles the individual to a care plan that is regularly reviewed by the professional.

If a person has a range of needs and is considered to have severe mental health problems, their care may be coordinated under a CPA and a CPA care coordinator will be appointed to oversee the assessment and planning process. The coordinator is usually a nurse, social worker or occupational therapist.

People with learning disabilities

For service users with learning disabilities, assessment is governed by the principles set out by the 'Valuing People' plan, which aims to improve services for people with learning disabilities by treating them all as individuals. This 'person-centred approach' considers the client's ability to exercise choice and control over their lives.

Other types of assessment include:

- **Needs-led assessment**: In this type of assessment the focus is on the individual's needs in a given situation.

- **User-led assessment or self-assessment**: The responsibility for decisions made about the care of an individual are shared between the care worker and the individual, but the person requiring the care is at the forefront in managing decisions. They assess their needs supported by a health professional and are proactive in determining issues surrounding their care.

- **Single assessment process**: All care agencies need to work together so that assessment and the resultant care plan are effective and coordinated. The Single Assessment Process (SAP) was introduced in the National Service Framework for Older People (2001) in Standard 2: Person-centred care, the aim of which was to ensure that the NHS and social care services treat older people as individuals, enabling them to make choices about their own care.

Many older people have wide-ranging needs and in recognition of that, care must be holistic and centre on the whole person. The requirement to develop a SAP was based on just this fact, so as to provide a person-centred health and social care framework, which includes entry into the system, holistic assessment, care planning, care delivery and review.

In working with partners to deliver care, there is always the potential for repetition of work and overlap of delivery. SAP aims to ensure that the individual's needs are assessed thoroughly and accurately, without duplication by different agencies. By sharing the information appropriately between all relevant agencies, SAP coordinates the assessment and ensures effective delivery care.

In undertaking an evaluation of risk, it is important not to lose sight of person-centred approaches to care and service user choice. (See Unit 508 for more information on risk assessment.) In this approach, risk is identified and assessed to establish the possibility of danger, harm or accident.

Develop others' understanding of the functions of a range of assessment tools

Your understanding of the assessment process is crucial to delivering care that is of a high quality. As a manager of a service you are responsible for ensuring that others, such as carers/family members, advocates and colleagues in your own service and other professionals outside your setting, also understand the process. You therefore need to be able to develop others' understanding of assessment and why it is beneficial to the service user, as well as how they can contribute.

Research it

3.1 Assessment tools

Research other types of assessment, including resource-led assessment.

There are a number of tools at our disposal which enable us to assess various functions and care activities. For example:

- Subjective Units of Distress Scale (SUDS) to measure anxiety levels
- pain assessment scales to determine severity and types of pain
- scales to measure activities of daily living
- scales to measure pressure area risk
- Patient Health Questionnaire – PHQ-9, which measures severity of depression.
- Glasgow Coma Scale (GCS) used to rate the severity of coma.

Evidence opportunity

3.1 Assessment and others' understanding

Consider the different forms of assessment used in your care setting and determine how useful they are and what changes might be made to improve what you are doing.

Undertake a staff training session to ensure that 'others' have an understanding of the assessment tools in use.

Research it

3.1 Assessment tools

Research a couple of the assessment tools discussed and identify their use in your assessment process.

Reflect on it

3.1, **4.1** Assessment

Reflect on the staff training session you undertook on assessment. What have you learned from it? What were the strengths and limitations of the session?

Your role as a manager

As a healthcare professional and as a manager, your duty is to provide safe care and to ensure that the staff are equally competent. Staff may therefore need to undertake further training on how to carry out assessments or may require assistance to do so and your role as manager is to support them in this. Job descriptions which clearly outline roles in the position for which staff are employed are invaluable in ensuring boundaries are not breached.

Maintaining health and care records in line with requirements

As we have seen in other units (see Units 502 and 503), it is essential to keep accurate and confidential records of the service user's health and care preferences. These:

- provide an account of the care given (although they do not show what the quality of that care was)
- give a record of continuous care (in the case of nursing and medical records)
- provide a source of reference for care
- provide an audit and quality assurance trail
- are a legal requirement.

As a manager, it is your responsibility to ensure that the systems for record keeping conform to the General Data Protection Regulation 2018 and that your policy for data protection and confidentiality is up to date and being used by staff.

Advance care planning and end-of-life wishes

Advance care planning is the process of discussing the service user's preferences and wishes about future treatment. The family and care team are involved in this discussion so that everybody is clear about what the service user wants. The plan will detail such things as where the service user wishes to be cared for, who needs to be consulted about the care and what treatments will be acceptable and which will not. If the service user becomes very sick and cannot speak or make decisions, this advance care planning directive can help care professionals to make decisions.

Escalating changes and getting treatment for symptoms may, of course, not be what the service user desires and we need to be clear about the sort of treatment they want when they are nearing the end of their life. A service user with a chronic condition may decline treatment that would prolong their life, and this needs to be clearly indicated in their notes and on their care plan. They may wish to put into place a Do Not Attempt Resuscitation form (DNAR) which means the medical team would not attempt cardiopulmonary resuscitation (CPR). As this directive only covers cardiac arrest, for other life-threatening conditions the service user may

decide they want no treatment to keep them alive. If so, they should look to completing an 'advance decision to refuse treatment', also sometimes called a 'living will' or 'an advance directive'. Either way, it is legally binding.

One of the main areas in which you can set yourself apart as a good leader is to support and facilitate your team. Giving care at the end of life requires staff to provide the most exemplary work for the families and the service user involved, and to do this they need to know that they are in an organisational environment that keeps them safe and gives them support.

As a leader, you need to ensure that supervision is available to address the care worker's emotional and development needs, and that staff have manageable workloads. You will also need to train staff so they have the correct skills to deal with the difficult emotions that can arise when working in end-of-life care. The team need to understand their roles in supporting people and be fully aware of issues around mental capacity, advance decisions and Safeguarding of Vulnerable Adults (SOVA), and this can be ensured by establishing systems and procedures that encourage information sharing and good communication.

At this time, staff may feel vulnerable and emotional and so a compassionate attitude is required to support them. Having empathy for how they are feeling and being aware of how this may affect performance at this time are useful qualities to exhibit.

You will also need to look at your agreed ways of working, as well as government guidance around end-of-life strategy.

End-of-life care does not finish when the person dies. In fact, this can be a time fraught with all sorts of issues that require other service involvement. For example, the death must be certificated and there may be a need to contact the coroner. Additionally, the service user may have expressed a wish for organ donation, so the team concerned with this will need to be contacted.

The way in which the body is handled and prepared for burial or cremation also requires sensitive handling and the staff dealing with this must be aware of cultural and religious differences. All of these factors must be considered and be a part of the care planning process and discussions before the service user dies. You can gain more information at www.gov.uk/government/publications/2010-to-2015-government-policy-end-of-life-care/2010-to-2015-government-policy-end-of-life-care.

Evidence opportunity

3.1 Systems and processes which enable early identification and assessment

Provide a written account critically evaluating your management systems and processes that enable early identification and assessment of an individual's current and emerging health and care needs. Include the topics we have covered.

You might like to identify all the management systems and processes in your setting which enable early identification and assessment of an individual's current and emerging health and care, and answer the following:

1 How do your staff recognise and record clients' or service users' current and emerging health and care needs?

2 Do they understand the importance of early identification and assessment?

3 What records are maintained with respect to advanced care planning and end-of-life wishes?

As a manager, you are responsible for ensuring that service users in your care remain safe at all time and this requires you to put into place systems and processes which enable early identification and assessment of an individual's needs. Staff need to be well-trained to use such systems confidently and they will need to feel supported. You also need to ensure that all methods and systems in use relate ultimately to person-centred care and outcomes.

AC 3.2 Implement and evaluate protocols for safe healthcare practice which actively promote positive outcomes

Here, you will be required to implement and evaluate protocols for safe health and care practices which actively promote positive wellbeing/outcomes for the areas we discuss in this section.

You will have processes and protocols in your setting to ensure safe health and care practices which actively promote positive wellbeing and outcomes for many aspects of individuals' lives. For example, you have a handwashing protocol to ensure that service users remain safe from infection and a protocol for resuscitation. Any protocol which is in place needs to be person-centred and many focus upon clinical needs, as shown in the example above. How do you ensure that individuals' psychological, social and spiritual needs are met?

Individuals' psychological, social and spiritual needs

A subjective view of psychological wellbeing would be to say that we are happy or satisfied with our lives. But this is fraught with difficulty since what makes you happy is unlikely to be the same for service users or other care workers. In order to feel really good and to have fulfilling lives, we need to experience purpose and meaning as well as positive emotions. Psychologist Carol Ryff has developed a clear model of psychological wellbeing that breaks it down into six key parts:

1 Self-acceptance.

2 Positive relations with others.

3 Autonomy.

4 Environmental mastery.

5 Purpose in life.

6 Personal growth.

Source: From Ryff's 1989 Psychological Wellbeing Inventory

If we are to lead practice that promotes social, emotional, cultural, spiritual and intellectual wellbeing, we need to be aware of the factors that can contribute to this.

Psychological wellbeing is about enabling service users to experience a well-rounded and balanced life and the emotions that go with this.

The Care Act 2014 definition of wellbeing

The DOH (2014) Care and Support Statutory Guidance, issued under the Care Act 2014 defines wellbeing as a broad concept, relating to the following areas:

- personal dignity (including treatment with respect)
- physical and mental health and emotional wellbeing, protection from abuse and neglect
- control by the individual over day-to-day life (including care and support)
- participation in work, education, training or recreation
- social and economic wellbeing, which refers to being actively engaged with life and with other people and having a positive standard of living based primarily on financial security
- domestic, family and personal issues
- suitability of living accommodation
- the individual's contribution to society.

Ensuring the wellbeing of our clients and even our staff requires us as managers to determine how we might measure the state of wellbeing. When things are not going well and our joy in life and general sense of calm are lacking, we start to experience stress, worry and anxiety. Our psychological wellbeing becomes compromised and this will inevitably lead to our quality of life being reduced. For the people in our care, this can lead to depression and its subsequent effects on physical wellbeing and health.

As a manager you need to implement and develop protocols which reflect how you can ensure that individuals in your care are able to experience a well-rounded life where they feel safe and free to make choices about how they live. We need to always keep in mind those processes that actively promote positive outcomes for all in our care. Social and economic wellbeing comes with being actively engaged with life and having a positive standard of living.

Maslow in his hierarchy of needs outlined the things that contribute to a person's wellbeing – see Figure 1.2 on page 5.

Individuals' physical health, mental health and mobility

In planning care for positive outcomes, the care worker needs to work with the client to ensure that the best services are offered to meet their needs. Care planning is about what the client needs and wants, not about what the care worker can arrange for them. Sometimes this may lead to conflict. For example, we, as care professionals, recognise that obesity can cause health issues and we may believe that it is in the service user's best interests to change their diet. However, the choice remains with them and we can only investigate services that may be of use to them; we are not at liberty to insist they use them.

Some of the things you may be asked to help with are outlined below:

- You may agree to therapeutic/development activities as requested by the service user.
- The service user may require help with assistive technology, for example in order to improve their communication, so we may need to find suitable help. They may need a variety of equipment to keep them mobile and we need to assess and assist in this.
- Service users who are unable to visit the GP or other health professional may require assistance to set up an appointment for health checks, for example, or may just require help to get to an appointment. Occasionally, a client may have a change in their cognitive function due to either mental health issues or dementia changes and will then require additional help.
- The service user may require help with administering prescribed medication/treatment. Any medication prescribed for the service user will need to be administered at the correct time but occasionally it may be in a form that is difficult for the individual to take so we can help by accessing easier ways in which medication might be administered.
- You may agree to promote/support healthy lifestyle choices. Service users may need additional help to undertake changes to their lifestyle and as health care workers we should be able to give information as to how change may be effected, such as providing information about diet, smoking and exercise.

The essential factor in any care planning and provision is to adopt a holistic approach, recognising that all service users – young, older or those with disabilities (either physical or a learning disability) – are individuals with needs that impact upon their lives (Figure 5.4). It is important to give individuals choice and doing so requires you to have information about services which are available. Assistive technology (AT) is improving all the time and we need to be up to date with what is available for our service users. For example, for older people, simply introducing amplification devices may make communication with everybody more effective. Those individuals with mobility issues may benefit from having a scooter so they can travel over distances. AT is anything that helps an individual to actively undertake daily activities on their own, allowing them to live more independently.

Your staff must be aware of all the options available and need to be able to give out that information in an unbiased way. You may be asked, 'What would you do or what would you choose?' In most cases the answer has to be, 'I am not you and it is for you to decide.' All these activities should be implemented in the context of safe health and care protocols, which may include following particular processes and recording decisions and outcomes.

▲ **Figure 5.4** Care workers should use appropriate ways to meet the care needs of individuals

Health and care practices

Typical health care procedures include blood sugar level testing, urine testing, catheter care, tissue viability and wound care. Those that involve invasive procedures require consent from the service user. This can be a simple verbal agreement, but the care worker must never assume that the practice can be carried out in the course of giving care. They need to specifically inform the service user what they want to do and ask if that is acceptable. Any refusal must be documented.

Active participation of individuals in working towards healthy outcomes

Active participation on the part of the service user can also be sought. For example, a service user who requires regular anticoagulation therapy can be taught how to give their own injections. They may also be willing to test their own blood sugar levels and to chart them themselves.

In managing this part of care work it is important to have in place policies which help staff to understand their roles. Training for staff may be needed in this.

To aid the client in active participation, the best way to proceed is to ask the questions, 'what would you like, what do you need, and how are you feeling at the moment?' By actively encouraging the client to voice their needs, concerns and how they would like their care needs met, a good rapport is developed and the client will feel actively involved in all decisions. Occasionally we may find that the client is not fully able to engage with the process due to conditions that prevent understanding or sensory impairments which may make the process difficult. In this case an **advocate** needs to be called in to act on their behalf and to ensure they are fully represented.

The NHS recognises that the patient is an expert in their own care and thus developed the Expert Patients Programme (EPP) (2007), which is specifically designed for those with chronic conditions. People living with conditions that are long term know more about their condition and the way in which to manage it than health professionals, and as such are more than able to communicate their needs and what support they may require. Go to www.nhs.uk/NHSEngland/AboutNHSservices/doctors/Pages/expert-patients-programme.aspx for more information.

KEY TERM

Advocates represent individuals or speak on their behalf to ensure that their rights are supported.

AC 3.3 Foster active participation of individuals

Here, you will be required to implement ways of working that ensure that individuals will be able use, develop, extend or relearn skills for daily activities and achievement of personal outcomes.

A study commissioned by the Joseph Rowntree Foundation and carried out by Wilcox et al. (1994) outlined ten key ideas about active participation and, in particular, community participation. Although this study is an old one, not much has changed with respect to participation, although SCIE has now adopted the term 'co-production' to describe working in partnership by sharing power with people using services, carers, families and citizens.

Co-production describes the key features of the concept as being the sharing of power within the care relationship. Individuals who use services in this are seen as assets with skills and are not merely told what is being planned or consulted about decisions. They work with peer and personal support networks alongside professional services and 'facilitate services by helping organisations to become agents for change rather than just being service providers'. It builds on service users' existing capabilities and breaks down the barriers between people who use services and professionals (New Economics Foundation, 2012).

One definition of co-production is:

> 'Co-production is not just a word, it's not just a concept, it is a meeting of minds coming together to find a shared solution. In practice, it involves people who use services being consulted, included and working together from the start to the end of any project that affects them.' (TLAP, 2011)

Evidence opportunity

3.2 Protocols

You will need to show your assessor how you implement and evaluate protocols for safe health and care practices that actively promote positive wellbeing/outcomes for the areas we have discussed here.

You could provide a written account evaluating the policies and protocols for safe health and care practices that actively promote positive wellbeing that apply to your setting.

How have they been implemented in your setting?

You need to say how you managed the implementation process. For example, new protocols may not be fully understood by staff, so you may have had to undertake some staff training and then had a trial run to see how it worked. In evaluating this process say what worked well and what did not, and why you think this was the case. How would you change the way in which you introduced the new protocols?

Provide evidence to show your assessor.

Systems and processes that promote active participation

The Wilcox et al. publication, *The Guide to Effective Participation*, identifies key ideas as follows.

A five-rung ladder of participation relating to the stance an organisation promoting participation may take is:

- **Information**: telling people what is planned.
- **Consultation:** offering options, listening to feedback, but not allowing new ideas.
- **Deciding together**: encouraging additional options and ideas, and providing opportunities for joint decision making.
- **Acting together**: not only do different interests decide together on what is best, they form a partnership to carry it out.
- **Supporting independent community interests**: local groups or organisations are offered funds, advice or other support to develop their own agendas within guidelines.

Your policies and procedures which are in place will support this.

Problems in participation

Problems in participation develop because of poor preparation within the promoting organisation – with the result that when community interest is engaged, the organisation cannot deliver on its promises. There needs to be a process or system in place to allow others to be involved and to allow the process to be controlled and monitored.

The initiator or person in control, and in your role as manager this may be you, can decide how much or how little control to allow to others – for example, just information, or a major say in what is to happen.

Many organisations fear loss of control and may be unwilling to allow people to participate. However, working together allows everyone to achieve more than they could on their own. The Wilcox guide emphasises the difference between power to and power over. People are empowered when they have the power to achieve what they want.

Many participation processes involve breaking new ground – tackling difficult projects and setting up new forms of organisations. Training may be needed or the opportunity to learn formally and informally, to develop confidence and trust in each other.

The above is adapted from the findings of *Community Participation and Empowerment: Putting Theory into Practice* by David Wilcox, published in 1994 by the Joseph Rowntree Foundation. Reproduced by permission of the Joseph Rowntree Foundation.

The process above is very much a social work model of practice and can be seen in initiatives such as the Sure Start programme. When arranging care packages for service users, it is important to involve as many partners in the community as possible in order to widen choice and options. By having an understanding of community developments, you are better able to refer service users to the right services.

Other systems and processes to support service users include policies and procedures. For example, risk assessment needs to form part of the systems and processes. You should also agree on how the care required is assessed in your workplace and how wishes, choices and preferences are agreed upon and met.

Participation in daily activities

In healthcare we use the term 'daily living activities' to refer to daily self-care activities such as:

- personal hygiene
- dressing and undressing
- self-feeding
- mobility and transfers (getting from bed to wheelchair, or the ability to get on or off the toilet, etc.)
- bowel and bladder management.

As professionals, we must assess our clients to determine their ability or inability to perform these daily living activities. By measuring in this way, we gain knowledge of the client's functional status and can determine how independent a client is. This has been impacted by law, which requires us to practise in safe and humane ways.

A managerial responsibility here is to determine the ways in which staff are enabling the clients in their care to actively participate in their care. This can be done by observing practice and through the appraisal system.

Evidence opportunity

3.3 Active participation

You will need to show your assessor how you implement ways of working that ensure that individuals will be able to use, develop, extend or relearn skills for daily activities and achievement of personal outcomes.

Show evidence of the systems and processes in your own work that promote active participation.

How effective are the systems and processes in ensuring that active participation is working?

AC 3.4 Maintain healthcare records in line with legislation and organisational requirements

Here, you will need to show you can ensure your service maintains health and care records in line with legislation and organisational requirements and review the need for further improvement(s).

The importance of good record keeping cannot be underestimated (Figure 5.5). Should an incident occur with a client/patient, you may be required to attend court if a claim for compensation is made or you are required to report on this incident. Records can be used in court as evidence to show compliance with policies and procedures. Unfortunately, we live in a highly litigious society and in order to protect ourselves when we are being held accountable for the care we give, we need to be aware of how important records are. If a complaint is made against us, we would be hard pushed to answer if we had inadequately prepared records. If negligence or a breach of health and safety is suspected in any care setting, any records and statements pertaining to the case will be taken and scrutinised.

If your records are less than accurate, you may find yourself in a difficult situation. Any records maintained need to be:

- accurate
- ordered
- up to date
- stored safely and securely.

▲ **Figure 5.5** Good record keeping is vital in a health and social care setting

Compliance with GDPR 2018

On 25 May 2018, the General Data Protection Regulation replaced the Data Protection Act 1998. This is a new regulation by which the European Parliament, the Council of the European Union and the European Commission strengthened data protection for all individuals within the European Union. It addressed the export of personal data outside the EU and gave citizens and residents control over their personal data. Go to https://ico.org.uk/for-organisations/data-protection-reform/overview-of-the-gdpr/accountability-and-governance for further details.

It is a legal requirement to protect any data we may have on our clients/patients and/or staff and to maintain it in a confidential way. Any unsuitable use of such information or any breach of confidentiality needs to be dealt with promptly and must be reported to you, the manager. The security of information is a safeguard for vulnerable service users and any breach of that security can be detrimental to those service users.

The National Fundamental Standards for care require that all organisation records relating to health and safety matters are accurate and kept up to date. Standard 10 requires good record keeping to be a vital part of good practice, with clear instructions given to all staff as to what information should be recorded and in what form.

You will be familiar with accident records and may have had to complete these from time to time. We can become blasé or relaxed about these, but we rely on these records, and if years later the case becomes part of a legal process, we need to be able to return to the records to remind us of what actually was done at the time.

Records, then, do the following:

- provide an account of the care given
- give a record of continuous care (in the case of nursing and medical records)
- provide a source of reference for care
- provide an audit and quality assurance trail
- are a legal requirement
- give evidence of compliance with health and safety guidelines and law.

Additionally, anything that is of a serious nature, such as a reportable disease, serious injury or death, must be reported under Reporting of Injuries, Diseases and Dangerous Occurrences Regulations (RIDDOR) (2013).

Dimond (1997) highlighted the major areas of concern in such care reports. She revealed that in many records there were major omissions.

Our responsibility with respect to record keeping is clear. We need to make records on service users, but the way in which we use and store that information is paramount. We must handle all information effectively and be aware of the need to maintain confidentiality of that information. The following checklist may be useful to ensure that you and your staff are aware of good record keeping. It also addresses major omissions that Dimond highlighted.

- Have I written legibly?
- Have I put information in time order, as it happened?
- Have I got dates and times in the record, and are they accurately recorded?
- Have I put in signs and symptoms? I might even have written how the service user/client is feeling, i.e. client details are recorded accurately.
- Did I carry out a risk assessment?
- Have I included names of other people involved, e.g. callers and visitors, and recorded information about them accurately?
- Have I written in a professional manner?
- Have I recorded things clearly? Are abbreviations clarified?
- Have I signed the forms/records?
- Have I completed records in time, without delay?

Evidence opportunity

3.4 Healthcare records

Supply evidence to show that the health and care records in your setting are maintained in line with legislation and organisational requirements. Is there anything that needs to be improved?

AC 3.5 Champion accountability when carrying out health and care procedures

Here, you will be required to show how you champion accountability when carrying out health and care procedures to include recommendations for developing practice with colleagues and others, including the areas we discuss here.

Being accountable means we take responsibility for the things we do. In healthcare, we take responsibility for any task we perform. As health service providers, we are accountable in law and must ensure that our activities meet legal requirements.

Ensuring staff understand their accountability when undertaking health and care procedures to include reporting any concerns

Employees are accountable to their employer and are duty-bound to work within their contract. Partners in care are also accountable and as a manager you need to ensure that those with whom you work in partnership also have accountability policies in place.

All practitioners in the care setting are duty-bound to perform competently and they should be able to feel they can inform somebody if they are concerned about any task

they do not feel able to do. A transparent and open system of being able to report any problems must be in practice if care work is to remain safe.

Management of care is inherently unpredictable and risky. It is not always possible to anticipate the outcome of interventions and, therefore, the requirement for safe and effective care cannot be focused on outcome alone. If called to account, the practitioner must be able to demonstrate that the activity was within their scope of knowledge and responsibility, that they had performed the activity based on best or accepted practice standards, that they had assessed the individual risks in this situation and tried to manage these appropriately, and had, wherever possible, involved and sought informed consent from the individual affected by the activity. Accidents and unfortunate outcomes still occur, but all reasonable action must have been taken to try to avoid them.

Good management demands that we hold people accountable for what they do or don't do and the way you do this can make or break the relationship.

When goals were not met due to something the employee has failed to do, then it is appropriate for them to be held accountable for this failure. But if we are trying to hold employees accountable for things that are out of their control, that is unreasonable, and we will lose the trust we have with the staff.

- **Be consistent**: The key ingredient is consistency and your staff will expect to be called to account if goals are not met or jobs are not done. The way in which you do this is also important – dealing with someone about a performance error in a firm but kind way in private is much better than berating or criticising them in public. Additionally, it is important that all staff are dealt with in the same way, otherwise the sense of injustice is great and trust is lost.
- **Build relationships**: As a manager there is a distance between you and your staff but those leaders and managers who take the time to build relationships will gain the trust of their staff. It is a wise manager who takes time to find out a little about their staff and to share a little about themselves. You are likely to remember a manager who takes an interest and asks about your family or is happy to share a few words, for example.
- **Be honest**: Trust builds respect and it is this that gets results. We can cultivate trust by being transparent and honest in what we are thinking and doing. We show ourselves to be trustworthy managers by being consistent and the sort of person who can be relied upon.

It is important to remember service users require staff who are confident and happy in their work and this can be achieved only if managers are able to encourage this in their team.

The importance of consent and maintaining confidentiality

The Health and Social Care Act 2008 (Regulated Activities) Regulations 2014: Regulation 11 refers to consent in care. Consent means that a person must give permission before they receive any type of treatment, examination or diagnostic test, and this must be done following explanation of what is planned. For consent to be valid, the person must have the capacity to make the decision and must do so voluntaril, although if the person doesn't have capacity the healthcare professionals treating them can go ahead and give treatment if they believe it to be in the person's best interests. It is reasonable to expect that advice is sought from the service user's friends or relatives before making these decisions.

As health professionals we are accountable for ensuring that the correct information with respect to the consent for treatment is given.

Information sharing and confidentiality

The DOH (2003) Confidentiality NHS Code of Practice identifies the best practice for information sharing and the guidance outlines the NHS commitment to the delivery of a first-class confidential service ensuring that all:

- patient information is processed fairly, lawfully and as transparently as possible so that the public:
  - understand the reasons for processing personal information
  - give their consent for the disclosure and use of their personal information
  - gain trust in the way the NHS handles information and
  - understand their rights to access information held about them.

Any patient information you keep may be passed on for a particular purpose with the patient's consent or on a need-to-know basis. You also need to ensure that the patient is fully informed about how the information about them may be used.

The guidance stresses the importance of anonymising personal information wherever possible to minimise the risk of security breaches in your systems. Threats to security can be accidental and due to human error or failure, due to

naturally occurring events such as fire, or from deliberate breaches from external hackers.

The responsibility for maintaining confidentiality lies with the manager and you need to be convinced that your policies and procedures are appropriate and operational within your area.

Before you read on, you should go to, Unit 503 AC 3.1 to read about Beauchamp and Childress' definition of confidentiality.

In addition to the text you referred back to, the Caldicott Report recommendations, which became part of the Data Protection Act in 1998, recommended the appointment of a person in every organisation to be responsible for the maintenance of confidentiality. In care homes this would be a senior staff member (or manager) who would be legally required to ensure that a policy was in place to protect the individual in the home.

The most important of the principles outlined were:

- The purpose of the information and the transfer of such should be clearly justified.
- Client-identifiable information should be limited if possible.
- Accessibility – staff should be permitted to access information on a need-to-know basis only.
- Staff should be made aware of their responsibilities with respect to confidentiality.
- All information kept on the client must conform to law.

From an ethical point of view, in maintaining confidentiality, health professionals explicitly or implicitly make a promise to their service users to keep confidential the information they receive, thus respecting the autonomy of the client. But problems arise when decisions need to be made about sharing certain personal information. For example, Article 10 of the Convention on Human Rights and Biomedicine states: 'Everyone has the right to respect for private life in relation to information about his/her health care' (European Parliament & Council of the European Union, 1995).

In gaining consent and maintaining confidentiality care staff are accountable for the way in which they proceed. Accountability is about taking responsibility for any actions and ensuring that you put service users'/clients' interests first and that you are competent to do the activity. This means that you need to be able to justify what you do and should be able to articulate why you are doing it.

Reflect on it

3.5 Consent and confidentiality

Reflect on the legal and ethical tensions between maintaining confidentiality and sharing information in your own workplace and write a short piece about them. How does this impact you in the setting?

How do you obtain consent from your clients within your role? What do you understand about the legal implications of doing so?

Consideration of other professionals and their responsibilities and limits relating to the health and care procedures

While we as individuals are accountable to our clients, to whom we owe a 'duty of care', we are also accountable to our employer and to the other people employed within the setting. In contracts of employment, the duties expected of care workers are laid out and we are duty bound to carry these out safely and effectively. As a manager, you need to support staff in their efforts but must also be prepared to invoke disciplinary measures should there be a failure in this respect. Your responsibility to staff and other professionals then is to ensure that:

- the boundaries of their role is clear
- agreed protocols to guide care delivery are available
- they have support and supervision
- they have opportunities to develop
- they understand the issues about delegation
- they are aware of the limitations of their roles as well as their responsibilities.

Accountability means complying with the code of conduct for healthcare workers and any codes your organisation has in place.

Ways to improve integrated working which fosters accountability, high standards of practice and seamless service provision

Your role as a team leader and a manager is a most important one, particularly in today's climate, which demands the delivery of quality care in a multidisciplinary way, working with partnerships from various parts of the care service. You are responsible for ensuring not only that staff morale remains high but that seamless service provision is given to the clients and service users. So how do you accomplish this?

There needs to be a high level of trust within the organisation so that staff feel supported and able to take initiative in what they do. Staff should also feel safe to take responsibility and be accountable for their actions. A good

team spirit and encouraging staff to work with the team and keep team members informed about the results of their work will go a long way to building trust and stability in the workforce. Staff must be aware that accountability is essential because when we don't practise accountability in our daily work then there is a tendency for things just not to get done. This will then have an impact upon the whole team and eventually the organisation. A missed deadline may become a habit and staff may start to miss deadlines for work more frequently. Accountability needs to become a team value and as a manager it is your duty to ensure that staff feel safe to express themselves when problems occur.

Evidence opportunity

3.5 Champion accountability when carrying out health and care procedures

Show your assessor how you champion accountability when carrying out adult care procedures. Include recommendations for developing practice with colleagues and others, and address the areas we have covered here.

KEY TERM

Accountability is taking responsibility and being liable or answerable for something.

Reflect on it

3.5 Championing accountability

What do you understand by the term accountability when carrying out health and care procedures? Write a short piece on how you ensure that your staff are accountable for their actions.

Give an example of how staff report concerns.

Consider (honestly) how you react to problems and concerns of staff.

Give one example from practice.

LO4 Champion equality, diversity and inclusion to achieve positive outcomes

The importance of understanding **equality**, respect for **diversity** and **inclusion** in care work cannot be overestimated. It is important that practice in your setting is reinforced by the principles of equality and diversity and that staff are aware of policies and procedures and it is your responsibility as a manager to ensure all of this. For example, this can be done through training and meetings.

KEY TERMS

Equality means treating individuals or groups of individuals fairly and equally irrespective of race, gender, disability, religion or belief, sexual orientation and age.
Diversity in this context is equal respect for people who are from different backgrounds.
Inclusion is positive behaviour to ensure all people have an opportunity to be included and not be unfairly excluded because of their individual characteristics.

AC 4.1 Investigate the legal context underpinning equality, diversity and inclusion relating to adult care services

In this section, within your own service area, you must show that you understand the impact and effectiveness of equality, diversity and inclusion legislation in preventing discrimination and exclusion on people using health and care services.

The manager has a key role in ensuring that equality and anti-discriminatory practice are promoted as core organisational values and that the law is complied with. Public sector organisations and other organisations that carry out public functions, such as in the health and social care sector, must have 'due regard' to eliminate conduct that is prohibited under the Equality Act.

The Equality Act 2010 provides for the protection of people and their different characteristics, with specific protections in respect of:

- age
- disability
- gender reassignment
- pregnancy and maternity/paternity
- race
- religion or belief
- sex/gender
- sexual orientation.

Legislation

The Equality Act 2010

The Equality Act (2010) clearly identifies that if a health or social care organisation provides goods, facilities, services or functions to the public then it must make sure that it does so within the requirements of the law. The act brought together a number of individual pieces of legislation into one law in order to make the law on equality, diversity and discrimination much clearer and simpler.

The Equality Act 2010 applies to any organisation that provides goods, facilities or services to the public or to a section of the public. The act applies to private, statutory and voluntary organisations, no matter their size. Equality law affects everyone running an organisation as well as applying to the staff and volunteers who might do something on behalf of the organisation.

The nine main pieces of legislation that merged to form the new Equality Act are:

- Equal Pay Act 1970
- Sex Discrimination Act 1975
- Race Relations Act 1976
- Disability Discrimination Act 1995
- Employment Equality (Religion or Belief) Regulations 2003
- Employment Equality (Sexual Orientation) Regulations 2003
- Employment Equality (Age) Regulations 2006
- Equality Act 2006, Part 2
- Equality Act (Sexual Orientation) Regulations 2007.

Human Rights Act 1998

Everyone in the UK is entitled to the same basic human rights and freedoms. The act supports individuals' rights to dignity and respect and to be treated fairly when accessing care or support services.

Special Educational Needs and Disability Act 2001

All education settings are required to make reasonable adjustments for people with disabilities so that they can be offered the same opportunities and choices as people who do not have disabilities, e.g. a specialist support person for an individual with a learning disability or the provision of teaching and learning materials in alternative formats such as in Braille for individuals with sight loss.

The Children and Families Act 2014 and the Special Educational Needs and Disabilities (SEND) Code of Practice 2014

These introduce new legislation regarding adoption and family justice. Part 3 includes a new Special Educational Needs and Disabilities (SEND) Code of Practice. This supersedes the Code of Practice from 2001 (but does not replace the Special Educational Needs and Disability Act 2001). You can find more information here: www.gov.uk/government/publications/send-code-of-practice-0-to-25.

Care Act 2014

This says that information and services for the provision of care and support should be made fairer and clearer to everyone involved. See Unit 504 AC 2.3 for more information.

The Mental Capacity Act 2005

Additionally, the Mental Capacity Act (MCA) 2005 empowers individuals who may lack the mental capacity to make their own decisions. The impact of this act for service users has been to liberate them from previous restrictive practices in which they had no say over their care or treatment. Forward planning can now be undertaken and advance statements about what will happen when the service users no longer have capacity to speak for themselves are put into place.

Evidence opportunity

4.1 Investigate the legal context underpinning equality, diversity and inclusion

Speak to your assessor, or provide a written account showing that, within your own service area, you understand the impact and effectiveness of equality, diversity and inclusion legislation in preventing discrimination and exclusion for service users.

Reflect on it

4.1 Impact of legislation and policy

Which law has had the most impact upon the care you give to your service users? For example, you may comment on how the MCA has changed the way you undertake assessment for care.

AC 4.2 Evaluate policies, systems, processes and practices that promote equality, diversity and inclusion

Here, you will be required to show you can lead practice with others in reviewing and evaluating current systems and processes and making improvements where required in respect of the above.

Your organisation's culture

The culture of an organisation will have a powerful and pervasive influence over the behaviour and practices of the people within that organisation (Mullins, 2009).

Organisations are complicated places, where complex interactions occur between individuals. The complexity and interdependency of relationships support an environment in which conflicts of interest and power differentials can be abused if appropriate policies, practices and safeguards are not in place to counteract this.

Formal power structures are necessary in most organisations. These structures are supported by policies and procedures which provide a framework to help everyone to understand expectations and responsibilities. Policies which highlight who's who in the organisation, lines of responsibility and lines of management give an idea of the power structure in a setting.

Power is exercised through management structures and is evident in an organisational hierarchy, role and position and sometimes by virtue of specialist knowledge or experience. Within this system, each layer has some exercise of power over those below and this is acknowledged and

Case study

4.1 The Equality Act 2010

In each of the following cases identify whether you think discrimination has occurred and whether there is a case to appeal to the law through the Equality Act (2010).

- Mary, 62, applies for a job as a care assistant. Despite having previous experience in this area of work, she is not offered an interview. She is told that she has not been shortlisted for the position because of her age.

- Parminder attends a day centre. She overhears another attendee making comments about her skin colour and dress to a member of staff.

- Gemma has a long-standing disability and uses a wheelchair. She is required to attend meetings for the care company she works for, but these meetings are always held in an upstairs room in an old building with no lift. She finds being carried

upstairs humiliating and has stopped attending the meetings. Her manager is adamant that she must attend.

- John has had a stroke and lives in a care home where he depends on care from others for his daily activities. He has cross-dressed for many years. Since his stroke, the care staff have refused to dress him in (his own) women's clothing because they feel it will cause upset to the other residents.

- Wendy, a white, middle-class woman aged 40, has applied for a post in a women's refuge set up specifically to cater for young Asian women. The refuge is funded by the local Asian community. The advertisement specifically identified being Asian as a necessary characteristic.

- Julie has been off sick with depression for five months. While on sick leave and a week before she is due to return to work, Julie is invited for an interview with her manager, who suggests that she should hand in her resignation.

understood by both those in leadership roles and those who are subordinates. Where individuals step outside the responsibilities of their role, those in leadership positions are legitimately empowered to take appropriate sanctions to ensure the smooth and effective running of the organisation. This type of power is legitimate and provides a framework for keeping the organisation running effectively. However, power operates also on an informal level.

Informal power is more difficult to understand because it is insidious, operates beneath the surface and is not formally acknowledged. Such power is not related to role or position – some people are natural leaders and have an innate ability to influence others, and this may be entirely independent of their position within the organisation. Where this is a positive, value-based influence it can be invaluable to the manager in spreading good practice. As manager, you might use your position to encourage your staff to adopt anti-discriminatory and non-judgemental attitudes in their work by challenging discrimination that may come to your notice.

Research it

4.2 Championing equality, diversity and inclusion

Research an organisation other than your own and comment upon how it has championed diversity, equality and inclusion.

This can be accomplished through the manager providing a good role model demonstrating fairness and anti-discriminatory practice to all staff and service users. Discrimination should be challenged at all levels of the staff structure and staff need to feel that they are able to report practices they believe to be wrong. Through training sessions and supervision as well as clear job descriptions, staff will understand their role in relation to equality, diversity and inclusion.

Powerful personalities on the team may lead others negatively, encouraging them to cut corners, bend rules or manipulate situations for their own advantage. The impact of this may mean that service users and other members of staff are treated in an unfair manner and this will compromise the equality, diversity and inclusion of the service and the manager must then find strategies to minimise their influence.

Training and supervision

You may need to remind your staff about issues surrounding equality, diversity and inclusion at team meetings and update them on the policies and procedures. You can also recommend training to remind them of their duty with respect to equality, inclusion and diversity.

Communication

When designing or updating a policy, it is important that a communication strategy is designed at the same time. A policy that nobody knows about is of no value. It is important that it is tailored to the different networks within the organisation to ensure all staff are alerted. It also needs to be clear who the policy is aimed at – staff in general, individuals or service users and visitors.

Many organisations have staff intranet sites, so a pop-up alert is a good way of raising awareness. This allows you to add a link to the policy and to highlight changes to existing policies. You can add information here, for example you could add a 'Frequently Asked Questions' page or examples of cases to illustrate how this policy may be applied in practice. You can also check out the effectiveness of your communication by doing informal and random checks to see whether staff are aware of the policy.

Training

Raising awareness, although crucial, is not enough. Equality, diversity and anti-discrimination policies need to be supported by staff training. This helps people to really think about their responses to different situations and assists people with different ways of responding to situations. It also ensures that staff are up to date with latest legislation and practice. Training can be provided as part of the staff development programme or via an online package.

Provide advice and support for staff when complaints are made

A reflective, learning organisation tries to identify issues before they become grievances or complaints. Consequently, a well-publicised and confidential opportunity to access advice, support and counselling should be a feature of how organisations engage with diversity and equality. One way is to recruit a number of advisers, trained to provide initial informal advice to any person who believes they are being discriminated against. They can talk through their situation and look at all the options before they take action. Often talking through the issue and being believed and supported is enough to enable the individual to draw on their own reserves and tackle the issue directly or change the situation indirectly.

Having champions for diversity will help to keep issues about equality on the agenda. Reflecting on best practice in your own and other organisations is valuable. It is not necessary for the manager to take on this role – it can be an opportunity for someone interested in this area to extend their skills and develop their role.

The aim of any activities that you instigate is to support compliance with equality legislation and to eliminate discriminatory behaviour.

For more on complaints procedures, see Unit 501 AC 2.5.

All policies

If it is communicated that equality and diversity are everybody's responsibility, it confers an obligation on employees to challenge or report discrimination if they encounter it. This can be daunting for employees who have to continue to work in an organisation in which an investigation, suspension or prosecution occurs as a result of the challenge. While the expectation is that individuals should raise challenges and concerns, it is imperative that they can do this in a supportive and protective environment. Most challenges should be able to be dealt with inside the organisation, which should, with appropriate guidance, allow you to resolve the situation or support sanctions. However, there are occasions when a practice is so widespread and resistant to change, or of such a serious nature, that a more radical approach is required. In such circumstances, staff who witness such activities will be protected by law for making this public. However, this does not mean that the individual has a right to go to the press or other public forum to expose an organisation without trying to resolve issues internally first.

The policies and systems discussed apply to staff as well as service users. Refer to Unit 501 AC 2.5 for more information on **whistle blowing**.

KEY TERMS

Whistle blowing means making a disclosure or revealing information that is in the public interest.
Disclosure is the release of information about something.
Obligation is an action or restraint from action that a person is morally or legally bound to owe to (an)other(s).

Protected disclosures

For a **disclosure** to be protected by the law, it should be made to the right person or authority and in the right way. Disclosure must meet the following criteria:

● The disclosure must be in good faith (honest intent and without malice).

● The whistle blower must reasonably believe that the information is substantially true.

● The whistle blower must reasonably believe they are making the disclosure to the right 'prescribed person'.

If a qualifying disclosure is made in good faith to an employer, or through a process that the employer has agreed, the whistle blower will be entitled to protection.

If a worker feels unable to make a disclosure to their employer, there are other 'prescribed people' to whom a disclosure can be made. Disclosure can be made to the person responsible for the area of concern such as a team leader or mentor.

To make a protected disclosure to 'others' rather than the employer, the whistle blower must:

1 Reasonably believe their employer would treat them unfairly if the disclosure was made to the employer or a prescribed person.

2 Reasonably believe that the disclosure to the employer would result in the destruction or concealment of information about the wrongdoing.

3 Have previously disclosed the same or similar information to the employer or a prescribed person.

If an employee loses their job and wants to claim compensation, an employment tribunal must be satisfied that the employee's actions to whistle blow and make the disclosure were reasonable.

Research it

4.2 How systems and processes promote equality and inclusion, and reinforce discrimination and exclusion

1 Look at the systems and processes that promote equality and inclusion or reinforce discrimination and exclusion in your workplace and comment on how effective they are.

2 Research and check whether you have a whistle-blowing policy in place and identify whether the responsibilities contained within it clearly identify for the worker what is expected of them in this situation.

Effectiveness of systems and processes in promoting equality, diversity and inclusion

It is important that you are not complacent about the effectiveness of policies and procedures that have been designed to support a culture that promotes and assures equality and respect for diversity and inclusion. Occasionally, a policy may be reinforcing discrimination and exclusion accidentally (without meaning to), or because of the language being used or out-of-date practices being continued. An annual audit of effectiveness is a good way of checking whether this issue remains at the forefront of people's minds and practice. The types of activities that can be used to monitor the effectiveness of your policies include:

● **User surveys**: You can use a quick questionnaire to assess how well the users of your service feel their differences are respected and equality is promoted by your staff.

● **Observation**: When you work alongside others and have an opportunity to witness staff interactions, you can use this as an opportunity to observe how well staff promote equality and respect diversity.

Reflective practice, including incident analysis (where we analyse an incident by considering what happened, how and why it happened, what might reduce the risk of it happening again and what we learned), allows you and your team to reflect on behaviours, interactions and incidents and to identify ways of enhancing or improving practice. Do not forget that reflective practice also allows you to identify good practice and share this more widely.

Evidence opportunity

4.2 Policies, systems, processes and practices that promote equality, diversity and inclusion

Look at the policies in your own setting that relate to equality, diversity and inclusion. Show your assessor that you can lead practice with others in reviewing and evaluating current systems and processes. Show and tell them how you make improvements where required in respect of what we have discussed in the LO so far.

You might, for example, review and evaluate the policies with your staff in team meetings and make improvements to them.

Evaluating means you are able to question why and how such things are in place. What do you think the strengths of the policies are? Would you change them in any way and if so how? How can they be improved?

Research it

4.2 Gaps, shortfalls and improvements

Undertake some research which identifies the gaps or shortfalls in systems and processes in your own setting and propose improvements to address these.

Reflect on it

4.2 Systems and processes

Think about the systems and processes that promote diversity, equality and inclusion in place in your organisation and reflect on how attitudes to these things have changed during your practice as a care professional. Give some examples of the changes you have noted and how they now affect your service users. Are there any improvements that can be made?

AC 4.3 Support others to challenge discrimination and exclusion in ways that are likely to achieve change and promote positive outcomes

Here, you will be required to show evidence of how you lead and foster an environment where any discrimination or exclusion is actively challenged and addressed, including for example the topics we discuss here.

Ensuring that equality, diversity and inclusion are effectively embedded within an organisation requires that all staff in all roles embrace and implement these principles. The role of the manager is crucial in identifying and removing barriers to the implementation of these principles. As a manager, you must lead and foster an environment where any discrimination or exclusion is actively challenged and addressed.

All organisations have their own culture or, as Thompson (2011, p. 199) suggests, a 'symbolic universe' in which a shared set of meanings, beliefs, values, norms and practices is based. It is, more simply, 'the way we do things'.

People's values, beliefs and attitudes are often deeply ingrained and are acquired through learning and upbringing. We are encouraged to believe that certain attitudes and behaviours are acceptable. It is only when these values, beliefs and attitudes are challenged, either by new information during training and education, or different experiences, that they may be seen to be flawed. Even when individuals' views can be shown to be discriminatory, deeply held beliefs may be resistant to change and this is termed prejudice.

A prejudice is an attitude or belief that is based on a faulty and inflexible generalisation which can lead to negative emotions and discriminatory actions. Prejudice can lead to unacceptable behaviours, including harassment, bullying and victimisation, as well as poor standards and abuse of power over others. Harassment, bullying and victimisation are all behaviours that individuals are protected against under the Equality Act (2010); remember, it is not just individuals and groups that can be prejudiced and discriminatory. Prejudice does not necessarily cause someone to discriminate unfairly, but examining such beliefs and values and questioning them is a first step in recognising and tackling prejudice.

Challenging discrimination and exclusion in policies and practice

Exclusion refers to the barring of somebody from a service or an activity or not allowing a group or an individual to join in due to a barrier of some sort. Whatever way it occurs, it is disabling and a form of discrimination. Discriminating against someone generally implies conferring disadvantage or oppression on that individual which impacts negatively upon their self-concept, their dignity, their opportunities or their ability to get justice.

Discrimination takes many forms:

- stereotyping
- marginalisation
- invisibilisation
- infantilisation
- medicalisation
- dehumanisation
- trivialisation.

Organisations must develop, implement and monitor policies and practices that support anti-discriminatory practice and exclusion. These policies help to raise awareness about unacceptable behaviours and provide a structure for individuals to challenge such behaviours. This includes the responsibility of management to ensure that all staff work within the policy and respect the difference of others. Most organisations will have equality and diversity policies which should also explicitly identify how staff seek redress when they believe there is non-compliance with the policy or law. For example, this can be accomplished through staff meetings and in supervision.

Why is challenging discrimination so important?

Discrimination causes people to feel devalued, worthless, angry, hopeless and powerless, and undermines confidence. From an organisational or managerial perspective, this can have a significant impact on the effectiveness of your workforce as well as the individuals they care for. Discriminatory practice is likely to result in poor performance, poor staff relations and a missed opportunity to benefit positively from the different attributes and potential of the staff employed.

Discrimination may be a result of individual prejudice or cultural or structural causes. Prejudice is a pre-conceived judgement that one group of people, or one person, is better or worse than others without any basis of knowledge or evidence.

False beliefs may be widely held and deeply ingrained; they are not easily changed, even in response to evidence to their contrary (Thompson and Thompson, 2008). If the false belief is not successfully challenged, it may be accepted as a fact and this may invoke an emotional response, which may be dislike or dismissal of the person or individuals associated with the belief.

Discriminatory, unfair behaviour often follows – inequitable treatment, exclusion, dismissal, becoming the butt of humour, being ridiculed or deliberately being marginalised

may be common outcomes. Threats and violence are extreme forms of discriminatory behaviour. Importantly, in the workplace much discriminatory behaviour may be covert and dressed up in the form of humour. Perpetrators may justify and trivialise the action with statements such as 'It's just a bit of fun', 'She's got no sense of humour', 'He's so sensitive'. This trivialisation may make it difficult to address; individuals or staff may not want to be seen to be making a fuss or unable to take a joke. This requires a clear policy that is carried forward into practice stating that singling out an individual's characteristics and using these to ridicule or humiliate them is completely unacceptable.

As a manager your role is to ensure that you are well-versed in the effects of discrimination and have at your disposal information about how you deal with or meet the needs of individuals in your care and workforce. You should also be aware of the effects of oppression.

The main outcome of inappropriate use of power is oppression. Oppression as a result of discriminatory practice results in significant harm. It may manifest as another's loss of confidence, or undermining one's self-belief and self-esteem; it may cause stress, anxiety or depression, all of which impact on work performance and subsequent work opportunity. If the individual is unable to successfully challenge the oppression, there is a risk that the prejudicial belief or disabling structure takes on the significance of 'fact' which then results in the oppressed person responding defensively by avoiding situations and people that discriminate against them by trying to keep a low profile, and a negative cycle begins. If nobody stops or challenges the above, then the perpetrators continue and the victimised learn strategies to cope. However, this is clearly unfair.

The impact of inclusion

So far much of the discussion has been focused on the impact of discrimination and strategies to redress unfairness. While this is extremely important, anti-discriminatory approaches are focused on the negative acceptance that discrimination is a fact of life and that energy should be spent on mitigating the effects. Inclusion, however, takes a more positive approach. A philosophy of inclusion is concerned with how things should and could be. Energies are spent on becoming better members of a community, by creating new visions for the community. The emphasis for inclusion is not on justifying reasons for why someone should be included and developing policies and procedures to support this; inclusion starts from an assumption that everyone has equal rights and opportunities and that these should differ only when there is an appropriate reason to do so.

Supporting others

The first step in supporting others to challenge discrimination and exclusion is to accept that they exist and to acknowledge that discrimination is a significant factor in inhibiting equality. As managers it is necessary to communicate to staff that discrimination is fundamentally wrong and that it cannot be tolerated within an organisation. We should also be quick to challenge any sort of discriminatory behaviour in order to send out a strong message of zero tolerance. However, challenging discrimination is not easy.

Few people are exempt from prejudice or exclusive practice. What is important is that individuals are open to recognising their prejudices and are committed to change. It takes practice and time. It will be helped by promoting policies that set out expectations of behaviour to others and that remind staff of disciplinary sanctions should they breach the policy. However, while it might be possible to get staff to comply with policies, that is only part of the picture. Policies alone do not change hearts and minds. The risk is that if only compliance is achieved, when not observed the behaviour will revert to that which perpetuated inequality. For many people, understanding the consequences and impact of their actions will cause a change in behaviour and encouragement for others to change, but we cannot assume this will be universal and managers must be vigilant.

We are all products of our culture, our experiences and our education. Discrimination and exclusion may not be intentional but may be the result of the belief that everyone experiences life in the same way. If we have never consciously experienced discrimination, we may not see it when it happens to others. Alternatively, we may be very conscious of discrimination and attitudes. A working mother, for example, may be very sensitive to individuals who make values-based assertions about the negative effect of working mothers on their children. One often needs to be able to relate to another person's experience in order to appreciate the injustice that is felt by others. It is not possible to be somebody else, but it is possible to ask them how it feels and to try to imagine what that must be like. Sometimes it is useful to assume the role of the impartial observer, setting aside emotion and experience and asking whether something is right or not.

Encourage reflection

It is imperative that we reflect critically on ourselves, our values, attitudes and behaviours towards others. Where do these come from? Are they consistent with the values that one would choose to have? Reflective practice is an excellent vehicle for critical self-reflection and as managers we need to be encouraging our staff to complete this task on a regular basis. By reviewing practice in this way, you can help staff to feel supported in their efforts to change practice. They will also feel empowered to challenge bad practice.

The simplest reflective model asks the participant to engage in three critical reflections:

- A detailed interrogation of the issue or situation.
- Why is this so or why did it happen?
- So what does this mean?

Gibbs' (1988) model of reflection (Figure 5.6) is particularly useful in reflecting on values because it requires the reflector to engage with their feelings and to consider and evaluate the morality of their thoughts and feelings.

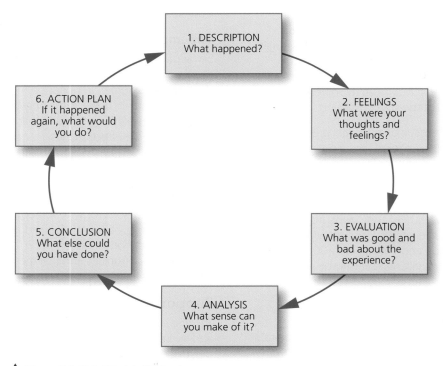

▲ **Figure 5.6** Gibbs' Model of Reflection

Reflect on it

4.3 Labels and assumptions

Using an incident analysis model of reflection, reflect on thoughts, feelings and behaviours from a situation where you may have labelled, or have been tempted to label, someone, or made assumptions about their capabilities or trustworthiness, or when you felt anxious or threatened by someone you did not know.

Reflect on what caused you to respond in the way that you did. Was your response reasonable? Could you have behaved differently? What risks would there have been if you had behaved differently? Can you think of strategies to prompt you to behave differently in the future?

Model good practice

Discriminatory behaviour is often hidden, even from ourselves, and unless we take the time to reflect and be sensitive, question and change our responses to others, evaluate the impact of our behaviours, service users will continue to be treated unjustly.

Managers must model good practice. You must be someone who positively challenges discrimination and supports others to do this. This requires you to be conscious of your own behaviour and to lead by example.

Dealing with discriminatory behaviour in staff and supporting others

Promoting equality and inclusion as positive concepts that are everybody's responsibility helps others to challenge discrimination when they encounter it. However, the way that the manager responds could determine whether the individual is willing to do this again in any future situation. Importantly, any challenge should be taken seriously and time must be made to listen to what the individual believes is occurring. The manager must investigate the situation impartially, trying to gain as much evidence as possible in order to ensure that they have the whole picture before they make any decisions. This includes talking to everyone involved, or to someone who has witnessed the potentially discriminatory behaviour, and taking statements.

Confidentiality should be maintained as these issues are often very sensitive. If the discrimination is found to be a reality, it is important to put in place an action plan to improve the situation and to provide managerial support to those affected. If discrimination has been proven, sanctions should be applied appropriately and proportionally. One purpose of investigating issues of concern is to resolve the particular situation, learn from it and, where possible, implement strategies to prevent something similar happening in the future. Where possible, actions should primarily be focused on enhancing and improving practice rather than on retribution or vengeance. Having clear processes that

Reflect on it

4.3 Challenging discrimination and exclusion

Imagine yourself in a world in which you are seen as an inferior being. You have similar capabilities to others and yet these are dismissed because your characteristics mark you out as being of lesser value. You are constantly overlooked, marginalised and given the worst and dirtiest jobs to do. You do not have access to the developmental opportunities afforded to others. You are good humouredly ridiculed for the amusement of others. If anything goes wrong, it is assumed that you are responsible.

What sanctions do you think are appropriate to improve the situation and bring about a more equal environment? What are the risks, if any, of imposing sanctions? How could you support others in a similar situation to challenge discrimination and exclusion?

You will also need to ensure that staff feel supported and are able to challenge issues safely. This can be achieved through staff meetings, CPD and supervision.

support individuals to raise concerns responsibly provides protection for those who wish to challenge discrimination and for those who may be under investigation.

Challenging discrimination and exclusion through training and development opportunities, staff induction/supervision and/or appraisal

One step in eliminating prejudice is to redefine beliefs and attitudes in the light of new information. We can do this through our staff induction processes and in supervision and appraisal, where we may be able to challenge attitudes that come to light.

Another step is to change behaviour in the light of that information, and also to challenge others who articulate similar prejudices. Training and development opportunities, staff appraisal and supervision can all be used as opportunities for achieving positive outcomes with respect to challenging discrimination.

None of these steps is easy, particularly the latter; however, challenging others can have a significant impact on breaking down discrimination and prejudice. Often prejudice is not only an individual issue but represents views that might be more widely held within a group or specific context. When a strong, widespread belief is apparent, challenging it is difficult and individuals who try to do so may fear ridicule, victimisation or reprisals if they stand up against the prevailing beliefs and practices. In an organisation, it is important that everyone is aware that prejudice and discriminatory practice cannot be tolerated. Individuals who become aware of such practice must be supported and protected to speak out.

Thompson (2011, p. 32) points out that significant structural barriers exist that discriminate negatively on individuals. For example, there may be an unfair unwritten policy and agreement that women in their 20s and 30s are not employed in managerial posts because of the potential for them to leave or take maternity leave. Alternatively, the organisation that fails to provide accessible facilities for those in wheelchairs is discriminatory and in breach of the law. Staff should be aware of such circumstances and feel confident in speaking out against them.

You can find more information on training in AC 4.2.

Management of complaints/service compliments and involvement and feedback from those in receipt of care and support

Creating a culture of discussion and tolerance is important in developing an open-minded community and in preventing abusive practice. We can ensure that our staff are acting in non-discriminatory ways by ensuring that we handle complaints and compliments in the organisation well. By involving service users and their families in evaluating care we are also able to see how the process is working.

Many organisations are constrained by the premises and resources available to them in developing completely fair facilities. However, this is not an excuse for doing nothing. The expectation is that reasonable adjustments must be made and while these adjustments may not be perfect, they must be fit for purpose. Failure to address such issues may oppress certain groups in society simply because they cannot access a building or a service, thus undermining confidence and self-esteem.

KEY TERM

Prejudice is an unreasonable, pre-conceived judgement or opinion that is not based on knowledge, evidence or experience.

Research it

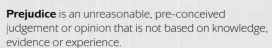

4.3 Support others to challenge discrimination and exclusion

Carry out a small-scale research study in your own setting which looks at diversity, equality and inclusion. Identify the strengths and limitations within your area of practice and make recommendations for improvement.

Look particularly at the following areas:

- Training and development opportunities
- Staff induction/supervision and/or appraisal
- Management of complaints/service compliments
- Involvement and feedback from those in receipt of care and support.

Evidence opportunity

4.3 Support others to challenge discrimination and exclusion

Show your assessor evidence of how you lead and foster an environment where any discrimination or exclusion is actively challenged and addressed, for example through:

- training and development opportunities
- staff induction/supervision and/or appraisal
- management of complaints/service compliments
- involvement and feedback from those in receipt of care and support.

LO5 Lead continuous improvement in carrying out health and care procedures where required

AC 5.1 Monitor, review and evaluate the implementation of person-centred practices and the achievement of positive outcomes for individuals

Here, you will be required to show that you can monitor, review and evaluate the implementation of person-centred practices and the achievement of positive outcomes for individuals within your area of service, to include robust feedback.

The appropriateness and 'usability' of systems and processes within an organisation determine whether those systems and processes help to promote positive outcomes in person-centred care. The first step is to ensure that clear and well-understood systems and policies set the standards of the behaviours expected of all employees in the workplace. When designing policies there are three requirements:

1 The policy with regard to person-centred practice and positive outcomes must be clear.
2 There should be no possibility of misinterpretation of what is intended.
3 It must address the issue directly and it must reflect current legal requirements.

Policies provide a framework for promoting positive outcomes but, if they are not monitored or staff are unclear about how they should be practising, then your service may not be offering person-centred care.

You must ensure that there have been no amendments, extensions or changes to relevant laws. A well-designed policy is essential in promoting a positive culture that celebrates person-centred care. All new policies should be agreed or designed in consultation with unions or employee representatives.

Policies should:

- give clear examples of what person-centred practice is and how it can affect positive outcomes
- give examples of what constitutes discrimination, harassment, bullying and intimidating behaviour, including cyber-bullying, work-related events and harassment by third parties
- state that if discriminatory behaviour has occurred it will be treated as a disciplinary offence.

Every policy should be monitored and regularly reviewed for effectiveness, including:

- records of complaints, why and how they occurred and who was involved – an analysis of trends will help you to identify if the policy is working or if there are any systemic problems
- individual complaints to ensure that action plans were implemented as intended, to identify resolution and to identify whether there was any evidence of victimisation for those involved.

Evidence of feedback from those in receipt of care and support

Our clients can provide us with first-hand knowledge about their care and how they perceive it and this can be facilitated by arranging service user meetings to be held where they are given an opportunity to speak out. Anonymous surveys can be used.

Additionally, 'complaints, compliments and comments' systems are a good way to audit practice.

Colleagues

Our colleagues need to have a safe avenue to comment upon care and practice and this may be achieved through appraisal and supervision but also staff meetings. As a manager you may want to stress that you have an open-door policy which enables people to come and express concerns at any time.

Contributions from others involved in supporting those in receipt of care and support

Carers and others who support clients should also be able to avail themselves of meetings with the manager. Although this might be time consuming, you may want to set aside a fortnightly meeting slot for all to come in to discuss needs. They may also be able to access the complaints, compliments and comments system and user surveys.

Evidence opportunity

5.1 Implementation

Collect evidence to demonstrate how you monitor, review and evaluate the implementation of person-centred practices and the achievement of positive outcomes for individuals within your setting. This should include robust feedback from those we have covered in this section.

AC 5.2 Use evidence-based research to identify best practice in outcomes-based and person-centred approaches

Here, you will be required to research up-to-date, reliable literature and/or other publications relevant to your area of study to establish best practice which supports the above.

Evidence-based practice is about incorporating evidence from research and making professional judgements as a result of the new knowledge and applying it to formulate care decisions.

As practitioners we are duty-bound to perform care in a safe way and in a way in which we are able to question our practice and be accountable for what we do. To 'do no harm' then is the essential premise of evidence-based practice and the need to be able to demonstrate that the care we provide is safe and effective is a reasonable expectation. It is no different in our practice with respect to supervision.

As an effective practitioner accountable for your own safe practice, you need to have access to and be up to date with the research related to your own area and be able to critically appraise such work. As a manager of staff in your setting, you are accountable when it comes to ensuring that the staff have embraced the notion of evidence-based practice.

In making a decision about how and what care is to be given, it is important to have an accurate picture of the research available and to construct sufficient evidence from it to support our actions. In supervising staff we need to ensure that their practice is based on good, sound evidence and that they are informed as to how they might be able to improve their practice consistent with new initiatives in care.

KEY TERM

Evidence-based practice (EBP) refers to using information from high-quality research and applying it within practice to make informed decisions about a service user's care.

Evidence opportunity

5.2 Use evidence-based research to identify best practice

Here you will be required to show your assessor that you have researched up-to-date, reliable literature and/or other publications relevant to their area of study to establish best practice that supports the above.

AC 5.3 Act on lessons learned from incidents that occur

Here, you will be required to show evidence of how any incidents that can or may have occurred have informed your leadership and management of service practice in respect of person-centred care, including the topics we discuss here.

Here you will be required to show evidence of how any incidents that can or may have occurred inform your leadership and management of service practice in respect of person-centred care.

Identifying mistakes or near mistakes and assessing whether or not these could have been avoided is an important activity. It is important that this is seen as a productive activity and not a punitive or disciplinary one. Its primary focus is about learning from an incident or set of behaviours in order that changes can be made to improve issues. The most significant examples of this are big public and government inquiries, which are called when serious failures and mistakes in public services are identified, such as Alder Hey, the Mid Staffordshire inquiry and Baby P. In each case, it has been identified that staff failed to follow procedures and protocols, that there were lapses in expected standards of care, and that there was a failure in anyone taking responsibility and reporting these lapses. Ideally, if organisations and individuals practise reflectively then public inquiries of this type should never be needed.

On a smaller scale, investigations into minor mistakes and accidents are designed to enable learning from reflection on the circumstances that allowed an accident or mistake to happen. Importantly, getting the balance between investigation, reflection and assigning blame is crucial. If staff feel they are going to be unfairly blamed or punished for mistakes, it may prevent them from reporting them or coming forward with concerns. An organisation that supports its staff to raise concerns, to acknowledge deficits and to report mistakes is much more likely to be a learning organisation than one where this is not the primary culture. An open organisation provides the conditions for someone to acknowledge and investigate and to reflect on how things can be improved or done differently.

Untoward incidents that occur in care work need to be fully investigated and reviewed. In recommending proposals for improvements to systems and procedures, you may for example start by taking a look at how you process complaints, what happens with the incident and accident reports and how care plans are used. You need to first of all ensure they are up to date and are useful for determining how well your safeguarding procedures are working.

Identified poor practice

Unsatisfactory work performance and poor practice might manifest in a number of ways. As a manager you may observe staff making frequent mistakes, or not following a job through, or some being unable to unable to cope with instructions or tasks.

Managing poor performance may require you to invoke formal procedures whereby you undertake an investigation of the reasons for poor performance, discussing this with the member of staff and then giving time to improve. Clear advice as to how improvement can be made and the provision of training and supervision must be offered and staff must also be aware of the consequences of failing to improve.

Accidents, and errors and 'near misses'

An audit of the accident record or the Datix system (a system which records accidents, near misses and complaints or concerns) will reveal whether anything connects to poor practice; this then needs to be addressed in a manner similar to above. Reflective practice, including incident analysis (where we analyse an incident by considering what happened, how and why it happened, what might reduce the risk of it happening again and what we learned), allows you and your team to reflect on behaviours, interactions and incidents and to identify ways of enhancing or improving practice. Do not forget that reflective practice also allows you to identify good practice and share this more widely.

Errors and 'near misses' may also be recorded and in the NHS there is widespread use of the Datix system on which all incidents are reported.

Concerns and complaints – informal and/or formal

Any complaint or concern that is brought to your attention needs to be dealt with in a structured way and you must document how the issue has been handled. You must not be complacent about the effectiveness of policies and procedures that have been designed to support a culture that promotes and assures equality and respect for person-centred practice. An annual audit of how effective such policies are and how complaints have been handled is a good way of checking whether this issue remains at the forefront of people's minds and practice.

There is a great deal of emphasis on evidence-based practice and best practice. This is another means of reflection. It has involved somebody identifying an issue and researching it in order to generate evidence. Best practice is to analyse the different ways of doing things in order to identify whether there is a preferred way of undertaking the activity. Access to up-to-date learning resources is important in supporting staff to keep abreast of new evidence and best practice.

Evidence opportunity

5.3 Acting on lessons

How are incidents that can or may have occurred dealt with in your setting? Show your assessor evidence of how any incidents that can or may have occurred inform leadership and management of service practice in respect of person-centred care. Include, for example, the topics we have discussed here.

Reflect on it

5.3 Lessons learned

Draw on a real example of a failure, a mistake of a standard of practice, or a practice that required change, and write a report that answers the following:

- What happened?
- Was the incident reported to senior staff?
- If the incident was reported to senior staff, who did they (senior staff) report it to and why that individual (or agency)?
- How was the individual perceived?
- What actions resulted from the incident?
- Are policies and protocols fit for purpose?
- If a similar thing occurred again, are you confident that employees feel sufficiently well supported to report the issue?
- What changes could you make in order to make it easier for staff to raise issues that can improve service and help to manage risks?

AC 5.4 Review the extent to which systems, processes and practice facilitate positive outcomes

Here, you will be required to review and update systems, processes and practices to ensure they facilitate positive outcome approaches to person-centred care.

As a manager, you must review and update systems, processes and practices to ensure they facilitate positive outcome approaches to person-centred care.

It is only by doing this that an organisation can grow and improvements can be made. In your own setting, for example, you might start by making a simple change to encourage all to invest in person-centred care. By putting up posters and giving out details via leaflets, individuals in your care and their families can be encouraged to ask questions and play a more active role in their treatment.

Additionally, you might encourage the team to identify what can be improved in the service to improve outcomes for clients and service users and then discuss the ways in which those changes can be made. It is important to have explicit aims, which means being clear about what it is the setting is trying to achieve in improving its approach to person-centred care. In this way the outcomes from the changes can be measured more readily.

AC 5.5 Plan and lead the implementation of improvements

Here, you will be required to show you can actively identify improvements, plan and implement changes to systems and processes.

The manager's role is to lead on improvements within the setting and you also need to be able to plan for and implement any changes required. The use of SMART objectives for staff, and ensuring that team objectives are set, will be a useful tool to develop improvement in the delivery of adult care.

LO6 Develop community relationships to provide integrated services

AC 6.1 Understand the importance of community involvement and promote own service within the wider community

Here, you will be required to critically evaluate how community involvement/activities support positive outcomes for those in receipt of care and support within their area of service, to include:

- *how their service is promoted within local communities*
- *how people using services and staff engage and integrate with the wider community*
- *how working with other community services supports the development of health and care provision within the community, e.g. GPs, hairdressers, chiropodists.*

The Local Government and Public Involvement in Health Act (2007) incorporated the recommendations of A Stronger Local Voice (DoH, 2006) and set out the government's plans to promote public and community influence in health and social care. The intention was to make NHS organisations more accountable to their local populations to strengthen the patient and service user voice.

The act states that the local involvement networks were developed for:

- promoting, and supporting, the involvement of people in the commissioning, provision and scrutiny of local care services
- reviewing and monitoring the commissioning and provision of local care services. (www.legislation.gov.uk/ukpga/2007/28/contents).

The development within each local authority of Health and Wellbeing Boards, which carry out assessments known as joint strategic needs assessments, involves the local community in this process and these enable service users and the public to influence and improve their local health and social care services.

The NHS Constitution, first published in 2009 and updated in 2013 in the light of the Health and Social Care Act (2012) and the findings of the Francis Report (2013), sets out the principles and values of the NHS and details the rights of patients, the public and staff. It states:

> *'The NHS aspires to put patients at the heart of everything it does. It should support individuals to promote and manage their own health. NHS services must reflect, and should be coordinated around and tailored to, the needs and preferences of patients, their families and their carers. Patients, with their families and carers, where appropriate, will be involved in and consulted on all decisions about their care and treatment. The NHS will actively encourage feedback from the public, patients and staff, welcome it and use it to improve its services.' (Section 1(4), p. 3)*

Patients come first is the message being sent here and in doing so it makes sense that we need to involve local organisations to ensure our service users get what they require, whether it be the local hairdresser, the dentist or the local sports centre.

How your service is promoted within local communities

As the population ages and we see more people living to greater ages we can anticipate that more care will take place out of hospital and in people's homes and the community. This will require support for people to manage long-term conditions together with a range of services within local communities. Your setting may have a role in the delivery of that care or may provide a service which helps people in the local community. How you market and promote your service with the local community is important in developing a sustainable service for the future.

How people using services and staff engage and integrate with the wider community

In line with government health policy on person-centred practice, it is the intention that health services must respond to individuals' wishes and choices to ensure positive outcomes. The Department of Health's 'Transforming Community services' (www.dh.gov.uk/prod_consum_dh/groups/dh_digitalassets/documents/digitalasset/dh_126111.pdf) programme showed that integrated care improves quality outcomes and efficiency through better use of resources. Individuals using your service and those of your partners, stakeholders and others in the community with whom you work will benefit from better resources and more positive health outcomes.

How working with other community services supports the development of health and care provision within the community

Working in tandem with other local services enhances the care the individual can expect to get. For example, the local GP service will offer primary care but will also be able to link in with physiotherapy, chiropody or leisure services should its service users need such care. Care homes may link in with local hairdressers or health clubs to provide services for the wellbeing of their clients. Private care companies may be engaged as partners to provide services the statutory sector cannot provide and this all enhances the service users' experience in care.

AC 6.2 Development of leadership and management practice

Here, you will be required to critically review current practice in respect of the above and make recommendations that inform strategic operational practice.

Person-centred care is about enabling people to have choice and control in their care and lives, and as wellbeing has been shown to link to social inclusion and active participation, it requires integration with local communities. As a manager and a leader, your focus will be on how you might improve the quality of the service and transform the current ways of working to ensure a more person-centred agenda is followed. This will require that you understand the role of local government and the wider community of health services such as the NHS, GPs, the private/independent sector, the voluntary sector and the local community.

The biggest challenge you may face will be to manage the day-to-day work of the service but also to lead the service through massive health policy changes.

Evidence opportunity

6.2 Development of leadership and management practice

Provide a written account critically reviewing current practice in respect of the above and make recommendations that inform strategic operational practice.

LO7 Managing concerns and complaints in adult care

AC 7.1 Monitor and review systems and processes to manage concerns and complaints and how these link to risk management and safeguarding

Here, you will be required to monitor and review systems and processes to manage concerns and complaints and how these link to risk management and safeguarding.

Evidence opportunity

6.1, **6.2** Community involvement

Provide a written account critically evaluating how community involvement/activities support positives outcomes for those in receipt of care and support within their area of service to include the areas we have discussed in this section.

You may for example show evidence of the involvement of the local community in your setting:

- How do you promote your service within local communities?
- How do your service users and staff engage and integrate with the wider community?

- How does working with other community services support the development of health and care provision within the community e.g. PAs, GPs, hairdressers, chiropodists?

Make a critical review of your current practice in respect of the above and make recommendations which inform your strategic operational practice.

In critical reviews, you need to look at the strengths and weaknesses of your current practice. For example, what are the strengths of having a partnership with the services in the community? How might you improve what you do for your clients with respect to engaging with more community services?

Review how systems and processes are visible and clear to all individuals receiving services and visitors to the setting

Systems and processes that function poorly, or are not used, make it difficult for people to deliver high-quality care and this may be because staff do not use the information or, more simply, cannot find it. It is important that concerns and complaints procedures are not only visible in the workplace, but that staff and visitors are using the systems to manage situations that may involve safeguarding and risk management issues. As the manager, you need to ensure not only that staff and visitors are aware of the policies, but that safeguarding is a policy that is a part of the cultural ethos of the setting and is embedded into the ways of working.

Embed assessment of risk within all person-centred approaches

As a manager you will be familiar with the need to conduct risk assessments, and it is important that they are conducted with the service user and their family in attendance. Adopting a person-centred approach requires that the choices and preferences of the service user are weighed against the risk being anticipated and discussed with all concerned. When we enter into a contract of care with an individual, we assume duties and obligations, and these include the respect for dignity and diversity, and the promotion of equality and fairness. A risk assessment and subsequent action plan to which all involved agree does not mean that all risks are eliminated but that they are managed according to safe guidelines to which all agree.

Provide individuals and their families with information on how to raise a concern

Service users and their families need to be clear about how they can make a complaint without feeling fear of recrimination. They also need to be reassured that any issue they raise will be dealt with rapidly.

Staff and individuals from other agencies must be informed of the information that all service users and their families are given and take responsibility for ensuring that they are well informed of the processes involved in safeguarding.

Understand their duty of care and duty of candour when managing complaints and concerns

Standard 3 of the code of conduct for healthcare support workers and adult social care workers outlines the duty of care to all those receiving care and support. As a legal requirement, staff are required to promote wellbeing and make sure that people are kept safe from harm, abuse and injury.

> ### Evidence opportunity
>
> **7.1** Monitor and review systems and processes
>
> Using a real work example, evaluate how you have conducted a risk assessment in the workplace.

AC 7.2 Learners ensure that the regulatory requirements, codes of practice and guidance for managing concerns and complaints are embedded within organisational systems and processes

Here, you will be required to show that you know and understand current regulatory requirements, codes of practice and guidance for managing concerns and complaints.

Health and Social Care Act 2008 (Regulated Activities) Regulations 2014

Regulation 16 of this act ensures that people can make a complaint about their care and treatment, and to do this you as the manager must ensure that the setting has effective systems for handling and responding to complaints from service users. Complaints must be investigated effectively and action taken rapidly.

Care Act 2014

The Care Act introduced a general duty on local authorities to promote an individual's wellbeing, and to have this in mind when planning and making decisions about them or their care.

Any service user who is not happy with their treatment or assessments is eligible to make a claim to social services, which should have a complaints procedure. If after following the complaints process the service user is unhappy with the outcome, then a complaint can be made to the local government ombudsman.

GDPR 2018 (replaced the Data Protection Act 1998)

The GDPR enables people to raise complaints about misuse of data through the courts.

Public Interest Disclosure Act 1998

The Public Interest Disclosure Act 1998 describes the meaning of whistle blowing and ensures that protected disclosure is afforded to all who make a complaint. Section 19 of the act introduces protection for whistle blowers from bullying or harassment by co-workers.

CQC Regulation 16

Regulation 16 of this act ensures that people can make a complaint about their care and treatment. When a complaint is made, the care provider must provide the CQC with a summary of complaints and their response.

Fundamental Standards

These standards state that a person in care must be able to complain about their care and treatment through the care provider's systems and that there will be a response to the complaint, which will be investigated.

Evidence opportunity

7.2

Describe how you inform staff and individuals and families of the procedure to be followed when making a complaint.

AC 7.3 Learners understand why service users may be reluctant to raise concerns or complaints

Here, you will be required to show you understand why those who use services may be reluctant to raise concerns or complaints.

Reasons why individuals using services or family members and friends may be concerned about reprisals if they make a complaint or raise a concern

Raising a complaint is difficult at any time, but in care the service user and their families and friends may feel they will be treated differently if they do so. They may fear recriminations and therefore be reluctant to divulge cases of poor care and ill treatment at the hands of staff. They need to be sure that a complaint will be dealt with fairly and confidentially. If there is not a culture of trust in the setting this becomes even more problematic, so complaints to an external agency may be necessary.

Evidence opportunity

7.3

How can you develop a culture of trust in which individuals using your service feel safe to raise complaints or concerns?

AC 7.4 Learners promote a culture where attitudes and approaches ensure concerns and complaints directly influence service improvement

Here, you will be required to show you promote a culture where attitudes and approaches ensure concerns and complaints directly influence service improvement.

All concerns and complaints are acted upon promptly, recorded, investigated and outcomes logged and reported

Complaints must be a priority for the manager as failure to address them can lead to failure of the business because people may then lose faith in the care delivery and the staff. They must be dealt with as a matter of urgency and recorded accurately according to the processes outlined by the organisation. Confidentiality must be maintained throughout the process. Records need to be logged and reports made to the CQC.

Using information on any concerns or complaints as a regular agenda item at team meetings, making explicit use of lessons learnt, trends and areas of risk

Having a regular agenda item that addresses complaints helps to keep staff mindful of the quality of their work and the need to address such issues responsibly and honestly. Rather than apportioning blame to those involved in a complaint, lessons need to be learned and addressed. Any trends that emerge need to be risk assessed and reviewed to determine whether changes to work patterns and ways of working need to be made. Your annual service review should address what happened and what changes were made to address the complaints.

Making explicit use of lessons learnt from concerns or complaints in service improvement plans, setting SMART targets and monitoring their achievement

SMART targets may be a useful way to address the concerns that arise. By setting specific and achievable goals about what needs to be done, and putting into place tools to measure achievement and timeframes, improvements can be more effectively monitored.

AC 7.5, 7.6 Learners support team members, service users and their carers to understand systems and processes relating to concerns and complaints

Here, you will be required to show you can support team members to understand systems and processes relating to concerns and complaints, as well as to ensure information and support are in place to enable individuals using services and their carers to raise concerns and make complaints when they wish to do so.

Dissemination of information on current requirements on how complaints and concerns can be raised, reported, recorded and monitored to resolution

Staff members and other professional and external agencies must be informed about the current requirements for complaints and concerns. Regular meetings addressing complaints and concerns, and discussions about how information is used, recorded and monitored, should be a transparent process within the organisation. In this way staff will be more willing to take responsibility for the process.

As with staff, the information that is available in policies and procedures must be available to all service users and their carers and family.

Monitoring of training on the importance of effective systems and processes

Staff training should be recorded on the member of staff's individual personal development plan and on the plan in the setting's training record. Any training undertaken needs to be accurately recorded and audited.

Acknowledging team members' anxiety about receiving concerns and complaints about their practice

Nobody likes to have complaints lodged against them and should this happen, a culture of no blame must be adopted.

As a manager you should discuss the complaint with the member of staff and check that they are supported to make changes. You may find an improvement performance tool may be useful. This starts with evaluating the employee's current performance to try to find out what might have gone wrong in this instance. Goals for improvement can then be set and performance monitored to see if their practice has changed. It is important that the member of staff takes responsibility for the complaint and the need to improve and for you to provide any necessary support to foster and facilitate this.

Acknowledging team members'/service users' anxiety about raising concerns and complaints about poor practice and the importance of whistle blowing

Staff may be anxious about the repercussions when making a whistle-blowing claim, particularly when it involves a member of the team. Developing a climate of trust will mean staff are open and honest about their dealings with each other. If they notice poor practice, they should be encouraged to talk to each other in the first instance and then take concerns to the manager if they feel no change has happened. Team meetings can instil in staff the need to be vigilant about noticing when staff are struggling in their work and when they require support. If poor practice is noticed it should be challenged and further support provided.

Showing an open-door policy and non-judgemental approach to team members/service users who wish to raise a concern or make a complaint

If staff need to talk further about their concerns, they need to understand that as the manager you will listen impartially and not judge them. An open-door policy means you are available at all times to discuss such issues and will do so confidentially. Service users and their families must also clearly understand that they can approach you when they feel the need to and that they are welcome to discuss any issues with you.

Reflective exemplar

An incident arose today at work which made me really think about how I was approaching personalised care. Mrs Casey, an 83-year-old diabetic client, was keen to use her new scooter to attend an art group in the town. She had arranged to meet her friend at the centre and was going to leave at 8.30 for a 9.30 start. I usually ensured that she had her insulin at about 7.30 each morning to ensure she could eat breakfast at 8.30. On the day in question we would need to review that arrangement and change the times. I was not concerned about that at all and felt it was fine to do that; however, my real worry was allowing her to go at all. Mrs C is rather forgetful lately and has only just learned to use her scooter. My worry is that she will not be in full control of the appliance and may forget the key or lose her way. I am also worried about her diabetes and have a concern that should she need help when at the group, she may be unable to articulate what she wants. I feel that I will need to arrange for somebody to be with her when she goes, and this is going to have staffing implications.

As I went through all these thoughts, it became clear to me that I had lost sight of the full picture. Mrs C is an individual with complete control over her own care and choice and I am merely there to ensure that she remains safe in the decision she makes. I spoke to my manager who said I needed to risk assess the event and then discuss with Mrs C anything she needed to help her to meet her goals.

Legislation

Act	Legislation
The Care Act 2014	The Care Act introduced a general duty on local authorities to promote an individual's wellbeing and to have this in mind when planning and making decisions about them or their care, thus strengthening the person-centred agenda.
The Equality Act 2010	This act has a process for complaints if a person is subjected to unlawful treatment (such as discrimination, harassment or victimisation). There is a variety of actions you can take to complain, which can be found on the DirectGov website.
The Mental Capacity Act 2005	The purpose of the MCA is to promote and safeguard an individual's right to make decisions by empowering them. It protects those who lack capacity by placing them at the heart of the decision-making process and also allows people to plan ahead for when they might lack capacity.
General Data Protection Regulation 2018	The General Data Protection Regulation (2018) replaced the Data Protection Act 1998. The GDPR enables people to raise complaints about misuse of data through the courts.
Carers and Disabled Children Act (2000) www.legislation.gov.uk	This act gives power to local councils to supply services direct to carers following assessment even where the person cared for has refused an assessment for community care services. The aim is to support carers in their caring roles and to help them maintain their own health and wellbeing.
Disability Discrimination Act (1995) www.legislation.gov.uk	Now replaced by the Equality Act, except in Northern Ireland, this act has made it unlawful to discriminate against people in respect of their disabilities in relation to employment, the provision of goods and housing.
Human Rights Act (1998) www.legislation.gov.uk	This act applies the human rights set out in the European Convention on Human Rights. These include: the right to life, the right to respect, privacy and family, the right to freedom of religion and belief. The Human Rights Act means you can take action in the UK courts if your human rights have been breached, so an individual who feels their right to personalised care has been breached may take action in court.
Mental Health Act (2007) www.dh.gov.uk	This act was introduced for children and young people. It brings the introduction of Independent Mental Health Advocacy and also the Deprivation of Liberty Safeguards (DoLS): humane and effective mental health legislation. It has been an attempt to ensure that people with mental health problems are not discriminated against in comparison with people needing treatment for physical illnesses.

→

Act	Legislation
Mental Health (Care and Treatment) (Scotland) Act (2003) www.legislation.gov.uk	The Mental Health (Care and Treatment) (Scotland) Act 2003 applies to people with a 'mental disorder' and safeguards them by giving them a right of access to independent advocacy, and the right to be able to choose a 'named person' to support them and protect their interests.
NHS and Community Care Act (1990) www.legislation.gov.uk	This act changed the way in which care is funded and transferred the responsibility of voluntary, private, residential and nursing homes from the Department of Social Security to local authority social services departments. This means that an individual's needs are assessed, and care is planned and provided. This includes the allocation of funds for places in nursing and residential homes as well as other services such as domiciliary care, thus a much more person-centred approach can be adopted.
The Health and Social Care Act 2012	Regulation 16 of this act ensures that people can complain about their care and treatment and that complaints must be investigated effectively and action taken rapidly.
The Data Protection Act 1998	This act was designed to protect any personal data stored on computers or in an organised paper filing system. Under the DPA 1998, individuals had legal rights to control information about themselves.

Suggestions for using the activities

This table summarises all the activities in the unit that are relevant to each assessment criterion.

Here, we also suggest other, different methods that you may want to use to present your knowledge and skills by using the activities. These are just suggestions, and you should refer to the Introduction section at the start of the book, and more importantly the City & Guilds specification, and your assessor, who will be able to provide more guidance on how you can evidence your knowledge and skills. When you need to be observed during your assessment, this can be done by your assessor, or your manager can provide a witness testimony.

Assessment criteria and accompanying activities	Suggested methods to show your knowledge/skills
LO1 Understand the principles and values of person centred outcome-based practice	
1.1 Reflect on it (page 134)	What do you think person-centred practice is? Describe its benefits. How is this positive practice? How is this used in your setting?
1.1 Research it (page 135)	Go to the Dimensions website. Evaluate the package and determine whether it would be useful in your setting.
1.1 Research it (page 136)	Go to the WHO website and research the Health Systems Framework. Undertake a small study to show how your own setting is 'fit for purpose'.
1.1 Evidence opportunity (page 136)	Give an example of how your setting uses each of the Common Core Principles to support the wellbeing of your service users. Evaluate their success and describe how the application of each principle can be improved.
1.1 Research it (page 136)	Research the reablement approach and biographical or life-story work. Critically review these approaches.
1.1 Reflect on it (page 138)	Write a reflective account of your views on this subject and describe how you meet these needs in your organisation.
1.1 Evidence opportunity (page 138)	Which approaches to person-centred practice do you favour? Give an account, evaluating its use. Which other model might be appropriate?
1.1 Reflect on it (page 139)	Consider how you might feel if you were a patient in hospital and never consulted about your treatment.
1.1 Research it (page 140)	Undertake a small-scale study of a group of individuals in your care and ask them to comment on how well active participation in their own care enhances their wellbeing and quality of life.
1.1 Evidence opportunity (page 140)	In your care setting, how do you promote a culture among the workforce that shows consideration of all aspects of individuals' wellbeing? Write a case study which shows the systems and processes in place that promote individual wellbeing.

Suggestions for using the activities	
LO2 Manage resources to facilitate positive outcomes for individuals	
2.1 Evidence opportunity (page 142)	Provide a reflective account on how you drive an organisational culture that values positive outcomes and person-centred practice.
2.2 Evidence opportunity (page 142)	Show your assessor how you develop, implement and evaluate plans to ensure colleagues have appropriate training, development and support to promote person-centred practice.
2.3 Reflect on it (page 143)	Reflect on an incident in which you and the team needed to adapt the care approach in response to one of your service user's changing needs or preferences. How did this affect the person-centred approach?
2.3 Evidence opportunity (page 143)	Provide evidence of how you manage the staff to work with those in receipt of care and support, ensuring that they adapt their approaches to meet an individuals changing needs.
2.4 Evidence opportunity (page 143)	Show your assessor how you manage resources to ensure that reviews of individuals' preferences, wishes, needs and strengths are valued within the achievement of positive outcomes.
2.5 Evidence opportunity (page 144)	Show your assessor how you manage resources to ensure that individuals are actively informed and supported to make healthy choices through a person-centred approach that maintains their wellbeing.
2.5 Reflect on it (page 144)	Write a short reflective account of how you have promoted the notion of good health and healthy choices in one aspect of your provision and how you engaged the staff with it.
2.5 Reflect on it (page 144)	Write a reflective account of the process undertaken here.
2.6 Evidence opportunity (page 145)	Provide a written account critically reviewing the systems in place by commenting upon the strengths and the weaknesses of the processes.
LO3 Lead practice in health and care methods to achieve person-centred outcomes	
3.1 Research it (page 146)	What early warning system is available for your staff? How are they required to document such changes?
3.1 Research it (page 148)	Research other types of assessment, including resource-led assessment. Consider the tools mentioned that enable us to assess various functions and care activities.
3.1 Evidence opportunity (page 148)	Consider the different forms of assessment used in your care setting and determine how useful they are and what changes might be made to improve what you are doing.
3.1 Research it (page 148)	Research a couple of the assessment tools discussed and identify their use in your assessment process.
3.1 Reflect on it (page 148)	Reflect on the staff training session you undertook on assessment. What have you learned from it? What were the strengths and limitations of the session?
3.1 Evidence opportunity (page 150)	Provide a written account critically evaluating your management systems and processes that enable early identification and assessment of an individuals current and emerging health and care. Include the topics covered.
3.2 Evidence opportunity (page 152)	Show your assessor how you implement and evaluate protocols for safe health and care practices that actively promote positive wellbeing/outcomes for the areas discussed here.
3.3 Evidence opportunity (page 153)	Show your assessor how you implement ways of working that ensure that individuals will be able to use, develop, extend or relearn skills for daily activities and achievement of personal outcomes.
3.4 Evidence opportunity (page 155)	Supply evidence to show that the health and care records in your setting are maintained in line with legislation and organisational requirements.
3.5 Reflect on it (page 156)	Talk to your staff and ask them what they understand by the term accountability. Write a reflective account about what you learn from your discussions.
3.5 Research it (page 156)	Research the GDPR 2018 and find out what it says about information sharing, consent and confidentiality.

Suggestions for using the activities	
3.5 Reflect on it (page 157)	Reflect on the legal and ethical tensions between maintaining confidentiality and sharing information in your workplace and write a short piece about them.
3.5 Evidence opportunity (page 157)	Show your assessor how you champion accountability when carrying out adult care procedures. Include recommendations for developing practice with colleagues and others, and address the areas covered here.
3.5 Reflect on it (page 157)	What do you understand by the term accountability when carrying out health and care procedures? Write a short piece on how you ensure that your staff are accountable for their actions.
LO4 Champion equality, diversity and inclusion to achieve positive outcomes	
4.1 Evidence opportunity (page 159)	Speak to your assessor, or provide a written account showing that, within your service area, you understand the impact and effectiveness of equality, diversity and inclusion legislation in preventing discrimination and exclusion of service users.
4.1 Reflect on it (page 159)	Reflect on which law has had the most impact upon the care you give to your service users.
4.2 Research it (page 160)	Research an organisation other than your own and comment upon how it has championed diversity, equality and inclusion.
4.2 Research it (page 161)	Comment on the effectiveness of the systems and processes that promote equality and inclusion or reinforce discrimination and exclusion in your workplace. Research and check whether you have a whistle-blowing policy in place.
4.2 Evidence opportunity (page 162)	Show your assessor that you can lead practice with others in reviewing and evaluating current systems and processes relating to equality, diversity and inclusion.
4.2 Research it (page 162)	Undertake research that identifies the gaps or shortfalls in systems and processes in your setting and propose improvements to address these.
4.2 Reflect on it (page 162)	Think about the systems and processes that promote diversity, equality and inclusion in place in your organisation and reflect on how attitudes have changed during your practice as a care professional. Give some examples.
4.3 Reflect on it (page 165)	Using an incident analysis model of reflection, reflect on thoughts, feelings and behaviours from a situation where you have been tempted to label someone, or to make assumptions about their capabilities or trustworthiness, or when you have felt anxious or threatened by someone you did not know.
4.3 Reflect on it (page 165)	Imagine yourself in a world in which you are seen as an inferior being. What sanctions do you think are appropriate to improve the situation and bring about a more equal environment?
4.3 Research it (page 166)	Carry out a small-scale research study in your setting that looks at diversity, equality and inclusion. Identify the strengths and limitations within your area of practice and make recommendations for improvement.
4.3 Evidence opportunity (page 166)	Show your assessor evidence of how you lead and foster an environment where any discrimination or exclusion is actively challenged and addressed.
LO5 Lead continuous improvement in carrying out health and care procedures where required	
5.1 Evidence opportunity (page 167)	Collect evidence to demonstrate how you monitor, review and evaluate the implementation of person-centred practices and the achievement of positive outcomes for individuals within your setting.
5.2 Research it (page 168)	Write down your findings and thoughts.
5.2 Evidence opportunity (page 168)	Take time to read the publications listed here, which are useful for best practice guidelines about person-centred care and positive outcomes.
5.3 Evidence opportunity (page 169)	Show your assessor that you have researched up-to-date, reliable literature and/or other publications relevant to your area of study to establish best practice.

→

Suggestions for using the activities	
5.3 Reflect on it (page 169)	Draw on a real example of a failure, a mistake of a standard of practice, or a practice that required change, and write a report.
5.4 Evidence opportunity (page 170)	Undertake a review and update of the systems, policies and practices you have in place to ensure they facilitate positive outcome approaches to person-centred care. Show evidence of this to your assessor.
5.5 Evidence opportunity (page 170)	Show your assessor how you actively identify improvements, plan and implement changes to systems and processes.
LO6 Develop community relationships to provide integrated services	
6.1 Evidence opportunity (page 171)	Provide a written account critically evaluating how community involvement/activities support positives outcomes for those in receipt of care and support within your area of service, to include the areas we have discussed in this section.
6.2 Evidence opportunity (page 171)	Provide a written account critically reviewing current practice in respect of the above and make a recommendation that informs strategic operational practice.
LO7 Managing concerns and complaints in adult care	
7.1 Evidence opportunity (page 172)	Using a real work example, evaluate how you have conducted a risk assessment in the workplace.
7.2 Evidence opportunity (page 173)	Show your assessor how you inform staff, individuals and families the procedure to be followed when making a complaint.
7.3 Evidence opportunity (page 173)	Explain how you can develop a culture of trust in which individuals using your service feel safe to raise complaints or concerns.
7.4 Evidence opportunity (page 174)	Set a SMART target to address a recent issue in your workplace.
7.5 Evidence opportunity (page 174)	Using a recent appraisal session, show how you demonstrated an impartial attitude to staff concerns about complaints. Write down how you ensured the member of staff felt safe to discuss their concerns.

References

Department of Health (2003) *Confidentiality NHS Code of Practice*. London: Crown Copyright. TSO.

Department of Health (2003) *Discharge from Hospital: pathway, process and practice*. London: TSO.

Department of Health (2006) *A Stronger Local Voice: A framework for creating a stronger local voice in the Development of Health and Social Care Services*. London: Department of Health.

Department of Health (2007) *Putting People First: A shared vision and commitment to the transformation of adult social care*. London: TSO.

Dimond, B. (1997) *Legal Aspects of Nursing*. Harlow: Pearson Education.

Health Foundation (2014) *Person-centred Care Made Simple*. www.health.org.uk/sites/health/files/PersonCentredCareMadeSimple.pdf

HSA (2015) http://helensandersonassociates.co.uk/outcomes/

Innes, A., Macpherson, S. and McCabe, I. (2006) *Promoting Person-Centred Care at the Front Line*. York: Joseph Rowntree Foundation/SCIE.

Maclean, I., Maclean, S. and Pardy-McLaughlin, L. (2002) *A Handbook of Theory for Social Care. Volume Two*. London: City & Guilds.

Mount, B. (1990) *Making Futures Happen: A manual for facilitators of personal futures planning*. St. Paul, MN: Governor's Council on Developmental Disabilities.

Mullins, L. (2009) *Management and Organisational Behaviour* (8e). Harlow: Prentice Hall.

New Economics Foundation (2012) Co-producing commissioning, unpublished but online: www.altogetherbetter.org.uk/Data/Sites/1/co-producing_commissioning_nef(3).pdf

O'Brien J. (1987) 'A guide to life-style planning', in B. Wilcox and G.T. Bellamy (eds) *A Comprehensive Guide to The Activities Catalog* (pp.175–89). Baltimore: Paul H. Brookes Publishing Co.

Public Health England (2016) *Local Wellbeing, Local Growth: Overview*. London: PHE Publications.

Renz, D. and Eddy, W. (1996) Organisations, ethics and healthcare: building an ethics infrastructure for a new era, *Bioethics Forum*, 12(2): 29–39.

SCIE (2003) *Summary Knowledge review 1: Learning and teaching assessment skills in social work education*. London: SCIE.

Smale, G.G., Tuson, G. and Biehal, N. (1993) *Empowerment, Assessment, Care Management and the Skilled Worker*. London: H.M. Stationery Office.

Taylor, B.J. and Devine, T. (1993) *Assessing Needs and Planning Care in Social Work*. Abingdon: Routledge.

Think Local Act Personal (2011) *Making It Real: Marking progress towards personalised, community-based support*. London: TLAP.

Thompson, N. (2011) *Promoting Equality: Working with diversity and difference* (3e). Basingstoke: Palgrave Macmillan.

Thompson, N. and Thompson, S. (2008) *The Critically Reflective Practitioner*. London: Macmillan Education.

Wilcox, D., Holmes, A., Kean, J., Ritchie, C. and Smith, J. (1994) *The Guide to Effective Participation*. York: Joseph Rowntree Foundation.

Further reading and useful resources

Care Quality Commission (2015) Guidance for Providers on Meeting the Regulations, Care Quality Commission, available on the CQC website.

Care Quality Commission (2015) How CQC Regulates: Residential Adult Social Care Services – Provider Handbook, available on the CQC website.

Care Quality Commission (2015) How CQC Regulates: Residential Adult Social Care Services – Appendices to the Provider Handbook, available on the CQC website.

Department of Health (2001) *Valuing People: A new strategy for learning disability for the 21st century; planning with people; towards person-centred approaches – accessible guide*. London: HMSO.

European Parliament & Council of the European Union (1995) Directive 95/46/EC of the European Parliament and of the Council of 24 October 1995 on the protection of individuals with regard to the processing of personal data and on the free movement of such data. Official Journal, L281, pp. 31–50.

Gov.UK (2016) *Joint Review of Partnerships and Investment in Voluntary, Community and Social Enterprise Organisations*. London: TSO.

Hunter, D.J., Perkins, N., Visram, S., Adams, L., Finn, R., Forrest, A. and Gosling, J. (2018) *Evaluating the Leadership Role of Health and Wellbeing Boards as Drivers of Health Improvement and Integrated Care across England*. Durham: National Institute for Health Research.

Public Health England (2017) *Reducing Health Inequalities: System, scale and sustainability*. London: PHE Publications.

SCIE (2016) *Dignity in Care, Social Care Institute for Excellence Practice Guide 9*. London: SCIE.

Skills for Care (2014) *The Care Certificate Standard 7: Privacy and dignity. What you need to know*, accessed from www.skillsforcare.org.uk/Documents/Learning-and-development/Care-Certificate/Standard-7.pdf

Code of Conduct for Health Care Support Workers and Adult Social Care Workers in England, Department of Health, Skills for Care and Skills for Health, 2013, available on the Skills for Health website.

Creating a Home from Home: A Guide to Standards, Residential Forum.

Delivering Dignity: Securing Dignity in Care for Older People in Hospitals and Care Homes (2012), Commission on Improving Dignity in Care, available on the NHS Confederation website.

Francis Report (2013) Report of the Mid Staffordshire NHS Foundation Trust Public Inquiry. Available at www.midstaffspublicinquiry.com

Books

Gibbs, G. (1988) *Learning by Doing: A guide to teaching and learning methods*. Oxford: Oxford Further Education Unit.

Harris, J., Foster, M., Jackson, K. and Morgan, H. (2005) *Outcomes for Disabled Service Users*. York: Social Policy Research Unit, University of York.

Roberts, G.W. and Machon, A. *Appreciative Healthcare Practice: A guide to compassionate, person-centred care*. Keswick: M&K Publishing.

Sanderson, H. and Lewis, J. (2003) *A Practical Guide to Delivering Personalisation: Person-centred practice in health and social care*. London: Jessica Kingsley Publishers.

Parker, A.H. (2013) *Hierarchy of Needs Counselling Care & Support: A person centred philosophy*. CreateSpace Independent Publishing Platform

Peters, S. (2012) The *Chimp Paradox: The mind management programme to help you achieve success, confidence and happiness*. London: Vermilion.

Journals and magazines

CMM Care Management Matters
Caring Times
Care Talk
Skills for Care, Care Magazine
Care Home Management
Expert Care Manager Magazine
The British Journal of Healthcare Management
Community Care
Caring UK

Websites

Age UK www.ageuk.org.uk

Equality and Human Rights Commission (EHRC) www.equalityhumanrights.com

Health & Care Professions Council (HCPC) www.hcpc-uk.co.uk

Social Care Institute for Excellence www.scie.org.uk

Dignity in Care Campaign www.nhsconfed.org/priorities/Quality/Partnership-on-dignity/Pages/Commission-on-dignity.aspx

Professional development, supervision and performance management

About this unit

People receiving care services must be confident that they can trust those who deliver care not to only know what to do but also to know how to do it well. This requires you to continually update and extend your knowledge and skills and, as a manager, to ensure that your team is also equipped with the appropriate knowledge and skills to fulfil their roles effectively. You also need to provide professional supervision to ensure staff are supported in their roles and enhance their skills and performance.

Personal professional development and supervision is a journey for the whole of your life; it does not end with the completion of a course or a specific activity but should, ideally, be an 'activity of daily living'. The secret of successful personal development is to learn to be reflective and questioning about both the things we know and the things we do not know.

This unit will help you to examine and assess your understanding of professional development, supervision and performance management, and the responsibilities that these concepts entail as a manager and leader. You will develop your reflective and individual planning skills to help you determine how you can most effectively support your own development and that of others.

Learning outcomes

By the end of this unit, you will:

1   Understand principles of professional development in adult care
2   Understand supervision in adult care
3   Provide professional supervision
4   Understand the management of performance in adult care settings

Getting started

Before you study the unit, think about the following:

- What does professional development mean to you?
- Why is professional development important when working in adult care settings?
- What types of support and resources are available to staff teams to support their professional development?
- What do you think are the key principles of formal supervision?
- How effective do you think current performance management processes are and do they work effectively for managers with their staff?

LO1 Understand principles of professional development in adult care

AC 1.1 Importance of continuously improving own knowledge and practice and that of the team

Here, you will be required to explain professional development in adult care in relation to the areas we discuss in this section.

What is professional development, and what is the manager's role in developing themselves and promoting the professional development of others?

Care is a complex, multi-dimensional activity and encompasses more than simply performing a skill. While technical competence gained through developing knowledge and skills is important, it is not sufficient on its own. Excellent care can be achieved only when technical competence is accompanied by appropriate attitudes and characteristics that relate to feelings, values and the way activities are carried out.

Professional development is a continuous process and care workers need to ensure they develop newer, up-to-date knowledge, understanding and skills to meet these changing needs and demands. In striving to improve quality of service and positive outcomes for service users, only the best possible practice will be acceptable. This can only be achieved with a workforce that continually updates knowledge and skills in line with any changes that occur.

This is not a new concept but has emerged as changes to the care system have developed. With moves to partnership working and new models of care which value personalisation and individualised healthcare, professionals have had to ensure that upskilling of the workforce has been a top agenda item.

The *Leitch Review of Skills* (2006) identified the need for the UK to upskill the workforce in order to be able to compete in a global economy that was undergoing rapid change. This has led to changes in education to ensure that the future workforce is sufficiently skilled in literacy, numeracy and new developments, together with moves to extend training in the workplace to ensure regular upskilling of the current workforce occurs.

Role of a manager and workforce development planning for those they manage

As a manager, you are responsible for ensuring that you complete a workforce development plan, which analyses your current skill mix to ensure that staff can fulfil the needs of the clients and service users in your care.

Workforce planning is the way in which an organisation's short- and long-term objectives are achieved by employing the 'right people with the right skills in the right place at the right time'.

Linked to the strategic business goals of the organisation and the planning process, it covers activities such as succession planning and flexible working, and can help you as a manager to develop work schedules and employee hours so that the business can run productively. With a good plan in place you can ensure that the needs of the organisation are met and that any staff gaps are filled. Additionally, you may be required to rethink job roles that may require change. As a manager, one of your roles is to ensure that your employees are satisfied in their work and this includes developing and putting into practice policies to help them carry out their roles in a safe and confident manner.

Source: Adapted from www.cipd.co.uk/knowledge/ strategy/organisational-development/workforce-planning-factsheet

In analysing your plans, you may need to upskill and retrain some staff to ensure that you are meeting current care needs and are planning for future ones also.

Also see section on personal development planning in AC 1.3.

CQC requirements

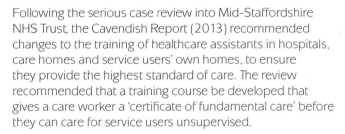

KEY TERM

CQC is the Care Quality Commission, the independent regulator and lead inspection and enforcement body of all health and social care services in England.

Following the serious case review into Mid-Staffordshire NHS Trust, the Cavendish Report (2013) recommended changes to the training of healthcare assistants in hospitals, care homes and service users' own homes, to ensure they provide the highest standard of care. The review recommended that a training course be developed that gives a care worker a 'certificate of fundamental care' before they can care for service users unsupervised.

The requirement for professional development is further reinforced in professional codes and standards of conduct, which articulate the standards that the public can expect from those delivering care. These are:

● Code of Conduct for Healthcare Support Workers and Adult Social Care Workers in England (2013)
● Health Professions Council (2016) Standards of Conduct, Performance and Ethics
● Nursing and Midwifery Council (2018) The Code: Professional standards of practice and behaviour for nurses and midwives

- National Occupational Standards
- Health and Social Care Act 2008 (Regulated Activities) Regulations 2014: Regulation 18

The Health and Social Care Act 2012 and the 2014 Care Act introduced the CQC as the lead inspection and enforcement body for safety and quality of treatment and care matters for people in receipt of a health or adult social care service. This body regulates all social care services in the UK including those provided by local authorities, private and voluntary organisations, as well as the National Health Service. It also provides protection to detainees under the Mental Health Act.

The CQC regulations ensure that providers have enough suitably qualified, competent and experienced staff to enable them to meet all the regulatory requirements described in the Health and Social Care Act 2008 (Regulated Activities) Regulations 2014. It also demands that staff must receive 'the support, training, professional development, supervision and appraisals that are necessary for them to carry out their role and responsibilities'.

CQC must refuse registration if providers cannot satisfy the body that they can and will continue to comply with this regulation.

In turn, the support, training, professional development, supervision and appraisals ensure that staff are able to develop and improve their knowledge. It is important that you as the manager also update your own knowledge along with that of your staff. For example, supervision and appraisals provide opportunities for staff to discuss the areas they would like to and need to develop, and areas where they need to improve their knowledge and practice. They can then find ways to improve this, which may include going on a training course for instance. Your support of your staff in this is very important and you should ensure they have regular supervision sessions and appraisals as well as training and professional development opportunities. This will ensure they are equipped with the most up-to-date knowledge and practice to provide the best possible support to those who use health and social care services.

Mandatory training

Mandatory training is compulsory. To run a safe service to all service users as well as staff, this training will need to be undertaken by the relevant people such as yourself and your staff.

Mandatory training is important, and is needed to comply with legislation, local and national policies as well as agreed ways of working within the setting. This might, for example, be offered to comply with health and safety legislation and help to reduce the risk of accidents in the setting. As a manager you must ensure that staff are given time to attend such training and are compensated if they are attending in their own time.

Mandatory training might include record keeping, hand hygiene, infection prevention and control, and medicines handling and management. The training offered will depend upon the staff role, so some staff may be required to attend more sessions than others depending upon the role they undertake in the organisation.

Whatever mandatory training is offered, however, is unlikely to be sufficient to meet the responsibility and breadth of expectations for personal and professional development implied in the law and in codes of conduct.

Processes involved to manage learning and development

Professional development is a process. This implies that it is an ongoing activity and needs to be thought about as something that is incremental, with the different elements contributing to a larger whole. It is important that you have processes in place to manage and advance your staff's learning and development. For example, in developing your staff you need to have a clear idea about the strategic direction of the organisation so that you can determine what skills and competences your employees will need to support that plan. A training needs analysis is a process by which you can clearly compare your staff's capabilities with your organisation's skill requirements. This will then highlight skills gaps and further development can be put into place.

If your staff are required to carry out different roles in the future to move a project along then the learning and development plan will need to include additional training and sometimes retraining to help staff to fill the gaps. Evaluation of training currently on offer needs to be undertaken to determine its effectiveness and value for staff.

Other processes include the need to prioritise some training and to allocate budget accordingly. Professional development and training enable an organisation to keep up to date and to change proactively so that its service is relevant and appropriate. It is important to note that to get the most out of investment in professional development it should be planned in line with an organisational vision. Ad hoc training may be useful but may only lead to staff undertaking a disparate set of activities that does not contribute to the greater whole.

Providing staff with a variety of skills-based training and one-to-one support is imperative if staff are to develop in a professional way. They are required to undertake training courses on an annual basis to ensure they remain up to date with skills and knowledge and this is all part of professional development.

The relationship between training and positive outcomes

It is recognised that those organisations that embed personal, professional development into their culture are best able to respond to day-to-day challenges and pressures and are more resilient and able to transform in response to changing situations and requirements (Schön, 1983, p. 28; Harrison, 2009).

Personal, professional development increases the capabilities of staff. If it is tailored to individual needs, it should bring about personal enhancements and opportunities as individuals expand their personal tool box of skills. The image of the 'Knowledge and Skills Escalator' articulated in *The NHS Knowledge and Skills Framework and Development Review Guidance* (DoH, 2004) is a powerful one. It effectively illustrates the idea of professional development being about continual movement. It generates the image of individuals having access to a range of education and development opportunities at different levels which can be individually selected and packaged in many different ways. It supports the idea that professional development can be undertaken in a traditional, linear way, starting at the bottom and moving through the levels to the top, but that it is equally valid for an individual to get off the escalator at any point and move around on that level in order to access a whole package of different activities before re-joining the escalator. The direction of travel may take an individual up a floor to extend previous knowledge, or down a floor to access new learning. It also suggests that there should be no limit to opportunities, that even if you start at the bottom you can move to the top. As a manager it is important that you and your organisation capitalise on the benefits that professional development brings by ensuring that it is purposive and planned to meet the individual needs of your staff and to address organisational needs.

Evidence opportunity

1.1 Importance of continuously improving knowledge/practice

Provide a written account explaining professional development in relation to the areas we have discussed in this section. Make sure you explain the importance of continuously improving your own knowledge and practice and that of the team you manage and lead.

You might want to explain how you undertake the process of professional development in adult care in relation to those you manage and your own professional development. You could evidence this by putting a copy of your professional development plan into your portfolio. Consider:

- the processes involved to manage learning and development
- how you undertake workforce development planning
- how you identify and provide mandatory training
- how you evidence that you support CQC requirements
- the relationship between training and positive outcomes.

Reflect on it

1.1 Training and positive outcomes

Write a reflective piece about the relationship between training and positive outcomes. How do you know this happens?

Reflect on it

1.1 The importance of continually improving knowledge/practice

What professional development activities have you and your team participated in over the last year?

- How do they reflect the changes that have impacted on your work in adult care? Make a list.
- Were they planned, and if so, by whom?
- Were they part of a development plan for the organisation or focused on individual needs?
- What is the evidence that they have resulted in positive outcomes?
- Give examples.
- How have they helped to improve knowledge and practice?
- Summarise the importance of improving knowledge and practice.

AC 1.2 Importance of reflective practice in improving performance and the use of models to support the reflective practitioner

Here, you will be required to critically evaluate the theory of reflective practice in improving individual performance with reference to the areas we discuss in this section.

As you learnt in Unit 501, AC 2.4, **reflective practice** is an essential element of personal development. It provides an opportunity to stop and take stock. Bolton (2010, p. 4) identifies a number of applications for reflective practice.

Go to Unit 501, AC 2.4 and the section on reflection and reflective practice to revise these points.

Reflective practice is a conscious activity that results in positive decisions. Reflection has gained significant weight in recent years in the healthcare arena and a number of models have been developed to assist practitioners to reflect.

KEY TERM

Reflective practice is the act of stopping and thinking about what we are doing in practice and analysing the decisions we make in the light of theory and the things we have learned. By doing this we are more able to relate theory to practice, helping us to generate new knowledge and ideas.

Donald Schön, 1983

The term reflective practice was first coined by Donald Schön (1983). He identified that learning in practice could be enhanced by two different kinds of activity: reflection in-action and reflection on-action:

- **Reflection in-action** requires practitioners to 'think ahead', to critically reflect on what one is doing while one is doing it and to revise actions in the light of that reflection (Greenwood, 1993). This is sometimes referred to as 'thinking on our feet' and being able to look at the experience and to say how we feel about it at the time. For example, something new that surprises us may happen in the course of our duty and we therefore have to think about how we approach this unique event. In care work this may require us to move outside of textbook-type responses and create new ways of doing things.

- **Reflection on-action** is a retrospective activity that requires practitioners to interpret and analyse recalled information from activities that they have been engaged with (Boyd and Fales, 1983; Fitzgerald, 1994; Atkins and Murphy, 1994). Using our example above this can be further explored by reflecting upon what we did in the new encounter and why we did it. In this way we start to develop questions and key ideas about the event and the experience. In doing so we are engaging with critical evaluation of a situation and can then build upon our knowledge of the practice and our responses.

One major criticism of the reflection in- and on-action theory is that of time and the notion that sometimes we need to make decisions quickly without much thought or reflection. We have to fall back on routine practice and carry out the task as set. However, this may set up some questions about why we are doing certain things in certain ways and this sort of reflection then becomes useful not only in moving practice forward but also for our own knowledge.

Reflection is, therefore, the art of thinking back and examining the things that happened, learning from them and avoiding those same mistakes. Schön's model encourages us to explore thoughts and feelings to become more self-aware and by doing so we can develop our practice. We should aim to ensure that we make sense of our learning and what we learn becomes practice.

D.A. Kolb's learning cycle

Kolb's (1984) cycle of experiential learning can be adapted well here. Kolb suggests that we need to recall our observation of an event, or the change in this case, reflect on those observations, develop and research some theories about what we saw and then decide on some action because of the process (Jasper, 2006).

Kolb's theory was based on the premise that learning is a process in which knowledge comes about through the transforming experience (Kolb, 1984).

Like Schön's theory, in this cycle the 'concrete experience' of the learning event (stage one) is followed by 'reflection' in which the learner thinks about what happened (stage two). Stage three is the process of thinking about how the learning can be used and, finally, the learner in stage four plans how to use the knowledge in the future.

G. Gibbs' six stages to reflective practice

Many models are constructed around the use of structured questions to prompt reflection in a logical and systematic manner (Johns, 1995). These questions are often focused on incident analysis as the key method of reflecting (Gibbs, 1988). Gibbs' model was developed from Kolb's four-stage experiential learning cycle (1984) and is sometimes referred to as an iterative model or learning through repetition as opposed to Kolb's experiential learning model described as learning through experience.

Gibbs' reflective cycle has six stages:

1. Description – Asking oneself 'what happened?'
2. Feelings – What did I think or feel here?
3. Evaluation – What was good or bad about what happened at that time?
4. Analysis – What does it mean, and can I make any sense of it?
5. Conclusion – How else might I have dealt with it? What else could I have done?
6. Action plan – What will I do next time?

This approach entails practitioners selecting a significant incident, writing about it in detail and then analysing what happened, asking why, and identifying what additional knowledge would have enabled the practitioner to behave differently. It requires the reflector to explore what evidence there is that similar things have been addressed by others more effectively and to establish what learning can be drawn from the experience.

It enables practitioners to be better prepared when faced with similar experiences in the future, as well as providing an opportunity to identify shortcomings in knowledge or skills which can be rectified.

As a learning tool, this theory can make the structure of how we write about an event easier. Occasionally, we may write in a purely descriptive manner and sometimes confuse evaluation and analysis, which leads to repetition. By using the stages shown above you can be sure that you are addressing each part of the learning cycle in a more constructive way.

Models of reflection are normally illustrated as cyclical activities, such as those depicted in Figure 6.1 and Figure 6.2.

Choose a model that suits your learning needs

Different models of reflection suit different learning styles and different purposes. A model is a tool to provide structure to an activity and it is important that you select one that suits your style. The significant thing to remember is that whichever model is selected, it is the learning that results from the activity that is the important thing. Learning that is either confirmation that behaviour is appropriate or learning that suggests a need to gain more information or change practice.

Evidence opportunity

1.2 Importance of reflective practice

Provide a written account critically evaluating the theories of reflective practice in improving individual performance, with reference to:

- Donald Schön
- Kolb's learning cycle
- Gibbs' six stages to reflective practice
- reflection for-action, reflection in-action, reflection on-action
- professionalism and reflection, individual responsibility
- relationship between professionalism and accountability
- barriers to effective reflective practice for organisations and individuals.

Remember, critical evaluation requires you to make positive and/or negative judgements about an experience and you do this by thinking about what went well or badly during the experience and perhaps commenting on how it ended.

Reflective practice improves performance because it helps us to challenge our assumptions about what we do on a daily basis. For example, it helps us to question why we practise in certain ways and do certain things and in doing so we can start to explore different approaches. We are also engaged in identifying our own strengths and weaknesses and are then in a position to address them.

Reflection for-action, reflection in-action, reflection on-action

Schön's theory identifies reflection in-action and reflection on-action as we explored earlier, but some writers have added a further stage: reflection-for-action. Killion and Todnem (1991) refer to the stages in Schön's model as occurring during (reflection in-action) and immediately after (reflection on-action) an event. Their addition of reflection for-action expects the learner to review the previous two processes and to reflect upon what has been accomplished and to identify guidelines to follow to succeed in the same task in the future. By undertaking this sort of reflection learners are encouraged to think about past experiences before rushing into completing the same actions in the future.

Professionalism and reflection, individual responsibility

Our fitness to work in adult care requires us to behave professionally and to do so means we need to demonstrate behaviour which shows we are open minded, reflective and take our duty of care seriously by engaging in life-long learning and self-improvement.

Professionalism is a core quality to be developed and demands that we work to defined standards within our codes of conduct and demonstrate a responsible attitude towards how we manage patients and their information. Our clinical judgement must be based upon evidence and research and we also must be mindful of ethical and moral consideration in our work.

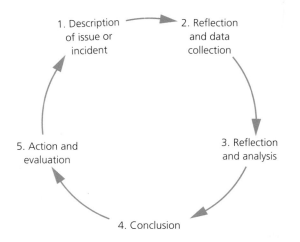

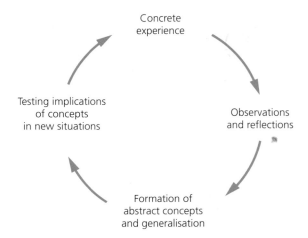

▲ **Figures 6.1 and 6.2** Models of reflection based on Gibbs and Kolb

Relationship between professionalism and accountability

Being a professional means that we behave in ways that do not bring the profession into disrepute, and we can accomplish this by keeping our professional development up to date through supervision as well as reflection on our practice. We are accountable for how we practise and how we approach the patients in our care and this accountability and professionalism come through regulation and the duty of care we owe the people we care for.

When times are difficult it may be necessary to reduce the amount of development that can be supported. Trying to do too much runs the risk of adding stress on staff and possible loss of good will. It is your responsibility to be able to justify decisions. Sorting your activities into priority categories with identification of associated risks if an activity is not done is one way of prioritising development.

Barriers to effective reflective practice for organisations and individuals

It is not difficult to mount a convincing argument for integrating professional development and reflective practice into organisational culture, yet when times are busy and challenging, it can be the first thing to drop off the agenda. However, reflective practice and staff development are essential requirements for any service seeking to provide care for others. The challenge for the manager, therefore, is to find ways of identifying, recognising, overcoming and reducing any barriers to reflective practice and professional development. Barriers are little more than hurdles to get around. While they may seem insurmountable, ingenuity, creativity and a positive attitude may be sufficient to overcome them. Barriers should be viewed as problems to be solved rather than as overwhelming obstacles.

Potential barriers to effective reflective practice

Boud and Walker (1993) classify barriers to reflective practice as being internal, or those coming from the learner themselves, and external, those coming from the environment and other forces that may impact upon the learner, such as stereotyping and culture.

A number of barriers from a personal perspective may become evident as we experience stress with the occurrence of negative events. In this case, we may avoid thinking about the situation and this then becomes a barrier because to revisit such raw feelings is painful. We become more inclined to lock them away rather than addressing the emotion and feeling inherent within reflection.

Also, we may be unaware of the existence of barriers. For example, journal writing is a major part of reflection and, for some professionals, group discussion, yet how many of your colleagues express their dissatisfaction with doing such activities, being unable to see the benefit of the activity? Getting down to writing the journal may also present a barrier as we may struggle to know what to write or how to write it. A further barrier is the environment in which to write because of potential interruptions, lack of space and time and the suitability of the place.

In addition, staff need to feel that reflecting is an activity valued for its own sake and is not just another chore to be squeezed in around more important routine activities. Consequently, staff need the encouragement to put their reflection and learning into practice.

Research it

1.2 Potential barriers to professional development

Research potential barriers to undertaking professional development and reflection in your workplace and then set up an action plan to overcome them. A table has been included to help you.

Potential barrier	Action to overcome barrier	Potential risk if not undertaken
e.g. journal writing		

Reflect on it

1.2 Barriers affecting outcomes for service users

Write a short reflective account of how the potential barriers to reflective practice affect the outcomes for service users.

AC 1.3 Mechanisms and resources that support learning and development in adult care settings

Here, you will be required to evaluate a range of sources and systems of support for professional development for the manager and their staff, including areas we discuss in this section.

Not all professional development will be achieved by attending formal training or education events. In fact, financial restraints often mean we need to be careful about where the money goes for training and it is clear that other in-house activities can be just as valuable and sometimes more cost effective. There are various forms of informal and formal support that are of significant value in developing others' capabilities.

Resources – internal financial support, access to publicly funded training opportunities

Inevitably, investing in opportunities to enable staff to keep up to date is associated with costs and it would be unrealistic and irresponsible not to consider these costs seriously.

There will be a budget for staff training (including for yourself, as manager) set aside but often this is inadequate and staff may need to be prepared to fund some of the cost for training themselves. Sometimes funding can be accessed from external sources. For example, grants and bursaries may be available to help with fees. The National Institute for Health Research also funds applied health research and provides training programmes for undergraduate level through to opportunities in leadership and research programmes.

However, the risk of not engaging in development activities may be very costly in terms of the long-term organisational plan, so it is important to balance these investment costs against this. While it might be tempting to see staff development as a luxury, non-essential activity when times are tight, in an environment in which treatments, practices and expectations are constantly changing, that would be a mistake. It is important to ensure that any development budget is spent appropriately and that key risks are prioritised over other, less important, activities.

See AC 1.5 for more information on what can happen if you fail to train staff.

Other factors include time and career goals and aspirations. Time is a factor that must be considered if staff need to go off site to attend training. Having a firm career plan in place can be a valuable asset in terms of choosing appropriate training activities.

Resources – access to books, journals

Access to books and journals may also be a source of learning for your staff, so a library of such might be a useful addition to the resources. In a small organisation, this may well be a luxury, but staff may be willing to donate books that they no longer have any use for and you might also check with other stakeholders about access to their book resources.

NHS trusts and CCGs often have links to local authorities, local colleges and universities so it is worth investigating the use of their resources. On-site facilities at hospitals and local colleges may house small libraries but can often obtain books and journals if requested.

Digital resources – e-learning

E-learning packages are an excellent way of ensuring that all staff undergo the same training and they can access these either at work or in their own time. They are also able to build their own e-portfolios without having to have a paper copy of everything and are able to upload reflective accounts, certificates and test results as well as essays and other pieces of information. These can then be accessed by tutors and assessors at a distance.

Many organisations have their own system of online training. The NHS, for example, now trains its staff using e-learning resources. Some of the partnerships you have may have access to such training and this might be shared. Staff are able to access this learning at any time. They can do so from home or when in work by simply logging into the system and undertaking the online modules.

Peer supervision , coaching, mentoring and buddying

Mentoring

Mentoring is an invaluable tool for supporting staff development and is a powerful means of individual empowerment. Clutterbuck and Megginson (1999, p. 17) describe mentorship as 'standing in front of a mirror with a trusted other, who can help you see things that you do not know how to see, or that have become too familiar for you to notice'.

Mentoring can be defined simply as a helping relationship between an individual with potential and an individual with expertise. The role of the mentor is to guide the mentee. Knowledge, experience and organisational perspective are shared candidly within a context of mutual respect and trust. It is an effective way of helping people to progress in their careers and is becoming increasingly popular as its potential is realised. A number of roles of the mentor have been listed by Bolton (2010, p. 193): role model, enabler, teacher, encourager, counsellor, befriender, facilitator, coach, confidant, supporter and 'un-learner'. We might also add peer supervision to this list and buddying.

> ### KEY TERM
>
> **Mentoring** is a relationship in which an individual with expertise can help another individual to progress in their career.

Peer supervision and buddying

Peer supervision is an arrangement in which peers work together for mutual benefit to provide support and feedback to each other, while buddying is a more informal arrangement, which also involves support and advice for the care worker. The buddy may be chosen by the person requiring the support and acts as a role model.

Coaching

Coaching, although sometimes used interchangeably with mentoring, is in fact a distinct activity, although there are some similarities.

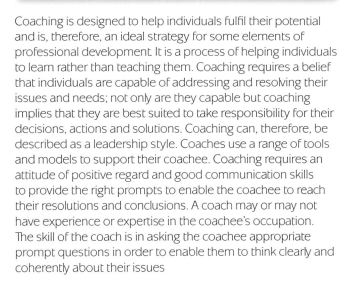

KEY TERM

Coaching is a process that supports and enables an individual to unlock and maximise their potential, to develop and improve performance.

Coaching is designed to help individuals fulfil their potential and is, therefore, an ideal strategy for some elements of professional development. It is a process of helping individuals to learn rather than teaching them. Coaching requires a belief that individuals are capable of addressing and resolving their issues and needs; not only are they capable but coaching implies that they are best suited to take responsibility for their decisions, actions and solutions. Coaching can, therefore, be described as a leadership style. Coaches use a range of tools and models to support their coachee. Coaching requires an attitude of positive regard and good communication skills to provide the right prompts to enable the coachee to reach their resolutions and conclusions. A coach may or may not have experience or expertise in the coachee's occupation. The skill of the coach is in asking the coachee appropriate prompt questions in order to enable them to think clearly and coherently about their issues

The 'GROW' model of coaching (Whitmore, 2002) provides a simple and structured model for the coach:

G = Goal setting asks questions to encourage the mentee to clarify what they want and where they want to get to. The coach will encourage the coachee to explore what achievement would look like to them.

R = Reality promotes questions that require reflection now. What is the situation currently? What is stopping you achieving your goals? What do you need to achieve your goals? What is a realistic time scale? What do you enjoy and why? What are the key risks?

O = Options. This stage of the model encourages the coachee to explore different means of achieving the goal. Questions that might be asked include: What are the different ways that you could achieve your goal? What else could you do? What are the pros and cons of different options? What would happen if ...? Which of the options would bring about the best result?

W = Way forward. Finally, the coach will encourage the coachee to make an action plan. Questions that might be useful include: What are you resolved to do, and by when? What support do you need? What commitment do you have? When should we/you review progress?

Coaching enables control and development to remain squarely with the coachee, with the effective coach acting merely as a key to help them unlock their potential.

These roles, although useful, do have their drawbacks. Some require additional training and others require time, always a scarce resource.

Use of external training providers

External training providers can offer experience and often challenge entrenched ways of thinking in an organisation. They are also specialists in their field and can, therefore, offer greater depth of knowledge. Additionally, an external company will bring in staff who are able to train others in an effective way. Often, in-house training relies on people who might be great managers but who may not necessarily possess good teaching skills. Unfortunately, external training providers are expensive and hidden costs, such as travel for the course trainers, accommodation as well as day rates for courses, can all add up and need to be factored into your own budget for an event. Also, you will want to ensure that most of your staff are at the event and this will then have an additional cost with staff being away from the workplace and cover being required.

Training needs analysis

It has been said that the richest resource that any organisation possesses is the people who work within it. Individuals are interested in, and motivated by, different things and this includes their motivation to learn something. Consequently, everyone's knowledge base and skill set are different, even when similar levels of formal training have been undertaken. If we could pool and share this knowledge, everyone, including the organisation, would benefit. A key role for a manager is to utilise the existing skill set within a team in order to enhance the knowledge and skills of others. This is achieved by having in place a *training needs analysis* in which you clearly set out what training must be accomplished and how this is best achieved. In AC 1.1, we defined training needs analysis as a systematic way in which we can understand what training is needed for our organisation. By identifying the skills of our employees and the gaps in their knowledge we begin to understand what training is needed to address the issues that have been identified.

Personal development planning

Formal support for development is organised and has learning objectives, the intention of which is to gain knowledge and skills. Informal support, meanwhile, may not be organised or planned, but may happen as a result of experience in the workplace. Again, it is important to understand which style suits the individual by discussing their *personal professional development*.

Appraisal

Appraisals are a key strategy for managers to assess performance and needs against organisational requirements and aims. An appraisal is a formally constituted, annual activity that should be booked with all staff. Appraisals are normally conducted by a manager but can be conducted by peers if their focus is on developmental needs rather than role performance. Whichever model is adopted, individuals need to be warned about what it will involve so that they can prepare. Ideally, they should see examples of any documentation that will be used so that they can plan responses to the questions that will be asked. Appraisal offers a vehicle for structured, personal development planning that can have positive outcomes for both individuals and the organisation. It may help develop a strategy for an individual to meet personal goals and objectives, both short and long term. It will help the manager to match individuals and their training needs against organisational aims and it will also enable managers to assess the fairness of the training and development allocation across the staff team. Where necessary, it also provides a process for managing staff performance, as it encourages managers to measure individual performance against role competency criteria.

Appraisal offers a vehicle for structured, *personal development planning* (PDP) that can have positive outcomes for both individuals and the organisation. It may help develop a strategy for an individual to meet personal goals and objectives, both short and long term. It will help the manager to match individuals and their training needs against organisational aims and it will also enable managers to assess the fairness of the training and development allocation across the staff team.

Appraisal is a shared activity, which takes time and effort and must be planned if it is going to have any significant impact on PDP. PDP can have a number of different purposes and it is important that the method you select for PDP meets your needs as a manager, as well as the individual staff member's needs. It is important that the tool you design or utilise addresses those purposes that you have identified as important for your organisation. If you do not have an appraisal process in your organisation, you may want to consider writing a proposal to implement one.

Of course, there are drawbacks to appraisals and if they are not carried out correctly they can be a negative experience, particularly as they may be somewhat subjective and potentially viewed as biased. Also, time is a major issue in carrying out this activity.

There is more information on appraisals in AC 2.5.

> ## KEY TERM
>
> **Appraisal**, sometimes referred to as performance appraisal, is the process by which employees and line managers discuss their performance, developmental needs and the support they need in their role. It is used to provide evidence and evaluation of recent performance and focus on future goals, opportunities and resources.

Support for staff with learning needs

You may have workers who have *specific learning needs* such as dyslexia or speaking English as an additional language. They may need extra help or different forms of learning. For example, some people with dyslexia report that text can appear to move or become blurred and that white paper or backgrounds make print hard to read. By changing the colour of the paper and the type of print you can help with this. For staff who have English as a second language we need to offer more creative ways to help them to learn not only our language but also the vocabulary that comes with care work. By using a more visual approach in training in the form of pictures and photographs, such learners can make sense of new information. We can also get learners to work with partners or in small groups to help them.

Older learners also may prefer a different style of learning to those who have just left school; for example, online learning may come more naturally to younger learners who have grown up with the internet. It is a case of knowing what fits each member of staff best and working with it.

Your role as a manager

As a manager it is your responsibility to ensure that staff development both meets organisational needs and priorities and supports and motivates individual team members' personal and professional development. A good development plan will fulfil both requirements. It will identify and prioritise development goals and targets to meet the standards and will address and avert potential risks resulting from knowledge or skills deficits. It will enhance service delivery and develop staff's personal and professional capacities. It should be realistic and recognise any limitations but also strive to be ambitious. It is important to achieve a balance between what can properly be supported and devising creative strategies to achieve more. It must be fair: opportunities must be fairly distributed across the team and across all levels of staff. It must result in tangible outcomes and staff who are developed must be enabled to share and/or implement their learning. Consequently, when designing your plan, you will need to build in evaluative measures to ensure that you are fulfilling your obligations and objectives.

See Unit 509 AC 4.2 for more information. It would also be useful for you to refer to ACs 1.5 and 2.5 for more information on SMART objectives.

Evidence opportunity

1.3 Mechanisms and resources that support learning and development

Look at the range of sources and systems of support for professional development below:

- Resources – internal financial support, access to publicly funded training opportunities
- Resources – access to books, journals
- Digital resources – e-learning
- Peer shadowing, coaching, mentoring, buddying
- Use of external training providers
- Training needs analysis
- Personal development planning

- Support for staff with learning needs (e.g. dyslexia; non-English speakers; the older learner; the young learner).

Provide a written account evaluating a range of sources and systems of support for professional development for the manager and their staff, including the ones above.

You might like to think about how you use each type of learning in your setting, taking into account how useful they are to staff members, which types specific staff would benefit from, how you can measure their success and how you can improve the planning and provision of systems of PD. For example, you might identify how each staff member would benefit from the types of learning above. You might also identify how peer coaching and mentoring are useful to your team.

Research it

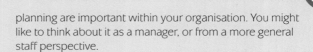

1.3 Comparing different sources/systems of support

Research sources and systems of support where you work. Think about which of the following functions of personal development planning are important within your organisation. You might like to think about it as a manager, or from a more general staff perspective.

Function of personal development planning	Tick	Does your PDP enable this function to be realised?	Comment here upon the strengths and weaknesses of these approaches
Assessment of competence to undertake a role against predetermined criteria (e.g. role descriptor)			
Opportunity to enhance effectiveness and performance			
Planning for the future (short, medium and long term)			
Clarification of values and behaviours			
Evaluation of service			
Means of enhancing service			
Increase staff motivation			
Opportunity for self-reflection			
Identification of strengths and areas for improvement			
Strategy to solve problems			
Provide a structure for and commitment to staff training and development			
Opportunity to manage and respond to change			
Increase team capabilities			
Manage underperformance			
Provide a structure for individual feedback			

AC 1.4 Technology used in supporting learning activities

Here, you will be required to analyse the effectiveness of digital technologies used in supporting learning activities with consideration of the areas we discuss in this section.

We live in a technological age where it is almost unthinkable that we can survive without our smartphones! All your staff are likely to use smartphones, computers, tablets and iPads for all sorts of activities. Using a device for training that a worker is familiar with will certainly help with adjusting to their own style of learning. They will also have access to digital textbooks that are constantly updated and are more cost effective than printed books. Apps are also now available to help with clinical work. For example, there are apps that provide medication guidance, and this might be useful for staff.

As discussed in AC 1.3 above, online and digital resources are valuable development aids if they are used wisely. However, you do need to consider how best to provide these to result in tangible outcomes and prevent users from being distracted.

Access to technologies

Computers are now a major part of health and care work and a lot of the systems for adult care are available in software packages. Our staff must be computer literate in order to be able to use adult care management and record systems and to be able to input patient changes to care plans. Additionally, the internet provides a wealth of information and guidance about adult care and we are able to access medication guidance and treatment protocols with ease.

The impact of e-learning packages in improving knowledge and skills and e-portfolios

E-learning packages are an excellent way of ensuring that all staff have access to the same learning programs and can therefore undergo training at home or at work. They are able to build e-portfolios without having to have a paper copy of all training and are able to upload reflective accounts, certificates and test results. This type of portfolio can also then be seen by managers and tutors if permissions allow.

Access to work-based internet

All staff should be able to access the internet at work for finding information and for research. The internet also offers opportunities to connect with other adult care workers and organisations for support and professional advice. It offers online training courses, and so the wealth of information and opportunities the internet offers should be exploited for the benefit of your staff and setting.

Webinars

A webinar is an online seminar, which might be a presentation, or a lecture or training session. For your staff it might be a useful way to access training at a distance but be able to interact with the trainer at the same time by asking questions. This is something that you and staff can access at home or in the setting, and so it can be time saving and cuts the cost of commuting to venues outside the setting. It offers opportunities to gain up-to-date insights into adult care, for example, and also to upskill. The Health Foundation has included and recorded many webinars on its website which are available for use. Go to www.health.org.uk/collection/webinars for more information.

Conference calling

Conference calling is a phone call involving several people at the same time. It can be set up so that each party may participate or that one party leads the call while the other participants listen. This system is often used in health and care when several providers in different locations need to be able to link in with each other to access information. For example, you may need to hold a conference call to discuss a change in a care package.

Recent developments

Skype is a way to make free computer-to-computer calls or reduced-rate calls from a computer to a phone and has been used in a number of trusts around the UK. Recently, new developments have involved GP consultations for patients who require a face-to-face consult with a medical practitioner for a small fee. Guidance for its use in healthcare work specifies that Skype can be used in some consultations, where quality of service and security are not paramount, but clinicians should be highly aware of the security risks associated with such technology. For your own use it might be useful to be able to have a face-to-face meeting at a distance with another care provider and as long as you are doing so in a secure way and patient confidentiality is not being compromised then this might be a useful technology.

Impact of using technologies to support professional development

The Wanless Report (2002) concluded that within 20 years the UK would need to devote substantially more resources to ensure high-quality services to meet public expectations and healthcare needs. In 2007, Wanless suggested that within the next two decades spending on technology would need to grow even faster to catch up with that of other countries, thus creating a challenge to develop an information strategy for the health service in this country (Wanless, 2007). Substantial progress has been made, so that today patient care is safer and more reliable as a result of the technological changes that have been made. We now have access to hand-held computers,

Evidence opportunity

1.4 Technology used in supporting learning activities

Provide a written account analysing the effectiveness of digital technology used in supporting learning activities with consideration of the areas we have discussed in this section.

You might like to think about the following questions:

- Access to technologies: How do staff access professional development technologies (e.g. online courses, apps, webinars) in your setting?

- The impact of e-learning packages in improving knowledge and skills: If you and your staff have access to e-learning, has it improved your staff training schedules? What other benefits have you seen? Are there any drawbacks? If you do not have access, how might you source them?

- Conference calling: How can conference calling or face-to-face communication via computers improve communication

with partners and between colleagues? What other advantages are there?

- Access to work-based internet: What are the pros and cons of accessing a work-based internet or intranet? If you do not have access, could it be an option? What would you need to do to make it successful?

- E-portfolios: Are these being used? If not, could they be? How?

- Webinars: Do you use these for sharing training? What are the advantages and issues? If you don't use them, how can you identify the potential benefits?

Reflect on the impact that using technologies to support professional development has on you, as the manager, staff members and service users.

What barriers have you found to the use of digital technologies in learning? How can you overcome them?

which record the medical history of patients and can check previous tests, vital signs and medicine orders. In 2016, the Health Secretary Jeremy Hunt outlined proposals to make it possible for patients to access their own GP electronic record online, including blood test results, appointment records and medical history, and this is becoming a reality.

Electronic databases contain large amounts of information used for medical research. Apps on smartphones mean that clinicians can access thousands of medical textbooks and online medical databases to improve treatment and diagnoses. Email, texting, videos, conference calls and social media are also useful means by which to consult with people all over the world. Search engines such as Google have opened medicine to the public, enabling people to access online NHS guidance.

Barriers to the use of digital technologies in learning

Time, lack of equipment and resistance to change are all barriers to integrating new technology into the way in which we deliver adult care. For example, we may have a great new computer program, which is designed to improve patient care by reducing the time it takes to access their information. If, however, time and training are not forthcoming, the likelihood of it being adopted will be low. Staff will simply see the new idea as unimportant. As a leader you will need to take the initiative and insist that time is given to developing its use.

AC 1.5 Potential barriers and constraints in relation to professional development in adult care

Here, you will be required to critically evaluate the potential barriers and constraints in your working environment in accessing professional development with consideration of the areas we discuss in this section.

Workforce development strategy and planning

You should have a workforce development strategy and plan in place to identify and prioritise development goals and targets to meet the standards and address and avert potential risks resulting from knowledge or skills deficits. This will enhance service delivery and develop staff's personal and professional capacities. It should be realistic and recognise any limitations but also strive to be ambitious. It is important to achieve a balance between what can properly be supported and devising creative strategies to achieve more. It must be fair: opportunities must be fairly distributed across the team and across all levels of staff. It must result in tangible outcomes and, consequently, staff who are developed in their roles must be enabled to share and/or implement their learning. Consequently, when designing your plan, you will need to build in evaluative measures to ensure that you are fulfilling your obligations and objectives.

Having identified strengths, deficits, training needs and ideas for service enhancements, it is important that these are transformed into tangible actions that can be articulated as objectives. Objectives are statements that describe what the end point of an activity will be. Objectives should be written with the **SMART** acronym in mind; that is, they should be **S**pecific, **M**easurable, **A**ttainable, **R**elevant and **T**imebound. Your plan must be able to deliver what you set out to do and you must evaluate how successful you have been. Consequently, having more information on which you can base your plan should secure the best chance of success.

You may find, however, that you meet barriers to your efforts and these may be due to fear of change and the sort of negative thinking that stops people from moving forward. New ideas are often met with fear of change and as a leader you need to outline a clear strategy and allow others not only to be heard but to contribute to the discussions. Also, in developing change in an organisation, it is not unusual for off-site workshops to be arranged at venues away from the workplace. This reduces interruptions, work phone calls and participants leaving the meeting to attend to work-related situations.

Financial budgets to support workforce development planning and delivery

Lack of finance can be a constraint in relation to professional development and is often the main reason for not supplying training. Inevitably, investing in opportunities to enable staff to keep up to date is associated with costs and it would be unrealistic and irresponsible not to consider these costs seriously. However, the risk of not engaging in development activities may be very costly in terms of the long-term organisational plan and the workforce development plan so it is important to balance these investment costs against this. While it might be tempting to see staff development as a luxury or non-essential activity when times are tight, in an environment in which treatments, practices and expectations are constantly changing, that would be a mistake. It is important to ensure that any development budget is spent appropriately and that key risks are prioritised over other, less important, activities.

For example, failing to ensure that staff gain appropriate training in relation to manual handling would leave the organisation vulnerable to litigation and potentially expensive compensation claims from both staff and possibly clients. Given the nature of care work that requires moving and handling to take place, it is highly likely that an incident will occur, and it is also likely to have a significant impact. This would result in a high-risk score on a risk assessment chart, which should alert the manager that there is a need to do something urgently to rectify the deficit. Risks can be plotted on a chart so that it is easy to get a visual image of where key areas need to be addressed.

Financial contributions of staff to support the costs of training and return on investment

This is potentially a major barrier as staff may be unable or unwilling to pay for their own training, so effective methods to enable this need to be sought. Training that staff wish to undertake for their own professional development, and for career enhancement, is usually paid for by themselves, and perhaps this is something that must be made clear to them. However, they can access bursaries and grants if they take the time to source these pockets of funding. You might also agree to fund part of the training, particularly if you can see that upskilling a member of staff in this way would be a useful addition to the training portfolio of the team. Staff may be able to cascade their knowledge to others so investing in their training may provide a better service for patients and improved training for other members of staff.

Poor time management and commitment of staff and quality of training delivery and support

Time is a factor that must be considered if staff need to go off site to attend training; for example, training days mean that staff are unavailable to work, and this requires payment for cover staff. Additionally, staff may not use the time in such training sessions wisely and merely see it as a day off from work. The training that staff are sent for also needs to be of good quality and staff might be asked to make some evaluation or provide reflective accounts of their learning to ensure they are gaining the most from such an investment. It also needs to be training that addresses the professional development needs of staff.

Insufficient or high turnover of staff

With insufficient staff in the department or team you may find attendance at training becomes impossible. Staff may be denied training if the department is busy and the setting would rather staff be in the setting than release them for training courses. Part of your workforce planning needs to address reasons behind the high turnover of staff in order to recruit sufficient numbers. The high turnover of staff may be due to stress and workload experienced in the workplace and knowing this means your recruitment process can look at introducing incentives to join your organisation.

Access to nationally recognised qualifications and/or apprenticeships

If staff are unable to access recognised qualifications, they may be unwilling to work for your organisation and this is a potential barrier to developing a well-qualified, resourceful team. You need to ensure that you are familiar with the apprenticeships and national awards available to staff and ensure that you advertise these as training you would be willing to source for potential applicants.

Levels of informal training, internally

Informal on-the-job training is an important part of resourcing our care work and as such may need to be addressed. Mentors and coaches in the workplace can provide support for staff in their daily duties so you may wish to invest in training for suitable staff to undertake these roles. This can also help to save on cost of external training. Staff can cascade what they have learnt through in-house training to other staff members.

Personal motivation and the impact on life balance for individuals

It is useful to know what type of learners your staff are to ensure that they are motivated and to understand how a course or training might impact their lives. A training course that might take three years of hard work with lots of written work and research may not be appealing to staff who already have to work hard and have families to consider.

Individuals learn in different ways and you should think about the method that suits your preferred learning style so that, where possible, you can select appropriate learning activities. Your understanding of what development activities suit each learning style means staff are likely to get more from their learning.

Lack of personal motivation can also be a barrier and constraint if workers do not feel motivated in their roles, and this can impact their work greatly. You need to be watchful of staff becoming burnt out in their roles and ensure that during supervision and appraisal you can honestly discuss the way forward for such people.

Other factors include time and career goals and aspirations. Having a firm career plan in place can be a valuable asset in terms of choosing appropriate training activities. As a manager it is your responsibility to ensure that staff development both meets organisational needs and priorities and supports and motivates individual team members' personal and professional development.

Levels of language, literacy, numeracy among workforce

Levels of language and literacy will affect how – and whether – staff learn. Everyone is different and professional development should be tailored to suit education levels, abilities, interests and experience. Think of the ways you prefer to learn. Do you like discussion and working with others? Do you prefer tutor guidance? Do you like exploring and learning on your own? Are computer programs a style of learning that you enjoy? If you enjoy the process of learning, you are more likely to stick with it, particularly if it is over a period of time. Staff may avoid learning and training courses if they struggle with basics of literacy and numeracy and this will be a potential barrier to

developing your workforce. Again, you should be mindful of how these staff might be helped by different technologies and ways of learning.

Level of IT skills

With new technology coming online all the time, new and possibly older staff may find this difficult to come to terms with. Time must be given to introducing new technology and staff who need help with IT skills must be supported in their learning.

Recommendations for practice

Guidelines for practice are available to us and need to be implemented into the way we work to deliver the best care possible. We are not in a position to ignore recommended ways of doing things and staff must be encouraged to change when required to do so.

> **Evidence opportunity**
>
> **1.5** Potential barriers and constraints for professional development
>
> Provide a written account critically evaluating the potential barriers and constraints in your working environment in accessing professional development, with consideration of the areas we have discussed in this section.
>
> You might like to create a table, and under each heading critically evaluate how you have understood and can address each barrier to accessing professional development in your workplace. Suggested headings are:
>
> - Workforce development strategy and planning
> - Financial budgets to support workforce development planning and delivery
> - Financial contributions of staff to support the costs of training
> - Return on investment – financially, improved service delivery
> - Poor time management and commitment of staff
> - Quality of training delivery and support – in-house, external
> - Insufficient or high turnover of staff
> - Access to nationally recognised qualifications and/or apprenticeships
> - Levels of informal training, internally
> - Personal motivation and the impact on life balance for individuals
> - Levels of language, literacy, numeracy among workforce
> - Level of IT skills
>
> What recommendations for your own area of practice will you make?

AC 1.6 Factors to consider when selecting and commissioning activities for keeping knowledge and practice up to date

Here, you will be required to explain the range of factors that impact on the selecting and commissioning of activities for personal and professional development within the work setting.

Some factors to consider here might be those of time, finance and availability of staff and in commissioning activities we need to recognise these as potential barriers. But we also need to recognise that without keeping up to date and investing in our staff, businesses will fail, and the public may simply boycott your organisation. For example, think for a moment about what you seek in a GP service. You are more likely to seek one in which the latest practices are available to you rather than one which lacks vision and urgency in its approach to your care.

Evidence opportunity

1.6 Factors to consider when selecting and commissioning activities

Provide a written account explaining the range of factors that impact on selecting and commissioning activities for personal and professional development within the work setting.

Remember that as a manager in a setting you need to be able to commission and develop new activities for staff development. Looking at the potential barriers to this in your own setting. You might like to think about the factors you now need to consider to engage staff in training to keep their knowledge up to date. You might like to consider the ones we have discussed in this section. How do these apply to your own setting? How have they constrained your practice and the practice of those that you manage?

LO2 Understand supervision in adult care

AC 2.1 Principles and scope of professional supervision

Here, you will explain the key principles and scope of supervision, including the areas we cover in this section.

What is professional supervision?

Supervision is a process whereby a manager or supervisor oversees, supports and develops the knowledge and skills of someone else (a supervisee). It is the way in which a manager can enable a worker to carry out their role in an effective manner.

Skills for Care (2007) defines supervision as 'an accountable process which supports, assures and develops the knowledge skills and values of an individual group or team'. It is, therefore, a process of learning, and a number of approaches and models are available for use.

SCIE's 2013 research paper quotes Morrison's work and defines supervision as:

> *'a process by which one worker is given responsibility by the organisation to work with another worker in order to meet certain organisational, professional and personal objectives which together promote the best outcomes for service users.*
>
> *'Further features of this relationship are that:*
>
> * *it occurs in a safe environment on a regular basis*
>
> * *it is based on a respectful relationship*
>
> * *the process is embedded in the organisation's culture and is understood and valued.'*
>
> **Source:** Lambley and Marrable, 2013

Carroll (2007) provides a fantastic potted history of the development of what we now know is supervision, from its inception during Freud's time to now:

> *'At its simplest, supervision is a forum where supervisees review and reflect on their work in order to do it better. Practitioners bring their actual work practice to another person (individual supervision), or to a group (small group or team supervision), and with their help review what happened in their practice in order to learn from that experience. Ultimately, supervision is for better quality service.'*

Research it

2.1 Models of supervision

There are three primary models of supervision:

1 Developmental models.

2 Integrated models.

3 Orientation-specific models.

You will also come across:

4 Managerial supervision.

5 Clinical supervision.

6 Professional supervision.

The first models are those primarily used in a counselling or psychotherapeutic context.

Research the various models and write down your findings.

As a care worker and manager, you will have your own ideas about how you see supervision. It is important, though, to focus on the purpose of the activity as well as the main principles.

Why supervision is necessary in adult care provision, management accountability and monitoring of the quality of care

Supervision has been introduced into practice to provide professional support and learning for staff, to enable them to develop knowledge, skills and competence in their work. This enhances the experience of the service user and in turn improves quality and safety in the care setting. As a manager, it is your responsibility to provide professional supervision for the staff to ensure they are supported in their roles and to enhance their skills and performance.

It is a practice that should provide regular, ongoing support for staff and as such time should be set aside for it (see Figure 6.3). Staff need to be clear about the need for supervision and what it is for and also given space to discuss issues in a confidential and safe environment.

All social care workers and managers in care settings are required to undergo supervision and meet particular standards and requirements. As managers we are accountable for the quality of the service and therefore need to have a good grasp of how staff are performing. Supervision is one way in which we can undertake this task.

▲ **Figure 6.3** Professional supervision involves supporting care workers to carry out their roles effectively

Reflect on it

2.1 What does 'supervision' mean to you?

Write a short account to answer the following questions:

a) What do you understand the purpose of supervision to be?

b) What policies and procedures are in place for your own supervision and how does it help you in practice?

As managers and members of care staff you are expected to:

> 'Meet relevant standards of practice and work in a lawful safe and effective way.
>
> 'Seek assistance from your employer or the appropriate authority if you do not feel able or adequately prepared to carry out any aspect of your work or you are not sure how to proceed in a work matter.'

Source: The General Social Care Council, 2010

To do this, there should be policies and procedures to enable such working to take place, as well as a vehicle for you to discuss your practice and to support you in changing any deficiencies in practice.

The whole purpose of this clear directive is to improve the quality of the work we do in order to achieve agreed objectives and outcomes. Our intention through supervision is to ensure that all people who use services in social care settings have the capacity to lead independent and fulfilling lives. It also ensures that staff themselves feel supported in their work and have recourse to a system of help should they require it.

The British Association of Social Workers and the College of Social Work (BASW/CoSW) England Code of Good Practice for Supervision in Social Work highlights the purpose as being:

> 'to support social workers to provide good quality services. Social work is a complex and demanding profession. Effective supervision of social workers enables social workers to maximise their effectiveness.'

Clinical supervision, therefore, allows the health professional access to professional supervision by a skilled supervisor.

The role of the manager within supervision to include care service outcomes, monitoring individual performance objectives, professional support and learning, feedback on skills, knowledge, behaviours

Performance management is the way in which managers and employees work together to set work objectives and to monitor and review how they contribute to the work of the organisation. It is the process of ongoing communication between a supervisor and a supervisee throughout the year and supporting the accomplishment of the strategic goals of an organisation.

The Chartered Institute of Personnel and Development (CIPD, 2006) describes the performance management cycle as 'a systematic approach', which includes:

- setting objectives
- using relevant performance indicators, objectives and other measures for determining output
- regularly monitoring and appraising individuals and teams to identify achievements and to provide ongoing support and feedback
- identifying training and development needs
- using the knowledge gained to modify plans.

This approach can be represented in a four-stage performance management cycle (see Figure 6.4).

Stage One – Plan

At the planning stage of the performance management cycle you will need to evaluate an employee's current role and performance in order to ascertain where areas of improvement may be needed and to set realistic goals and aims.

Stage Two – Develop

The focus is on improving expertise by allowing the employee to develop new skills and knowledge through CPD.

Stage Three – Perform

At this stage staff are enabled to practise or 'perform' new skills and new roles that they have learned. Job satisfaction and improved staff morale come with doing the job well. A good manager will ensure that staff are working to their strengths in order to achieve this.

Stage Four – Review

The final stage is evaluation by both parties to consider what has been done and what has been achieved. It is here that we can ascertain whether the goals have been reached. By assessing the results of the planned changes, it is possible to determine what next needs to be done, hence the cyclical nature of the process.

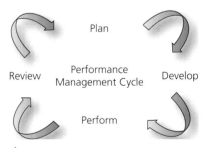

▲ **Figure 6.4** The four-stage performance management cycle

Care service outcomes and monitoring individual performance objectives

These can be readily achieved if they are part of the supervision and performance management cycle. In constructing personal development plans and using supervision events, the outcomes of the organisation and for the service user may be incorporated into personal objectives of staff.

Professional support and learning and feedback on skills, knowledge, behaviours

Supervision is also the optimum time for providing staff with the support they need and feedback on how well they are doing. This means assessing their knowledge, skills and behaviours and advising on how they may improve these.

The importance of confidentiality, boundaries and accountability

Effective supervision is about sharing experiences in a safe environment, and informality will enable both parties to feel comfortable and safe. It is important to set boundaries, such as how the session will be conducted and what can be discussed, as well as addressing confidentiality, at the outset of the process. In doing so the worker can feel confident that the session is being taken seriously and is not just a tick box exercise.

Without such a structure in place there is a danger that supervision sessions will not be viewed as meaning much and learning may not occur at all.

The best way to impose structure on the proceedings is to first ensure there is a supervision policy in place. If so, then you will be expected to undertake this aspect of staff development and there will be guidelines as to how you can do this.

The whole process of supervision needs to be 'owned' not only by the organisation but also by the supervisee. Everybody needs to feel part of the process if the merits of such an activity are to be appreciated.

Thompson (2006) writes:

> *'Some people unfortunately adopt a narrow view of supervision and see it primarily... as a means of ensuring that sufficient quantity and quality of work is carried out... a broader view of supervision can play a significant role in promoting learning and developing a culture of continuous professional development.'*

A possible framework

You may wish to adopt the following framework to manage your supervision sessions:

- Establish ground rules and boundaries, reminding the supervisee of these at the start of each session.
- Remind the supervisee of the need for confidentiality of information on both sides and agree the boundaries of such and areas that may have to be divulged.
- To ensure the supervisee is confident that the whole process will take place in a calm and confidential manner, the room must afford privacy and you will need to ensure that mobile phones are switched off or landlines re-routed to another line for the duration of the meeting.

- Agree that the session will not be interrupted unless an emergency occurs and agree what constitutes an emergency. This will really help to confirm the importance of the process.
- Agree the appropriate reason for cancelling the session.
- Identify the agenda for discussion at the start of each session and agree an action plan following each item discussed. Both you and the supervisee should agree on this. This should fit within the categories of:
  - clinical issues/reflections on role and accountability
  - what support is needed/professional issues
  - educational issues/workload discussions
  - management issues.
- Ensure appropriate allocation of time and agree that you, the supervisor, should act as timekeeper.
- A brief record of the contents of the session should be kept by the supervisor.
- Conduct the session in a non-judgemental/ non-discriminatory manner.

Accountability, when it comes to confidentiality, means we need to take responsibility for personal data and employees working in adult care are bound by a legal duty of confidence to protect personal information. This is a legal requirement. You and your setting will need to be aware of legislation such as the General Data Protection Regulation 2018 and make sure you comply with it.

Research it

2.1 Your supervision policy

Obtain a copy of your supervision policy and write a short piece about how you might change it to fit what you have learned about supervision to date.

Roles and responsibilities of the supervisor and supervisee

With a policy in place, together with a supervision agreement, you can then look at the roles and responsibilities in more detail.

The supervisor, who is likely to be you in your own area, is usually a skilled professional who assists staff to develop their skills and helps them to attain knowledge and professional values. You are also required to give advice in supervisory situations and to counsel staff on practice guidelines and policy. Supervisors require training in the process and should provide a good role model for the supervisee.

The person being supervised, or the supervisee, is a practitioner who receives professional advice, support and guidance from a supervisor who is engaged in observing and assisting staff in delivering good quality care and then giving feedback. In the case of an experienced person, the supervisor may impart support and guidance on reflective practice. We occasionally manage people who have more experience than ourselves and in this case we may be used more as a source of support in their practice.

Some of the more 'practical' roles and responsibilities of each party must also be established. For example, you must agree on the frequency and location of the supervision. How often you meet will depend upon the policy in your organisation, but you may agree to meet regularly on a fortnightly or monthly basis for 1–2 hours.

Both of you need to be prepared for each session and topics for discussion may be arranged in advance. An action plan may require the supervisee to do something before the next meeting and to bring it with them. For example, the supervisee may require some support in course work, and so they could bring with them copies of work, course content and reflective accounts of their learning so far, which you could discuss during the meeting. However, you will need to ensure that you do not fall into the trap of becoming a 'surrogate course tutor' for the supervisee but allow them to reflect on how their learning is affecting or changing their practice.

In preparing for the supervisory meeting, staff need to be aware of the agenda set at the previous meeting. If this required work to be completed, they should get into the habit of bringing with them evidence to support the work done.

The evidence you require a member of staff to bring to supervision will depend on the agreement you have made and the agenda set at the last meeting. The evidence will be linked to the supervisee's objectives and may include reflective accounts of critical incidents that have occurred, assessments undertaken, observations and service user surveys.

All of this will be recorded in the supervisee's personnel file and will become part of their PDP.

The importance of recording and constructive feedback to improve performance

Performance can only be affected when the person receiving feedback is clear about what they need to do. Your clarity in detailing what they need to do to improve their performance in a given task will elicit a change if they understand and have support to make the change. For example, a staff member may be required to work with service users who have a degree of dementia. Without some training in this special area of work they may find it difficult to improve their performance.

Evidence opportunity

2.1 Understand the purpose of supervision in adult care

Provide a written account explaining the key principles and scope of supervision, including the topics we have discussed in this section.

- Explain why supervision is necessary in adult care provision, and what accountabilities you have as a manager with regard to professional supervision and monitoring quality of care that is provided.
- Explain what your role is as a manager with regard to professional supervision, thinking about some of the things that we have discussed in this section.
- Make sure you consider the importance of confidentiality, boundaries and accountability.
- What is the role of the person you supervise? What are their responsibilities? What are the role and the responsibilities of the supervisor?
- Make sure you also consider the importance of recording, and constructive feedback, to improve performance.

- How have you ensured that you protect others during supervision? Again, think about the things that we have discussed in this section. How does supervision enable reflective practice?
- You could produce evidence of a supervision session you have carried out with a staff member.
  - How did you go about agreeing confidentiality, boundaries, roles and accountability with the supervisee?
  - How did you explain the roles and responsibilities of the supervisor and supervisee?
  - How did you explain the importance of recording and constructive feedback to improve performance?
  - What sources of evidence did you request the supervisee to bring?
  - What was the supervisee expected to do to prepare?
  - How did you encourage reflective practice in the session?

Training courses and dates by which these should be attended, in addition to goals to be achieved, must be recorded and then monitored.

Protection of others, e.g. carers, individuals in receipt of care, families, supervisors and supervisees

During supervision you may become party to knowledge about individuals in your care and may be brought into confidential discussions. You and the supervisee need to be clear, however, that in such cases the protection of the service users, their family and other carers is very important but if that safety is compromised then the confidentiality of the supervision session may need to be breached. For example, your supervisee may express concern about the treatment of a service user by others in the team. In supervision, such discussion would be confidential but in cases where there may be a safety issue it is your duty to ensure that the information is shared with the appropriate agencies to deal with this. This would need to be discussed with the supervisee.

Enabling reflective practice

Reflective practice is invaluable as a staff development tool. The ability to reflect on practice is a most important element of anybody's work and supervision should allow and encourage that to happen. Once individuals learn to be reflective, they can begin to take responsibility for their learning and to identify their learning needs. Some supervisees may want to ask for advice and guidance and others may simply want to offload their dissatisfaction with the organisation. It is important that this does not become a session whereby you are being asked to answer and account for management decisions as this is clearly not relevant to the objectives of the supervision. Supervision should allow the supervisee to reflect on what has happened in their work and to be allowed to question their practice and to learn from various experiences. You might ask questions in the session about how the person felt at the time of the activity they are talking about or what they did and why they did it. You might also ask them about how they might act differently if a similar situation arose. These types of questions focus them on their strengths and limitations and also help them to come to solutions for their own practice. It is easier for the staff member to go away and write an account of the incident having verbally reflected on it in the session.

AC 2.2 Theories and models of professional supervision and developing policies

Here, you will be required to critically evaluate theories and models of professional supervision to help inform practice, including those we discuss in this section.

Professional supervision in the past has been likened to the apprentice system or the 'student learning at the feet of a master'. Clinical and professional supervision is now recognised as a complex exchange between supervisor and supervisee, with supervisory models and theories developed to provide a framework for it. It is an ethical requirement of professions where one-to-one contact with clients is an ongoing process and the models that have been developed lend themselves more to this type of process.

While there are a number of models for supervision, including one-to-one supervision, group supervision and peer group supervision, the approach chosen will depend on a number of factors, including personal choice, access to supervision, length of experience, qualifications and availability of supervisory groups.

Cognitive behavioural supervision

Cognitive behavioural theory is based upon the idea that our thoughts, beliefs and emotions influence our behaviour. In other words, we may believe certain things about ourselves, which are based upon what we have been told. For example, a child who is persistently told that they are stupid or lazy may grow up with that belief and act accordingly.

In cognitive behavioural supervision a similar model is practised and the supervisor attempts to correct faulty beliefs or misconceptions brought by the supervisee by examining the thoughts related to his or her skills and understanding how these may influence the work with the client. For example, a supervisee may struggle with a certain task simply because they hold the belief that they do not have the ability to do it. The supervisor then would be able to question the assumptions behind this.

Liese and Beck (1997) suggest a structure for supervision sessions that is similar to a cognitive behavioural therapy session. They suggest that at the start of the session there is a general checking in, in which the agenda is set. Enquiries are then made about the previous supervision sessions and previously supervised cases (this is called 'bridging').

Any homework, such as reading or researching a case study, is then referred to and individual cases or topics may be discussed, perhaps using 'direct instruction' and 'guided discovery'. Finally, new homework tasks are assigned and a summary is applied to the session. This is a highly structured didactic (a more educational, or instructive) approach, with the supervisor being viewed as the 'teacher'. Liese and Beck (1997) identified the following learning goals for therapists:

- diagnosis of problems
- associated cognitive models
- cognitive case conceptualisation
- basic counselling skills
- structuring therapy
- cognitive techniques and behavioural techniques.

In summary, the supervisor needs to enable or teach the supervisee to define and diagnose problems, and use a variety of frameworks, models and counselling skills to structure each session to help the client to get as much out of it as possible.

This approach could be adapted to fit the work of care professionals. There would still be a diagnosis of work problems, and you might refer to health models (such as the Health Belief Model, or Social Cognitive Theory), how the person conceptualises what the problem is, the skills they can bring to solutions and the techniques they will use to structure their work in the future. A drawback might be associated with the task of changing thought to adjust behaviour and this would require skill on the part of the supervisor so more training would be necessary.

Integrated development model

Developmental models of supervision simply define progressive stages of supervisee development from novice to expert (Bernard and Goodyear, 1998). This has been a dominant model for many years and focuses on stages within the process (Hogan, 1964; Holloway, 1987).

Stoltenberg and Delworth's (1987) developmental model has three levels for supervisees – beginning, intermediate and advanced – and the focus at each level is on the development of self-awareness, motivation and autonomy.

Supervisees at the beginning or novice level have limited skills and are presumed to lack confidence. The supervisee is likely to be highly dependent upon the supervisor and may feel quite insecure.

The supervisee starts working in a dependent manner, imitating the supervisor in their role and becoming more self-assured as they gain in confidence. They move to the intermediate level when they are depending on the supervisor only for more difficult work cases. Conflict may happen in this stage as the supervisee's self-concept is threatened when they start to question the supervisor's actions.

At the intermediate level, supervisees have built on their skills and confidence and they may tend to question more and move between feeling dependent and autonomous. The supervisee is likely to demonstrate problem-solving skills and reflection, is more confident and begins to integrate theory into their practice. They are able to reflect on why they are practising in the way they are.

Independence occurs at the advanced level when supervisees start to be accountable for the decisions they make.

The supervisor must have an accurate picture of the current level of the person being supervised and be able to facilitate progression to the next level. The term **scaffolding** has been used to describe this (Stoltenberg and Delworth, 1987; Zimmerman and Schunk, 2003). It means the supervisee uses knowledge and skills they already have to produce new learning. They are encouraged to incorporate these skills along with some from the next stage and, in doing so, build a more advanced repertoire. This continuous growth is a two-way process in that the supervisor–supervisee relationship changes as they both progress in their learning.

Integrative models utilise a number of theories and models and tend to integrate several types of approach. Many of these models refer to the supervision that exists for counsellors and the requirement they have to seek supervision in order to maintain their practice.

Some examples of integrative models are those developed by Bernard (1979) with the discrimination model and Holloway (1995) and the systems approach to supervision.

Bernard's discrimination model was published in 1979 and later developed in 1998. It identified three parts of supervision, namely intervention, conceptualisation and personalisation, and three possible supervisor roles, that of teacher, counsellor and consultant. It focuses on the relationship a counsellor would have with their supervisor and promotes effective skill building through the three areas shown above.

Within the roles taken on by the supervisor, the 'teaching' role occurs when the supervisor lectures or instructs the supervisee. In a care setting this might happen in the clinical setting or during a shift when a situation arises and can then be further discussed at supervision. Counselling happens when the supervisor assists supervisees in noticing how they may be responding to a client's issues and need to be more objective in their approach. They may have been caught up in a client's problem: they feel empathy but cannot move on. The consultant role occurs when co-therapy is required, and the supervisee works with the supervisor and the client.

In addition to the three roles taken on by the supervisor, there are within these three different types of supervision:

- **Intervention**, where the supervisee's intervention skills are the main focus.
- **Conceptualisation**, or how the supervisee understands what is going on in the session.
- **Personalisation**, or how the supervisee deals with the potential issues of counter-transference responses, the process whereby emotions are passed on from one person to another, and how they deal with their personal issues.

In a care setting you, as the manager, may well act as a teacher and consultant but may not act as a therapist. The counselling part of this model may not, therefore, be appropriate but you may be able to assist a supervisee who is perhaps feeling emotional about a case and may need to talk about how they are feeling.

Systems approach to supervision

In Holloway's systems approach model, the emphasis is on the relationship between the supervisor and the supervisee. Holloway describes seven aspects of supervision, which are represented as six wings connected by the supervisory relationship at the centre. These aspects or 'wings' are the functions of supervision, the tasks of supervision, the client, the trainee, the supervisor and the institution (Holloway, from Smith, 2009). This model is an integrative one in which relationships are a central feature, with the characteristics of the supervisor, supervisee and the organisation all deemed to be important. It looks closely at the skill and knowledge of a worker, recognising that their performance is a result of these being utilised in the organisational setting in which they are working. For example, if we are improving safety in the workplace we need to understand where in the work setting errors are more likely to happen, and how we can support workers to accomplish their tasks successfully. By using a systems model it can help us in settings to identify the factors in the work environment that are supporting or damaging good practice.

Reflect on it

2.2 **Which model of supervision do you use?**

Which model of supervision do you use in your own practice? Highlight how you undertake the process and determine where it fits with the models shown. Write a reflective piece to show your understanding of the models and frameworks.

AC 2.3 Ways in which legislation, codes of practice and agreed ways of working inform supervision

Here, you will be required to explain why supervision could be informed by current legislation, codes of practice and agreed ways of working, compliments and complaints.

Current legislation, codes of practice and agreed ways of working

In AC 2.1 we discussed why supervision is necessary and here we cover some of the legislation that informs this practice.

Current legislation

The Care Act 2014

Under the 2014 Care Act, safeguarding individuals in various settings requires that supervision be a fundamental process, with the focus on 'good outcomes for adults in need of care and support'. The act further states that as managers are responsible for the standard of safeguarding practice, they need to ensure that supervision is used not only to constructively challenge practice, but to identify barriers to effective practice. The recommendation is that sessions may be one-to-one or in groups, but should be flexible enough to allow supervisees to raise issues they are most immediately concerned about (Adult safeguarding practice questions SCIE 2015; www.scie.org.uk/care-act-2014/safeguarding-adults/adult-safeguarding-practice-questions/).

According to the British Association of Social Workers and the College of Social Work (BASW/CoSW) England Code of Good Practice for Supervision in Social Work, the purpose of supervision is:

> 'to support social workers to provide good quality services. Social work is a complex and demanding profession. Effective supervision of social workers enables social workers to maximise their effectiveness.'
>
> **Source:** The General Social Care Council, 2010

As the manager, it is also your responsibility to ensure that staff are aware of the legislation that they must abide by in the setting. For example, this will include being aware of:

- The General Data Protection Regulation (GDPR) 2018
- Health and Safety at Work etc Act 1974
- The Equality Act 2010
- The Human Rights Act 1998.

You will also need to ensure that your staff are up to date with changes to legislation, codes of practice and agreed ways of working.

Clinical supervision, therefore, allows the health professional access to professional supervision by a skilled supervisor.

The Care Certificate also identifies supervision as a key role for workers, insisting it be supportive rather than judgemental.

The focus of supervision is for the care professional to practise in such a way as to meet legal requirements and to ensure codes of practice and local policy are being followed.

The policies and procedures within your own work setting will reflect the legal position and any guidelines that need to be followed and you need to make a thorough analysis of these policies to ensure you understand how these may impact upon your work as a supervisor. Analysing your policies and codes of practice in line with legislation will ensure that staff are being given the best supervision experience in line with legal requirements.

You may also want to recap your learning from AC 2.1 now.

Codes of practice and agreed ways of working

The Code of Conduct for Healthcare Support Workers and Adult Social Care Workers in England (2013)

As a healthcare support worker or care professional you are duty-bound to deliver high-quality care and support to vulnerable individuals. Codes of conduct not only provide guidance as to how this should happen, you can also gain some reassurance that you are providing safe and compassionate care of a high standard.

With respect to supervision, the guidance within the Code of Conduct for Healthcare Support Workers and Adult Social Care Workers states that you must:

> 1 *Ensure up-to-date compliance with all statutory and mandatory training, in agreement with your supervisor.*
>
> 2 *Participate in continuing professional development to achieve the competence required for your role.*

3 Carry out competence-based training and education in line with your agreed ways of working.

4 Improve the quality and safety of the care you provide with the help of your supervisor (and a mentor if available), and in line with your agreed ways of working.

5 Maintain an up-to-date record of your training and development.

6 Contribute to the learning and development of others as appropriate.

Source: Skills for Care 2013 *Code of Conduct for Healthcare Support Workers and Adult Social Care*

KEY TERM

Continuing professional development (CPD) is the planned process of improving and increasing capabilities of staff and is an ongoing process.

Again, as a manager, you must ensure that all staff are clear about how the legislation feeds into the practice and policy within their area of work. Without such clarity staff may fail to see the point of some of the things they are expected to do and simply fail to do them.

CQC regulations

In 2013, CQC published a paper entitled 'Supporting information and guidance: Supporting effective clinical supervision' following the recommendations made from the Winterbourne View serious case review. It sets out what effective clinical supervision should look like, and although it was developed primarily for people with a learning disability, it does provide a useful guide for all care sectors and settings. As a result of this case, codes of practice have changed and ways of working mean that staff are required to undertake realistic workloads and are entitled to training and regular skills updates.

From a legal point of view, supervision is a requirement for all staff. The Skills for Care Council in its document *Providing Effective Supervision* (2007) states that:

> 'High quality supervision is one of the most important drivers in ensuring positive outcomes for people who use social care and children's services. It also has a crucial role to play in the development, retention and motivation of the workforce.'

In your own care setting, the implementation of the CQC regulations will ensure that you are not only complying with the law but also monitoring staff performance to ensure that there are no breaches of standards in your setting.

Research it

2.3 CQC guidance and professional supervision

Look at the 'Supporting information and guidance: Supporting effective clinical supervision' document at www.cqc.org.uk. You will need to search for the document on the website.

The document describes effective clinical supervision and applies to registered providers, registered managers and staff across all care sectors and settings.

How can you use the guidance within your own setting to influence the supervision practice you currently have in place?

It would also be useful for you to research recent stories to understand the importance of supervision.

Not only is it good practice to supply supervision, the National Minimum Standards for Care Homes for Older People and for Adults also make this a requirement. Standard 36 states the following:

36.1 The registered person ensures that the employment policies and procedures adopted by the home and its induction, training and supervision arrangements are put into practice.

36.2 Care staff receive formal supervision at least six times a year.

36.3 Supervision covers:

- all aspects of practice
- philosophy of care in the home
- career development needs.

36.4 All other staff are supervised as part of the normal management process on a continuous basis.

36.5 Volunteers receive training, supervision and support appropriate to their role and do not replace paid staff.

While the standards outline the minimum requirements, it goes without saying that you may well need to see and supervise staff on other occasions. Effective management demands that you support your staff to develop areas of practice in which they are deficient or not coping well.

The Care Certificate

The Care Certificate also identifies supervision as a key role for workers, insisting it be supportive rather than judgemental.

The focus of supervision is for the care professional to practise in such a way as to meet legal requirements and to ensure codes of practice and local policy are being followed.

The policies and procedures within your own work setting will reflect the legal position and any guidelines that need to be followed and you need to make a thorough analysis of these policies to ensure you understand how these may impact upon your work as a supervisor. Analysing your policies and codes of practice in line with legislation will ensure that staff are being given the best supervision experience in line with legal requirements.

Safeguarding procedures

A core responsibility and ultimately one role of supervision is to deliver healthcare that is safe for all and ensures that all who receive care are safeguarded. It is imperative that we examine and analyse how we manage such performance. As managers of health services, we are responsible for the safety and wellbeing of our service users, but for those individuals who are less able to protect themselves from harm, neglect or abuse, or those with impaired mental capacity, there is a greater need for diligence. Safeguarding, therefore, is how harm and abuse to patients is prevented through the provision of high-quality care. Additionally, any allegations of harm or abuse should be responded to effectively and according to policy.

Agreed ways of working

These are the ways in which your work setting wants you to work in accordance with policy or procedure. With supervision it is easy to forget the importance of this practice and sometimes it can become an activity that is not taken seriously enough or not given time to. As a manager it is, therefore, vital that you practise in accordance with the supervision policy and devote time to its implementation and use.

> ### KEY TERM
>
> **Agreed ways of working** are your setting's policies, procedures as well as guidelines for the care and support you provide for service users.

Compliments and complaints

Our compliments and complaints systems will help us to identify where the practice is working and where it is falling short.

Our intention through supervision is to ensure that all people who use services in social care settings have the capacity to lead independent and fulfilling lives. It also ensures that staff themselves feel supported in their work and have recourse to a system of help should they require it. By using the compliments and complaints system within our sessions we can start to address the failings and the successes of our work.

> ### Reflect on it
>
> **2.3** Compliments and complaints
>
> Write a short reflective piece about how compliments and complaints have informed supervision where you work. These could be compliments and complaints from those who use care services, or you may even like to think about compliments and complaints that you have received with regard to supervision. How have these impacted supervision? Have they led to an improvement in supervision practice? How? Have they led to improvements in the care services that your setting offers to individuals? How? What did you do to address these compliments and complaints?

> ### Evidence opportunity
>
> **2.3** Ways supervision can be informed
>
> Provide a written account explaining why supervision could be informed by current legislation, codes of practice and agreed ways of working, compliments and complaints.

AC 2.4 Impacts of research findings, critical reviews and inquiries and how these can be used within professional supervision

Here, you will investigate relevant research and inquiry outcomes that have informed management supervision practice in adult care settings.

Evidence-based practice is about incorporating evidence from research and making professional judgements as a result of the new knowledge, applying it to formulate care decisions. In supervision, staff need to be informed of how they can research and review new information and should be made aware of how inquiries inform guidelines and standards.

We must perform care safely and in a way in which we are able to question our practice and be accountable for what we do. To 'do no harm' is the essential premise of evidence-based practice and the need to be able to demonstrate that the care we provide is safe and effective is a reasonable expectation. It is no different in our practice regarding supervision.

As an effective practitioner accountable for your own safe practice, you need to have access to and be up to date with the research related to your own area and be able to critically appraise such work. As a manager of staff, you are accountable for ensuring that staff members have embraced the notion of evidence-based practice.

KEY TERM

Evidence-based practice (EBP) refers to using information from high-quality research and applying it within practice to make informed decisions about a service user's care.

In deciding how and what care is to be given, it is important to have an accurate picture of the research available and to construct sufficient evidence from it to support our actions. When supervising staff, we need to ensure that their practice is based on good, sound evidence and that they know how they might improve their practice consistent with new initiatives in care.

From an ethical viewpoint, practising in an informed way means we can be assured that staff are delivering enhanced care that is safe. Each member of staff should be aware of the need to contribute to their knowledge base by accessing continuing professional development and knowledge updates to ensure safe practice. This will reduce the number of incidents surrounding patients and their care and risks in the workplace and thus the potential for litigation. It can also raise the profile of the organisation.

Research on critical reviews and inquiry outcomes will help improve the practice in care settings. For example, without research we would not have developed changes to treatments or procedures and adult care would fail to grow. You will be aware of the way in which sepsis has become a major issue within care work and how research has developed our responses as adult care workers to those who present with the potential life-threatening signs and symptoms. As a result of this research, we are now more adept at treating signs of sepsis more quickly and more successfully.

Also, the work carried out in response to critical reviews and inquiries, such as the Review by Professor Sir Bruce Keogh, the NHS Medical Director at NHS England, into the Quality of Care and Treatment Provided by 14 Hospital Trusts in England; The Cavendish Review, which made an Independent Review into Healthcare Assistants and Support Workers; and the report by the Children and Young People's Health Outcomes Forum by Lewis and Lenehan have all led to change in child and adult care and the way in which we as care workers respond to potential cases of abuse. They have also changed the way in which care workers communicate with and respond to each other. These are all things which may be addressed in supervision to ensure that staff are not only aware of the changes these reports have had on care but have incorporated these changes into their practice.

Research it

2.4 Inquiry outcomes

Download and read the relevant research and inquiry outcomes mentioned in the section above or others that you have found useful in your setting and that have informed management supervision practice in adult care settings.

Identify how you have translated this into practice in your setting.

Evidence opportunity

2.4 Impacts of research findings, critical reviews and inquiries

Investigate relevant research and inquiry outcomes that have informed management practice in adult care settings. Provide a written account documenting your findings.

You might like to consider the impact of research findings, critical reviews and inquiries and how these can be used within professional supervision.

AC 2.5 Uses of professional supervision in performance management

Here, you will critically evaluate the principles of performance management with regard to the areas we discuss in this section.

In AC 2.1 we looked at the performance management cycle.

By using a performance management cycle, you impose structure and process on the management of staff and their training and development needs, and also through supervision.

In any organisation, the aim is to produce and deliver high-quality services and to ensure that all opportunities for improvement, change and innovation are clearly identified and worked towards. To achieve that end, the organisation must realise its potential against performance targets, and equally ensure that the performance management systems in place get the best out of people in the workplace and deliver the best for people who use services. This can be monitored through the supervision process.

Existing systems and procedures

All healthcare systems in this country are required to provide safe and good quality healthcare, improving the patient experience, as well as continually update practice and systems in the light of evidence from research. The scandal of the Mid Staffordshire NHS Foundation Trust, for example, highlighted the treatment of patients and led to yet another inquiry into failings in the system. The Francis Report and a response by the government to improve the safeguarding and the quality of care is another example of the need to monitor performance in a structured and effective manner. As Robert Francis stated in his report:

> '*The extent of the failure of the system shown in this report suggests that a fundamental culture change is needed.*'
>
> **Source:** Robert Francis QC, 2014

Performance management systems identify organisational goals, measuring the achievement of those goals through different systems, which control employee behaviour and performance. Target setting, 360-degree appraisal and personal development plans together with supervision are designed to measure the performance of your staff. Advantages of these approaches are that they are less subject to personal bias and provide information and evidence. A disadvantage is that the collection of such information can be time consuming.

Standards and policies to support performance management

The essential standards of quality and safety consist of 28 regulations (and associated outcomes) that are set out in two pieces of legislation: the Health and Social Care Act 2008 (Regulated Activities) Regulations 2014 and the Care Quality Commission (Registration) Regulations 2009. Together with national occupational standards and codes of practice, they are helping to change the performance management framework in the social care sector and this is something to celebrate. The inspection process and even the supervisory framework you adopt should be seen as an opportunity to improve performance and service delivery rather than be used as a punitive or disciplinary measure to be feared. Critics argue that performance management is not a good thing for this very reason and there are also some people who do not value supervision. However, effective performance management and supervision can promote good quality service delivery and result in more highly motivated staff (SCIE, 2007).

As a supervisor, there is a need to measure performance against results and not merely focus on behaviours and activity. Think for a moment about the member of staff who always seems to have a lot to do but rarely accomplishes what should be done. In this instance, the employee needs to be made aware of the organisational goals together with methods by which those goals may be achieved. This can be done through good supervision, continuing professional development and effective line management.

The role of individual supervision and performance indicators

Individual supervision can be both formal and informal, but both support the professional development of members of your staff to develop knowledge and competence in their work.

As we have seen, supervision is an important part of professional development and managing the performance of staff. It is key to set SMART objectives so that each individual can show they have reached the desired standards, and you, as manager, can be satisfied that the safety and wellbeing of service users are maintained.

A good way in which to do this is to have a set of performance criteria made up of measures and standards that clearly state the level of performance required in different areas. We need to ensure that the setting's organisational performance indicators are used to focus on what the organisation wants to achieve.

These might be:

- deadlines or delivery
- cost or budgets
- colleagues' and service users' views of your performance
- the quality that is expected
- how much is expected or the quantity.

You also need to ensure that the objectives you set are:

- consistent with the member of staff's job description
- consistent with the organisational goals
- clearly expressed
- supported by measurable performance criteria
- challenging.

Setting objectives is not an easy task by any means, but objectives that are specific, measurable, achievable, relevant and time bound, or SMART, are a useful way to start.

Specific – being specific means we have a much greater chance of success and the way to set such a goal is to plan with these questions in mind:

- Who: is involved?
- What: do I want to accomplish?
- Where: will this happen?
- When: in what timescale?
- Which: requirements and constraints do I need to identity?
- Why: do we need to do this?

Example: Tina Tilmouth to rewrite the Safeguarding Policy by the end of (date).

Although we have not specified here the reason for doing this, it can be assumed that safeguarding being a huge area in care work is a firm enough reason.

Measurable – to ensure your target is measurable, you might ask questions such as:

- How much?
- How many?
- How will I know when it is accomplished?

In the case of our example (the writing of the safeguarding policy) we will know it is done when it is written. We might also add how much we would expect to be written; we could, for example, specify a word count.

Achievable – an achievable target for a member of staff is one which they agree is needed and one they can actually do. In helping a member of staff in this part of target setting, you could identify small steps towards the larger goal and outline dates by which they should achieve this.

Realistic – to be realistic, the member of staff and you as the manager must believe that the person can actually accomplish the task. It is wise to check that the individual has done something similar in the past and is given the opportunity to identify what they might need in terms of support to accomplish the target.

Time bound – without a timeframe, the target loses urgency and momentum. By setting a date for completion, there is a given point when the task is to be completed and delivered.

Having a large number of performance indicators will result in little progress being made and it is important to be wary of this. By measuring practice using SMART objectives, the information you obtain may then be used in staff appraisals. The facts obtained provide firm evidence for performance and will show improvement or limitations. As a manager, it is crucial to focus your staff on essential areas for improvement.

Setting organisational performance indicators to improve and monitor the performance of individuals

Your organisation's objectives are the starting point when it comes to setting targets for performance. You will also be aware of the staff's job descriptions and the competencies required to carry out certain roles. In order to maintain high-quality care in your organisation you need to create a performance management system which:

- identifies areas of best practice and focuses on continuous improvement

- sets organisational and individual performance indicators to improve and monitor the performance of individuals.

For example, a PI is a performance measurement that helps you understand how your organisation or team member is performing and whether you are achieving the strategic goals. You might need to know what percentage of your staff receive regular supervision, so a target will be set which may be measured against appraisal, supervision and personal development records when audited. This will help to, for example:

- deliver better outcomes for those using the services
- improve health services by acting upon new initiatives and information
- ensure that organisational activities are linked to the overall goals of the organisation.

Helping individuals set and achieve meaningful goals in respect of their practice

One of the most important functions you have as a manager is to ensure that staff are fully aware of the organisational strategy and targets, and to link those with individual objectives. In supervising staff, performance management is an issue that needs to be part of the agenda. Staff must be clear about the aims and focus of their job role in relation to the wider aims of the organisation, and it is the supervisor's responsibility to ensure that staff are clear about how they can achieve these objectives.

Staff appraisals, performed at the end of an annual cycle for managing staff, are a vehicle for reviewing the goals set throughout the supervision process and planning for the year to come:

- Review the job description and role.
- Look at individual performance and achievement and reward (performance-related pay or other incentives).
- Plan ongoing professional development.
- Give feedback.

The object of appraisal is to set goals for the coming year and to identify ways in which the staff member can improve their performance over the next year. It should be a positive process in which the member of staff can be given details about their performance and can start to plan for the forthcoming year. Staff who have been underperforming should have been made aware of this during supervision and an appraisal will identify ways in which they can meet the required standards in the year to come. They should not be surprised to learn of the problems with their performance at this stage in the proceedings since they will have received feedback in the previous supervision sessions.

The process of appraisal is similar to supervision. For example, you could check in with how they are going about their own CPD and whether the work they are doing is within their expertise or if they need to develop their skills further. You may also want to look at how the employee dealt with the workload and what they achieved with the service users.

There is more information on appraisals in AC 1.3.

For individual staff in an organisation, one method of measuring performance may be management by objectives (MBO) developed by Peter Drucker. The process involves the manager and employee identifying employee goals together with a list of the resources and a timeframe necessary to achieve the goals. Meetings to evaluate the outcomes and to discuss progress are held regularly and during these meetings goals may be reset. The employee's performance is measured by how many goals have been accomplished within the timeframe. (For more information see http://communicationtheory.org/management-by-objectives-drucker.

The development and measurement of a quality workforce with shared values and behaviours, aspiring to become an effective leader and manager with individuals and teams

A quality workforce requires a positive culture, which reflects values such as trust, transparency, openness and respect. In developing this culture, our recruitment of staff needs to ensure that they also demonstrate those values. This can be measured by testing the values at interview and asking candidates to demonstrate how they understand them and then by developing these values in the workplace. We can do this by ensuring that our workforce themselves feel valued and respected and are treated with openness and trust. As an effective leader and manager, you will seek opportunities to integrate the organisation's values into training, supervision and appraisal. Your staff may follow you simply because you are the manager, but you will not inspire them to give of their best. If you aspire to be an effective leader and are passionate about what you do and fully believe in that vision, then your enthusiasm will encourage staff to see the meaning in their roles and the purpose of what they do. Communication is a big part of ensuring that a quality workforce is achieved.

Addressing conduct and performance and key performance indicators (internal/external), CQC regulations

The Health and Social Care Act 2008 (Regulated Activities) Regulations 2014 provided fundamental requirements and standards for healthcare, below which care must never fall. The CQC regulations provide guidance to managers in healthcare settings in following these regulations.

In order to be able to assess conduct and performance we need to understand how performance management is measured. There are a number of ways of doing this, but primarily performance management is defined as being a cycle of continuous process, which involves:

- **planning and developing** – at this stage there should be a clear indication about what needs to be done and to what standard. The employee's ability and competence to perform the task needed are looked at. If training or skills development are needed, these are also planned for here
- **progress reviewing** – at this point the employee has the chance to determine their progress so far and can gain feedback about whether any changes might be needed
- **evaluating** – this stage is all about what was done, how, what might have been done differently to engage with a better outcome and what has been learned.

The aim of a performance management system is to ensure that the organisation's goals are met, and that staff are effective and productive. To achieve this, there needs to be a clear strategy to support the vision and mission statement of the organisation. This then needs to be translated into specific objectives and targets for the department, and finally individual job goals and targets. In evaluating performance there needs to be a clear process through which the staff will be monitored and evaluated. Such performance objectives will be set in supervision and appraisal through open discussion between the supervisors and the supervisee, with progress towards the goals being monitored regularly.

In 2001, annual performance ratings for the NHS were measured by means of the 'star rating system for English NHS trusts', with each trust being given a rating from zero to three stars. This has now gone out of use but targets for performance remain. While targets have been somewhat beneficial, the ways in which some targets have been met have come under criticism and scrutiny. For example, to meet A&E targets of emergency department waiting times, more staff may have been brought in at the expense of operations being cancelled elsewhere. (For more information see www.lse.ac.uk/newsAndMedia/news/archives/2006/GwynBevan.aspx)

In the NHS, key performance indicators (KPIs) are a means of measuring how far progress has been made towards organisational goals and they focus on a range of areas. They measure things such as length of stay in hospital, mortality rates, readmission rates and day case rates. For example, a local trust may notice that its discharge rates for certain procedures are above the national benchmark and patients are requiring more lengthy stays as a result. It may, therefore, wish to investigate this and make changes to bring it in line with national protocols. (For more information see www.institute.nhs.uk/quality_and_service_improvement_tools/quality_and_service_improvement_tools/performance_ management. htm. This webpage may have been removed so you should search using your browser.)

The aim of any performance management system is to ensure that the organisation's goals are met and that staff are effective and productive. To achieve this, there needs to be a clear strategy to support the vision and mission statement of the organisation. This then needs to be translated into specific objectives and targets for the department, and finally individual job goals and targets. In evaluating performance there needs to be a clear process through which the staff will be monitored and evaluated. Such performance objectives will be set in supervision and appraisal through open discussion between the supervisor and the supervisee, with progress towards the goals being monitored regularly.

The Institute of NHS Quality states:

> 'Performance management enables organisations to articulate their business strategy, align their business to that strategy, identify their key performance indicators (KPIs) and track progress, delivering the information to decision-makers.'

It also provides a performance management tool which may be downloaded from its website to help the process. Go to: www.institute.nhs.uk/quality_and_service_improvement_tools/quality_and_service_improvement_tools/performance_management.html#sthash.efKrswZI.dpuf

Indicators of poor performance

What is likely to indicate to you that a member of staff is performing badly in their role? Perhaps they are failing to complete tasks on time or making more mistakes when doing so. Maybe they consistently break rules or do not follow procedure, and you find you need to spend more time with them because of this. Perhaps they are having excessive amounts of time off sick or their personal life is encroaching upon their time at work and causing issues with other staff members. Have you noticed that they are arriving late or leaving earlier than they should, or spending more time at break and lunch? All these are indicators that a person may not be coping in their job.

Poor performance can be a problem and it needs to be managed in a sensitive manner, with the facts of the poor performance clearly recorded.

Reflect on it

2.5 Poor performance

Think about how you have managed poor staff performance in the past and describe your feelings about this part of the management role.

Evidence opportunity

2.5 Professional supervision in performance management

Write a piece critically evaluating the principles of performance management with regard to the areas we have discussed in this section.

Remember to address topics like the role of individual supervision, setting organisational and individual performance indicators in improving and monitoring the performance of individuals, and how you help individuals to set and achieve meaningful goals in respect of their practice. In critically evaluating this piece, you might for example comment on how useful the role of professional supervision is in your setting and what the drawbacks may have been. Say how you might begin to improve the performance indicators to make them more useful to measuring performance. What is good about setting personal goals?

AC 2.6 Factors that can result in a power imbalance in professional supervision and how to address them

Here, you will explore management supervision practice with regard to some of the areas we discuss in this section.

Addressing possible power imbalances in formal supervision

In most organisations, there will be people who have more power than others simply because they are in a higher position in a hierarchy. This may bring about a power imbalance in the adult care setting and may be a barrier to adult care and also to staff relationships. In formal supervision staff need to know that, despite the existence of a hierarchical difference between supervisor and supervisee, their input is valued and shared decision making is possible. Power that comes with positions in adult care can be used in a positive way, but often the concept of power has negative connotations of abuse and harassment and this type of thinking can lead us to distrust anybody who is in a position of power. In this way, power can be perceived as influencing or controlling somebody negatively. This can affect supervision.

If you are the manager in a work setting, you are already in a position of power. It is possible that you may even have recruited the people you manage. You have influence and authority over those people. Furthermore, the concept of 'master–apprentice' in supervision evokes a hierarchy of power that favours the master and this is likely to affect the supervisory relationship.

Two main types of power, personal and organisational, are worthy of further investigation here. When we refer to personal power, we are noting the knowledge, skills and competence associated with an individual that make them an expert. As an expert, the individual can exert a certain amount of power in various situations. Think about the teacher–learner relationship.

Organisational power can be of four types:

- **Reward power** – the manager's ability to give inducements such as pay, promotion or praise to move an organisation forward.
- **Coercive power** – the use of punishment such as disciplinary procedures.
- **Legitimate power** – that which comes with a rank in an organisation that gives authority.
- **Information power** – based on access to information or data that is valued and not open to all (from Gopee and Galloway, 2009).

Power imbalance is common between employer and worker and supervisor–employee relationships simply because we may be affected by a person who has greater authority than ourselves. But power imbalance can be healthy or not and conflict has the potential to arise when imbalance occurs.

Factors that result in power imbalance

Being the manager means you invariably supervise the work of the team and this may lead to power imbalance and occasionally conflict. Supervision in care has become one of the ways in which it is possible to monitor employees' work, ensuring that performance indicators are being met, and this can lead to conflict, so we need to look at ways to address the imbalance.

How to address power imbalance in own supervision practice

If you recognise that a power imbalance exists in the supervision relationship, then you can start to address it. What do we mean by this?

Evidence opportunity

2.6 Factors leading to power imbalance and how to address these

- What factors might you see resulting in a power imbalance in professional supervision in your setting?
- How do you deal with power imbalance in your own setting?
- What sorts of actions do you take, for example, when an important decision needs to be made which you know is likely to be unpopular?
- Give an example from your workplace.

Case study

2.6 Power imbalance

James was the manager in a large care organisation but found his role a difficult one. He always blamed the unpopular decisions he had to make on higher management with the line 'it's not my decision, it's what they have told me to do' and then took credit for the more palatable ones. In time, he lost credibility with staff who saw his lack of integrity.

What do you think was the problem here and how might James gain the staff's trust again?

James was clearly trying to be popular with the staff while failing to accept that he would sometimes have to make unpopular decisions. It seems he was not comfortable with that and did not want to adopt an authoritarian approach or an approach in which he would be seen to be dictating and directing matters. Unfortunately, staff are likely to lose confidence in this type of manager and conflict arises.

As a manager with responsibility for the smooth running of a department or organisation, your staff will be looking to you to lead with respect for them and honesty. You will always have the power in the relationship by virtue of the fact that you are accountable for the actions of the staff, that is, the buck stops with you. However, you are responsible for addressing power imbalances and there is no need to take an authoritarian approach to how you lead. Having a conscious awareness of how being 'in charge' can make or break a relationship means you can take control of decisions and set the tone for the work group. While it is good to be 'one of the team' and adopt a friendly manner towards staff, there is a fine line between this and taking control of the situation when you need to. It is always best policy to act with honesty, integrity, fairness and respect for others – this will help to ensure a positive relationship between the supervisor and the supervisee.

Managing difficult situations and disagreements during formal supervision and managing conflict in formal supervision

Difficult situations and conflict that arise in the workplace can cause the team to feel insecure and as their manager you need to establish stability. By reminding them about how you value their work, you should offer the opportunity to talk about concerns they have in a professional manner. In approaching conflict in this way, you are giving an example of how each person involved in the conflict should behave. By showing each other respect, conflict can be quickly diminished.

What is a conflict situation and why does it occur?

In supervision, the potential for conflict arises when there is a disagreement about a point of professional practice or the values and goals of the supervisor do not fit with those of the supervisee. For example, the supervisor may challenge the member of staff and this could cause some opposition.

You may come across two types of conflict:

● **Task-based conflict** – disagreements related to approaches to work, processes and structural issues within the team and the organisation.
● **Relationship-based conflict** – conflicts between individual members of the team, usually caused by differences in personal values and beliefs.

Specific areas of conflict that you may come across during supervision include:

● lack of clarity around team roles and responsibilities
● unfair distribution of work
● lack of clear vision on the part of the supervisee
● lack of understanding of the role of others
● poor communication.

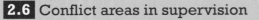
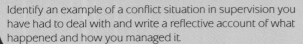

Reflect on it

2.6 Conflict areas in supervision

Identify an example of a conflict situation in supervision you have had to deal with and write a reflective account of what happened and how you managed it.

Effects of conflict

Conflict can disrupt performance but within teams it is a common occurrence. When the resolution of the conflict is effective, it can have a positive effect, leading to personal growth and development.

If managed effectively it can be 'creative and productive and creative solutions to difficult problems can often be found through positive conflict resolution' (Tilmouth et al., 2011).

How to deal with conflict situations

Resolving conflict in a team is done most effectively by the people concerned having a constructive conversation. LaFasto and Larson's (2001) CONECT model for resolving conflict by conversation is useful – see page 122.

It would also be useful for you to read about Thompson's RED approach to managing conflict covered in Unit 504, page 122.

Research it

2.6 Conflict management

For your next team meeting, agenda an item on conflict management.

Collect information about how staff manage conflict in their roles with service users and with other staff members.

Collect the information to provide a record of types of conflict experienced and ways in which it is managed.

In resolving conflict, when people's needs are discovered then a solution can be found. We may be tempted to compromise, but compromise means that people's needs are still not fully met and this can lead to resentment (West, 2004).

Ensuring that conflicts are addressed in the right manner means that relationships are maintained and can function smoothly.

Reflecting on practice

A conflict situation is never pleasant but by reflecting on the circumstances that led to the event and thinking about how it might have been handled in a different way we can sometimes find more useful ways of managing conflict should it arise again.

In dealing with any challenging situation, your supervisees must be directed to the policies in the workplace and should be given the opportunity to undergo training. Any challenging behaviour, by a visitor, another staff member or a service user, can be frightening and staff need to be given the opportunity to talk about the situation and to discuss the triggers that may have led to the outburst.

It is a good idea to discuss this with new staff and to remind experienced staff of the types of challenging behaviour your setting might come across and to ensure they are aware of how they are to deal with such incidents. By reflecting on these incidents, the staff can learn from challenging situations and can also start to be more aware of how they felt in such instances.

By evaluating the event in this way, staff can start to appreciate how they might have been affected by a situation and how others may also be affected. They will also see how circumstances at the time may have led to the event and this sort of examination can be useful in planning for a different reaction the next time it happens.

Reflect on it

2.6 Challenging behaviour

Remind yourself of your policies with respect to how you would help staff to deal with challenging behaviour.

Managing challenges arising during and after professional supervision

Occasionally, difficult situations within supervision and team management arise. You may have to deal with cases of poor individual or team performance or complaints from members of the public about staff. It is likely that at times of staff shortages, you may have to respond to the worries or complaints of team members who are unhappy about the situation they are in.

The fact that conflict exists, however, is not necessarily a bad thing: as long as it is resolved effectively, it can lead to personal and professional growth. If managed well, conflict can be creative and productive, and creative solutions to difficult problems can often be found through positive conflict resolution. However, conflict within the team or among staff should not impact upon the wellbeing of the service user.

Support systems available to them after formal supervision

Staff need to be aware that they can receive support after formal supervision should they so wish it. They can be directed to your manager if they feel they wish to discuss a grievance or can simply talk to a mentor or a peer to discuss what happened. In an organisation that values and respects its employees, everybody should feel able to discuss challenging situations in a responsible and open manner.

Current appraisal processes used alongside supervision to manage and improve performance with those they manage

Alongside supervision there will also be appraisals, which may be an annual event although ideally discussing performance should be a regular event at team meetings and on an individual basis. Regular updates on progress towards targets and goals that have been set are likely to be more meaningful than a yearly meeting. See ACs 1.3 and 2.5 for more information on appraisals.

We covered task-based and relationship-based conflict earlier, but there is also conflict with carers and service users over service decisions. Whatever the cause of the conflict, the related emotions can be quite damaging to the care being delivered and, if badly managed, ineffective care emerges. People may start to avoid each other, with rifts developing as teams take sides. In the midst of this happening the service user suffers as care starts to disintegrate into ineffectiveness.

One of the crucial things to remember here is that challenging behaviour may be the only way a person can communicate at that time, and it is important for us as managers to find out what the 'function' of that behaviour is. For example, a member of staff in a supervision setting may start to lose their temper and shout at you. This can be because they are frustrated in some way or cannot articulate well enough what they are feeling. Although the behaviour is potentially threatening to us, by trying to understand the reason for that behaviour we can help to change the situation. It is easy to shout back or to manhandle somebody, but by standing back and trying to determine what led to the behaviour and what is being communicated by that behaviour we can go a long way towards defusing the situation.

If we describe behaviour in a negative manner we are likely to deal with it as such. But if we view it as a way of getting attention to a problem, we might have a different reaction to it. By working out what the 'function' of the challenging behaviour is and what it helps the person to achieve in a given situation we can then start to help the individual to deal with the situation they find difficult in more constructive ways.

We might use the following as a guide:

- Get the facts first and ask questions – we often race to find a solution, but it is more useful to gather information and ask questions to really understand what is happening.
- Ask questions that get to the core problem and try to stop the person going into too much detail.
- Listen carefully.
- Reflect on the answers you are given and do not be too quick to jump in with a solution. Do not be tempted to think you know the answer and pre-judge the person. Avoid making such a judgement, as it may be wrong.
- Act professionally.
- Aim for a balanced solution. We do not want people to feel that they have lost a battle and that management has won! Negotiate to find a solution in which both parties feel heard and have a solution both are happy with. This may not always be possible but careful negotiation can be useful.

Case study

2.6 Dealing with challenging situations

Nadia is a member of staff who has worked in the same role for three years. She is undertaking a foundation degree at the local university and has recently been off sick for at least one span of duty per fortnight. There seems to be a pattern developing and you are wondering what is going on. In your regular supervision session, Nadia becomes very defensive and starts to lose her temper with you. You remain calm – you are aware that this is uncharacteristic but is something you need to address.

How will you deal with this situation?

Reflect on it

2.6 Challenging behaviour and policies

Remind yourself of your policies with respect to how you would deal with challenging behaviour shown by a member of your staff and how power imbalance might be addressed.

Reflect on it

2.6 Managing and reflecting on conflict situations

What sort of conflict have you managed in your own practice? Identify an area of conflict you have been involved in with a member of staff and write a short piece showing how you managed that situation.

Evidence opportunity

2.6 Factors that can result in a power imbalance

Write a piece exploring management supervision practice with regard to some of the areas we discussed in this section.

LO3 Provide professional supervision

AC 3.1 Establish agreement with the supervisee on key areas

Here, you will plan and undertake professional supervision to include the areas we cover in this section.

Actions to be taken in preparation for supervision by the supervisor and supervisee

Prior to a supervision session, the supervisor and supervisee must ensure they have records in place and have taken time out of their day to be present. As a supervisor you should be mentally prepared to listen and respond to concerns and challenges from the supervisee. Additionally, you will want to discuss previously set goals and how the person is performing to reach those goals. You might also expect the supervisee to come with written summaries or records, which help them to discuss certain cases. Having the necessary records to hand and any agenda you need will also help. Refer to AC 2.1 for more details about how to prepare for a supervision and what to expect.

Adherence to ensuring confidentiality, setting boundaries, roles and accountability

Confidentiality is a requirement, so that the supervisee feels they are able to discuss with you things that are troubling them. Breaching confidentiality can lead to a lack of trust

and a workforce that fails to give care that is of high quality. The assurance of confidentiality needs to be established at the very first session, with boundaries being set and accountability clearly shown. Refer to ACs 1.2 and 2.1 for more information.

Frequency, location and environmental considerations of supervision sessions

As a manager, you must ensure there is clarity about when supervision is to take place, how often, where it will be held and how the environment is to be managed. For example, it should be a quiet, well-lit place where there should be no interruptions and any enquiries should be directed elsewhere. You also need to be strict about the duration of the session.

Evidence opportunity

3.1 Establishing agreement with the supervisee on key areas

Here, you will need to show you can plan and undertake professional supervision to include the areas we have covered in this section.

Reflect on it

3.1 Supervision meetings

Write about the way you set boundaries, ensure confidentiality and agree location and times for meetings. Ensure you first have your supervisee's permission, and that names and other identifying details are changed. In your supervision meetings, what are the actions that you take to prepare? What are the factors that you consider in terms of how often you have the meetings and where you have the meetings?

AC 3.2 Support supervisees to reflect on their practice using the range of information available and their own insights

Here, you will be required to support supervisees to reflect on their practice using the range of information available and their own insights, to include the areas we discuss in this section.

Sources of data and evidence available and their own insights used to inform supervision

The evidence you require a member of staff to bring to supervision will depend on the agreement you have made and the agenda set at the last meeting. The evidence will be linked to the supervisee's objectives and may include reflective accounts of critical incidents, assessments undertaken, observations and service user surveys.

An action plan may require the supervisee to do something before the next meeting and to bring the finished piece. In preparing for the supervisory meeting, staff need to be aware of the agenda set at the previous meeting. If this required work to be completed, they should get into the habit of bringing with them evidence to support the work done. See AC 2.1 above for more ideas about how information such as a supervisee's coursework can be supported during a session.

Analysis of information from a range of perspectives to build an evidence-based understanding of the supervisee's performance to date

In order to analyse information, the supervisee needs to be able to undertake the process of reflection. This is extremely important since it enables us to bring together practice and theory. Reflection on practice enables us to take a step back from what we are learning and assess what was good and what we might have done differently in any one situation.

In helping your staff to be more reflective about their work, there are a number of useful reflective tools, such as the one developed by Gibbs (1988). See AC 1.2 for more information on Gibbs.

By using a range of information available from other sources and from any learning they have undertaken, supervisees can reinforce their own insights that they have gained from reflecting. For example, when they engage with the art of reflecting in a meaningful way, reflection can clarify the learning that they have gained from a training course and also from situations that arise in experience gained in the workplace. Following a training session, a member of staff may have learned a new skill, for example taking blood. In developing this skill, they need to practise and also reflect upon the successes and failures they may have with undertaking this skill. In this way, they gain a better insight and are able to build evidence about their own performance.

Evidence opportunity

3.2 Supporting supervisees to reflect on their practice

Prepare a PowerPoint presentation detailing the process of reflection and showing the key elements of this for your staff.

You may have highlighted the key elements of reflection as follows:

- **Reflection** helps us to achieve a better understanding of ourselves and the roles we carry out. We actively analyse experience, attempting to 'make sense' or find the meaning in it.

- **Stand back.** It can be hard to reflect when we are caught up in an activity. 'Standing back' gives a better view or perspective on an experience, issue or action.

- **Undertake repetition.** Reflection involves 'going over' something, often several times, in order to get a broad view and check nothing is missed.

- **Gain a sense of deeper honesty.** Reflection is associated with 'striving after truth'. Through reflection, we can acknowledge things that we find difficult to admit in the normal course of events.

- **'Weigh up'.** Reflection involves being even-handed or balanced in judgement. This means taking everything into account, not just the most obvious.

- **Achieve clarity.** Reflection can bring greater clarity, like seeing events reflected in a mirror. This can help at any stage of planning, carrying out and reviewing activities.

- **Gain understanding.** Reflection is about learning and understanding on a deeper level. This includes gaining valuable insights that cannot be just 'taught'.

- **Make judgements.** Reflection involves an element of drawing conclusions in order to move on, change or develop an approach, strategy or activity.

KEY TERM

Reflective practice is the act of stopping and thinking about what we are doing in practice and analysing the decisions we make in the light of theory and the things we have learned. By doing this we are more able to relate theory to practice, helping us to generate new knowledge and ideas.

Evidence opportunity

3.2 Support supervisees to reflect on their practice

Here, you will be required to support supervisees to reflect on their practice using the range of information available and their own insights, to include the areas we discuss in this section. Demonstrate this to your assessor or obtain a witness testimony.

AC 3.3 and AC 3.4 Provide constructive feedback that can be used to improve practice and support supervisee to identify their own development needs

Here, you will be required to provide feedback to the supervisee, which covers the areas we discuss in this section.

Constructive and developmental feedback to improve practice

KEY TERM

Feedback is an open two-way communication between two or more parties.

Feedback needs to be provided on a regular basis and should be a daily part of your work as a manager. In a formal supervision session, the best way to approach feedback is to ask the supervisee how they perceived their performance of a task before you launch in with your assessment. By linking the feedback to their professional development, the member of staff will be able to focus more on what they need to change. In this way, you can see what they understand about how well they are doing their job and you are also encouraging them to be reflective about their performance.

Occasionally, we are very critical about what we do, and it is therefore nice to hear some positive praise for how we have completed a particular job. Positive feedback is often not forthcoming and yet it is motivating when it is genuinely felt. Thanking somebody at the end of the day for a job well done or acknowledging a person's work during a shift builds respect and ensures that the member of staff is secure in their work.

Think about the following. Your manager wants to give you some constructive feedback and has called a meeting for that purpose. How are you feeling? You are probably approaching the meeting in a negative way, thinking that you are about to be criticised in some way. The term 'feedback' is often confused with criticism and how we might have done a job in a better way, and for that reason we view the whole concept less than positively.

So if that's how you feel about it, chances are your staff and supervisees share the same negative vibes. We cannot go through life without making any mistakes and without requiring some guidance on aspects of our work, and although the content of feedback may be negative, it can always be given in a constructive and encouraging manner. When done in such a way, you can help the member of

staff to solve a problem, or even to address a part of their behaviour and work towards organisational goals.

Constructive feedback must be based upon what you have observed about somebody's performance and you should not fall into the trap of giving praise or criticism which comes from a place of personal judgement. Instead, you should provide information that is specific to the issue in question. You need to give the message clearly and get right to the point and not give mixed messages. What you want to be done needs to be clear to the person receiving the message. For example, telling Sarah that she 'needs to improve her handover reports' is vague – she will need to be told how she can improve. Also, informing Sarah that her handover was 'quite good' on Monday and adding the word 'but' or however' is not clear. She hears the praise but may fail to hear the real message, which is that she needs to improve. You need to give clear, constructive feedback. Emphasise the positives but be clear on how the supervisee can improve.

Unambiguous feedback that clearly sets out any issues

If we need to give negative feedback it should be done in such a way that the person is clear about what has to be done. The tone of voice in such a delivery is important, showing concern but never anger or frustration. The message needs to be helpful to the person and they need to know that it is sincere. Focus on what you have observed and be clear, focusing on the facts of the situation. This shows a non-judgemental approach, and it means the issue does not become personal. For example, 'I have noticed that you are not using the hand gel on patients' bedsides before you approach them, and our guidelines specify that we should be doing this every time. Please make sure that you build this into your routine'. It is clear what you require as a manager and the member of staff is left with a clear message about what needs to improve.

Feedback that supports the supervisee to identify their own development needs

Ongoing staff development is just one discussion you will have with your supervisees during the supervision session. These needs are likely to reflect their job role and the long-term goals of the organisation. Supervisees should be encouraged to reflect on their practice with respect to this and their future career development.

If the member of staff is seeking new responsibilities in the work setting, they may be helped to identify courses to enable them in a new role. It is important that you as a manager and supervisor are up to date with policy changes, national initiatives and legal requirements for the setting in order to specify the sort of training they need.

Reflect on it

3.3, **3.4** Positive and constructive feedback

Provide a written account detailing an example of positive and constructive feedback you have used to help improve the performance of a member of staff. Record a real supervision session and anonymise it for your coursework. Then explain how you have supported a supervisee to identify their own development needs. How have you provided feedback that is unambiguous and clearly sets out any issues?

Evidence opportunity

3.3, **3.4** Providing constructive feedback and support supervisee

Here, you will be required to provide feedback to the supervisee that can be used to improve performance and covers the areas we discuss in this section. You will also need to show that you can support your supervisee(s) to identify their own development needs.

Support supervisee to identify their own development needs

As a manager, you will support staff to identify their professional development needs in different ways, such as appraisals and the setting of SMART objectives as we have discussed.

AC 3.5 Review and revise targets to meet objectives of work settings and individual objectives of supervisees

Here, you will be required to review and revise targets with the supervisee that meet objectives of work settings and meet the objectives of the individual.

It is not enough to set targets; we should also plan when to review progress. Review is about reflecting upon experience, making sense of it and determining what has been learned from the outcomes. Without reviewing targets, we cannot move on with development, as we will not be able to clarify what has been achieved or be able to measure the success or failure of a project. Also, the supervisee will lose interest in the plan and may start to feel devalued as a result. Time needs to be spent on going over what has happened since the target was set and what has been achieved. Through the review we can then help to make revisions to targets and set new objectives.

Meet objectives of work settings

In supervision, the objectives of the work setting should be part of the targets that are set for each individual. For example, one of the organisational objectives may be to ensure that all new members of staff be made aware of the values of the settings and a target may be that your supervisee is involved in training to help new staff understand the work of the setting and its values.

Meet the objectives of the individual

In addition to working towards the organisation's objectives your supervisee may have their own individual objectives. For example, they may wish to undertake further courses to improve their career prospects. Professional development requirements attached to various roles and required by regulatory bodies such as the NMC or HCPC (Health and Care Professions Council) change over time and your supervisee may want to undertake their own further development to ensure that they keep up to date.

Reflect on it

3.5 Development needs

Provide evidence of how you support supervisees to identify their own and the organisation's development needs. Using an anonymised personal development plan, show how you set targets and monitor these. What do you think is good about the system you are using? Is it fit for purpose? How might you improve it?

Evidence opportunity

3.5 Review and revise targets to meet objectives

Show your assessor that you can review and revise targets with the supervisee that:

- meet objectives of work settings
- meet the objectives of the individual.

Reflect on it

3.5 Your review process

Using the same evidence from AC 3.4, critically evaluate your own review process. Was it successful? Or maybe you need to make a change to ensure that it is?

Make some notes about how you might improve this aspect of your supervision.

AC 3.6 Support supervisees to explore different methods of addressing challenging situations in their work

Here, you will be required to support supervisees to explore different methods of addressing challenging situations in their work practice, agree suitable methods in any actions to be taken forward, reflect on own strengths and resilience in addressing challenges, understand own responsibilities and own role when facing work challenges.

Explore different methods of addressing challenging situations in their work practice

See AC 2.6 for information on supporting supervisees to address challenging situations. There is a saying that 'if we always do the same thing we will always get the same results'. Occasionally, those results are not what we need or want and we therefore repeat the behaviour and get into a spiral of non-achievement.

In challenging situations, you need to address the incident quickly to ensure it does not become practice. Some ways to do this may include:

- Describe the behaviour – 'I noticed you did … or did not do …'
- Say how this feels or how it impacts the team – 'I felt … or this means the team cannot do …'
- Say what needs to be done – 'Instead … I need you to do …'
- Gain commitment – 'Do you think you can do this?' or 'Is there anything I need to help with?'

By undertaking a simple approach like this you deal with a situation in a factual and non-emotive way.

Evidence opportunity

3.6 Support supervisees addressing challenging work situations

Show your assessor how you support supervisees to explore different methods of addressing challenging situations in their work, taking into account the topics we have discussed in this section.

Agree suitable methods in any actions to be taken forward

Agree with staff the way in which you wish to handle any situations that may be challenging. You may decide to adopt the simple strategy shown above.

Reflect on own strengths and resilience in addressing challenges

Think about how you handle challenges and the feelings that emerge when something happens. What are you good at in these situations and how might you improve where you have weaknesses?

Understand own responsibilities and own role when facing work challenges

Each member of staff needs to be clear about where their authority ends with respect to challenging situations. For example, a complaint from a relative may be dealt with at a higher level than the team and this needs to be made clear. Staff must be aware of their limitations in dealing with certain areas of challenge.

Evidence opportunity

3.4 , 3.5 , 3.6 Development needs, objectives and challenging situations

Show evidence of how you support supervisees to identify their own development needs and how you work with them in challenging situations. How have you reviewed and revised targets to meet objectives of work settings and individual objectives of supervisees? You could write a reflective account to detail all of this.

AC 3.7 Record agreed supervision decisions

Here, you will be required to show that you are able to record supervision meetings and decisions agreed in line with workplace policies and procedures.

All supervision meetings need to be properly recorded to identify and support agreed actions and their completion within agreed timescales. Without records we cannot be sure we have actually set tasks and actions, and this can lead to confusion. You will need to record the decisions and plans made in line with your organisation's policies and procedures.

However you choose to record the meeting, the following are points to consider:

- Record decisions and actions which you agree on and ensure that these are signed and dated.
- Have clear timescales.
- Detail responsibilities.
- Ensure copies are filed in a safe place and supervisees know that other managers may have access to them.

Organisational procedures

In your setting, there may be a specific system by which supervision is recorded, perhaps in staff files or online using software, and such procedures must be followed.

Ways to record which can be owned by the supervisee

The supervisee may have a personal development plan which is on their online continuous professional development training system or you could simply undertake to record their sessions in a way they wish to.

Ways to record agreed actions which can be referred to at the next supervision

However records are to be kept, there needs to be mutual agreement as to how they can be accessed and measured.

AC 3.8 Adapt personal approaches to professional supervision in light of feedback from supervisees and others

Here, you will be required to critically evaluate your working practice and use feedback from a range of people to improve your performance as a supervisor.

One way you can evaluate your work as a supervisor is to ask for feedback; however, this may be quite difficult to do. Nevertheless, if you are to improve your practice, you need evidence of what you can do to achieve this.

You might decide to ask staff to complete an anonymous questionnaire about your work. The following questions might be useful:

1 How did you find my approach to the session?
2 Was it positive?
3 How might I have improved it?
4 What was the best aspect of my approach?
5 And the worst?
6 What are the areas I need to improve?

Supervision requires that you are conforming to standards as set out in guidance supplied by governing bodies such as CQC, which provide us with minimum standards. By working in line with such guidance we will be able to measure our performance against standards and we can highlight areas for improvement in our practice.

Good supervision goes a long way to ensuring that staff and managers maintain a healthy working relationship. Gaining feedback from staff keeps the relationship healthy since we can learn and adapt our style and as a result change our practice to more efficient ways of working. Supervisors who are reflective will be able to change, develop and improve their practice for the good of their supervisees.

It is likely that you may approach a range of people for feedback on performance. For example, you might ask colleagues you work with in the setting and those who work in other teams, such as physiotherapists or occupational therapists. Anyone who has an input into your work setting would be able to provide feedback on performance and you might also approach service users for their comments about staff performance. You will, of course, also need to reflect upon and evaluate your own performance as a manager and supervisor of staff.

Supervision is a two-way process and supervisees should be able to contact their supervisor in between sessions if they need to. Agreement can be made as to the method of that contact, either via email or phone or additional appointments.

Demonstrate that you take feedback seriously and set yourself any actions to improve, and seek feedback on any improvements made

Any feedback given helps improvement and should be worked on. Feedback can be positive or negative and both are valuable in learning. Any feedback needs to be reflected upon and then plans put in place to make changes. When improvement has been made this can then be taken back to supervision and demonstrated.

Develop any personal skills and approaches to improve supervision by training and reflection

Personal skills development occurs through additional training, which may be sought as a result of learning in supervision and also through reflecting upon feedback.

Reflect on it

3.7, **3.8** Feedback

Anonymise a copy of the supervision carried out with the member of staff to show how you record the supervision meetings in your workplace.

Ask a member of staff you supervised to comment on your work. Collect the data and reflect on the comments.

How have you gathered and used the feedback gained from colleagues and other staff including the supervisee about your approach?

How have you adapted your approach according to the feedback you received about your style?

Provide a written account detailing this information.

Evidence opportunity

3.7, **3.8** Record agreed supervision decisions and adapt personal approaches to professional supervision

Here, you must show you can record supervision meetings and decisions agreed in line with workplace policies and procedures, including, for example, organisational procedures, ways to record which can be owned by the supervisee and ways to record agreed actions which can be referred to at the next supervision.

Then provide a written piece, critically evaluating your working practice, and use feedback from a range of people to improve your performance as a supervisor. For example:

- Actively seek feedback from the supervisee on own performance as a supervisor.
- Then demonstrate that you can take feedback seriously and set yourself any actions to improve.
- You will then need to show you can develop any personal skills and approaches to improve supervision by training and reflection.
- Then show you can seek feedback on any improvements made.

Research it

3.8 An evaluation sheet

Prepare an evaluation sheet for your supervisees and other staff members to enable you to gain feedback on your approach to the supervision process. Collate the information gained and say how you will adapt your approach in light of feedback from supervisees and others.

Reflect on it

3.8 Feedback and changes

Reflect on the comments and identify any changes you intend to make as a result of your feedback.

LO4 Understand the management of performance in adult care settings

AC 4.1 Procedures which address performance management and related issues

Here, you will be required to evaluate your role with regard to your organisation's performance management systems and procedures to include the areas we discuss in this section.

How to address conduct and performance issues with individuals

In being constructive about performance there must be a valid set of measures that can support our judgement. This is where a good performance management system must be in place, and if you have confidence that the performance is clearly not up to standard, then you can set up a performance review where you meet the member of

staff to address the situation and help them improve their performance. Be aware that the employee is likely to feel under threat at such an interview, so you need to approach this with care.

Finding out what is causing the poor performance is a useful starting point in this meeting, and a copy of the job description is needed here. You might be able to go through what is expected of the employee and the standard of work expected, and it is likely that at this stage the reason will become clear and can be remedied.

Some reasons for poor performance are that the employee is unclear about their role, job description or what it is they are trying to achieve. They may feel they lack training or are having some personal issues that are causing them concern. It may simply be that the employee is not suited to this type of work.

By discussing the reason in a calm and clear way, the poor performance can quickly become a thing of the past.

See AC 2.5 on indicators of poor performance.

KEY TERM

Constructive feedback focuses on the issue in question and provides specific information. It is firmly based on observation and provides supportive evidence. There are two types of constructive feedback. One is positive or favourable and this is when we praise a performance or effort or outcome. The other is more negative and may be seen as unfavourable, when we criticise a performance or outcome.

Discipline and grievance procedures and the impact of a performance management system

The impact of an effective performance management system is successful achievement of organisational goals and strategies and a healthy and reliable workforce. It helps to motivate and retain staff members and is useful in identifying top performers among staff but also those who are struggling or simply not doing what they should be. One of the ways we do this in the health service is by identifying KPIs, which we have discussed in AC 2.5.

With respect to disciplinary procedures, policies to support the staff need to be put into place, as well as a process for raising grievances at work. However, an approach that sensitively deals with such conflict is a more humane approach to performance.

If a member of staff is struggling with their work, then competency and capability to do the job may be in question. In this instance, it is best not to go down the disciplinary route. The best course of action would be to determine what the staff member would need to do to be able to function more efficiently and this may then reveal that further training might be the solution.

The feedback to the member of staff and the performance data collected mean you will be in a position to see where you are in relation to the achievement of objectives within the workplace. For example, if you are aiming to market your service as outstanding and you have members of staff who underperform, the feedback you receive might lead you to re-evaluate staff members' roles and provide additional training. In doing so, the next review meeting may well show a marked increase in performance that clearly meets the objectives of the organisation.

Evidence opportunity

4.1 Procedures that address performance management

Provide a written account evaluating your role with regard to your organisation's performance management systems and procedures, to include the topics we have covered in this section.

AC 4.2 Meeting current legislative and regulatory requirements

Here, you will be required to critically evaluate your organisation's disciplinary and grievance procedures and consider recommended changes to these processes to ensure they meet current legislative and regulatory requirements.

The Employment Act 2008 replaced the minimum statutory Disciplinary and Grievance Procedures with a new ACAS Code of Practice on Disciplinary and Grievance Procedures (the 'ACAS Code' 2015). Although the Code is not legally binding, the principles within it are considered by a tribunal when addressing the cases of dismissal and fairness. One of the things the Code stresses is that it is far better to try to resolve disputes in a less formal manner rather than going straight to law. The procedures in this Code are flexible in

that they encourage employers and employees to resolve disputes in a less formal way.

As a manager, you need to be fully aware of how the Code works. Cases that go to tribunal may be costly in terms of compensation as the tribunal has the power to adjust the compensation by up to 25 per cent if they find the Code has not been followed correctly by either the employer or the employee.

The government website at www.gov.uk/disciplinary-procedures-and-action-at-work clearly sets out the statutory minimum disciplinary procedures and your disciplinary procedure should include the following steps:

- A letter to the member of staff setting out the reasons or reasons why disciplinary action is being taken.
- A meeting to discuss the issue.
- A disciplinary decision or the outcome of the hearing which might be no action being taken, a verbal or written warning, a final warning, demotion or dismissal.
- A chance to appeal this decision.

Reflect on it

4.2 Your organisation's disciplinary and grievance procedures

Obtain a copy of your organisation's disciplinary and grievance procedures and summarise the main points.

Identify the strengths and the weaknesses of the policies. For example, why do you need to have these policies in place? How do they protect the workforce and the employer?

Discuss how these policies have been used in your workplace and what the outcomes have been.

What changes might you recommend to ensure they meet current legislative and regulatory requirements?

How have the policies been measured in the past? Are they linked to KPIs?

Evaluate your role as a manager with respect to discipline and grievance and say how this affects the workforce.

Comment upon the effects on staff morale and staff turnover. Provide a reflective account.

Evidence opportunity

4.2 Meeting current legislative and regulatory requirements

Provide a written account critically evaluating your organisation's disciplinary and grievance procedures and consider recommended changes to these processes to ensure they meet current legislative and regulatory requirement.

AC 4.3 Possible outcomes in disciplinary cases

Here, you will consider potential outcomes in disciplinary cases, both internally and externally, as well as on the future management of service delivery teams, including consideration of the areas we discuss in this section.

If there is a disciplinary case to be answered then a formal meeting will be set up with the staff member, their manager and a representative possibly from the staff member's union. The outcome of such an event could be one of the following:

● That the allegation is upheld and minor, serious or gross misconduct has occurred.

● Sanctions will then be put in place to address the outcome and these can be in the form of written warnings at various levels or even dismissal or redeployment.

Information about how to appeal will also be given at this meeting.

Impacts on service provision and impact on staffing

If there are issues with staff performance or capability there is likely to be impact upon other members of the team. For example, if staff have to attend further training in order to improve their performance this is likely to affect other staff who have to take on their workload. Also, staff under pressure may leave and turnover therefore increases. The way in which you deal with such issues will also affect staff morale and possibly turnover. It is essential then to ensure that such situations are dealt with fairly and efficiently to reassure other staff in the team. You need to ensure that you have good capability procedures in place should a situation arise where formal disciplinary measures need to be taken.

Adapted from: www.throgmorton.co.uk/resources/business

Appeals procedures and future management support and training and development required

As a manager, you must inform the member of staff of their right to appeal any decision that is made. If staff think that the decision was wrong or unfair procedures were used, they are at liberty to take this further. They may also appeal if they consider the punishment or sanctions to be too harsh.

The process is similar to the grievance process in that the staff member needs to write a letter giving reasons for appealing and asking for a meeting, usually with a more senior manager.

Following this, the manager needs to ensure that support is in place to help the member of staff. If the appeal is upheld the manager should enable the staff member to return to work with additional support by means of further training or mentoring to develop and improve their performance.

Legal implications – e.g. employment

If there is anything left unresolved with the disciplinary hearing or the member of staff feels aggrieved at the outcome, then they need to be informed of their right to make a claim. They may feel they have not been treated lawfully and have been dismissed unfairly or discriminated against in some way. They must be told how to make a claim, which should be done within three months of the disciplinary hearing, although as a manager you would be wise to attempt to resolve the grievance in a more open and friendly way if possible.

Evidence opportunity

4.3 Possible outcomes in disciplinary cases

Provide a written account considering the potential outcomes in disciplinary cases, both internally and externally, as well as on the future management of service delivery teams, including consideration of:

● impacts on service provision

● impact on staffing

● appeals procedures

● legal implications – e.g. employment tribunals

● future management support and training and development required.

Reflect on it

4.3 A disciplinary case you may have been involved in

Using a flow chart, show the disciplinary and grievance procedure in place in your setting.

Ensure that you show the stages of the disciplinary hearing and the appeals procedure.

Consider a disciplinary case you have been involved with.

● What would you consider to be the drawbacks of the event, particularly with respect to the impact it had on other members of staff and their morale?

● Did it affect staff turnover?

● How did it affect the service provision? Was there an improvement in practice?

● How did you explain to the member of staff the appeals process and the use of employment tribunals? Comment upon the process you went through.

● Reflect on how the whole event made you feel as a manager having to undertake this task. Provide a written account.

If you have not been involved with a disciplinary case, think about how you might handle this. Refer to your setting's agreed ways of working and speak to your own manager for further guidance.

Reflective exemplar

During my course I have been told I need to write a reflective journal and to some extent this scares me. It has been explained to us that reflection is important if we are to improve our practice and also the practice of those in the team. As a manager I am a little concerned that I may not be reflecting on the right things and not able to answer questions properly. I wrote a small journal piece about a staff appraisal I did at work and then asked my tutor to read it.

During the appraisal I realised that I was quite concerned about the impact my lack of confidence would have on the member of staff. I have only completed a couple of staff appraisals and so was trying hard to ensure that I had all the relevant paperwork and was completing the documents correctly. This led to me not really listening to the member of staff and I missed a lot of what he was saying because I had my head in the writing! I found I was trying too hard to present myself as a confident manager when in fact I felt less worthy than that. Following that particular session, I had a bit of a panic! I wondered what the staff would think of me and if I would ever get this part of my job right.

Feedback from the tutor

This account is descriptive but there is some evidence of reflection. At the start you refer to a past event – a staff appraisal – but you have not considered how other prior experiences such as your own appraisals could have impacted upon your own attempt here. Have you perhaps learned to document appraisals in this way because of your own experience?

You do comment upon how you felt at this time which is good, but it might have been useful here to say what the member of staff thought of the appraisal session. Did you ask him? After the session you say you felt panicked and I was left wondering what this was like and what impact it had on you as a team leader? Did you ask the staff member what he felt like at the end of the appraisal? How did you think it might affect the other staff? What made you immediately consider that this part of your job was not right? Did you even consider that this was a good appraisal?

Legislation

Act	Key points
The Health and Social Care Act 2012 and the 2014 Care Act	These introduced the Care Quality Commission (CQC).
General Data Protection Regulations GDPR (2018)	In May 2018, the GDPR came into force. This provides detailed guidance to organisations on how to govern and manage people's personal information.

Suggestions for using the activities

This table summarises all the activities in the unit that are relevant to each assessment criterion.
Here, we also suggest other, different methods that you may want to use to present your knowledge and skills by using the activities. These are just suggestions, and you should refer to the Introduction section at the start of the book, and more importantly the City & Guilds specification, and your assessor, who will be able to provide more guidance on how you can evidence your knowledge and skills. When you need to be observed during your assessment, this can be done by your assessor, or your manager can provide a witness testimony.

Assessment criteria and accompanying activities	Suggested methods to show your knowledge/skills
LO1 Understand principles of professional development in adult care	
1.1 Evidence opportunity (page 184)	Provide a written account explaining professional development in relation to the areas we have discussed in this section. Make sure you explain the importance of continuously improving your own knowledge and practice and that of the team you manage and lead.
1.1 Reflect on it (page 184)	Write a reflective piece about the relationship between training and positive outcomes and how you know this happens.
1.1 Reflect on it (page 184)	What professional development activities have you and your team participated in over the last year? Make a list. Address the questions in the activity and provide a reflective account.
1.2 Evidence opportunity (page 186)	Provide a written account critically evaluating the theories of reflective practice in improving individual performance, with reference to the topics we cover in the section.

Suggestions for using the activities	
1.2 Research it (page 187)	Research potential barriers to undertaking professional development and reflection in your workplace and then set up an action plan to overcome them. Complete the table or write down your findings.
1.2 Reflect on it (page 187)	Write a short reflective account of how the potential barriers to reflective practice affect the outcomes for service users.
1.3 Evidence opportunity (page 191)	Provide a written account evaluating a range of sources and systems of support for professional development for the manager and their staff, including the ones we cover in this section.
1.3 Research it (page 191)	Write down your findings and complete the table.
1.4 Evidence opportunity (page 193)	Provide a written account analysing the effectiveness of digital technology used in supporting learning activities considering the areas we have discussed in this section.
1.5 Evidence opportunity (page 195)	Provide a written account critically evaluating the potential barriers and constraints in your working environment in accessing professional development, with consideration of the areas we have discussed in this section. See the activity, which suggests you could also create a table.
1.6 Evidence opportunity (page 196)	Provide a written account explaining the range of factors that impact on selecting and commissioning activities for personal and professional development within the work setting.
LO2 Understand supervision in adult care	
2.1 Research it (page 196)	Research the various models and write down your findings.
2.1 Reflect on it (page 197)	Answer the questions in the activity and provide a written account.
2.1 Research it (page 199)	Obtain a copy of your supervision policy and write a short piece about how you might change it to fit what you have learned about supervision to date.
2.1 Evidence opportunity (page 200)	Provide a written account explaining the key principles and scope of supervision, including the topics we have discussed in this section.
2.2 Evidence opportunity (page 202)	Provide a written account critically evaluating theories and models of professional supervision to help inform practice, including the ones we discuss in Section 2.1.
2.2 Research it (page 202)	Research a couple of the models and provide a written account about your findings.
2.2 Reflect on it (page 203)	Write a reflective piece to show your understanding of the models and frameworks.
2.3 Research it (page 204)	Write down your findings.
2.3 Reflect on it (page 205)	Write a short reflective piece about how compliments and complaints have informed supervision where you work.
2.3 Evidence opportunity (page 205)	Provide a written account explaining why supervision could be informed by current legislation, codes of practice and agreed ways of working, compliments and complaints. Or you could explain this to your assessor.
2.4 Research it (page 206)	Write down your findings.
2.4 Evidence opportunity (page 206)	Provide a written account documenting your findings. You could explain these to your assessor.
2.5 Reflect on it (page 210)	Provide a written account.
2.5 Evidence opportunity (page 210)	Write a piece critically evaluating the principles of performance management with regard to the areas we have discussed in this section.
2.6 Evidence opportunity (page 211)	Explore management supervision practice with regard to some of the areas we discuss in this section. Provide a written account keeping the questions in the activity in mind.

➜

Suggestions for using the activities	
2.6 Case study (page 211)	The case study will help you to think about some of the issues around power imbalance.
2.6 Reflect on it (page 212)	Provide a written account.
2.6 Research it (page 212)	Write down findings from your research.
2.6 Reflect on it (page 212)	You could provide a reflective account.
2.6 Case study (page 213)	Write a response to the question thinking about what you have learnt in this section.
2.6 Reflect on it (page 213)	Provide a reflective account based on your own experience.
2.6 Evidence opportunity (page 214)	Write a piece exploring management supervision practice with regard to some of the areas we discussed in this section.
LO3 Provide professional supervision	
3.1 Evidence opportunity (page 214)	Show your assessor you can plan and undertake professional supervision to include the areas we have covered here.
3.1 Reflect on it (page 214)	Provide a reflective account addressing the questions in the activity.
3.2 Evidence opportunity (page 215)	Prepare a PowerPoint presentation as instructed, or you could provide a written account.
3.3, 3.4 Reflect on it (page 217)	Provide a written reflective account addressing the questions in the activity.
3.3, 3.4 Evidence opportunity (page 217)	Show your assessor that you can support your supervisee(s) to identify their own development needs.
3.5 Reflect on it (page 217)	Provide evidence of how you support supervisees to identify their own and the organisation's development needs. Using an anonymised personal development plan show how you set targets and monitor these. Provide a reflective account addressing the questions In the activity.
3.5 Evidence opportunity (page 217)	You will need to show your assessor that you can review and revise targets with the supervisee which • meet objectives of work settings • meet the objectives of the individual.
3.5 Reflect on it (page 217)	Write down your response to the activity.
3.6 Evidence opportunity (page 218)	Show your assessor how you support supervisees to explore different methods of addressing challenging situations in their work taking into account the topics we have discussed in Section 3.6.
3.4, 3.5, 3.6 Evidence opportunity (page 218)	You could write a reflective account to detail all of the questions in the activity.
3.7, 3.8 Reflect on it (page 219)	Provide a written account detailing the information requested in the activity.
3.7, 3.8 Evidence opportunity (page 220)	Here, you must show you can record supervision meetings and decisions agreed in line with workplace policies and procedures, including for example organisational procedures, ways to record which can be owned by the supervisee, ways to record agreed actions which can be referred to at the next supervision. Then provide a written piece, critically evaluating your working practice and use feedback from a range of people to improve your performance as a supervisor, considering the areas we have covered in this section.
3.8 Research it (page 220)	Prepare an evaluation sheet/write down your findings.
3.8 Reflect on it (page 220)	Provide a reflective account.

Suggestions for using the activities	
LO4 Understand the management of performance in adult care settings	
4.1 Evidence opportunity (page 221)	Provide a written account evaluating your role with regard to your organisation's performance management systems and procedures to include the topics we have covered in this section.
4.2 Reflect on it (page 221)	Provide a written account addressing the points in the activity.
4.2 Evidence opportunity (page 221)	Provide a written account critically evaluating your organisation's disciplinary and grievance procedures and consider recommended changes to these processes to ensure they meet current legislative and regulatory requirement.
4.3 Evidence opportunity (page 222)	Provide a written account addressing the points in the activity.
4.3 Reflect on it (page 222)	Write about your own experience or how you might feel if you were in such a situation.

References

Atkins, S. and Murphy, K. (1994) Reflective practice, *Nursing Standard*, 8(39): 49–54.

Bernard, J.M. and Goodyear, R.K. (1998) *Fundamentals of Clinical Supervision* (2e). Needham Heights, MA: Allyn and Bacon.

Bolton, G. (2010) *Reflective Practice: Writing and professional development* (3e). London: Sage.

Boud, D. and Walker, D. (1993) 'Barriers to reflection on experience,' in *Using Experience for Learning*. Buckingham: SHRE/Open University Press.

Boyd, E. and Fales, A. (1983) Reflective learning: The key to learning from experience, *Journal of Humanistic Psychology*, 23(2): 99–117.

Care Quality Commission (CQC) (2013) Registration under the Health and Social Care Act 2008. Supporting information and guidance: Supporting effective clinical supervision.

Carroll, M. (2007) One more time: what is supervision? *Psychotherapy in Australia*, 13(3), May.

Cavendish Review, (2013) An Independent Review into Healthcare Assistants and Support Workers in the NHS and social care settings.

CIPD (2006) *Coaching Supervision: Maximising the potential of coaching*. Bath: Bath Consultancy Group.

Clutterbuck, D. and Megginson, D. (1999) *Mentoring Executives and Directors*. Oxford: Butterworth-Heinemann.

Department of Health (2004) *The NHS Knowledge and Skills Framework and Development Review Guidance – Working Draft Version 7*. London: Department of Health. www.dh.gov.uk

Department of Health (2013) *The Cavendish Review: An independent review into healthcare assistants and support workers in the NHS and social care settings*. London: HMSO.

Fitzgerald, M. (1994) *Theories of Reflection for Learning*. Oxford: Blackwell Scientific.

General Social Care Council (2010) *The General Social Care Council – Code of Practice*. London: GSCC.

Gibbs, G. (1988) *Learning by Doing: A guide to teaching and learning methods*. Oxford: Oxford Further Education Unit.

Gopee, N. and Galloway, J. (2009) *Leadership and Management in Health Care*. London: Sage.

Greenwood, J. (1993) 'Reflective Practice: a Critique of the Work of Argyris & Schön', *Journal of Advanced Nursing*, 27: 13–17.

Harrison, R. (2009) *Learning and Development* (5e). London: Chartered Institute for Personnel and Development.

Health Professions Council (2016) *Standards of Conduct, Performance and Ethics*. London: HPC.

Hogan, R.A. (1964) Issues and approaches in supervision, *Psychotherapy, Theory, Research and Practice*, 1: 139–4.

Holloway, E.L. (1987) Developmental models of supervision: Is it development? *Professional Psychology: Research and Practice*, 18(3): 209–16.

Jasper, M. (2006) *Professional Development, Reflection and Decision-Making*. Oxford: Blackwell Publishing.

Johns, C. (1995) Framing learning through reflection within Carper's fundamental ways of knowing in nursing, *Journal of Advanced Nursing*, 22: 226–34.

Keogh, B. (2013) *Review into the Quality of Care and Treatment Provided by 14 Hospital Trusts in England: Overview report*. NHS England.

Killion, J. and Todnem, G. (1991) 'A process for personal theory building'. *Educational Leadership*, 48(7): 14–16.

Kolb, D. (1984) Cycle of experiential learning, in Tilmouth, T., Davies-Ward, E. and Williams, B. (2011) *Foundation Degree in Health and Social Care*. London: Hodder Education.

Lambley, S. and Marrable, T. (2013) *Practice Enquiry into Supervision in a Variety of Adult Care Settings Where There Are Health and Social Care Practitioners Working Together*. London: SCIE.

LaFasto, F.M.J. and Larson, C.E. (2001) *When Teams Work Best: 6,000 team members and leaders tell what it takes to succeed*. Thousand Oaks, CA: Sage Publications.

Leitch, S. (2006) *Leitch Review of Skills*. London: HM Treasury.

Liese, B.S. and Beck, J.S. (1997) Cognitive therapy supervision, in Watkins, C.E. *Handbook of Psychotherapy Supervision*. Hoboken, NJ: John Wiley & Sons, pp. 114–33.

Morrison, T. (2005) Staff supervision in social care, in SCIE (2013) *Effective Supervision in a Variety of Settings*. London: SCIE.

Nursing and Midwifery Council (2018) *The Code: Professional standards of practice and behaviour for nurses and midwives*. London: NMC.

Schön, D. (1983) *The Reflective Practitioner: How professionals think in action*. New York: Basic Books.

SCIE (2007) *Providing effective supervision. A workforce development tool, including a unit of competence and supporting guidance*. London: SCIE.

Skills for Care and CWDC (2007) Providing effective supervision: A workforce development tool, including a unit of competence and supporting guidance. SCF01/0607, accessed from www.skillsforcare.org.uk/Document-library/Finding-and-keeping-workers/Supervision/Providing-Effective-Supervision.pdf

Smith, K.L. (2009) A brief summary of supervision models, www.marquette.edu/education/grad/documents/breif-summary-of-supervision

Stoltenberg, C.D. and Delworth, U. (1987) *Supervising Counsellors and Therapists*. San Francisco, CA: Jossey-Bass.

Thompson, N. (2006) *People Problems*. Basingstoke: Palgrave Macmillan.

Tilmouth, T., Davies-Ward, E. and Williams, B. (2011) *Foundation Degree in Health and Social Care*. London: Hodder Education.

Wanless, D. (2002) *Securing our Future Health: Taking a Long-Term View, A report*. Accessed from www.yearofcare.co.uk/sites/default/files/images/Wanless.pdf

Wanless, D. (2007) *Our Future Health Secured? A review of NHS funding and performance*. London: The Kings Fund. Accessed from www.kingsfund.org.uk/sites/default/files/field/field_publication_file/our-future-health-secured-review-nhs-funding-performance-full-version-sir-derek-wanless-john-appleby-tony-harrison-darshan-patel-11-september-2007.pdf

West, M. (2004) *Effective Teamwork: Practical lessons from organizational research*. London: Wiley and Sons.

Whitmore, J. (2002) *Coaching for Performance: GROWing people, performance and purpose*. London: Nicholas Brealey.

Zimmerman, B.J. and Schunk, D.S. (eds) (2003) *Emotional Psychology: A century of contributions*. Mahwah, NJ: Lawrence Erlbaum Associates.

Websites

Skills for Care, www.skillsforcare.org.uk

Social Care Institute for Excellence – Effective supervision in a variety of settings, www.scie.org.uk/publications/guides/guide50

Code of Conduct for Healthcare Support Workers and Adult Social Care Workers in England, www.skillsforhealth.org.uk/images/services/code-of-conduct/Code%20of%20Conduct%20Healthcare%20Support.pdf

About this unit

In an adult care setting, 'resources' include the finances, staff and materials at our disposal to deliver good healthcare. However, effectively managing resources can be tricky to master and there are concerns that a lack of such resources is causing problems in care work today. Careful and effective management of resources is, therefore, essential in order to run a successful care setting and, as a manager, you will play a key role in ensuring this.

Mismanagement or not managing resources effectively can result in budget overspend, lack of resources for people using health and care services, and even the closure of the organisation. In this unit you will understand the principles of effective resource management and the principles of effective human resource management. You will be required to demonstrate your ability to manage resources within your care setting.

Learning outcomes

By the end of this unit, you will:

1 Understand principles of effective resource management
2 Understand principles of human resource management

Getting started

Before you study the unit, think about the following:

● What resources are available in your workplace?

● How can you as a manager learn to trust staff enough to delegate or assign tasks?

● What do you think effective resource management is?

● As a manager, what are you accountable for?

LO1 Understand principles of effective resource management

AC 1.1 National, local and organisational strategies and priorities on resource planning and management

Here, you will be required to explain the impact of different strategies and priorities on resource planning and management, including financial, physical and human resources.

National strategy

The NHS *Five Year Forward View* was published in 2014 by various government bodies including NHS England, NHS Improvement (Monitor and the NHS Trust Development Authority), Health Education England (HEE), The National Institute for Health and Care Excellence (NICE), Public Health England (PHE) and the Care Quality Commission (CQC). These bodies set out a vision for the future of the NHS and looked closely at spending within the NHS, providing a review to 'restore and maintain financial balance' and 'to deliver core access and quality standards for patients' (DoH, 2015a).

In 2017, *Next Steps on the NHS Five Year Forward View* (see page 229) was published and this outlined the progress the NHS had made towards the targets, concluding that the NHS has to evolve to meet new challenges such as our ageing population and the complex health issues we have due to this.

National priorities for 2016/17 to 2020/21 were set out and a requirement for the NHS to produce a five-year Sustainability and Transformation Plan (STP) and one-year Operational Plans for 2016/17 was established. This plan identified nine 'must dos' for 2016/17 for every local system and these included the need for an STP, the delivery of efficiency savings and various plans to look at general practice, waiting times in A&Es across the country, and referrals to specialist and mental health services.

National strategy for adult care settings

For adult care settings it was the Care Act 2014 that set out the law for market development in adult social care. It details the duties and responsibilities for the Department of Health, CQC and local authorities to promote efficient and effective adult care and support.

In 2016, The House of Lords select committee published *The Long Term Sustainability of the NHS and Adult Social Care,* which describes the changes needed to address failures in the NHS and adult care and the need for radical transformation to both the NHS and adult social care systems.

Research it

1.1 National strategy

Take a look at the following reports (or search for them online):

- www.england.nhs.uk/wp-content/uploads/2015/12/planning-guid-16-17-20-21.pdf This report identifies the five-year forward plan

- *Next Steps on the NHS Five Year Forward View* at www.england.nhs.uk/wp-content/uploads/2017/03/NEXT-STEPS-ON-THE-NHS-FIVE-YEAR-FORWARD-VIEW.pdf This is a follow-up report that tracks the progress of the five-year forward plan

- www.gov.uk/government/uploads/system/uploads/attachment_data/file/434202/carter-interim-report.pdf This report looks at efficiency savings in the NHS. It is sometimes referred to as the Carter Review

- Department of Health and Social Care 2017 Adult social care market shaping

- A Vision for Adult Social Care: Capable Communities and Active Citizens, Department of Health, 16 November 2010.

- Transparency in Outcomes: A Framework for Quality in Adult Social Care

- The Association of Directors of Adult Social Care (ADASS) – How to Make Best Use of Reducing Resources: A Whole System Approach

- Making a Strategic Shift to Prevention and Early Intervention 2008 (Putting People First)

- Think Local, Act Personal, January 2011

Write a short piece to show how each report has influenced your own organisation with respect to resource planning in relation to:

- financial resources
- physical resources
- human resources.

Another report, *Improving England's Mental Health: The First 100 Days,* published in 2015, sets out a number of practical actions the government will take to ensure mental and physical health are valued equally.

With poor mental health costing £105 billion annually in England, and businesses losing £26 billion due to mental health issues every year, the report highlighted the need to ensure that resources by means of increased funding were made available.

Research has shown poor mental health as a contributor to wider health inequalities, being associated with increased health-risk behaviours and increased morbidity and mortality from physical ill health. Promoting good mental health, therefore, has significant potential benefits – not only the improvement to health outcomes and life expectancy, but also improving educational and economic outcomes.

This research recognising mental health issues and the effects on physical health further highlights the impact this has on care settings. Additional resources will, therefore, be required to ensure that mental health issues are not only recognised but are adequately resourced to manage the increased risk to physical health. This is likely to further impact upon already scarce financial and staffing resources.

The national strategy to resource care services, both in hospitals and in adult social care, is devolved to five regional teams that are responsible for covering and financing healthcare commissioning and delivery in their regions. The regional teams support the local care strategy groups and work with Clinical Commissioning Groups (CCGs), local authorities (which are responsible for commissioning publicly funded social care services), Health and Wellbeing Boards as well as GP practices providing leadership on finance, nursing and medical professionals, the commissioning of new services and hospitals, patients, human resources, quality assurance and care delivery.

For adult social care it is the local authority that is responsible for services provided to people in their homes and residential care services.

Research it

1.1 Mental Health: The First 100 Days

Take a look at the following link to see the document: http://nhsconfed.org/ resources/2015/05/the-first-100-days-and-beyond

Look at the five priority areas for action and write down how you might use these in your setting.

Local strategy

Local strategies for care set out the strategic priorities for the development and delivery of healthcare in local areas, bringing together health and social care organisations with the CCG, HWBs, GPs and local councils. In this way, the financial, physical and human resources in a local setting can be looked at in a holistic way to ascertain the most efficient way in which to resource the care for a diverse population of people. Not all areas are the same and some locations in the country will have different care needs according to the population demographic. For example, an area where there is a larger elderly population will require different care services, which may need to be resourced. Financial, physical and human resources are clearly identified in the local strategic plan, which should identify the action needed to address deficits.

Organisational strategy

The local strategy and the groups involved (such as the CCG, HWBs, GPs and the local council) will allocate finance to organisations within their area that have responsibility for delivering care within the budget. The organisational strategy will be outlined in a strategic plan but will support the national and local priorities for healthcare.

Budgets and financial resources

Effective businesses need business plans and as a manager you may have been asked to prepare such a document, although many managers in social care will have no involvement in preparing business plans as this is something the owner or director of the business would undertake. The Department of Health requires all care establishments to have business and financial plans in place for external inspection.

You may have been asked to present financial accounts to the Care Standards Commission to demonstrate that clients' fees are being used in an effective way towards their care and that you are providing the best value in your service delivery (again, this is something that not all or many managers would be involved in). To do this, you need to be aware of how to set budgets and also monitor the expenditure of your own department. This expenditure is likely to be in relation to supplies, staffing, equipment and overhead expenses.

A budget refers to the allocation of finances for specific purposes and will form a part of your action plan for the future. If you are part of a large organisation, you will be allocated a small part of the overall financial income and will be expected to audit the expenditure you undertake and to keep within the limits of your budget for a specific length of time, usually known as the financial year. If, however, you work within a small care home and are in total control of the whole income and outgoings, then you need to ensure that the budget is carefully allocated to various areas and to avoid overspending.

Budgeting is a continuous process and to manage the process effectively requires the ability to see beyond the barriers of the yearly divisions and to project future trends with respect to the business. In preparing a budget, the expected income for the year needs to be predicted, along with the predicted expenditure for the year.

Whichever way you choose to set your budget, variations may occur – the cost of services may be far more expensive than it was last year, for instance – and you need to be aware of the potential to overspend. Accuracy is the key to managing the finances effectively.

You may also need to undertake a cost–benefit analysis, which is weighing the effectiveness of the resources and services you wish to purchase against alternatives. For example, you may have decided that the setting needs to be updated and decorated and new furniture purchased. However, if the washing machine breaks down and a new one is needed, you might have to change the plans or at least reassess the needs with respect to the decorative update. Planning, therefore, needs to be on both a long-term and a short-term basis.

The flowchart in Figure 7.1 may be helpful in the planning process.

▲ **Figure 7.1** The planning process

Evidence opportunity

1.1 **Reviewing effectiveness of approaches to resource management**

Write an account explaining the impact of different strategies on resource planning in your setting in relation to:

- financial resources
- physical resources
- human resources.

You could also think about how you ensured staff were kept aware of how they can contribute to the financial stability of the organisation.

Would you make any changes in the next year and if so, why?

Regular reviews and monitoring of budgets

Regular review and monitoring of the budget is essential as the amount you spend throughout the year is likely to vary. In the winter time, the expense of heating and lighting is likely to be much more than during the summer months, so seasonal fluctuations need to be considered. Such planning is called budgetary profiling and if you do not take this into account, you are likely to introduce cash flow problems, which can be most stressful. Your staff may not understand how the budget is set and why sometimes they are unable to purchase certain items or undertake activities with clients.

It is important, therefore, to ensure that the team is aware of how the budget functions. You will need to discuss changes with your team and clarify the costs of any changes. For example, some staff may not understand why they are now being asked to finance their own university courses when in the past these costs have been met by the organisation. Clear discussions in an open and transparent manner can help to clarify this for them.

Physical resources

The physical resources of any care service, hospital, GP surgery or a care home refer to the land, buildings, clinical, care and administration equipment owned by the organisation.

At national, local and organisational levels these resources need to be managed and maintained in order to keep the care system safe and efficient. In your setting you will be responsible for maintaining perhaps a residential care setting or part of one. You will have a budget that will require careful balancing to reduce the financial pressures on an already depleted social care service.

As a manager, you will be responsible for the maintenance of equipment and monitoring the use of it and ensuring that equipment and premises remain fit for purpose.

Human resources

This is by far the biggest resource in the care service today. The state of the adult social care sector and workforce report in England (2018) reports that:

- in 41,000 care establishments providing or organising adult social care in England in 2017, 25,300 of these services were CQC regulated
- the number of adult social care jobs in England in 2017 was estimated at 1.6 million
- direct care employees numbered 1,220,000, which represents 76 per cent of the total workforce
- managerial numbered 119,000, which represents 7 per cent
- regulated professional carers numbered 83,000, which represents 5 per cent
- other staff numbered 180,000, which represents 11 per cent.

Source: Skills for Care, 'The size and structure of the adult social care sector and workforce in England, 2018'

Go to www.skillsforcare.org.uk/NMDS-SC-intelligence/ Workforce-intelligence/documents/State-of-the-adult-social-care-sector/The-state-of-the-adult-social-care-sector-and-workforce-2018.pdf for further statistics about adult social care.

In March 2017, the NHS employed:

- 106,430 doctors
- 285,893 nurses and health visitors
- 21,597 midwives
- 132,673 scientific, therapeutic and technical staff
- 19,772 ambulance staff
- 21,139 managers
- 9,974 senior managers.

Source: NHS Digital, NHS Workforce Statistics – March 2017, provisional statistics

These numbers, in both the NHS and social care, represent an increase on previous years and yet news reports are consistently reporting staff shortages, with Health Education England estimating a shortfall in nursing staff of approximately 8.9 per cent, while in adult social care, Skills for Care estimates 8.0 per cent of roles in the adult social care sector vacant, or 110,000 vacancies at any one time.

One of your key responsibilities at a more local level will be to ensure that you have addressed your staffing needs and developed a **workforce plan**. Additionally, as a major resource for your area you must ensure that you retain the staff you have and develop them to meet the needs of future developments in healthcare.

> **KEY TERM**
>
> **Workforce planning** is the process whereby the staff with the necessary skills are allocated to the task when they are needed in order to deliver organisational objectives.

As a manager, you will be well aware of the need to determine what skills each staff member has and to ensure that during a span of duty you have the right people in place for the care that needs to be given. You also need to develop trust in the team so that you can be confident that delegated tasks will be undertaken. Developing trust is dependent upon certain behaviours such as listening to your staff, seeking input from them in decision making, recognising good work, giving praise and giving them the opportunity to develop. When there is trust in a team, staff will feel secure and empowered to undertake delegated tasks.

In developing your workforce development plan, you will need to:

- analyse your current workforce and identify the skills mix required in your setting to deliver the sort of service you provide
- ensure staff receive any training that is required to meet service user needs.

It is not only about your current provision, though. You need to be aware that changes in the future to the type of service user or the number of service users coming to your setting will need to be considered so that your plan can highlight gaps to be filled.

In developing your plan, it is useful to consider the stages outlined by the SCIE. See www.scie.org.uk/workforce/peoplemanagement/leadership for further information.

Audit of current provision – where the business is now

You need to have up-to-date records of all staff working in your setting, with details such as working hours, training undertaken, retirement ages and turnover. You would also do well to look at the diversity of your staff to see whether the workforce matches that of the clientele you have. If not, you may wish to plan for future campaigns to bring in more diverse staff.

The context of your service – the current trends and changes

In this section of the plan you make reference to the trends in the business, whether it is expanding or otherwise, the changing needs of service users, new regulations or national and local initiatives that may change the service delivery.

Forecasting – or what will we need in the future

This refers to the identification of gaps in the service that you have identified from stages one and two. You may have realised that with the growth of the elderly population in your area, not only will more staff be needed but there may be a need to recruit qualified nurses if these clients have chronic conditions requiring nursing care.

Planning – action plan

Three areas are necessary in this part of your plan:

1 Recruitment and succession planning (i.e. replacing staff who leave or retire).
2 Career development plans for staff and retention plans.
3 Changes to remuneration packages, pay increases or benefits to staff.

Implementation – putting it into practice

In this stage, the plan needs to be integrated into the strategic plan of the organisation and should then be reviewed in line with it.

Workforce development helps to identify current trends and forecast future workforce structures to meet service delivery requirements. The healthcare system is concerned with productivity and outcomes, and with changing structures in health and social care, workforce development planning is critical to maintaining a good service and achieving positive outcomes for people.

Skills for Care also offers advice and guidance on workforce planning in its free guide. Go to www.skillsforcare.org.uk/Documents/Leadership-and-management/Workforce-planning/Practical-approaches-to-workforce-planning-guide.pdf which refers to the constant changes within adult social care. Staffing is mentioned as the most important asset and having the right people in post with the right skills and knowledge ensures a sustainable business for the future.

Strategic planning

Your organisation will have at its heart a strategic plan or a vision, which will identify a corporate strategy and will highlight the way in which the business will run and how resources will be allocated.

The first part of the strategic plan should identify a mission statement, which outlines the direction in which the company wishes to go. There will then be short-term, long-term and operational plans:

- **Short-term plans** cover the day-to-day operation of the organisation and have specific timeframes in place. These can then be measured by conducting research to check whether the deadlines have been met and plans been fulfilled. A simple checklist or survey can be carried out to assess this.
- **Long-term plans** link to finances, how profitable a business is and how the business can survive in the long term. They are linked to the overall strategic planning process and operational planning.
- **Operational plans** detail the specific objectives and milestones for a business and consider the budgetary, physical and human resources needed for the success of the organisation.

The strategic plan in your organisation will have been put together with reference to national organisational strategies and priorities on resource planning and management, and with consideration of government-led spending reviews and plans.

Reflect on it

1.1 **Resources and your setting**

Think about how your own service has changed with respect to the resources at its disposal. Why do you think this change has come about? If you are new to the setting, and are unaware of how the organisation has changed, you could ask a colleague to find out. How has the organisation evolved?

AC 1.2 Roles, responsibilities and accountabilities for resource management

Here, you will be required to explain your role and responsibilities regarding resources management in your service with reference to how potential improvements are implemented.

The role you undertake as a care manager will vary according to the setting you are in but with respect to managing resources you are required to ensure that the financial, physical and human resources within the area are all covered efficiently.

You might manage budgets and report to a financial committee to justify your spending, although not every manager or organisation will have a financial committee. You will need to monitor expenditure and costs. Your budget planning needs to ensure that you:

- plan your income for the year
- plan your expenditure for the year
- review the spend at given points in the year
- keep records of costs.

Physical resources will require you to maintain quality standards in the setting and ensure health and safety is complied within the use of equipment and the fabric of the building and furniture. In managing the physical resources, you need to:

- allocate finances to ensure you can update and renew equipment, furniture and decoration if needed
- draw up a resource plan at the start of the year to determine what you need in terms of equipment, materials, furniture or other items
- monitor the use of physical resources to determine wastage and stock.

For staffing and human resources, your role is to recruit, train and supervise staff to ensure they deliver quality care. This goes beyond these three areas, and also includes more nuanced responsibilities of ensuring the wellbeing of your staff, looking at workloads and opportunities for development within their roles and the setting.

In managing your human resources your responsibilities include ensuring that your budget allows for additional training should it be required so that you can invest in current staff.

Responsibilities and accountability

As a manager in an adult care setting, you are responsible for ensuring that the financial, physical and human resources for your department are meeting the national standards of care and also the strategic and operational plans for the organisation. This means that being in charge of your setting you will be responsible for the failure or success of the operations within it. It is your responsibility to

see that the quality of the care setting is not compromised with potential shortfalls in funding and staffing. Should this happen you will need to be aware of how you can improve the situation. For example, at times staffing becomes problematic and you may be required to look carefully at workloads and employ agency staff as a short-term measure. If staffing issues are unresolved then you will be responsible for escalating concerns to higher management and putting together a case for additional staff.

Being accountable is something different and it means that you are answerable for the success or failure of something. If you are held accountable for something, then you will be expected to explain why you acted in a certain way and why that action failed or succeeded.

If you are accountable for the financial, physical and human resources within your setting then you can be asked to justify the reasons, for example for overspending on budgets or failing to train staff to required standards. You can also make improvements to the current state of affairs if you have both control of your budget and an understanding about how you might save on the use of physical resources. By undertaking a resource planning exercise at the start of the year, you will be able to see where improvements to staffing, physical resources and finances can be made at certain points in the year. For example, you may wish to allocate funds to train a member of staff to undertake mandatory training for all staff, which means you save on employing external companies that offer the same training at elevated costs.

> ### Evidence opportunity
>
> #### 1.2 Roles, responsibilities and accountabilities
>
> What is your role and responsibility with respect to resource management in your own service? How do you address concerns and implement potential improvements? Provide a written account explaining this.

AC 1.3 Importance of accurate forecasting for resource management

Here, you will be required to critically analyse the role of forecasting in resource management. This must include reference to maintaining accuracy, validity and reliability.

It is easy to come to work every day and take for granted that our shift will run smoothly and we will have access to stock we need, food for the people in receipt of services and a full team of staff for the care required that day. This requires accurate and reliable planning. As a manager, you will be responsible for the duty rota and, according to guidelines, are required to ensure that the correct number of staff is available to look after the patients in your care for every shift. This means you need to have knowledge of the staffing resources at your disposal and the needs of the people in receipt of services on every shift. Different service areas will have different staffing needs, for example, according to the type of people in receipt of services being cared for.

Resource management

Resource management is the way in which you manage the organisation's physical, financial and human resources and you will need to do this in the most efficient way possible. These resources include stock and equipment, your budget and the staff at your disposal.

SCIE gives a definition of resource management as the practice of:

> 'balancing competing priorities for resources while still delivering good outcomes for people who use services, e.g. resourcing personal budgets and support for disabled adults and children, safeguarding services for adults and children, preventative strategies to promote well-being, and workforce costs.'

Source: www.scie.org.uk/workforce/Peoplemanagement/
staffmanagement/resourcemanage/

Forecasting

The strategic plan for the whole organisation will have forecast how the service will function in the year ahead. It will set out the budgets available and plans for how these will be spent in order for the service to be sustainable in the short term and how it will grow and develop in the long term. Devolved to your section of the service will be part of the budget and you are expected to manage that by predicting demand and supply of your own service and doing so in an accurate and valid manner. For example, you may feel, and it is likely your staff will agree, that you require many more staff to accomplish a quality service. If, however, you spend money on more staff early on in the year, by the end of the year you may have a redundancy situation because you no longer have the budget to pay them. However, if you work in a smaller organisation, such as a care or nursing home, you will have a smaller budget but will be responsible for setting a budget for all the resources in the setting.

It is important to forecast in a quantitative and qualitative manner and you may find you are referring to the forecasts on a weekly basis. Staffing will be your biggest budgetary spend so your forecast will show 'how many' and 'when' you need those staff as well as what the desired personal qualities and role-related qualifications are to fulfil those needs.

Forecasting is an important part of resource management. It means thinking ahead to build a clear picture of what future expenses are likely to be, and how the setting might allocate the money that is available to them. For example, we may look at equipment to see what needs to be replaced or repaired or staffing needs and would budget accordingly. Human resources forecasting involves looking at the staff that we need in the coming years and months based upon growth of the organisation or changes to roles within the team.

Accuracy

Forecasting must be done in an accurate manner and this requires a critical analysis of the needs of the organisation. This can be done by looking at how the setting met targets in the previous year and what plans there are for the future. Typically, we may assume that the future is going to be like the past and simply plan according to last year's data. But this would not produce an accurate result. If, for example, your service is changing or growing in some way then you may need to accurately plan for more staff, more equipment and more financial support to meet this need. Your forecast will be based upon last year's budget, with adjustments due to inflation and costs to cover new services. If the service is to remain the same, you will still need to forecast for inflation.

Validity and reliability

The data you collect to forecast your future resource needs must be valid, which means it must be based upon data that is correct and reliable. Reliability simply means that it is precise and sound. For example, a reliable forecast is one that takes into account expenditure from the last year, cash flow for the next year, and an accurate analysis of the staff needed to ensure a quality service is delivered. This is just one example. Forecasting does involve some subjective judgement because we are looking at uncertainty in the future. We cannot know for certain what might happen, so our prediction may fall short of the actual outcome. This might be because the demand for our service changes, inflation may rise more than we had anticipated, meaning cutbacks are inevitable, and there may also be changes in legislation which impact upon how our service is to be run. All these are factors that can result in different outcomes to the ones that had been planned.

Evidence opportunity

1.3 Importance of accurate forecasting

Provide a written account critically analysing the role of forecasting in resource management in your setting. You must refer to maintaining accuracy, validity and reliability.

You might also like to use your own strategic/service plan and analyse how you undertook the role of forecasting in resource management. Ensure that you make reference to how you maintained the following:

- **Accuracy**: How accurate are you likely to be with your planning? For example, will there be major changes to your service or is it remaining the same?
- **Validity**: What sort of data are you going to use and do you consider it valid?
- **Reliability**: How reliable was your planning last year?

AC 1.4 Value of using assets and resources outside traditional services and in the community

Here, you will be required to evaluate the use of alternative resources and assets. This could include volunteers and voluntary services, alternative non-traditional therapies, community and educational resources.

Partnership working

The idea of partnership working developed as a result of acknowledging that it was impossible for one healthcare provider to provide all care for a service user. To that end, there are valuable resources that can be accessed in the community via voluntary groups, alternative therapies and education and in other parts of the service area.

Working in this way is now integral to the way local authorities have developed community strategies, with a huge number of people all delivering services at different areas and locations. Joint working with other health professionals is paramount if the service user is to receive the best service.

The Five Year Forward Plan you looked at in the AC1.1 Research it has moved this agenda on with the development of the Building Health Partnerships programme, which is intended to support **Sustainability and Transformation Partnerships (STPs)** to engage more effectively with other providers and people necessary to meet their plan objectives.

KEY TERM

Sustainability and Transformation Partnerships (STPs) are drawn up by senior people in the local health and care system to develop proposals that improve health and care.

Working with other organisations

You may already be working with other agencies within the wider multidisciplinary team such as advocacy agencies or other healthcare teams. An advantage of working closely with other organisations is that they may be able to offer advice on specific issues. They may also have access to equipment which your service does not have and could share this resource with you. A disadvantage of purely relying on other organisations is that some may be affected by lack of funding, which may make it difficult for the sector to fund their work.

In developing links with other services we can improve the experience and outcomes of people who use services as we can then access other resources in terms of staff expertise, advice and even shared physical resources. It might also be possible to access technological services that your own service may lack. For example, shared equipment such as computer software or training may be available to you.

Volunteers and voluntary services, alternative non-traditional therapies

Voluntary and other non-traditional or alternative therapy services and organisations make a great contribution to the health service and as such are part of the resources you may call upon to enrich your own service. Such services may be able to deliver preventative services that reduce the visits people make to the GP or the A&E department. For example, day care centres and lunch groups may help isolated individuals to meet up with others on a daily basis. Your care setting may also receive volunteers and other services that enhance the wellbeing of your service users, but alternatively it could be that your setting provides a day care service for others in the community. New initiatives of care homes working closely with their local primary schools encourage a reciprocal arrangement for service users and young people to enjoy the benefits of each other's company.

The Department of Health launched the Voluntary Sector Strategic Partner Programme in April 2009 to improve communication between the department and voluntary health and social care organisations. It enabled voluntary sector organisations to work in equal partnership with the Department of Health, NHS and social care for the benefit of the sector and has improved health and wellbeing outcomes.

Community and educational resources

Other agencies within the wider multidisciplinary team include social groups, community exercise or walking groups, befriending services, and counselling, advocacy agencies or other healthcare teams and these may all be available to help your own service. These partnerships need to be part of resource planning and forecasting decisions. For example, if the service you work with is under threat of closure, you need to make plans for the deficit this will create in the service you offer.

The use of these services may well enrich the quality of your own service, but you need to justify their use and inclusion in your care offer. As the manager you must, therefore, evaluate their effectiveness in supplying value for money and provide evidence of what they offer to your service users. An analysis of the strengths and limitations of the service they offer will provide valid and reliable evidence to include in your resource planning.

Evidence opportunity

1.4 Value of using assets and resources outside traditional services

Write a piece evaluating the use of alternative resources and assets. This could include, for example:

- volunteers and voluntary services
- alternative non-traditional therapies
- community and educational resources.

You could think about what voluntary, alternative non-traditional therapies, community and educational resources services your service links or partners with and evaluate how these are useful to your service users. Consider the strengths and the weaknesses of the alternative resources and assets and make arguments for and against their use.

AC 1.5 The role technology plays as a resource in service delivery and service management

Here, you will be required to evaluate the use of different technologies within your service provision, including your use of digital technology and use by people in receipt of services, team members and other stakeholders.

The role technology plays as a resource in service delivery and service management

In 2015, the DoH published a paper, 'Using technology to improve delivery of health and care services', which commented on how integrated data and technology are beginning to improve the delivery of health and care services.

For people in receipt of services this has meant that nearly 6.5 million patients are now booking online appointments for their GPs and can order repeat prescriptions online (DoH, 2015c). Additionally, a move to enable people to access their own GP records online saw 3 million patients registering for online access. There has also been the development of healthcare apps such as 'NHS Smokefree' and 'One You, Drink Less', as well as exercise apps such as 'Couch to 5K'. The NHS website also offers healthcare programmes for weight loss, plus advice on coping with stress and other health concerns. Also, other digital technologies are enabling people to take control of their health and wellbeing.

Research it

1.5 NHS digital offers

For more information, go to: www.gov.uk/government/speeches/using-technology-to-improve-delivery-of-health-and-care-services

Also look at: www.nhs.uk/oneyou/apps/ and explore other digital offers and apps that are available online, as well as those offered by the NHS.

Write down what you find out. Also think about how you can ensure that you keep up to date with the latest digital developments and offers, and how this can help you in your role as manager.

Use of digital technology in the setting, use by team members, those who use services, and stakeholders, and your use

For care professionals such as yourself, team members and your stakeholders, the use of technology has started to improve the quality of the service we can offer. Technology is increasing the efficiency of the way in which we do things. For example, we are now able to access online up-to-date lifesaving information wherever a patient is, which means you and your team members are able to link into algorithms for care such as resuscitation and sepsis guidelines, thus reducing the waiting time for life-saving care if you are required and trained to do so as part of your role. You can also access the British National Formulary (BNF) online and software such as Medusa, which gives information about medication – again, if this is part of your role as an adult care worker.

As a manager, however, you will need to ensure that your staff are aware of the ways in which digital technologies can be used to work efficiently, and how these resources can be used for professional development. There may be training that you can discuss with them and arrange. They will also need to be aware of the dangers around using technology in the workplace, such as security of systems and files that are stored digitally, and so they will need to be aware of how they can ensure information remains secure. As a manager, you will also need to ensure that you have robust systems in place to project the setting's systems and data that is stored electronically. This might mean ensuring your computer systems are firewall protected, that passwords are used and that information is backed up externally or, for example, online in the 'cloud'. Protecting individuals in your setting when it comes to technology will also be one of your responsibilities. You will need to ensure, as a manager in an adult care setting, that information about the dangers of being online is readily available, and that your staff are trained in and have an understanding of this, so they are able to confidently advise those they provide care for. This might mean being aware of issues such as cyber-bullying, online data protection, online fraud and identity theft, as well as safety issues around meeting or befriending people online.

Technology is having a huge impact upon the way services are now delivered in healthcare and in the management of services. Software is available to help us to conduct staff reviews and appraisals, for example, in a more efficient manner and we can order most things online and receive them by next-day delivery. Information can be shared immediately, reducing the time for treatment to be delivered. For example, patient notes can now be emailed using encrypted software systems to speed up access to treatment.

We now see the use of mobile phones, computers, social media, electronic health and patient records, an NHS-wide network of evidence-based health and healthcare information, as well as access to telemedicine and telecare. These systems are available for our personal use and also for our service users. It enables us to communicate with team members and stakeholders from any location. Our work can still be conducted when we are commuting with the use of laptops and hands-free phones in our cars.

The advantages of this are clear. It is quicker, paperless and we can respond to consumer healthcare needs more efficiently. The disadvantages surface when the technology fails to work or breaches arise in the system, which puts confidential patient data at risk of being lost or shared.

Technology certainly has a part to play in developing our social care services. There are many online training courses, which you can access to help you learn about staying safe online. You may even run a training course about this for your staff, or offer guidance through leaflets and posters on notice boards.

Also at your disposal is the NHS Spine (developed by the Health and Social Care Information Centre), which allows information to be shared securely through national services such as the Electronic Prescription Service, Summary Care Record and the e-Referral Service. It also enables healthcare professionals to share child protection information and allows easier access to demographic data.

AC 1.6 Sustainability in terms of resource management in adult care

Here, you will be required to analyse the use of sustainable resources within adult services, with particular reference to own service provision.

You will be familiar with the term sustainability as this is a much-used term in healthcare. But what exactly does it mean?

SCIE has worked with the NHS Sustainable Development Unit (SDU) to promote sustainable healthcare development across social care. It describes sustainable healthcare as a system:

> *'achieved by delivering high quality care and improved public health without exhausting natural resources or causing severe ecological damage.'*

Source: SDU, 2014

Sustainability is about making savings where possible and reducing waste.

However, with the ever-changing demands upon the health care system and social care, such as increasing population numbers and the needs of an ageing population, the delivery of a sustainable health and social care or adult care service is a challenge.

The 'Fit for the Future' 2009 report, which was commissioned by the SDU, is an important one for healthcare in the UK as it looks at scenarios for the healthcare system in England in 2030. It is aimed at helping healthcare organisations understand and prepare for their role in the future and to help create a 'low-carbon' and more efficient NHS to provide the best possible quality of healthcare (SDU, 2009). It identifies climate change as the biggest global health threat of the 21st century and recognises that for the healthcare systems to survive and meet the demands for care in the future, key steps must be taken which ensure that preventative care and helping people take more responsibility for their own health are top agenda items. For social care, an immediate threat is the increasing demand from an ageing population and, together with cuts to local authority funding places, this puts a lot of pressure on adult social care services. Subsequently, with shortfalls in social care places, people are forced to access the NHS.

The SDU gives a definition of sustainable health and care:

> *'A sustainable health and care system works within the available environmental and social resources protecting and improving health now and for future generations. This means working to reduce carbon emissions, minimising waste and pollution, making the best use of scarce resources, building resilience to a changing climate and nurturing community strengths and assets.'*
>
> **Source:** SDU, 2014

In 2016, the SDU published the *Sustainable Development Management Plan (SDMP) Guidance for Health and Social Care Organisations*, which guides organisations in the production of their own SDMP.

You may find it useful to look at the *Sustainable Development Management Plan (SDMP) Guidance for Health and Social Care Organisations* (January 2017) document. You can search for it on the SDU website: www.sduhealth.org.uk

For example, one trust in London reduced electricity consumption by installing software that automatically shut down computers that were not being used and made savings of £100,000 per year. Although this may not be such an issue in your own setting, reducing electricity can be as simple as turning off lights and computers when not in use and asking staff to be mindful of waste. You might also consider where the food you serve comes from and could reduce your carbon footprint by buying locally, thereby sustaining the local economy at the same time.

In adult care, for example, the Local Government Association (LGA) undertook research to transform the health and care system to one that was personalised, responsive and value for money for service users and carers. Working with partner organisations, the research that was developed identified our understanding of what a more sustainable system might look like in the future (LGA, 2016).

AC 1.7 Processes for acquiring resources

Here, you will be required to evaluate the processes for acquiring adequate resources, to include stock, stock management and auditing, storage of invoices.

Acquiring stock

You will have a system in place for how you order and acquire stock and, as the manager, you are responsible for checking the process and ensuring it is fit for purpose.

You should monitor where the stock comes from and also check that it compares favourably to other services on offer. For example, you may have a contract with a local stationery firm but may find that their service is slow, meaning you have to wait for stock. You could either talk to them about improving this side of their service or find another firm that can deliver more quickly. This example may also apply to other areas of stock acquisition/management in your setting.

Stock management

Once stock arrives there must be a system to manage it and ensure that it is not wasted. A large stock of food, for example, which can potentially go out of date quickly must be monitored carefully. This is the same with medication and you need to ensure that staff are making checks on expiry dates regularly and also detailing low supplies of essential resources.

Auditing

An audit of stock is a systematic examination of any records and documents you have to ensure that the stock system is maintained as required by law. For example, you are required as a manager to have in place checks on equipment to show that it is in good condition.

Storage of invoices

The invoices provide a trail of evidence of purchases and as such need to be stored safely and securely. Again, you will need to establish that there are systems in place to ensure that these are handled, maintained, processed and stored consistently and that staff are aware of the process and follow it.

As with all processes, you will need to determine the strengths and the weaknesses of how you currently acquire, manage and store the stock. By checking the systems you have in place, you can determine whether they are useful or require developing. For example, good record systems provide evidence of processes and can help you to make decisions in the future. If something is working well you can continue the practice, and faulty systems can be improved and changed.

Evidence opportunity

1.7 **Processes for acquiring resources**

Provide a written account evaluating the processes for acquiring adequate resources to include stock, stock management, auditing and storage of invoices. You will also be required to analyse the factors that can impact on recruitment and retention and how to overcome potential challenges.

You might like to provide evidence of how you order, manage and audit the stock in your own service. What is the invoice storage system you use? What are the processes that work well and not so well? How would you improve them?

LO2 Understand principles of human resource management

AC 2.1 Factors and approaches known to improve recruitment and retention of adult care staff

Here, you will be required to explain a range of approaches for retention and recruitment of staff. This includes formal training routes, local recruitment drives and social media.

Staff are the biggest resource in an organisation and a large percentage of your budget will go towards paying their salaries. It is crucial that you develop your workforce to ensure that you attract the right staff and, more importantly, retain them. The recruitment process can be costly so if you find that there is a high staff turnover in your setting, in other words more and more people are leaving their jobs and you need to hire new people to replace them more frequently, then this is something that you will need to look at so that you can find out why staff are not staying in your setting. One of the ways in which you might recruit staff is to offer the opportunity to access some of the things we discuss below. These are just examples.

Formal training routes

These can include a promise to train staff by offering to fund courses such as the Care Certificate, Level 2, 3, 4 and 5 Diploma qualifications, or, for more qualified staff, foundation degrees or management training. Training allows staff to enhance and develop their skill set by gaining new skills, offering them opportunities to grow in their role, as well as to develop their career. As a manager, you will need to ensure that there are such opportunities for your staff, so that they remain motivated and driven in their roles, and also to meet legal requirements.

Local recruitment drives

In advertising for staff, a useful method is through a recruitment drive where people are invited to open days. Using local newspapers and social media such as Facebook, Twitter and emails, such events and vacancies can be quickly advertised to a great number of potential recruits.

Some organisations advertise one-day events with a promise of a potential job at the end of that day. This works when there are many posts on offer and can be a most useful way of getting staff into the organisation. During the day, the applicants are interviewed and given an initial induction to the organisation which outlines its values and attitudes and what it is looking for in staff members. Applicants can undertake any tests that may need to be completed, have paperwork and certificates checked and are then given a conditional offer of a role at the end of the day. For the candidates, such a day will highlight to them very quickly whether they would feel comfortable working in the organisation and they can then decide for themselves whether to accept the role.

Social media

Social media such as Twitter or Facebook can be a most efficient way to advertise for staff due to its accessibility by thousands of people. By advertising for staff and asking people to share the advert, you can contact thousands of potential candidates. Social media is also a good way to engage employees and make them feel that they are part of a team, as you are able to share news that they may not always be aware of. Some teams set up closed Facebook groups where messages and posts can only be seen by the team. In that way, social events and requests for information or just news can be shared. Email is another way to reach many potential candidates quickly.

Job advertisements, recruitment agencies and job centres

These are also useful for recruiting staff. Local job centres serve the local community and recruitment agencies may be able to widen your search for staff outside the local area.

Analysing the factors that can impact on recruitment and retention and how to overcome potential challenges

A number of factors impact recruitment. Recent health planning has revealed a shortage of GPs in rural areas. Here there are fewer doctors and this has impacted the services that are offered in these areas. As a means of improving this, the government offered a 'golden handshake' to encourage more GPs to apply. You may even live in an urban area but find that there are also fewer GPs or waiting times for appointments are longer at your surgery.

In an adult care setting, a recent survey showed a shortfall of social care workers, with seven in ten people commenting that a care career is undervalued by society and more than two in ten believing that care work is not valued by the government (Anchor, 2018). According to the sector skills agency, Skills for Care England's adult social care sector has 90,000 vacancies on any one day and an average turnover rate of 28%.

Suggestions for recruiting and retaining staff include a public awareness campaign to raise the profile of social care work and a call for the government to demonstrate how it values social care work.

Research it

2.1

Go to: www.skillsforcare.org.uk/NMDS-SC-intelligence/Workforce-intelligence/publications/The-state-of-the-adult-social-care-sector-and-workforce-in-England.aspx

Read the report by Skills for Care (2018) on the state of the adult social care sector and workforce in England.

Both internal factors – such as budget, size of organisation, whether it plans to expand and grow and the recruitment policy – and external factors affect recruitment, although external factors, which we discuss below, are more difficult to control. However, as mentioned in the example of the 'golden handshake', external factors can have positive outcomes.

Location may be an issue, requiring people to travel a greater distance to get to work. There may also be fewer people in the area to choose from or perhaps your organisation has a poor reputation in the area (deserved or not), which will put people off applying. You may also be in an area where there are a number of competitors who are also recruiting from perhaps a diminished workforce in the area. Overcoming such factors can be difficult.

As a manager, you face a number of challenges in recruitment and the external factors affecting your service need to be addressed. For example, if your recruitment

package offered the opportunity for further training, then you need to deliver on this and budgetary demands sometimes make this a challenge. You must be clear on your offer to potential staff and a compromise may be offered. For example, training courses will be available but substantial courses are offered on the proviso that staff stay for two years following the course or pay the cost in full. You could also offer to pay for half of the course fees.

Reflect on it

2.1 Your own role

What was it that attracted you to your current job role and why have you stayed?

Make a list of some of the reasons that made you apply to this particular organisation.

AC 2.2 Importance of recruitment, selection and induction processes in the organisation and learners' role in this process

Here, you will be required to evaluate the recruitment, selection and induction processes within your own service provision.

Recruiting and retaining staff

While an increase in salary may be a factor in applying for a role, that might not be the only reason people apply for the roles and jobs that they do. Perhaps it is the reputation of the company for its fair dealings with people or the fact that it also offers **CPD** opportunities (opportunities to develop) or a career progression route. When you applied for your own role, for example, you might have been impressed with the way in which the setting delivered the care to service users or maybe it was the atmosphere of the place or the values and ethos declared in the mission statement.

KEY TERM

Continuing professional development (CPD) is the planned process of improving and increasing capabilities of staff and is an ongoing process. It includes training and education activity to ensure staff remain fit to practise.

The staff you wish to recruit will also have a number of reasons for applying for a new role. The recruitment and selection process, therefore, must be one that attracts candidates with the appropriate skills, values and attitudes for the role you wish them to do. They need to be able to fit well into the team and the team culture and to deliver the sort of care that gives the best quality to those who use the service.

At the same time, you need to think about how you will retain the staff once they are recruited. An unhappy person will leave the job very quickly or be demotivated and so unlikely to perform to the best of their ability, so you need to ensure that you have in place a retention strategy. Methods of keeping staff happy could include the following:

- Formal training routes and career development.
- Terms and conditions may be offered so that potential new staff are likely to want to work for you.
- Benefits such as family-friendly hours or maybe crèche facilities for staff with children.
- A benefits scheme may make your organisation a more attractive place to work.

The selection process

When you have a post to fill, the outcome you want is to find the right person for the job. That person must not only have the skill to do the job but must be committed to the team and the organisation and share the same values and attitudes.

The selection process is your opportunity to collect evidence about the candidate and to identify their strengths and weaknesses. This process is helped by having documents in place such as a job description, which shows the key tasks and responsibilities of the job, and a person specification, which sets out the characteristics needed for the role and is clearly described in terms of competencies that can be measured. You might consider using the National Occupational Standards in drawing up the documents to develop a core competency framework.

At the point of interview, it is most important that all candidates are offered the same opportunities to present themselves. A consistent approach to interview must be followed, with pre-determined questions, which clearly enable candidates to give information about themselves. This will enable the interview panel to assess their strengths and potential weaknesses.

Skills for Care documents and guidance

You will find it useful to refer to the Skills for Care 'Values-based recruitment' and 'Finding and keeping workers' documents. The 'Values-based recruitment' document mentions recruiting people for their values and behaviours to ensure that the right people are attracted to a setting. People who are committed to high-quality care and who have strong values are more likely to be retained in the workplace. Skills for Care provide a values-based recruitment and retention toolkit, which has practical tools and templates to help support managers in their values-based recruitment. It also offers free workshops.

The 'Finding and keeping workers' document supports social care providers with recruitment and retention problems, and the site supplies videos, case studies and a resources library to help you deal with some of the most common issues.

Research it

2.2

Go to the Skills for Care website and access the above documents. Consider how you might be able to use the suggestions for enhancing your current recruitment strategies.

Induction

Induction is the opportunity for new staff to become familiar with their new role and working environment. Every organisation should invest in a well-considered induction programme, which should not be just a tick box exercise of reading policies and signing to say they have done so. It should provide information that new staff need and should be conducted in a way that does not overwhelm them.

Each care worker starting in a new role should also be enrolled upon the Care Certificate, which an employer must provide to meet the essential standards set out by the Care Quality Commission. Alongside your own induction programme, this certificate provides training that focuses on the specific skills and knowledge needed for care work.

The whole induction process can involve orientation to the site on which they are to work, introductions to the team and maybe external partners, and receiving information about the relevant policies. This might be covered in a day or over a length of time and the member of staff may be required to complete paperwork that specifies what they have learned, and this provides you as their manager with an audit trail.

As the manager in a small organisation, you might be responsible for setting up the recruitment process from start to finish and might, therefore, wish to delegate some tasks to team members. In a larger organisation, you may well work alongside the HR team.

Evidence opportunity

2.2 Recruitment, selection and induction processes

Provide a written account evaluating the recruitment, selection and induction processes within your own service provision.

You might like to:

- explain the approaches for retention and recruitment of staff in your organisation and identify areas that might present a challenge to the process. What are the strengths and weaknesses of this particular approach?
- think about the areas that we have discussed in this section
- evaluate the recruitment, selection and induction processes within your own service provision and determine a case for change. Highlight the effective or positive parts of the process and the parts you believe require change and why.

AC 2.3 Importance of ensuring employment practices are free from discrimination and harassment

Here, you will be required to explain the importance of ensuring all employment practices are free from discrimination and harassment in line with current legislation, including the Equality Act, the Care Act, the Employment Rights Act, and own policies and procedures.

KEY TERMS

Discrimination occurs when you treat people differently from others. It can be unlawful and refers to the unfair treatment of a person usually based on their race, age, sex or disability.

Harassment is unwanted behaviour towards another person that is designed to intimidate or degrade.

The recruitment and selection process must be a fair one and you are legally responsible for ensuring that no unlawful **discrimination** on the grounds of sex, age, race, disability, sexual orientation, and religion or belief occurs. We must also be careful not to use any comments or language that might offend or humiliate somebody as this might be construed as **harassment**. This also applies to employment practices more generally, as staff must be allowed to perform their roles without fear of discrimination and harassment and be offered equal opportunities and be judged based on their performance and not on characteristics such as race and religion.

Equality of opportunity is a major part of the recruitment and selection process, and it is, therefore, acceptable for you to advertise for applications from those groups that are under-represented in the organisation as well as those that are not. For example, your workforce may be under-represented in people with protected characteristics (such as those of a different race or religion) and if you are trying to address this you may choose a candidate who has a protected characteristic over one who does not.

The laws that apply to recruitment and selection are as follows.

The Equality Act 2010

The Equality Act became law in 2010. This act outlines what is needed to make the workplace a fair environment. It offers protection to individuals regardless of age, disability, gender, gender reassignment, race, religion or belief, sexual orientation, marriage and civil partnership and pregnancy and maternity. The Equality and Human Rights Commission (EHRC) offers guidance for employers regarding changes to recruitment, in particular in relation to questions about health and disability, and you might wish to look at these to remind yourself of this.

The Equality Act 2010 calls for people to be treated with dignity, which cannot happen if we are harassing and discriminating.

The Employment Rights Act 1996

The Employment Rights Act (ERA) 1996 updated the Contracts of Employment Act 1963, the Redundancy Payments Act 1965, the Employment Protection Act 1975 and the Wages Act 1986.

Within this act dismissal, unfair dismissal, parental leave, and redundancy and the rights of employees are addressed. In 1997, an amendment to the act introduced the right to request flexible working time. Additionally, the act deals with employees' rights to contracts, suspension, dismissal and the notice that needs to be given, unfair dismissal, redundancy and employer insolvency issues.

Own policies and procedures

You will of course have your own policies and procedures for dealing with fairness in your recruitment and selection process. As the manager in the setting you are duty bound to ensure that all employment practices are free from discrimination and harassment.

Your policies may include: Recruitment and Selection; Bullying and Harassment; Anti-discrimination; Equality; Code of Conduct; Dignity and Respect; Disclosure and Barring Service (DBS); whistle blowing and others, all of which cover the need for staff to be clear about how they should work in an anti-discriminatory manner.

Staff need to be aware of how they should conduct themselves in the workplace and how they should report any infringements with respect to harassment or discrimination. Treating people with dignity and respect should be a major part of your team values.

Below is a list of other acts that may have been covered in your own documentation.

- Rehabilitation of Offenders Act 1974
- Sex Discrimination Act 1975 (now see Equality Act 2010)
- Race Relations Act 1976 (now see Equality Act 2010)
- Disability Discrimination Act 1995 and Regulations 2005 (now see Equality Act 2010)
- General Data Protection Regulation 2018 and previously Data Protection Act 1998
- Part-Time Workers (Prevention of Less Favourable Treatment) Regulations 2000
- Flexible Working Regulations 2002–2006
- Employment Equality (Sexual Orientation) Regulations 2003
- Employment Equality (Religion or Belief) Regulations 2003
- Employment Equality (Age) Regulations 2006
- Health and Social Care Act 2008
- Protection of Children Act 1999

More recently

The issue of discrimination and harassment is a topic that has been highlighted more in the media in recent years. Gender discrimination and harassment have been highlighted as major issues in the film industry, for example, with equal pay also being discussed more and more. Discrimination on the basis of race and religion has also been a prominent issue. As a manager, you will need to ensure that your setting provides an environment that promotes inclusion and diversity and is one where discrimination and harassment are not an issue; that everyone understands the importance of respecting each other and their differences; that policies and procedures are in place to ensure they do so; and such issues are confronted and tackled if instances of discrimination and harassment do appear in your workplace.

Research it

2.3 Discrimination in the workplace

Conduct some research online around discrimination in the workplace. You might like to read the following news stories:

www.bbc.co.uk/news/uk-england-london-38751307

www.bbc.co.uk/news/uk-northern-ireland-41741178

How can you make sure that such discrimination is not an issue in your workplace? Discuss this with a colleague and provide a written account of your discussion.

Evidence opportunity

2.3 Employment practices that are free from discrimination and harassment

Provide a written account explaining the importance of ensuring all employment practices are free from discrimination and harassment in line with current legislation, including the legislation we have covered above.

You might like to think about the process of recruitment and selection in your workplace. How do you ensure that the employment practices are free from discrimination and harassment in line with current legislation? Think about the legislation we have discussed in this section. How do you ensure this through your setting's policies and procedures?

You might show copies of your policies here.

AC 2.4 Processes to identify the numbers and patterns of staffing required to provide a person-centred, outcomes-based service

Here, you will be required to evaluate processes that are used in your own setting to ensure effective staffing numbers and patterns and how these ensure the services are providing person-centred, outcomes-focused care; this includes continuity of care and support, importance of flexibility, varying skills sets, identification of and adaptation to changes, use and management of agency workers.

Impacts of funding

The media constantly remind us about how funding deficits have affected the social care system over the last ten years. The National Audit Office reported a £461 million net deficit by NHS trusts and NHS foundation trusts in the first three months of 2016–17. Additionally, NHS trusts, NHS foundation trusts and clinical commissioners need to make £14.9 billion in savings by 2020–21 to help close the estimated £22 billion gap between patients' needs and resources (National Audit Office, 2016).

In social care, a similar funding crisis persists. From 2009–10 to 2014–15, the total spending for adults' services fell by 8 per cent despite a rise in the number of people with care and support needs.

In managing these deficits in funding, local authorities reduce spending by targeting staffing costs, reducing services, cutting back on environmental and regulatory services such as waste disposal, and introducing efficiency measures.

Decisions about which services and treatments will be provided (known as 'rationing') are largely made by the CCGs in local authorities but may also be made at a national level, by local commissioners and providers, and by individual clinicians. Some decisions are made as a result of law or policy, but others may be based on individual judgements and a range of factors are evident including national policy initiatives, clinical guidelines, local priorities and needs and what has been provided in the past, individual clinical judgements and conversations with patients (The King's Fund, 2016).

Additionally, by targeting inefficient treatments, savings can be made. The King's Fund report states that by reducing overused and ineffective treatments there are benefits to patients and money can be saved. For example, in 2017 NHS England set out a draft consultation for CCGs to reduce ineffective and over-priced drug prescriptions. The document stated that 'patients are often prescribed drugs proven to be ineffective or in some cases dangerous', and highlighted 18, including homeopathy and herbal treatments, which should no longer be prescribed in primary practice. Prescriptions for these treatments cost the taxpayer £141 million each year (Univadis.co.uk).

Productivity can be improved by implementing new ways of working and new service models.

Consequently, there is a range of ways that social care can respond to financial pressures, some of which can have a positive impact on the care of patients and service care users.

The impact of budget reduction is narrowed down to four options:

1 To go into deficit (which is not sustainable), in other words constantly work with an overdraft, which can only get worse year on year.
2 To improve productivity (which has helped the NHS meet its efficiency targets).
3 To restrict access to services.
4 To dilute the quality of services (The King's Fund, 2016).

Your role as a manager is to effectively manage the impacts that funding can have, and maintain an effective workforce with a variety of skills to ensure that the services being provided are person-centred and outcome-focused. Staff need to be clear about the importance of continuity of care and support.

Research it

2.4 The King's Fund

Go to www.kingsfund.org.uk/publications/six-ways and read the report that details the NHS finances and shows how funding growth has slowed down with the rising demand, making it difficult for the health service to live within its means. With this in mind, write a report to show how budget cuts and deficits have affected your ability as a manager to sustain the numbers and patterns of staffing required to provide a person-centred, outcome-based service in your setting.

Continuity of care and support

You will need to use the budget available to ensure that person-centred and outcomes-focused care is not disrupted. This can be managed by looking at the staff you need, the staff you have, and how flexible you are in delivering the current services you have.

Varying skill sets and importance of flexibility

A skill set is a particular group of skills or abilities to perform the role. A qualified nurse in your employment will offer different skills to the health care assistant and the administration staff will also have a different set of skills to perform their tasks.

In AC 2.2, we discussed the recruitment process and the need to have person specifications in place to show the skills required for a role. For example, if a position requires somebody with excellent computer or communication skills, then your person specification needs to highlight these as part of the required skill set. Of course, the person who can be flexible and shows willingness to develop the skills beyond those required in their role will improve their chance of employment.

Identification of and adaptation to changes

As job roles evolve we need to adapt to the changes that become evident. New treatments emerge all the time and we might be required to undertake procedures we are unfamiliar with (as long as we have had the training). A service user may come into our care with complex needs, which require a different approach. Staff training, therefore, becomes important and there may be funding issues around this. As the manager, you must identify the changes that are needed to sustain the service and determine the means to adapt to the change.

Use and management of agency workers

The use of agency staff is a huge expense but a necessary one. In controlling your budget and to ensure that the skill mix is sufficient on each shift you may have to access agency workers. It is useful to develop a good relationship with the agency staff who fit the team profile well and who are valued by other staff in the team. For example, you may require nursing staff and have to contact agencies to fill the shortfall in your team on a temporary basis. As such, they will still require management and you need to be very clear about what they can and cannot do in the workplace. An agency will supply you with a clear idea about the roles the staff can undertake and the competency level of each. You will have to manage a short induction to the area to orientate the member of staff to the work setting.

Evidence opportunity

2.4 Processes to identify the numbers and patterns of staffing required

Provide a written account evaluating the processes you use in your setting, or that are used in your setting to ensure effective staffing numbers and patterns and how these ensure the services provide a person-centred, outcomes-focused care. You could, for example, consider:

- impacts of funding
- continuity of care and support
- importance of flexibility
- varying skill sets
- identification of and adaptation to changes
- use and management of agency workers.

AC 2.5 Manage and adjust staffing levels

Here, you will be required to manage staffing patterns and adjust them to meeting changing circumstances.

The range of circumstances where staffing patterns will need to be adjusted include the following.

Short-, medium- and long-term, and emergency cover

Staffing for care delivery in any setting may be subject to short-, medium- and long-term changes. In the short term, we may need to cover staff who are attending a day release course which will mean one day a week requires cover. Medium- and long-term changes may apply to covering sickness and maternity leave. These times can be planned for in advance but occasionally an emergency may occur and this might be when agency cover is the only option available. You will need to think about the following aspects.

Type and number of staff required

Your role as the manager is to ensure that the above circumstances are planned for with the correct number of staff and the correct skill set. You may have established that each shift requires a qualified nurse to oversee medications. If one of your qualified staff is to be absent for a long time, then you will need to look again at skills that staff have and numbers to determine how this might be covered.

According to the Health and Social Care Act 2008 (Regulated Activities) Regulations 2014 and the Care Standards, employers are required to provide sufficient numbers of suitably qualified, competent, skilled and experienced staff to meet the needs of the people using the service at all times (cqc.org.uk). Your staff must be supported, and be provided with training, professional development and supervision.

You should refer to KLOEs in Unit 501 AC 2.1.

Impact on other resources such as training and equipment

Absences for any length of time may require you to address the training and equipment budget. A budget that has not planned for contingencies such as staff absence may mean cuts to training for staff and this is short sighted. Your responsibility is to ensure that staff absence does not mean training needs are cancelled so plans must reflect this.

Managing staffing requests for changes to established working patterns

Managers who are flexible and open to different ways of working are going to get the best out of their staff. Your shifts may be eight hours in length, but some staff may be open to working 12-hour shifts in order to get more days

off. Staff with children may wish to work within school hours only. If you can accommodate such requests, you will have a workforce who not only are happier but whose motivation will improve.

Staffing levels

The Health and Social Care Act 2008 (Regulated Activities) Regulations 2014: Regulation 18 identifies the staffing levels which are required to ensure that suitably qualified, competent and experienced staff are on each shift to enable them to meet all regulatory requirements. You might find it useful to visit www.cqc.org.uk/guidance-providers/regulations-enforcement/regulation-18-staffing for more information.

The regulation states that there should be 'sufficient numbers of suitably qualified, competent, skilled and experienced staff to meet the needs of the people using the service at all times' and that staff receive 'support, training, professional development, supervision and appraisals so that they can carry out their role and responsibilities'. Additionally, staff must be able to access any other qualifications to help them to meet the professional standards they need to continue to practise (Health and Social Care Act 2008 (Regulated Activities) Regulations 2014: Regulation 18).

In the UK, nurse staffing levels are locally set and there is currently compulsion for providers to follow recommended staffing levels set by the Department of Health and professional organisations such as the RCN or NMC.

The *Guidance on Safe Nurse Staffing Levels in the UK* highlights the methods for planning or reviewing staffing level (RCN, 2010) and includes reference to care homes.

The Health and Social Care Act 2008 (Regulated Activities) Regulations 2014, Regulation 18 states that: 'Sufficient numbers of suitably qualified, competent, skilled and experienced persons must be deployed in order to meet the requirements of this Part' but does not indicate what safe staffing levels are or should be. Staffing levels need to be determined based on the needs of service users and number of beds, taking into account the nature of the premises and staff training requirements. You need also to look at the skills of the staff as well as the needs of the service users (www.ridout-law.com/so-what-are-safe-staffing-levels-in-care-homes).

Evidence opportunity

2.5 Manage and adjust staffing patterns

Demonstrate to your assessor how you manage staffing patterns and adjust them to meet changing circumstances. Remember to consider the range of circumstances where staffing patterns will need to be adjusted:

- short term
- medium term
- long term
- emergency cover

- the type of staff and number of staff required
- the impact on other resources such as training and equipment
- managing staffing requests for changes to established working patterns.

You might like to also think about and evaluate the methods you have used to overcome funding cuts, skill mix issues and supply of staff to roles by first describing what you did and then commenting upon the effects of your actions. What went well and what needs to change?

Reflective exemplar

I have just compiled my first report which shows my resource planning forecast for the coming year and details the financial, physical and human resources. Not an easy task! I understand the principles of effective resource management and managed to collect the data from last year's report which has helped me to forecast what we will need in terms of staffing and physical resources next year but the financial part is a little more tricky, particularly as my manager has informed me that my budget is not likely to exceed that which I had this year. This has concerned me greatly as I know we are in need of new furniture for the day room and if we spend on this for the patients' comfort then it is likely that we will have to make some cuts in another area. I am worried that we may have to lose a member of staff to cover this. Although I have learned a great deal in undertaking this exercise I now realise that it has opened up a whole new area of potential conflict. But it has also focused my mind on what I need to do next and that is to prepare an argument for an increase in funding to ensure that all staff are safe, that redundancies are not an option and to inform staff that we will need to make some budget cuts elsewhere. I intend to ask them to help me in deciding what is best to do.

Legislation

Act	Key points
The Equality Act 2010	The act brings together, simplifies and strengthens all the legislation related to discrimination on grounds of: • race • sex • sexual orientation (whether being lesbian, gay, bisexual or heterosexual) • disability • religion or belief • being a transsexual person and 'gender reassignment' • pregnancy and post pregnancy • being married or in a civil partnership • age.
The Care Act 2014	This replaces previous laws to provide a 'coherent' approach to adult social care. It set out new duties for local authorities and partners, and new rights for service users and carers. It aims to ensure that: • fairer care and support are given to individuals • support for physical, mental and emotional wellbeing is offered to the person needing care and their carer • prevention and delay of the need for care and support are avoided • people are in control of their care.

Suggestions for using the activities

This table summarises all the activities in the unit that are relevant to each assessment criterion.

Here, we also suggest other, different methods that you may want to use to present your knowledge and skills by using the activities.

These are just suggestions, and you should refer to the Introduction section at the start of the book, and more importantly the City & Guilds specification, and your assessor, who will be able to provide more guidance on how you can evidence your knowledge and skills. When you need to be observed during your assessment, this can be done by your assessor, or your manager can provide a witness testimony.

Assessment criteria and accompanying activities	Suggested methods to show your knowledge/skills
LO1 Understand principles of effective resource management	
1.1 Research it (page 229)	Write a short piece to show how each report has influenced your own organisation with respect to resource planning and in relation to financial, physical and human resources.
1.1 Research it (page 229)	Write notes to document your findings.
1.1 Evidence opportunity (page 230)	Provide a written account explaining the impact of different strategies and priorities on resource planning and management, including financial, physical and human resources.
1.1 Reflect on it (page 232)	Write a reflective account addressing the points in the activity.
1.2 Evidence opportunity (page 233)	Provide a written account explaining your role and responsibilities regarding resources management in your service with reference to how potential improvements are implemented.
1.3 Evidence opportunity (page 234)	Provide a written account critically analysing the role of forecasting in resource management in your setting. You must refer to maintaining accuracy, validity and reliability.
1.4 Evidence opportunity (page 236)	Write a piece evaluating the use of alternative resources and assets. This could include, for example: • volunteers and voluntary services • alternative non-traditional therapies • community and educational resources.
1.5 Research it (page 236)	Write down what you found out. You could also discuss this with a colleague and write notes to document your discussion.
1.5 Evidence opportunity (page 237)	Evaluate the use of different technologies within your own service provision, including own use, that of people in receipt of services, team members and other stakeholders. Provide a written account to evidence this.
1.6 Research it (page 238)	Make notes to document your findings.
1.6 Evidence opportunity (page 238)	Analyse the use of sustainable resources within adult care services, and in particular refer to your own. Provide a written account.
1.7 Evidence opportunity (page 239)	Provide a written account evaluating the processes for acquiring adequate resources to include stock, stock management, auditing and storage of invoices. You will also be required to analyse the factors that can impact on recruitment and retention and how to overcome potential challenges. You could discuss this with your assessor.
LO2 Understand principles of human resource management	
2.1 Research it (page 240)	Read the report and make notes.
2.1 Reflect on it (page 240)	Write a reflective account addressing the questions in the activity.
2.2 Research it (page 241)	Consider the suggestions.
2.2 Evidence opportunity (page 241)	Provide a written account evaluating the recruitment, selection and induction processes within your own service provision.
2.3 Research it (page 243)	Discuss this with a colleague and provide a written account of your discussion. You could also discuss this with your assessor.

➞

Suggestions for using the activities	
2.3 Evidence opportunity (page 243)	Provide a written account explaining the importance of ensuring all employment practices are free from discrimination and harassment in line with current legislation, including the legislation we have covered above. You could explain this to your assessor and you might show copies of your policies here.
2.4 Research it (page 244)	Read the report at www.kingsfund.org.uk/publications/six-ways and write a report as instructed in the activity. You could also discuss your findings with your assessor.
2.4 Evidence opportunity (page 244)	Provide a written account evaluating the processes you use in your setting, or that are used in your setting to ensure effective staffing numbers and patterns and how these establish services providing person-centred, outcomes-focused care.
2.5 Evidence opportunity (page 246)	Demonstrate to your assessor how you manage staffing patterns and adjust them to meet changing circumstances. Remember to consider the range of circumstances where staffing patterns will need to be adjusted, including the points in the activity.

References

Anchor (2018) Social care sector unites to warn of an impending workforce crisis and raise the perception of care. Available at: www.anchor.org.uk/media/social-care-sector-unites-warn-impending-workforce-crisis-and-raise-perception-care

Centre for Mental Health, the Mental Health Foundation, Mental Health Network, Mind, Rethink Mental Illness and the Royal College of Psychiatrists (2015) *Improving England's Mental Health: The First 100 Days.* The Mental Health Policy Group. Accessed from https://www.nhsconfed.org/-/media/Confederation/Files/public-access/MHPG-the-first-100-days-and-beyond.pdf

Department of Health (2015a) *Delivering the Forward View: NHS planning guidance 2016/17 – 2020/2.* London: The Stationery Office.

Department of Health (2015b) *Review of Operational Productivity in NHS Providers. An independent report for the Department of Health by Lord Carter of Coles.* London: The Stationery Office.

Department of Health (2015c) *Using Technology to Improve Delivery of Health and Care Services.* London: Office for Life Sciences.

House of Lords Select Committee on the Long-term sustainability of the NHS (2016) *The Long Term Sustainability of the NHS and Adult Social Care.* Accesses from https://publications.parliament.uk/pa/ld201617/ldselect/ldnhssus/151/151.pdf

Institute for Voluntary Action Research (2017) Self-care – A New Chapter for the Building Health Partnerships programme. Available at: www.ivar.org.uk/live-project/self-care-a-new-chapter-for-the-building-health-partnerships-programme/

King's Fund, The (2016) Six ways in which NHS financial pressures can affect patient care. Available at: www.kingsfund.org.uk/publications/six-ways

LGA (2016) Efficiency opportunities through health and social care integration. Delivering more sustainable health and care. London: LGA.

National Audit Office (2016) Local government report by the Comptroller and Auditor General – the impact of funding reductions on local authorities. London: National Audit Office. Available at: www.nao.org.uk/report/financial-sustainability-of-local-authorities/

NHS Digital, NHS Workforce Statistics – March 2017, Provisional statistics.

RCN (2010) *Guidance on Safe Nurse Staffing Levels in the UK.* London: RCN.

Skills for Care (2018a) The size and structure of the adult social care sector and workforce in England, 2018. London: Skills for Care. www.skillsforcare.org.uk/NMDS-SC-intelligence/Workforce-intelligence/documents/Size-of-the-adult-social-care-sector/Size-and-Structure.pdf

Skills for Care (2018b) The state of the adult social care sector and workforce report in England. London: Skills for Care. www.skillsforcare.org.uk/NMDS-SC-intelligence/Workforce-intelligence/publications/The-state-of-the-adult-social-care-sector-and-workforce-in-England.aspx

Social Care Institute for Excellence (2018) www.scie.org.uk/workforce/Peoplemanagement/staffmanagement/resourcemanage/

So what are safe staffing levels in care homes. Available at: www.ridout-law.com/so-what-are-safe-staffing-levels-in-care-homes

Sustainable Development Unit (SDU) (2009) *Fit for the Future. Scenarios for low-carbon healthcare 2030.* London: SDU. www.sduhealth.org.uk/policy-strategy/what-is-sustainable-health.aspx

Sustainable Development Unit (SDU) (2014) *Sustainable Development Strategy for the Health and Social Care System 2014–2020* (gateway No 01011). London: SDU.

Sustainable Development Unit (SDU) (2016) *Sustainable Development Management Plan (SDMP) Guidance for Health and Social Care Organisations.* London: SDU.

Safeguarding, protection and risk

About this unit

The purpose of this unit is to enable you to engage with issues related to the protection and understanding of this area of work.

The unit will introduce you to the legal framework and the best practice with respect to handling situations where abuse may be suspected as well as systems and processes that safeguard vulnerable adults and children and young people. You'll gain a better understanding of restrictive practice and its potential impact. You'll also gain a better understanding of the role and responsibilities of adult care practitioners in ensuring the safety and wellbeing of children and young people and how to promote health and safety in the workplace.

Learning outcomes

By the end of this unit, you will:

1 Understand safeguarding legislation, local and national policies
2 Lead the effective application and review of safeguarding policies, procedures and protocols
3 Understand restrictive practice and potential impact
4 Understand the role and responsibilities of adult care practitioners in ensuring the safety and wellbeing of children and young people
5 Promote health and safety in the workplace

Getting started

Before you study the unit, think about the following:

● What do you understand by the term 'safeguarding'?
● How much do you know about wider aspects of danger, harm, abuse and/or exploitation?
● How are you supporting all work colleagues to be vigilant?
● Why is it crucial that managers in adult care services have an understanding of their responsibilities in safeguarding children and young people?

LO1 Understand safeguarding legislation, local and national policies

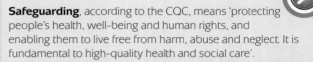

KEY TERM

Safeguarding, according to the CQC, means 'protecting people's health, well-being and human rights, and enabling them to live free from harm, abuse and neglect. It is fundamental to high-quality health and social care'.

Safeguarding and protection, while often used synonymously, are different concepts and since the introduction of the personalisation agenda perceptions have changed. The main difference between the two concepts is that 'protection' implies decisions are made by care professionals rather than allowing individuals to safeguard themselves and make choices as to the risks they take. If the service user has the capacity to make decisions about their care, then they should be enabled to safeguard themselves and to make calculated risks if they choose to do so.

A vulnerable adult is defined as an individual aged 18 or over who:

● depends on others for assistance with respect to the performance of basic functions, or
● has a severe impairment in their ability to communicate and, therefore, reduced ability to protect themselves from assault, abuse or neglect.

There is a debate about the differences in definitions that seem to surround this subject.

The Department of Health's definition of a vulnerable adult refers to a person who:

> *'may be in need of community care services by reason of mental or other disability, age or illness; and who is or may be unable to care for him or herself, or unable to protect him or herself against significant harm or exploitation.'*
>
> **Source:** DoH, 2000, pp. 8–9

This definition seems to identify groups of people such as older adults as being vulnerable and we may find this unacceptable. It is, after all, the situation in which the person finds themselves that makes them vulnerable, not the actual individual. There are many older adults who would be most upset to be termed vulnerable just by virtue of the fact that they happen to be aged over 65, for instance.

CSCI, in its 2008 document *Raising Voices: Views on safeguarding adults*, further addressed the issue, going as far as commenting that such a lack of clarity with respect to the terms used also led to confusion over the roles and responsibilities of care workers responding to concerns (McKibbin et al., 2008).

There does not seem to be a commonly accepted definition for 'safeguarding adults' and as such, your own policies need to clarify the terms for your staff in order to ensure that a shared understanding is at least possible for your workplace.

AC 1.1 Legislation relating to safeguarding adults

Here, you will provide evidence of key aspects of legislation which apply to safeguarding in adult care services in your management and leadership role.

Examples of relevant legal requirements and provisions are discussed here.

Our work in the care system is governed by the legal system and you will be familiar with the laws under which we work.

The Care Act 2014

With the passing of the Care Act 2014, adult safeguarding became an important part of public services, with the key responsibility put on local authorities in partnership with the police and the NHS. This was a major move to put adult safeguarding into a legal framework.

Under the Care Act 2014, LAs are responsible for:

- setting up local Safeguarding Adults Boards (SABs), with core membership from the local authority, the police

and the NHS Clinical Commissioning Groups and other relevant bodies

- arranging independent advocates to represent and support adults who are the subject of a safeguarding enquiry or Safeguarding Adult Review (SAR)
- following up any concerns about actual or suspected adult abuse.

The key message of the new legislation highlights six principles of safeguarding:

- **Empowerment**: The emphasis is on person-led decisions and informed consent.
- **Prevention**: Taking action before harm occurs.
- **Proportionality**: The need to risk assess and apply proportionate and least intrusive responses.
- **Protection**: Support and advocacy for those with the greatest needs.
- **Partnerships**: To seek local solutions through services working with their communities.
- **Accountability**: Accountability and transparency in delivering safeguarding.

In line with the personalisation agenda this law advocates a person-centred approach and a move away from process-led care. In addition, there is a recognition of the key role of carers in relation to safeguarding.

The whole concept of partnership working in order to achieve safety for vulnerable adults is the highlight of the act, recognising that safeguarding requires joint working with police, the NHS and other key organisations as well as awareness of the wider public. The statutory guidance also introduces Designated Adult Safeguarding Managers (DASMs) in organisations concerned with adult safeguarding.

Historically, the law provided guidance as to the rights and requirements for service provision, but there was limited mention of protection until the Care Standards Act was published in 2000, which led to the development of the National Minimum Standards. This act set out the Protection of Vulnerable Adults (POVA) scheme, which was then implemented on a phased basis from 26 July 2004.

Local SABs came about as a result of the Care Act 2014 and are in place to safeguard adults with care and support needs by ensuring that local safeguarding arrangements are in place and that the safeguarding practice offered is person-centred and outcomes-focused. They are a collaborative group comprised of various agencies led by social services.

The Safeguarding Vulnerable Groups Act (2006)

As a result of this act, changes to the reporting system by way of the Vetting and Barring Scheme ('the Scheme') were introduced. The changes followed the publication of the Bichard Inquiry (2004), which was commissioned following the well-publicised murders of Holly Wells and Jessica Chapman in 2002 and revelations that certain checks had been missed. The inquiry recommended a new scheme under which everyone working with children or vulnerable adults should be checked and registered.

It was the POVA scheme that went further to protect those in care from abuse by care providers. Central to the POVA scheme is the POVA list of care workers who have harmed vulnerable adults in their care. In appointing people to care work, it became a legal requirement from July 2004 to undertake checks through the Standard or Enhanced Disclosure application process from the Criminal Records Bureau (CRB).

Recognising the need for a single agency to vet and register individuals who want to work or volunteer with vulnerable people, the Independent Safeguarding Authority (ISA) was set up and the CRB was made responsible for managing the system and processing the applications for ISA registration. The Bichard Inquiry also led to the Safeguarding Vulnerable Groups Act 2006 and the Safeguarding Vulnerable Groups Order (Northern Ireland) 2007, which set up the scheme.

While these policies have been instrumental in ensuring that all people working with children and vulnerable adults undergo strict checks if they are to work with these groups, it has been criticised for being expensive and time consuming. It has led in some cases to potential staff in these sectors deciding not to volunteer as the checks required are too onerous and costly to undertake.

The Disclosure and Barring Service (DBS) replaced the CRB and ISA in 2012. The DBS helps employers make safer decisions regarding recruitment and prevents unsuitable people from working with vulnerable groups, including children. It acts as a central access point for criminal records checks for all those applying to work with children and young people.

The Mental Capacity Act

The main aspects of the Mental Capacity Act can be found in Unit 504, AC 2.3.

With respect to safeguarding, the Mental Capacity Act (MCA) 2005 protects and restores power to those vulnerable people over the age of 16 who lack capacity. It empowers those in health and social care to assess capacity themselves to work out the best interests of the individual concerned.

The Mental Health Act 1983 (amended 2007)

The main aspects of the Mental Health Act are covered in Unit 502 AC 1.1.

The Mental Health Act 1983 (amended 2007) gives health professionals the powers to detain, assess and treat people with mental disorders in the interests of their health and safety or for public safety and thus ensures that appropriate treatment is arranged to safeguard individuals who suffer with mental health problems.

Deprivation of Liberty Safeguards

These safeguards are explained in Unit 502 AC 1.1.

The Deprivation of Liberty Safeguards (DoLS) are an amendment to the Mental Capacity Act 2005 which allows for restraint and restrictions of adults to be used if they are in a person's best interests. The DoLS are put into place to safeguard a vulnerable person and to prevent harm coming to them if it is deemed necessary to deprive them of their liberty. To do so requires compliance with assessment and requests for authorisation from the Court of Protection. In July 2018, a Mental Capacity (Amendment) Bill was put forward by the government that, if passed in law, will reform the DoLS. It will replace them with Liberty Protection Safeguards (LPS), a key feature of which includes more guidance on the timing of deprivation of liberty. This currently stands at a maximum of one year, but under LPS, this can be renewed initially for one year, but after that for up to three years.

The new bill broadens the scope to treat people and without gaining prior authorisation to deprive them of their liberty, in a medical emergency. You should keep up to date with the changes and most recent legislation.

The Sexual Offences Act

The Sexual Offences Act 2003 revised the law of sexual offences in order to safeguard a wider range of society and to address the growing concern about child sexual abuse and to provide clarity about new forms of sexual abuse. Individuals who lack capacity may be vulnerable to sexual abuse and this act added a number of different offences, which may apply where consent was not given by them. Individuals who suffer with mental disorders are also safeguarded under this act.

The Health and Social Care Act 2012

The key points of the Health and Social Care Act are outlined in Unit 502 AC 1.1. For particular information relating to safeguarding see pages 46–47.

This introduced the role of the Care Quality Commission, set up to ensure the Essential Quality Standards were being implemented and regulated. Safeguarding and protection of individuals are specifically mentioned in these laws to address concerns about abuse. One of the intentions of this act is to safeguard people who use care services from suffering any form of abuse or improper treatment while receiving care and treatment and to meet the requirements under this act providers must demonstrate zero tolerance of abuse, unlawful discrimination and restraint.

Role of the Court of Protection

The Court of Protection is in place to ensure that decisions on financial or welfare matters for people who lack mental capacity are fair and just.

The Court is available to:

- decide whether someone has the mental capacity to make decisions for themselves
- appoint deputies to make ongoing decisions
- give people permission to make one-off decisions on behalf of someone else who lacks mental capacity
- handle emergency applications when a decision must be made on behalf of someone else
- make decisions about a lasting power of attorney or enduring power of attorney
- consider applications to make statutory wills or gifts
- make decisions about when someone can be deprived of their liberty under the Mental Capacity Act.

Source: www.gov.uk/courts-tribunals/court-of-protection

Prevent duty 2015

The Prevent duty is part of the Counter-Terrorism and Security Act 2015 and places a duty on certain bodies to exercise their functions, to have 'due regard to the need to prevent people from being drawn into terrorism'. While counter-terrorism is ultimately the responsibility of the UK government, health, education and local government are included in the authorities that also have a role to play.

The Prevent duty aims to stop people becoming terrorists or supporting terrorism.

There are three specific strategic objectives:

1 Respond to the threat and challenge of terrorism from those who promote it.

2 Prevent people from being drawn into terrorism or 'radicalised' and ensure that they are given appropriate advice and support.

3 Work with sectors and institutions where there are risks of radicalisation that we need to address.

This is to be done is through effective leadership and working in partnership with specified authorities, to establish strategies for understanding the risk of radicalisation and ensuring that staff understand the risk and build the capabilities to deal with it.

The government advises the need for organisations and schools to clarify what the Prevent duty means and to outline in detail what they can do to help safeguard children from the risk of radicalisation. Advice upon how social media is used by extremist groups is also part of safeguarding measures for schools to be aware of.

The Counter-Terrorism and Security Act 2015 places a duty on all schools and children's homes to prevent people being drawn into terrorism. Statutory guidance has been published stating that school leaders (including governors) must have robust safeguarding policies that identify children and young people at risk, intervening where appropriate, and a need to provide staff with training so they understand the 'Prevent duty'.

Modern Slavery Act 2015

This act was introduced to counter the trafficking of human beings into this country and also to ensure that people who find they are enslaved, exploited and forced to work in this country can seek help through this law. Additionally, there are cases of slavery with respect to vulnerable adults in this country who find themselves being forced to work in inhumane conditions and for little gain. Adults with additional care and support needs, as well as children, are vulnerable too, and can become victims of modern slavery. Safeguarding these people requires carers to recognise signs that might indicate a person is in need of help. For example, healthcare workers should be alert to warning signs such as adults who do not seem to have access to their legal documents such as passports and bank account details and who are withdrawn, frightened, unkempt or malnourished in appearance and have old untreated injuries. With respect to children, health and adult care workers should be alert to all of the above and additionally, changes in behaviour at school.

You can find out more at www.legislation.gov.uk/ukpga/2015/30/contents/enacted.

The Public Interest Disclosure Act 1998

This act is also known as the 'Whistle blowers Act'. The safeguarding of individuals in care has been enhanced by this act. Any care worker who is concerned about individuals in their care, who exhibit signs of neglect or abuse which they believe is ongoing at the hands of relatives or other staff members, for example, must be able to voice such concerns in a safe environment without feeling they will be victimised because of that disclosure. Additionally, concerns about other staff members who are exhibiting signs of being radicalised in any way are covered here and staff must be able to report their concerns.

KEY TERM

Disclosure is the release of information about something.

Other legislation you may be aware of and which are relevant to protection and safeguarding include:

- National Assistance Act 1948
- Theft Act 1978
- Mental Health Bill 2004
- Chronically Sick and Disabled Persons Act 1986
- Disability Discrimination Act 1995
- Public Interest Disclosure Act 1998
- NHS Community Care Act 1990
- Criminal Justice Act 2003
- Safeguarding Adults 2005 (Safeguarding Adults – A National Framework of Standards for good practice and outcomes in adult protection work)
- Fraud Act 2006
- Adult Support and Protection Act (Scotland) 2007
- Equality Act 2010
- Law Commission Review of Adult Social Care (2011), which sought to promote the wellbeing of the individual and focus on their needs rather than those of the local authority or service provider and was accepted in 2012 by government
- Statement of Government Principles on Adult Safeguarding 2011 and the introduction of the six principles of empowerment, protection, prevention, proportionality, partnership and accountability, which are now enshrined in the Care Act 2014.

As a manager of a healthcare setting you are duty bound to ensure that the setting complies with legislation, and that staff are compliant with it. It is imperative that staff are regularly updated with respect to change and are aware of and are complying with their legal duties with respect to safeguarding.

Research it

1.1 Legislation

Choose two or three of the following legislation or policy documents (both old and more recent) and find out more about them. How do these legislation and useful policy documents shape care work, or how have the older pieces of legislation shaped care work? If they continue to do so, how?

Adults

The Human Rights Act 1998

Our Health, Our Care, Our Say (2006)

Putting People First (2007)

No Secrets (2000) and In Safe Hands (2000)

Vetting and Barring Scheme/Independent Safeguarding Authority from the Safeguarding Vulnerable Groups Act (2006) and DBS

Modernising Social Services 1998

Valuing People: A new strategy for learning disability in the 21st century (2001)

Children and young people

The Children Act 1989, 2004

The Every Child Matters (ECM) initiative 2003

The Children's Plan 2007

Working Together to Safeguard Children 2010, 2015

Special Educational Needs and Disability Act 2001 (SENDA)

The Children and Families Act 2014

SEND Code of Practice 2014 (Part three of the Children and Families Act includes a new Special Educational Needs and Disabilities Code of Practice)

Evidence opportunity

1.1 Impact of policy documents and legislation

All of the above legislation and guidelines changed the way in which care was being delivered, recognising the real threat of abuse and its impact.

You will need to provide evidence of key aspects of legislation that applies to safeguarding and whistle blowing in adult care services in your management and leadership role, including the examples of relevant legal requirements and provisions such as the ones we have discussed in this section.

Reflect on it

1.1 Your setting and legislation

Think about and evaluate the impact of the legislation and policies on your work in your care setting and how it affects the standards by which you work. Provide a written account.

AC 1.2 National and local guidance and agreed ways of working

Here, you will be required to explain current national and local guidance and agreed ways of working in respect of safeguarding in adult care services.

KEY TERMS

National guidance describes a full range of provision for care settings, formal and informal settings, and provision in the public, private, voluntary and charitable sectors.

Local guidance describes the way in which national guidance translates to a local area.

Agreed ways of working are the policies and procedures in your setting. They are set by your employer. As a manager, you will need to ensure that staff are aware of the agreed ways of working in your setting and comply with these. They need to be aware that non-compliance is not an option and would be a disciplinary matter.

National guidance

Dignity in Care 2006

The Human Rights Act (HRA) 2000 had a direct impact on the way in which care is delivered in this country and in meeting the fundamental rights of individuals. Rights that relate to dignity in care include:

- the right to life
- the right not to be subjected to inhuman or degrading treatment
- the right to a family life.

These rights were first recognised by the European Court of Human Rights (ECHR) when it acknowledged that the protection of human dignity was 'inviolable' and to be protected and respected (Dupre, 2011).

The Dignity in Care campaign started in 2006 as a response to negative media reports about how people were being treated in health and social care services.

The Dignity Challenge led by the Department of Health states that high-quality care services that respect people's dignity should (among other things):

- treat each person as an individual by offering personalised services

- enable people to maintain the maximum possible level of independence, choice and control.

In practice, enabling people to have more independence is not an easy option in care but it can be achieved through simple changes to practical care. For example, we should be ensuring that people are fully involved in all decisions that affect their care. These could be personal decisions about what they want to eat, wear and what time they wish to go to bed. They might also be included in making decisions about the wider functions of the place in which they are resident. If they are in a care home, for example, they could be included in decisions about menu or activity planning or even the home décor. People need to feel that they have a purpose in life and must be able to participate as fully as they can at all levels of the service. As a manager, you will need to ensure that staff are aware of and implement person-centred care.

Adult Social Care Outcomes Framework

The Adult Social Care Outcomes Framework (ASCOF) collects data on the outcomes for adult users of local authority-funded social care and support (including carers) for each local authority area. It describes outcome measures from four domains and details the achievements within the care sector. You can access your own authority's latest data on the ASCOF website: www.gov.uk/government/uploads/system/uploads/attachment_data/file/664582/20171129_ASCOF_Handbook_of_Definitions_17-18.pdf

Such information can inform your own ways of working and local policies. For example, if your setting is not meeting a national standard you can put into place new ways of working to ensure that this is corrected. For example, Domain 1 is about 'Enhancing quality of life for people with care and support needs' and in 2016–17, it stated that 77.7 per cent of service users in England reported they have control over their daily lives. If your setting falls below this level you are able to improve this by changing the ways in which you work (NHS Digital, 2017).

Francis Report

The Francis Report (2010) highlighted the experiences of the patients at the Mid Staffordshire NHS Trust and recommendations for change were made. The report detailed how a failure to put the patient first led to poor care and in a number of cases neglect and failure to safeguard patients. It also highlighted shortcomings in the management in the setting and the training of staff. The recommendations addressed the need for a culture change within the organisation to one in which staff put the patient first and all worked towards a set of fundamental standards of care. Training of staff and high cost area supplements (HCAS) were also mentioned. It also recommended the need for openness, transparency and candour about concerns as this had been sadly lacking before, with staff feeling unable to report wrongdoing or poor care.

Care Quality Commission Fundamental Standards

The following are standards which care must never fall below. Every service user has the right to expect these standards:

- **Person-centred care**: This is the right for people to have care that is tailored to their own needs and preferences.
- **Dignity and respect**: This means that every service user in your setting has a right to expect to be treated with dignity and respect at all times, having privacy when they need it and being treated as an equal. They must also be supported to remain independent and involved in their local community.
- **Consent**: This means that before any care or treatment is given, the person or anybody acting on their behalf must give consent.
- **Safety**: Any person in your care must be cared for in a safe manner. This means that all care providers need to assess the risks to health and safety and ensure that staff are qualified, competent, and have the right skills and experience.
- **Safeguarding from abuse**: In the care setting, neglect or degrading treatment are outlawed and freedom should not be limited.
- **Food and drink**: Making sure that adequate food and drink (nutrition/hydration) are provided for service users and that any dietary requirements are met is vital.
- **Premises and equipment**: All equipment in the care setting must be clean, cared for and used properly.
- **Complaints system**: This must be in place so people are able to complain about inadequate care or service so that service can be imporved.
- **Good governance plans**: Plans that ensure that standards are met should be in place and there should be systems to check on the quality and safety of care to ensure that the service can improve and any risks may be reduced.
- **Staffing**: Staff must be suitably qualified, competent and experienced to meet these standards and should be given support, training and supervision to help them.
- **Fit and proper staff**: Recruitment procedures must be in place to enable the employment of people who can provide care and treatment appropriate to their role. Safeguarding checks must also take place at this time.
- **Duty of Candour**: The adult care provider needs to be open and transparent about all care and treatment, and

if something goes wrong you have a duty to report what has happened, provide support and apologise.

- **Display of ratings**: The CQC rating must be displayed in the setting as well as on the service's website.

CQC Regulations

The CQC has provided guidance on how providers may meet the fundamental standards within the Health and Social Care Act 2008 (Regulated Activities) Regulations 2014 and Care Quality Commission (Registration) Regulations 2009 (Part 4).

This guidance was developed in response to Section 23 of the Health and Social Care Act 2008 (HSCA 2008), which made it clear that the CQC should produce guidance to help providers to comply with the regulations made under this act.

The fundamental standards, outlined above, are similar to the idea of a national minimum standard. If an inspection finds care falling below a standard, the service will be required to take the appropriate actions to become compliant with the standards. This then requires the care setting to readdress its ways of working.

Nothing Ventured Nothing Gained

This provides guidance on best practice in assessing, managing and enabling risk for people living with dementia. It is published by the Department of Health and can be downloaded at www.gov.uk/government/uploads/system/uploads/attachment_data/file/215960/dh_121493.pdf. It presents a framework for managing the risk in a positive way by enabling and supporting people with dementia and their carers and helping settings to agree ways of working that focus upon improved outcomes for people living with dementia.

Winterbourne View: Transforming Care

This review responded to the criminal acts of staff at this care setting and called for a culture change in the way of working to enable staff to challenge poor practice and promote compassionate care. Not only were changes to the regulatory framework made making care home owners, directors and board members accountable for any abuse or neglect found to be happening, it also drew attention to wider issues in the care system, that of people with learning disabilities or autism staying too long in hospital or residential homes. As a result, councils and local authorities were tasked with finding different and new agreed ways of working with these people.

Domestic Violence and Abuse Guidance

The government definition of domestic violence and abuse describes controlling, coercive, threatening behaviour as well as physical, sexual, psychological and financial abuse and recognises that young people of 16 and 17 can be victims of domestic abuse.

The recognition in law of coercive and controlling behaviour extends previous legal powers to bring to justice individuals who inflict this sort of psychological control over others.

The Domestic Violence Disclosure Scheme gives individuals the right to ask police to check whether a new or existing partner has a violent past. Disclosure by the police can be made if the records show that there may be a risk of domestic violence from a partner.

Care workers may become aware of people who are exposed to domestic abuse and need to respond in an appropriate way, by listening and empathising with the person, validating their decision to come forward and disclose, and indicating their willingness to help. The safeguarding policy in the setting will identify how to work in such situations and informing the designated safeguarding officer should be an agreed way of working.

The Care Certificate

The Care Certificate is covered in Units 501 and 503. Standard 10 of the Care Certificate relates to the principles of safeguarding adults and describes the ways of working to safeguard adults in the setting. The Care Certificate is a response to the need for upskilling staff in care work to ensure that vulnerable people have access to qualified and skilled staff. As a manager, you need to ensure that your policies and procedures meet the Care Quality Commission's Fundamental Standards of Quality and Safety and that your care staff follow the Code of Conduct for Healthcare Support Workers and Adult Social Care Workers in England (www.skillsforhealth.org.uk/code-of-conduct).

Healthcare Professions Council – whistle-blowing guidance

The Public Interest Disclosure Act 1998 gave protection to those raising concerns by making a 'protected disclosure' against victimisation or dismissal and this has translated into practical guidance for staff about how to raise concerns. Effective whistle-blowing policies and practical guidance for staff should also be in your agreed ways of working.

Importance of partnership working; showing an awareness of aspects

Multi-agency working was summarised in the *No Secrets* (2000) and also the *Safeguarding Adults* (2005) documents and resulted in local authority planning and the development of Safeguarding Adults Boards and safeguarding procedures. The statement of government policy on Safeguarding 2011 further built on these documents and highlighted principles for care.

Local Safeguarding Adults Boards are made up of the local social services authority, the police, the NHS and all groups involved in protecting at-risk adults. In order to ensure that the public are able to have a say in decision making, the boards also include members of the local community.

The Standards outlined in the Safeguarding Adults National Framework specifically detail how the partnerships should work and be set up. The onus is on the local authority to establish a multi-agency partnership to lead 'safeguarding adults' work and to include representation from all the appropriate statutory agencies such as adult social services, housing, welfare rights/benefits, education services, legal services, primary care trusts, other NHS care trusts, the Commission for Social Care Inspection, the Health Care Commission, the Strategic Health Authority and the Department for Work and Pensions.

Boundaries are in place in care work to ensure there is clarity about what your role and responsibilities are. With clear boundaries, all members of staff in the partnership will be clear about where their roles begin and end (Figure 8.1).

- **Information sharing and recording information**: In partnership, there must be a safe way of sharing information and confidentiality must not be breached. Systems need to be in place to ensure that all partners are aware of how they may accomplish this. Record keeping should also be standardised where possible across the partnership so that records are consistent.
- **Limits of authority**: As with boundaries, all partners must know where their authority ends and is taken up by another service.
- **Decision making**: Clarity with respect to who makes final decisions in certain areas of the service should be established at the outset of the partnership.
- **Areas of responsibility**: Like boundaries, each partnership member needs to be clear about what they are responsible for with respect to the care the service user requires. You will need to have an understanding of all of these areas.

▲ **Figure 8.1** You will need to agree ways of working when working in partnership

Research it

1.2 Agreed protocols

Research the agreed protocols for working in your partnerships and write notes documenting your findings.

The established partnership then brings together an executive management team to oversee strategic development of the work in the form of a strategic/forward plan. The strategic plan includes:

- safeguarding adults policy – development and review
- safeguarding adults procedures for reporting and responding to concerns of abuse or neglect – monitoring, development and review
- equal access strategy
- information-sharing agreement – development and review
- training strategy for all staff and volunteers
- training strategy for service users and carers
- strategy to disseminate information about adult abuse and 'safeguarding adults' work to staff, volunteers, service users, carers and members of the public
- a commissioning strategy for services for people who are at risk of or have experienced abuse or neglect
- a commissioning strategy for responses to and services for perpetrators of abuse/neglect
- strategies for reducing risk of abuse and neglect across a range of settings, including care settings and the community
- review of the strategic plan and publication of an annual report.

Source: Safeguarding Adults – A National Framework, October 2005

See AC 2.7 for more information on partnership working and the importance of this here with regard to these policies and safeguarding.

Vulnerable Adults Risk Management

The Vulnerable Adults Risk Management (VARM) protects adults who are suffering with severe self-neglect or for whatever reason are refusing to engage with services. It is also for people who are being targeted by an unknown third party; so, for example, a carer who cares for a vulnerable person may believe that abuse is happening at the hand of another person, a family member or a neighbour.

Local safeguarding boards are required to produce policy statements which provide agencies with a framework to help them work with adults who have mental capacity but who are at risk of serious harm or death through self-neglect. This may also include individuals who engage in risky behaviour such as self-harm. You may find it useful to refer to guidance on how to work within (VARM) procedures which is provided by local safeguarding boards.

Multi-Agency Safeguarding Hubs (where operative)

These were set up as a result of a government report published in 2014, which highlighted several cases of child abuse including the death of four-year-old Daniel Pelka. The report identified the risks involved in information not being shared between care agencies and resulted in the establishment of Multi-Agency Safeguarding Hubs (MASHs) to address the risk of anyone slipping through the safeguarding net (The Home Office, 2014).

MASHs include police, local authorities and other agencies that work together to ensure that safeguarding agencies and their data are located in a single secure research and decision-making unit enabling effective information sharing.

In your setting, you may need to refer to them when you have concerns about the safety of a child or vulnerable person under the age of 18 years.

Shared training opportunities

You can read more about the potential for shared training opportunities in Unit 506 Professional development and Unit 501, specifically AC 2.4 and AC 5.4.

With partnerships, shared training for staff will ensure that all parties are aware of the protocols to protect people in care. The failures in the past where information has not been shared have led to untimely deaths of children and adults.

Safeguarding Adult Boards

Safeguarding Adults Boards were set up as a result of the Care Act 2014 which described their role and duties and how boards should operate.

Section 43 of the act specified the need for Safeguarding Adults Boards in each local area and outlined their objectives. Membership of SABs involves many agencies and key partnerships as well as consultancies of specialist advisers when needed. The needs of the local community must be considered when forming SABs and selecting the agencies needed for partnership working.

Winterbourne View: Transforming Care

In May 2011, the BBC *Panorama* programme aired a documentary showing undercover footage of abuse and humiliation carried out by a team of carers at the Winterbourne View Hospital. As a result of this programme, a Serious Case Review (also known as **Safeguarding Adults Review**) was undertaken, leading to 11 employees being charged and the closure of Winterbourne View, as well as criticism of the CQC for its failure to act when complaints had been made. Lessons learned from this serious breach of human rights led to a review of management structures by the providers of the care at Winterbourne as well as the launch of a new strategy for quality.

This case highlights the need for quality assurance, regulation and inspection procedures to be in place and monitored to ensure that safeguarding is foremost in our care giving.

As a manager, you may find that you are expected to run a service with smaller budgets and fewer staff and this is where good practice may suffer. Your role is to be vigilant and to challenge poor practice before it results in abuse or neglect.

Agreed ways of working

The failings at the Mid Staffordshire NHS Trust highlight the need for agreed ways of working to ensure that standards of care and the safeguarding of people in care are not compromised in any way. This can be achieved only if staff are aware of and work with policies and procedures that are up to date and reflective of the legislation.

For example, one of the policies your workplace will have is a risk assessment specifically for examining potential cases of abuse and a safeguarding policy. (There will also be policies for induction, training and CPD and an equal opportunities policy to ensure recruitment procedures are adhered to.)

A risk assessment of this type will examine the potential causes of harm to vulnerable adults, staff, volunteers or others in your organisation with respect to the activities and services provided, as well as the interactions with and between vulnerable adults and the wider community.

In your organisation's risk assessment there should be details of the risk of harm that might be posed in different situations such as:

- threatening behaviours or intimidation
- behaviours which might result in injury, neglect or exploitation by self or others

- the use and misuse of medication
- the misuse of drugs or alcohol
- aggression and violence
- suicide or self-harm
- the type of impairment or disability of individuals in your setting
- the potential for accidents, for example while out in the community or participating in a social event or activity.

Each local authority has established a multi-agency partnership to lead 'safeguarding adults' work and the set of standards outlines the multi-agency framework within which planning, implementation and monitoring of 'safeguarding adults' work should take place, including a list of suggested partner agencies. Your organisation will have a copy of that policy and as a manager you need to be aware of its contents.

AC 1.3 Ways in which legislation, guidance and agreed ways of working impact on day-to-day leadership and management practice

Here, you will be required to analyse how current legislation, guidance and agreed ways of working impact on your day-to-day leadership and management practice within your work setting, to include the topics we cover in this section.

Safeguarding legislation and guidance will inform the policies in place in your work setting and you will need to regularly review your policies and ways of working to ensure that they still meet the requirements of the Care Act 2014. This will include ensuring that your service is one which has a safeguarding system which prevents abuse and neglect and, if it happens, then staff address it immediately. You, therefore, need to ensure that your staff are well-versed in what they need to do if they believe an adult with care and support needs may be at risk of abuse or neglect.

See AC 1.1 for more information on legislation, and AC 1.2 for information on current national and local guidance and agreed ways of working.

Management and operational strategy for safeguarding and whistle blowing

At this level, the establishment of Safeguarding Adults Boards may require you as a manager to represent your setting alongside members of the local authority, NHS and police. You may also be required to carry out Safeguarding Adults Reviews.

Staff induction, employees, volunteers

For staff and anybody who comes into your setting, the safeguarding agenda needs to be clearly outlined and the setting has a duty to ensure that the care given is safe and of a high standard. This therefore requires that staff who are employed have undergone induction training which clearly outlines how they are expected to behave towards people in the setting and that they can recognise what constitutes poor care, neglect and abuse. They need to be clear about what they can do should they experience or see anything that detracts from a person's wellbeing and follow the policies and protocols which translate the legislation into agreed ways of working.

Staff training and development

Staff require training in safeguarding and this may need to be updated on an annual basis. They also need to be aware of what it means to whistle blow and when to do so. Policies must clearly address the agreed way of working with respect to both areas.

Individuals who use adult care and support services

Those people who use the service and those who support them should be clear about how staff will work with them to meet safeguarding needs. The policies should be made available to them and transparency with respect to how they can expect to be treated and cared for must be clear. Any concerns must be dealt with through a complaints procedure, which is both robust and fair.

Any external workers or visitors to the organisation

Stakeholders, partners and other agencies as well as families who work alongside us should all be aware of how the setting handles safeguarding and how it promotes transparency and openness in its approach to dealing with any issues. The current legislation and guidance impact upon how you as a manager work with others in the setting, ensuring that anybody who enters the premises is fully aware of the behaviour expected of those who care for the service users and the ways of working in the setting. A zero-tolerance policy towards neglect, abuse or mistreatment must be promoted and monitored.

AC 1.4 Methods of promoting and supporting safeguarding in the work setting

Here, you will be required to use methods to effectively promote and support safeguarding in the work setting.

In promoting and supporting safeguarding, policies must be in place which enable your workforce to ensure they are working in a safe way. A risk assessment policy specifically for examining potential cases of abuse and a safeguarding policy are an important start, as are policies for induction, training, CPD and an equal opportunities policy to ensure recruitment procedures are adhered to, for example, and suitable care workers are employed.

A risk assessment will examine the potential causes of harm to vulnerable adults, staff, volunteers or others in your organisation with respect to the activities and services provided, as well as the interactions with and between vulnerable adults and the wider community.

Active and visible working practices to support staff with their responsibilities towards safeguarding and whistle blowing

The policies in place which define the agreed ways of working, together with additional training, need to be available to staff to ensure that they are conversant with their responsibility with respect to safeguarding and whistle blowing.

Training for all staff in their responsibilities towards safeguarding and whistle blowing

Staff training should be available to all staff to ensure they are aware of their responsibilities and should be delivered on an annual basis to update them in new legislation and guidance.

Review of any issues as a regular agenda item at meetings with internal and external stakeholders

A regular agenda item dealing with safeguarding is good practice and helps inform staff in the setting and those stakeholders who work outside of the setting.

Open door approach for whistle-blowing issues and reporting of safeguarding concerns

Staff need to feel secure in the knowledge that they can approach you as their manager at any time with concerns about a safeguarding issue. Having an open-door policy for this type of thing will make it easier for staff to voice concern and know that it will be dealt with appropriately.

Information provided for all relevant individuals on how to raise a concern or make a complaint

A complaints procedure must be available in the setting to ensure that all who enter can raise concerns should they need to.

LO2 Lead on the effective application and review of safeguarding policies, procedures and protocols

AC 2.1 Review safeguarding policies and procedures that reflect current legal, national and local requirements

Here, you will be required to provide evidence of how your setting's policies and procedures to support safeguarding and whistle blowing reflect national and local requirements and how these are reviewed to ensure currency.

A policy statement makes it clear to everyone in the setting – staff, service users, stakeholders and others – what you and your organisation will do to keep people safe. There are many policies available online that might be of use if you are updating or re-writing your own policy. (See e.g. www.qcs. co.uk or www.careukgroup.com)

Any sample policy statement can be used as a guide, and with amendments you can personalise the policy to fit your own setting. All safeguarding policies need to acknowledge the duty of care your setting must safeguard to promote the welfare of service users. The agreed ways of working within the setting must reflect legal responsibilities, government guidance and guidance of your regulatory body.

The policy should be reviewed annually, and changes made according to current guidance and practice. The policy may need to reflect changes to working practices, which may have emerged as the result of experience.

AC 2.2 Show how individuals and/or families are included in reviewing policies and procedures

Here, you will need to provide evidence of how others are involved in reviewing and/or updating the adult care service safeguarding policies and procedures, including those in receipt of care and support, employees and others.

Those in receipt of care and support

Good practice and personalisation demand that the service user is the 'central' part in the process of care and is part of the decision-making process. A review of the *No Secrets* document in the SCIE 'Report 47: User involvement in adult safeguarding' (2011) made a firm recommendation for the involvement of service users in strategic planning. It highlighted the notion that service users and their representatives should be seen as key partners in safeguarding and strategic planning, with all views being taken into account.

The review further recommended the involvement of service users in training staff and in making staff appointments. In 2001/2, the Department of Health reviewed social work education, consulting people who used such services. This review found that service users were able to state what they wanted from social workers, emphasising qualities such as empathy, respect and non-judgemental attitudes as being important. As a result, the DoH brought in a new requirement for social workers to be educated to degree level and for user and carer involvement to be integrated into the design and delivery of the degree programme (SCIE, 2011).

The Care Act 2014 takes the process further:

> *'It signals a major change in practice – a move away from the process-led, tick-box culture to a person-centred social work approach which achieves the outcomes that people want. Practitioners must take a flexible approach and work with the adult all the way through the enquiry and beyond where necessary.'*
>
> **Source:** Briefing: Care Act implications for safeguarding adults, Skills for Care, p. 2

Individuals using care services can also be included in reviewing and updating safeguarding policies. They are the ones in receipt of care and could usefully give an indication of how they expect to be safeguarded. Your role as a manager might include here the means by which service users can be more active in developing policy within the setting.

Employees

It is the duty of employees to make sure they are working within policy and are up to date with what are the agreed ways of working in the setting. They may also be called upon to be part of the review of policy and this is something you as a manager may wish to instigate within the course of appraisal sessions or team meetings. Staff should be encouraged to reflect upon how the policies are working and whether and how changes can improve the quality of care.

Others

Family and other agencies may also be a useful source of information about how a policy change might improve the care being given.

Evidence opportunity

2.2 **How individuals and/or families are included in reviewing policies and procedures**

Provide evidence to your assessor of how others are involved in reviewing and/or updating the adult care service safeguarding policies and procedures, including those in receipt of care and support, employees and others.

Reflect on it

2.2 **Reviewing and updating policies**

How might you involve individuals and/or family members in reviewing and updating policies and procedures in your own setting? What evidence can you provide of how others are involved in reviewing and/or updating the adult care service safeguarding policies and procedures?

Write a short report which shows how you include individuals or family members when it comes to reviewing policies and procedures with regard to the care of vulnerable adults in your care. Describe the process. For example, sometimes the individuals you care for may exhibit challenging behaviour, so how do you build relationships and provide positive support to help them to avoid behaving in challenging ways? It might be that you have developed physical interventions to help in such cases or have put in place individual support plans that will detail the de-escalation strategies for each service user. Include some examples in your report.

How did you involve individuals and family members to improve the policies? Did this improve the process? Provide a written account.

AC 2.3 **Support individuals to understand and be able to apply the policies and procedures in their day-to-day work**

Here, you will be required to provide evidence of how relevant safeguarding information is disseminated to all employees and non-care staff, and to those in receipt of care and support services, e.g. families, carers. You will also be required to provide evidence of how relevant safeguarding information is checked in respect of your knowledge, understanding and expected behaviours which apply to your role/practice, and actioned in the event that knowledge in relation to care/practice was not current and/or inaccurate.

How relevant safeguarding information is disseminated or passed on

Information about safeguarding must not be restricted to policy but needs to be actively shared among employees and those who work in partnership with your setting. You might schedule safeguarding as a permanent agenda item for discussion at each team meeting and in this way, you can ensure that all staff are firmly aware of their role in practice. For non-care staff, support services, families and service users, the information must be made available on the setting's website and perhaps in hard copy by means of a prospectus about the setting.

You can obtain feedback about how safeguarding information is being disseminated and received through appraisals and supervision sessions. Additionally, when working in partnership with other agencies, families and carers, information must be recorded and shared safely, and confidentiality must not be breached. Systems need to be in place to ensure that all partners are aware of how they may accomplish this. Record keeping should also be standardised where possible across the partnership so that records are consistent.

As the manager, you need to ensure that everyone connected to the service is supported in their efforts to apply the policies and procedures. Training and guidance may be required to help the people involved in care of service users to understand policies and to question the content if they need to.

How safeguarding information is checked in respect of knowledge, understanding and expected behaviours

As a manager, you will need to ensure that checks to monitor safeguarding are undertaken regularly to ensure best practice is being implemented. Staff must be under no illusion as to their role in completing paperwork and records correctly and any issues of concern must be reported to you as the manager.

Annual training on safeguarding will ensure that staff are helped to update their knowledge and to expand upon how they are expected to behave with respect to this area of work. Many organisations focus on safeguarding by including it in mission statements and the values of the organisations. Annual performance review requires staff to demonstrate how they implement their knowledge into their practice and to give examples of having done so. Nurses, for example, are required to reflect upon practice and to give examples of how they safeguard the patients in their care.

How safeguarding information is actioned in the event that knowledge in relation to care/practice was not current and/or inaccurate

In our day-to-day work we have a duty to safeguard and promote the welfare of every individual we care for and this means we need to be very clear about the organisation's policy and procedures for safeguarding. When concerns are expressed about the welfare of anybody in our care, you must report these concerns immediately to the designated safeguarding officer. If a member of staff reports concerns to you, as the manager you will be required to make a written, dated note of their concern and inform the safeguarding officer as soon as possible. This person will then take the matter forward. For concerns related to historical abuse or cases where there has been inaccurate recording of safeguarding issues you need to be aware that any allegation of abuse or neglect might lead to a criminal investigation and, therefore, you as the manager and your staff must not do anything that may jeopardise a police investigation. No attempt must be made to investigate the allegations yourself.

Evidence opportunity

2.3 Safeguarding information and the people you work with

Provide evidence to your assessor of how you ensure that safeguarding information is disseminated, passed on or circulated safely to employees, non-care staff, those in receipt of care and support services, e.g. families, carers.

How do you check staff with respect of their knowledge, understanding and expected behaviours which apply to their roles/practice in safeguarding?

Finally, provide evidence of how relevant safeguarding information is actioned in the event that knowledge in relation to care/practice was not current and/or inaccurate.

AC 2.4 Provide effective support for individuals where danger, harm or abuse is suspected or disclosed

Here, you will be required to explain how to investigate and manage individual and/or group allegations where danger, harm or abuse is suspected or disclosed, including support that is provided for team members/employees/volunteers, and support that is provided for those in receipt of care and support services.

The legal and internal processes for managing complaints

Any suspicion of abuse or complaint made which indicates abuse or discovery of abuse happening must be dealt with immediately. It may also transpire that an individual approaches you or a member of your staff and tells you/ them that they are being abused. Abuse might be reported through your complaints procedure and should, therefore, be taken seriously.

This is called 'disclosure'. You are duty-bound to believe what you are being told and act on it. If the person wants to tell you in confidence, you need to inform them that if they are at risk of harm, you have a duty to put a stop to it and will need to inform others in order to help them. You cannot keep abuse a 'secret'. In addition, reviewing care plans and assessments may highlight issues with respect to care and may raise questions as to potential neglect and abuse. In the Winterbourne View care home case, abuse was suspected and disclosed to higher management, the local authority and the CQC but there was a failure at each stage to take the allegations seriously. There have since been reviews to ensure this failure never happens again.

As a manager, a disclosure of abuse sets into motion a time-consuming process of meetings and writing reports, and this can distract you from the day-to-day running of the setting. It is so important, therefore, that you have put into place processes that comply with legal regulation and that you ensure that staff are fully cooperating with these processes.

The Care Act 2014 sets out a clear framework for how local authorities should deal with abuse and you as a manager must comply with the processes set out by your local Safeguarding Adults Board.

Support provided for team members/ employees/volunteers and those in receipt of care and support services

Support provided for team members/employees/ volunteers

When an allegation of abuse by a member of staff has been made, the team are likely to feel vulnerable and upset. This will affect morale and may lead to employees leaving the team or simply becoming stressed and ill. This may, therefore, affect the actual running of the team and require you to employ more agency staff to cover shifts. Your team may find it hard to motivate themselves to work so your role as a manager will be to ensure that, as much as possible, they are supported and can express their concerns at any time. You may wish to provide additional supervision at this time or give staff the opportunity to discuss what has happened in team meetings.

Staff need to be able to voice their concerns to management about the need for additional help without fear of repercussions and steps should be taken to address these issues. A culture of openness and transparency is to be encouraged.

There is more information on this in AC 2.5.

Support for those in receipt of care and support services

If you or your staff are in a position where you suspect that the individual is in danger of harm or abuse or where they have disclosed this, you will need to make sure that you and your staff respond appropriately. As a manager, you will need to ensure that your staff are aware of the policies and procedures to follow in such situations. For example, if an individual has told you that they are being abused, you or your staff will need to:

- seek advice from the nominated safeguarding officer immediately
- reassure the person but listen and avoid questioning before taking a detailed report
- use open questions to ensure that they understand what they are being told
- inform the person that the information must be passed on but that only those that need to know about it will be told
- identify the parties who will be informed
- report the disclosure immediately to a senior person, or as a manager, act according to your setting's agreed ways of working or policy
- access the procedures in your workplace for dealing with suspected abuse
- write down when the report was made to you, date, who was involved, names of witnesses, what happened and the facts of the conversation
- not discuss the incident further with anybody else. The matter is confidential and will be discussed only with relevant people who need to know what has happened.
- keep the report safe until it can be investigated further by the team involved in dealing with the issue
- keep the individual who reported the abuse or suspected abuse safe by reassuring them that the matter will be taken seriously and investigated fully and that they have done the right thing by revealing their concerns.

This is just guidance and you should consult your setting's agreed ways of working for more information on how you should handle such situations.

Staff, family and others must be informed about the steps that need to be taken if abuse is suspected.

Why those in receipt of care and support may not complain

Both staff and service users need to feel able to complain when things are not right because they may not do this if they feel their complaint may not be taken seriously or if they feel that further harm may come to them.

It is crucial that you operate a system of transparency with staff and service users who are confident that as a manager you will not only take them seriously if they make a claim of abuse but that they will be supported in their decision to do so. You can do this by ensuring that your setting is open about the complaints procedure, that this is available on notice boards, for example; that your staff know how they can support individuals in the complaints procedure; and that individuals feel that they can make a complaint or discuss issues that are concerning them.

Recommendations to improve management practice

Any allegation of abuse made by a service user or anyone outside the setting against a member of your staff, or by a member of staff on another member of staff, will have an impact upon you as a manager. You may feel upset or angry about what has happened or is alleged to have happened and want to put a stop to this immediately. The way in which you respond may affect outcomes so you need to adopt an objective approach to the incident and follow procedure to the letter. Putting aside your emotions can be hard to do but a professional approach must be developed here and gossiping or discussing the incident will be damaging to the team and the investigation. You may want to seek supervision to discuss how you are feeling about the incident or seek advice from higher management or the HR team, although not all adult care setting will have an HR team.

Evidence opportunity

2.4 Effective support for individuals where danger, harm or abuse are suspected or disclosed

Provide a written account explaining how to investigate and manage individual and/or group allegations where danger, harm or abuse is suspected or disclosed.

Make sure you address each of the topics we have discussed in this section and think about how this applies to your practice and the practice in your setting:

- What are the legal and internal processes in your setting for managing complaints?

- How can you as a manager provide support for team members, employees and volunteers when they suspect abuse, or if they have disclosed this?

- How can you as a manager provide support for those who receive care when you suspect abuse, or if they have disclosed this?

- Why might an individual not complain?

- What recommendations to improve your management practice might you make to ensure that when there are allegations of danger, harm or abuse you support staff and service users?

AC 2.5 Provide effective support for team members where danger, harm or abuse is suspected or disclosed

Here, you will be required to critically evaluate how you have supposed or would support others who have had a disclosure of alleged/suspected abuse made to them, and what they would do if a colleague had an allegation made against them.

Supporting others who have had a disclosure of alleged/suspected abuse made to them

When an allegation is made, action must be swift. Your role here is to ensure that the investigation is carried out in a professional manner and that each part is dealt with according to the policy and procedures your own setting outlines. Discussing the case with others in your team who are not involved is not helpful and may damage the investigation, but you may need to inform the team of what has happened without giving any specific details. It is important at this time to ensure that team morale is not damaged in any way and you need to be available to help them.

You may also want to recap your learning from AC 2.4.

Remember, this is just guidance and your setting's agreed ways of working will provide more information and the steps to follow.

Table 8.1 has been compiled from Standards 6, 7, 8 and 9 of the Safeguarding Adults (ADDS, 2005) document. This includes examples of actions to take and the time frame for these when there are concerns about abuse or neglect. Again, this is just guidance and you should refer to your setting's agreed ways of working.

What to do if a colleague has an allegation made against them

Sometimes, an allegation may be made against you as the manager or against a colleague.

If this happens, it is recommended that you involve your own manager as soon as possible and document the complaint. Taking yourself out of the situation (removing yourself from that specific situation) will help and discussing it with your next in line will be most useful. In the case of a colleague, you will need to ascertain the facts and start an inquiry. It may be that you take the colleague out of the situation by reassigning them or perhaps giving them leave until the investigation has been dealt with. It is imperative that claims like this be dealt

Table 8.1 Guidelines from the Safeguarding Adults document

	Action	Time frame
Alert	Report concerns of abuse or neglect which are received or noticed within a partner organisation. Any immediate protection needs should be addressed. Ensure the individual is safe. Seek medical attention if needed.	Immediate action to safeguard anyone at immediate risk.
Referral	Ensure other agencies are given information and made aware of the concern.	Within the same working day.
Decision	Deciding whether the 'Safeguarding Adults' procedures are appropriate to address the concern.	By the end of the working day following the one on which the safeguarding referral was made.
Safeguarding assessment strategy	Formulate a multi-agency plan for assessing the risk and address any immediate protection needs.	Within five working days.
Safeguarding assessment	Coordinate the collection of the information about abuse or neglect that has occurred or might occur. This may include an investigation, e.g. a criminal or disciplinary investigation.	Within four weeks of the safeguarding referral.
Safeguarding plan	Coordinate a multi-agency response to the risk of abuse that has been identified.	Within four weeks of the safeguarding assessment being completed.
Review	Review the plan.	Within six months for first review and thereafter yearly.

Source: adapted from www.adass.org.uk/adassmedia/stories/publications/guidance/safeguarding.pdf

with sensitively and in privacy. Your colleague must not feel that any blame is being apportioned but that an allegation has been made which requires investigation. They need to be reassured that the situation will be dealt with in a confidential manner and as swiftly as possible.

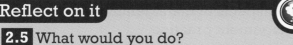

Reflect on it

2.5 What would you do?

What would you do if you or a colleague had an allegation made against you?

Evidence opportunity

2.5 Providing effective support for team members where danger, harm or abuse are suspected or disclosed

Using your own workplace as a possible case study, provide a written account critically evaluating how you have supported or would support others who have had a disclosure of alleged/suspected abuse made to them, or what they would do if a colleague had an allegation made against them.

You might like to think about what was useful about the approach you took and what you might have done better. If you have not been in such a situation, what would you do?

Identify the strengths of the approach you take in dealing with these matters. How could you improve the manner with which such cases are dealt?

Reflect on it

2.5 Effective support for team members where danger, harm or abuse is suspected or disclosed

Highlight how you as a manager address cases of suspected abuse. Be sure to detail the measures that you take with your staff to avoid abuse taking place as well as the steps taken in the case of suspected or alleged abuse. How do you make sure that you provide information on all of these areas to individuals, staff and families?

Write a short piece to show your understanding about this crucial area of work.

Then write down how you have dealt with situations where allegations have been made against you or a colleague. If you have not been in this situation, find out from your own manager or agreed ways of working what you would need to do.

AC 2.6 Analyse how the findings from recent Serious Case Reviews have impacted the provision of adult care services

Here, you will be required to critically evaluate lessons learned from a recent national or local inquiry or Serious Case Review (SCR), showing how these have brought changes to local or national safeguarding requirements in adult care services.

Serious Case Reviews (now known as Safeguarding Adults Reviews) have shown that abuse in care has been ongoing for a number of years and, despite a number of government initiatives, it still continues today. This includes abuse occurring in institutional settings and in the home by care staff, relatives and friends in the form of:

- sexual and financial abuse
- abuse of medication to control and sedate
- physical abuse
- neglect
- behaviour designed to degrade and humiliate.

This has been highlighted through media coverage and reporting.

For example, Orchid View was a nursing home registered as a care home with nursing for up to 87 people in the categories of old age and dementia. Opened in November 2009, it closed in October 2011 following revelations of a number of safeguarding alerts and investigations and possible criminal offences. In October 2013, an inquest found that five people had

> *'"died from natural causes attributed to neglect" and that several other people "died as a result of natural causes" with "insufficient evidence before me [the reviewer] to show that this suboptimal care was directly causative" of their deaths ... this suboptimal care caused distress, poor care and discomfort to residents and the families of people who were not the subject of the Inquest.'*
>
> **Source:** Orchid View Serious Case Review, June 2014

Research it

2.6 Serious Case Reviews

Look at some of the serious case reviews such as the Orchid View case, the Francis Report or Winterbourne View and describe what we have learned from such cases.

How have these cases brought changes to local or national safeguarding requirements in adult care services?

Evidence opportunity

2.6 Analyse how the findings from recent Serious Case Reviews have impacted the provision of adult care services

Provide a written piece analysing and critically evaluating lessons learned from a recent national or local inquiry or Serious Case Review, showing how these have brought changes to local or national safeguarding requirements in adult care services.

For example, the Francis Report recommended that healthcare workers should undertake training and the Care Certificate is one of the responses. Also, that there should be transparency when dealing with service users and if mistakes are made health professionals are now duty bound to tell the service user what has happened and apologise. These are just some of the changes. How do you think this will ensure that care is improved? What changes have been made in your own setting and have they been useful? What else will you need to do to bring your setting up to the required standard?

AC 2.7 Critically evaluate the effectiveness of safeguarding policies, procedures and protocols

Here, you will be required to show how you effectively disseminate and implement safeguarding policies and procedures.

Internal policies and procedures relating to all aspects of management and non-management practice

This has been covered in earlier sections, specifically ACs 1.3 and 2.1.

The strategic plan of your organisation will specify how safeguarding will be practised and the policy will ensure that abuse and neglect are prevented and explain how services users will be protected.

The policy should include details about effective joint working and should identify the agencies and professionals with whom you share this responsibility. There must be clear lines of accountability within the organisation for safeguarding and staff need to be aware of the role of the local Safeguarding Children Boards' and Safeguarding Adults Boards' strategies.

The policy should also identify the arrangements for staff training and continuing professional development as well as safe working practices with respect to recruitment and vetting and barring procedures.

See ACs 2.4 and 2.5 for more information.

Whistle-blowing guidance for staff

The expectation in any organisation is that individuals should raise challenges and concerns, but they must be able to do this in a supportive and protective environment. Most challenges or complaints should be dealt with inside the organisation, which should, with appropriate guidance, allow you to resolve the situation or support sanctions. However, there are occasions when a practice is so widespread and resistant to change or of such a serious nature that a more radical approach is required. In such circumstances, staff who witness such activities will be protected by law for making this public. However, this does not mean that the individual has a right to go to the press or other public forum to expose an organisation without trying to resolve issues internally first.

The policies and systems discussed apply to staff as well as service users.

A **whistle blower** is protected by law for disclosure if they:

- are a 'worker'
- believe that malpractice in the workplace is happening, has happened in the past or will happen in the future
- are revealing information of the right type (a 'qualifying disclosure'), which refers to information that the worker believes is a criminal offence, a miscarriage of justice or failure to comply with a legal **obligation**. This may have taken place in the past, or may happen in the future
- reveal it to the right person and in the right way (making it a 'protected disclosure'). This is where workers bring information about a wrongdoing to the attention of their employers or a relevant organisation, and in doing so they are protected in certain circumstances under the Public Interest Disclosure Act 1998.

As the manager of a care setting you need to ensure that you have created an environment where staff can report concerns knowing that you will act upon them and investigate. Staff must be confident about this so having an open culture will help. Your whistle-blowing policy should be promoted to staff to make it clear that they can go outside their normal line management to raise concerns and that they will have the protection of the Public Interest Disclosure Act as long as disclosure is not untrue

or malicious. You as a manager may also wish to raise such concerns and can make disclosures to report concerns.

Without a whistle-blowing policy, there is a possibility that bad practice will go unchallenged as staff will not feel confident about their rights to make a disclosure.

Your whistle-blowing policy might cover the following points, for example:

- The identity of the person the whistle blower made the disclosure to (e.g. disclosing to a relevant professional body may be more likely to be considered reasonable than, say, one made to the media).
- The seriousness of the wrong-doing.
- Whether the wrong-doing is continuing or likely to occur again.
- Whether the disclosure breaches the employer's duty of confidentiality (e.g. if information was made available that contains confidential details about a client).
- If the whistle blower made a previous disclosure, whether they followed any internal procedures then.

It is important to note that the term 'worker' includes agency workers and people who aren't directly employed but are in training with employers. Some self-employed people may be considered to be workers for the purpose of whistle blowing if they are supervised or work off-site.

Making a disclosure

For a disclosure to be protected by the law, it should be made to the right person or authority and in the right way. Disclosures must meet the following criteria:

- The disclosure must be in good faith (honest intent and without malice).
- The whistle blower must reasonably believe that the information is substantially true.
- The whistle blower must reasonably believe they are making the disclosure to the right 'prescribed person'.

If a qualifying disclosure is made in good faith to an employer, or through a process that the employer has agreed, the whistle blower will be entitled to protection.

If a worker feels unable to make a disclosure to their employer, there are other 'prescribed people' to whom a disclosure can be made. Disclosure can be made to the person responsible for the area of concern such as a team leader or mentor.

To make a protected disclosure to 'others' rather than the employer, the whistleblower must:

1   Reasonably believe their employer would treat them unfairly if the disclosure was made to the employer or a prescribed person.

2   Reasonably believe that the disclosure to the employer would result in the destruction or concealment of information about the wrong-doing.

3   Have previously disclosed the same or similar information to the employer or a prescribed person.

Whistle blowers should not become the subject of an internal investigation, or be ridiculed or dismissed as a result of raising concerns. In health and care organisations, the law requires a **Duty of Candour**, which protects individuals from poor or unsafe care. The Duty of Candour (2014) requires transparency about failures or lapses in respect of care.

KEY TERM

Duty of Candour requires providers to be open and transparent with service users about their care and treatment. If treatment goes wrong the care provider must inform the service user about the incident, provide support and offer an apology.

Protocols relating to partnership working

The most important thing you can do to develop effective working relationships is to build your reputation as being a professional who is trustworthy and inspires confidence and respect in your team as well as between all team members. In this way, you can show that you provide other professionals with information, advice and support within the boundaries of your role and expertise and as such can develop protocols for partnership working that are fair to all parties involved.

Records of any issues raised and action taken in line with agreements and legislative bodies

It is important that any action taken or any disclosure is documented accurately and as soon as possible after the event. You need to inform HR of this and they can advise on the legal agreements and protocols.

Many smaller settings do not have an HR department. Here, you will need to act upon policy that is in the setting or you can obtain further information from Citizens Advice or other settings. Your stakeholders may also be able to provide information for you, as can the Care Quality Commission.

Clearly visible processes for raising concerns and making complaints

Policies need to be available to all staff and stakeholders as to the process of making complaints and disclosure in the event of malpractice. Staff must be made aware through the induction process and training of how they can action this and what process they need to go through.

LO3 Understand restrictive practice and potential impact

AC 3.1 Terminology relating to restrictive practice

Here, you will be required to explain what is meant by the terms mental capacity, restrictive practice, restraint, hidden restraint, risk and risk-averse culture and practice, and positive risk taking.

Mental capacity

This is the ability to make decisions for oneself and those people who are unable to do so are said to 'lack capacity'. There may be a number of reasons for this to happen, including mental health problems, physical injury, a learning disability, or dementia. People who lack capacity may be unable to give consent to restriction being applied in their care and this means they need to be assessed with respect to the deprivation of their liberty (DoLS). See AC 1.1 for more information on mental capacity.

Risk and risk-averse culture and practice

Care settings vary in type and as such the risks associated with them will differ (Figure 8.2). The rights of individuals in our care can occasionally be in conflict with health and safety issues and we need to be prepared to address such occasions. For example, a new service user in a care home may wish to go out shopping by themselves or may wish to go along to the local pub in the evening. The service user is clearly not imprisoned in the home and there should be no reason to deny them that right, but at the same time the staff may well have some concerns as to the service user's safety when they are not in their care. The CSCI (Commission for Social Care Inspection) document *Rights, Risks and Restraints: An exploration into the use of restraint in the care of older people* (2007), although concerned mainly with how some older people have been restrained in some care settings, makes some useful points:

> *'Respecting people's basic human rights to dignity, freedom and respect underpins good quality social care. People may need support in managing their care and making decisions but they have the right, whether in their own home or in a care home, to make choices about their lives and to take risks.*
>
> *Social care services have responsibilities to keep people safe from harm and to ensure their safety. It is this need to balance people's rights to freedom and to make choices with ensuring people are safe that is at the heart of this exploration into the use of restraint in the care of older people.'*

It is a case, then, of balancing your duty of care and the client's safety while also respecting their rights. The individual is at the forefront of any decision made and the risk assessment should enable rather than hinder. While workers might be afraid that they are neglecting their responsibilities when it comes to risk assessment, by putting measures in place and enabling risk, care can be transformed. One way in which this has been addressed is through the setting up of 'risk enablement panels'. The emphasis for the panel is on supporting **positive risk taking** while maintaining duty of care.

Positive risk taking

> ### KEY TERM
>
> **Positive risk taking** means identifying the potential risks and then developing plans and actions that reflect the potential benefits and harm of exercising one course of action over another. It is a way of seeing the risk in a positive way that enhances the quality of life for an individual.

Think about the risks you take on a daily basis. Did you pull out into a busy road in the path of an oncoming car? Perhaps you had to run to catch the bus and didn't look carefully at the road? Maybe you stood on a chair in order to retrieve something from a high cupboard?

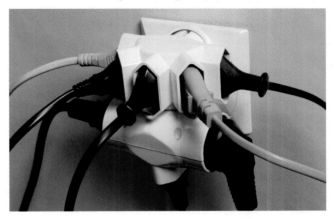

▲ **Figure 8.2** It is important to assess the environment for risks to individuals

Our attitude to risk is likely to be different when it comes to risking our personal safety. As care professionals, though, we are bound by law and have a duty of care to our service users and this is likely to change our attitude to risk management. We may be more careful when dealing with service users and take the view that as 'vulnerable adults' they need to be protected in some way. But is this a fair assessment of the people we care for or merely a stereotypical view? Titterton (2005), in his work *Risk and Risk Taking in Health and Social Care*, takes the view that care workers tend to focus on what the service users cannot do and therefore take what he calls a 'safety first approach' to risk.

This type of approach focuses on the person's physical problems and disability and tends to ignore other needs. This leads to loss of self-esteem and denies the right to choice and to an increase in independence. There is a danger that the care worker becomes more controlling of the service user and person-centred approaches become less of a reality.

Risk in this instance is thought of in terms of danger, loss, threat, damage or injury and the positive benefits of risk taking are lost. Therefore, a more balanced approach needs to be adopted.

The Department of Health's 2007 paper, 'Independence, Choice and Risk: A guide to best practice in supported decision making', makes the point that a 'safety first approach' may 'not be necessarily the best option for the person and may be detrimental to quality of life and a risk to maintaining independence'.

A more intelligent option is that proposed by Titterton in his Positive Risk approach. In this approach, risk is seen as positive and enhancing, and recognises the needs of individuals. It demonstrates that choice and autonomy are important and promotes the rights of vulnerable people. Steve Morgan (2004) summarises the approach:

> '*Positive risk-taking is: weighing up the potential benefits and harms of exercising one choice of action over another. Identifying the potential risks involved, and developing plans and actions that reflect the positive potentials and stated priorities of the service user. It involves using available resources and support to achieve the desired outcomes, and to minimise the potential harmful outcomes. It is not negligent ignorance of the potential risks … it is usually a very carefully thought-out strategy for managing a specific situation or set of circumstances.*'

If we are to provide real choice and control for our service users, we need to enable individuals to take the risks they choose, with support from the staff. This means allowing the individuals using our service to define their own risks and to plan and monitor any activity they wish to undertake that may entail some form of risk.

Restrictive practice, restraint and hidden restraint

Restrictive practice is defined by any practice which restricts a person's right to choose, or restricts their privacy or freedom. An example would be sectioning under the Mental Health Act or may be the act of locking doors to prevent people from leaving a building. Skills for Care identifies the use of restrictive practice as something that must be used only to prevent serious harm and must be ethically and legally justified.

Restrictive practice or any form of restraint of an individual must always be carried out with dignity and respect. You can find guidance in the Skills for Care documents on restrictive practice and restraint.

Its definition of such practice is: 'Making someone do something they don't want to do or stopping doing something they want to do' (*A Positive and Proactive*

Workforce, Skills for Care, April 2014) and it defines restrictive interventions as 'deliberate acts on the part of other person(s) that restrict an individual's movement, liberty and/or freedom to act independently' (*Positive and Proactive Care: Reducing the need for restrictive interventions*, DoH, April 2014).

In 2014, the publication of *A Positive and Proactive Workforce. A guide to workforce development for commissioners and employers seeking to minimise the use of restrictive practices in social care and health* advocated the use of a framework designed to 'radically transform culture, leadership and professional practice to deliver care and support which keeps people safe, and promotes recovery' and to ensure that restrictive practice was being used safely and not being misused as seen in such cases as the incidents at Winterbourne View Hospital.

New approaches, then, are to reduce the use of restrictive practice where possible.

The Mental Capacity Act 2005 states that anybody who uses or threatens to use force to make someone do something they are resisting is using restraint measures.

We can restrain people in a number of ways, such as through the use of medication, or through the use of keypad systems so they are unable to leave premises. We may also restrain somebody unintentionally, such as leaving a patient without means to mobilise and this might be termed hidden restraint. Hidden restraints are those activities that restrain somebody without actually seeming to do so. For example, putting an older adult into a chair that is low to the ground may make it more difficult for them to mobilise since they are unable to get up from the chair. While not physically restraining the individual, we are still preventing them from moving freely.

In some circumstances restraint is the right thing to do but it should always be consensual, part of a care package and used only if the individual lacks capacity and is unsafe.

Evidence opportunity

3.1 Terminology around restrictive practice

Write down the meanings of the following terms:

- Mental capacity
- Restrictive practice
- Restraint
- Hidden restraint
- Risk and risk-averse culture and practice
- Positive risk taking

How do these apply in your setting and your role?

AC 3.2 Legal requirements around restrictive practice

Here, you will be required to reflect on your understanding and application of the legal requirements and implications relating to restrictive practice in adult care services and be aware of recent case law and codes of practice, including the ones we discuss in this section.

Deprivation of Liberty Safeguards

The Mental Capacity Act 2005 (MCA) and its Code of Practice introduced Deprivation of Liberty Safeguards. You can find more details about the safeguards in AC 1.1 in this unit, and in Unit 502. It is important to understand what restraint means and to enable staff to recognise the situations in which it would be safe to use.

Provision for obtaining informed consent

It is vital that when we are considering the use of restraint we obtain consent from the individual themselves or from their advocate or next of kin. As a manager, it is important that a policy is in place and that staff are aware of this and are supported in their action. Anyone who is involved in carrying out a restrictive practice should complete training in the Mental Capacity Act, which covers the learning outcomes of the QCF Unit MCA01, 'Awareness of the Mental Capacity Act 2005' (level 3), so staff must be given the opportunity to undertake this training.

Assessing mental capacity, including the work of independent mental capacity advocates

In determining a lack of mental capacity, the care professional needs to be able to demonstrate that the person lacks the capacity to make a specific decision when they need to. Such an assessment must never be based on factors such as age, appearance, physical disabilities, learning difficulties or temporary conditions such as drunkenness. The decision must be clearly documented together with the rationale for the decision you have made.

The role of the independent mental capacity advocate (IMCA) was introduced in the Mental Capacity Act 2005 to represent individuals when there is nobody to do so. They provide a legal safeguard to aid decision making when a person lacks capacity to do so and has nobody close to them to help.

Best interests assessments and *P v Cheshire West* case

The Mental Capacity Act 2005 states that '[a]n act done, or decision made, under this Act for or on behalf of a person who lacks capacity must be done, or made, in his best interests'.

What the act does not do, however, is to prescribe in detail what 'best interest' means and therefore it lacks clarity. It does supply a checklist and a process to apply to ascertain an individual's capacity but when applied in this way it is possible that two people may come up with very different views about what a person's best interest actually is.

In the case of *P v Cheshire West*, a landmark Supreme Court ruling threw out previous judgments that had defined deprivation of liberty more restrictively. Under the Deprivation of Liberty Safeguards, strict control of a person's living space had meant that many individuals might have been deprived of their liberty unlawfully and without safeguards in settings including care homes and supported living placements.

P had lived in a supported living bungalow with other residents since 2009, receiving substantial one-to-one care and supervision. His behaviour, which was to tear his incontinence pads and put the pieces in his mouth, was managed by physical intervention. In 2011 the Court of Appeal had ruled that this was not a deprivation of liberty because P's life was as normal as possible for someone with his level of disability and he would require the same level of supervision in any other setting.

However, this ruling was rejected by the Supreme Court, which said that people with a disability should not face a tougher standard than people without a disability. Being constantly monitored and not being able to go out without supervision was depriving the person of their liberty.

Reflect on it

3.2 Your own practice

What do you think about the information in the section above? How might it change the way in which you work?

Evidence opportunity

3.2 Legal requirements around restrictive practice

Write a piece reflecting on your understanding and application of the legal requirements and implications relating to restrictive practice in your adult care setting and adult care settings generally. Make sure you refer to the case law and codes of practice we have discussed in this section; for example, Deprivation of Liberty Safeguards, provision for obtaining informed consent, assessing mental capacity, including the work of independent mental capacity advocates, best interests assessments and the *P v Cheshire West* case.

How do you or would you apply these in your setting and in your role?

AC 3.3 Impacts of restrictive practice

Here, you will be required to critically analyse the potential impact and outcomes of applying restrictive practices, and cover the topics we discuss in this section.

Impact of restrictive practice on those in receipt of care and support services

A restrictive practice is designed to keep individuals safe and sometimes when service users become distressed or confused they may lack understanding of their situation and may need restrictive interventions to keep them or other people around them safe. The impact of this may be disturbing to them or loved ones but a carefully planned restriction can be explained and carried out in a compassionate and caring manner.

The need to restrict the person needs to be fully explained where possible and must be justified as being necessary to prevent harm to the person. Your staff must show empathy and compassion during such procedures.

Impact of restrictive practice on all staff

For staff, the decision to use restrictive practices will involve assessing whether the person has the mental capacity to make a specific decision and they must be sure that what they are proposing to do is necessary to prevent harm and not merely for staff convenience. While restricting the liberty of a person may go against the person-centred ethos for some staff and will be a difficult choice to make, they must be reassured that any restrictive practice is legal and ethical.

Impact of restrictive practice on others such as families, carers

For families and carers, to see a loved one being restrained in some way can be a very distressing event, so they need to be clear about what is happening and how the practice will be of help. If the use of restrictive practices can be planned in advance and involve the individual and their family, this will reduce the stress. For example, a person with increasing dementia may require safety in the near future and may need to be restricted in their movements. A discussion about what would happen to ensure safety in the future would be positive and useful.

The impact if restrictive practice is used incorrectly

People must be treated with compassion, kindness and dignity so any restrictive practice that falls short of this would be unethical and legally wrong. The impact upon the individual, their family and also staff in the setting is likely to be most damaging and might be seen as abusive and neglectful.

Evidence opportunity

3.3 Impacts of restrictive practice

Provide a written account critically analysing the potential impact and outcomes of applying restrictive practice for those in receipt of care and support services, for all staff, and for others such as families and carers, and the impact if restrictive practice is used incorrectly.

You might like to think about restrictive practice impacts upon service users, staff, family and others. What are the positives for its use and the limitations of such practice? Give an example of when you have had to use a restrictive practice and identify what went well in the process. What might you improve next time? What is the impact if restrictive practice is used incorrectly?

AC 3.4 Demonstrate ways of minimising restrictive practices through person-centred practice

Here, you will be required to demonstrate how person-centred practice can help to minimise the use of restrictive practices, including the areas we discuss in this section.

By creating a positive person-centred environment, you can minimise the need for restrictive practice and the use of restraint. Person-centred care requires that the rights of the individuals we care for are paramount, the individual's needs and wishes are at the centre of the care we offer and that as care workers we respect them and nurture them. We need to understand that the behaviour of our service users is a form of communication and can change and be influenced by medication, how they may be feeling, the people they are with or even the space they occupy in the setting. While we develop care plans that offer choice and control, sometimes it may not be possible for an individual to make a decision and it is then a 'best interests' decision should be made and restraint may be required in the interest of safety.

The main reason for the use of restraint is the risk to the individual's safety and that of others. By ensuring that the environment is supportive and offers activity and variety for service users, the risks are minimised. If the physical space within a care setting is one which is pleasant to be in with colourful decoration and good seating areas, offering some outside space and a variety of activities for the enjoyment of the residents, then a sense of wellbeing can be instilled and the use of restraint will be minimised.

Comply with legislative and organisational requirements at all times

Restrictive practices are still evident in care work and as such you must be fully aware of your own policy with respect to this. There are legal guidelines that apply and your own setting policy will give details of your practice guidelines. If, for example, your setting opts for no restrictive practice then to do so would be against the policy and may result in sanctions being taken against you.

Demonstrate/role model how an individual's behaviour is understood and valued

A role model is someone whose behaviour is seen by other people as a good example. In modelling good behaviour, high standards are set and passed on to others to guide their behaviour. For example, to create a person-centred organisation, role models will help others to see how they take time with their service users and include them in decision making and care planning. They will emulate how they value their service users.

Managers who are good role models encourage team work, support and recognise the positive behaviours of their staff.

Demonstrate/role model how to value an individual's unique needs, aspirations and strength to enhance their quality of life

'Unique needs' refer to needs which are different from everybody else's. Each person we meet in our daily lives has their own identity, beliefs and values which enhance the quality of their lives and care professionals need to respect and value this. When it comes to providing support for our service users, a 'one size fits all approach to care shows a disrespect for others' needs and aspirations.

Demonstrate/role model how to effectively involve and enable active participation of individuals, their families, carers and advocates

Person-centred values are the principles that put the interests of the service users at the centre of their own care journey. By actively engaging people in a partnership where choice and participation in their care are encouraged we can ensure that staff and those cared for retain their individuality and dignity.

Demonstrate/role model how to treat individuals with compassion, dignity and kindness

Care professionals have a responsibility to provide care that is respectful and compassionate. This is more than just providing care with a successful outcome or a procedure which is performed to a high standard. While people will be grateful for the skill of the care worker, they go away from an experience with much more when the care worker has treated them with compassion. We should never forget the significance of events for people, which for care workers are just a daily routine. We need to consider ways in which we can show our respect for the people we care for by offering them kindness and dignity in the care we give.

Demonstrate/role model how to support and protect positive relationships between the people who deliver services and the individuals they support

Positive relationships are built by accepting that everybody is different and celebrating those differences. Work relationships are important to finding job satisfaction. Developing positive work relationships requires a willingness to listen to others and to communicate openly. We must show respect and offer support for those who may require it.

AC 3.5 Methods of managing policies and procedures related to positive risk taking

Here, you will be required to explain how team members are made aware of the policies and procedures of the setting, to include how restrictive practice would be managed by the registered manager, the deputy, and others such as team members, supervisors and volunteers.

The registered manager

The registered manager must ensure that clear policies outlining the organisational approach to restrictive intervention reduction are in place and that staff training opportunities are planned for. As a manager, you are responsible for ensuring that staff receive training, including updates and refresher courses, and that the policies include guidance on the safe use of restrictive interventions to be used as a last resort.

You are also responsible for ensuring that recording and reporting arrangements are in place and that you review and monitor the use of restriction. Additionally, you need to ensure that your staff can access support when they feel the need to and will be offered post-incident debriefing when situations arise. As the manager in a setting you will be required to manage risk positively and this means ensuring that policies and procedures that weigh up the potential benefits and harms, and identify the potential risks, are in place.

The deputy

The deputy needs to support the manager in the above practices and deputises when necessary. The deputy manager also requires knowledge of the methods to manage risk positively and should support the manager in developing plans and arranging for available resources and support to minimise risk in the workplace.

Others – team leaders, supervisors, volunteers

Staff or even volunteers who may be subject to experiencing challenging behaviour, which may require restrictive responses, must have specialised training and need to be assured that they have the support of the manager and the deputy in the way they handle situations.

There must be a collective understanding by all involved that restraint is the last resort and that should it be necessary, clear guidelines have been made available to ensure safe application of restrictive interventions. The risk policies and procedures should be available to all people who come into the service and they should be encouraged to adhere to them.

Evidence opportunity

3.5 Methods of managing policies and procedures related to positive risk taking

You will be required to explain and show how team members are made aware of the policies and procedures of the setting, to include how restrictive practice would be managed by the registered manager, the deputy, and others including team members, supervisors and volunteers. Consider the methods of managing policies and procedures related to positive risk taking.

You might like to consider how you manage restrictive practice in your setting. How about the registered manager? The deputy? Others such as team leaders, supervisors and volunteers? Provide a copy of the policy that is in place for your assessor.

Discuss this with your assessor and provide a written account detailing your discussion.

AC 3.6 Demonstrate positive approaches to risk assessments

Here, you will be required to show that you can work with service users, family members and colleagues to adopt a positive approach to risk assessment, which covers the areas we highlight in this section.

KEY TERM

Risk management is the forecasting of potential risks and minimising them or avoiding them altogether. Your policies should identify how you undertake risk assessment in your area and how you intend to manage risks that arise.

Assessing the seriousness of risks and supporting others in doing this

Care workers are duty bound to adopt a positive approach to risk assessment which balances individual choice with the duty of care to protect. Managing risks is a process that identifies the factors which may prevent care workers from providing safe, efficient care. If we believe that patient safety may be compromised in any way we need to identify and report our concerns to ensure safety controls can be put into place to reduce the chance of the risks occurring again. We do this by helping family and service users to weigh up the potential benefits of a course of action against the harms of exercising it and also to look at alternative actions. Service users, family members and others involved in care can all be a part of the process to assess risk.

In assessing the seriousness of risk, you may want to address the following aspects in your workplace:

- the sorts of factors that increase exposure to risk, e.g. environmental, social, financial, communication and recognition of abuse
- the existence of support to minimise risk
- the nature, extent and length of time of the risk
- the impact the risk may have on the individual and on others.

In addition to the above, you are bound by law as stated in Section 3(1) of the Health and Safety at Work Act 1974, which clearly states:

> *'It shall be the duty of every employer to conduct his undertaking in such a way as to ensure, so far as is reasonably practicable, that persons not in his employment who may be affected thereby are not thereby exposed to risks to their health or safety.'*

Unfortunately, this can make us risk averse and you may have staff who err constantly on the side of caution and fail to allow service users to undertake certain activities that they consider to be a risk to safety. This sort of professional risk aversion will undoubtedly lead to a lack of choice for the service users, together with a loss of control and independent living. This will, of course, have an adverse effect on care and is potentially bad practice. Staff, then, need to be supported in carrying out risk assessment that they feel confident about. Balancing the risk against the benefits and the rights of an individual can significantly improve a person's quality of life.

You will need to show that you can work with service users, family members and colleagues to adopt a positive approach to risk assessment and cover the areas we highlight below.

Adopt a positive approach that manages policies and processes and their implementation

The policies and processes of the setting must be implemented and adhered to, to ensure that a positive approach to risk is developed and managed well.

Adopt a positive approach that balances individual choice with the duty of care to protect

Balance between people's choice to do everyday activities and the duty of care owed by services to their staff and to users of services must be considered. The dangers associated with the risk and the potential benefits of risk taking must be identified.

Adopt a positive approach that ensures positive outcomes for individuals in receipt of services

A positive approach to risk taking means involving everybody working together to achieve positive outcomes for the service user. Identifying and managing risk should promote the independence and social inclusion of adults and older people with disability, health conditions and mental health problems.

Adopt a positive approach that enables positive risk taking in support of the individual's wellbeing

Risks change, just as the care of an individual may change, and therefore they need to be reviewed on a regular basis just as you would review a care plan or care package. Although we may think of risk in terms of danger or injury,

risk taking can have positive benefits for individuals' wellbeing. Balance must, therefore, be exercised in meeting the desires of people to undertake activities that may require thought and planning to minimise risk.

Adopt a positive approach that acknowledges and considers the views of family members and colleagues

Conflict may occur when families disagree with the service user as to their choice of activity. They may be risk averse, so the care staff can help them to understand the process of how the decision has been arrived at. Involving the family in discussions whereby decisions made are based on clear reasoning regarding legislation, policies and procedures will help.

Adopt a positive approach to the management of concerns and complaints, risk management and safeguarding

Safeguarding of the individual receiving care is paramount and in handling decisions about risk, information should be shared in accordance with the setting protocols.

Developing a simple approach to identify, assess and manage risk will enable staff and service users to seek clarification if they are unsure about what to do if complaints or concerns are raised.

Evidence opportunity

3.6 Demonstrate positive approaches to risk assessments

Show your assessor you can work with service users, family members and colleagues to adopt a positive approach to risk assessment, which includes the areas we have covered in this section.

AC 3.7 Demonstrate ways of assessing effectiveness of risk management practice

Here, you will be required to show that you actively follow policies and procedures and show how you evaluate their effectiveness in respect of risk and management practices, including the sections we cover here.

To assess risk, we need to look at what is involved in the proposed course of action and identify the potential benefits and harm that could result. For example, a patient with dementia may wish to continue to live at home with his wife. While his wife can support him during the day, at night her husband becomes confused, wanders and is, therefore, a falls risk. His constant getting out of bed is worrying his wife and if it continues she may also become ill. In determining the risk here, the potential benefits of staying at home must be weighed against the safety of a care setting where both may be looked after. While this may seem an obvious solution, the couple's choice is to stay in their own home and this, therefore, requires further planning to ensure they are given the help needed here and to ensure that risks are minimised. Plans must be developed which reflect the positive wishes and priorities of the service user and his wife and resources made available to achieve the best outcomes for them and at the same time minimise potential harm.

Practice that uses organisational policies and processes to ensure risk management is monitored and reviewed regularly

Some settings may view policies and processes relating to risk management as mere documents to be read then forgotten. This is short sighted as policies provide valuable insight into needs to be monitored and taken into consideration in the assessment of risk.

This makes for a safer environment and as the manager you need to ensure that staff are not simply ticking boxes when it comes to complying with the risk assessment policy.

Risk and management practice that supervises the practice of others

Risk from whatever source can cause uncertainty in any setting and some staff may require supervision to help them to manage risk confidently. As the manager, you might start to consider ways staff can supervise their peers so that the principles of risk become embedded in daily practice.

Risk and management practice that evaluates own practice in leading others

Risk management practice involves developing strategies that prevent negative events occurring and minimising harm. Your responsibility as the manager is to ensure that your own practice is sound and this will require you to evaluate that practice and to establish that a risk management plan which documents identifiable risks in the setting, together with responses to these, is made available to staff.

Risk and management practice that reviews and updates policies and processes

Compliance with respect to legislation will require you as the manager to ensure that policies and processes are up to date and reflect current safe practice. Failure to do so is breaking the law.

> ### Evidence opportunity
>
> **3.7** Demonstrate ways of assessing effectiveness of risk management practice
>
> Show your assessor how you actively follow policies and procedures and show how you evaluate their effectiveness in respect of risk and management practices with consideration of the topics we have discussed in this section.

> ### Reflect on it
>
> **3.6, 3.7** Positive approaches to assessing effectiveness of risk assessment practice
>
> Provide an account of your own practice to show how you promote a balanced approach to risk taking for your own setting. Think about how you have helped individuals, staff and others such as family members to carry out risk assessments that support a positive risk-taking approach. How did you help them to understand the balance between risk and rights? Say how this practice has improved the care in your area. Determine how you might help an employee to understand the balance between risk and rights.
>
> How might you change your risk assessment policy in the light of what you have learned?
>
> For practice, you could critically evaluate the effectiveness of your policies and procedures in respect of risk management practices. In critical evaluation, you might want to identify the good points about the policy and state what its strengths are. Is there any improvement that might be made or are there gaps in the policy that must be rectified?

LO4 Understand the role and responsibilities of adult care practitioners in ensuring the safety and wellbeing of children and young people

AC 4.1 Reasons adult care practitioners need to be aware of national and local requirements that seek to ensure the safety and wellbeing of children and young people

AC 4.2 Ways in which team members are supported to understand their role in safeguarding children and young people from danger, harm, abuse or exploitation

As an adult care professional, you may not work directly with children, but you will come across children, families and carers in your work. As the manager in an adult setting, you and your staff are required to have some understanding of the safeguarding protocols and procedures when working with children and must be aware of the national and local requirements with respect to safeguarding children and young people. These can be found in *Working Together to Safeguard Children: Guide to inter-agency working* (2015), which gives guidance to local authorities responsible for promoting the welfare of and safeguarding all children and young people in their area.

You will also be recruiting staff and are obliged to carry out checks on their suitability to work within environments where there may be children present. There is a requirement, then, to ensure that all staff know what their roles are with respect to reporting abuse or suspicions of abuse, and preventing harm to children, whether by sexual exploitation, the risk of radicalisation, domestic violence or from individuals who have been known to have abused children in the past. Additionally, we should have knowledge of practices such as female genital mutilation and child trafficking.

We live in a multicultural society and are faced with many different cultures and religions on a daily basis. Our knowledge of these cultures is crucial to care practice.

Reporting suspicions or disclosures of danger, harm, suspected abuse

There are certain protocols you need to follow in reporting abuse at work and it is important that you act according to the setting's policy. Failure to do so may lead to a poor outcome for the person involved. All suspicions of abuse have to be followed up in a formal way. As a manager, it is your responsibility to ensure that staff are aware of the need to respond to allegations or suspicions in line with safeguarding policies and procedures.

The staff need to know:

- what to do if they suspect abuse is taking place
- who they should report it to in the first instance
- what to do if it is not appropriate to raise the concerns with that person for whatever reasons
- what to do if they feel their concerns have not been addressed.

Preventing radicalisation

The government's counter-terrorism strategy 'CONTEST' (2011) and the prevent strategy (2015) are a response to the threat of extremist activity and aim to stop people from becoming radicalised or becoming terrorists or supporting terrorists. The NHS is a partner in the Prevent strategy and focuses on working with vulnerable individuals who may be at risk of being exploited or drawn into terrorist activity.

As the manager, you are responsible for ensuring that staff are aware of policy which identifies how such situations must be managed. Any concerns about a member of staff, a service user or somebody in their family becoming radicalised must be shared with the person who is leading safeguarding in your setting.

Preventing child sexual exploitation

All staff in care work have a responsibility to safeguard children they meet. As a manager, your role will be to ensure that your staff are aware of how to recognise unsafe situations for children or signs of maltreatment that will require investigation. This includes grooming where children are befriended and emotionally and sexually abused.

You and your staff need to be aware of protocols and procedures and work in partnership with those that may have expertise, including the police. You should also know how you can support staff to then support individuals who have been abused and exploited in this way and inform them of how they may make a disclosure to a Local Safeguarding Children Board or with whom they may share safeguarding concerns.

Preventing female genital mutilation (FGM)

Although FGM is practised in some countries, in the UK the practice is illegal and FGM is child abuse. The NSPCC offers guidance on what to do and the steps to take if you or a member of your staff suspect that a child may be about to be taken abroad to undergo FGM. You might have a section in your safeguarding policy to cover this more fully.

You will also need to know who you and your staff can consult about this. This might be your Local Safeguarding Children Board or the police.

(See www.nspcc.org.uk/preventing-abuse/child-abuse-and-neglect/female-genital-mutilation-fgm/preventing-protecting for more information.)

Preventing child trafficking

The Modern Slavery Act 2015 consolidates current offences relating to trafficking and slavery of children and adults and has increased the maximum penalty for such offences. As care workers, we may come into contact with people who have been brought to this country for the express purpose of child sexual exploitation, forced marriage, benefit fraud or simply domestic labour for which little money is given. Children are trafficked into the UK from abroad, but can also be trafficked from one part of the UK to another.

This sort of criminal activity is becoming more prevalent and as a manager in a setting your policies with respect to safeguarding need to reflect an awareness of this and should help staff to know what to do and to whom reports must be made. Again, the NSPCC has useful information on its site.

Preventing domestic violence

Domestic violence is

> 'any incident or pattern of incidents of controlling, coercive, threatening behaviour, violence or abuse between those aged 16 or over who are, or have been, intimate partners or family members regardless of gender or sexuality.'
>
> **Source:** www.gov.uk/guidance/domestic-violence-and-abuse#domestic-violence-and-abuse-new-definition

The children in the family, as well as the person experiencing the abuse, are also victims and need support. Witnessing such abuse is scary for a child and can result in serious harm.

Any suspicion you or a member of staff have about this happening needs to be brought to the attention of safeguarding officers and boards. A number of government strategies are in place to prevent the violence escalating and to address the problem (see Bellis et al., 2012).

Monitoring adults who are known to have abused children and young people

Once an individual has been identified as presenting a risk to children, all agencies are responsible for working together to monitor and manage the risk of harm to others. Where an offender is given a community sentence, offender managers need to make sure that they monitor the individual's risk to others and inform partner agencies as necessary. As a manager of a care setting you may become party to such knowledge only if you are recruiting to posts and need to

check the vetting and barring systems or if concern about potential harm to children has been expressed in the local area.

How all relevant and appropriate information is disseminated to new staff, agency staff and non-care staff

New staff to an area must be offered the opportunity to undertake induction training, which will help them to become familiar with the ways of working in the setting. Even agency staff who may be brought in for just a couple of shifts must be given a short introduction to the setting and be able to access policies if they need to. It is a useful practice to link them with a member of the regular team who they may be able to speak to if they need information during the shift. For new staff, statutory training must take place soon after joining the team and they need to be involved with team meetings from the outset of their employment. Information can also be made available to all staff by means of a website or an online training provision to ensure that new policies and procedures are available to be viewed. Such induction training and information can be used to support new staff, agency staff and non-care staff to understand their role in safeguarding children and young people from danger, harm, abuse and or/exploitation.

Evidence opportunity

4.1, 4.2 Reasons adult care practitioners need to be aware of national and local requirements and their role in safeguarding children

Write an account explaining why you need to be aware of and understand national and local requirements, protocols and procedures when working in partnership with other local agencies in relation to safeguarding children and young people, including the topics we have covered in this section.

Also explain how all team members are supported to understand their role in safeguarding children and young people from danger, harm, abuse and/or exploitation, including how relevant and appropriate information is disseminated to new staff, agency staff and non-care staff.

Reflect on it

4.1, 4.2 Safeguarding children

- How often do you come into contact with children and young people in your work?
- How do you ensure that staff understand their roles with respect to safeguarding children?
- What is your role as a manager in ensuring that children are safeguarded?

AC 4.3 National and local requirements for reporting suspicions or disclosures of danger, harm, abuse or exploitation of children and young people

Here, you will be required to explain the requirements for reporting suspicions or disclosures of danger, harm, abuse or exploitation of children and young people, including the topics we cover in this section.

Information Sharing: Advice for Practitioners Providing Safeguarding Services to Children, Young People, Parents and Carers, July 2018

To effectively safeguard children, information sharing is vital but when done poorly may result in missed opportunities to take action that keeps children safe.

The government advice document supports practitioners to make vital decisions and to share information to reduce the risk of harm to children.

Working Together to Safeguard Children and your role and responsibilities as a leader and manager

The government published 'Working Together to Safeguard Children: A guide to inter-agency working to safeguard and promote the welfare of children' in 2015 and recently updated this in 2018 to help local authorities to understand what they need to do to safeguard children.

It clearly details the legal requirements, outlining the roles of various people in organisations to ensure they know what to do to keep children safe. Your role as a manager in a care setting is to ensure that you follow the guidance and that staff are acting in an efficient way to safeguard children.

Your responsibility is to ensure that you are operating an effective safeguarding system, and to use the guidance to make sure that all professionals who work in your setting and who come into contact with children and families are alert to their needs and put those needs and wishes first. There is also a directive for all professionals to share appropriate information with others involved in the care of the child and to discuss any concerns about an individual child with colleagues and local authority children's social care services.

Research it

4.3 Recent changes

Look at the following document to learn about some of the recent changes:

www.gov.uk/government/uploads/system/uploads/attachment_data/file/683115/Changes_to_statutory_guidance-_Working_Together_to_Safeguard_Children.pdf

Your team's and other colleagues' roles and responsibilities

You and your staff have a responsibility and duty of care to act in order that the appropriate agencies can investigate and take any necessary action to protect a child and this will be set out in your organisation's child protection or safeguarding procedures.

When a child makes an allegation, you need to listen to them and ensure they feel that their allegations are taken seriously, they feel reassured and that you believe what they are saying. Following the information you have been given, you will need to decide what to do next (in consultation with other professionals) and whether further investigation is needed.

The DFES guidance entitled *What to Do If You're Worried a Child is being Abused – Summary* supplies useful information on how to deal with such a situation. It highlights the following points that everyone working with children and families should familiarise themselves with:

- Follow your organisation's procedures and protocols for promoting and safeguarding the welfare of children.
- Know who to contact in your organisation to express concerns about a child's welfare.
- Remember that an allegation of child abuse or neglect may lead to a criminal investigation, so do not do anything that may jeopardise a police investigation.
- Do not ask a child leading questions or attempt to investigate the allegations of abuse.
- Ensure that you are aware of who is responsible for making referrals.
- If you are the person who makes the referral, make sure you know who to contact in the police, health, education, school and children's social care.
- Record full information about the child at first point of contact, including name(s), address(es), gender, date of birth, name(s) of person(s) with parental responsibility (for consent purposes) and primary carer(s), if different.

- Keep this information up to date.
- Record in writing all concerns, discussions about the child, the decisions that were made and the reasons for those decisions.

If you are concerned in any way that a child is in danger, then you may want to take advice, for example from the NSPCC. While we do have concerns about protecting data and maintaining confidentiality you need to ensure that you protect the child in much the same way as you might a vulnerable adult, which may mean you have to share information with others. Ensure that you follow your policy about alerting children's services.

Others' responsibilities – e.g. those in receipt of care, carers, families, visitors

One of the key principles of the safeguarding directives from the government is that everybody has a responsibility with respect to safeguarding children and as such those who receive care, together with family, friends, carers and visitors, are required to be alert to the possibility of children being at risk of harm and should know what to do if they suspect this.

Your website information might include details of what staff and others can do should they suspect that a child is at risk in any way.

Research it

4.3 NSPCC

Access the NSPCC website and familiarise yourself with the guidance it gives on how to deal with abuse. How would you respond to evidence or concerns that a child or young person has been abused or harmed in the light of this new learning?

You could also go to www.nice.org.uk/guidance/cg89/evidence/full-guideline-243694621 and read the NICE guidelines on what to do if you suspect maltreatment.

Reflect on it

4.3 Actions to take

Describe the actions you would take if a child or young person alleged harm or abuse in line with the policies and procedures of your setting. What national and local requirements for reporting suspicions or disclosures of danger harm, abuse or exploitation of children and young people would you need to follow? What would your responsibilities be? Think about the various people we have discussed in this section, such as colleagues, carers, families, visitors. What are their responsibilities? Write a reflective account.

Evidence opportunity

4.3 National and local requirements for reporting suspicions or disclosures of danger, harm, abuse or exploitation of children and young people

Provide a written account explaining the requirements for reporting suspicions or disclosures of danger, harm, abuse or exploitation of children and young people including, for example:

- your role and responsibilities as a leader and manager
- your team's and other colleagues' roles and responsibilities
- others' responsibilities – e.g. those in receipt of care, carers, families, visitors.

Cover relevant requirements, including:

- Working Together to Safeguard Children (most recent version)
- Information Sharing: Advice for Practitioners Providing Safeguarding Services to Children, Young People, Parents and Carers.

AC 4.4 Tensions between maintaining the safety of team members and others with the duty of care to adults who are known to have abused children and young people

Here, you will be required to explain the potential tensions between maintaining the safety of team members and others with the duty of care to adults who are known to have abused children and young people.

While we may not share the same values or beliefs as some of the people in our care, we do have a duty to treat them with respect. Sometimes this may be difficult. Tension and conflict are likely when we are faced with individuals who have perpetrated crimes or acts we find difficult to understand or to come to terms with. This may make us less inclined to deal with people fairly or with kindness. However, our codes of practice demand that we approach each person in our care with a professional attitude.

The concept of unconditional positive regard (UPR) is one that we need to adopt. A term coined by Carl Rogers (1951), it describes the acceptance and support of a person regardless of what the person says or does and requires us to set aside our personal opinions and biases. This is used extensively in counselling therapy. Rogers believed that by approaching individuals in this way we can help them to accept and take responsibility for themselves. UPR is dependent on our ability to isolate the behaviour from the person. In other words, while we disagree with their behaviour, it is the person we are caring for. We may, for example, have a person in our care setting who has served a prison sentence for a crime against a child. Some staff may find it difficult to treat the person with compassion but as a manager you have to ensure the person is safe and is receiving the care required. It is important, therefore, to allow staff to talk to you about their feelings and to reassure them of their duties, of the **6Cs** in health and social care, and your support.

KEY TERM

6Cs are the values that underpin health and social care. These are care, compassion, commitment, communication, courage and competence.

Reflect on it

4.4 Unconditional positive regard (UPR)

Write a short reflective piece about how you would help staff understand the importance of UPR.

Evidence opportunity

4.4 Tensions between maintaining the safety of those with the duty of care to adults who are known to have abused children and young people

Provide a written account explaining the potential tensions between maintaining the safety of team members and others with the duty of care to adults who are known to have abused children and young people.

Reflect on it

4.4 Tensions between maintaining safety of team member and others and your duty of care to adults who have abused

Have you come across situations in your setting where you had a duty of care to someone who abused another individual or a child, but you had to balance your duty with maintaining the safety of staff and others? What did you do? What kinds of things did you have to take into account? If you have not been in this situation, what would you do? Discuss your thoughts with your assessor and make notes to document your discussion.

AC 4.5 Responsibility of the Designated Officer

Here, you will be required to explain the role of the Designated Officer.

The Care Act mentions the appointment of a Designated Adult Safeguarding Manager (DASM) responsible for the management of cases where allegations are made or concerns raised about a person, whether an employee, volunteer or student, with respect to safeguarding. This was adopted into policy and guidance and the Working Together to Safeguard Children (2015) document introduced the role of the Local Authority Designated Officer (LADO). The local authority DASM works closely with the children's services LADO to ensure sharing of information and development of best practice.

The LADO is an important role since it provides a point of contact throughout the case, from the initial allegation through to the conclusion of the proceedings, being available to discuss any concerns and to provide assistance.

However, in 2015 the Department of Health stated that the DASM role had never been a requirement and is seeking to cut the role following concerns raised by councils and other stakeholders that the role duplicated others already being carried out within authorities.

Community Care magazine (2015) stated that as of 2016 the government will no longer ask councils, NHS commissioners and police forces to appoint DASMs under the Care Act 2014. This move was welcomed by ADASS (the Association of Directors of Adult Social Services) (www.communitycare.co.uk/2015/11/03/government-scraps-designated-adult-safeguarding-manager-role/).

In the 'Care and Support statutory guidance: changes in March 2016', the Department of Health removed the need to have a DASM.

Research it

4.5 Up-to-date guidance

Go to www.gov.uk/government/publications/care-act-2014-part-1-factsheets/care-and-support-statutory-guidance-changes-in-march-2016 and familiarise yourself with the changed guidance.

Evidence opportunity

4.5 The role of the Designated Officer

Provide a written account explaining the role of the Designated Officer, or you could explain this to your assessor.

AC 4.6 Ways of critically evaluating practice

Here, you will be required to critically evaluate your leadership and management practice(s) in respect of protecting children and young people, to include any future recommendations.

It is important to review the way in which you manage and lead your team with respect to safeguarding children and young people and to take time to critically evaluate the way in which you manage this area of your work. While you may not have direct access to children in your care role and setting, they will be part of the families of the services users, visitors and your own staff. It is everybody's responsibility to ensure that children remain safe and there may be times when you recognise a need to invoke safeguarding procedures on behalf of a vulnerable child. You therefore have a duty to keep up to date with recommendations with respect to child safeguarding. In evaluating your role, you may ask yourself what you would do should you have concerns about the child of a member of staff. How might you handle the behaviour of a visitor towards a child in your setting? What would you do if you suspected that a member of your staff with two small children was the victim of domestic violence? It may be that your own manager can offer you support with this and arrange training for you to attend. You must, however, know how to approach such situations as a manager and leader in your setting.

Evidence opportunity

4.6 Critically evaluate leadership and management practice

Prepare a report for your assessor critically evaluating your leadership and management practice(s) in respect of protecting children and young people, including any future recommendations.

You could evaluate how you as a manager in an adult care setting protect children and young people. What are your strengths and weaknesses, for example?

After you have evaluated your practice, what recommendations will you make to improve your management of this area of work?

LO5 Promote health and safety in the workplace

AC 5.1 Reviewing health and safety policies and procedures to reflect current legal, national and local requirements

Here, you will be required to explain how health and safety policies and procedures are reviewed and updated, including relevant legal and national regulations.

KEY TERMS

Policy is a plan or principle of action proposed by an organisation, also known as guidelines or codes.

Procedures state how policies will be carried out or actioned in the setting.

Health and safety is ensuring people are safe and come to no harm in the workplace. This will inform policies such as Control of Substances Hazardous to Health (COSHH), infection control, safe handling of medicine, moving and handling, and fire safety.

The **Health and Safety Executive (HSE)** is the regulator or official supervisory body for the health, safety and welfare of people in work settings in the UK.

As a manager and leader in healthcare, your knowledge of the law and how it is translated into practice through **policy** and implemented by your staff must underpin your practice. Undoubtedly, you will already have a good working practice in the legal aspects of care work, but it is wise to revisit this from time to time.

In your role as manager you will need to ensure you offer strong induction activities and training for staff. Staff need to understand their roles and responsibilities with regard to **health and safety** record keeping and reporting and must also be aware of the necessity of complying with policies, **procedures** and practice. Any breaches must be dealt with effectively and quickly to avoid unsafe practice. By monitoring compliance, ensuring that checks / audits take place and that risk assessments are updated you will be practising safely with respect to this part of your management role.

Relevant legal and national regulations

Under the Health and Social Care Act 2012 (and mentioned in the 2014 Care Act) the CQC is the lead inspection and enforcement body for safety and quality of treatment and care matters involving service users in receipt of a health or adult social care service from a provider registered with the CQC.

The Health and Safety Executive (HSE) and local authorities are the lead inspection and enforcement bodies for health and safety matters involving service users who are in receipt of a health or care service from providers not registered with the CQC.

The process recognises that certain bodies may be more appropriate to deal with specific cases. So, for example, the CQC will be called to investigate an incident where a service user is seriously injured or dying after being physically restrained by staff, but the HSE and LA may be asked to investigate a manual handling injury to an employee.

All the laws will be enshrined in the policies and procedures you are required to follow in your workplace. A variety of relevant laws will be covered.

Policies set out the arrangements you have for complying with the law and procedures and identify what you need to do in order to implement the policy. As a manager, one of your roles is to ensure that staff are aware of the importance of carrying out practice according to policy. Failure to do so can have major consequences for the client, the organisation and the member of staff, as we shall see in the next section.

The Health and Safety at Work Act

The Health and Safety at Work Act 1974 (HASAWA) is the main piece of UK health and safety legislation. It places a duty on all employers 'to ensure, so far as is reasonably practicable, the health, safety and welfare at work' of all their employees. Additionally, it requires:

- 'The safe operation and maintenance of the working environment, plant (equipment) and systems
- maintenance of safe access and egress to the workplace
- safe use, handling and storage of dangerous substances
- adequate training of staff to ensure health and safety
- adequate welfare provisions for staff at work.'
- written policies to be in place.

Source: www.hse.gov.uk/legislation/trace.htm

Management of Health and Safety at Work Regulations (1999)

These **regulations** further highlight and detail in greater depth what employers are required to do to manage health and safety under HASAWA. The main requirement is the need to carry out a risk assessment. Employers with five or more employees need to record the significant findings of the risk assessment.

Other regulations to be followed

Table 8.2 outlines some examples of responsibilities. These are just examples and your job spec/agreed ways of working will offer more information. It will be up to you and your setting to be aware of your full duties and responsibilities with regard to legislation.

KEY TERM

Regulation is a rule or order which is underpinned by law. In health care settings, apart from those concerned with health and safety care, regulations with respect to health protection and control of disease are also available.

Table 8.2 Legislation, purpose, practice and examples of your responsibilities.

Legislation	Purpose	Practice: examples of your responsibilities
The Care Act 2014	The act will help to improve people's independence and wellbeing.	Local authorities must provide or arrange services that help prevent people developing needs for care and support, or delay people deteriorating such that they would need ongoing care and support. The responsibilities of the manager are, for example, to ensure that your staff are operating fully in line with the Care Act through the policies developed in house and that they are trained accordingly.
Health and Safety (First Aid) Regulations 1981	To ensure that everybody has access to immediate first-aid care in the workplace.	To maintain first-aid training of designated first aiders and to supply resources for first aid.
Mental Health Act 1983	The MHA allows compulsory action to be taken, where necessary, to ensure that people with mental health disorders get the care and treatment they need for their own health or safety or for the protection of other people.	Staff need to be aware of the rights of individuals under this act and the choices the service user has.
Mental Capacity Act 2005	The MCA (2005) provides a legal framework for acting and making decisions on behalf of adults who lack capacity to make particular decisions for themselves.	To ensure that staff are fully informed of issues such as informed consent and legal application. This should be clearly stated in job descriptions and contracts of work.
Electricity at Work Regulations 1989	To minimise the risk due to electricity in the workplace.	To maintain upkeep and ensure regular safety checks are made. As a manager, you will be required to keep records of regular testing that is undertaken.
Food Safety Act 1990	To minimise the risk due to food handling in the workplace, such as contamination. To minimise the risk due to moving and handling food.	Ensure any hazards are identified and controlled. Ensure good personal hygiene procedures are upheld.

Legislation	Purpose	Practice: examples of your responsibilities
Food Hygiene Regulations 2006	To show how to identify and control food safety risks in the process of preparing and selling food and set out basic hygiene principles.	Staff who handle food are required to undertake training and food hygiene courses so as their manager you will need to ensure compliance with this.
Food Information Regulations (FIR) 2014	To combine existing rules on general food labelling and nutrition into a single regulation to enable consumers to make an informed choice.	All staff must be trained in checking for any allergens contained in the food served in the setting. Staff need to be aware of the contents of the food that is served in order to comply with service users' choice.
Manual Handling Operations Regulations 1992 (MHOR)	To reduce the risk of injury in manual handling.	A risk assessment for manual handling, moving and handling must be in place and monitored. You must ensure staff are trained in moving and handling protocols.
Lifting Operations and Lifting Equipment Regulations (LOLER)	Businesses and organisations whose employees use lifting equipment are subject to these regulations (LOLER), which place duties on organisations that own or operate lifting equipment to ensure that any lifting operation must be planned by a competent person, supervised and carried out safely. The equipment must also be maintained regularly, with records being kept of all examinations and defects reported.	Staff are required to undergo manual handling training to include use of lifting equipment on an annual basis. As their manager, you will be required to ensure that staff are compliant with the training and the use of the equipment.
Workplace (Health, Safety and Welfare) Regulations 1992	To minimise the risk due to working conditions in the workplace.	Ensure that standards for heating, lighting, sanitation and building upkeep are maintained.
Personal Protective Equipment at Work Regulations 1992 (PPE)	To minimise the risk of cross-infection in the workplace.	To ensure staff are aware of infection-control procedures and are trained in dealing with potential cross-infection. To supply work wear and PPE. As a manager, your role is to ensure staff comply with infection control procedures. There should be regular spot checks as well as annual training to ensure infection risk is kept to a minimum.
Reporting on Injuries, Diseases and Dangerous Occurrences Regulations 1995 (RIDDOR)	Ensure that procedures are in place for the reporting of injury and illness to the HSE or local authority where appropriate.	Maintain the policy in the workplace and ensure that accident forms and reports are in place.
Provision and Use of Work Equipment Regulations 1998 (PUWER)	Risks due to the use of equipment must be minimised.	Train staff in use of equipment and ensure equipment is maintained and safe to use. This links with the LOLER regulations.
Data Protection Act 1998	Ensure that personal information is kept private and safe.	Check policy on confidentiality and arrange to undertake regular risk assessments.
General Data Protection Regulation (GDPR) 2018	Replaces the Data Protection Act 1998.	Replaced the Data Protection Act 1998 and redefined how organisations approach data. See Unit 502 for more information on GDPR.
Management of Health and Safety at Work Regulations 1999 (MHSWR) Amended 2003 and 2006.	This revokes and replaces the 1992 regulations of the same title. The 2003 amendment allowed claims to be brought against employees by third parties who were affected by their work activity, e.g. members of the public. The 2006 amendment changed the civil liability provisions in the regulations so as to exclude the right of third parties to take legal action against employees for contraventions of their duties under these regulations.	Carry out risk assessments to minimise any risks to safety with respect to fire and safe handling of substances hazardous to health. Fire safety training is an annual process and you as the manager need to ensure staff are up to date with the training.

Legislation	Purpose	Practice: examples of your responsibilities
Control of Substances Hazardous to Health Regulations 2002 (COSHH)	Minimise the risk from the use of substances that may be hazardous to health.	Carry out risk assessments and ensure staff are trained in use of hazardous substances.
Regulatory Reform (Fire Safety) 2005	Minimise fire hazards.	Regular checks of fire-safety procedures in the workplace.
Corporate Manslaughter and Homicide Act 2007	If a death occurs in suspicious circumstances, then an organisation may be convicted of negligence.	Ensure staff are aware of duty of care and are following policy.
Health and Social Care Act 2008, 2012	Highlighted significant measures to modernise and integrate health and social care.	The changes that were introduced in 2012 mean that practitioners need to understand the reforms and how these may impact them and their service users. As a manager, you need to be aware of the changes and be able to direct staff to better understanding.
Human Medicines Regulations (2012)	Replaced most of the Medicines Act 1968 and 200 statutory instruments with a simplified set of rules. The new regulations set out a regime for the authorisation of medicinal products for human use; for the manufacture, import, distribution, sale and supply of those products; for their labelling and advertising.	Ensure a medicines policy reflects the law and staff are continually trained and updated in this role. You as manager are responsible for ensuring that medication is safely stored and administered. There are different policies operating in different settings and agency staff may need to be made aware of this. For example, controlled drugs differ. In some settings Oramorph is not classed as a controlled drug and is stored in the usual drug trolley. This will make a difference to who may administer the drug and how it is administered.
Equality Act 2010	Brought together over 116 separate pieces of legislation into one single act that provides a legal framework to protect the rights of individuals and advance equality of opportunity for all. The main pieces of legislation that have merged are: • Equal Pay Act 1970 • Sex Discrimination Act 1975 • Race Relations Act 1976 • Disability Discrimination Act 1995 • Employment Equality (Religion or Belief) Regulations 2003 • Employment Equality (Sexual Orientation) Regulations 2003 • Employment Equality (Age) Regulations 2006 • Equality Act 2006, Part 2 • Equality Act (Sexual Orientation) Regulations 2007	To ensure policies and procedures reflect the act and staff are aware of duties of care with respect to equality and diversity. This also relates to safeguarding as you will need to ensure service users are treated fairly and given safe treatment regardless of any differences.
Health and Safety Information for Employees Regulations (1989)	These set out the general duties which employers have towards employees and members of the public, and employees have to themselves and to each other.	Ensure that staff are aware of the arrangements for implementing the health and safety measures identified by the risk assessment. Be aware of emergency procedures. Have clear information and training. Be aware of the need to work together with other employers in the workplace. HASAWA risk assessment – managing health and safety requires you to control the risks in your workplace. There should be audits and reviews of the risk assessments. See LO2 for more information on risk assessments.

Research it

5.1 Legislation, policies and procedures

Look at the legislation listed in Table 8.2 and for each one think about your setting. Find out the purpose and related policies and procedures in your setting; the practice of your responsibilities; and examples of how legislation is implemented in your setting.

Evidence opportunity

5.1 Reviewing health and safety policies and procedures to reflect current legal, national and local requirements

Provide a written account explaining how health and safety policies and procedures are reviewed and updated, including how the policies cover relevant legal and national regulations.

How do you review health and safety policies and procedures to reflect current, legal, national and local requirements?

AC 5.2 Supporting all team members to understand and be able to apply the policies and procedures in their day-to-day work

Here, you will be required to explain how health and safety information is disseminated to all colleagues, to include any agency staff and non-care staff.

Health and safety training is an annual event, with all staff requiring updates. As their manager, it is important to establish that staff can access the training and also that you are recording that activity. With respect to staff who are not regularly on site, there should be displays of health and safety legislation available to them and they must be made aware of what is expected of them via a mini induction session that should be undertaken with them at the start of a shift. You may also wish to ensure they are trained and check their credentials when they arrive at the setting.

See AC 4.2 for more information.

Evidence opportunity

5.2 Supporting all team members to understand and be able to apply the policies and procedures

Provide a written account explaining how health and safety information is disseminated to all colleagues, including any agency staff and non-care staff. How do you ensure that all staff are aware of the policies in place with respect to health and safety? How do you support all team members to understand and be able to apply the policies and procedures in their day-to-day work?

AC 5.3 Applying policies and procedures

Here, you will be required to critically evaluate the application of health and safety policies and procedures in your workplace in respect of the topics we discuss in this section.

Safeguarding

Care providers must provide a safe environment for their service users and a health and safety incident may overlap safeguarding protocols. For example, if a service user is harmed in an incident where manual handling equipment was faulty or they were scalded in a hot bath, while these are both reportable under the HSE guidance there is also a safeguarding issue to be answered. In this case, the HSE may wish to further investigate the incident and include the local safeguarding team. As a manager, you will need to know about the policies and procedures for safeguarding and ensure staff are taught and trained in these.

Staff training and development

Not only is the need to train staff in health and safety a legal requirement for all employers, it is also part of the Care Certificate regulated by the CQC. Although settings may differ in what they offer in care, health and safety training is mandatory and some certifications require updating annually.

Person-centred care

Person-centred care means ensuring that individuals/ service users are at the centre of all the care they receive and that care that is given is based on their needs, wishes and preferences. With respect to safety, we need to ensure that any care we give protects not only the physical state of the person but also the mental and emotional state. We need to show respect for each individual and ensure they are treated ethically and with dignity. Again, as a manager, you will need to ensure that your staff are aware of how they can apply a person-centred approach when they care for individuals.

Safety

People in care and undergoing treatment in hospital are vulnerable and we must ensure that we take steps to reduce risks to their safety and address any environmental issues that may pose dangers to them and others.

Risk management practices, leadership and management practice

One of your responsibilities as a manager is to ensure the health and safety of your workplace so you must control the risks to those who use services, their carers and families, as well as staff. By giving thought to what might cause harm to people and conducting risk assessments, you can ensure that you are taking reasonable steps to prevent harm. You are required to carry out risk assessments in/for your setting by law.

Compliance with the Safety Representative and Safety Committee Regulations (1977) and the Health and Safety Consultations with Employees Regulations (1996) (www.hse.gov.uk) is part of the employer's role and, as a manager, you need to ensure that everyone in your team understands that they are responsible for their own safety and also that of anybody with whom they interact in the workplace, and that staff are aware of their responsibility when it comes to compliance with the legal aspects of health and safety.

Future practice

It is important to keep up to date with changes to the legislation surrounding health and safety, which is why annual updates need to form part of your training schedule.

In order to demonstrate good practice as a manager, you can also do the following, for example:

- **Make health and safety and safeguarding a part of the agenda**: Health and safety and safeguarding should be a regular agenda item for your team meeting. In this way, staff can be updated on training opportunities, risk assessments and their outcomes, and general safety in the workplace issues. A poster giving details of the staff who are designated safety officers and first aiders is useful since it displays relevant information for staff and visitors to the area.

- **Be a good role model**: By demonstrating good practice in a consistent manner, you will inspire others to follow your lead. For example, by ensuring that you take part in regular training updates for health and safety and manual handling with the staff you will be sending positive messages with respect to good practice.

- **Be aware of your responsibility to staff and others**: You need to ensure that visitors to the site are aware of the systems in place for fire safety, infection control and COSHH. You might also want to include information about how challenging behaviour will be dealt with should this occur.

As a manager, it is important that you monitor that staff are complying with the policies and procedures the setting has in place with respect to health, safety and risk management. Care setting failures have shown that although these policies may have been in place, lack of staff compliance led to poor performance and quality of care suffered.

Evidence opportunity

5.3 Applying policies and procedures

Provide a written account critically evaluating the application of health and safety policies and procedures in the workplace in respect of the topics we have discussed in this section.

Reflect on it

5.3 Applying policies and procedures

How do you ensure the application of health and safety policies and procedures in the workplace in respect of the following happening in your setting?

Go through each of the headings in turn and justify how they are used.

- **Safeguarding**: e.g. look at incidents where an accident has been reported, then determine how it impacted upon safeguarding. What was done about it and how might it have been prevented?

- **Staff training and development**: e.g. look at your staff training plans and evaluate how they might be improved. What is good about the training on offer and what gaps might need to be filled?

- **Person-centred care**: e.g. determine how staff perceive person-centred care and demonstrate that patients are safe. What might be improved?

- **Safety**: e.g. look critically at the accidents that are reported in your setting, then determine how you might make the place safer. What needs to be introduced to ensure these accidents do not reoccur?

- **Risk management practices**: e.g. look at the last risk assessment that was carried out. Was it useful? How might you improve it?

- **Leadership and management practice**: e.g. how are you ensuring that staff comply with health and safety legislation and, as a manager, what have you put into place to check and audit this practice?

- **Future practice**: what plans are in place to ensure that you have a safe environment for the future?

Legislation

See ACs 1.1, 1.2, 3.2 and 5.1 for information on legislation relevant to this unit.

Suggestions for using the activities	
This table summarises all the activities in the unit that are relevant to each assessment criterion.	
Here, we also suggest other, different methods that you may want to use to present your knowledge and skills by using the activities.	
These are just suggestions, and you should refer to the Introduction section at the start of the book, and more importantly the City & Guilds specification, and your assessor, who will be able to provide more guidance on how you can evidence your knowledge and skills.	
When you need to be observed during your assessment, this can be done by your assessor, or your manager can provide a witness testimony.	

Assessment criteria and accompanying activities	Suggested methods to show your knowledge/skills
LO1 Understand safeguarding legislation, local and national policies	
1.1 Research it (page 253)	Write down your findings and thoughts.
1.1 Evidence opportunity (page 253)	Show your assessor, or include in your portfolio, evidence of key legislation that applies to safeguarding in adult care services in your management and leadership role.
1.1 Reflect on it (page 254)	Provide a reflective account.
1.2 Research it (page 257)	Write notes documenting your findings.
1.2 Reflect on it (page 258)	Write down your thoughts.
1.2 Evidence opportunity (page 258)	Write down your responses to the activity. You could also explain to your assessor current national and local guidance and agreed ways of working in respect of safeguarding in adult care services.
1.3 Evidence opportunity (page 259)	Provide a written account analysing how current legislation, guidance and agreed ways of working impact on your day-to-day leadership and management practice within your work setting to include the areas we have covered in this section for example.
1.3 Reflect on it (page 259)	Provide a reflective account and address the questions in the activity.
LO2 Lead the effective application and review of safeguarding policies, procedures and protocols	
2.1 Evidence opportunity (page 260)	Provide evidence to your assessor of how your policies and procedures to support safeguarding and whistle blowing reflect national and local requirements and how you review these to ensure they are current.
2.1 Reflect on it (page 260)	Make notes/write down your responses to this activity.
2.2 Evidence opportunity (page 262)	Provide evidence to your assessor of how others are involved in reviewing and/or updating the adult care service safeguarding policies and procedures, including those in receipt of care and support, employees and others.
2.2 Reflect on it (page 262)	Provide a reflective account.
2.3 Evidence opportunity (page 262)	Provide evidence to your assessor of how you ensure that safeguarding information is disseminated, passed on or circulated safely to employees, non-care staff, those in receipt of care and support services, e.g. families, carers.
2.4 Evidence opportunity (page 264)	Provide a written account explaining how to investigate and manage individual and/or group allegations where danger, harm or abuse are suspected or disclosed. Make sure you address each of the topics we have discussed in AC 2.4 and think about how these apply to your practice and the practice in your setting.

→

Suggestions for using the activities	
2.5 Reflect on it (page 265)	Write a reflective account.
2.5 Evidence opportunity (page 265)	Provide a written account critically evaluating how you have supported or would support others who have had a disclosure of alleged/suspected abuse made to them, and what they would do if a colleague had an allegation made against them.
2.5 Reflect on it (page 265)	Provide a written account.
2.6 Research it (page 266)	Write down your findings.
2.6 Evidence opportunity (page 266)	Provide a written piece analysing and critically evaluating lessons learned from a recent national or local inquiry or Serious Case Review (SCR), showing how these have brought changes to local or national safeguarding requirements in adult care services.
2.7 Reflect on it (page 267)	Write down your responses to the activity.
2.7 Evidence opportunity (page 268)	Provide a written account critically evaluating the effectiveness of safeguarding and whistle-blowing policies, procedures and protocols. Show your assessor how you effectively disseminate and implement safeguarding policies and procedures and consider the topics we have covered in this section.
2.7 Reflect on it (page 268)	Look at the processes that promote safeguarding and whistle blowing in your workplace and reflect on how effective they are. Provide a written account.
LO3 Understand restrictive practice and potential impact	
3.1 Evidence opportunity (page 270)	Provide a written account explaining the meanings of the terms, or you could explain these to your assessor.
3.2 Reflect on it (page 271)	Provide a reflective account.
3.2 Evidence opportunity (page 271)	Write a piece reflecting on your understanding and application of the legal requirements and implications relating to restrictive practice in your adult care setting and adult care settings generally. Make sure you refer to the case law and codes of practice we have discussed in this section.
3.3 Evidence opportunity (page 272)	Provide a written account critically analysing the potential impact and outcomes of applying restrictive practice for those in receipt of care and support services, for all staff, and for others such as families and carers, and the impact if restrictive practice is used incorrectly. Or you could discuss this with your assessor and provide a critical analysis.
3.4 Evidence opportunity (page 273)	Demonstrate to your assessor how person-centred practice can help to minimise the use of restrictive practices, including the areas we have discussed in this section.
3.4 Reflect on it (page 273)	Provide a reflective account.
3.5 Evidence opportunity (page 274)	Provide a written account explaining how team members are made aware of the policies and procedures of the setting to include how restrictive practice would be managed by the registered manager, the deputy and others including team members, supervisors and volunteers.
3.6 Evidence opportunity (page 275)	Show your assessor you can work with service users, family members and colleagues to adopt a positive approach to risk assessment, which covers the areas we have looked at in this section.
3.7 Evidence opportunity (page 276)	Show your assessor how you actively follow policies and procedures and show how you evaluate their effectiveness in respect of risk and management practices, with consideration of the topics we have discussed in this section.

Suggestions for using the activities	
LO4 Understand the role and responsibilities of adult care practitioners in ensuring the safety and wellbeing of children and young people	
4.1, 4.2 Evidence opportunity (page 278)	Write an account explaining why you need to be aware of and understand national and local requirements, protocols and procedures when working in partnership with other local agencies in relation to safeguarding children and young people, including the topics we have covered in this section. Also explain how all team members are supported to understand their role in safeguarding children and young people from danger, harm, abuse and/or exploitation, including how relevant and appropriate information is disseminated to new staff, agency staff and non-care staff.
4.1, 4.2 Reflect on it (page 278)	Provide a reflective account.
4.3 Research it (page 279)	Write down your findings.
4.3 Research it (page 280)	Provide a written account of your findings.
4.3 Evidence opportunity (page 280)	Provide a written explanation.
4.3 Reflect on it (page 280)	Write a reflective account.
4.4 Reflect on it (page 281)	Write a reflective piece about how you would help staff understand the importance of unconditional positive regard (UPR).
4.4 Evidence opportunity (page 281)	Provide a written explanation, or you could explain this to your assessor.
4.4 Reflect on it (page 281)	Provide a reflective account.
4.5 Research it (page 281)	Write down your findings.
4.5 Evidence opportunity (page 281)	Provide a written account explaining the role of the Designated Officer, or you could explain this to your assessor.
4.6 Evidence opportunity (page 282)	Prepare a report for your assessor critically evaluating your leadership and management practice(s) in respect of protecting children and young people, including any future recommendations. You could also discuss your critical evaluation with your assessor.
LO5 Promote health and safety in the workplace	
5.1 Research it (page 286)	Write down findings from your research.
5.1 Evidence opportunity (page 286)	Provide a written account explaining how health and safety policies and procedures are reviewed and updated, including how the policies cover relevant legal and national regulations. You could also explain this to your assessor.
5.2 Evidence opportunity (page 286)	Provide a written account explaining how health and safety information is disseminated to all colleagues, including any agency staff and non-care staff. You could also discuss this with your assessor.
5.3 Evidence opportunity (page 287)	Provide a written critical evaluation.
5.3 Reflect on it (page 287)	Provide a reflective account.

References

ADSS (2005) *Safeguarding Adults – A National Framework*. Accessed from www.adass.org.uk/AdassMedia/stories/Publications/Guidance/safeguarding.pdf

Bellis, M.A., Hughes, K., Perkins, C. and Bennett, A. (2012) *Protecting People*. Liverpool: Department of Health.

CSCI (2007) *Rights, Risks and Restraints: An exploration into the use of restraint in the care of older people*. London: CSCI.

CSCI (2008) *Raising Voices: Views on safeguarding adults*. London: CSCI.

Department of Health and the Home Office (2000) *No Secrets: Guidance on developing and implementing multi-agency policies and procedures to protect vulnerable adults from abuse*. London: DoH and the Home Office. Accessed from www.dh.gov.uk/en/Publicationsandstatistics/Publications/PublicationsPolicyAndGuidance/DH_4008486

Department of Health (2007) *Independence, Choice and Risk: A guide to best practice in supported decision making*. London: HMSO.

Department of Health (2010) *Nothing Ventured, Nothing Gained: Risk guidance for dementia*. London: TSO.

Department of Health (2012) *Promoting Health – A public health approach to violence prevention for England*. Leeds. DoH.

Department of Health (2014) *A Positive and Proactive Workforce. A guide to workforce development for commissioners and employers seeking to minimise the use of restrictive practices in social care and health*. Leeds: DoH, www.skillsforcare.org.uk

Dupre, C. (2011) What does dignity mean in a legal context? The *Guardian*, March.

Gov.UK (2015) *Working Together to Safeguard Children. A guide to inter-agency working to safeguard and promote the welfare of children*. London: TSO.

Home Office, The (2014) *Multi Agency Working and Information Sharing Project Final Report*. London: TSO.

McKibbin, J., Walton, A. and Mason, L. (2008) *Leadership and Management in Health and Social Care for NVQ/SVQ Level 4*. London: Heinemann.

Morgan, S. (2004) Positive risk-taking: an idea whose time has come, *Health Care Risk Report*, 10(10): 18–19.

NHS Digital, NHS Workforce Statistics – March 2017, Provisional statistics.

Rogers, C. (1951) *Client-centered Therapy: Its current practice, implications and theory*. Boston, MA: Houghton Mifflin.

Titterton, M. (2005) *Risk and Risk Taking in Health and Social Care*. London: Jessica Kingsley Publishers.

Titterton, M. (2010) *Positive Risk Taking*. Edinburgh: Hale.

Further reading and useful resources

Owen, T. and Meyer, J. (2009) *Minimising the Use of Restraint in Care Homes: Challenges, dilemmas and positive approaches*. London: SCIE.

The West Sussex Adult Safeguarding Board (WSASB) (2014) Orchid View Serious Case Review.

Websites

Community Care www.communitycare.co.uk/2015/11/03/government-scraps-designated-adult-safeguarding-manager-role

Skills for Care www.skillsforcare.org.uk/Topics/Restrictive-practices/Restrictive-practices.aspx

Managing self

About this unit

In your role, you will need to know how you can most effectively manage yourself and your own behaviour as well as effectively manage others. In this unit, you will understand the key principles and behaviours that are required to effectively manage yourself and your wellbeing. You will consider different strategies which you can use and which you can identify through self-reflection and reflective practice. This will include exploring ways in which you manage stress and pressures that you will face when managing a care service.

You will explore the importance of self-awareness, and how you can manage your personal and professional behaviour in your role. You will explore your own professional development needs and see how these affect and impact the work you do. As a manager, you will manage various workloads and you will also learn about workload management here, as well as how you can undertake professional development.

Learning outcomes

By the end of this unit you will:

1 Understand the importance of self-awareness
2 Manage personal and professional behaviour
3 Manage workloads
4 Undertake professional development

Getting started

Before you study the unit, think about the following:

- How do your belief systems and experiences affect your current work practice as a manager?
- How do your professional actions reflect a high standard of personal integrity?
- What is meant by work–life balance and how is this achieved or how do/can you achieve this?
- What opportunities for professional development are there to support your role?

What is self-awareness?

For Goleman (1995), self-awareness is about knowing our own emotions and recognising those feelings as they happen. So, we may feel angry at something somebody has said, but as a manager and leader, showing that anger inappropriately will have a negative effect on relationships.

Social awareness refers to the empathy and concern we have for others' feelings; the acknowledgement that people under threat in an organisation may show aggression and anger. Decisions affecting people's jobs may have to be made, and the manager who sees only the task in hand is failing to acknowledge the effect this is having on those at risk and those who have to continue to work in such a climate of change.

Research it

1.1 Goleman

Goleman was famous for his theories about emotional intelligence and this links to self-awareness. Undertake a search on Goleman's theory and write a short account to show how it can help us to become more self-aware.

LO1 Understand the importance of self-awareness

AC 1.1 Emotions affecting own behaviour and behaviour of others

Here, you will need to critically evaluate how your own emotions affect your behaviour and the behaviour of others.

1.1 What do we mean by self-awareness?

Can Goleman's theory help us to manage others in a more effective manner? Think about what you know about yourself and the qualities and strengths you possess. Reflect also upon your limitations. How can this knowledge help you to grow as a person and as a manager?

How your emotions affect your behaviour and the behaviour of others, your role as leader and manager, and your style

What sort of mood are you in today? Have you come to work feeling happy, sad, angry or frustrated? How do you think the way you feel will affect how you work and behave?

The way you feel and the emotions you have will affect the decisions you make and as a manager working with vulnerable people, sometimes challenging people and staff, you need to be aware of how your emotions affect your work.

Emotions give way to, or influence, your feelings and thoughts. For example, think about how you feel when you are talking to a difficult member of staff or you are required to address a problem with a visitor. This might cause you to feel anxious and it is good to recognise what is going on for you and how you are feeling at this time. Do you allow the anxiety to get the better of you so that in future you try to avoid the situation? The emotion you are feeling at this time and the anxiety that goes with it are worth investigating and you should reflect on how you are feeling. As a result of thinking about, reflecting and critically evaluating how your emotions affect your behaviour, and the behaviour of others, you will develop self-awareness. For example, is the anxiety a reaction to the person or to your own feelings and emotions? Perhaps you fear failure in this situation, which gives rise to anxiety? Perhaps it is not the person causing the anxiety but the situation you are in.

Dealing with difficult situations when working with colleagues, service users, other professionals, family/carers

At some point in your work life, you will have difficult conversations with difficult people and this can be a challenge. It may be that you find it hard to talk to some people who do not share your values and beliefs, and this might be colleagues, individuals you provide care and support to, other professionals such as GPs or doctors, and families and carers of the individuals. For example, if you value diversity and are highly tolerant of people's

beliefs and religious views it may be quite difficult to talk to somebody who lacks this. This can sometimes make situations uncomfortable but as a manager you will need to overcome this and manage the emotions you experience in a professional and respectful way.

Dealing with difficult situations

The things we value and believe are sometimes tested when we are working in difficult situations. For example, in a busy environment when resources are low and demand on your service is high you may find you are unable to give the care service users require and this may go against your beliefs about healthcare and rights of individuals. The current crisis the NHS is facing in accident and emergency departments around the country is showing clearly how difficult situations at work affect staff in many ways. In high-pressured environments, emotions may run high and this can affect the behaviour of those working in the area as well as the behaviour of others such as those in receipt of care and support and other professionals, family/carers.

1.1 Difficult work situations

Do some research around some of the issues affecting adult care currently, and some of the difficult work situations that may arise as a result. You may find either of the following links a useful starting point:

- www.theguardian.com/social-care-network/2018/jan/03/social-care-2018-future-workforce
  This article highlights a green paper on care and support for older people (2018) in which the government will set out plans to improve care and support for older people and tackle the challenge of an ageing population.

- https://publications.parliament.uk/pa/ld201617/ldselect/ldnhssus/151/151.pdf
  This website takes you to a government paper on the long-term sustainability of the NHS and an Adult Social Care document, which describes the changes needed to address failure in the NHS and adult care.

- www.bbc.co.uk/news/uk-scotland-44991592

Managing positive and negative emotions within yourselves and others

What is a positive or a negative emotion? If we feel happiness, joy, love and contentment we are showing positive emotions, and these affect the way in which we address and relate to others and the way in which we carry out our work. Not only do we feel good, but others in our company are also likely to feel similarly. Negative emotions, on the other hand, like sadness, anger, or even being self-critical and fearful, can be difficult, even painful at times, and when brought into the workplace can really have a negative effect on others around us too. It is, therefore, important to be aware of the impact that emotions can have and manage them in a way so that they do not impact negatively on you and others.

Sometimes, the emotions we feel, particularly in pressured situations, are experienced as stress and at times you need to be aware of the staff you manage and how they are experiencing their workloads. For example, people behave differently and approach tasks in different ways. For some, a project they have to complete will trigger anxiety until it is completed. They may constantly be on edge until they have completed the task. For others, the stress may become apparent as the deadline approaches, but this may also have the effect of motivating them to get on and do the task. Recognising how emotions affect your staff will be a real help in your decision making.

Reflect on it

1.1 The effects of emotions

How do your emotions affect your behaviour? Think about an emotion that crops up in situations at work, such as anxiety or anger, and write a short reflective piece about how it affects your behaviour.

Evidence opportunity

1.1 How your emotions affect your own behaviour and behaviour of others

Critically evaluate how your emotions affect your behaviour and the behaviour of others in respect of:

- your leadership and management role and style
- dealing with difficult situations when working with colleagues, those in receipt of care and support, other professionals, family/carers
- managing positive and negative emotions within yourself and others.

Have a professional discussion with your assessor to critically evaluate how your own emotions affect your behaviour and the behaviour of others in respect of the topics we have discussed in this section. You might like to record or document your discussion.

To critically analyse, you will need to ask questions about the emotions you are experiencing, how they affect you, and how this compares to how others experience these emotions.

AC 1.2 Values, belief systems and experiences affecting working practice

Here, you will need to analyse your own value and belief systems which affect your working practices and how these have been shaped by various life experiences.

Our values and beliefs describe what we believe to be important and as such will influence the decisions we make in our life, our work and our behaviour. Sometimes, these values and beliefs support our decisions but on occasion they can cause conflict, and this may distress us. For example, if you are good at managing your time and value meeting deadlines you may become conflicted if you become too busy at work and find that this is becoming impossible to do.

Environmental factors

Where we are born and where we live may have some effect on the way our beliefs and values are formed. A child born in an overcrowded and deprived environment may be more prone to illness and, therefore, their education may suffer as a result and may shape the way in which they view their world and the choices they have in life. Your upbringing and the area and family environment in which you lived will have taught you your values and belief systems which you have brought to the way in which you work. You will also have been shaped by various experiences as you have grown up. For example, some areas of the country are poorly supplied with healthcare services and schools and this may affect the life chances of a child being brought up in such an area.

Countless governments have tried to tackle this so-called health postcode lottery but still it persists. A *Which?* analysis (www.which.co.uk/news/2018/04/which-reveals-nhs-care-funding-postcode-lottery/) found that the latest 2017–18 figures show huge differences in funding between regions when it comes to the proportion of patients whose care costs are fully funded. In your role as a manager in healthcare this is likely to affect the care that you can give.

Family/family relationships

The way in which we are introduced into the world by our family and our upbringing, together with the experiences we have had in life through our education and work, all help us to formulate our personal system of values and beliefs. We learn through our parents and through observation of what is happening around us about what we feel is 'good'. We are taught how to behave in a manner that is polite and acceptable to others in our family and in wider society. This will carry into our working lives and as managers we are likely to work alongside people who have very different values to ourselves. Your role in this respect is to ensure that we promote British values of respect, tolerance and democracy to ensure that we embed such values into the healthcare culture.

Social interactions including peers

As we grow older, the different social influences and interactions increase and our friends and peers may become more important to us. As you learn, meet new people and experience new things you could find some of your personal values are challenged and they may change to incorporate new thinking. In the healthcare setting this will affect not only our care workers but also the people who use the service and in our role as managers we need to ensure that we respect or even challenge the changes that may occur. For example, some people are divided on political issues such as those brought about by the Brexit vote and this may affect the way in which they view some groups in society.

Culture and religion(s)

Parents or caregivers in the early years and family culture help to influence beliefs, and this includes adopting a religion or certain cultural practices. Being exposed at a young age to a religious upbringing or traditions will affect our personal beliefs, and such exposure to the culture helps to shape our values.

The culture in which we are brought up also teaches us to value different things. For example, some cultures teach respect for the environment, which can directly influence personal belief about how we use natural resources. Some religions teach that modern medicine is to be avoided. Your culture and religion will influence the way in which you work and as a manager you need to be aware of differences of others and be tolerant of these.

Media

The internet, Facebook, Twitter, Instagram and other forms of media are all useful additions to the way in which we gain information. However, a rising concern has been the use of such media to target vulnerable individuals with the intention to 'radicalise' them or to persuade them to adopt increasingly extreme political, social or religious views. Additionally, 'fake news' has become an issue whereby news stories supported by little evidence, or often completely made up, are presented as fact. Violence is also a major part of what people may be seeing through the media and this can influence behaviour and change attitudes. As a manager in an adult care setting, it is important that you do not let your personal views that may have been influenced by the media affect your interactions with those you manage, colleagues, individuals you provide support to as well as others you work with. In addition, you must be acutely aware of how your staff are engaging with social media and ensure that they are not displaying unacceptable views or posting comments which may be considered inflammatory or damaging to others.

Education, professional career and working environment(s)/situations

In response to the media, and sometimes family influences, which may negatively affect the way in which children behave and their belief systems, education now has a wider remit via the 'Prevent' and safeguarding agendas to address these issues. The introduction of *Promoting fundamental British Values* in 2015 aims to promote respect for British law, democracy, mutual respect and tolerance for those from different beliefs and faiths and individual liberty (DfE, 2014). By being exposed in schools and colleges to the beliefs of others and to different attitudes and values, young people are being challenged to rethink their values and are exposed to alternative belief systems, which may offer wider choice and solutions. This sort of socialisation continues into the workplace, with employers in local authorities and working with people in healthcare, education and the justice system now bound to deliver the Prevent strategy, the government response to terrorism and radicalisation, to employees for their safety.

Such exposure to different points of view, values and beliefs of others can help us to analyse our own value and belief systems and help us to make sense of how they affect our working practices and how we live our lives. Your role will be to ensure that you are embedding the British Values into training of staff and into the ethos of the setting.

Reflect on it

1.2 How your values and beliefs have developed and/or changed through your working practice(s)

Think about a personal value you hold and try to trace it back to your very first experience of it. How did you acquire it?

What values and beliefs have changed as a result of your work and the exposure you have had to training? For example, think about something you have learned through the course of your work, which has made you question something you may have grown up believing.

Or you could list some examples of personal values you hold about the following:

- Environment family/family relationships
- Social interactions including your peers
- Culture
- Religion(s)
- Media
- Education
- Professional career and working environment(s)/ situations.

Think back to the first time in your life you were aware of them.

Think about how your values and beliefs have developed and/or changed through your working practice(s).

What changes have you made to your beliefs as a result of the work you now do?

Write a reflective account.

How your values and beliefs have developed and/or changed through working practice(s)

Perhaps you believe that all humans are equal or perhaps that men are superior to women. You may have a firm belief that 'what will be will be' and you are subject to whatever fate brings you. In other words, you take the view that there is no point in giving up smoking since you may well be subject to another condition anyway! Some universally accepted values highlight honesty and respect for others. It is possible that within your family you may have been brought up in a religion and, therefore, hold certain views about how you should live your life. We may also hold beliefs that certain groups of people are not to be trusted and these beliefs or stereotypes can affect us in our work. We make decisions about others at an unconscious level and because of the biases and stereotypes we may treat people in the workplace in different and less positive ways. We may find we prefer some people to others and unconsciously deal with them in a different manner. It may lead to poor decisions being made and different behaviours to some groups being displayed. Some organisations are challenging this and training their staff in 'unconscious bias', which addresses the negative attitudes we have about others but may fail to realise at a conscious level. By encouraging questioning of our beliefs through education we can start to develop our self-awareness and this can lead to changes in attitudes and bias.

Indeed, as you have grown and lived through many new experiences you may have started to question particular views and values and could have changed your outlook. By paying more attention to how you feel about something, or by reflecting on experiences and being truthful to yourself about how you feel, you can start to become a more self-aware person. This process can then help you to start to choose your own values rather than merely reflecting those of others and those you learned in childhood.

You may experience this sort of process within your career as a healthcare worker. Having your values and beliefs challenged is not always a comfortable process, but it can be very liberating. For example, if you have always held the belief that certain groups of people cannot be trusted then a challenge to that belief can be quite uncomfortable. This might lead you to either dismiss the challenge and continue with your former belief or you may challenge it yourself. You can do this by analysing what caused you to believe this in the first place and where and how you learned it. You may also ask yourself if it is valid or whether there has been a time when this belief was not true. You may even find that you have a close friend who is part of this particular group!

The answers you come up with will help you to see that the belief is not as strong as you thought it was and you can then start to change it, or it may be that your belief is strengthened.

AC 1.3 Socialisation processes that inform values and beliefs

Here, you will analyse the impact of different socialisation factors in relation to the development of values and beliefs.

Socialisation, values and beliefs

Socialisation is the process through which we are taught the norms, customs, roles, values and beliefs of our society. If we want our society to function well, then we need to find our place within it. We are also guided by family, teachers, the community and the media to a certain extent about these norms, values, beliefs and how we are to live.

Primary socialisation occurs from birth where we learn from our family and significant others such as caregivers, teachers and peers. Secondary socialisation occurs throughout life, and we may change as a result of the influences of new situations, places or people we encounter whose norms, customs, assumptions and values may differ to those we hold.

Working in the adult care service is a privilege. We are caring for vulnerable groups of people who, for example being disabled by illness, find themselves in less than satisfactory circumstances. If you have ever been seriously ill and in need of expert help you will appreciate this. Being at the receiving end of care can be quite distressing and may be made all the more so if the person delivering the care is less than sympathetic and does not appear to value you. What is it about this particular 'carer' that makes them treat others without respect?

Our behaviour is a direct result of our personal values that guide us. The decisions we make are based on knowledge, morals and ethics. The values we have learned throughout our lives become part of our personality and make-up. When we are faced with a decision or have a choice to make, we will always look to what we value the most in the making of that decision. If we value comfort over fashion, then we may choose the more sensible shoe when deciding what to buy. That's a simple example. Things become a little more demanding when we are making more important life decisions.

Gender roles

Gender roles refer to what it means to be a male or female and gender socialisation is the process of learning how society expects each gender to behave. Males and females behave differently and according to sociologists it is because they learn different social roles. For example, even today we find that girls learn to do and are expected to perform different household chores than boys. Although things are changing and stereotypes are being broken down, in many countries and cultures it is still the case that girls learn to cook and clean, and boys learn to help with the garden or the car. Despite years of feminist thought and action and the approach to address inequality due to the way in which boys and girls are socialised, we still find that parental attitudes, schools, how peers interact with each other, and the media all influence the way in which we view gender and such stereotypes. More work must be done.

Norms and values of family and peer groups, cultural beliefs, influence of school, work environment and government

See AC 1.1 for more information about these areas.

Theories of learned behaviour

Our value system has developed over a long time and all sorts of influences affect our learning. We may acquire our values in a conscious or an unconscious way. We are taught certain things by our parents and teachers and even by religious instructors but occasionally we are subject to more subtle influences that become part of our value system. For example, you may have come across children who do not seem to value their education, constantly truant or take time off sick from school, they do not engage with homework and rarely participate in lessons; teachers may not meet the parents as they do not have contact with the school. You may then discover that their family do not consider education to be useful or something to aspire to. The response 'it never did me any good' has been passed into the value system of these children who perpetuate the same response. A similar situation can arise in the learning of prejudiced attitudes. While we may not overtly teach children our own prejudices, the way we behave can lead them to model that behaviour. In the work setting, staff may hold similar attitudes and fail to engage with training and, as the manager, you may need to address these and encourage your staff to engage in a meaningful way in order to develop.

Bandura (1977) followed up on the work of earlier psychologists and posited the theory of social learning. This theory suggests that prejudice is learned in the same way we learn other attitudes and values through association, reinforcement and modelling.

- **Association**: We learn to associate a particular group with bad traits. For example, we may see elderly people as weak and senile.
- **Reinforcement**: Taking part in the telling of racist or sexist jokes, just because others laugh and think it's fun.
- **Modelling**: Children may imitate the prejudices of their family and friends.

This process of learning is known as 'socialisation' and it occurs throughout our lives. The socialisation that occurs within the family is referred to by sociologists as 'primary socialisation' and it is within this close-knit group that you are likely to learn the values your family hold. Secondary socialisation begins at school and continues throughout our lives, shaping our thinking and often causing us to question our values and beliefs.

> ### Evidence opportunity
> **1.3** Socialisation processes that inform values and beliefs
> Analyse the impact of different socialisation factors in relation to the development of values and beliefs, such as the topics we have discussed in this section. Provide a written account.

1.4 Strategies for keeping aware of own stress levels and for maintaining wellbeing

Here, you will evaluate the psychological and physiological effects of work-related stress.

When the demands of work and life become too much, we may become stressed. Being aware of how we behave in times of stress and what triggers us to feel overwhelmed is useful for us to know so we can then develop strategies to help us to overcome this.

We may well notice in colleagues signs of stress such as unhappiness, tiredness, being less communicative than usual, having trouble eating or sleeping, or even eating more and perhaps showing anger towards others. We should be able to recognise these sorts of behaviours in ourselves to enable us to put into place ways in which we can overcome the stress to avoid serious health issues. By addressing our work–life balance, we may find we are working too hard to maintain a good balance and this may indicate that a step back from work to take stock of what we are doing will help. With our employees and staff, we would put into place strategies to help them to redefine their work–life balance and so we also need to apply this to ourselves at times.

The relationship between pressure, anxiety and stress

When we feel under pressure, we usually use the term 'stress' to describe it. We may feel unable to cope with the demands being put on us and this can lead us to feel anxious. This may well affect our work and can have an impact upon the people we work and live with. It might also affect the service users in our care. Even though we feel stressed it would be inappropriate to take this out on those we care for but may even escalate if left unchecked. A care worker under stress and pressured to work more quickly may leave out parts of care that are essential for the wellbeing of others.

Psychological stress includes symptoms of anxiety and tension, and there may be a tendency for the sufferer to worry about things over which they have no control. People who are irritable and distracted may also be unable to concentrate. The mind–body connection means that once these psychological symptoms are in place, physical symptoms of stress soon emerge and these can include difficulty in sleeping, loss of appetite or even a tendency to overeat, tiredness, and also aches and pains.

Stress affects us all in different ways and is a normal reaction when we are under pressure. It is often caused by something we think is harmful or poses a danger or threat to us. In such situations, when we are overwhelmed, tense or emotional, our body will react with the 'fight or flight' mechanism. The raised heart and breathing rates signify to us that our body is preparing us to meet the challenge and is recognised biologically and psychologically. On a positive note, it is telling us that our body is working well to help us. This helps us to guard ourselves or fight and the body begins to secrete adrenaline to help us to do this. This can be harmful if the body remains in this state for long periods of time, however.

As a manager, you'll need to understand the causes of stress so that you are able to manage this in yourself and others.

Work-related stress is not something that magically disappears when we return home and its continual presence can affect health and wellbeing and become chronic. This can lead to time off dealing with health issues including high blood pressure, sleep problems and even heart disease and depression.

In dealing with the first signs of stress it is a good idea to be aware of your stressors by identifying any situations at work that seem to create the most stress for you and by analysing how you respond. For example, did you lose your temper, or find some other distraction to alleviate the feelings?

By looking at our diet and exercise regimes we can start to develop healthy responses to alleviating stress. Also, we should think about our work–life balance by setting boundaries with respect to how often we check work emails and make work phone calls when at home. Finding ways to switch off from work is important and taking time to relax is also helpful. Finally, you should seek support from work colleagues or your line manager and maybe have discussions with a counsellor for additional help.

The causes of stress for leaders and managers, and stress triggers

Stress comes about as a response to many situations and can be triggered as a result of external stressors such as managing difficult situations and people as well as the pressures associated with the day-to-day running of a department. Internal stressors come about as the result of the emotions and thoughts that sometimes cause us to feel uneasy, as we mentioned in AC 1.1. External pressures come from the workplace itself and the situations which develop daily with the individuals within the setting. They may be more mundane issues such as the duty rota or people calling in sick or even equipment not working but they can all lead to pressure. These sources of stress are quite common and becoming aware of how they affect you and what situations may trigger them is the first line of defence in handling them. For example, if you find giving presentations to senior management or having difficult conversations with people in your team cause you anxiety, you can be forewarned about this and take some time out to understand just how you are feeling and develop ways that are useful for dealing with such situations.

Stress triggers

These are the thoughts and feelings that may stimulate a stress response in us. These triggers can come from external events or internal thoughts. For example, any major life change, even positive ones, such as promotion at work or moving house, or negative ones, such as illness or a divorce, can trigger feelings of anxiety. At work, we may feel overburdened by an ever-increasing workload, or endless emails and urgent deadlines. Our internal thoughts may also trigger stress in us at times. Our beliefs, attitudes and even our fears come into play here. A fear of failure, for example, may cause stress to develop when we feel uncertain about what is happening around us, and maybe feeling we are losing control.

It is important to be aware of what triggers your stress levels, how they then affect your mind and body, so that you can better deal with stress. You may, for example, feel your heart rate increase slightly when there are work pressures or your workload has increased. If you are aware of these changes, then you can start to think about strategies to overcome them. You might, for example, take some time out, or go for a walk. You will find it useful to visit www.nhs.uk/conditions/stress-anxiety-depression/understanding-stress/ for more information.

There is more on strategies in this section on page 299.

Signs and symptoms of stress

Signs and symptoms of prolonged stress include the following:

- problems with thought processes and only seeing the negative in life
- memory and concentration issues
- constant anxiety and worry
- irritability
- mood swings
- depression and isolation
- unexplained aches and pains
- upset digestive tract causing diarrhoea or constipation
- nausea, dizziness
- chest pain, rapid heartbeat
- loss of sex drive/libido
- frequent infections
- poor sleeping habits
- using alcohol, cigarettes or drugs to relax
- low energy
- insomnia.

Only you can say how your own stress manifests itself and you need to be aware of the symptoms. Stress has a tendency to slowly accumulate so you are unaware of it happening until it is too late and you suddenly feel overwhelmed. If you are aware of the signs and symptoms you can ensure that you are able to implement strategies to manage the stress and maintain your own wellbeing and that of the people you support.

The relationship between stressful thoughts and behaviour

Anxiety starts with a thought and when we are faced with a situation which may have triggered stress in the past, the thoughts at that time will trigger a similar response this time. For example, not everybody relishes public speaking and if the last time you did this you were concerned that you would forget what to say, or that you would dry up or visibly shake, then being faced with a similar situation may start with that thought and lead to anxious feelings. This may lead to you shaking when speaking and noticing that your mouth is dry and that you are stumbling over your words. The way you are behaving has been shaped by a previous experience, which can be physical or emotional. Having the thought then can lead onto a physical reaction, which repeats again and again when a similar situation occurs unless the pattern is interrupted. By understanding this we also have the opportunity to change by choosing another way in which to behave. If we recognise that this is our usual response we can start to think about alternative behaviours

and make a conscious decision to not behave in this way. For example, we can start to analyse what it is about the situation that is scary and reframe it in our minds. Perhaps we are afraid of looking foolish or forgetting our train of thought. Perhaps we see a sea of faces looking stern and unsympathetic. By changing those thoughts and viewing the situation perhaps from the audience's perspective we start to think differently about the whole event. It might be that the audience is concentrating on what you are saying. They may even be grateful it's you there and not them! They may even be enjoying what you are saying. By looking at it from a different angle you can start to change the way you react.

Effective coping strategies in the management of stress (including emotional resilience)

Having good emotional health gives us the ability and the tools for coping with difficult situations and maintaining a positive outlook. In traumatic circumstances we are able to remain focused and flexible enough to deal with adversity in a more positive way. This is resilience: the ability to recognise our emotions and express them appropriately and divert depression, anxiety or other negative moods. In addition to this, a protective factor to help is a strong network with people we rely on for support and encouragement.

The notion of resilience is often used to describe an individual's ability to recover from difficult or stressful situations. While it appears to be a quality that some people possess in abundance and others lack, emotional resilience is a trait that involves actions, thoughts and behaviours that can be learned and developed by anybody.

A resilient person is generally positive, optimistic and aware of their emotions. If they fail at a task they can bounce back quickly and use the failure as feedback to do better next time.

Some effective ways to cope with stress include exercising, which helps to release endorphins and sparks positive feelings; helping others by becoming a volunteer; and ensuring you put measures in place to establish a work–life balance.

The meaning of wellbeing and work–life balance

Mental wellbeing is about taking action and making small changes to our lives to increase our resilience. You will know people who always seem to bounce back from bad situations, are able to be positive in adversity and carry on with their lives despite difficult times. It is possible that you will also be aware of people who become very stressed at hardship and believe they cannot cope.

The fact is, we all experience hard times and painful situations. Disappointments, loss and change are a part of everybody's lives and they cause stress and anxiety even in the healthiest individuals. It is the individual who has good mental and emotional health who is able to cope with this anxiety and they do this by seeing the setback for what it is, and maintaining their emotional balance in dealing with it. It is about developing a good relationship with our work–life and making sure we take time out to gain balance in our lives. Is this something we can teach ourselves and others to adopt as a strategy?

The manager has a crucial role in helping with the demands of work and ensuring that employees are encouraged to develop a useful work–life balance. You may be in a position to offer rewards for work or time off in lieu when the pressure is on. Also, arranged activities with staff to help them to relax may improve team spirit and resilience to cope with the stresses in the workplace, and can positively impact general wellbeing.

A review of current stress management strategies and work–life balance

As the manager in a setting where stress may be an issue you will need to ensure that you have stress management strategies for staff in place. You can do this by ensuring that employees know how to manage their time effectively and that job activities are shared fairly among the team. Staff need to be aware that if they are feeling stressed, they have a good support system in place.

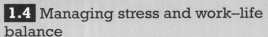

Reflect on it

1.4 Managing stress and work–life balance

Think about how you manage stress in your role and maintain a good work–life balance. Write a reflective account detailing this.

Evidence opportunity

1.4 Stress

Evaluate the psychological and physiological effects of work-related stress. Think about each of the areas that we have discussed above, for example, and what your role as the manager is. Provide a written account.

To evaluate the psychological and physiological effect of stress, for example, you will need to collect information from external sources and make judgements about what you have read.

You might think about the psychological effects of stress that you notice in your staff. How does their anxiety affect their behaviour? How do you help them to manage this and what are the advantages and disadvantages of the strategies you suggest for them? How do they help?

AC 1.5 Methods of using feedback from others and own reflective practice to increase self-awareness

Here, you will critically evaluate the benefits of self-reflection to increase your self-awareness.

Reflective practice is a tool that can be used by all practitioners, individually, to enhance their practice. It can also be used as a management tool, enabling managers to guide and support staff to reflect on key elements of their role and their performance. Prompts such as 'You did that really well. What was it that made that such a successful activity?' are useful. This approach develops individuals' self-esteem, confidence and a questioning and critical approach to their work. Reflection provides an ideal vehicle of learning that can be shared within the wider team. Teams can reflect as a group, particularly if they are keen to examine or change an aspect of practice which they have in common, and can also share their learning with others.

Reflective practice as a tool to improve performance

Inevitably, when we reflect, no matter how candid we try to be, it is difficult to see the world from anything other than our own perspective. Reflection may require that we seek opinions and information from others to validate our reflections and to help us to see whether any change is required. While information gained in this way can be seen as threatening, if managed and used sensitively, 360-degree feedback can be illuminating and can challenge and refocus our perceptions of reality.

Obtaining feedback on your performance and behaviours

As a manager of a team, teaching and encouraging staff to be self-reflective is important. It is also a crucial tool to use for our own wellbeing and self-awareness. Reflection can be a powerful tool. It can be used to improve practice by supporting us to question our routine work as we carry it out. In doing so, we can measure our behaviour against our values and those of the organisation to ensure that these are consistent. Alternatively, reflection may encourage us to try a new approach to an activity and evaluate its success. Encouraging staff to become self-governing and to take responsibility for their work standards is an important element of a successful learning organisation. Reflective practice provides an opportunity for all practitioners to check their own standards of work and enhance practice.

360-degree reflection

360-degree reflection asks us to reflect on our behaviours and performance once we have gathered information from a range of individuals, both those in positions of authority and those over whom you have authority. You should gather information from people who will be honest but who can be trusted to feed back responsibly and constructively. It is important that you do not only ask your friends – they are more likely to tell you what you want to hear rather than what you need to know. To gain the most from the activity, you need to know how different people experience you and your actions. Learning about how others perceive and experience you, your actions, attitudes and behaviours can be empowering and being self-aware leads to growth, both personally and professionally. Getting all-round 360-degree feedback may provide you with insight about the following:

- **A façade** – information that suggests that you are better or worse at something than you think you are.
- **A blind spot** – information that you did not know about yourself.
- **A suggestion** about something that you could easily do which would make a positive difference.
- **An opportunity** to stop doing something.

360-feedback is usually built around a questionnaire as this helps the individual to control the areas on which they want feedback.

The criteria for choosing the wording of questionnaires for 360-feedback reflect general principles when designing performance appraisal systems and criteria, and include the following points:

- Questions should be relevant to the recipient's job.
- Each question should be concise, use plain English and omit qualifiers, such as 'when appropriate' and 'as necessary'. Vague and complex questions rarely produce clear feedback.
- Each question should relate to a clearly defined competency or function to avoid muddled feedback. It must be specific.
- Questions should set clear and appropriate standards. For example, 'makes decisions' is a poor criterion as the decisions made could be unclear, late or wrong. A better statement might be 'makes timely and effective decisions'.
- Open questions provide the opportunity to add comments in support of the answers to the rated questions and, as such, can be particularly helpful. The recipient is able to look for frequently used words or phrases and for common themes. When wording such questions, it is important to use clear language, for example, 'what does the recipient do well?' and 'what does the recipient need to improve?'

Source: CIPD Factsheet 360 Degree Feedback, www.cipd.co.uk/hr-resources/factsheets/360-degree-feedback.aspx#link_furtherreading

Additionally, you can gain feedback via other sources at your disposal such as appraisals, supervision and at performance reviews. Appraisals are an opportunity for the employee and manager to get together to reflect and discuss their achievements over the past year, the aim of which is to have a shared view of the performance of the employee at the end of the meeting. Supervision is an ongoing process in which the manager oversees, supports and develops the knowledge and skills of the employee. By using a variety of methods, you are able to gain much-needed information about a person and also enable them to develop their self-awareness.

Reflect on modelling a healthy diet and exercise programme patterns

Personal wellbeing and team welfare are currently embedded into our working cultures and we are expected to ensure our employees are cared for in the workplace. For example, we are required to ensure that fresh drinking water is available to staff on duty and some organisations subscribe to local gyms to help their staff to maintain a fit lifestyle. In general, restaurants and cafes in many companies are required to offer healthy eating options to encourage a healthy diet. As a manager, you will need to consider your role in not only modelling good behaviour with regard to healthy diet and exercise, but also ensuring your setting caters for such facilities.

Reflect on it

1.5 Reflecting on your wellbeing

Compile a diary, which shows a review of your diet and exercise regime and reflects how you are developing a more self-aware view/becoming more aware of your own wellbeing. Provide a reflective account detailing how you could increase the amount of exercise you do each day. What change might you make to your diet to encourage you to eat a healthier option?

Maintaining regular work breaks and time management strategies

Managing time is an important component of your work and taking regular breaks will enhance your work–life balance and the way in which you do your job. It will help maintain motivation and morale in the team.

Planning and prioritising what you need to do on a daily, weekly and monthly basis is a good start to managing the stress that may arise due to the lack of time.

Trying to do too much runs the risk of adding stress on yourself and this will inevitably affect the staff you are managing in a negative way.

Your staff also need to understand how they prioritise their workload and manage their time. You may notice that some staff tend to eat at their desks rather than taking lunch breaks and also fail to take breaks. There may also be a tendency for them to leave late and take work home. As their manager, you must ensure that they are encouraged to think about their welfare and to take regular breaks to maximise their efficiency.

Covey's (1989) matrix provides a useful strategy by which you can determine important and urgent tasks as opposed to non-urgent and non-important tasks.

Time management matrix		
	Urgent (time pressure)	**Not urgent** (no time pressure)
Important (significant impact on service user/ work/setting)	1 These activities usually get done as top priority	2 These activities are high impact and should be made a priority
Not important (no significant impact)	3 These activities are deceptive – don't confuse urgent and important	

▲ **Figure 9.1** Covey's matrix

By compiling an activity log, you can prioritise your workload and can see at a glance what tasks need to be done and what tasks can be left. It will help you determine which items on your list require urgent attention now or can wait until a more convenient time. For example, an urgent important task may be to prepare the team for a quality inspection happening within the next two days. A task that might be non-urgent but important may be to compile an agenda for the next team meeting.

Considering the benefits of coaching and mentoring support

Coaching and mentoring are similar in nature. Gallwey defined coaching as unlocking a person's potential to maximise their performance. It is helping them to learn rather than teaching them (Gallwey, 1986; Whitmore, 2002). Mentoring is a professional relationship and is about following in the route of a colleague who can pass on knowledge and experience of a role. Both roles are in place to enable individuals to flourish in their work and personal lives.

Successful coaches, according to Parsloe (1999), require knowledge and understanding of process and have at their disposal a variety of styles, skills and techniques. A coach, therefore, may not have direct experience of your formal occupational role but will be able to use a process to help you to make the changes you desire. A successful mentor will be somebody who has been in the job and can impart knowledge and best practice from their own experience about care in the adult sector.

Considering the benefits of alternative therapies and/or other support mechanisms

In managing stress in the workplace or determining ways in which you can access a balanced way of working you might also seek help from other professionals in your own time. Counselling is not only for mental health problems but can help with things like managing time or relationship issues. In addition, you might avail yourself of alternative therapies such as massage or reiki therapy as such therapies can help you to relax. Relaxing in this way can also certainly help you to reflect on your work and your experiences.

Evidence opportunity

1.5 Methods of using feedback from others and own reflective practice to increase self-awareness

Critically evaluate the benefits of self-reflection to increase your self-awareness by exploring, for example, the areas we have looked at in the section above.

Provide a written account or have a professional discussion with your assessor about this. You could also write a reflective account about this.

You could, for example, undertake a project in which you gain the following information and then provide a reflective account of what you now know about yourself:

- Ask your colleagues about your performance and behaviours – you might include 360-degree feedback from colleagues, management performance reviews, self and organisational appraisals.
- Reflect on yourself modelling a healthy diet and exercise programme.
- Think about how you maintain regular work breaks and time management strategies.
- Consider the benefits of coaching and mentoring support.
- Consider the benefits of alternative therapies and/or other support mechanisms.

LO2 Manage personal and professional behaviour

AC 2.1 Professional behaviour

Here, you are required to analyse the link between personal and professional behaviour and values and the vision and function of the service. This must include management of situations where team members are not acting in a manner that promotes the vision of the service.

As a healthcare professional, you are expected to perform your duties within the code of conduct specified by your own professional body. Figure 9.2 shows the code for a healthcare support worker or adult social care worker. You are also expected to meet the expectations set down by your employers through the policies and perhaps their own standards and codes.

As a Healthcare Support Worker or Adult Social Care Worker in England you must:

1 Be accountable by making sure you can answer for your actions or omissions.

2 Promote and uphold the privacy, dignity, rights, health and wellbeing of people who use health and care services and their carers at all times.

3 Work in collaboration with your colleagues to ensure the delivery of high quality, safe and compassionate healthcare, care and support.

4 Communicate in an open and effective way to promote the health, safety and wellbeing of people who use health and care services and their carers.

5 Respect a person's right to confidentiality.

6 Strive to improve the quality of healthcare, care and support through continuing professional development.

7 Uphold and promote equality, diversity and inclusion.

▲ **Figure 9.2** Professional code of conduct, Skills for Care and Skills for Health (2013)

AC 2.2 Learning from feedback

Here, you will be required to reflect on how you respond to feedback from a range of sources. This will include a positive attitude towards change and a willingness to review your behaviours and attitudes.

See Unit 506, AC 3.3 for more on feedback.

Change is inevitable in adult care work and sometimes we may not find this palatable. However, a positive approach to the required changes will make the transition to new ways of working easier and more likely to be accepted by the staff we work with. If we view all feedback as a way in which we can develop and grow we will receive it in good grace and accept it openly and learn from it (Figure 9.3). Negative feedback, although sometimes hard to hear, if given in the right way can have a positive impact upon the receiver if they are willing to accept it as a learning experience.

▲ **Figure 9.3** How does feedback from others help you to improve your performance?

AC 2.3 Links between emotional intelligence and professional conduct

Here, you are required to explain the links between emotional intelligence and professional conduct, including the topics we discuss here.

Relationship management is the ability to handle relationships competently in order to best deal with conflict, and to develop collaboration in the workforce.

In a management situation our awareness of the impact of our actions and responses can go a long way towards defusing situations that might be potentially threatening. We may not be feeling very happy or friendly ourselves, but being in a position of authority demands that we have some awareness of the feelings of others. A good manager is one who has a level of emotional intelligence.

Emotional intelligence is the capacity some of us have for managing our own emotions and for being able to recognise the feelings others may be having. We may feel angry at something somebody has said, but as a manager and leader, showing that anger inappropriately will have a negative effect on relationships. If, in addition, we are socially aware then we are able to show empathy and concern for others' feelings and are then able to acknowledge that staff who, for example, have a large workload may feel stressed, and those that may be feeling under threat or harassed may show aggression and anger. As an emotionally intelligent manager, you should acknowledge the effects these situations will have on your staff and try to understand the reasons for their behaviour.

The range of emotions

The range of emotions we can experience may manifest itself in a positive or negative way and we need to be aware of these feelings and the impact emotions have on the people around us. Positive emotions can affect the workforce and their impact will be shown in a more productive and upbeat workplace.

Evidence opportunity

2.2 Responding to feedback

Reflect on how you respond to feedback from a range of sources, including a positive attitude towards change and a willingness to review your own behaviours and attitudes. Provide a written account or explain this to your assessor.

You might like to provide a reflective account on how you respond to feedback, demonstrating how you show willingness to review your own behaviours and attitudes to change. Think about how you react to both positive and negative feedback.

How do you respond to feedback from those senior to you? How do you respond to feedback from those you manage? How do you respond to feedback from individuals in your setting and their families? How do your reactions differ based on the people who give the feedback?

How do you ensure you learn from the feedback you are given and maintain a positive attitude towards change? Are you willing to review your behaviours and attitudes?

Emotional responses under stress

When we feel stressed, we feel under threat from many sources. Stress is a response to overwhelming situations and this will undoubtedly affect the emotions we have. As managers, we need to be able to deal with the stress we may be feeling in a productive manner and should have some strategies we can use to help us to respond appropriately to staff. See AC 1.4 for more information.

Negative emotions

These must be recognised as unhelpful and, as a manager, although we may experience such emotions from time to time, we need to try to develop our emotional intelligence to ensure we are not affecting our workforce.

As a manager, you will need to adapt the way you communicate to suit your audience. This requires a professional response to all situations. You must be respectful of your audience at all times, no matter how negative the situation is, and whatever emotions the person you are communicating with exhibits. By being open, honest and clear in our communication, we show empathy for the feelings of others.

Case study

2.3 Emotional intelligence

A member of staff has recently undergone a traumatic separation from her husband. She has three small children and is struggling to make ends meet. She finds it difficult to get to work on time and has been late a number of times recently. You know she does not have family in the area to help her get the children to school.

When you ask to see her to try to resolve some of her issues, she is aggressive and quite rude. This may make you feel angry, particularly when you are trying to come up with a solution. However, fighting anger with anger does not work and you need to consider how you might approach this problem in a different manner.

How might you deal with this situation?

Perhaps you will have empathised with the staff member's plight and asked her how she might see a way forward. It is likely that she has been unable to take time out to note the decline in her work or her lateness. You might suggest a change in hours to help her to get to work on time, or a reduction in her hours of work until she can settle her children into a more favourable routine. Perhaps she might work the same number of hours but at times when the children are at school.

The way you deal with the situation will have an effect on the whole workforce, as they will be aware of the situation. The trust and rapport you have with the team can be strengthened or weakened depending upon the way in which you deal with this member of staff.

How can this example help you to understand the links between emotional intelligence and professional conduct?

Passive-aggressive behaviour

Expressing anger is not an acceptable emotion, so a person who is showing passive aggression will mask that anger by adopting other hostile behaviours. It might be described as a more covert or hidden anger and is demonstrated by a variety of responses. In the workplace this can have negative effects on the staff. For example, staff who are aggrieved in some way at a decision you have made may respond by not communicating with you, disengaging from work or just being sulky or obstructive. They may also accept a task but then take a long time in completing it.

This type of behaviour may have been learned in childhood and needs to be addressed for harmony in the workplace to be restored. As a manager, you can resolve this issue by avoiding passive-aggressive behaviour, and instead discuss the issue with the staff member and ask them to identify what it is they are aggrieved or angry about and then discuss possible solutions.

Victimhood

This sort of behaviour can be just as destructive as the passive-aggressive type and is another way in which people may show emotions. It may be unintentional and can occur as a result of being unable to express one's emotions. The victim will fail to take responsibility for their work and will endeavour to get you to pity them. It is always somebody else's fault that they have been unable to do the job you asked them to do or they may be persistently late coming in or they are having to leave early every day. In dealing with this behaviour you will need to ensure that limits are set that are not negotiable and you may have to be firm about the time they are taking up.

People may react in this way simply because they have had useful results in the past and they may have gained sympathy for their behaviour. It may be that they have legitimate reasons for such behaviour, and there may be issues outside of work troubling them. Changing this behaviour can be accomplished by building the person's self-confidence and helping them to take responsibility for their own actions.

Evidence opportunity

2.3 Links between emotional intelligence and professional conduct

Explain to your assessor the links between emotional intelligence and professional conduct, including:

- the range of emotions
- emotional responses under stress
- negative emotions
- passive-aggressive behaviour
- victimhood.

AC 2.4 Adapt communication in response to the emotional context and communication style of others

Here, you will need to adapt and extend your communication and responses to suit needs of others and situations.

See page 72 for a definition of communication.

Level of formality of situation and differences between personal and professional relationships

Communication is the basis of interaction, so skills in speaking, writing and, in particular, listening are essential in adult care. As a manager, you will be interacting and communicating with a range of people within adult care settings, including service users (who may be vulnerable) and their families as well as staff, visitors and other professionals. You may sometimes communicate with people who are going through personal crises or are feeling upset, and this requires skill in making sure they feel supported and valued. The level of formality you will adopt in such situations will change with the audience. For example, you may adopt a more formal manner of speaking to a relative than you would to a member of staff for example or somebody you know on a personal level. This is because you recognise that there is a difference between personal and professional relationships and will, therefore, use different communication skills in each. Addressing a personal issue with somebody we know will require a different set of communication skills and responses than if we were addressing a professional issue. Our body and verbal language will change and will be informal and friendlier. A professional discussion will of course require a different set of skills and is likely to require a more formal response. You will, therefore, need to ensure you can adapt and extend your communication and responses to suit the level of formality and situation and adapt this to personal and professional relationships.

Different factors affecting communication

The effectiveness of your communication skills as a manager and leader will affect the success of the organisation and the team with which you work. There are factors that affect communication that should be recognised.

Age, developmental age and pre-existing communication differences/sensory loss

As humans, we will go through different stages of growth as we progress and age from infants to adulthood. We develop and grow in various ways; we grow and change physically but also intellectually, emotionally, and there will also be changes in terms of our social relationships. There will be changes at different ages. There will be milestones – for example, for babies it may be the ability to crawl, walk, talk and read; for teenagers it might be going through puberty. As a manager, and in situations where you need to communicate generally, it is important to take into account the age of the individual and developmental age.

As people get older their hearing and sight may begin to fail. The way in which we communicate will mean we need to be mindful of these changes. We may use simple ways at first in which to help: by allowing them to have access to larger print or to allow them to sit nearer to you so they can hear better; by slightly raising the volume of your voice or enabling them to sit opposite you so they can lip read. As things get progressively worse you may adopt methods such as sign language, Braille, Makaton, assisted technology and other non-verbal methods of communication as useful aids for those service users who cannot communicate verbally. As a manager, you will need to ensure that staff are equipped to support service users who may need to use such methods. You may also need to be aware of your staff and their communication needs. Conversations with younger staff will require a different approach to those with adults or more senior staff and it is important not to patronise. A good approach is to reflect the words the younger staff use in our own responses and to check in on meaning.

Our choice of words is important, and we should be careful not to use jargon and abbreviations or language that is too complex. Keep in mind the person you are speaking to and tailor your language to them.

Assisted communication refers to use of aids such as picture and symbol communication boards and electronic devices, which help individuals who have difficulty with speech or language problems to express themselves. Many people who come into our services may have pre-existing conditions such as a learning difficulty, or may have suffered a stroke, which make communication more challenging, so we need to be aware of resources that might help with this.

Gender

Mohindra and Azhar (2012) conducted research into gender differences in communication and bring attention to the differences in male and female communication skills. They comment about the way socialisation in early childhood plays a part, with subsequent effects later in life. For example, girls are told to play quietly and to adopt 'ladylike' politeness whereas boys are encouraged to 'play loudly, and be rambunctious'. If a girl shows her feelings and starts to cry, she is nurtured, but boys are told that it is not macho to cry. According to Mohindra and Azhar, these early differences are later seen in the workplace where women develop a relational style of interaction whereas the men develop a competitive style of interaction. For women, communication is about building rapport in a tactful, caring way whereas men are seen as more direct and competitive in building relationships (Mohindra and Azhar, 2012). In your managerial role, you should ensure that when you are dealing with each gender you treat everyone equally and communicate in a balanced way.

Culture

When we talk about 'fostering equality and diversity' and the importance of respecting the differences we may come across in people, we are not talking only about language differences, but also about cultures and the differences in values that people hold. This can have a huge impact on our ability to communicate, not only because verbal and non-verbal communication can have different meanings across different cultures but also our understanding of different cultures can impact our interactions with people from those different cultures. It is important to be aware of the differences across cultures and how communication is interpreted. For example, some cultures may interpret certain hand gestures differently, so it is important to be aware of the differences and nuances around this and be sensitive to the needs of others.

Living in a society that is made up of various different cultures, it is important to be culturally aware in our interpersonal interactions. Miller (2006) says that defining the term culture is complex. When we talk about race, we often confuse the term with ethnicity and culture. Ethnicity, gender and social class, while all being relevant, should additionally include religious beliefs, sexuality, rationality, skin colour and experience of oppression (Miller, 2006). Miller suggests that by developing a respectful curiosity about the beliefs and practices within all service users' lives, we are able to communicate in more meaningful ways. In your role as manager you have a responsibility to ensure that your staff uphold and actively promote the British Values of democracy, law, tolerance and respect as set out in the Prevent strategy 2011. Having respect for the differences presented by cultural diversity, we can more readily adapt our responses and communication accordingly.

▲ **Figure 9.4** How do you adapt your communication skills and responses to suit needs of others and situations?

Level and complexity of language used/use of jargon

Differences in learning and the education a service user has had in the past affect the way in which people communicate. Some people may find it hard to understand certain words (particularly if the person speaking is using complex and difficult words). Also, the use of jargon may not be helpful. For example, a person with a knowledge of healthcare may have a better understanding about what is happening to them in the care setting whereas those without this sort of knowledge will struggle. Staff need to be trained to use language that is accessible to service users and understand that the jargon we might use as adult care workers is often not understood by others (Figure 9.4).

Background experiences

The background and experience of the person to whom we are speaking are also important. Some people who come into care services may have had a bad experience in the past and this may have an effect on whether or not our message gets across. They may be fearful of what is about to happen and not listen to instructions or not concentrate on the information being given to them. For example, a bad experience at the dentist as a child may rear up when in a clinical setting and this fear the person is now feeling may affect their ability to listen and to understand what is going on. It is important that staff understand how the individual is affected and as a manager you may need to bring the staff's awareness to this.

Audience

Every day in care we meet with varied audiences with whom we need to communicate and we have to adjust our language to suit diverse groups of people. We welcome a diverse range of services into our organisations and need to recognise how this affects communication. This demands we use a variety of communication skills, all highly dependent on the position and education level of the person and the context in which the communication takes place. Many barriers to communication arise as a result of inappropriate language and terminology being used, which effectively means the message is lost. For example, the delivery of factual information can be quite impersonal and may be totally inappropriate when dealing with a vulnerable child or adult who requires an empathetic response to a problem. However, a member of the medical staff may require just such a response. Therefore, in order for the message to be received and understood, you must match appropriate communication with the individual to whom you are speaking and the circumstances in which the interaction takes place.

So, effective communication is crucial. As well as our communication skills, how we develop our relationships with others is paramount to getting the message across effectively.

In management roles, we communicate with people who may be in a subordinate position, those in more senior roles, peers and others such as visitors or other service providers. They will all have different communication needs and, as the manager in the setting, you need to ensure that there is clarity in the words and actions you are using which reinforce the vision and values of the service, and that you and your staff are aware of the ways in which communication needs to be adapted.

Research it

2.4 Factors affecting communication

Research different factors affecting communication. Choose one factor and undertake a review of articles. For example, look at gender or culture and make notes on how these might need to be reviewed in your setting to ensure you are matching the vision and value of the service.

Reflect on it

2.4 Communication diary

Keep a communication diary for one span of duty. Use the questions below to show how you have adapted and extended your communication and responses to suit the needs of others.

1   Who were the groups or individuals whose communication needs were addressed in the diary?
2   In what context did the communication take place?
3   What purpose did it have?
4   How successful was it?
5   How did you ensure the communication was effective? What did you do?
6   How did you adapt and extend the way in which you conversed with people of different ages, genders, cultures, those with pre-existing communication differences, and those with different education levels and background experiences? For example, what else did you have to do to ensure that the message you were relaying was understood and clearly given? Did you need to use other forms of communication to get your message across?

Evidence opportunity

2.4 Adapting communication

Show your assessor how you adapt and extend your communication and responses to suit the needs of others and situations. How do you adapt communication in response to the emotional context and communication style of others? Make sure you consider the sections we have covered above.

AC 2.5 Challenge views, actions, systems and routines that do not match the vision and values of the service

Here, you will be required to challenge views, actions, systems and routines that do not match the vision and values of the service.

Use monitoring systems to check that systems and processes match the vision and values of the service

One way in which this might be monitored is through appraisal and supervision sessions where, as the manager, you can check workers' understanding about the vision of the organisation and challenge and undertake to check that their views match that vision. This might reveal that staff require further training in order to develop their understanding.

Visibly and explicitly challenge views that do not match the vision and values of the service

Stakeholders may have limited awareness about the vision of your organisation, but you need to ensure that they have an understanding about what it is you are trying to achieve through the systems and routines you develop. You may need to challenge views that do not match the values you are trying to instil in your staff.

Reflect on any lessons learned and provide training and guidance

It is wise to offer staff and stakeholders training about the vision of the organisation so that all can be working towards the same ends. It is important that you, your staff and stakeholders reflect on the lessons that you have learned from all of this. It may even be that you discuss such matters during team and one-to-one meetings. Ensuring that the vision and values of the service are followed is of utmost importance if your setting is to offer effective care.

Evidence opportunity

2.5 Challenge views, actions, systems and routines

Show your assessor how you challenge views, actions, systems and routines that do not match the vision and values of the service. Consider the topics we have discussed in this section.

LO3 Manage workloads

AC 3.1 Use strategies and tools to identify priorities for work

Here, you will be required to select and use strategies and tools to identify operational management priorities in setting clear priorities and goals for your work team(s).

Business efficiency

An efficient business is a successful one and every part of the organisation should recognise how it fits into the success of the organisation. It requires that every employee recognises their part in working together to reach the ultimate mission statement of the business. For example, employees need to be aware that strategic objectives are linked to departmental and team objectives and that their part in meeting team objectives is crucial to success. Organisations therefore need to take time to implement processes that reinforce this.

Organisational and staff structures

For any business to be efficient there need to be good systems, processes and structures in place. The staff structure and the way in which each department works towards the whole vision of the organisation need to be linked in such ways that there is a seamless connection between each department. There are different ways in which an organisation may be structured and these determine how the business will operate. Within the structure there must be the allocation of responsibilities for how management will work and what operational standards and routines need to be developed.

Systems and procedures

Systems and procedures refer to the rules and regulations an organisation must follow and provide us with day-to-day operations for the organisation to run efficiently and safely. They also improve safety levels in a workplace by establishing rules that meet workplace regulations.

The systems, and this includes policies, help to guide employees by describing the rules of operation and the consequences for breach of those rules. Procedures detail the actions that an employee can take to undertake tasks.

Working practices and responsibilities

Working practices should be prioritised in ensuring the delivery of quality. They also need to be safe and clearly communicated and understood by all.

For example, staff are required to keep up-to-date, accurate records about the care they deliver by updating care plans and computer systems. This will link into quality audits, which show key performance indicators. As the manager, you are able to check where staff may be falling short of their tasks and can then set clear goals for staff to achieve and support them to prioritise their work to ensure compliance.

Work culture – are people receptive to change?

Work culture refers to the beliefs and attitudes of the employees and the ideologies and principles of the organisation. A healthy work culture is one in which employees follow the rules and regulations and adhere to the existing guidelines and as a result are satisfied employees who respect each other and are valued by the employer. Change happens rapidly within healthcare systems and our response can often be negative if we do not understand why it is happening. People tend to be more receptive to change if the reasons for implementing it are clear and if the benefits are laid out.

Costs vs revenues

Costs to the organisation are the result of operating the business and purchasing of assets needed. Revenue refers to the sales of the services. In an adult care setting this will be the cost of staff, buildings and equipment. As the manager, you will be responsible for managing your budgets and ensuring that your costs do not exceed the revenue.

A management priority at the start of each financial year will be to set clear priorities and goals for your work team by devising a team resource plan to help you to identify what resources you have, where they are used and how much they cost.

Quality management

In managing quality, there needs to be a quality plan, a quality assurance process, quality control and quality improvement.

As the manager of an adult care service, you need to ensure that a quality management process is in place and it describes the processes and measures that will be used to determine success. Quality assurance ensures that all staff are using the procedures and standards set out consistently, and that they have the correct knowledge and skills to do so. Quality control is the inspection and measurement that determine if the plan is successful, and quality improvement is a term which describes how the information gained from the processes above drive improvements in efficiency and effectiveness.

Research it

3.1 Your strategic plan and operational management priorities

Obtain a copy of the strategic plan and identify your organisation's mission and values.

Identify the operational management priorities within the plan and describe the priorities and goals you have set for your work team.

Use the headings above to complete the piece of work.

Workforce planning

Workforce planning is about addressing two basic premises in terms of the workforce: how many staff and what sort of staff you need. As a manager, you will be well aware of the need to determine what skills each staff member has and to ensure that during a span of duty you have the right people in place for the care that needs to be given.

In developing your workforce development plan, you will need to:

- analyse your current workforce and identify the skills mix required in your setting to deliver the sort of service you provide
- ensure staff receive training required to meet service user needs
- look carefully at the working practices and the responsibilities of each staff member
- look at costs of staff and determine how these can be optimised.

It is not only about your current provision. You need to be aware that changes in the future to the type of service user or the number of service users coming to your setting will need to be considered so that your plan can highlight gaps to be filled.

See Unit 507 for more information on developing your workforce development plan.

Research it

3.1 Skills for care

Go to www.skillsforcare.org.uk/Documents/Leadership-and-management/Workforce-planning/Practical-approaches-to-workforce-planning-guide.pdf

The guide describes how effective workforce planning can ensure that your setting is delivering personalised, safe and good quality services to the service users. Recruiting and retaining a workforce that reflects the attitudes, values and skills of your organisation underpins workforce planning.

KEY TERM

Workforce planning is the process whereby the staff with the necessary skills are allocated to the task when they are needed in order to deliver organisational objectives.

Evidence opportunity

3.1 Strategies and tools to identify priorities for work

Select and use strategies and tools to identify operational management priorities in setting clear priorities and goals for your work. You could, for example, consider the topics we have discussed in this section:

- Business efficiency.
- Organisational and staff structures.
- The systems, procedures and working practices and responsibilities that are in place.
- The current working culture – are people receptive to change?
- Show an understanding of the budgetary control of costs vs revenues. What systems do you have in place to ensure balance?
- Quality management.

Demonstrate this to your assessor and discuss the various topics with them.

You might like to develop a workforce development plan for your setting. Start by giving evidence of the strategies and tools you use to identify the operational management priorities in setting clear priorities and goals for your teams. Think about the above points when developing this.

AC 3.2 Plan ways to meet responsibilities and organisational priorities while maintaining own wellbeing

Here, you will be required to plan to meet your own and your organisational priorities while maintaining your own wellbeing.

Operational planning and related priorities

In the AC 3.1 Research it activity you were asked to obtain a copy of the strategic plan and it is important that you understand the difference between an 'operational plan' and a 'strategic plan'. While the strategic plan sets a direction for the organisation, the operational plan is a tool for managing an organisation and provides the manager with information about the work that needs to be done to carry out the goals and objectives. For example, you may need to undertake further training of staff in order to implement newer ways of working and you will need to plan this effectively in order to meet such objectives. In doing this, you will be enabling staff to undertake more responsibility in their roles and you can then delegate tasks, which will reduce your workload, ensuring you are maintaining your wellbeing.

The operational plan, therefore, details the strategies and tasks that must be undertaken and identifies the people who are responsible for each of those tasks. It also gives a timeline in which tasks must be completed and provides financial detail as to resources to be provided to complete tasks. It identifies organisational objectives that feed down into your team as well as your personal objectives. Your role as manager includes checking timelines and measuring the performance as well as assigning responsibilities and resources to a project. You will be ensuring that the organisational objectives are being met alongside those set for the team and the personal ones you also want to meet.

Time management strategies to prioritise work activities

Stephen Covey (1989) produced a useful time management tool in his 'urgent versus important' matrix. We mentioned this above in AC 1.5.

The matrix helps to identify which tasks are most important and urgent as opposed to those which are important and yet non-urgent and may be left. It helps you to prioritise work activities into management and leadership responsibilities and individual and/or service demands. Your day may be busy and feel quite overwhelming at times, but taking a step back and looking carefully at the tasks you are currently doing and prioritising those tasks into the important and unimportant may reveal that you are using valuable time to deal with tasks which are not increasing productivity but rather hindering it. It will be most important to prioritise your management responsibilities and the meeting of organisational objectives over other less demanding operational ones. For example, when staffing levels are low it is tempting to try to resolve this by helping staff with their

Reflect on it

3.2 Time management

Having completed the time management exercise above you will be in a better position to notice just how much more time you really have.

Think about how the time saved can be used towards better management of individuals in the workplace and the service demands of the organisation.

work. This would be counterproductive as it takes you away from your own work and not only could be detrimental to your wellbeing but it will also not provide a long-term solution to meet the demands of your setting.

Using different resources to identify the key priorities for your own professional development

In your role as a manager you need to be able to work in ways in which you keep yourself safe and your wellbeing protected. You should prioritise the work you do to ensure that you meet the operational plans of the organisation as well as the general management of the day-to-day business at ground level. Good time management is the key to success along with the ability to prioritise your workload. A balanced approach will ensure that you are also mindful of your own wellbeing in what can be a very stressful profession.

Having a mentor would also be a useful resource as this is a person who understands the pressures of the role and can work with you, providing support when needed. In addition, training can help you to develop skills that you may require.

Research it

3.2 The Covey matrix

Research the Covey matrix.

Then undertake a time management analysis by using the Covey matrix.

- In Quadrant 1 (top left) write down all the **important, urgent** items that you need to deal with immediately. A lot of people work solely in this area, but this is not a good place to be. By addressing this you reduce your risk of burnout.

- In Quadrant 2 (top right) write down the **important but non-urgent** items that do not require your immediate attention but still need to be planned. This is a good place to be because here you have the time to spend on important tasks.

- In Quadrant 3 (bottom left) highlight **unimportant but urgent** items that can be minimised or eliminated.

- In Quadrant 4 (bottom right) write down the **unimportant and non-urgent** items or the things that should be minimised or eliminated as these are the true time wasters.

Examples to help you are given below.

Important/urgent	Important/non-urgent
e.g. responding to a service user's needs	e.g. responding to interruptions from people knocking on your door
Unimportant/urgent	Unimportant/non-urgent
e.g. arranging a staff meeting	e.g. surfing the net or on Facebook

Using different resources to address any personal wellbeing issues (work–life balance; management of work-related and personal stress)

A good work–life balance means that you can switch off from work when you go home and not allow work to intrude upon your home life. You need to set yourself boundaries so that you work within those timeframes, and to ensure that you do not spend time working at home, for example answering work emails. This might mean ensuring you leave work on time and do not stay late. As a manager, you might feel that you are in a senior role and need to take work home with you. This might be something that you need to do at times. However, this should not be something you should make a habit of. Also, if the demands of work are starting to creep into your home life and leisure time then you are at risk of developing issues around stress. There may be training that you can attend which can help with time management and working smartly.

Maintaining wellbeing

What do we mean by wellbeing? A subjective view of psychological wellbeing would be to say that we are happy or satisfied with our lives. However, what makes you happy is unlikely to be the same for other adult care workers.

The Department of Health (2014) Care and Support Statutory Guidance; Issued under the Care Act 2014 defines wellbeing as a broad concept. Although it was specifically designed for service users we can still identify with the concepts it outlines and apply them to our own experience. Wellbeing relates to the following areas:

- personal dignity (including treatment with respect)
- physical and mental health and emotional wellbeing, protection from abuse and neglect
- control by the individual over day-to-day life (including care and support)
- participation in work, education, training or recreation
- social and economic wellbeing, which refers to being actively engaged with life and with other people and having a positive standard of living based primarily on financial security
- domestic, family relationships and personal issues
- suitability of living accommodation
- the individual's contribution to society.

Ensuring our wellbeing and that of our staff requires us as managers to determine how we might measure the state of wellbeing. When things are not going well, we start to experience stress, worry and anxiety. Our psychological wellbeing becomes compromised and this will inevitably lead to our quality of life being reduced. For us and the people in our care and staff, this can lead to depression and its subsequent effects on physical wellbeing and health.

In order to promote psychological wellbeing, we need to engender a culture that promotes wellbeing in our day-to-day practice. By valuing the concept of positive wellbeing, you can ensure that staff are reminded about the need for positive outcomes. Training and ongoing staff development during supervision can also ensure that staff fully appreciate the need to constantly raise their awareness about how their wellbeing can be improved.

Evidence opportunity

3.2 Planning ways to meet responsibilities and organisational priorities while maintaining own wellbeing

How do you plan to meet your own and staff organisational priorities while maintaining your own wellbeing with consideration of the things we have discussed in this section?

Explain this to your assessor or demonstrate to them how you do this. You could also write down how you are able to do this.

AC 3.3 Use digital technology to enhance own efficiency

Here, you will be required to critically evaluate the application of different types of technology, which can enhance your efficiency at work and work plans.

Email

Email has certainly transformed business. Messages are fast and can be sent at any time of the day, and as long as you have access to a digital device such as a laptop or a phone, you are able to send and receive email anywhere. You are able to send large files inexpensively and to multiple recipients, cutting out postage costs.

The disadvantages, however, are that emails can leave you open to viruses and spam, which can result in time wasting. There are also security issues that you must consider – you can have software in place to ensure that your systems are not easily open to hacking. As a manager, you will need to ensure that you use email efficiently, and equip your staff with the skills to do so too. This might, for example, include ensuring that emails are checked only at certain times of the day. They must also be aware of the threats that emails can pose.

▲ **Figure 9.5** How does email enable you to be more efficient in your communications, and how do you promote efficiency in your staff by using digital technology?

Electronic reporting systems and specialist software for care plans/auditing

In care work, the use of reporting systems via computers, specialist software for logging service users' observations and e-learning software has changed the way in which we operate. There is also a wealth of auditing software, which can help organisations to perform health and safety assessments and quality assurance tests.

It is now possible to inform other services of a service user's status simply by logging their current observations, results and status into a handheld device which is then able to be accessed via a similar device elsewhere. A disadvantage may be that handheld devices belonging to staff may malfunction. Also, internet or broadband speed can cause delays.

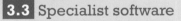

Research it

3.3 Specialist software

Research some of the specialist software that is available for care plans and auditing in adult care settings. You might, for example, wish to explore Vital packs.

e-learning software

A good example of an e-learning platform is 'Aptem' from Corndel Management College, a resource tool providing video, audio and text for students on diplomas in management and apprenticeships (www.corndel.com).

One of the advantages of using e-learning software is that it can be accessed at various locations, which means you can undertake a course from your own home. Some courses are self-explanatory and can be offered without a tutor, meaning that you do not have to pay for someone to teach the course. A disadvantage is that sometimes the internet may be unreliable and broadband access may be slow in some areas. This can be frustrating when access is unavailable.

Social media systems

Social media can be an effective way to engage and motivate staff if you use it appropriately. One advantage is that private groups can be set up on Facebook where discussions can be held about various topics on adult care in the news and best practice can be debated, which can ensure that staff are more efficient during working hours when putting this into practice. Social media can also be used to organise social gatherings.

The disadvantages are that not all staff may want to be part of such groups on social media or may in fact not be able to access the sites for various reasons. Also, there is a danger that confidential matters about individuals in your setting may be discussed in such groups. This is not the forum for such discussions.

Electronic conferencing

Electronic conferencing such as Skype, Facetime and Zoom has also meant that we are able to speak face to face with people in different locations. The advantage of this has been to reduce the need to travel to meetings in various locations, which has vastly reduced cost. However, the disadvantages are that sometimes the internet cannot be relied upon to work when needed and not everyone has access to Skype or similar software.

Evidence opportunity

3.3 Digital technology

Critically evaluate the application of different types of technology which can enhance your efficiency at work and your work plans. Examples may include the ones we have discussed in this section. Provide a written account.

You might like to look at the headings above and compile a list of how these different types of technology have improved the efficiency of your way of working. In each case, say which systems you use and how they have enhanced your work.

In critically evaluating, you will need to ask questions such as 'why' and 'how' the different types of technology have proved effective or otherwise for your business. Consider the strengths and weaknesses of each type.

If you haven't used any of the ones we have discussed in this section, then research how they might help you to enhance efficiency.

AC 3.4 Delegating responsibilities to others

Here, you will be required to explain how delegating is a part of effective team management.

Delegation is the giving of a task to another member of staff to complete on your behalf. For example, you may delegate the task of compiling the work rota to another care worker, enabling you to do other things, which may be a more effective use of your time. You will need to use your judgement to ensure that you pick the right people to delegate the tasks to; who has the skills and knowledge to complete the task safely and effectively. It may be that you need to give them clear instructions, or even training if this is a bigger task. You must also ensure that the person you have delegated the task to has agreed to accept the task and supervise them if needed. As the manager, you are accountable for delegating the activity and must undertake to oversee the member of staff carrying out the task. You might find it useful to visit http://rcnhca.org.uk/46-2/accountability-and-delegation/delegation/ for more information.

Delegation is a good way to empower employees, making them more motivated if they have been given tasks that managers would normally do. However, you should also be aware that it can have the opposite effect if they are being given mundane tasks to carry out that simply add to their workload rather than enhance their role.

> ## Evidence opportunity
>
> ### 3.4 Delegating responsibilities to others
>
> Provide a written account explaining how delegation is a part of effective team management. You might like to explain how you delegate tasks and how you monitor the process. How is this a part of effectively managing your team?

AC 3.5 Revise plans to take account of changing circumstances

Here, you will be required to adjust your work to take account of changes in operational circumstances.

Staff absence and sickness

Every day we are faced with challenges ranging from staff sickness to major incidents and everything in between. How you deal with such unexpected demands upon your time is a useful measurement of how successful you are as a manager. Some managers are immediately stressed by any change; others do not deal well with staff who phone in sick. We may also have been fortunate to work with managers who seem to be unfazed by emergencies and deal with them efficiently and with calm and ease. Which sort of manager do you aspire to be and how will you attain this?

Staff sickness demands that a manager respond by reallocating tasks, responsibilities and workload and perhaps liaising with agencies to access temporary staff. If the staff sickness is to be long term you may need to contact Human Resources to inform them of your needs as a team, find out what your options are and also to understand what your responsibilities are with respect to handling the member of staff who is off sick.

Needs and challenges presented by individuals in receipt of care and support and unscheduled and unexpected demands from others – internal and external

One of the challenges with managing an adult care provision is that circumstances change rapidly. The needs of our service users are ever changing and we may also be subject to unexpected situations arising from stakeholders and other services.

For example, if an emergency arises with one of the service users then redeployment of staff may be required, placing demands upon the setting. Staff may be required to escort service users to other settings, leaving staffing short on your site.

Additionally, you may be asked to accommodate service users from other settings at short notice and this will also increase demands upon staff.

As the manager, you need to be flexible and manage change in a calm and efficient manner. Plans may need to be adjusted and staff may need to be redeployed to accommodate changes.

> ## Evidence opportunity
>
> ### 3.5 Revise plans to take account of changing circumstances
>
> You will need to show your assessor how you adjust your work to take into account changes in operational circumstances, like the ones we have discussed in this section. You could also request a witness testimony.

> ## Case study
>
> ### 3.5 Changing plans, revising circumstances
>
> You come on duty and have two staff off sick, a complaint from a relative about care of their mother and a deadline to meet on a report, which has proved very challenging to fulfil. How will you plan your day?
>
> Provide a written account detailing your response to the above scenario. Then explain how you revise plans to take account of changing circumstances, including:
>
> * staff absence and sickness
> * needs and challenges presented by individuals in receipt of care and support
> * unscheduled and unexpected demands from others – internal and external.

LO4 Undertake professional development

AC 4.1 Evaluate own knowledge and performance

Here, you will be required to critically evaluate your own professional skills, knowledge and behaviours against standards and benchmarks, feedback from others and organisational appraisal.

Reflect on it

4.1 Reflecting on your own role

Think about how much you have learned as a result of your course and your role. Look back to the start of your course and reflect upon how you have made changes to your management style as a result of what you have learned. Provide a reflective account.

Standards and benchmarks

Individuals working in the care industry will be subject to a range of professional codes, expectations and standards of performance that are set by external organisations. All staff need to demonstrate that they are working to these standards. The requirement for professional development is reinforced in professional codes and standards of conduct, such as:

- Code of Conduct for Healthcare Support Workers and Adult Social Care Workers 2013.
- Regulations, for example, General Data Protection Regulation 2018, the Data Protection Act 1998 or the Mental Capacity Act 2005.
- Minimum/essential standards refer to the quality and safety of care and identify the experiences individuals are expected to have as a result of the care they receive.
- National Occupational Standards describe the skills, knowledge and understanding required to undertake a particular task or job to a nationally recognised level of competence.
- Health Professions Council (2008) Standards of Conduct, Performance and Ethics highlight the standards of practice for individuals to be fit to practise as healthcare professionals.
- Nursing and Midwifery Council (2018) The Code: Standards of conduct, performance and ethics for nurses and midwives identifies standards for nurses to maintain registration.
- This new version of the code is similar to the 2015 version, but has added new responsibilities for the regulation of nursing associates. Nursing associates will be registered under this code.

These documents articulate the standards that the public can expect from those delivering care. All codes and standards of practice make explicit reference to the need for those providing care to work within their levels of knowledge and experience and to address any knowledge deficits.

Evaluating your own knowledge and performance

Each individual is also accountable for their professional development and you may be required to identify to your managers, to your profession and/or to a legal authority how you have maintained this. You need to be able to evaluate and examine your knowledge with respect to practice so that you are able to identify any gaps in knowledge and your strengths and areas for development. It is most important that you can provide evidence of your knowledge and skills and how you have maintained these. As a manager and leader of others, it is your responsibility to ensure that those you manage are appropriately equipped to effectively fulfil their roles. This requires you to assess each individual's capabilities against their job description to ensure that they have the skills that are necessary to do their job.

As well as identifying the standards of care to be achieved, codes of practice articulate the manner in which care should be delivered. All recipients of care should expect to receive competent care. An organisation that strives for excellence will also ensure that attention is paid to the value base of care provision, which facilitates good and excellent practice as opposed to merely competent or safe practice.

Evaluating your own performance requires you to supply an examination of your practice showing that your knowledge and skills are based on sound learning and that you always work within the standards required. You need to show that you are a lifelong learner and continually update your practice.

Feedback from others

360-degree feedback is a system by which employees receive anonymous feedback from the people who work around them. These can be other managers, stakeholders and peers. By asking others about your performance you can gather valuable insight into how others see your professional skills and behaviour. This can then help you to evaluate how you are developing in your role and identify any gaps in your learning. Remember that feedback does not have to be anonymous. It can be an open and honest discussion with staff members, where you ask for their thoughts on your performance. Remember to take feedback and criticism in a constructive manner, and not be offended by it. You should use it to improve your performance and practice, and not to affect your performance or self-esteem negatively. See AC 1.5 for more information on 360-degree feedback.

Organisational appraisal

Just as we conduct appraisals on individual performance, so we can expect our organisation to undergo an organisational appraisal in which information is gathered and the performance of the company is assessed.

An organisational appraisal helps the management team to check how effective the organisation is by checking:

- whether policy and procedure are being complied with
- the effectiveness of leaders and staff
- how well resources are being used
- how well your monitoring systems are working.

By undertaking such a process your skills, knowledge and behaviour within the organisation come under scrutiny and you will gain valuable experience into how well you understand the company for which you work and where you may require development.

Evidence opportunity

4.1 Standards and benchmarks

Provide a written account critically evaluating your own professional skills, knowledge and behaviours against standards and benchmarks, feedback from others and organisational appraisal.

You might, for example, like to make a list of the codes and standards that guide and govern your role.

- When did you last review and reflect on your work against these standards?
- How is your work influenced by these codes and standards?
- Evaluate your performance in the light of these standards, taking into account the standards and benchmarks you are required to work within.

Research it

4.1 360-degree feedback

Conduct a 360-degree feedback exercise to assess your professional skills, knowledge and experience. See Unit 501 for more information on what a 360 evaluation entails.

Also try CIPD (2011) CIPD Factsheet 360 Degree Feedback, www.cipd.co.uk/hr-resources/factsheets/360-degree-feedback.aspx#link_furtherreading

AC 4.2 Establish own learning style

Here, you are required to establish your own learning style/s using a recognised assessment tool/s.

How do you like to learn? Individuals learn in different ways and you should think about the method that suits your preferred learning style so that, where possible, you can select appropriate learning activities.

Think about different learning activities you have participated in. Do you like discussion and working with others? Do you prefer tutor guidance? Do you like exploring and learning on your own? Are computer programs a style of learning that you enjoy? If you enjoy the process of learning, you are more likely to stick with it, particularly if it is over a period of time. Your understanding of what development activities suit your learning style means you are likely to get more from your learning.

Having identified your strengths, deficits, training needs and ideas for service enhancements, it is important that these are transformed into tangible actions that can be articulated as objectives. Objectives are statements that describe what the end point of an activity will be. Objectives should be written with the **SMART** acronym in mind; that is, they should be **S**pecific, **M**easurable, **A**chievable, **R**elevant and **T**ime bound. When writing your objectives you should have the end in mind before you start. Think of it as a journey – it is not often that you set out on a journey not knowing where you want to end up. Your plan must be able to deliver what you set out to do and you must evaluate how successful you have been. Consequently, having more information on which you can base your plan should secure the best chance of success.

Honey and Mumford (1992) developed a questionnaire that enables participants to distinguish between four key ways of learning:

- **Activists** – prefer to work intuitively, be flexible and spontaneous, generate new ideas and try things out. They like to learn from problem solving, discussion, group work and experience.
- **Reflectors** – like to watch/listen and reflect, gathering data and taking time to consider options and alternatives. They like lectures, project work and information research.
- **Theorists** – prefer to go through things thoroughly and logically, step by step. They like guidelines and prefer to learn from books, problem solving and discussion.
- **Pragmatists** – learn by 'trying things out'. They are practical and realistic, and like work-based learning and practical application in real settings.

There may be a dominant style that fits your way of learning, but it's equally possible that more than one method is appropriate for you.

Barbe et al. in 1979 identified the VAK model of learning styles, which suggests that we learn better depending upon our most dominant sense. For example, a visually dominant person will learn better by seeing pictures, graphs and diagrams, whereas those who favour the auditory sense will prefer to listen and hear from others. They may learn better by listening to auditory books or lectures. The kinaesthetic

Research it

4.2 Learning styles

Undertake some research on the VAK learning style and try to ascertain where your preference is.

If individuals can be matched with their preferred style it will make learning easier for them. Inevitably, this cannot always be fully accommodated, but knowing someone's style will help you to plan appropriately.

Evidence opportunity

4.2 Establish your own learning style

You will need to establish your own learning style/s using a recognised assessment tool/s. Have a professional discussion with your assessor about this.

- You might like to think about what your preferred learning style is.
- Try to remember your most satisfying and least satisfying learning experiences. What was it that made them satisfying or not?
- What assessment tool did you use to establish your own learning style?
- Is it helpful to identify your preferred style?
- Think about the characteristics of your team. Can you identify their different learning styles?
- Think about the learning opportunities and development objectives that best reflect the preferred styles of learning.

learner is one who prefers to do things and have a more hands-on approach to learning, preferring to experience things and to undertake experiments.

AC 4.3 Prioritise own development goals and targets

Here, you will be required to select and prioritise your own goals and targets.

Once you understand how you prefer to learn, you then need to articulate what you need to learn and identify how this can be achieved. Identifying needs and areas for improvement can amount to nothing more than a wish list. Time spent reflecting on these wishes will help you to prioritise your development needs. Once you have identified your needs these must be articulated as objectives. It is important that objectives are prioritised and committed to paper in the form of a plan.

Developing a formal plan serves a number of purposes. It enables you to:

- structure and prioritise your learning and development
- set short- and long-term goals (using the SMART model)

- address those things that you must do, such as update your knowledge and skills
- start to devise a more creative and personalised plan.

Remember, the short-term goals may or may not contribute to the longer-term ones. Writing your objectives in a plan adds weight and structure to them and you are more likely to act on them, especially if the plan is shared with another person such as a line manager who may commit to supporting it.

Use of tools (for example, SWOT analysis)

You might undertake what is known as a SWOT analysis (Figure 9.6). This is an acronym for identifying four key areas about yourself and asking yourself questions. For example:

Strengths

- What are you good at in life and in the workplace?
- Which part of your job do you do well and why?
- What are the values and attitudes that you live by and that help you?
- What do others see you as an expert in?
- How do others value you?
- What qualifications do you have and could you make more use of them?

Weaknesses

- What areas of your job do you least enjoy?
- What makes you stressed?
- What would others say your weaknesses are?
- Are there skills you wish you had?

Opportunities

- What new skills are needed in your job role that you could learn?
- Do you have any skills that could be used to improve your performance which you currently do not use?

Threats

- During appraisal, have you been made aware of anything your manager is concerned about respecting your performance?
- Is your job role changing and can you handle that change?
- What makes it harder for you to perform at work?

Strengths	**W**eaknesses
Opportunities	**T**hreats

▲ **Figure 9.6** SWOT analysis

Setting SMART targets with realistic short- and long-term goals

In prioritising your own development goals, the setting of SMART targets help you to identify what it is you want to achieve, how you will do it, how you will know you have done it, and the specific time scale in which it will happen.

Concentrating on the crucial activities

The SMART targets can further be prioritised into the crucial activities you need to accomplish and those that can be left for later. For example, a long-term target might be to finish your degree course but in the short term the target may be to successfully accomplish the first year.

Setting deadlines and managing interruptions

You will need to ensure that deadlines are set and met and any interruptions to your plans must be dealt with flexibly. For example, interruptions can take many forms – illness, additional workload, personal issues – and these need to be addressed within your planning. You will need to ensure that the deadlines that are set are realistic and attainable, and that there are milestones in place, when/where needed, in order to meet those deadlines.

Managing multi-tasking

Multi-tasking is the ability to manage our time well and to focus on each task equally. You will need to check out how you can use your time effectively. You may also need to determine whether multi-tasking is the right thing to do in certain situations, or whether you can delegate certain tasks to others.

Evidence opportunity

4.3 Prioritising your own development goals and targets

For this AC, you will be required to show that you can select and prioritise your own goals and targets. You might, for example, have a professional discussion about this with your assessor or prepare a presentation for them about this.

You could, for example, undertake a SWOT analysis and use this tool to prioritise your goals and targets.

Research it

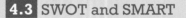

4.3 SWOT and SMART

Look at the SMART model and compare it to SWOT. What are the differences? Provide a written account.

AC 4.4 Use personal and professional development planning

Here, you will be required to implement, establish and reflect on a personal and professional development plan.

When prioritising your objectives, think about how much you want to do something. Before embarking on development activities, you should be clear about what you are prepared to invest in achieving the goals that you set. This may include decisions about your personal motivations and the time you are prepared to make available, which is likely to be in addition to anything your employer will provide. You must be realistic about resources and in particular the financial burdens and who will be responsible for them. It is also important to acknowledge the potential impact that education and development can have on those around you, both at home and at work. This can be as a result of support that others must provide or the change that may occur in you as a result of the development. You must be realistic about these factors, but that does not mean you should not also have aspirations and set an ambitious plan.

A successful professional development plan will:

- clearly specify how the objectives will be achieved
- identify the timeframes and milestones against which progress can be measured
- suggest criteria against which the activity can be evaluated.

Personal goals for staff should be part of an organisation's goals. Although there may be barriers to developing the staff, plans must be put in place to overcome those barriers and these plans need to be reviewed and changed if necessary. It is a requirement of the CQC that settings have systems in place for staff development.

Clarify aims to ensure the plan is designed to improve the effectiveness and impact of practice

In developing goals for the success of the setting you must establish a plan that will have a positive impact upon practice. There must be clarity about what it is you are trying to achieve and how you are going to do this.

Identify areas for improvement and development of skills

The plans should highlight the areas that need to be improved in the first instance and the skills that will be required of staff to achieve those goals. For example, you may feel that you need to improve your grasp of resource management recording and you notice that Excel spreadsheets are a good way of doing this. You recognise that your lack of skills in the use of Excel currently limits your use of spreadsheets, so you will need to seek some help with this.

Establish SMART objectives that are time bound

The SMART targets that are set should have deadline dates applied to them to ensure that the development is kept to target and accomplished. Without this, the plan will fail.

Identify support and training needed to achieve the objectives (including costs)

A business case may need to be developed in order to ensure that any support required to meet the targets is costed and resources and finances are available to support the objectives.

Identify how and with whom the plan will be reviewed

The date for review and the person doing the review need to be identified at the outset.

Evidence opportunity

4.4 Use personal and professional development planning

Have a professional discussion with your assessor about how you implement, establish and reflect on a personal and professional development plan. Address the areas we have discussed in this section.

If you have not developed your plan, you might like to use a template similar to the one below to develop your professional development plan. Ensure that you write objectives that can be measured and evaluated. Clearly articulate the evidence that will demonstrate whether or not you have achieved your objectives.

Overall learning development need		What specifically do you need to know/learn?			
Objectives		**Date for achievement**	**How will you achieve your objective?**	**Support required**	**Evidence and outcomes**
What specific end or steps do you have in mind? You must include a measurable verb in each objective statement in this column, e.g. Pass an accredited first-aid course.		When will you assess progress? When will you have achieved your objective, e.g. dates of course/training?	How will you demonstrate that you have met the objective, e.g. attend a first aid course?	Human? Financial? Time? Learning resources?	What evidence will you have to confirm your achievement, e.g. certificate of competence?
Avoiding barriers and blockers		**What positive steps can you take to avoid barriers?**			
Objective 1 Example Develop IT skills to enable effective forward planning and publication of staff rotas for off-duty cover.		September this year.	Complete course on using Microsoft Excel.	Either day release to attend course or time to undertake online programme.	Publication of all off-duty rotas using computerised support packages. Staff cover will be effective and planned and produced four weeks in advance.

What positive steps can you take to avoid barriers and blockers?
Identify need and actual and potential benefits for the organisation. Research and present different methods of achieving goal, with pros and cons identified. Discuss with and gain commitment from line manager through signed agreement or financial support to enable attendance/completion of the course. Report progress.

How this plan improves the effectiveness and impact of your practice

By undertaking a professional development plan you can be sure that you will be developing your skills and keeping up with changing trends in your role. Additionally, you can enhance your position in the job field and perhaps move on to higher roles within or external to your organisation.

Legislation

Legislation	Key points
Mental Health Act 1983, 2007 Mental Capacity Act 2005	While legislation relevant to mental health and capacity is not wholly relevant here, you should be aware of the issues around mental health and wellbeing for yourself, your staff, individuals in your setting and others you work with.

Suggestions for using the activities

This table summarises all the activities in the unit that are relevant to each assessment criterion. Here, we also suggest other, different methods that you may want to use to present your knowledge and skills by using the activities. These are just suggestions, and you should refer to the Introduction section at the start of the book, and more importantly the City & Guilds specification, and your assessor who will be able to provide more guidance on how you can evidence your knowledge and skills. When you need to be observed during your assessment, this can be done by your assessor, or your manager can provide a witness testimony.

Assessment criteria and accompanying activities	Suggested methods to show your knowledge/skills
LO1 Understand the importance of self-awareness	
1.1 Research it (page 292)	Write a short account of Goleman's theory and how it can help us to be more self-aware.
1.1 Reflect on it (page 293)	Write a reflective account addressing the questions in the activity.
1.1 Research it (page 293)	Write down your findings.
1.1 Reflect on it (page 294)	Write a reflective account and answer the questions in the activity.
1.1 Evidence opportunity (page 294)	Have a professional discussion with your assessor or provide a written account.
1.2 Reflect on it (page 295)	Address the points in the activity. Provide a reflective account.
1.2 Evidence opportunity (page 296)	Provide a written account detailing your response.
1.3 Evidence opportunity (page 297)	Provide a written account.
1.4 Reflect on it (page 300)	Provide a reflective account.
1.4 Evidence opportunity (page 300)	Provide a written account. You could also prepare a presentation.
1.5 Reflect on it (page 301)	Compile a diary and provide a reflective account as instructed in the activity.
1.5 Evidence opportunity (page 302)	You could provide a written account, have a professional discussion or provide a reflective account.
LO2 Manage personal and professional behaviour	
2.1 Research it (page 303)	Write down your findings.
2.1 Reflect on it (page 303)	Provide a reflective account.
2.1 Evidence opportunity (page 303)	Provide a written account or have a discussion with your assessor.
2.2 Evidence opportunity (page 304)	Provide a written account, a reflective account or have a discussion with your assessor reflecting on how you respond to feedback.
2.3 Case study (page 305)	Read the case study and provide a written account detailing how you might deal with the situation.
2.3 Evidence opportunity (page 305)	Explain the links between emotional intelligence and professional conduct. Provide a written account so this relates to the requirement.
2.4 Research it (page 308)	Write down your findings.

➜

Suggestions for using the activities	
2.4 Reflect on it (page 308)	Keep a communication diary. Write down your answers to the questions in the activity.
2.4 Evidence opportunity (page 308)	Show your assessor how you adapt and extend your communication and responses to suit the needs of others and situations.
2.5 Evidence opportunity (page 308)	Show your assessor how you challenge views, actions, systems and routines that do not match the vision and values of the service.
LO3 Manage workloads	
3.1 Research it (page 309)	Provide a written account.
3.1 Evidence opportunity (page 310)	Demonstrate this to your assessor and discuss the various topics with them.
3.2 Research it (page 311)	Undertake the time management analysis as instructed.
3.2 Reflect on it (page 311)	Write a reflective account.
3.2 Evidence opportunity (page 312)	Explain this to your assessor or demonstrate to them how you do this. You could also write down how you are able to do this.
3.3 Research it (page 313)	Write a short account detailing your findings.
3.3 Evidence opportunity (page 313)	Provide a written account. You could also prepare a presentation for your assessor.
3.4 Evidence opportunity (page 314)	Provide a written account. You could also have a professional discussion with your assessor.
3.5 Evidence opportunity (page 314)	You will need to show your assessor how you adjust your work to take into account changes in operational circumstances, like the ones we have discussed in this section.
3.5 Case study (page 314)	Provide a written account detailing your response to the scenario.
LO4 Undertake professional development	
4.1 Reflect on it (page 315)	Provide a reflective account.
4.1 Evidence opportunity (page 316)	Provide a written account addressing the points in the activity.
4.1 Research it (page 316)	Write up your findings.
4.2 Research it (page 317)	Discuss your findings with your assessor or write them up.
4.2 Evidence opportunity (page 317)	Have a professional discussion with your assessor.
4.3 Evidence opportunity (page 318)	For this AC, you will be required to show that you can select and prioritise your own goals and targets. You might, for example, have a professional discussion about this with your assessor or prepare a presentation for them about this.
4.3 Research it (page 318)	Provide a written account with your findings.
4.4 Evidence opportunity (page 319)	Have a professional discussion with your assessor.

References

Bandura, A. (1977) *Social Learning Theory*. New York: General Learning Press.

Barbe, W.B., Swassing, R.H. and Milone, M.N. (1979) *Teaching Through Modality Strengths: Concepts and practices*. Columbus, OH: Zaner-Bloser.

CIPD (2011) *CIPD Factsheet 360 Degree Feedback*. Available at: www.cipd.co.uk/hr-resources/factsheets/360-degree-feedback.aspx#link_furtherreading

Covey, S. (1989) *The 7 Habits of Highly Effective People*. New York: Simon & Schuster.

Crawford, P., Brown, B. and Bonham, P. (2006) *Communication in Clinical Settings*. Cheltenham: Nelson Thornes.

DfE (2014) *Promoting Fundamental British Values as Part of SMSC in Schools. Departmental advice for maintained schools.* London: TSO.

Gallwey, T. (1986) *The Inner Game of Tennis*. London: Pan.

Goleman, D. (1995) *Emotional Intelligence*. New York: Bantam Books.

Honey, P. and Mumford, A. (1992) *Learning Styles Questionnaire*, Peter Honey Publications Ltd.

Miller, L. (2006) *Counselling Skills for Social Work*. London: Sage.

Mohindra, V. and Azhar, S. (2012) Gender communication: A comparative analysis of communicational approaches of men and women at workplaces, *IOSR Journal of Humanities and Social Science (JHSS)*, 2(1) (Sep–Oct.): 18–27. www.iosrjournals.org

NHS Executive (1998) *Information for Health. An information strategy for the modern NHS 1998–2005*. London: NHS Executive.

Parsloe, E. (1999) *The Manager as Coach and Mentor*. London: Chartered Institute of Personnel & Development, p. 8.

Skills for Care (2013) *Code of Conduct for Healthcare Support Workers and Adult Social Care Workers in England*. London: DoH.

Whitmore, J. (2002) *Coaching for Performance: GROWing people, performance and purpose*. London: Nicholas Brealey.

Websites

www.apa.org/helpcenter/road-resilience.aspx#

www.gov.uk/government/publications/care-act-2014-part-1-factsheets

www.psychologytoday.com/basics/resilience

www.scie.org.uk/workforce/Peoplemanagement/leadership/workforcedev/index.asp

www.sonoma.edu/users/d/daniels/lewinnotes.html

www.which.co.uk/news/2018/04/which-reveals-nhs-care-funding-postcode-lottery

http://rcnhca.org.uk/46-2/accountability-and-delegation/delegation

Corndel Management College www.corndel.com

Decision making in adult care

About this unit?

In your role as manager or supervisor, you will make decisions daily on various issues relating to staff, budgets, the setting and the people who use care services. Decision making is, therefore, a key part of adult care work and management and will be a key part of your role so it is important that you understand how to make decisions effectively, ones that consider the best interests of those that will be affected by them.

In this unit, you will understand what it means to make choices, identify the decisions that need to be made and gather the information that is needed to inform effective and positive decisions in your role. You will gain a better understanding

of what it means to make thoughtful decisions by carefully organising the information you have and considering alternatives. You will explore models and methods of decision making and understand how you can apply these to your own management practice. You will understand how you can use and analyse qualitative and/or quantitative data to inform your decision making and how you can justify decisions. You will also learn how to evaluate your own management of the range of situations in which decisions are required and to reflect and critically evaluate your skills in decision making and recommendations to enhance your future practice.

Learning outcomes

By the end of this unit, you will:

1   Understand how to make effective and positive decisions
2   Carry out and reflect on effective decision making

Getting started

Before you study the unit, think about the following

- What safeguards are in place for the decisions managers make? In other words, what in law protects us when we make decisions on behalf of others? When do you think it is right to make a decision based on intuition?
- What are the potential challenges to decision making when working with difficult situations and if there are disagreements? Have you experienced these?
- How does legislation impact on decision-making processes?

LO1 Understand how to make effective and positive decisions

AC 1.1 Elements of management decision making

Here, with examples from your own practice, you will be required to critically evaluate:

- *the meaning of effective decision making at senior management level*
- *what constitutes an effective management decision*
- *the effects of not making timely decisions in management*
- *the impact that making a management decision has on others, e.g. for colleagues, teams, others*
- *the impact that not making a management decision has on others, e.g. colleagues, teams, others*
- *the relationship between decision making and accountability.*

Effective decision making at senior management level and what constitutes an effective management decision

What decisions have you made today? What to have for breakfast? What to wear? How to get to work? You had to go through a process to make those decisions. In your role as manager you will be making decisions daily. Some of those may be life changing for somebody, so you need to be aware of the impact of the decisions you are making.

Reflect on it

1.1 The decisions you make

What decisions do you make on a daily basis in your management role? Make a list of some you have made today and then say how you feel about this as part of your management role. What are the pros and cons of making a list of the decisions you have made? What are the pros and cons of reflecting on how these decisions are part of the management role?

Peter Drucker (2015) highlighted seven elements of decision making.

1 Determining whether a decision is necessary

This sounds simple but if a decision does not need to be made then a lot of time and resources may be wasted. It is important then that you are able to distinguish between necessary and unnecessary decisions.

2 Classify the problem

As a manager, you will face varying types of issues. Some will be of a general nature, which can be answered with reference to policy and procedure. For example, if somebody asks for a decision about annual leave you might direct them to the policy in place. Occasionally, though, an event may occur that cannot be answered in this manner, such as an emergency situation. When this happens, a decision must be made. Drucker refers to these events as 'unique' problems requiring a unique solution but makes the point that these are rare occurrences and should be carefully examined and defined.

3 Define the problem

Sometimes, we may look at a problem and jump to a conclusion. This is dangerous. For example, we may make the assumption that the problem lies with the service user but in reality it is how the staff dealt with the service user that was really the issue.

Sometimes, what the problem appears to be is not what it really is. So, how can you make an effective decision here? Drucker suggests asking questions to define the problem:

- What is this all about and what's going on? Here you will need to think about the situation as it is happening and the people or resources surrounding the situation. For example, you may be faced with an emergency and need to make a decision quickly. You will need to evaluate in that moment what you are actually seeing and what is happening here.
- What is key to this situation? In this case, you want to know what the priority is in this situation.

4 Decide on what is right

The next step is to form the decision. It is here that you need to decide who in the wider organisation might be affected. You will start to think about what your manager may think about your decision or how the finance team might view it. Perhaps a compromise is needed. Making a decision implies that there are alternatives that may need to be considered, but those alternatives should be ones which fit with the goals and values of the organisation and any compromise also needs to reflect those values.

5 Get others to buy into the decision

This is when you form the decision and start to 'sell' it to the organisation. For example, a new way of working is sometimes not received well. In this case, you will need to explain to staff why the change is necessary and good for the organisation. Staff need to understand that the decision has been made with the wider organisation's objectives in mind and therefore has meaning and purpose. Also see the section below on page 325 about the impact that making a decision has on others.

6 Build action into the decision and make it happen

If this is missing, then the decision simply remains an idea. You now need others to do something to move the action forward and this requires more than just a memo informing staff of a change. You will need to identify the following:

- Who needs to know of this decision?
- What action has to be taken and who is to take it?
- What do they have to do?

As the decision maker, you must be assured that the staff who are involved in making it happen are not only capable of doing so but are aware of how they will show that they have accomplished the action. They will be impacted by the decision and therefore you should be aware of how that decision may affect them. Almost any decision may involve some conflict or dissatisfaction and you need to be ready to justify your decision.

7 Test the decision against actual results

Finally, the results of a decision that has been made may be seen in the future – you may not see the results immediately, but there should be monitoring and reporting built into the decision to provide evidence of its progress.

Source: Adapted from Drucker, 2015

What constitutes an effective management decision

A good decision is one where the choice made has been considered against other alternatives. In making a good decision we will be aware of the positives and negatives of the options we have and think about the outcome by weighing up the options. For example, we may have two members of staff who need to attend a training course but there is only one place left. Our decision will depend on the information we have about the members of staff and perhaps who might benefit from it more or who can wait until the next course is available. We may make the decision based on the need of the organisation and send the most experienced member of staff who will be able to cascade what is learned to the rest of the team. The decision, then, will be based upon a number of factors but will require information gathering to make it a good one.

The impact that management decision making has on others

If we look at our example above, the decision we make will impact upon at least one member of staff; that is, the one who will not at this time attend the training. This can be negative and will require careful handling, but a well-reasoned and informed choice will ensure that staff understand why you made the decision. You need to justify what you have decided.

Sometimes, not making a decision can also have an impact on others because the decision may be taken out of our hands and made for us. If this happens it may not lead to the best result for your team. Ignoring the need to make a decision will not make it go away, it will simply make somebody take the decision for us.

The effects of not making timely decisions

It is tempting sometimes to leave a decision alone and to simply not make one. We procrastinate. Perhaps we hope the problem will go away or that if we leave it long enough it will magically get better. However, putting off making a decision may result in somebody else making the decision for you and that may not be palatable. The team around you may start to lose confidence in you if they are waiting for a decision to be made and you are seen to be 'dragging your feet'. The impact may be that you have a team of very demotivated staff who feel you are unable to lead them.

The relationship between decision making and accountability

Being 'accountable' means we take responsibility for our actions. It is the same in making decisions. Any decision we make in the course of our work must be accompanied by the fact that we are liable for what we have done. Therefore, a good decision-making process will ensure we can stand by the decisions we make and can justify why we made them. Sometimes, though, we may make a bad decision and we must take responsibility for this also. In these cases, we need to look back at the process we went through and the choices we made to determine what went wrong.

Evidence opportunity

1.1 Effective decision making

With examples from your practice, critically evaluate:

- the meaning of effective decision making at senior management level
- what constitutes an effective management decision
- the effects of not making timely decisions in management
- the impact that making a management decision has on others, e.g. for colleagues, teams, others
- the impact that not making a management decision has on others, e.g. colleagues, teams, others
- the relationship between decision making and accountability.

Provide evidence of a decision you have had to make at work and show the process you went through and how effective it has been.

How have you measured its effectiveness and what impact has it had on the staff and the service providers? What would be the consequences of not making this decision?

How did you justify the decision you made and who were you accountable to in making the decision?

Make sure that you record your thoughts. You could provide a reflective piece.

AC 1.2 Purpose of management decision making

Here, you will analyse the purpose of:

- *making management decisions*
- *managers having to make independent decisions without consultation – negotiable vs non-negotiable*
- *managers making collaborative team decisions*
- *managers having to make decisions on behalf of others.*

As we mentioned in AC 1.1, as a manager, you are making decisions for many different reasons and purposes on a daily basis. Some require a negotiable, collaborative approach with members of the team, whereas others are made independently or on behalf of somebody in your team or in your care.

Decision making is a primary function of management, the purpose of which is to drive the organisation forward and to ensure that goals are achieved. It involves the process of deciding what is important in a situation and acting upon it.

Making management decisions

Making management decisions supports the organisation's strategic plan and objectives, including those that are sometimes difficult to make. Occasionally, a decision may be unpopular among staff but, as manager, you will ensure that you can supply a rationale for why the decision has been made and how it will help the organisation to move forward.

Managers making independent decisions without consultation – negotiable vs non-negotiable

As a manager, you will have certain rules that are simply non-negotiable. For example, some settings have protected mealtimes, where every activity except eating and helping service users with their food stops until the meal is finished. All traffic through the area is discouraged and staff are employed in helping the service users to get the food they need. Other tasks are postponed until the meal is completed. As a manager, you may have developed this rule to ensure that the service users are well nourished and this may be a value you hold and will not waver from.

You may also have rules that are negotiable, or you may be prepared to undertake discussion on. For example, you may be prepared to discuss the off-duty rota and negotiate shift changes among the staff.

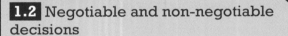

Reflect on it

1.2 Negotiable and non-negotiable decisions

What are your non-negotiable and negotiable rules, or the negotiable and non-negotiable decisions you make? Which would you be prepared to change?

Managers making collaborative team decisions

Although this is considered to be a time-consuming exercise, with clearly defined goals, good communication and the right people in the group, collaborative team decisions are those which are generally more acceptable to employees than those decisions made in a 'top-down' manner. Collaboration on a problem helps the team to accept the outcome of the decision more readily than if a decision is made without their input. Although it is easier for a manager to present a decision to a team, it may not be accepted and staff may be reluctant to 'buy in' to that decision. By involving the staff in the process of making the decision, you may find that the time it takes is well spent and produces a better outcome in the long run.

Evidence opportunity

1.2 Purpose of decision making

Identify the purpose of all the decisions you make on a daily basis.

Analyse the purpose of:

- making management decisions
- managers having to make independent decisions without consultation – negotiable vs non-negotiable
- managers making collaborative team decisions
- managers having to make decisions on behalf of others.

Provide a written account.

Managers having to make decisions on behalf of others

Sometimes, you need to make a decision that may have an effect on the team and is made on their behalf. Errors in doing so can lead to consequences so you must have good decision-making processes in place to ensure that you are clear about what you are doing and why you are doing it. When managers make decisions on behalf of the staff, it is important to define the problem clearly to have a good understanding of it. Only then can you determine alternate solutions to the problem, weigh the pros and cons of each decision, and then opt for one you feel is beneficial to all. You need to be aware that your choice will result in change at some level and may not be a popular one, so you should be able to justify the choice made, such as a change to the time you start and end your shift.

AC 1.3 Reasons for decision-making management practice

Here, you will be required to explain the reasons, purpose and benefits of why managers:

- *make decisions about strategy, policies and procedures in adult care practice that might and might not involve others*
- *make decisions for those in receipt of care and support*
- *might struggle with making management decisions in respect of the above.*

Strategy, policies and procedures in adult care practice are in place to ensure the organisation functions well. Sometimes, you will make decisions that involve others in the process or that others will simply have to accept. Decisions made on behalf of those in your care, however, need to be shared.

As the manager, it is important that you keep others 'in the loop' with regard to your decisions and inform them about these to help them to understand why decisions have been made. It may be that you need to comply with legislation or regulation to address the day-to-day running of the organisation. The rationale behind the decision is important. You will be expected to make decisions on various issues, whether they are to do with staffing issues and deciding you need emergency cover in an employee's absence, for example, or broader decisions with regard to strategy. It may be that an unpopular change to work practice may be ill received; however, as mentioned, if you inform staff as to why it needs to be made, they can then start to understand.

Decisions also need to be made for and with patients in your care. When needs change, decisions must be made about how the care will be delivered in the future. Research has shown that patients who have been actively involved in their own care, treatment and support have improved outcomes which help them to stay well and manage their own conditions in a more productive way. NHS England has made a commitment to support shared decision making, which involves letting patients review all the treatment options available to them to make the 'best interest' decisions that work for them.

NHS England in the *Next Steps on the Five Year Forward View* (2017) has made a commitment to give more power to individuals to manage their own care and support to make their own informed decisions. This will have an impact on how you deal with this process in your own setting. As the manager, you may need to guide the service user and their family in this decision making. Unwise decisions may be made at this point and the family and service user may need to be informed of all the facts in order to make a choice that is rational and feasible.

Make decisions about strategy, policies and procedures in adult care practice that might and might not involve others

Strategies and policies provide guidelines for decision making and are different from rules or procedures. Policies allow for discretion and judgement to be exercised within certain limits whereas rules must simply be followed. For example, 'No Smoking' is a command with no room for negotiation or discretion. We simply follow that command. A policy, on the other hand, is a guide that establishes certain boundaries in which we can exercise judgement. The purpose of policies, which are formulated by managers, is to ensure that decisions made will meet the organisation's objectives and these will be part of the organisation's strategy. Some policies may be generated at team level and will be more applicable to your specific department.

Make decisions for those in receipt of care and support

People with mental capacity can make decisions about their own health and care. However, occasionally this may be compromised and it falls to care professionals to make decisions on their behalf and this must be assessed carefully. As far as possible, a person in your care should be helped to make their own decisions, but if deemed to lack capacity the decision made on their behalf must be in the person's best interest and according to the law must be the least restrictive option (MCA, 2005).

A person-centred approach

The systems you have in place to ensure that the personalisation agenda is met in your setting need to show regard for the service users' views and their needs. Your systems must hold the service user at the centre of the decision making if this is to work. Care planning is a good example of a system we have in place to ensure that care is individualised. The development of these systems puts the service users at the centre of the process.

Decision making about the day-to-day running of the adult care setting and the general state of repair and decorations should not only be left to the staff but should include the service users as well. Most care establishments now run a weekly or monthly service user meeting in which such things can be discussed.

You should also refer to Unit 507 on Partnership, AC 1.4.

Why managers might struggle with making management decisions in respect of the above

It is difficult to make a decision on somebody else's behalf, particularly when there may be a moral or ethical principle involved. For example, without **advance directives** in place, individuals may be subject to treatment that could be considered very invasive and not of much benefit. In making such decisions, we would need to ask close relatives to make the decision on behalf of the individual, but difficulty arises if we are not in full agreement with their choice. From a management point of view, we might need to take advice from other health professionals and may even have to involve the courts in these cases (MCA, 2005).

KEY TERM

Advance directive (also known as a living will) is a legal document that specifies what actions should be taken for a person if they cannot make decisions for themselves because of illness or incapacity.

▲ **Figure 10.1** How do you ensure you involve others when making decisions?

AC 1.4 Models and methods of decision making

Here, you will be required to investigate models and methods of decision making and analyse their relevance to you in your leadership and management role.

It is useful for you as a manager to have options with respect to the types of models available to you in decision making. Adair (2009) makes the point that a decision is like a cake that can be shared. If we view decision making as a continuum, at one end of that line the manager has all the 'cake' and makes the decision without consultation. As we move along the line the 'cake' can be shared as the manager starts the process of explaining why a decision is needed. As Adair says, the more you move along the line, the more people become involved in the process, sharing the 'cake' and thus being more motivated to carry out the decision-making process.

For example, you may have been asked to introduce a new directive which has been developed by higher management. This is a change in shift patterns introducing internal rotations, which means that permanent night workers of whom you have six in the team will lose their favoured way of working. How will you share this? Perhaps you will meet with the night staff first to outline the change, then the rest of the team who will need to rotate onto nights, and last perhaps you could meet with all staff together to discuss how this can be made more palatable by involving all in finding the best way forward.

Group decision making

This approach to making a decision can sometimes be time consuming as you are trying to gain the consensus or agreement of everybody in the team (Figure 10.1). The decision that is made affects all participants, who each have a say in the process and are given the opportunity to speak and voice their opinion. The manager leads the discussion but ultimately wants all in the room to buy into the decision and commit to a joint decision. If we use our example above, we would involve the whole team at some point to discuss the change and to develop a strategy which all agree on or at the very least are willing to compromise on.

Descriptive, normative or prescriptive, rational and intuitive decision making

If we use a **descriptive model** to make a decision we tend to focus on how we would make a decision in our everyday life. It is simply a theory about how decisions are actually made.

For example, decisions made using this model in the adult care setting are likely to be made from a personal perspective. Individuals will bring into the decision their own values and beliefs.

A **normative model** is about how decisions should be made and whether we need to allow the team to participate in those decisions. The model describes various strategies that may be adopted, from a wholly autocratic style, such as when you the manager make the decision, to consulting the team and then making the decision based on feedback, to democratic styles where you allow the team to make the decision. This might work with our example above. You can make the decision, or you can ask the team to feed back their ideas and then make the decision based upon the feedback, or you can ask the team to come up with their decision alone.

A **rational approach** is one that is based on analysis and facts. In this approach, in a care setting we would try to lose the emotion in the decision and adopt a rational approach or one that is based upon facts and figures. If we use our example about the new internal rotation directive above, this approach would be based upon the facts about the change proposed and how it might benefit the service and patients.

A **prescriptive model** is one in which the decision is made by higher management and the team are given no role in the decision-making processes. They simply follow the decision that has already been agreed.

Mind mapping – aims and purpose

Mind mapping was developed by Tony Buzan in his 1972 book *Use Your Head*, and is a technique for problem solving and project planning. It is useful in making decisions since it allows the sharing of ideas. Diagrams are used and information is connected by drawings or words. You might use such an approach for staff who require more than just discussion. To see the problem outlined in a pictorial way can sometimes be a useful tool for those who require a visual representation.

'Gut' instincts and related risk and implications without facts

We sometimes have a 'feeling' about something which we cannot quite put our finger on, but instinctively know that to follow that feeling is the right or the wrong thing to do. For example, in an emergency we have to act quickly, but what if we observed somebody about to do something or make a decision that we feel uneasy about? Perhaps we feel that the action or decision is wrong, and this may bring about an emotion in us that might be described as fear. We may feel fear because this could have a very poor outcome. We have no rational reason to feel this and in that moment we may not even have any facts to support our views, but there is something that does not add up. These feelings generally follow from an emotion we have and we call them 'gut instincts', which can be defined as 'an innate, typically fixed pattern of behaviour in animals in response to certain stimuli' (www.lifehack.org/articles/lifestyle/5-gut-instincts-you-dont-want-ignore.html).

How safe would it be to make a vital decision on that basis, particularly one that might affect a lot of people in the workplace? What would you do about the situation described? Accept it without voicing concern or speak out?

If your gut instinct or your feelings tell you something is wrong, or off kilter, you should listen to it. You have a wealth of experience that has been developed over your lifetime and it is this that makes this an important lesson. In some situations, you will need to listen to what you are feeling, which after all is subjective and potentially biased, but then back up the decision with a factual analysis to support it. This might, for example, be when you are required to make an 'on the spot' decision.

Sometimes, you need to weigh up the related risk and implications of making decisions without facts. If we said nothing in the emergency situation above, then a service user might suffer or even the individual about to carry out the action. There is not enough time in this situation to reason, deliberate or seek out facts and we need to act quickly, so relying on our gut instinct seems acceptable. More complex decisions may also bring up an impulsive gut reaction, but if we have time to check this out we can make a more informed decision, which is based on reasoned facts.

Professional judgement(s)

We may have heard people refer to the term 'professional judgement' in making a decision, but what does the term actually mean?

Professional judgement is more commonly known as professional wisdom and is based upon knowledge that is gained through experience and practice in a profession. It is not taught in colleges and universities but gained as a result of reflection, relationships and communication with peers.

Care workers and medical professionals possess special education, knowledge and skills in the area of care and are also duty bound to follow a code of conduct for care. As such, they can be deemed professionals.

The word judgement is defined as:

> *'an opinion or decision that is based on careful thought; the act or process of forming an opinion or making a decision after careful thought; the act of judging something or someone; the ability to make good decisions about what should be done.'*
>
> **Source**: *Merriam Webster Dictionary*, 2015

In all areas of care practice and management, adult care professionals use their judgement to form opinions and make good decisions about what should be done to provide safe, competent care. Professional judgement is about using our knowledge, skills and values, which have been informed by a code of conduct or standards to make decisions on behalf of our service users and staff. In your management role you would use your professional judgement in dealing with staff as individuals. For example, a staff misdemeanour may be dealt with by invoking the disciplinary policy immediately or you may use your professional judgement to deal with it more constructively and develop a way with the member of staff to work through the issue.

Logical and justifiable decision making

In making decisions based upon our professional judgement, as a manager in an adult care setting you should be making logical and justifiable decisions, which are based upon skill and knowledge as well as experience. In order to practise ethically we would ensure that any decision made can be justified according to such knowledge and skill. We are accountable for all we do in our practice as managers, so any decision made must be responsible and able to be justified. Without such justification, we cannot support our decisions;

staff may, therefore, lose trust in our decisions if we cannot justify them, and we are even likely to make errors.

The difference between informal and formal decision making

We have established that, as a manager, you make a number of decisions on a daily basis and you lead your team by operating a decision-making process that is sound and fair based upon the information that is available at the time.

These are the formal processes within the detail of making a decision and in the section below we address the stages of formal decision making.

In formal organisations, designated decision makers may make all the decisions without recourse to anybody else. This can be useful as roles are well defined, but if the decision maker is not available then progress with a decision may stop and here is where the weakness lies. In addition, the decisions made in such formal organisations are sometimes not well received by staff, who may feel powerless, and this can lead to low morale. If decisions are constantly being made without staff involvement, the 'buy in' will be low. Formal decisions may need to be made at times, perhaps in emergency situations or when deadlines loom and there is no time to agree consensus.

An informal organisation is less structured and decisions are usually made when consensus in a group is received. Although this can be time consuming, the decision made may be more palatable to staff. They are likely to feel more empowered and valued in the workplace.

Informal decisions may be made at team level. Perhaps a minor change to a way of working can be discussed and built into the working day. As a manager, you may agree to a member of staff working a different set of hours on one day of the week to accommodate childcare arrangements. This is an informal decision and as long as you can justify the change to higher management it can be an effective decision to make.

Reviewing the decision-making process

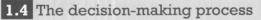

Research it

1.4 The decision-making process

Research the various processes others in your setting use to make decisions or look at ones discussed online.

Makes notes detailing your findings.

Let's review the steps in making a decision. The processes will vary for different people, but here is a popular one:

1 We have a problem so need to state and explain what it is in order to make it clear. First, think about the purpose of the decision and the timing of it. Why does it need to

be made and when? Is it an urgent one or can it be left until you have more facts?

2 Examine, analyse and look carefully at the problem. Remember, the problem you see may not be the actual problem, so don't assume you know what it is until you have investigated it. For example, staff morale seems low. You believe it is to do with pay cuts. They, in fact, are fed up with the poor communication in the team.

3 What might be the limiting factors that stop you from making a decision? It might be you procrastinating, for example.

4 Is there anyone else that might influence the decision you want to make? Who else needs to know? Who drove the last decision you made? It might be people in the team who resist the change you want to make.

5 Identify potential alternatives and other means to solve the problem if you are unable to agree on a decision. Start by looking at the formal process and determine who or what might be involved in agreeing the decision.

6 Analyse the alternatives. Look closely at what you have and decide if the alternatives are feasible. Are they viable, or justifiable? Can everyone agree on the alternatives?

7 Choose the best alternative. Think about whether this is the best way forward. Does it effectively respond to the issue at hand?

8 Whatever the decision that has been agreed on, you must now implement the decision and justify its purpose. Make an action plan showing the way forward and make sure deadlines and dates for completion are in place. It is useful to consider whether deadline dates are realistic and achievable.

9 Put into place a system to measure and evaluate the decision. What are the markers you will set? How will you know that the decision has been implemented effectively and successfully?

An effective decision maker is somebody who is thoughtful about the process, the purpose and the timing of a decision. Keeping the lines of communication open and being prepared to discuss the reason for the decision are imperative. The timing of a decision may also be important. If we try to introduce too many changes at one time, the team may well reject the decision and morale will be low. Remember, we are accountable for the decisions we make.

Evidence opportunity

1.4 Methods of decision making

Look at/investigate the models and methods of decision making. Analyse their relevance to you in your leadership and management. Think about the things that we have discussed in this section (i.e. the headings we have explored). Write a reflective account to evidence this.

LO2 Carry out and reflect on effective decision making

AC 2.1 Evaluating range, purpose and situation for effective decision making

Here, you will evaluate your management of the range, purposes and situations for which your individual decisions are required in your service and draw conclusions in respect of your decision-making practice. You will need to ensure that you include at least five of the topics/headings we cover below.

As a manager, you will be required to make decisions on a range of issues and in a range of situations. The following headings outline your areas of responsibility as manager of a setting.

Quality management and improvement and the role of evidence-based decisions

An evidence-based decision is made by critically thinking about the information or facts you have that either support or contradict what it is you are making a decision about. Research is at the heart of this type of management and in developing the quality of, and improving, your service you should focus upon the way in which you use quality assurance processes to achieve consistent results.

Estates management

This is about managing the day-to-day operations within the setting. In a care setting you may also be managing the domestic, catering and laundry staff and services, which means ensuring that all these services are able to fulfil their roles and that they meet the service users' needs. In this area of work you will be making decisions about how the budget is spent on laundry facilities and other resources. It is also possible that you will have to update premises and buy furniture or decorate areas, so you will be making decisions as to how to fund such large capital expenditure.

Financial planning

As a manager, you will have a budget and as such are responsible for managing how that money is spent. The way in which you financially plan will feed into all other areas of your role. Without finances you cannot, of course, pay for staff or services, so a plan needs to be put into action, and you will be responsible for financial decisions. Go to Unit 507 for more information on financial resources and responsibility.

Care planning and partnership working

Although the team will be involved in the individual care plans of service users and patients, you will need to have an overall understanding about how the care is being delivered on a daily basis and may be required to make decisions about changes that need to be made. While you may not be involved in individual plans, your role will be to coordinate the care in the adult care setting.

Care plans that are negotiated well and include partners from other services mean that individuals are able to live lives that are meaningful despite having serious physical or mental health issues. Any activity that can contribute to developing a care plan that helps with a person's wellbeing will be an important part of their care. In working with partners, you are able to offer more services to achieve this. For example, you may work closely with a team of physiotherapists or counsellors and have a partnership deal with them. Their expertise can add to the quality of the care planning you offer your service users.

Policy and procedures

As a manager, you need to ensure that staff are working within the policies of the organisation and you may also be the person who ensures that the policies and procedures remain up to date and relevant. You may, of course, make a decision to delegate this role but ultimately you have responsibility for ensuring that all staff are aware of their roles with respect to the policies.

Staffing – recruitment

In recruitment, decisions must be made as to what staff are needed, what roles they must undertake and how you will recruit the team. You need to be clear about the type of person you want to fulfil a particular role in the organisation and you will have some responsibility in a small organisation for drawing up a job description and person specification. In larger organisations, your role will be to work with the HR team on this, but you will still need to make decisions about the staff needs in your area.

Environmental factors

All organisations are subject to changes in the internal and external environments. The internal environment may refer to the staffing and the way the setting works to meet the needs and mission of the organisation. It might also include other resources in its vicinity that are needed for it to function effectively. As a manager, you will have control over this and will also be responsible for this. It will be in the scope of your role to be able to make decisions to effect change and to ensure the smooth and effective running of your setting. The external environment is less pliable as there will be factors that you will not be able to control. This will include your organisation's competitors, economic conditions, policies and procedures that are determined by legislation, and changes to legislation itself. As environment factors that are external to the organisation are not in your control in the same way that internal environmental factors are, you will need to ensure that you keep up to date with any changes that will require action to ensure the smooth running of the organisation.

Safety and security and risk assessments

Managing safety and security within your organisation requires decisions about the risks you need to manage and control in the setting. This means you must think about potential hazards that exist and that may cause harm to people and undertake risk assessments to identify the steps to prevent such harm. We cover risk assessment in Unit 508.

Advocacy issues, deprivation of liberty issues and best interest issues

Advocacy, **Deprivation of Liberty Safeguards (DoLS)** and best interests issues provide legal safeguards for people who are in your care in either a hospital or an adult care setting. These safeguards are part of the Mental Capacity Act, so as the manager in the setting you must be aware of the implications of this act for your service users and staff. Decisions about the best interests of patients are often made particularly towards end of life and also when mental capacity is at risk. You may be required to make assessments and decisions on behalf of patients.

> ### KEY TERM
>
> **Deprivation of Liberty Safeguards (DoLS)** protect the rights of individuals who may need to be detained in a hospital if they lack mental capacity.

Health and safety issues and safeguarding issues

Any health and safety decision you make must be in line with the law and also the policy of your organisation; so too with safeguarding. As a manager, you will be required to ensure that the policies with respect to safeguarding of service users in your care are followed and that any issues are quickly dealt with for the safety of the individual, the members of staff and the organisation.

You can appreciate that the range of your decision making as a manager is vast and perhaps you are starting to evaluate just what is essential to your role and what might be delegated or shelved. The Reflect on it activity will help you to identify the decisions that need to be made for you to evaluate the range (are you a designated decision maker or can you seek feedback from others to support your decisions?), purpose (what are the reasons for the decisions you make and who do they affect?) and situation in which you manage.

AC 2.2 Providing support to engage others in the decision-making process

Here, you will need to critically evaluate situations in which others may need to be engaged in decision making, including the topics we cover in this section.

Team meetings

A meeting is an opportunity to communicate with the whole team present and can be a useful vehicle through which to encourage staff to discuss the overall aims of the team, share ideas with the shared vision in mind and engage the team in the decision-making process.

Meetings afford the opportunity for the team members to get to know each other and to open discussion and make action points. The success of a meeting can depend on the way it is chaired, and this is an important role for the manager to learn.

As the chair leading the meeting, you need to ensure that you encourage participation from the entire group using open questions and occasionally directing your attention to one person in particular. In this way, you are giving everybody in the team the chance to express what they know and to demonstrate their skills, which may be useful for achieving the whole team's outcomes. It is very important to come away from the meeting with some action points or objectives, if appropriate.

When a planning activity is required the team meeting can be a useful vehicle for this. If all team members understand the background to the project and its relevance to the organisation, they will be more focused on the changes needed and be motivated to ensure a successful outcome.

At the meeting there can be a collaborative approach to the collection of data such as service user requirements, and timescales can be set which are clear and achievable. With the project broken down into manageable tasks and assigned to team members for completion, the planning process can reach a successful conclusion in a timely manner. You will need to ensure that timescales are achievable and that the team are aware of the need to meet deadlines, otherwise the project may falter.

One of the best ways to get staff involved in planning is to allow time during the regular team meeting for them to express their views and to communicate their opinions or ideas. So often, our team meetings become mere information-giving sessions, without an adequate venue for the exchange of ideas. If this is the case, then valuable expertise, the skills and knowledge of the staff will not be accessed. Through a mentoring process, team members can learn a great deal from each other, and the expertise each one possesses as a result of their experience and training can be used as a valuable resource for planning.

Staff supervision, staff appraisals

In this setting you can engage with your staff to share decisions about certain areas of their work, such as how they engage with the other members of staff or how well they perform in their tasks with service users. As part of the performance appraisal system, these are meetings where staff can be involved in decisions about their careers and professional development in their roles. This is also an opportunity to deal with any negative behaviour or poor performance.

Care assessments and reviews and carer/advocate and/or family meetings

Decisions are required in all aspects of care and it should not simply be the remit of the manager to make the final decision. When we enter into meetings with carers/

advocates and families in the care assessment process we need to encourage them to engage with making their own decisions in order to achieve ownership of the final product. For example, it is easy to put into place a care plan for somebody which we as carers may decide is the best course of action. We may have made a decision that the person will engage in activities in the setting and leave a meeting believing that this was a shared decision. Unfortunately, the person may agree at the time that this is the best decision but then not comply with it. Decisions that have been made on our behalf and without our engagement are not likely to sit well with us and yet we may be guilty of doing this in our own care practice.

The document *Making Shared Decision-making a Reality. No decision about me without me* (Coulter and Collins, 2011) sets out the government's plans to make shared decision making the norm in the NHS.

It highlights a process in which clinicians and patients work together to select appropriate care packages based upon clinical evidence and the patient's informed preferences. The rationale for this is the 'compelling research evidence that suggests that patients who are active participants in managing their health and health care have better outcomes than patients who are passive recipients of care'. You can read more about this here: www.kingsfund.org.uk/sites/default/files/Making-shared-decision-making-a-reality-paper-Angela-Coulter-Alf-Collins-July-2011_0.pdf

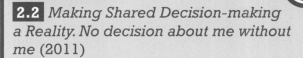

Research it

2.2 *Making Shared Decision-making a Reality. No decision about me without me (2011)*

Make notes on what you found out from reading the *Making Shared Decision-making a Reality. No decision about me without me* (2011) document: www.kingsfund.org.uk/sites/default/files/Making-shared-decision-making-a-reality-paper-Angela-Coulter-Alf-Collins-July-2011_0.pdf

Partnership working

For others in the care process such as stakeholders, partners, families and carers, shared decision making reduces the variation in practice across services and duplication. There are many situations in which others will need to be engaged in decision making and we discuss these below. In meetings with stakeholders and others such as families or carers, you can support each other in decisions that need to be made and provide clarity about what needs to be done for the care package to be delivered. As a manager, your role will be to ensure that the care provided by all partners is seamless and does not overlap any part of the service. Repetition of care is a wasted resource and by analysing the care process you can identify any potential issues which may arise and determine a way forward.

Lessons learned from the above in providing support and encouragement to others

You make decisions on a daily basis in your role as manager, but it is important also to ensure that you empower others to take their own decisions. For example, it is easy for staff to come to you with a problem and for you to make a decision for them. This increases your workload enormously and does not encourage or empower staff to take decisions for themselves. Encouraging them to act in an autonomous way, making decisions based upon their own professional judgement, and supporting them in this, will help you to take a step back.

You can do this by listening to what the member of staff is saying and asking them what they feel they ought to do and what the consequences might be. Ask them if there is an alternative course of action and how this might work. If they get into the habit of engaging with this sort of decision-making process, they will start to build this into their daily routine.

Reflect on it

2.2 Engaging others in the decision-making process

Think about a decision you made for somebody else. How well was it received and what happened? What have you learned as a result of this? How can you involve others and support them to engage in the decision-making process?

Evidence opportunity

2.2 Providing support to engage others in the decision-making process

Critically evaluate situations in which others may need to be engaged in decision making, including the areas/topics we have discussed in this section.

You might like to give an example for each and say what decision was discussed in each situation. Provide a written account detailing all of this and say what worked and what did not work. Look at the pros and cons of each action you took and say how you might change this in future.

What lessons did you learn from providing support and encouragement to others in the various situations?

AC 2.3 Using factual data, recommendations, suggestions and ideas in a logical and purposeful manner to inform decision making

Here, you will evaluate how you use and analyse qualitative and/or quantitative data to inform your management decision making which is sourced from the areas we discuss below.

Qualitative and quantitative data to inform management decision making

Informing your decisions will require you to produce evidence in the form of factual data. You will already have this sort of data in the form of surveys or evaluation forms, appraisals and audits. Data that is **quantitative** in nature will focus on answering questions such as 'how many' and 'how often' and is likely to be presented in terms of numbers and statistics.

The methods include surveys, experiments and statistical data. You might also use **qualitative** methods to gain information, particularly if your decision means you need to gain a greater understanding and depth about what is happening in a given circumstance.

It is important in your role as manager to use all forms of data and information to help you make sound decisions. Whether it is quantitative or qualitative in nature you also need to ensure that it is both reliable and valid. There is more information on qualitative and quantitative research on page 336.

KEY TERMS

Quantitative data is data that is numerical in nature. It will answer questions such as 'how much' or 'how many'.
Qualitative data is gained through observation and is descriptive in nature. It will be collected through interviews and observations and will try to find a meaning in certain phenomena.

Using digital technology to research data and information relevant to adult care service

By conducting online searches, you can gain valuable insights into how others in the care system work. You can also access government documents, care standards and guidelines as well as media reports that can all give useful information to help you to make a decision that is informed. Remember, the sites you access should be reliable and credible. You may need to conduct thorough research to ascertain the reliability and validity of the research and opinions you find online.

The URL at the end of the website address can give you a good idea about the source of the document. For example, if the site ends with .edu then it is an educational setting; .gov is a government website and is useful for reports and legal documents; and .org refers to an organisation, so you need to be aware of possible bias, particularly if the organisation sponsors political or large companies with an agenda to promote a product. For example, you may find useful articles about pain management but need to be mindful of the sponsor who may be marketing a type of dressing and using the research data to support their product.

You are also able to access online journals and magazines which can give insight into the issue you are researching and help you to form opinions and make decisions on the basis of information that has been researched.

National reports and regulatory findings

Reports about healthcare can often be found on government websites or the NHS, CQC or Health Foundation websites. These also comment upon findings that are linked to regulations and guidelines and are good sources of factual data.

Company/internal formal report

Other organisations similar to your own may also supply useful information about how they may have overcome issues and problems and reading company reports can help decision making. You do not have to restrict yourself to other health settings though. Sometimes, ideas from different sectors – for example, education, manufacturing and customer service – can supply useful information and can be adapted to adult care. For example, the safety checklists used in aviation have been compared with safety in healthcare and the UK government has set up an Independent Patient Safety Investigation Service to investigate this further (Kapur et al., 2016). A criticism might be that the aviation sector is too different from healthcare to provide a valid measure.

Media reporting

This type of reporting sheds light on issues in adult care. We have all seen recent investigative journalism reporting upon the waiting times and corridor queues in the country's emergency departments. We are also aware of the shortcomings and failings in adult care that have been investigated and have led to national inquiries and changes to the law and practice. While the issues these reports highlight may not be an issue in your setting, they could help to inform your decision making. Such journalism may at times be biased so you need to bear this in mind. Remember, check where the information is from and that it is from a reliable and valid source to make an informed decision.

Validity

This refers to whether a study measures or examines what it claims to measure or examine. A researcher who is trying to measure people's attitudes to pregnant women and smoking, for example, needs to construct a tool that he/she knows is measuring that specific attitude. In this way, the results can be accurately applied and interpreted for a test to be valid.

Reliability

Reliability refers to the extent to which an experiment, test or other measuring procedure gives the same results in repeated experiments. Other researchers must be able to perform exactly the same experiment under the same conditions and generate the same results in order to reinforce the findings. This is called replicating findings.

Reflect on it

2.3 Validity and reliability

Think about the two terms and then write a short piece to show your understanding.

Complaints

Your own complaints system can be a valuable source of information in making decisions or justifying something. There may be an area of practice that is constantly complained about and evidence to support a change may be useful here. You will need to carefully explore the issue(s) being complained about, weighing up the positives and negatives, perhaps by having a discussion with the complainant, and determine whether it is a reasonable complaint or simply a subjective point of view. If something can be done about it, then you can start to gather other information to help the situation.

Quality/service provision surveys undertaken which have been completed by others

Surveys are useful if you want to learn what a larger sample of people think and you need to keep the costs of research down. Surveys tend to have a different way of questioning than interviews and are most useful for gathering data through a wide variety of methods such as emails, post or face-to-face interviews to provide useful statistical data. The disadvantage of using this type of method is that poorly written questions can limit the types of responses you get and may also affect reliability and validity of the study if the questions are biased in any way. There may also be a low response rate and the answers are subjective. Types of surveys include interview, postal, telephone, internet or online surveys.

Quantitative research

If your research is focusing on questions such as 'how many' and 'how often', then you are likely to present your data in terms of numbers and statistics and it will, therefore, be quantitative in nature.

Originally developed to study natural phenomena, this was the method of choice of natural scientists but is now widely used in education and healthcare. The methods include surveys, experiments and statistical data.

Strengths of the quantitative approach

- Subject to rigorous controls and checks throughout the process.
- An objective approach to data collection is favoured, and therefore the results are often thought to be more accurate.
- Large numbers of participants (samples) are used in this type of research, therefore a large amount of information can be obtained.
- The findings can be generalised to the wider population.
- Studies can be replicated or repeated, and therefore the results obtained can be more readily compared with similar studies.
- In this type of work it is also possible to reduce personal bias, simply because researchers are able to keep their 'distance' from participating subjects.
- This type of research is well–controlled, and the methods and instruments used, such as questionnaires, are standardised.

Weakness of the quantitative approach

- Some of the methods involve the use of laboratory conditions, and this is not entirely appropriate when studying human subjects.
- The validity of the study is questionable.
- The way in which questionnaires or survey methods are written may not elicit responses that are useful or real.
- Misunderstanding about the questions can occur.
- The relationship between what somebody says and actually does cannot always be truly tested.
- We all have own unique experiences and this can certainly change the manner in which we behave. In other words, we may all bring a different way to behave to an experiment, which is not useful for quantitative research.
- Gathering primary data can result in data unreliability.

Qualitative research

Qualitative research methods were developed in the social sciences when it was felt that the study of social and cultural phenomena required a different means of enquiry.

This approach seeks to gain insight into people's lives. Their attitudes, behaviours and value systems are the areas of interest for the qualitative researcher, who wants to seek out the 'why' of a particular topic. Rather than merely trying to describe a certain phenomenon, this approach attempts to gain greater understanding and depth about what is happening in a given circumstance.

Using the phenomenological approach, as posited by sociologists in an attempt to study the experience of the subjects and how they interpret their world, the researcher becomes an interpreter and attempts to reveal concealed meaning. The four major qualitative approaches are ethnography, phenomenology, field research and grounded theory.

Strengths of the qualitative approach

- Produces some very in-depth work and rich data about phenomena which are impossible to collect from sets of statistics.
- Enables the researcher to look far more closely at the meanings within behaviour and to understand what is happening in settings, and to question participants' responses to certain issues.
- Enables the study of people in their own settings where there are naturally occurring events that provide rich data for study.
- Enables collection of information in areas where there has been little knowledge in existence in the past and where the issues under study may be sensitive.
- Enables the researcher to get close to the material under study and to gain in-depth data which can later be subjected to quantitative research.

Weakness of the qualitative approach

- It can be very time consuming to conduct this type of research to gain a valid response.
- Collecting and analysing the material which is often unstructured in nature can also be time consuming.
- Finding themes in reams of notes can at the very least be a little daunting, and trying to find meaning in the materials can also take time.
- The sample size is usually quite small, with just a few participants taking part.
- Some critics are concerned that the type of study lacks rigour since variables cannot be controlled.
- Results produced cannot be readily generalised to the population as a whole.
- This type of research lends itself to small-scale study and therefore data obtained, while rich, is too small to allow valid conclusions.

Table 10.1 compares the two types of research.

Table 10.1 Comparison of quantitative and qualitative research

Quantitative	Qualitative
Quantitative analysis is thought to be objective.	Qualitative data is generally thought to be more subjective.
Thought to have little human bias attached to it.	As it is dependent on people's opinions and assumptions, there are biases present.
Lack of bias is seen as the data collected relies on the comparison of numbers according to mathematical tests.	Bias is thought to occur because the researcher interprets people's statements or other communication, and this might be influenced by the way the researcher sees the world or approaches the work.

Evidence opportunity

2.3 Using factual data, recommendations, suggestions and ideas to inform decision making

Evaluate how you use and analyse qualitative and/or quantitative data to inform your management decision making which is sourced from the areas we have discussed in this section. Provide a written account.

You may wish to include an example of a recent decision you had to make in the workplace and show what qualitative and/or quantitative data informed that decision. Evaluate the sources by saying what the strength of the source was and what limited its use for you. What was good about the information, and what was missing perhaps? Was it relevant or biased in some way?

Highlight the sources you used and justify your choice.

AC 2.4 Reviewing available information and making valid decisions

Here, you will need to explain and reflect on how the above has enabled you to present a rationale and conclusions to justify your decisions to stakeholders in order to gain support from internal and external stakeholders.

Internal stakeholders in the setting and external stakeholders

Partnerships, both internal and external, are key in any organisation, and these partnerships form a big part of our work life. This might include internal staff/adult care workers who are involved in the organisation on a daily basis, and external stakeholders who also have an interest in the running of the organisation; these may include medical care workers, resource suppliers, or advocates and families of service users receiving care. As a manager, the decisions that you make will affect the different stakeholders, but the different stakeholders will also influence the decisions and decision-making process. It may be that these stakeholders are affected by the decisions that are made on a day-to-day basis, or it may be that they have a financial stake.

You will find that projects that you are working on for your setting, as well as policies and procedures, are often carried out across multidisciplinary boundaries; in other words, alongside other disciplines, organisations and professionals. For example, it may be that internal stakeholders may be involved in a new strategy in the setting, or in the local health and wellbeing strategy, and may be responsible for organising and planning the project, arranging meetings, sourcing the resources and funding needed. They may be involved in developing the project, organising and managing it. Individuals or service users, families/carers and the local community, who are external stakeholders, may also want to contribute their views and guidance. It is important to choose stakeholders who can make valuable contributions, which will enhance the overall project and the outcomes.

Making decisions with stakeholders in mind must have the support of relevant information and data (such as that we discussed in AC 2.3) if support is to be gained from them. By undertaking a thorough search for evidence to support your topic you can present stakeholders with relevant information and justify the decisions you have made. It is important that stakeholders can see and understand the rationale for your decisions as they need to be fully informed in order to give their support. Without this they may fail to understand the importance of the reasons for the decision you have made, and this might compromise care.

Evidence opportunity

2.4 Review available information and make valid decisions/justify your decisions

Provide a written account explaining and reflecting on how the above (what we discussed in AC 2.3) has enabled you to present a rationale and conclusions to justify your decisions to stakeholders in order to gain support from internal and external stakeholders.

Or, following on from the Evidence opportunity activity in 2.3, prepare a PowerPoint presentation for internal and external stakeholders to justify the decision you made. Present the case with researched evidence and conclusions as to the possible outcomes for the change you wish to make. (This can be a real or fictitious account.)

AC 2.5 Reflecting on your own decision-making practices and areas for further development

Here, you will need to critically evaluate your own strengths and weaknesses in the management decision-making process.

As a manager, you make decisions on a daily basis, some of which may not always be palatable. For example, you may have to have a difficult conversation with a member of staff and decide to leave that off the urgent list in the hope that they will rectify their actions before you talk to them. This, of course, may not be the best action to take, not the best way forward. As we have learned, decisions can be based on intuitive processes, gut instincts, and we can also gather information for analysis before we make our decisions. You will, therefore, need to reflect on your approach, how you make decisions and think about the strengths and the weaknesses of your style. Do you always act on intuition and is it always the right choice? What is good about that approach and how can it sometimes go wrong? Do you prefer to get all the facts before you make your move, but does this sometimes hinder the process? As a manager, you should continually reflect not only on your decision making and decision-making process but generally on your practice to identify areas where you could develop further and therefore ensure that you are able to be as effective as possible in doing so.

Evidence opportunity

2.5 Reflect on your decision-making practices and areas for further development

Critically evaluate your own strengths and weaknesses in the management decision-making process. Provide a written account.

You may wish to refer to Unit 509 where you carried out a SWOT analysis. Remind yourself of how to do this now. Complete a SWOT analysis for the way in which you conduct the management decision-making process. How will you turn your weaknesses into strengths?

Include any recommendations to enhance your future practice.

Case study

LO1, LO2 Effective decision making

You have received notification that your budget is to be cut by 20 per cent from the next calendar month. You are already struggling with under-staffing and are now at risk of losing yet more staff. One of the rooms in the adult care setting requires redecorating and you are already in the process of obtaining quotes and are about to employ a local firm to do the job.

1   What will you do?

2   How can you ensure that the service delivered to your clients remains safe and efficient?

3   What action plans can you put into place?

4   How will you ensure your decisions are effective and positive?

Reflective exemplar

Today I worked with a member of the team and my own manager to select a candidate for the Health Care Assistant role. Together we drew up a shortlist of candidates and invited two for interview. One candidate had one year's experience in a care work setting different to our own and the other was new to care work entirely. We appointed the one with more experience after much discussion. Although I was involved in the decision-making process I was not sure that we were making the right decision. I had a gut feeling that this was not really the right choice but allowed myself to listen to the other two members of the panel and agreed to appoint the experienced member of staff despite them not really having the correct skills for the job we offered.

I now wonder what it was that led me to this outcome. I realised that gut instinct and feelings were not a useful or factual argument to put forward and therefore did not feel I could argue my point well enough. In future I need to pinpoint exactly what my reasons for rejecting a candidate are and why. I have to learn to justify my judgements in a more meaningful manner.

Legislation

Legislation	Key points
Mental Capacity Act 2005	This act informs individuals about what they can do to plan and ensure that someone else can make decisions for them if they ever lack capacity to do so for themselves.

Suggestions for using the activities

This table summarises all the activities in the unit that are relevant to each assessment criterion. Here, we also suggest other, different methods that you may want to use to present your knowledge and skills by using the activities. These are just suggestions, and you should refer to the Introduction section at the start of the book, and more importantly the City & Guilds specification, and your assessor who will be able to provide more guidance on how you can evidence your knowledge and skills. When you need to be observed during your assessment, this can be done by your assessor, or your manager can provide a witness testimony.

Assessment criteria and accompanying activities	Suggested methods to show your knowledge/skills
LO1 Understand how to make effective and positive decisions	
1.1 Reflect on it (page 323)	Write a reflective account.
1.1 Evidence opportunity (page 325)	Provide a written account of your critical evaluation.
1.2 Reflect on it (page 326)	Provide a reflective account.
1.2 Evidence opportunity (page 326)	Have a discussion with your assessor or provide a written account identifying the purpose of all the decisions you make on a daily basis. Address the points outlined.
1.3 Evidence opportunity (page 328)	Provide a written account explaining the reasons for your decision making. Make sure you address the points outlined.
1.4 Research it (page 330)	Make notes detailing your findings. You could also put together a PowerPoint presentation.
1.4 Evidence opportunity (page 330)	Write a reflective account, or you could have a discussion with your assessor.
LO2 Carry out and reflect on effective decision making	
2.1 Reflect on it (page 332)	Provide a reflective account.
2.1 Evidence opportunity (page 332)	Provide a written account evaluating your management of the range, purposes and situations for which your individual decisions are required in your service and draw conclusions in respect of your decision-making practice. You will need to ensure that you include at least five of the topics/headings we covered in this section.
2.2 Research it (page 333)	Make notes detailing your findings.
2.2 Reflect on it (page 334)	Respond to the questions. Write a reflective account.
2.2 Evidence opportunity (page 334)	Critically evaluate situations in which others may need to be engaged in decision making, including the areas/topics we have discussed in this section. Provide a written account.
2.3 Reflect on it (page 335)	Write a short piece about validity and reliability, thinking about what we have discussed in this section so far.
2.3 Evidence opportunity (page 337)	Provide a written account addressing the points in the activity. You may also wish to have a discussion with your assessor.
2.4 Evidence opportunity (page 337)	Provide a written account and/or PowerPoint presentation as outlined in the activity. You could also have a discussion with your assessor.
2.5 Evidence opportunity (page 338)	Provide a written account. You may wish to refer to Unit 509 as outlined in the activity.

References

Adair, J. (2009) *Effective Leadership – How to be a successful leader*. London: Pan Books.

Buzan, T. (1972) *Use Your Head*. London: BBC.

Coulter, A. and Collins, A. (2011) *Making Shared Decision-making a Reality. No decision about me without me.* London: King's Fund.

Drucker, P.F. (2015) *The Elements of Effective Decision Making*. Available at: www.linkedin.com/pulse/elements-effective-decision-making-peter-f-drucker-muharemovic-mba

Kapur, N., Parand, A., Soukup, T., Reader, T. and Sevdalis, N. (2016) Aviation and healthcare: A comparative review with implications for patient safety, *JRSM Open*, https://doi.org/10.1177/2054270415616548

Merriam Webster Dictionary (2015) Definition of Professional, www.merriam-webster.com/dictionary/professional

Further reading and useful resources

Age UK (2018) Deprivation of Liberty Safeguards. www.ageuk.org.uk/globalassets/age-uk/documents/factsheets/fs62_deprivation_of_liberty_safeguards_fcs.pdf?dtrk=true

Cohen, D. (2015) What is Professional Judgment? www.collegeofdietitians.org/resources/professional-practice/what-is-professional-judgment-(2015).aspx

Hansson, S.O. (1994) *Decision Theory – A Brief Introduction*, cited at: http://people.kth.se/~soh/decisiontheory.pdf

Mental Capacity Act (2005) www.legislation.gov.uk/ukpga/2005/9/contents

NHS England (2017) *Next Steps on the NHS Five Year Forward View*. London: TSO.

Website

www.lifehack.org/articles/lifestyle/5-gut-instincts-you-dont-want-ignore.html

Service improvement, entrepreneurship and innovation

About this unit

This unit is about the importance of entrepreneurship and innovation within adult care services and how you can contribute to change and growth within your service area. You will learn about the theories of entrepreneurship and change management, how market forces operate to improve services and how to develop a vision for the future of adult care services. You will also understand how you can work with others to support an entrepreneurial culture.

This unit will be assessed by portfolio.

Learning outcomes

By the end of this unit, you will:

1 Understand the provision for the adult care services market
2 Understand the principles of effective change management
3 Understand how to develop a vision for the future of the service
4 Work with others to support an entrepreneurial culture

Getting started

Before you study the unit, think about the following:

- What is meant by having a 'future vision' in adult care services?
- What do you think makes a successful entrepreneur?
- Why are **evidence-based approaches** key to supporting best practice?
- What role can 'innovation' have in the management of service provision?

Reflect on it

Think about the future in adult care services. What might it look like? Write a short reflective piece. You might like to think about current practice – what works well, what could be improved – and current trends and how these might affect the future of adult care services.

KEY TERMS

Entrepreneurship refers to organising and managing a new business or idea for profit. Innovation is a part of this.
Evidence-based approaches are informed by thorough objective research and evidence. (see Unit 5.5, AC 5. 2.)
Innovation includes new ideas, methods, ways of doing things.

LO1 Understand the provision for the adult care services market

AC 1.1 Importance of entrepreneurial theory and skills in adult care services

Here, you will be required to critically evaluate the importance of entrepreneurial skills within yourself, others and your own service provision in respect of some of the areas we discuss in this section.

The differences between 'entrepreneurship' and 'innovation'

Entrepreneurship, theory and skills are key in adult care settings if we are to provide high-quality care to the most vulnerable people and ensure the smooth and efficient running of our care settings. It is therefore important that you understand the importance of entrepreneurial theory and skills.

The words 'entrepreneurship' and '**innovation**' in a business context have very different meanings. An entrepreneur is somebody who is innovative and puts into practice creative and unique answers to situations or problems. To innovate means to create something that is unique or to identify creative and new solutions. In recent times, people like James Dyson and Richard Branson are good examples of people who have shown entrepreneurship and innovation. In an adult care setting, you too will be able to, and will be required to, show entrepreneurial and innovative qualities in your day-to-day role in the way you manage the setting and introduce innovative ways of working for the benefit of those who use the services as well as for your staff.

What is meant by an 'entrepreneurial culture'?

An entrepreneur will turn a good idea into a creative one, an even stronger one in order to maximise its strengths and make it right for the target user, and will also consider the risk that is involved. For example, you may wish to open a care home in an area where there are many already; this might be a risk. How will you ensure that your establishment will be able to offer a competitive edge?

In creating an entrepreneurial culture, you will be asking staff to display skills of creativity, innovation and calculated risk taking. To do this, you ensure that you motivate staff and empower them so that they feel they are able to be innovative and to put forward ideas for change. They should feel that they are able to implement and take the lead on such ideas with your guidance and support. In this way, not only will they gain more experience in different areas, but the organisation will benefit from a motivated and innovative workforce. Ideas and such innovation must, of course, be in line with the setting's vision and overall strategic plans, and you must also be astute in recognising those in your workforce that are able to take a lead but also ensure that everyone feels empowered and is given the opportunity to contribute.

What is meant by an 'innovative culture'?

Innovation in an organisation supports new ideas and the implementation of those ideas. An innovative organisation is one that encourages its workforce to be creative and to understand the value of creativity and thinking competitively and commercially. Leaders and managers in such organisations will offer training and empower their workforce to think creatively and develop solutions to problems affecting the setting. As a manager, you will lead others to recognise and value the importance of change to address the many challenges you are faced with in an adult care setting, and to offer enhanced and better quality of care to those using the service. This might be through reviewing and changing the procedures you use in the setting. This might seem like a difficult task for staff to adjust to, but this will all be part of an innovative culture, and just as with creating an entrepreneurial culture as we discussed above, staff should be empowered to offer innovative solutions.

How to develop a culture that supports innovation, change, redevelopment and/or growth

If we always do the same things, we will always get the same results and this applies to any area of our lives. In the workplace we cannot expect a different result if we carry out the same processes.

An innovative culture involves the workers in planning and embraces their ideas and views. Their creative thinking about solutions to problems and change is encouraged and, more importantly, they are given the time to develop new ways of working. It is important that in your role as manager you support and encourage innovation, change, redevelopment and growth of the organisation and foster and promote such a culture. This means creating forums where staff feel empowered to contribute ideas and shape ways of working. This could perhaps be through meetings, and suggestion and ideas boxes or even competitions. This in turn will ensure a collaborative workplace culture, staff who are happier in their roles, and higher retention rates. Again, such innovation can help to drive forward more efficient ways of working and improved practice in adult care.

Maher et al. (2009), writing for the NHS Institute for Innovation and Improvement, cited the characteristics of highly innovative organisations. The common themes across various studies into innovation are brought together in Table 11.1.

Table 11.1 Characteristics of highly innovative organisations (adapted from Maher et al. (2009), with extra points added)

Risk taking	• Emotional support – *give staff the support to engage with risk.* • Balanced assessment – *assess each risk in a balanced way.* • Learning from failure rather than punishing – *view failure as feedback.* • Trying new things – *encourage staff to engage in innovative ways of doing things, trying out new ideas in practice rather than practising in the same way all the time.*
Resources	• Funding – *budget for additional funds that can be used for new ideas and practice. Free up finance to move a new project in a different direction.* • Time – *allow staff time off the job to engage with a new project or idea and develop it further.* • Authority to act – *empower them to make decisions. Give staff some freedom to make a change and to try things in a new way.*
Goals	• What, but not how – *describe what is needed.* • Specific call for innovation – *ask staff to be creative.* • Tie to strategic plan – *link to organisation's overall vision.* • 'Stretch' – *challenge staff to put forward creative ideas.* • Clear case for need – *demonstrate the rationale for change. Ensure there is clarity about why change would be a good thing and get staff to 'buy in' to the future.*
Rewards	• Aligned with organisational goals – *plan rewards in line with the goals met.* • Recognition – *ensure the staff are recognised in some way for their effort.* • Intrinsic motivation – *identify the staff's motivation for their work. What are your staff motivated by: recognition, time off, additional pay?* • Individualised – *recognise differences in staff and respect these.*
Relationships	• Honouring everyone's input – *reward and praise the effort and encourage team ownership.* • Diversity – *recognise difference in people and their input.* • Trusting, open environment – *develop a no-blame culture.* • Team-based work – *encourage a team approach and identify team roles based on individual strengths and weaknesses.*
Knowledge	• Wide scope search – *embrace research.* • Uncensored, unfiltered, unsummarised – *allow all ideas and encourage the voicing of those, however 'off the wall' they may seem.* • Free-flowing – *do not stifle creativity and give staff free rein to think and talk about ideas.*
Tools	• Flexibility – *allow time for the creative phase to be fully developed.* • Deliberate process – *make time for activity to be tried out and reviewed and monitored as to its effectiveness.* • Training – *supply additional help and support.* • Encouragement for skills development – *train and develop staff skills. Invest in training if the project identifies a skills gap.*

How to positively encourage and exploit entrepreneurship and innovation in others and maintain a culture that supports growth and change

As the population of those aged over 85 grows, there is a need for more care provision, yet research has indicated that individuals view the prospect of moving into a care organisation as 'a last resort' and one to be avoided. If there were ever a time for an innovative solution to care for older adults it is now.

Clearly, the structure of existing care organisations and roles needs to change in order to create a culture based on putting the service user first and changing the way in which care is delivered. As a manager in a traditional type of care setting, one of your roles will be to consider ways in which change can be achieved in order to respond to the **future vision** of adult care. See the above sections on innovation and entrepreneurship for how you can positively encourage

KEY TERMS

'Future vision' refers to the innovative work going on in the NHS. It is providing new ways of thinking about healthcare delivery. Future vision is a response by government and healthcare bodies to the growing financial and workforce pressures to meet the needs of the population and to realise the vision set out in the NHS *Five Year Forward View*.

and exploit entrepreneurship and innovation to benefit the care service and maintain a culture that supports growth and change.

Maher et al. (2009) discuss and show how organisations might encourage a more entrepreneurial spirit and maintain the culture of change.

● **Risk taking**: Staff should feel free to try out new ideas. Risk taking encourages the leaders in innovative organisations to demonstrate that they are more 'interested in learning from failure than in punishing it'.

- **Resources**: Create a climate where staff are able to act autonomously and with authority to move forward on innovative ideas. They should feel empowered and that they have resources at their disposal to help them to create change.
- **Goals**: These need to be linked to the strategic priorities of the organisation.
- **Rewards** for innovation: Recognise innovative behaviour.
- The **relationships** theme: Looks closely at how we interact as teams and how innovative ideas are formed over time and through such interactions. The development of an environment where staff are encouraged to be exposed to a wide range of people from a variety of backgrounds provides growth for innovation.
- Broad-based **knowledge**: Refers to any information that can generate new ideas, wherever it is from. The act of filtering or rejecting the knowledge without consideration is seen as damaging to innovation.
- **Tools**: Refers to how leaders can build capability and capacity in staff to ensure creative thinking becomes a valued and deliberate structure. Within Maher et al.'s document there are tips for developing this sort of training.

Evidence opportunity

1.1 Entrepreneurship and innovation, and the importance of entrepreneurial theory and skills in adult care services

Download a copy of the document *Creating the Culture for Innovation* at www.institute.nhs.uk/innovation and make some notes on the importance of entrepreneurial skills in your own service provision.

Give a written account of how your own organisation is developing a culture that supports innovation, change, redevelopment and growth.

Explain how you encourage and exploit entrepreneurship and innovation in others for the benefit of your service(s) and maintain a culture that supports growth and change.

In your written account, critically evaluate the importance of entrepreneurial skills for managers, other staff and your own service or setting. Think about all of the points we have covered in this section. To critically evaluate, think about the strengths of promoting an innovative culture and the disadvantages to developing such a culture, for example.

Economic theories – providing incentives to achieve

As far back as 1999, the government White Paper *Modernising Government* highlighted the idea of taking a more creative approach to financial incentives for public service staff (HMSO, 1999). As noted above,

entrepreneurship and economic growth can happen only when we have staff who feel valued and are committed to moving the organisation forward. As a manager, you should understand what it is that staff are motivated by. Incentive schemes such as staff benefits schemes which enable staff to purchase items at lower prices or offers on restaurants and cinemas are often used, as are lease car schemes and overtime payments.

Financial rewards/money as an incentive must be considered but these are surprisingly low on the list for most people. Any change that requires low-paid staff to do more for little recompense is likely to be viewed negatively and staff will feel undervalued. If more pay cannot be part of the agreed changes, then other incentives and packages can be implemented. Some organisations offer time off or cut-price gym membership, car-leasing schemes and discounts for local shops as part of their incentive scheme.

Psychological theories – a vision and ability to manage opposition to change

In adult care, change happens for various reasons:

- New research in practice becomes available.
- New policies and regulations appear.
- There is overspending on budgets.
- The need to update buildings or premises leads to disruption in the working day.
- The turnover of staff constitutes a change to team working.

Any change is a challenge and can cause anxiety for some, so managers need to be aware of how to minimise this and keep the team focused. Managing change requires a planned and systematic approach to ensure that the team's motivation is maintained.

John P. Kotter (1996) devised 'eight steps to successful change', which provide a useful starting point. Each stage recognises how individuals respond to and approach change, and Kotter identifies this through how we see, feel and then act towards change.

Research it

1.1 Lewin's change theory

We are going to look in some detail at Kotter's theory here, but you might like to compare it to Kurt Lewin's change theory.

Research the three stages of: 1. Unfreezing, 2. Moving to a new level or changing 3. Refreezing. This is also covered in AC 2.3 in this unit. Compare it to Kotter's eight-stage theory.

Write a short account of your findings.

Kotter's model shows well how managers can motivate people to buy into the change by 'owning' the change and this is the important element of any successful change.

We can reduce the eight-steps model down to four major factors:

- **The urgency factor**: The pressure to change is on the organisation. You need to get the team behind you to ensure successful outcomes.
- **The vision factor**: A clear shared vision is an imperative and, as a manager, it is necessary to ensure that team members are with you and not against you. Motivation is the key here and you need to be aware of what motivates your team.
- **The resource factor**: The resources you need to implement change have to be identified before you proceed and you need to ensure these are provided. Without the necessary tools, your team cannot be expected to do the job.
- **The action factor**: When all else is in place, the next part of any change is to act. Having planned for change and implemented it, you then need to check that it is working and act if it is not.

If the change is working, then maintaining the effectiveness and appropriateness of the change is good practice. By monitoring and analysing data produced you are in a position to evaluate the success or otherwise and to keep the team informed of progress.

The fear of the consequences of change can have a damaging effect on the team's morale. Ensuring that staff feel secure in their roles is a management task to maintain motivation. Honest and open communication is essential, and it should be provided on a continuous basis.

Change raises the level of stress and takes us out of our comfort zone. We start to fear not only for our jobs but also for the upset in our routine and the status quo. As a manager, communicating to the team that the change will bring about a new 'comfort zone', once implemented, will be most welcome.

Sociological theories – how values influence motivations, behaviours and beliefs in decision making

In developing entrepreneurship in an organisation, we need to develop a culture in which the values, beliefs and customs of the organisation are embedded in the structures and processes of the workplace. Staff need to share those values and make decisions accordingly.

Sociological theory shows how values and attitudes influence the way in which we behave and theorists such as Durkheim (1897) and Weber (1905) explained how society functioned and changed. More recently, Schwartz

(1992) developed new thinking on values, resulting in the identification of ten personal values that are recognised across cultures together with an explanation of where they have emerged from. Fundamentally, values are beliefs linked to feelings, goals and standards and have different levels of importance among individuals.

Values are the things that we believe to be important in the way we live and work and may be defined as preferences which help us to determine whether a course of action is right or wrong for us. For example, we may believe that all people must be treated with respect but if we are working in an environment which does not share this as a value, then this misalignment can cause us unhappiness. Such values and beliefs will influence our motivation, behaviour and decision-making process, as we are likely to be respectful and fair towards other when we are making decisions that will affect them, for example.

Entrepreneurship innovation theory – foresight, creativity

Joseph Schumpeter (1883–1950) was an economist and sociologist who developed theories of capitalist development and business cycles. His theory was that entrepreneurs help the process of development in an economy by being innovative and creative. The innovation would mean that a new product would be introduced with a new method of production for a new market. Furthermore, new sources of supply and demand would also be introduced. The theory mainly applies to large businesses and it was generally found that smaller organisations would imitate rather than innovate. In your workplace/adult care setting, then, this might mean that you adapt a practice you see in a large organisation to fit your ways of working rather than come up with innovations. However, you should of course still drive forward an entrepreneurial and innovative culture in your setting.

Theory of achievement motivation – doing things new and in a different way, high achievers

McClelland's (1988) motivation theory identified three types of motivational need:

1 Need for achievement or achievement motivated, in which the desire for excellence and the need to do a good job and to advance one's career are the motivational force.
2 Need for power/authority motivated, in which the desire to lead and the need for job status and influencing others are important.
3 Need for affiliation/affiliation motivated, in which the need to be liked and having good relationships within a team rate highly as the motivating factors.

According to McClelland, the need for achievement is the highest among entrepreneurs who like to seek new and better ways of doing things, and they were able to make decisions even in situations where there was high level of uncertainty. He maintained that people who were achievement motivated were more likely to become entrepreneurs and were not necessarily influenced by money or external incentives, but considered profit to be a measure of success and competency (McClelland, 1988; McKibbon et al., 2008). In care work, this sort of motivation and innovation are seen in the development of new ways of working, such as a new social care model called 'Shared Lives'. As a result of budget cuts in care, this innovation was developed to ensure that young people or adults who needed extra support were linked to a carer who opened up their home and family life to provide that support. You can find out more at http://sharedlivesplus.org.uk/images/6innovationsinsocialcare1.pdf

▲ **Figure 11.1** What motivates you and your staff in your roles?

Needs theory of motivation – factors that motivate individuals' behaviours

In Abraham Maslow's hierarchy of needs theory, he proposed that fulfilling five basic needs were motivators that influence behaviour and cause us to take action. The needs are shown in Figure 1.2 on page 5.

The needs are structured hierarchically, suggesting that lower-level needs must be met before higher-level needs. Once satisfied, that need is no longer a motivator because an individual will take action only to satisfy unmet needs.

The needs theory of motivation is a development of this theory into leadership and management theory. It was believed that if organisations could satisfy the needs of their employees when at work then they would benefit from higher levels of motivation. The levels in the hierarchy would be addressed in turn, with the lower needs being met first. For example, people require food and shelter to survive so a basic pay level would satisfy this. The next level of safety and security can be met by addressing the safety needs of the employee and ensuring that health and safety and

financial security are in place. The need to belong is often met by team-building activities and social events. Self-esteem needs are met by ensuring that our workers feel praised and respected at work and that they are valued. At the top of the hierarchy we are self-actualised and in work terms this means that people are motivated in their work and are using their skills and knowledge. It is when people experience job satisfaction from their work that they are empowered and trusted. As a manager in an adult care setting, you will need to understand the factors that drive people so that you can effectively motivate your staff and cater to their needs.

AC 1.2 Factors and drivers likely to have an impact on the service provision

Here, you will analyse factors and drivers that could influence growth and change in service delivery, and evaluate the impact that areas we discuss in this section might have in respect of supporting an entrepreneurial and innovation culture within your service and related delivery.

Political drivers, regulation, local government initiatives and influence of the media

Political drivers are related to government policy, regulations and initiatives that affect change. New legislation or regulatory changes can have a major impact upon the way in which your organisation develops and failure to heed such drivers may result in a failure of the actual setting or business.

One of the key drivers of recent years has been the need to improve quality in the NHS, with revelations of unacceptable treatment of patients highlighted by the media. The media was a key driver for demanding change when it published reports of demeaning and cruel treatment of patients with learning disabilities at Winterbourne View private hospital, poor management and care at Mid Staffordshire NHS Foundation Trust, and other care establishments where quality of care was lacking. This resulted in government inquiries being set up and reviews published to effect change within the sector. You will be familiar with some of the reviews such as:

- Mid Staffordshire NHS Foundation Trust Public Inquiry (Francis, 2013)
- The Cavendish Review (2013) An Independent Review into Healthcare Assistants and Support Workers in the NHS and social care settings
- Berwick Review into Patient Safety (2013)
- The Keogh Mortality Review (2013) which looked at the quality of care and treatment provided by those NHS trusts and NHS foundation trusts that were persistent outliers on mortality indicators
- Transforming Care: A National Response into Winterbourne View Hospital (2012).

As a result of the above reviews, new drivers for improving quality in the NHS and across the sector are being put forward and these include a drive for transparency in the NHS and an improvement in quality.

In 2013, NHS Improving Quality published 'The new driving force for improvement across the NHS in England: How NHS IQ intends to support excellence in elective care'. The intention was to set up an NHS improvement organisation with the remit to 'provide improvement and change expertise to support improved health outcomes'.

The programme focused on the five domains of the NHS Outcomes Framework:

1 Preventing people from dying prematurely.
2 Enhancing quality of life for people with long-term conditions.
3 Helping people to recover from episodes of ill health or following injury.
4 Ensuring that people have a positive experience of care.
5 Treating and caring for people in a safe environment and protecting them from avoidable harm.

As a manager, these factors, political drivers, regulations, local government initiatives all have an influence and impact upon service delivery, including the policies that govern your setting and the procedures you follow. The way in which we respond to this can be innovative and entrepreneurial if we develop a culture of empowerment and trust within our teams. By allowing workers to take ownership of decisions and developing cultures of trust and openness, employees are more likely to try to develop new ways of working that can lead to innovation and an entrepreneurial spirit.

More recently, in 2018 NHS England published the *Commissioning for Quality and Innovation (CQUIN) Guidance for 2017–2019*, in which the focus to deliver clinical quality improvements and drive transformational change was updated. Two main parts are highlighted and these are to:

- improve quality and outcomes for patients and NHS staff, reduce health inequalities, and encourage collaboration across different providers

- support local areas – through increased funding and the development of Sustainability and Transformation Partnerships (STPs) and Integrated Care Systems (ICSs).

Internal directorates, access to resources – human, physical

Internal directorates are responsible for the development of internal policies that match the political drivers. In organisations such as the NHS, various clinical areas are divided into directorates. These work to ensure that structures and processes are in place to allow the clinical area to work as a team internally and to link into the wider strategies demanded by the organisation as a whole. They also allow physical and staff (human) resources to be shared, enabling access to a wider range of resources. Entrepreneurship can be encouraged in such areas only when there is trust and staff are encouraged to make decisions and are valued for their ideas.

The responsibilities of an internal directorate are to ensure that staff working in the area are aware of the wider political agenda and the organisational objectives. Each internal directorate will have some autonomy to manage its own budget and resources but will be responsible for auditing its work and justifying its action to a higher authority.

For example, your team in the setting may be likened to an internal directorate and, as the manager, you are responsible for the way the budget is used, how the stock is ordered and monitored and how you staff the team. Actions you take in the way you manage the team must be justified at board level.

The team being part of a larger organisation benefits from having access to resources from elsewhere in the setting and this can influence the way in which the service delivery is improved and quality raised. For example, a staff member seconded from a different area might bring new skills and ideas to the team, impacting upon the culture within the team. New ideas and innovation may come from sharing physical resources and applying them to the way in which the team works, changing service delivery.

Gaps in current market provision within service locality and beyond, funding

The media constantly inform us of disparity between services offered in some parts of the country and those areas where services are lacking. This disparity leads to gaps in the market, which need to be addressed.

Tackling health inequality has been a major government driver for many years. Public Health England (PHE) in its 2014 document *Tackling Health Inequalities* highlighted the problem.

'Where you live, what you earn and how long you stay in education may all affect your health.'

Source: PHE, 2014

For example, people who live in the poorest areas of the country are more likely to die on average seven years earlier than those who live in more affluent areas. This gap may be due to lack of services being offered in certain areas or due to other factors such as poor lifestyle choices or lack of education. More commonly, however, it has been seen to be a gap between the health of the rich and the poor. The CQC's annual equality information report of 2014, *Equal Measures*, supported this, showing that variation in access, experience and outcomes in many health and social care services has been an issue (CQC, 2014). The examples cited within the report suggest that some ethnic groups use certain hospital services more than other groups, which would suggest that access could be an issue. Additionally, people with dementia seem to have poorer outcomes than those without dementia going into hospital for the same health conditions and people with visual impairment and hearing loss within care homes are sometimes overlooked.

The CQC's report (2017) shows that the quality of care has been maintained despite very real challenges with health and care services working at full stretch trying to meet the needs of people with complex, chronic or multiple conditions, which are on the increase.

It has also been suggested that discrimination experienced by staff in the workplace affects the quality of care provided. The CQC, therefore, has determined to assess this in its inspections to ensure that service providers are protecting their staff with respect to equality in the workplace, which it believes will drive quality of care. The equality objectives for April 2017–19 are to review evidence of inequality in health and social care and in the CQC workforce, to set priorities, and to look at the impact of the inequality.

A paper published by Public Health England (2017), *Understanding Health Inequalities in England*, reported further on inequalities across socio-economically deprived areas and provided a report focusing on ethnic groups and the differences in health behaviours and outcomes. Innovative strategies involving working with external stakeholders to build more collaborative approaches to tackle the issues have resulted in the publication of guides to help local areas give children a good start in life, together with guidance on parenting, transition to schools and movement into work. The promotion of a 'health in all policies' approach to help local government improve wellbeing and growth has led to a Healthy Places programme. This sees PHE collaborating with housing and health partnerships and drives forward a communities-based approach to reducing health inequalities (PHE, 2017).

Change and improvement for any service inevitably involve a need for more money, and financial constraints can be a key driver of change. With the drive for new and innovative models of care such as the implementation of preventative services, the demographic challenge of an ageing population and increasing numbers of people with long-term conditions, the health service and social care needs financial change as well as the injection of more government revenue to deliver the care required (Health Foundation, 2014). As a manager in a care service, where funds are often scarce, innovative and entrepreneurial ways of working may be the way forward. NHS England is supporting staff to record innovation and improvement practice as CPD. This is to establish new networks of entrepreneurs and innovators, allowing clinical staff to use the points gained in revalidation. By encouraging your staff to undertake innovative care to improve quality of care and service user outcomes, you will be helping to reduce variation in care and developing the entrepreneurial spirit in the adult care setting.

Research it

1.2 Innovation and the NHS

Do some online research around innovation and adult care settings. Think about how you might encourage and motivate your staff to engage with this activity.

Evidence opportunity

1.2 Growth and change in your organisation

Identify the factors and drivers that influence the growth and change in your own service delivery. What impact have these had on your organisation with respect to developing an entrepreneurial and innovative culture within your service?

Provide a written account analysing the factors and drivers we have discussed above that could influence growth and change in service delivery.

In order to analyse, think about how the factors and drivers are influential in change.

Analysis requires you to break down the subject matter and to examine each part. Look closely at the factors and drivers and identify the main issues and then show how each is related to your area of work and what impact it will have.

Then evaluate the impact the factors and drivers we have discussed above might have in respect of supporting an entrepreneurial and innovative culture within the service and related delivery. In order to evaluate these, think about the effects these factors have on innovation and the strengths and the weaknesses, for example.

AC 1.3 Wider markets and potential future demands

Here, you will analyse and compare the wider market in respect of similar care service provision, with consideration of the areas we discuss in this section.

National care services, (their role and market position) and local services (public, private, not-for-profit and charitable sector and market position)

There is growing pressure on the national health and social care systems in our country to change to meet the challenges they face now and in the future. Already, we require additional hospital beds if we are to reduce the waiting list for operations and investigations. Local public and private healthcare organisations must consider how they can deliver healthcare that meets the needs of an ageing population with complex health needs. Community services are urged to improve and GP services are also undergoing major change to make stronger ties with the community services. The impact upon the NHS inevitably puts pressure on the adult social care system. With hospital beds in demand, the need to discharge patients earlier means stretching the adult care system even more.

The charity and voluntary sector, or the 'not-for-profit sector', describes a range of organisations that are neither public nor private sector. It includes voluntary and community organisations, registered charities associations, self-help groups and community groups, social enterprises and co-operatives.

One governmental aim is to increase the connection with the voluntary sector and local government to help keep people connected with their own community. Better care can be given if all services work together and share resources.

On managing a care setting, you need to think about local groups and charities that might add value to the service you give to your service users. For example, you need to consider how local charities and associations may be of benefit to your service users and how they might be encouraged to work alongside you in supplying care. They might, for example, offer group support services, or additional advice on dementia care that your setting may not necessarily offer. You will need to be aware and stay up to date on additional services that are available and how they may benefit your setting and those individuals receiving care, as well as staff, who may also benefit from the knowledge and advice these services offer.

How national and local services are commissioned, procured and funded and how this informs service availability

Taxes and national insurance contributions fund areas like the NHS and are underpinned by legislation. The Health and Social Care Act 2012 gave responsibility to NHS England, NHS Improvement and the Department of Health for pricing services. The NHS had a budget of approximately £124.7 billion in 2017/18.

These funds are allocated to Clinical Commissioning Groups to commission hospital, community and mental health services and areas with greater healthcare needs are given a bigger budget.

Commissioning refers to the process of planning, agreeing and monitoring health services. This is carried out by CCGs, which are groups of general practices in each area that commission the best services for their patients and local population. These boards are required to involve local people in the preparation of joint strategic needs assessments and health and wellbeing strategies. The availability of care services will depend on the type of care required according to the population demographic. This may mean a reduction in some services in certain areas and funds allocated to other more necessary services. This can, of course, have an impact upon your setting and you may find a change to your budget.

At a national level, NHS England has five regional teams which are accountable to one board and which commission specialised services, primary care, public health services, offender healthcare and some services for the armed forces. You should refer to www.england.nhs.uk/commissioning/ for more information.

The CCGs and NHS England are supported by commissioning support units (CSUs) whose role is to look at redesigning services, managing contracts within services and externally, and monitoring information and risk.

Overall, it is the Department of Health that leads all the groups and provides government funding for healthcare. While NHS England has responsibility for the commissioning of public health services, it does so with evidence produced by PHE, whose role is to improve and protect the nation's health and to address health inequalities.

While the NHS is free at the point of delivery, it is a different case with adult social care. People pay for their own care, or services are supplied by the local government, but in most cases, it is a mixture of the two. Care and support are not free services. Any adult who has 'eligible' needs, such as medical or mental conditions, is assessed by the local authority and support is supplied as a result of this.

In the November budget in 2018, the government announced further funding for social care of £240 million to ease pressure on the NHS by preventing unnecessary admissions and to get people home more quickly.

The local authority and council will be able to decide how best to spend the funds, which may be used for domestic services or for adapting homes.

How your service relates to the wider market and is able to meet potential demand

Adult social care is part of a system of public services and forms of support which include:

- health services, such as GP, counselling, district nursing and care homes
- housing, such as supported housing, warden schemes and assisted living
- welfare and benefits, such as advocacy, care and professional support, Citizens Advice
- leisure and wellbeing, such as sports facilities, libraries, education and transport.

Research it

1.3 National Audit Office 2018

You will find it useful to look at the *Adult Social Care at a Glance* document, July 2018 at www.nao.org.uk/wp-content/uploads/2018/07/Adult-social-care-at-a-glance.pdf or you can search for this online.

Your challenge as a manager of such a service is to ensure that all parts of the system are working together and that you are accessing wider services for the benefit of the people to whom you provide a care service. For example, with better medical management of long-term conditions a person may be able to stay independent for longer and not have to rely on additional care or support. The adult care sector continues to change and continues to request more money to support the growth it is experiencing. However, this money cannot always be forthcoming so smarter ways of working and innovation are necessary. Challenges with respect to the demand for additional services from an increasing elderly population might be envisaged in future and you therefore need to be aware of how your service will continue to supply services. You may be required to increase the number of beds offered, with subsequent effect on resources and staffing, or to look at ways of supplying care in a patient's home, therefore changing the way in which your service currently works.

Reflect on it

1.3 Working within the wider market

How does your own service relate to the wider market just referenced above and what do you see are the major challenges to your own setting's sustainability within the wider market?

Evidence opportunity

1.3 Wider markets and potential demands

Analyse and compare the wider market in respect of similar care service provision, considering the areas we have discussed in this section, for example. Provide a written account.

What do you think the wider market in adult care means to your service provision and what are the future demands with respect to your own service?

AC 1.4 Express vision in a way to engage and inspire others

Here, you will be required to express the vision of the service succinctly in a way that covers the areas we discuss in this section.

Engage and inspire external and internal stakeholders

External and internal stakeholders contribute to the success and development of the organisation and the way in which you communicate plays a major part in the way they perceive you. Changes in social media have led to more sophisticated means of communicating and forward-thinking organisations and settings have embraced this. Regular contact with stakeholders, keeping them abreast of current news about your setting, can now be achieved without resorting to weekly or monthly board meetings to go through accounts and progress. Electronic newsletters via email or Facebook, or Twitter updates, blogs, webinars and instant messaging are newer ways of engaging colleagues. The use of conference calls and video teleconferencing or Facetime means face-to-face contact can still be maintained for stakeholders or families of service users who are located outside the setting.

Expressing the vision of the service succinctly in a way that is clear to individuals in receipt of services and their families

Information giving is the first step in marketing your services and your vision to individuals and their families and they need to be clear about the mission statement and the vision of the setting, your principles and strategies.

Expressing the vision of the service succinctly as a 'statement of purpose'

The organisation's mission and statement of purpose can be widely advertised through marketing materials and in the policies and procedures of the setting. A statement of purpose describes what your service does, where and for whom. It must include clear details of aims and objectives and the service you provide. It also needs to highlight to others what needs your service meets.

Expressing the vision of the service to meet legislative requirements

The vision of the organisation needs to comply with legislation and should not imply that other services are offered. As a manager, you must communicate the importance of the organisation's goals not only by words but also in the way you behave. What you do can inspire and engage others to believe in the vision and to share it. Our employees, as well as stakeholders and service users and their families, want to engage with a service that is making a difference in the care sector so we need to communicate with enthusiasm and conviction. Positive feedback from our service users, stakeholders and staff should be shared and success celebrated. People who are engaged in this way find more enjoyment in their work, and really want to be part of a successful organisation.

Evidence opportunity

1.4 Express vision in ways to engage and inspire others

Provide a written account or tell your assessor about your vision of the service, in a succinct way, taking into account the areas we have covered in this section, for example.

LO2 Understand the principles of effective change management

AC 2.1 Importance of embracing and inspiring change within adult care services

Here, you will consider both 'imposed' and 'self-created' change relevant to your area of service, undertaking a critical evaluation of the impact this may have.

Research it

2.1 Self-change model

The self-change model (Prochaska and DiClemente, 1983) describes how people modify a problem behaviour or transform it into a positive behaviour. It was originally directed at health behaviour changes such as those relating to smoking and diet.

Research the model and make notes about how this might help your staff to embrace change in a more positive way.

Any change we make in our lives brings about uncertainty and the tendency to ask ourselves the 'what if' question. What if I am wrong to do this? What if everything goes wrong? We sometimes get into a cycle of negative thinking about our own intentions. Even if the source of change is our own choice, it can still be scary. Self-created change may cause us anxiety but the motivation to make the change was entirely our own. This is different from the changes that might be imposed from external sources.

The impact of legislative changes

Because of the growing and ageing population and the way in which disease patterns are changing we need to make changes to the way in which care is delivered. For example, epidemic diseases like cholera, smallpox and malaria have largely been eradicated with the use of vaccines but chronic conditions such as respiratory and heart disease may have increased due to lifestyle changes.

The changes that might be imposed upon us from the government will include those due to legislative changes and, as a result, service providers are duty bound to amend their ways of working.

The benefit of changes in the law may be that we make cost savings if we change the way in which we work. For example, by involving people in their own health and care by offering the information and support they need to manage their medical conditions, we may be reducing the need for a hospital visit. A disadvantage of legislative changes is that we usually have no choice about them. We may also not be privy to the reason behind the change, which can make it even more difficult, particularly if we believe it is unnecessary or we cannot see any benefit to it, even though there is obviously a benefit and clear rationale for it. In these circumstances we have not had the time to process what is going on and to reflect upon the change and it is then we may start to feel anxious and try to resist the change. However, it is important to embrace the positives and focus on how such legislation can bring about positive change.

The impact of regulatory/inspection changes

'Change' is also part of the inspection experience and can be a process that can cause anxiety among staff. Prior to an inspection we may expect staff to make changes to how they are working (i.e. 'self-created') but also inspection may bring about (or 'impose') the need to make changes to the ways in which care is being delivered in order to meet standards, which can be advantageous and beneficial as it can lead to improved ways of working.

Revenue/funding changes and staffing/ workforce changes

Changes to the way in which care is funded or even budgetary cuts will impact upon staff and service users and may lead to staffing and workforce changes, which are necessary. This can, of course, impact negatively on the workforce, causing anxiety and concern about job losses and reduction in salaries. The benefits may result in a more streamlined staff who are working more efficiently, but such change requires careful handling and sensitivity.

Managerial strategy and operational objectives and changes in service/business ownership, mergers

New policies as a result of inspection or legislation or changes to strategic objectives which may come about as a result of change to the business or a merger or new ownership may at first be viewed negatively by staff until they are fully versed on the reasons for the changes and the need for them. Change, which is imposed, can feel threatening and may be a cause of stress.

All of the points above may create feelings of anxiety among our staff and, as the manager, you need to appreciate why this is so. Any change, whether it is self-created or imposed, is likely to cause stress. If we choose to move to a new house, we may be excited about the prospect but we may also fear the unknown that comes with such a big life decision. With imposed change, we may try to ignore it or actively resist it by not buying into that change. What is the emotion behind resisting change? Think back to your self-imposed change and the thinking that went on. What if it's the wrong decision? The emotion that is foremost is one of fear and any change that your staff have to deal with will invariably expose their fear in a variety of ways.

They may fear being unable to adapt to the change or that they lack the ability to undertake new work. For example, the implementation of a new IT system may have meant that staff at a local hospital had to reorganise the way they admitted service users to the setting. This change may have been met with anger, frustration and disapproval by staff for the way in which they were being treated. The underlying fear may also have been due to the loss of a system they felt worked well but may also have been due to concern about potential job losses.

Fredrickson (1998) argued that the negative emotions result in a fight or flight type of response which limits our thoughts and actions. We become overly concerned with the threat and want to run away. Change in organisations is inevitable and by establishing positive ways of dealing with it we can help staff to embrace it rather than fear it. If we feel good about something we take more interest in it and are curious about what might happen. By taking a more positive view of change and recognising how it can bring about better working conditions, we can help staff to embrace it.

Reflect on it

2.1 Changes in the setting

What was the last major change you had to deal with in your setting?

How did you feel about it and how did it impact your thinking?

Evidence opportunity

2.1 Imposed changes

Look at the following list and undertake a critical evaluation of how these imposed or self-created changes have impacted your service. Consider the impact on your staff.

Consider what the strengths and weaknesses of each change are and how they have impacted your work. Provide a written account.

- Legislative changes.
- Regulatory/inspection changes.
- Revenue/funding changes.
- Staffing/workforce changes.
- Managerial strategy and operational objectives.
- Changes in service/business ownership, mergers.

AC 2.2 Role of leadership in change management

Here, you will critically analyse the role your leadership has in the following areas.

Driving changes in service strategy and operational delivery and business development and related opportunities

Business development refers to the tasks and processes that grow a business. It refers to the identification and the management of organisations outside of the company which can help the business to reach goals. This is different to sales development, where the business development team will engage in activities to expand the organisation into new markets.

Service strategy differs from operational delivery and, as a manager, you need to be clear about each of these terms.

Your organisation might have in place a strategic plan together with key performance indicators for staff and services offered. These goals will provide a three- to five-year plan to help the organisation to reach a level to meet service users' needs for now and the future. The strategic plan will look closely at what we do at operational levels and try to plan for change, which will ensure the service remains sustainable and competitive in the future. It will also give an indication of how the business will develop and evolve over the years to ensure that it remains fit for purpose in the future. Your yearly business plan will feed into the wider organisational plan. You should be mindful of the political and legislative drivers that will change the service provision, the market trends as well as demographic changes happening, so that in the five-year span we will be evolving the organisation to meet all these needs we may want to serve.

The operational part of the business is concerned with the everyday activities and work that move the service forward on a daily basis and as we tend to focus more on getting through the day and providing the care that's needed, we may be forgiven sometimes if we forget the bigger picture that is the strategic strategy.

We need to have both streams working together and our staff must be aware of where the organisation is heading and how what they do is linking into that. Focusing just on what we do now to get through the day is foolhardy and a number of care homes fell into this trap 20 years ago. When mandatory training for care staff was cited in legislation, some managers/owners of homes buried their heads in the sand and decided it was not for them. They failed to see the bigger picture, which meant that inspection strategy was also changing. At the next inspection, many found they did not meet the requirements for trained staff and they did not receive a favourable inspection grading.

It is imperative that the operational part of the organisation works closely with the strategic plan, that staff are fully aware of the threats and opportunities that exist and are able to offer their solutions to the everyday problems, in order to be part of shaping the future.

In managing change, leaders have to ensure that employees buy into the vision for the organisation and this requires good communication, with clear and consistent information. You must also show understanding if there is resistance to change. People need to feel included in decisions and, as a manager, your role will be to help the staff to overcome any resistance.

Leading by example – setting best practice, incorporating, inspiring and encouraging others to recommend changes in care service provision

In a leadership role, others will look to your behaviour and be guided by it. This gives you great responsibility because it begs the question: 'What behaviour am I displaying?'

Take a moment to reflect upon somebody you have worked with whom you admired. What characteristics did they have that you liked and would like to copy? For me, I have worked with various people who under pressure managed to keep a perspective that meant everybody around them felt calm and in control. They dealt with challenging situations in a rational way and managed to keep a sense of humour in the process. You may, therefore, take that example and try hard to emulate that in your daily work. You may have also worked with people who under stress would snap at staff and become completely unapproachable until the situation was in control. This is a behaviour that you certainly do not want to copy as it can completely change the team spirit. When managing change, a positive attitude towards it can be inspiring for others who may otherwise feel anxious.

As managers we need to be setting examples that move the organisation's strategy forward and at the same time inspire and encourage the staff to do the same. We can go a step further in this and ask and encourage staff, as well as those who use such services to recommend changes for developing an entrepreneurial spirit and innovation. See AC 1.1 for more information on entrepreneurship and innovation and Unit 501, AC 1.1 for more information on Kouzes and Posner's (2003) leadership challenge model for good leaders.

Overcoming resistance and barriers to change

We have looked at why people dislike the idea of change and suggested that fear is at the heart of it. Think of the last time a change occurred in your workplace in which you had no say and had been given no information about why it was needed. How did you feel?

Lack of understanding about why a change is necessary can be a real barrier to people committing to the change. Also, if there is no leadership to help you through the change it will be difficult to be inspired to make it work. If staff issues about the change are not defined and addressed, staff will not engage with the change and morale will plummet. Worse still, they may simply ignore the change and hope that it goes away (NICE, 2007).

To overcome such barriers, the NHS Improvement quality group has published a document to help managers to elicit the changes needed. One of the sections, entitled

'Engagement to mobilise,' suggests ways in which staff can be included and helped through times of change. For example, by understanding who is involved in and affected by the change, we can start to understand what motivates those members of staff to support it. The document suggests asking questions and helping staff to connect with their values and to gain commitment through a shared purpose (NHS QB, 2013). For example, staff engaged in healthcare are, on the whole, committed to delivering quality of care. If, as managers, we can demonstrate how a change will improve that delivery and be better for the patient, staff are more likely to buy into a new way of doing something.

Another crucial factor in eliciting commitment to change is to keep channels of communication open and to ensure that the team understands the vision and strategic direction. Team meetings with agendas giving team members opportunities to offer their ideas should be set up and other forms of communication, such as email, may also be useful, but you should consider the advantages and disadvantages of these. Communicating through discussions and appraisals is a good way to ensure that all are aware of the changes and how they might be affected. Suggestions from staff should be encouraged and considered.

In working with others, as managers, we need to promote a shared vision in the team by ensuring that everyone is involved in decision making and is aware of any change and the need for the change.

Evidence opportunity

2.2 Change management

Provide a written account critically analysing the role your leadership has in the following areas we discussed in this section.

You might like to think of a change you have had to make in your care setting and critically analyse the way in which you led the team in each of the following areas. Examine each heading to determine how effective your change was. Give one example for each heading.

- Driving changes in service strategy and operational delivery, e.g. what was the change?
- Business development and related opportunities. How would the change affect the business?
- Overcoming resistance and barriers to change. What resistance did you get and how did you handle it?
- Leading by example – setting best practice. How do you lead by example?
- Incorporating, inspiring and encouraging others to recommend changes in care service provision, e.g. teams, those in receipt of care services. How do you inspire your team?

AC 2.3 Theories, models and tools of change management

Here, you will investigate and critically evaluate change management theories and models, focusing on their relevance and application in your current leadership and management practice.

K. Lewin – Change Management Model

Kurt Lewin's three-stage theory of change is commonly known as Unfreeze, Change, Freeze (or Refreeze), but also includes something you may be familiar with in today's healthcare setting – the use of Force Field analysis.

1 Unfreezing

This stage is about preparing for the change and making sure there is shared understanding about the nature and rationale for the change. Deadlines need to be created because this motivates us towards the change. If there is no deadline there will be no action. Force Field analysis comes into play in this stage: this is the time to weigh up the pros and cons of change before any action is taken. If there are more positive factors for the change then staff are more likely to move with it and be motivated. Think about the last major change you made at work. Maybe you decided to change a process of working or a method of delivering care. Such big decisions require the listing of the advantages (pros) or disadvantages (cons) of such a change and the staff need to be on board with the developments. This is where Force Field analysis and the unfreezing take place.

2 Change

The change or transition is the process of making the change or moving towards the change. As we start to implement the change there is a steep learning curve and staff need to be given some time to understand what is happening.

3 Freezing

Once the first two stages have successfully been negotiated, freezing or refreezing, as it is sometimes referred to, happens. In this stage, the change becomes the norm and staff can now start to feel comfortable in new routines. This has been criticised by some writers as being a little simplistic because change is happening so rapidly, particularly in healthcare settings, that we are not given the luxury of becoming comfortable in new routines. What we can do is to support staff and reinforce the change whenever we can.

The advantages of the Lewin model are its simplicity and the number of steps involved. It is easy to plan for and implement. The disadvantages are the time it takes to 'unfreeze' current thinking and practice. Some critics also point to the lack of instructions as to how to accomplish each step. Your role as manager will be to engage staff in this activity by training them in the use of Force Field analysis. Your staff will need support to ensure they have a clear picture of what the end result following an implemented change is likely to look like. This will require clear communication and explanation during each stage.

D. Kolb – the learning cycle

Kolb (1984) developed a cycle of experiential learning and this has led to the development of models of reflective practice. Kolb recommends that we need to recall our observation of an event, reflect on the observations, develop and research some theories about what we saw and then decide on some action as a result of the process (Jasper, 2003). With respect to change, similar processes are utilised and his model, written with Frohman, is a lengthier version of Lewin's and is shown in Figure 11.2.

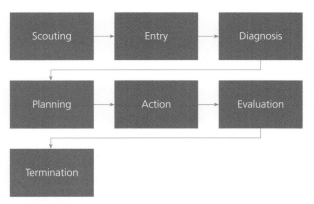

▲ **Figure 11.2** Kolb and Frohman's change model

This model looks at the stages of organisational change as a relationship between an organisational consultant (designer) and his or her client (user).

- **Scouting**: The consultant and client look at each other's needs in order to decide if there is a fit.
- **Entry**: A starting point for the project is selected, with initial goals and objectives set. Commitment to the project is also declared. The two parties build a trust relationship and a 'contract' for who will lead the project.
- **Diagnosis**: Data gathering begins and the problem is clearly defined. The consultant and client look at the available resources (including commitment) to see if it is feasible to continue.
- **Planning**: Planning begins with the consultant and client defining clearly the specific objectives and examining alternative ways to accomplish these. Any proposed solutions are judged as to the impact they will have, and an action plan is then put into place.
- **Action**: The consultant and client put into practice the best solution.
- **Evaluation**: The action plan is assessed as to its level of achievement of the goals set and the consultant

and client decide whether more work is needed or to terminate the plan.

- **Termination**: The consultant and client make sure that all involved with the change have mastered new ways of working and have control of the new systems which are in place.

(Adapted with the use of the *Journal of Engineering Studies and Research* 19(2) article by Buşe, F., Mangu, S-I., Buşe G-F, Slusariuc, G-C. (2013))

The advantage of using Kolb's learning cycle lies with its effectiveness in improving performance in **experiential learning**, but a disadvantage of it is that the experiential learning model does not always fit with all situations. Staff may already be aware of this model as an experiential learning cycle and a way of reflection and in managing change in your setting, your role as manager will be to show how it can be used as a way to introduce change in practice.

KEY TERM

Experiential learning is the process of learning through experience.

D. McGregor – theory 'X' (authoritarian) vs 'Y' (participative)

The two models discussed above focus on how to make changes. McGregor's theory is about the type of leaders who are able to move change forward. Lewin identified two types of leadership style: autocratic/authoritarian and democratic. McGregor defines these as X and Y.

The X type believe that workers are in need of micro managing and will lead in a rule-orientated way, believing the workers to be inherently lazy, working only for the money. This type of leader will not seek out an opinion or acknowledge achievement. Often, threat is part of the package to achieve what the leader wants. While we can see the negatives in this style, there are some benefits, particularly in a situation where there is an emergency and you need somebody to take the lead and direct people.

The Y style of leadership is about sharing responsibility and decision making. The leader demonstrates trust in their team and promotes a culture of mutual respect. This type of leader is of the opinion that the team thrive on achievement and want to be involved. Innovation, and the sharing of creative ideas, are encouraged. The downside is that decisions take a long time to be made.

F. Herzberg – two-factor theory (motivation–hygiene)

Herzberg's theory of motivation identified motivators or factors that brought high morale to staff as being achievement, recognition, responsibility and the promotion prospects within the role and the nature of the job. These factors can motivate staff if they are present and increase job satisfaction. Alternatively, hygiene factors such as pay, company policy, type of management, benefits and relationship with colleagues are, according to Herzberg, likely to lead to job dissatisfaction if they are ignored or absent. They were not considered to be 'true' motivators but rather were expected conditions of normal working life.

Herzberg found that to increase motivation in workers, dissatisfaction had to be avoided and this was accomplished by addressing the hygiene factors, meaning workers were not negative about their jobs. This led to people who were calmer in their workplace and happier. He determined that by addressing the motivators, job satisfaction could be increased and when managing a team this is worth investing in. For example, you may have no control over the pay somebody gets but you can address the way in which they are perceived and valued in their role.

The advantage of Herzberg's theory lies with the factors that motivate and demotivate groups of employees and, as a manager, you will have some control over these. A disadvantage of Herzberg's theory is that factors that motivate can change; they may also be different for some people. Employees may have very different views as to dissatisfaction and satisfaction at work and, as a manager, you need to work towards achieving no dissatisfaction at work. This means, for example, addressing the hygiene factors in the workplace and ensuring that working conditions, pay relationships and company policy all benefit the employees. As a result, staff are likely to be more positive at work and job satisfaction can then be worked upon by introducing the motivators such as responsibility, recognition and achievement.

Kubler-Ross – five-stage model – the change curve

You might be familiar with Kubler-Ross' five stages of grief in her book *On Death and Dying,* which were said to represent the normal range of feelings people experience when dealing with bereavement.

As managers, we can appreciate change involves some sort of loss, so the five-stage model has been applied to managing change.

Kubler-Ross' five stages of grief (Figure 11.3) are:

1 Denial
2 Anger
3 Bargaining
4 Depression
5 Acceptance.

Kubler-Ross explained that these are normal reactions we have to tragic news and called them defence or coping mechanisms that we need to move through in order to manage change. Any change in the workplace may see staff going through similar stages.

These stages evolved into what Kubler-Ross terms the change curve, which shows the levels of emotion or energy experienced by people as they deal with change. Even though it depicts a linear process, individuals move in and out of stages and it does not follow that we can expect somebody in shock and denial to move straight into anger. They may well do, but they may also simply move straight on to acceptance.

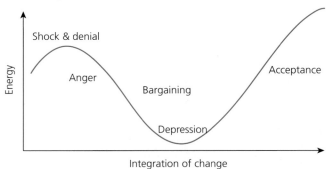

▲ **Figure 11.3** Kubler-Ross change curve

When we use this model, we can identify and understand how our staff are dealing with change and also have a better understanding of the reactions we are seeing and why staff are behaving in a particular way.

As a change model, one advantage is that it identifies how others are dealing with and reacting to change and, in this way, we are able to see why our colleagues may be behaving in a particular way. A disadvantage is that it does not describe the wide range of emotions that people may feel. It assumes that we all react similarly, but cultural differences may bring about different emotional reactions.

Evidence opportunity

2.3 Change management models

Having looked at the theories of change, evaluate the change management theories and models in terms of their relevance and how you apply them or would apply them in your current leadership and management practice.

Remember to critically evaluate these and to consider the strengths and weaknesses of each theory.

You may also wish to investigate other change management theories and models. Make sure you critically evaluate them as you have done with the above. What other ones did you find?

AC 2.4 Innovation and business development

Here, you will consider how change management theories and models support your own innovation and business development in respect of the areas we discuss in this section.

If a business is to remain viable and competitive it needs to develop new products and processes and in care work this may mean it needs to look at new ways of working. This requires changing the way we do things and as we noted previously this might be unsettling.

Service vision and service strategy

The vision of a service sets out its direction and its broad aims and distinguishes it from other organisations. For example, your vision might be 'to provide the highest quality adult social care provision in the county'. The service strategy determines how the organisation intends to reach that vision. There are a number of ways in which you can reach the vision but innovation and entrepreneurial strategies are likely to give you the edge over other similar providers. As the manager, you need to develop a culture of curiosity and openness within the team to encourage new ways of thinking about providing care.

Operational planning and delivery

With a strategic plan in place it is a managerial task to develop an operational plan which details the day-to-day tasks needed for the smooth and efficient running of the organisation or setting and for the people who work there. It will outline, for staff, their roles and responsibilities and duties so that everyone is aware of what is expected of them. These will be in keeping with the overall objectives of the organisation or setting. The operational plan will focus on such details as the 'what', 'who', 'when' and 'how much' to ensure these areas are clearly explained so that everyone is aware of their role within the organisation and how the organisation will operate.

An operational plan changes over time and managers need to be able to manage those changes. For example, in a competitive field of work, change may be required because of new updates and guidance from government or there may be changes to finances. As the manager, you need to be able to manage the change and to help others to see the advantages of it. High levels of competition require organisations to move forward by embracing change and adapting new technology and methods for the service user.

Evidence opportunity

2.4 Innovation and business development

Write a piece about how change management theories and models support your own innovation and business development in respect of:

- service vision
- service strategy
- operational planning and delivery

- service quality
- integration and integrated services/the wider adult care system.

You might find it useful to show evidence of innovation and business development you have been a part of in your workplace and consider the theory you have used. Use the table to say how change feeds into the following areas.

	Define; say what each of these terms mean to your setting	Change theory utilised for each of these concepts, i.e. what is the change theory utilised for service vision, service strategy, etc.?	Comment on how it supported your work
Service vision	e.g. what is your service vision or mission?	e.g. how has it been developed or changed over time and how was it delivered to staff?	e.g. what areas did it support?
Service strategy			
Operational planning and delivery			
Service quality			
Integration and integrated services/the wider adult care system			

Service quality

Within the operational plan there will be reference to how the quality of the service is to be monitored and maintained. Audit tools will be available and quality measures need to be adhered to. Changes may need to be made as a result of surveys and audits to improve the delivery of quality care.

Integration and integrated services/the wider adult care system

With the inclusion of the wider care services around us we must ensure that other services are made fully aware of any changes. Changes may come about as a result of working with external stakeholders when operations become more complex. Managing the changes may involve transitioning staff, groups and projects from one way of working to another.

Change management theories and models, when correctly implemented, can support innovation and business development in your area by empowering staff to improve their practice. By involving them in the development of new ways of working, staff who are informed and supported throughout the change are likely to offer less resistance.

LO3 Understand how to develop a vision for the future of the service

AC 3.1 Define personal role in relation to developing a vision for services

Here, you will be required to explain the aims and objectives of your vision for your service area, with consideration of the areas we discuss in this section.

The business planning process – maintenance and potential growth

In developing your business plan for your setting, you will have answered two questions: What is the current state of play or where are we now and where do we want to go or be in one, three or five years' time? You will then define what needs to be done and by when to accomplish the goals of the organisation. It is important that you as a manager are aware of the changes that may be happening to the business as new guidelines are developed and as the competition around you changes. Without such knowledge, your organisation will not grow and could even fail.

Research it

3.1 Business planning

Look at a variety of articles dealing with business planning. Think about what your role is in this process and make notes.

Competition/market competitors – national and local – and risks – actual and potential

Our business, like any retail or customer care service, needs to be sustainable and provide the best quality of care. A potential risk of not doing so may be the closure of a service. For example, if a GP service is not providing good care which patients are happy with, it may find it loses patients to other services. The failing GP practice will ultimately lose the contract for providing primary care service in that area. A care home that is continually rated 'needs improvement' or 'inadequate' by CQC in inspections may share a similar fate, with service users moving elsewhere. So, we need to be aware of the competition and what is referred to as the market economy in the national and local areas and understand the strengths and weaknesses of each competitor. In addition, we should be aware of the risk competitors pose for our service and we may need to act to diminish this.

A 'market economy' describes an exchange of goods between buyers and sellers and in adult care it means service users have more choice about who provides their care.

Aside from the risk posed by competitors in the field, adult care managers also need to acknowledge the risks of several factors that can damage a business if they are not considered or prevented. For example, we are at risk of cyber-attacks when computer systems are targeted and data breaches result. There has also been an increase in telemedicine and other innovative ways in which people can access healthcare. Infection risk is another area of concern. As a manager there is a growing need for you to be aware of these risks to your business and so you will need to think about ways in which these can be managed.

Service redesign

Having seen the competition and what they offer we may decide to redesign our services to improve the way in which care is given or to move ahead of the competition. For example, it may not simply be a case of redesigning the care space but maybe the way in which the care is delivered. You may also consider redesigning how the workforce is used and could look at developing new roles. If staff training has been an issue it may be that you develop a mentor system to ensure new staff are trained when working. However you plan to develop the area, it is the aims and objectives of the service area and the wider organisation together with the mission and vision statement that need to be prioritised.

Local and national data that informs your service area

In AC 1.2 we looked at factors and drivers likely to have an impact on service provision and determined that these are often driven by national data and legislation and also local need. Your own local area will have different demographical details that will inform how your service runs. For example, there may be a greater number of older adults or young people and this will mean a different approach to the services you offer.

Needs of individuals requiring care and support services and needs of local communities

The types of people in a population, the age demographic and the needs they have are all data the Clinical Commissioning Group collects. These needs then need to be met with the development of services. As mentioned previously, a high number of older adults with complex needs will require different services and support than those in an area where there is a mental health need.

As a manager, it is important that your aims and objectives for the future are aligned to the vision of the organisation. The business planning process should clearly address needs for the future to ensure your setting is sustainable; you should be aware of the market economy, potential competition and changes to service delivery, which will affect your service users.

New trends in digital technologies and innovations

Telemedicine, for example, is a new concept whereby people can access doctors by phone or online rather than waiting in a GP surgery. There is a cost, but it is rapidly becoming a means by which we can access healthcare. Your role as a manager may be to embrace such technology within your own service.

Your influence or not in respect of engaging in change and/or growth and staffing needs in support of the above

Change will either bring about growth or it can contribute to its failure. In moving your service forward, you must not only be aware of the changes that are happening but also need to move with them. You can have real influence in engaging in change and growth. This may mean you require more staff to grow as a business and to rival competition. Or you may need to retrain staff to fulfil the needs of the service. Perhaps your staff are unfamiliar with the use of new digital technologies and therefore require upskilling.

AC 3.2 Recognise areas within own service that require improvement in order to provide person-centred care

Here, you will critically evaluate areas within your own service that require improvement in order to provide person-centred care, taking into consideration the areas we discuss in this section.

As a manager, you will be responsible for identifying and recognising the areas within your own service that require improvement, so you can continually offer enhanced person-centred care that meets the needs of those who use adult care services.

Service planning and delivery

Current services may still be using outdated models of service delivery, which fail to recognise the individual. This may be due to funding which is allocated to a service and, therefore, may provide a cheaper option to deliver care. As the manager, you need to take a critical look at how your service is delivering care and then think about ways in which improvements can be made to meet person-centred ideals.

Staff views and views of those in receipt of support and care services and other stakeholders

Your staff and stakeholders as well as service users may all have excellent suggestions as to how the person-centred agenda may be delivered. By eliciting responses from them for change you can gain a wealth of knowledge about the service and the improvements that can be made.

Formal compliments/complaints

The complaints and compliments system can provide valuable insight about how well or poorly a service is being delivered. By analysing these things, you will be able to see clearly where improvements can be made. For example, a persistent complaint is a clear sign for you as a manager that a change needs to be made. But if you are getting compliments about either a care practice or a member of staff, then you can also learn valuable lessons from this, as this is something that you can exploit further to offer even better care. Again, as a manager, you will play a key role in recognising the improvements that need to be made and capitalising on good practice to offer even better service.

Reflect on it

3.2 Your compliments and complaints procedures

Are there any ways that you could improve the compliments and complaints procedure in your setting? What do your staff think about this?

Evidence opportunity

3.2 Areas that require improvement to provide person-centred care

Critically evaluate each of the areas that we have covered above, including service planning and delivery, staff views, views of those in receipt of support and care services, other stakeholders, formal compliments/complaints.

When critically evaluating each of these, think about strengths and weaknesses of each area and how they have impacted upon your work, for example.

Provide a written account of your critical evaluation.

AC 3.3 Review drivers relating to areas of service that require improvement

Here, you will investigate and review national and/or local drivers relating to areas of your service that inform service improvement.

A wealth of policy and guidance has been published and has influenced how health and adult care is delivered in this country. It is important to keep up to date with these and to work with them to strengthen your edge in the service industry.

Government reports and public inquiries and outcomes

Government policy reforms and reports have significant health impacts and managers need, therefore, to review these to determine how they affect their own service areas. Additionally, public inquiries and the outcomes of reviews, which may have been held in cases of serious incidents in care, give us much needed guidance into how we need to work together to safeguard and promote the welfare of members of the public. This can all help us to improve our service delivery.

CQC reports/findings/recommendations

CQC reports and inspections may point out the need to change our practice in order to effect improvement. Such reports can give guidance as to what needs to be changed to ensure safe and high-quality care is given.

The Care Certificate

The development of a set of standards has meant that all workers in care have an opportunity to complete a qualification and this has directly influenced the way in which care is improving. There are e-learning modules online to support the training for this (Health and Skills for Care).

Media reports

News alerts us to poor practice more so than good practice. Keeping up to date with news and changes in health or adult care can have a massive impact upon whether we deliver a quality service or not.

Internal quality assurance reports/reviews

Our own internal inspections and quality audits are a useful way to ensure service delivery is of a high quality. We are able to grasp things that may need to change in the light of an audit or survey.

Formal service user reviews and evaluations

By undertaking surveys of service users' opinions, we are able to gain a wealth of information about how we function and whether we can improve.

Internal business strategies and objectives

If objectives set are being achieved, then we can gain useful information about how the business is performing and whether change may be required to improve the service in the future.

Changes in digital technologies

Information technology and other media tools change rapidly but we can use them to advance our business and to check on quality. Simple surveys can be sent to service users and stakeholders to ascertain their feedback on how well our staff and service are performing for them.

Community need

The communities in which we live and work change over time, so we need to keep track of the changes so we can determine how our business needs to adapt. Are you living in an area where life expectancy is particularly high or low? Are there certain illnesses that a great number of people suffer from in your area?

With all these factors and drivers, the manager's role is one of keeping ahead of the changes that may occur. Failure to be up to date may result in missing vital clues as to how your service needs to improve in order to stay viable and safe.

AC 3.4 Evaluate research findings to formulate options for the future direction of services

Here, you will evaluate findings to formulate options for the future direction of your care service. The options for the future could inform the areas we discuss in this section.

You will also be required to ensure options formulated are bold, innovative and embody the core values of adult care.

- **Strategy design**: There is little doubt that healthcare design and strategy have to change in the future to meet the growing needs of an increasing elderly population, for example.

- **Operational delivery**: As we discussed previously, we may need to think about different ways in which healthcare can be delivered to meet needs and also to offset the rising cost.

- **Internal policy and procedures**: As change occurs and as more research and government reports are being compiled, policies and procedures will need to be updated to accommodate change.

- **Recruitment and workforce training and development**: The way in which we recruit staff will be done according to the changes that have been identified in the strategy design and operational delivery. So, too, training and development may well be revised as a result of newer, more innovative ways of working.

- **Quality monitoring**: Without monitoring quality, we cannot be sure we are delivering the best and most efficient care required by our service users. This activity of monitoring and scrutinising must become a major part of the daily work we undertake.

- **Service user involvement**: Service user involvement in care has already undergone great change but must move forward even more to enhance the care service users receive. Allowing service users to be part of team meetings and to engage more in the running of the care

setting may be a way forward, particularly for those who are in settings for the long term.

- **Innovations for change by self and/or others**: A staff who are autonomous and empowered are likely to be innovative and bold in their thinking and are not afraid to voice their opinions.

LO4 Work with others to support an entrepreneurial culture

AC 4.1 Recognise aspects of the organisation that need to be improved in order to be effective in providing a person-centred service

Here, you will be required to evaluate aspects of the organisation that are no longer effective in providing a person-centred service.

National Voices, a coalition of charities, reported in 2017 on the extent of person-centred care in the care system. Its conclusions were that while some areas have improved, there is still evidence that coordination of person-centred care is not measured and there is some inequality in the delivery of such care within some groups. For example, only 3 per cent of people with a long-term health condition stated that they had a written care plan in place.

You will need to conduct research to determine how effective you are in providing person-centred care in your own setting. If you conclude that certain areas are being carried out ineffectively, you can then put into place improvements.

Evidence opportunity

4.1 Recognise aspects of the organisation that need to be improved

Provide a written account evaluating aspects of the organisation that are no longer effective in providing a person-centred service.

You may wish to identify the strengths and the weaknesses of this process in your setting, and possibly conduct a survey to determine how well person-centred care is being carried out. Look at care planning, decision making and involvement with the service user and their family and the way in which all this is measured. Conclude your account by showing which aspects of the organisation are no longer effective in providing a person-centred service.

You might like to think about why they are no longer effective, and how they could be improved in order to be effective and provide person-centred care.

AC 4.2 Identify opportunities for growth and development

Here, you will work with others to identify opportunities for growth and development or redesign in your setting as a service and as a business.

The future of health and adult care services requires change to keep up with the needs of an ageing population, the changes in disease patterns and also the changes in public expectation of what healthcare should offer. These changes, although challenging, also provide opportunities to develop your setting and redesign the way in which you are delivering your care.

Bolder and more innovative management of staff and care services is needed, and traditional models of care should be overhauled to bring in newer strategies. Working alongside internal and external stakeholders, staff and families to address changes to develop newer ways of working will highlight areas of growth for the organisation and a redesign of delivery of care can be agreed upon. Failure to embrace change in this way will mean failure for the organisation moving forward.

Evidence opportunity

4.2 Identify opportunities for growth and development

Show your assessor how you work with others to identify opportunities for growth and development or redesign in your setting as a service and as a business.

AC 4.3 Maintain a culture that supports innovation, change and growth

Here, you will be required to show you maintain a culture that supports innovation, change and growth in relation to the service provided and recognises the resource available in the expertise of those using or working in the service.

An innovative culture requires a vision and a positive style of management. At the heart of every organisation there are values that staff are expected to hold. The NHS Constitution has at its core person-centredness and responsiveness and staff need to conduct themselves in their daily work with these in mind. Your staff will also need to be aware of the 6Cs of commitment, care, compassion, competence, communication and courage. In your own setting, you will have identified values to which your staff are working and, as their manager, your role is to ensure that the message you give out in your conduct and behaviour reflects those values. Also, the way in which you treat your staff and support them is crucial to the success of growth and innovation. Treating staff with compassion and respect will ensure that staff subsequently treat each other and their patients in a similar manner. Aggressive leadership styles disempower staff and diminish morale and reduce job satisfaction. Positive leadership and management encourage staff to engage with change more readily.

The aims and objectives of the organisation must be clearly shared by everyone to give direction to the work. Staff who are unaware of their goals in their daily work may feel stressed and overworked. Members of staff should be aware of their personal goals with respect to their work and how these align with the mission and vision of the organisation.

Another feature of cultural innovation is the investment in staff. Staff are your biggest and most expensive resource and asset and improvements in quality care will be sustained, ensuring your staff are well trained, up to date and working effectively as a team. A culture where openness and honesty are key words is instrumental in maintaining a culture of high-quality care.

Evidence opportunity

4.3 Maintain a culture that supports innovation, change and growth

Show your assessor that/how you maintain a culture that supports innovation, change and growth in relation to the service provided and recognises the resource available in the expertise of those using or working in the service.

Tutors have the opportunity to use a wide range of delivery techniques; these could include group discussions, lectures and active learning tasks.

For AC 4.3, investigations should be relevant, recent and from accurate and reliable sources.

Suggestions for using the activities	
This table summarises all the activities in the unit that are relevant to each assessment criterion. Here, we also suggest other, different methods that you may want to use to present your knowledge and skills by using the activities. These are just suggestions, and you should refer to the Introduction section at the start of the book, and more importantly the City & Guilds specification, and your assessor, who will be able to provide more guidance on how you can evidence your knowledge and skills. When you need to be observed during your assessment, this can be done by your assessor, or your manager can provide a witness testimony.	

Assessment criteria and accompanying activities	Suggested methods to show your knowledge/skills
LO1 Understand the provision for the adult care services market	
1.1 Evidence opportunity (page 344)	Give a written account of how your own organisation is developing a culture that supports innovation, change, redevelopment and growth. You could also explain this to your assessor.
1.1 Research it (page 344)	Write a short account of your findings about Lewin's change theory.
1.1 Evidence opportunity (page 346)	Look at some of the theories and reflect on the one you favour the most. Write a short account of theories of entrepreneurship and decision making and how they could be applied to adult care management. You could also explain this to your assessor.
1.2 Research it (page 348)	Do some online research around innovation and adult care settings.
1.2 Evidence opportunity (page 348)	Provide a written account analysing the factors and drivers we have discussed above that could influence growth and change in service delivery.
1.3 Research it (page 350)	Write down your findings.
1.3 Reflect on it (page 350)	Provide a reflective exemplar.
1.3 Evidence opportunity (page 350)	Provide a written account analysing and comparing the wider market in respect of similar care service provision.
1.4 Evidence opportunity (page 351)	Provide a written account of your vision of the service.
LO2 Understand the principles of effective change management	
2.1 Research it (page 351)	Research the model and make notes about how this might help your staff to embrace change in a more positive way.
2.1 Reflect on it (page 352)	Provide a reflective account or make notes in response to the questions in the activity.
2.1 Evidence opportunity (page 352)	Provide a written account undertaking a critical evaluation.
2.2 Evidence opportunity (page 354)	Provide a written account critically analysing the role your leadership has in the areas we discussed in this section.
2.3 Evidence opportunity (page 356)	Having looked at the theories of change, evaluate the change management theories and models in terms of their relevance and application in your current leadership and management practice. Remember to critically evaluate these and to consider the strengths and weaknesses of each theory.
2.4 Evidence opportunity (page 357)	Write a piece about how change management theories and models support your own innovation and business development in respect of the areas we discuss in this section.
LO3 Understand how to develop a vision for the future of the service	
3.1 Research it (page 358)	Make notes based on your research and remember to think about your own role in business planning.
3.1 Evidence opportunity (page 359)	Write a piece that explains the aims and objectives of your vision for your service areas. Remember to comment on all of the different areas, such as the business planning process, competition, service redesign, local and national data, that we have covered in this section, as examples.

→

Suggestions for using the activities	
3.2 Reflect on it (page 360)	Are there any ways that you could improve the compliments and complaints procedure in your setting? What do your staff think about this?
3.2 Evidence opportunity (page 360)	Critically evaluate each of the areas that we have covered, including service planning and delivery, staff views, views of those in receipt of support and care services, other stakeholders, formal compliments/complaints, for example.
3.3 Evidence opportunity (page 361)	Provide a written account detailing your investigation and review.
3.4 Evidence opportunity (page 361)	Provide a written account evaluating your findings to formulate options for the future direction of your care that could inform the areas we have discussed here. Remember that you should ensure options formulated are bold, innovative and embody the core values of adult care.
LO4 Work with others to support an entrepreneurial culture	
4.1 Evidence opportunity (page 362)	Provide a written account evaluating aspects of the organisation that are no longer effective in providing a person-centred service. You could also discuss this with your assessor.
4.2 Evidence opportunity (page 362)	Show your assessor how you work with others to identify opportunities for growth and development or redesign as a service and as a business.
4.3 Evidence opportunity (page 362)	Show your assessor that/how you maintain a culture that supports innovation, change and growth in relation to the service provided and recognises the resource available in the expertise of those using or working in the service.

References

Buşe, F., Mangu, S.-I., Buşe, G.-F. and Slusariuc, G.-C. (2013) The strategy and implementation and integration of the decision support systems having in view achievement of a performance management at S.C. Energetic complex Oltenia S.A, *Journal of Engineering Studies and Research*, 19(2).

Care Quality Commission (2014) *Equal Measures: Equality information report for 2014*. London: CQC.

Durkheim, E. (1897/1964) *Suicide*. Glencoe, IL: Free Press.

Fredrickson, B. (1998) What good are positive emotions? *Review of General Psychology*, 2(3): 300–19.

Health Foundation (2014) *More Than Money: Closing the NHS quality gap*. London: Health Foundation.

Jasper, M. (2003) *Beginning Reflective Practice*. Oxford: Nelson Thorne.

Kolb, D. (1984) Cycle of experiential learning, in Tilmouth, T., Davies-Ward, E. and Williams, B. (2011) *Foundation Degree in Health and Social Care*. London: Hodder Education.

Kotter, J.P. (1996) *Leading Change*. Brighton, MA: Harvard Business School Press.

Kouzes, J.M. and Posner, B.Z. (2003) *The Leadership Challenge* (3e). San Francisco, CA: Jossey-Bass.

Kübler-Ross, E. (1969) *On death and dying*. London: Tavistock Publications.

Lewin, K. (1947) Frontiers of group dynamics, *Human Relations*, 1: 5–41.

Maher, L., Plsek, P. and Bevan, H. (2009) *Creating a Culture for Innovation: Guide for executives*. Coventry: NHS Institute for Innovation and Improvement.

McClelland, D. (1988) *Human Motivation*. Cambridge: Cambridge University Press.

McKibbon, J., Walton, A. and Mason, L. (2008) *Leadership and Management in Health and Social Care*. London: Heinemann.

NHS England (2018) *Commissioning for Quality and Innovation (CQUIN) Guidance for 2017–2019*. London: TSO.

NHS QB (2013) Quality in the new health system – maintaining and improving quality from April 2013. Department of Health and Social Care. Accessed from https://assets.publishing. service.gov.uk/government/uploads/system/uploads/ attachment_data/file/213304/Final-NQB-report-v4-160113. pdf

National Institute for Health and Clinical Excellence (2007) *How to Change Practice. Understand, identify and overcome barriers to change*. London: NICE.

Prochaska, J.O. and DiClemente, C.C. (1983) Stages and processes of self-change of smoking: Toward an integrative model of change, *Journal of Consulting and Clinical Psychology*, 51: 390–5.

Public Health England (2014) *Tackling Health Inequalities*. London: PHE Publications.

Public Health England (2017) *Reducing Health Inequalities: System, scale and sustainability*. London: PHE Publications.

Schwartz, S.H. (2011) *An Overview of the Schwartz Theory of Basic Values*. New York: The Berkeley Electronic Press.

Weber, M. (1905/1958) *The Protestant Ethic and the Spirit of Capitalism*. New York: Scribner's.

Further reading and useful resources

Department of Health (2015) *Public Health Commissioning in the NHS 2016 to 2017*. London: TSO.

Department of Health (2018) *Health Inequalities Annual Report 2018*. London: TSO.

Durkheim, E. (1912/1954) *The Elementary Forms of Religious Life*. Glencoe, IL: Free Press.

Hartley, J. (2013) *The New Driving Force for Improvement across the NHS in England: How NHS IQ intends to support excellence in elective care*. London: NHS IQ.

http://study.com/academy/lesson/the-needs-theory-motivating-employees-with-maslows-hierarchy-of-needs.html

HMSO (1999) *Modernising Government*. White Paper. London: HMSO.

National Voices (2017) *Person-centred Care in 2017*. London: National Voices.

Nuffield Trust (2013) *The Francis Public Inquiry Report: A response*. Policy response, accessed from www.nuffieldtrust.org.uk/files/2017-01/francis-public-inquiry-report-web-final.pdf

Schwartz, S.H. (1992) Universals in the content and structure of values: Theory and empirical tests in 20 countries. In M. Zanna (ed.) *Advances in Experimental Social Psychology* (Vol. 25, pp. 1–65). New York: Academic Press. http://dx.doi.org/10.1016/S0065-2601(08)60281-6

Websites

https://scholarworks.gvsu.edu/cgi/viewcontent.cgi?referer=&httpsredir=1&article=1116&context=orpc accessed on 29/9/18

www.volarisgroup.com/blog/article/fostering-an-entrepreneurial-culture-within-your-organization

Glossary

6Cs are the values that underpin health and social care. These are care, compassion, commitment, communication, courage and competence.

Accountability is taking responsibility and being liable or answerable for something.

Action orientation is a type of leadership in which practical action is taken to deal with a problem or situation.

Active listening is listening clearly and ensuring that you understand what the sender intends to communicate and the content of the message.

Active participation is a way of working where the individual is an active partner in their care rather than a passive one. It is the core principle of person-centred care. It enables individuals to be included in their care and to be able to voice how they wish to live their life and obtain their own care.

Advance directive (also known as a living will) is a legal document that specifies what actions should be taken for a person if they cannot make decisions for themselves because of illness or incapacity.

An **advocate** is an individual who acts for or on behalf of another, particularly if the person lacks capacity in some way or simply requires help to speak out.

Advocates represent individuals or speak on their behalf to ensure that their rights are supported.

Agreed ways of working are your setting's policies, procedures and guidelines for the care and support you provide for service users.

Appraisal, sometimes referred to as performance appraisal, is the process by which employees and line managers discuss their performance, developmental needs and the support they need in their role. It is used to provide evidence and evaluation of recent performance and focus on future goals, opportunities and resources.

Assistive technology refers to the use of aids such as picture and symbol communication boards and electronic devices, which help individuals who have difficulty with speech or language problems to express themselves.

Authoritarian/autocratic is having total authority and control over decision making; keeping everything under close scrutiny.

Brexit is a term that has been used to denote the United Kingdom leaving the European Union. The EU was formed by France and Germany after the end of World War Two to ensure that they would never again go to war with each other. The European Union currently consists of 28 countries of which the UK is one. The countries in the EU trade with each other and also discuss political issues like climate change. In 2016, UK voters decided that they no longer wanted the UK to be a member of the EU. There are a number of EU laws that are in place in the UK. At the time of printing, it is uncertain how these laws will be affected when the UK finally leaves the EU.

Capacity in this context refers to the ability of a person to do or understand something.

A **care or support plan** is a written document or something recorded in patient notes which is an agreement between a service user and an adult health professional to help manage their day-to-day health and care needs.

Coaching is a process that supports and enables an individual to unlock and maximise their potential, to develop and improve performance.

Colleagues are people you work with to provide care services. They may be in similar job roles to you or may have a different status. For colleagues to work in partnership, there needs to be collaboration and commitment to the service user to ensure best practice.

Conflict is a disagreement or argument.

Consent means to give permission for something to happen. It may be verbal, written or implied but always needs to be addressed.

Constructive criticism is offering positive and negative comments about another person's work in a friendly rather than a confrontational way. In doing so, we want to improve the outcome so well-reasoned and valid facts are given to help the person to change.

Constructive feedback focuses on the issue in question and provides specific information. It is firmly based on observation and provides supportive evidence. There are two types of constructive feedback. One is positive or favourable and this is when we praise a performance or effort or outcome. The other is more negative and may be seen as unfavourable, when we criticise a performance or outcome.

Contingency theories state that there is no one best style of leadership. In this case the leader's effectiveness is based on the situation.

Continuing professional development (CPD) is the planned process of improving and increasing capabilities of staff and is an ongoing process. It is training and education activity to ensure staff remain fit for practice.

CQC is the Care Quality Commission, the independent regulator and lead inspection and enforcement body of all health and social care services in England.

A **critical incident** is an unintended event that occurs when an individual in health care is involved in something that results in a consequence to him or her; for example, a fall.

Culture is the customs, attitudes and beliefs that distinguish one group of people from another.

Democratic/participative is a sharing type of leadership in which employees' participation in the decision making is favoured.

Deprivation of Liberty Safeguards (DoLS) protect the rights of individuals who may need to be detained in a hospital if they lack mental capacity.

Disclosure is the release of information about something.

Discrimination means treating people unfairly or unlawfully because they have a disability, or are of a different race, gender or age for example.

Diversity is equal respect for people who are from different backgrounds.

Duty of Candour requires providers to be open and transparent with service users about their care and treatment. If treatment goes wrong the care provider must inform the service user about the incident, and provide support and an apology.

Emotional intelligence is being aware of and having the ability to control our own emotions, so as to handle interpersonal relationships empathetically (to think about and understand how others are feeling and see things from their point of view).

Empathy is being able to understand and share the feelings of another person or having the ability to experience another person's condition from their perspective.

Empowerment is giving someone authority.

Entrepreneurship refers to organising and managing a new business or idea for profit. Innovation is a part of this.

Equal opportunity is the principle of having opportunities in life that are fair and similar to those of other people and ensuring people are not discriminated against on the basis of individual characteristics.

Equality means treating individuals or groups of individuals fairly and equally irrespective of race, gender, disability, religion or belief, sexual orientation and age.

Evidence-based approaches are informed by thorough objective research and evidence.

Evidence-based practice (EBP) refers to using information from high-quality research and applying it within practice to make informed decisions about a service user's care.

Experiential learning is the process of learning through experience.

Feedback is an open two-way communication between two or more parties.

'Future vision' refers to the innovative work going on in the NHS. It is providing new ways of thinking about healthcare delivery. Future vision is a response by government and healthcare bodies to the growing financial and workforce pressures to meet the needs of the population and to realise the vision set out in the NHS *Five Year Forward View*.

GDPR refers to the General Data Protection Regulation. This is a set of data protection laws that protects individuals' personal information. This superseded the Data Protection Act 1998 in May 2018.

Governance procedures and **mechanisms** refer to the monitoring of actions, practices and policies which guide the decisions of organisations and their stakeholders.

Harassment is unwanted behaviour towards another person that is designed to intimidate or degrade.

Health and safety is ensuring people are safe and come to no harm in the workplace. This will inform policies such as Control of Substances Hazardous to Health (COSHH), infection control, safe handling of medicine, moving and handling, and fire safety, for example.

The Health and Safety Executive (HSE) is the regulator or official supervisory body for the health, safety and welfare of people in work settings in the UK.

Inclusion is positive behaviour to ensure all people have an opportunity to be included and not be unfairly excluded because of their individual characteristics.

Innovation includes new ideas, methods, ways of doing things.

Integrated care and support is a means to improving the experiences and outcomes of individuals and their communities and at the same time allowing people to be true partners in their own care. A good example of integrated care is the work of the Health and Wellbeing Boards (HWBs) and local authorities which link the NHS, public health and social care with employers, the police and the criminal justice system, schools, and the business and voluntary sectors.

Interlinked work is work that is connected and that has similar objectives.

Laissez faire is the leadership style that favours leaving things to take their own course, without interference.

Lasting Power of Attorney (LPA) is a legal document which allows anybody over the age of 18 to appoint one or more people to support the decision-making process should the individual become unable to do so. The person must have the mental capacity to undertake this step. This has replaced the Enduring Power of Attorney (EPA) which was a legal document that appointed one or more people to make financial decisions.

Lay carer is a person who is not a health professional but gives care to somebody, usually in their own home.

Local guidance describes the way in which national guidance translates to a local area.

Mentoring is a relationship in which an individual with expertise can help another individual to progress in their career.

Multidisciplinary groups have people with different specialist skills. For example, the group may have people with medical and care expertise, and there may be people who have specialist knowledge on housing and other services.

National guidance describes a full range of provision for care settings, formal and informal settings, and provision in the public, private, voluntary and charitable sectors.

Negotiation is taking part in a discussion which aims to reach an agreement.

Obligation is an action or restraint from action that a person is morally or legally bound to owe to (an)other(s).

Other professionals include people who are from different agencies and disciplines but still part of the wider healthcare team. They may be advocates for the service user or from social care agencies or other health disciplines such as physiotherapists and mental health workers, etc.

Others refers to those people who may not come under the umbrella of health professionals. They could be family, carers and friends, or children and young people.

Outcomes-based practice, also referred to as outcomes management and outcomes-focused assessment, is one approach to achieving desired patient care goals. It refers to activity that benefits patients and involves team work and quality assurance measures.

Outcomes management is a means to help service users, funding services and providers make care-related choices based on knowledge of the effects of these choices on the service user's life.

Partnership working is the use of inclusive and mutually beneficial relationships in care work that improve the quality and experience of care. It refers to the relationships between individuals with long-term care conditions, their carers, and service providers and care professionals.

Perception awareness is our ability to recognise how and what we are communicating to others through our non-verbal communication. How we present ourselves to others can communicate much about us.

Personalisation refers to the way in which individuals are helped to become the drivers in developing systems of care and support designed to meet their unique needs.

Person-centred practice is a process of life planning for individuals based around principles which respect their individuality, rights, choice, privacy, independence and dignity.

Policy is a plan or principle of action proposed by an organisation, also known as guidelines or codes.

Policy drivers are documents, research, acts of parliament and information that can lead to change in practice and drive forward new types of treatment and procedures.

Positive outcomes are the end results of services for individuals.

Positive risk taking means identifying the potential risks and then developing plans and actions that reflect the potential benefits and harm of exercising one course of action over another. It is a way of seeing the risk in a positive way that enhances the quality of life for an individual.

Prejudice is an unreasonable, pre-conceived judgement or opinion that is not based on knowledge, evidence or experience.

Procedures and policies are agreed ways of working that employees in an organisation are required to follow. Procedures state how policies will be carried out or actioned in the setting.

A **protocol** is a set of rules that explain the correct procedure to be followed in a situation.

Qualitative data is gained through observation and is descriptive in nature. It will be collected through interviews and observations and will try to find a meaning in certain phenomena.

Quantitative data is data that is numerical in nature. It will answer questions such as 'how much' or 'how many'.

Reflective practice is the act of stopping and thinking about what we are doing in practice and analysing the decisions we make in the light of theory and the things we have learned. By doing this we are more able to relate theory to practice, helping us to generate new knowledge and ideas.

Regulation is a rule or order which is underpinned by law. In healthcare settings, apart from those concerned with health and safety care, regulations with respect to health protection and control of disease are also available.

Risk management is the forecasting of potential risks and minimising them or avoiding them altogether. Your policies should identify how you undertake risk assessment in your area and how you intend to manage risks that arise.

Safeguarding, according to the CQC, means 'protecting people's health, well-being and human rights, and enabling them to live free from harm, abuse and neglect. It is fundamental to high-quality health and social care'.

Safeguarding Adults Reviews (previously known as Serious Case Reviews) take place after a person is seriously injured or dies, particularly if abuse or neglect is thought to have been a causative factor. It looks at what we might learn from the occurrence in order to help prevent similar incidents from happening in the future.

Scaffolding is the process of moving students progressively towards better understanding and independence in their learning using various instructional techniques (adapted from http://edglossary. org/scaffolding).

Self-awareness is the ability to notice the self and to be able to recognise our own behaviour and personality. It is to be aware of our own character and feelings and sometimes this can be difficult for us. Being self-aware means that we know our own emotions and recognise the feelings arising from those emotions when they happen. We are therefore in control of what is going on within us and we are able to use our emotions appropriately. We may feel angry or sad at times but it might be inappropriate to show those feelings at work.

Serious Case Review takes place after a person who should be safeguarded is seriously injured or dies, particularly if abuse or neglect is thought to have been a causative factor. It looks at what can be learned from the situation to help prevent similar incidents in the future.

Service teams are teams within the multidisciplinary groups such as the primary care team, hospital, housing and other services used within your own setting.

SMART targets are those objectives which are specific, measurable, achievable, realistic/relevant and time-related.

Stakeholders include any person, or group, that has an interest in what is happening in your organisation. For example, in a care home for elderly people, stakeholders may be relatives, the residents themselves, local businesses and the board of directors.

Stigma implies that a characteristic held by some people or groups is deviant from social expectations. For example, some people will not admit to being depressed because of the stigma of mental health in our society.

Sustainability and Transformation Partnerships (STPs) are drawn up by senior people in the local health and care system to develop proposals that improve health and care. Note: STP can also stand for Sustainability and Transformation Plan.

SWOT analysis involves defining strengths, weaknesses, opportunities and threats and can be undertaken as part of your professional development, to evaluate your setting or a particular project you are working on. It will help you to identify things that you are good at and doing well, things that you are not doing so well and could improve, areas that present opportunities and things that could threaten or are troublesome. The aim is to improve performance and the quality of care.

Systems leadership is the way in which beneficial change is affected across interconnecting systems, for example health and social care, and characterised by a belief that leadership is the responsibility of teams, not individuals, and is collaborative in nature.

Trust is having confidence in something or someone.

A **values-based** culture is one in which the goal is to work by a common set of values that guides behaviours.

Whistle blowing means making a disclosure or revealing information that is in the public interest.

Workforce planning is the process whereby the staff with the necessary skills are allocated to the task when they are needed in order to deliver organisational objectives.

Index